More Than Just a Textbook

Stay Connected
at Glencoe.com

Internet Resources

Step 1 Connect to **History** **ONLINE** at <u>glencoe.com</u>.

Step 2 Connect to online resources by using *QuickPass* codes. You can connect directly to the chapter you want.

TAJEY7158c1

Enter this code with the appropriate chapter number.

For Students

Connect to <u>glencoe.com</u> to find all of these resources:

- Online Student Edition
- Test Practice
- Multi-language Glossary
- Interactive Maps
- Workbooks
- Section Spotlight Videos
- Study Central™ and Study-to-Go™
- . . . and more

For Teachers

Connect to standards correlations and professional development content at <u>glencoe.com</u>.

Welcome to Glencoe Online

A whole new world of learning opportunities is just a click away.

Indiana Edition

The American Journey

Early Years

Joyce Appleby, Ph.D.

Alan Brinkley, Ph.D.

Albert S. Broussard, Ph.D.

James M. McPherson, Ph.D.

Donald A. Ritchie, Ph.D.

NATIONAL GEOGRAPHIC

McGraw Hill Glencoe

Authors

Joyce Appleby, Ph.D., is Professor of History at UCLA. Dr. Appleby's published works include *Inheriting the Revolution: The First Generation of Americans; Capitalism and a New Social Order: The Jeffersonian Vision of the 1790s;* and *Economic Thought and Ideology in Seventeenth-Century England,* which won the Berkshire Prize. She served as president of both the Organization of American Historians and the American Historical Association, and chaired the Council of the Institute of Early American History and Culture at Williamsburg. Dr. Appleby has been elected to the American Philosophical Society and the American Academy of Arts and Sciences, and is a Corresponding Fellow of the British Academy.

Alan Brinkley, Ph.D., is Allan Nevins Professor of American History at Columbia University. His published works include *Voices of Protest: Huey Long, Father Coughlin, and the Great Depression,* which won the 1983 National Book Award; *The End of Reform: New Deal Liberalism in Recession and War; The Unfinished Nation: A Concise History of the American People;* and *Liberalism and Its Discontents.* He received the Levenson Memorial Teaching Prize at Harvard University.

Albert S. Broussard, Ph.D., is Professor of History and Graduate Coordinator at Texas A&M University. Before joining the Texas A&M faculty, Dr. Broussard was Assistant Professor of History and Director of the African American Studies Program at Southern Methodist University. Among his publications are the books *Black San Francisco: The Struggle for Racial Equality in the West, 1900–1954* and *African American Odyssey: The Stewarts, 1853–1963.* Dr. Broussard has also served as president of the Oral History Association.

Donald A. Ritchie, Ph.D., is Associate Historian of the United States Senate Historical Office. Dr. Ritchie received his doctorate in American history from the University of Maryland after service in the U.S. Marine Corps. He has taught American history at various levels, from high school to university. He edits the Historical Series of the Senate Foreign Relations Committee and is the author of several books, including *Doing Oral History, The Oxford Guide to the United States Government,* and *Press Gallery: Congress and the Washington Correspondents,* which received the Organization of American Historians Richard W. Leopold Prize. Dr. Ritchie has served as president of the Oral History Association and as a council member of the American Historical Association.

James M. McPherson, Ph.D., is George Henry Davis Professor of American History at Princeton University. Dr. McPherson is the author of 11 books about the Civil War era. These include *Battle Cry of Freedom: The Civil War Era,* for which he won the Pulitzer Prize in 1989, and *For Cause and Comrades: Why Men Fought in the Civil War,* for which he won the 1998 Lincoln Prize. He is a member of many professional historical associations, including the Civil War Preservation Trust.

The National Geographic Society, founded in 1888 for the increase and diffusion of geographic knowledge, is the world's largest nonprofit scientific and educational organization. Since its earliest days, the Society has used sophisticated communication technologies, from color photography to holography, to convey knowledge to a worldwide membership. The School Publishing Division supports the Society's mission by developing innovative educational programs—ranging from traditional print materials to multimedia programs including CD-ROMs, videodiscs, and software. "National Geographic Geography & History," featured in each unit of this textbook, was designed and developed by the National Geographic Society's School Publishing Division.

Contributing Author

Dinah Zike, M.Ed., is an award-winning author, educator, and inventor known for designing three-dimensional hands-on manipulatives and graphic organizers known as Foldables®. Foldables are used nationally and internationally by teachers, parents, and educational publishing companies. Dinah has developed over 150 supplemental educational books and materials. She is the author of *The Big Book of Books and Activities,* which was awarded *Learning Magazine's* Teachers' Choice Award. In 2004 Dinah was honored with the CESI Science Advocacy Award. Dinah received her M.Ed. from Texas A&M, College Station, Texas.

 Students with print disabilities may be eligible to obtain an accessible, audio version of the pupil edition of this textbook. Please call Recording for the Blind & Dyslexic at 1-800-221-4792 for complete information.

The McGraw-Hill Companies

 Glencoe

Send all inquiries to:
Glencoe/McGraw-Hill
8787 Orion Place
Columbus, OH 43240-4027

ISBN: 978-0-07-881090-9
MHID: 0-07-881090-6

Printed in the United States of America.

2 3 4 5 6 7 8 9 10 071/043 12 11 10 09

Academic Consultants

Christopher McGrew
Christopher McGrew is the former social studies coordinator for the Indiana Department of Education and Past President of the Council for State Social Studies Specialists. He also teaches an economics class for future teachers for the School of Management at Purdue University. He is a former secondary school teacher of world history and economics at Carroll Junior/Senior High School in Flora, Indiana. His research interests include examining exchange programs concerning civic and economic education, specifically in China and Russia.

Laura Belmonte, Ph.D.
Associate Professor of History
Oklahoma State University
Stillwater, Oklahoma

David Berger, Ph.D.
Broeklundian Professor of History
Yeshiva University
New York, New York

Keith S. Bohannon, Ph.D.
Professor of History
University of West Georgia
Carrollton, Georgia

David Canton, Ph.D.
Jacob & Hilda Blaustein Assistant Professor of History
Connecticut College
New London, Connecticut

Jaime Cardenas, Jr., Ph.D.
Associate Professor of History
Seattle Central Community College
Seattle, Washington

Jeffrey A. Davis, Ph.D.
Associate Professor of History
Bloomsburg University of Pennsylvania
Bloomsburg, Pennsylvania

Allison Gough, Ph.D.
Assistant Professor of History
Hawaii Pacific University
Honolulu, Hawaii

Melissa Klapper, Ph.D.
Associate Professor of History
Rowan University
Glassboro, New Jersey

Daniel Lewis, Ph.D.
Professor of History
California State Polytechnic University
Pomona, California

Teacher Reviewers

Lysa Augustin
Davis Hills Middle School
Huntsville, Alabama

John Brandt
Cumberland County Middle School
Cumberland, Virginia

Stephanie Doyle
Breckinridge Middle School
Roanoke, Virginia

Teresa Gallup
York Suburban Middle School
York, Pennsylvania

Tina Gersdorf
Jefferson Middle School
Champaign, Illinois

Michael Gordon
Barrington Middle School
Barrington, Illinois

Timothy Gray
Doe Creek Middle School
New Palestine, Indiana

Dawn Grindley
Westlake Middle School
Thornwood, New York

Chris Hartlieb
Highland Middle School
Highland, Illinois

Susan Hawes
Elm Middle School
Elmwood Park, Illinois

Thomas Joice
Clark Middle School
Vincennes, Indiana

Tom Kish
Zimmerman Middle School
Zimmerman, Minnesota

Steven Miller
Blue Ridge Middle School
Purcellville, Virginia

Lisa Ray
Chapin Middle School
Chapin, South Carolina

Christopher R. Renner
Lynhurst 7 & 8 Grade Center
Indianapolis, Indiana

Terry Robinson
Alden Middle School
Alden, New York

Kathleen Shaeper
Allegany-Limestone Middle School
Allegany, New York

Karan Stubbs
Bixby Middle School
Bixby, Oklahoma

Stephanie Sumick
Thompson Middle School
Middletown, New Jersey

Lynn Voorhees
Creekside Middle School
Carmel, Indiana

Susan Yurkovic
Brownsburg West Middle School
Brownsburg, Indiana

Contents

NATIONAL GEOGRAPHIC Reference Atlas

Unit 1

The Americas: Worlds Meet 1

Contents

Features

Primary Sources
INTERPRETING
POLITICAL CARTOONS

People IN HISTORY

YOU DECIDE

YES NO

Chance & Error in History

Skills Handbook

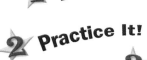

Critical Thinking Skills

Social Studies Skills

1 Learn It!

2 Practice It!

3 Apply It!

Documents of American History

Primary Source Quotes

Bartolomé de ▶
Las Casas

◀ Dolley Madison

Frederick Douglass ▶

Robert E. Lee ▶

Maps

Maps In MOtion Maps, charts, and graphs with this logo have been enhanced by In Motion graphics in the StudentWorks™ Plus CD-ROM and the Presentation Plus! CD-ROM. These In Motion graphics allow students to interact with layers of data and listen to audio components.

War in the West, 1862–1863

NATIONAL GEOGRAPHIC

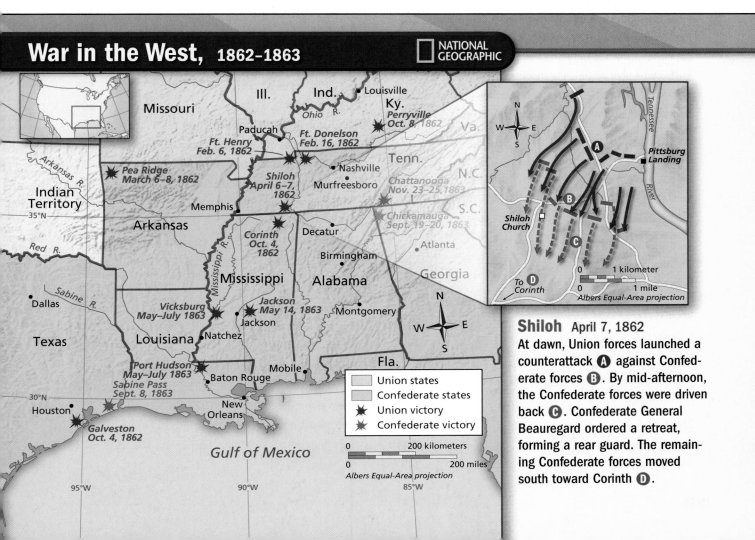

Union states
Confederate states
★ Union victory
✦ Confederate victory

0   200 kilometers
0   200 miles
Albers Equal-Area projection

Shiloh April 7, 1862
At dawn, Union forces launched a counterattack **A** against Confederate forces **B**. By mid-afternoon, the Confederate forces were driven back **C**. Confederate General Beauregard ordered a retreat, forming a rear guard. The remaining Confederate forces moved south toward Corinth **D**.

Charts, Graphs, & Diagrams

Scavenger Hunt

The American Journey contains a wealth of information. The trick is to know where to look to access all the information in the book. If you complete this scavenger hunt exercise with your teachers or parents, you will see how the textbook is organized and how to get the most out of your reading and study time. Let's get started!

1. How many units and how many chapters are in this book?

2. Where would you look to quickly find facts about each state, including the capital and the year it was admitted into the Union?

3. You want to read the Declaration of Independence. How will you find it?

4. What time period does Chapter 16 cover?

5. In Chapter 4, what information will the *Foldables* activity help you organize?

6. What Reading History skill will you practice in Unit 2?

7. Where can you find the Essential Questions for each chapter?

8. What is the History Online Web Activity for Chapter 12?

9. Where in the back of the book can you quickly find the meaning of important vocabulary words such as *federalism*?

10. Where can you learn about and practice critical thinking and social studies skills?

Focus on Indiana

Correlations to Grade 8 Indiana Academic Standards for Social Studies

Indiana Academic Standards	Student Edition Pages
Standard 1 **History** *Students will examine the relationship and significance of themes, concepts, and movements in the development of United States history, including review of key ideas related to the colonization of America and the revolution and founding era. This will be followed by emphasis on social reform, national development and westward expansion, and the Civil War and Reconstruction period.*	
Historical Knowledge *The American Revolution and Founding of the United States: 1754 to 1801*	
8.1.1 Identify major Native American Indian groups of eastern North America and describe early conflict and cooperation with European settlers and the influence the two cultures had on each other.	16, 20, 21, 22, 46, 47, 49–52, 61, 66, 69, 78, 81, 82, 105–106, 107, 112, 261, 262
8.1.2 Explain the struggle of the British, French, Spanish, and Dutch to gain control of North America during settlement and colonization.	50–52, 59, 60, 73, 74, 75, 77–82, 104, 105, 106
8.1.3 Identify and explain the conditions, causes, consequences, and significance of the French and Indian War (1754–1763), and the resistance and rebellion against British imperial rule by the thirteen colonies in North America (1761–1775).	100, 101, 107, 108–112, 122–125, 126–129, 133–137
8.1.4 Identify fundamental ideas in the Declaration of Independence (1776) and analyze the causes and effects of the Revolutionary War (1775–1783), including enactment of the Articles of Confederation and the Treaty of Paris.	111, 112, 133–137, 138, 139, 141–142, 146–149, 152–159, 160–165, 168–173, 174–178, 180–181, 186–189, 190
8.1.5 Identify and explain key events leading to the creation of a strong union among the thirteen original states and in the establishment of the United States as a federal republic.	187, 188, 189, 197, 198–199, 200–201, 204–210
8.1.6 Identify the steps in the implementation of the federal government under the United States Constitution, including the First and Second Congresses of the United States (1789–1792).	197–199, 200, 201, 202–203, 253, 263

Indiana Academic Standards	Student Edition Pages
8.1.7 Describe the origin and development of political parties, the Federalists and the Democratic-Republicans, (1793–1801) and examine points of agreement and disagreement between these parties.	264, 265, 266, 267, 268, 270, 271
8.1.8 Evaluate the significance of the presidential and congressional election of 1800 and the transfer of political authority and power to the Democratic-Republican Party led by the new president, Thomas Jefferson (1801).	277, 278, 279
8.1.9 Describe the influence of important individuals on social and political developments of the time such as the Independence movement and the framing of the Constitution.	102, 103, 125, 132, 133, 135, 136, 139, 140, 141, 142, 156, 161, 164, 165, 176–177, 194, 197, 210, 253, 255, 256, 257, 265, 266, 267
8.1.10 Compare differences in ways of life in the northern and southern states, including the growth of towns and cities in the North and the growing dependence on slavery in the South.	89–90, 92, 93, 94, 95, 389–393, 394–399, 400–403, 406–412, 476
National Expansion and Reform: 1801 to 1861	
8.1.11 Explain the events leading up to and the significance of the Louisiana Purchase (1803) and the expedition of Lewis and Clark (1803–1806).	280, 281, 282, 283, 284, 285
8.1.12 Explain the main issues, decisions, and consequences of landmark Supreme Court cases.	279, 324, 344, 349, 458–459, 540, 602–607
8.1.13 Explain the causes and consequences of the War of 1812, including the Rush-Bagot Agreement (1818).	293, 294, 295, 296, 297, 298, 325
8.1.14 Examine the international problem that led to the Monroe Doctrine (1823) and assess its consequences.	325, 326, 611
8.1.15 Explain the concept of Manifest Destiny and describe its impact on westward expansion of the United States.	363, 364–365, 371, 373, 374, 376, 377, 379, 380, 381, 382, 383
8.1.16 Describe the abolition of slavery in the northern states; conflict and compromises associated with westward expansion of slavery, such as the Missouri Compromise (1820), The Compromise of 1850, Kansas-Nebraska Act (1854); and the continued resistance to slavery by people such as Frederick Douglass, Harriet Tubman, William Lloyd Garrison, and Harriet Beecher Stowe.	322, 323, 324, 326, 327, 371, 409, 411, 421, 424, 425, 426, 427, 428, 429, 430, 431, 432, 433, 435, 449, 450, 451, 452, 453, 454, 455, 456–461, 475

Focus on Indiana

Indiana Academic Standards	Student Edition Pages
8.1.17 Identify the key ideas of Jacksonian democracy and explain their influence on political participation, political parties, and constitutional government.	336, 337, 338, 339, 340, 341
8.1.18 Analyze different interests and points of view of individuals and groups involved in the abolitionist, feminist and social reform movements, and in sectional conflicts.	340, 341, 418–421, 424, 425, 426, 427, 428, 429, 430, 431, 432, 433, 434, 435, 436, 437, 438, 449–451, 454, 455, 464, 465, 468–469, 486, 487
8.1.19 Explain the influence of early individual social reformers and movements.	418–421, 424, 425, 426, 427, 428, 429, 430, 431, 432, 433, 434, 435, 436, 437, 438, 486, 487
The Civil War and Reconstruction Period: 1850 to 1877	
8.1.20 Analyze the causes and effects of events leading to the Civil War, including development of sectional conflict over slavery.	451, 453, 454, 455, 457, 458, 459, 460, 461, 462, 463, 464, 465, 466
8.1.21 Describe the importance of key events and individuals in the Civil War.	466, 475–479, 480–487, 492, 495, 496, 497, 499–505, 507–512
8.1.22 Explain and evaluate the policies, practices, and consequences of Reconstruction, including the Thirteenth, Fourteenth, and Fifteenth Amendments to the Constitution.	509, 519, 520, 521, 523, 524, 525, 526, 527, 529, 530, 531, 535, 536, 537, 538, 539, 540
8.1.23 Describe the conflicts between Native American Indians and settlers of the Great Plains.	361, 362, 547–548, 615
8.1.24 Identify the influence of individuals on political and social events and movements such as the abolition movement, the *Dred Scott* case, women rights, and Native American Indian removal.	342, 343, 344, 345, 346, 347, 418–421, 424–431, 432–433, 434–438, 458–459, 460, 461, 486, 487, 523, 524
8.1.25 Give examples of how immigration affected American culture in the decades before and after the Civil War, including growth of industrialism in the North; religious differences; tensions between middle-class and working-class people, particularly in the Northeast; and intensification of cultural differences between the North and the South.	395, 397, 398, 399

Indiana Academic Standards	Student Edition Pages
8.1.26 Give examples of the changing role of women and minorities in the northern, southern, and western parts of the United States in the mid-nineteenth century, and examine possible causes for these changes.	396, 397, 435, 436, 437, 438, 492, 493, 496, 497, 501, 523, 524
8.1.27 Give examples of scientific and technological developments that changed cultural life in the nineteenth-century United States, such as the use of photography, growth in the use of the telegraph, the completion of the transcontinental railroad, and the invention of the telephone.	306, 307, 308, 309, 315, 316, 389, 390, 391, 392, 393
Chronological Thinking, Historical Comprehension, Analysis and Interpretation, Research, and Issues–Analysis and Decision–Making	
8.1.28 Recognize historical perspective and evaluate alternative courses of action by describing the historical context in which events unfolded and by avoiding evaluation of the past solely in terms of present-day norms.	7, 8, 9, 68, 127–128, 140, 176–177, 202–203, 266, 364–365, 368–369, 468–469, 502, 589
8.1.29 Differentiate between facts and historical interpretations recognizing that the historian's narrative reflects his or her judgment about the significance of particular facts.	70–71, 127, 128, 129, 130–131, 310–311, 368–369, 404–405, 488–489
8.1.30 Formulate historical questions by analyzing primary sources and secondary sources about an issue confronting the United States during the period from 1754–1877.	140, 202–203, 218, 263, 266, 278, 354, 364–365, 436, 468–469, 502, 515, 590, 592, 610–616
8.1.31 Obtain historical data from a variety of sources to compare and contrast examples of art, music, and literature during the nineteenth century and explain how these reflect American culture during this time period.	351, 408–409, 421, 422, 427, 428–429, 488–489

Standard 2

Civics and Government

Students will explain the major principles, values, and institutions of constitutional government and citizenship, which are based on the founding documents of the United States and how three branches of government share and check power within our federal system of government.

Foundations of Government

8.2.1 Identify and explain essential ideas of constitutional government, which are expressed in the founding documents of the United States, including the Virginia Declaration of Rights, the Declaration of Independence, the Virginia Statute for Religious Freedom, the Massachusetts Constitution of 1780, the Northwest Ordinance, the 1787 U.S. Constitution, the Bill of Rights, the Federalist and Anti-Federalist Papers, *Common Sense,* Washington's Farewell Address (1796), and Jefferson's First Inaugural Address (1801).	66, 68, 100, 101, 138, 140, 141, 142, 146–149, 187, 188, 189, 190, 191, 193, 198, 200, 201, 205–206, 209, 210, 214–223, 224–245, 254, 255, 610, 611

Indiana Academic Standards	Student Edition Pages
8.2.2 Identify and explain the relationship between rights and responsibilities of citizenship in the United States.	208, 215, 217, 222, 223, 236–237, 238, 240, 241, 245, 254, 255
8.2.3 Explain how and why legislative, executive, and judicial powers are distributed, shared, and limited in the constitutional government of the United States.	204, 207, 208, 216, 217, 218, 219, 220, 221, 223, 225–233
8.2.4 Examine functions of the national government in the lives of people.	206, 207, 208, 216, 218, 219, 221, 222, 223, 496, 497
Functions of Government	
8.2.5 Compare and contrast the powers reserved to the federal and state government under the Articles of Confederation and the United States Constitution.	187, 188, 189, 193, 197, 198, 200, 201, 206, 207, 208, 210, 211, 216, 233–234, 266, 267, 270, 579
8.2.6 Distinguish among the different functions of national and state government within the federal system by analyzing the United States Constitution and the Indiana Constitution.	206, 207, 208, 210, 213, 216, 233–234, 266, 267, 270, 545
Roles of Citizens	
8.2.7 Explain the importance in a democratic republic of responsible participation by citizens in voluntary civil associations/nongovernmental organizations that comprise civil society.	208, 222, 223, 425, 426, 431, 435, 436, 520, 531
8.2.8 Explain ways that citizens can participate in political parties, campaigns, and elections.	222, 223, 277, 337, 338, 339, 340, 552–553
8.2.9 Explain how citizens can monitor and influence the development and implementation of public policies at local, state, and national levels of government.	215, 223, 419–421, 425–431, 432–433, 435–438, 523, 551–553, 563–566
8.2.10 Research and defend positions on issues in which fundamental values and principles related to the United States Constitution are in conflict, using a variety of information resources.	202–203, 214–223, 224–245, 254, 468–469, 593

Indiana Academic Standards	Student Edition Pages
Standard 3 **Geography** *Students will identify the major geographic characteristics of the United States and its regions. They will name and locate the major physical features of the United States, each of the states, and major cities, and use geographic skills and technology to examine the influence of geographic factors on national development.*	
The World in Spatial Terms	
8.3.1 **Read maps to interpret symbols and determine the land forms and human features that represent physical and cultural characteristics of areas in the United States.**	20, 21, 44, 67, 74, 78, 134, 156, 157, 158, 181, 258, 277, 283, 291, 296, 306, 308, 313, 314, 315, 324, 344, 360, 362, 370, 374, 376, 379, 389, 401, 433, 449, 450, 454, 458, 465, 482, 484, 503, 510, 511, 519, 525
Places and Regions	
8.3.2 **Identify and create maps showing the physical growth and development of the United States from settlement of the original thirteen colonies through Reconstruction (1877) including transportation routes used during the period.**	Ref 26, 190, 262, 283, 291, 306, 308, 313, 314, 315, 324, 362, 370, 389, 401, 433, 450, 454
Physical Systems	
8.3.3 **Identify and locate the major climate regions in the United States and describe the characteristics of these regions.**	17, 19, 22, 88, 92, 93, 94
8.3.4 **Name and describe processes that build up the land and processes that erode it and identify places these occur.**	Ref 17, 7, 8
8.3.5 **Describe the importance of the major mountain ranges and the major river systems in the development of the United States.**	44, 51, 52, 74, 81, 180, 181, 306, 360, 362
Human Systems	
8.3.6 **Identify the agricultural regions of the United States and be able to give reasons for the type of land use and subsequent land development during different historical periods.**	79, 80, 89, 92, 93–94, 95, 401, 402, 403, 407, 408, 538, 539, 542, 543
8.3.7 **Using maps identify changes influenced by growth, economic development, and human migration in the eighteenth and nineteenth centuries.**	Ref 26, 190, 262, 283, 291, 306, 308, 313, 314, 344, 362, 370, 379, 389, 401, 433, 450, 454

Indiana Academic Standards	Student Edition Pages
8.3.8 Gather information on ways people changed the physical environment of the United States in the nineteenth century using primary sources and secondary sources including digitized photo collections and historic maps.	Ref 18–Ref 20, 258, 259, 315, 316, 542, 543, 593
8.3.9 Analyze human and physical factors that have influenced migration and settlement patterns and relate them to the economic development of the United States.	7, 8, 60–61, 62–63, 74, 91, 95, 259, 281, 283, 284, 285, 306, 309, 313, 314, 315, 316, 317, 343, 344, 345, 347, 359, 361, 362, 363, 367, 370, 374, 379, 380, 381, 382, 389, 393, 397, 398, 399, 433, 532
Environment and Society	
8.3.10 Create maps, graphs, and charts showing the distribution of natural resources—such as forests, water sources, and wildlife—in the United States at the beginning of the nineteenth century and give examples of how people exploited these resources as the country became more industrialized and people moved westward.	Ref 28–Ref 29, 285, 309, 476, 487, 587, 588
8.3.11 Identify ways people modified the physical environment as the United States developed and describe the impacts that resulted.	18, 19, 89, 90, 315, 316, 317, 379, 380, 382, 390, 393, 397, 398
Standard 4 **Economics** *Students will identify, describe, and evaluate the influence of economic factors on national development from the founding of the nation to the end of Reconstruction.*	
8.4.1 Identify economic factors contributing to European exploration and colonization in North America, the American Revolution, and the drafting of the Constitution of the United States.	14, 29, 30, 31, 33, 35, 36, 37, 39, 44, 45, 47, 52, 60, 73, 74, 79, 123–124, 125, 128–129, 161, 164, 177, 191–192, 579, 594
8.4.2 Illustrate elements of the three types of economic systems, using cases from United States history.	50, 52, 99, 307
8.4.3 Evaluate how the characteristics of a market economy have affected the economic and labor development of the United States.	305, 307, 308, 309
8.4.4 Explain the basic economic functions of the government in the economy of the United States.	228, 229, 256, 257, 322, 323, 497

Indiana Academic Standards	Student Edition Pages
8.4.5 Analyze contributions of entrepreneurs and inventors in the development of the United States economy.	306, 307, 308, 309, 314, 315, 389, 390, 391, 392, 393, 423
8.4.6 Relate technological change and inventions to changes in labor productivity in the United States in the eighteenth and nineteenth centuries.	305, 306, 308, 309, 395, 396, 401, 402, 403
8.4.7 Trace the development of different kinds of money used in the United States and explain how money helps make saving easier.	189, 191, 192, 228, 497
8.4.8 Examine the development of the banking system in the United States.	255, 256, 257, 266, 349, 350, 352
8.4.9 Explain and evaluate examples of domestic and international interdependence throughout United States history.	50–51, 88, 90, 91, 99, 256–257, 287, 289, 368, 373, 380, 403, 408
8.4.10 Examine the importance of borrowing and lending (the use of credit) in the United States economy and list the advantages and disadvantages of using credit.	192, 408, 530, 531, 539
8.4.11 Use a variety of information resources to compare and contrast job skills needed in different time periods in United States history.	89, 90, 305, 309, 396, 579, 593

Correlations to the Grade 8 Indiana Academic Standards for Social Studies by Chapter

Unit	Chapter	Indiana Academic Standards
Unit 1	Chapter 1 pp. 4–25	8.1.1, 8.1.28, 8.3.1, 8.3.3, 8.3.4, 8.3.9, 8.3.11, 8.4.1
	Chapter 2 pp. 26–55	8.1.1, 8.1.2, 8.3.1, 8.3.5, 8.4.1, 8.4.2, 8.4.9
	Chapter 3 pp. 56–85	8.1.1, 8.1.2, 8.1.28, 8.1.29, 8.2.1, 8.3.1, 8.3.5, 8.3.6, 8.3.9, 8.4.1
	Chapter 4 pp. 86–115	8.1.1, 8.1.2, 8.1.3, 8.1.4, 8.1.9, 8.1.10, 8.2.1, 8.3.6, 8.3.9, 8.4.2, 8.4.9
Unit 2	Chapter 5 pp. 120–145	8.1.3, 8.1.4, 8.1.9, 8.1.28, 8.1.29, 8.2.1, 8.3.1, 8.4.1
	Chapter 6 pp. 150–183	8.1.4, 8.1.9, 8.1.28, 8.3.1, 8.3.5, 8.4.1
	Chapter 7 pp. 184–213	8.1.4, 8.1.5, 8.1.6, 8.1.9, 8.1.28, 8.2.1, 8.2.2, 8.2.3, 8.2.4, 8.2.5, 8.2.6, 8.2.7, 8.3.2, 8.3.7, 8.4.1, 8.4.7, 8.4.10
Unit 3	Chapter 8 pp. 250–273	8.1.1, 8.1.6, 8.1.7, 8.1.9, 8.1.28, 8.1.30, 8.2.1, 8.2.2, 8.2.5, 8.2.6, 8.2.10, 8.3.1, 8.3.2, 8.3.7, 8.3.9, 8.4.4, 8.4.8, 8.4.9
	Chapter 9 pp. 274–301	8.1.8, 8.1.11, 8.1.12, 8.1.13, 8.2.8, 8.3.1, 8.3.2, 8.3.7, 8.3.9, 8.3.10, 8.4.9
	Chapter 10 pp. 302–329	8.1.12, 8.1.13, 8.1.14, 8.1.16, 8.1.27, 8.1.29, 8.1.31, 8.3.1, 8.3.2, 8.3.5, 8.3.7, 8.3.9, 8.3.11, 8.4.2, 8.4.3, 8.4.4, 8.4.5, 8.4.6, 8.4.11
Unit 4	Chapter 11 pp. 334–355	8.1.12, 8.1.17, 8.1.18, 8.1.24, 8.1.31, 8.2.8, 8.3.1, 8.3.7, 8.3.9, 8.4.8
	Chapter 12 pp. 356–385	8.1.15, 8.1.16, 8.1.23, 8.1.28, 8.1.29, 8.3.1, 8.3.2, 8.3.5, 8.3.7, 8.3.9, 8.4.9
	Chapter 13 pp. 386–415	8.1.10, 8.1.16, 8.1.25, 8.1.26, 8.1.27, 8.1.29, 8.1.31, 8.3.1, 8.3.2, 8.3.6, 8.3.7, 8.3.9, 8.4.5, 8.4.6, 8.4.9, 8.4.10, 8.4.11
	Chapter 14 pp. 416–441	8.1.16, 8.1.18, 8.1.19, 8.1.24, 8.1.26, 8.1.31, 8.2.7, 8.2.9, 8.3.1, 8.3.2, 8.3.7, 8.3.9, 8.4.5
Unit 5	Chapter 15 pp. 446–471	8.1.12, 8.1.16, 8.1.18, 8.1.20, 8.1.21, 8.1.24, 8.1.28, 8.3.1, 8.3.2, 8.3.7
	Chapter 16 pp. 472–515	8.1.10, 8.1.16, 8.1.18, 8.1.19, 8.1.21, 8.1.22, 8.1.24, 8.1.26, 8.1.28, 8.1.29, 8.1.31, 8.3.1, 8.3.10, 8.4.4, 8.4.7
	Chapter 17 pp. 516–545	8.1.12, 8.1.22, 8.1.24, 8.1.26, 8.2.7, 8.2.9, 8.3.1, 8.3.6, 8.3.9, 8.4.10

Correlations to Grade 8 Indiana Academic Standards for English/Language Arts

ELA Academic Standards	Student Edition Pages
Standard 1 **READING: Word Recognition, Fluency, and Vocabulary Development** *Students use their knowledge of word parts and word relationships, as well as context (the meaning of the text around a word), to determine the meaning of specialized vocabulary and to understand the precise meaning of grade-level-appropriate words.*	
Vocabulary and Concept Development	
8.1.3　**Verify the meaning of a word in its context, even when its meaning is not directly stated, through the use of definition, restatement, example, comparison, or contrast.**	6,16, 28, 34, 42, 48, 58, 64, 72, 76, 88, 98, 108, 122, 126, 132, 152, 160, 168, 174, 186, 194, 204, 252, 264, 276, 280, 286, 304, 312, 320, 336, 342, 348, 358, 366, 372, 378, 388, 394, 400, 406, 418, 424, 434, 448, 452, 462, 474, 480, 490, 498, 506, 522, 528, 534
Standard 2 **READING: Comprehension and Analysis of Nonfiction and Informational Text** *Students read and understand grade-level-appropriate material. The selections in the **Indiana Reading List** (www.doe.state.in.us/standards/readinglist.html) illustrate the quality and complexity of the materials to be read by students. At Grade 8, in addition to regular classroom reading, students read a variety of nonfiction, such as biographies, autobiographies, books in many different subject areas, magazines, newspapers, reference and technical materials, and online information.*	
Structural Features of Informational and Technical Materials	
8.2.2　**Analyze text that uses proposition (statement of argument) and support patterns.**	68, 140, 202, 266, 364, 468, 502
8.2.7　**Analyze the structure, format, and purpose of informational materials (such as textbooks, newspapers, instructional or technical manuals, and public documents).**	5, 6–22, 27, 28–52, 57, 58–82, 87, 88–112, 121, 122–142, 151, 152–178, 185, 186–210, 251, 252–270, 275, 276–298, 303, 304–326, 335, 336–352, 357, 358–382, 387, 388–412, 417, 418–438, 447, 448–466, 473, 474–512, 517, 518–540

ELA Academic Standards	Student Edition Pages
Analysis of Grade-Level-Appropriate Nonfiction and Informational Text	
8.2.3 Find similarities and differences between texts in the treatment, amount of coverage, or organization of ideas.	39, 80, 81, 102, 136, 164, 197, 267, 284, 322, 323, 346, 375, 392, 427, 437, 508, 509, 530
8.2.4 Compare the original text to a summary to determine whether the summary accurately describes the main ideas, includes important details, and conveys the underlying meaning.	10, 75, 103, 112, 142, 155, 169, 178, 223, 248–249, 257, 270, 279, 285, 290, 293, 298, 309, 321, 341, 363, 393, 452, 486, 487, 497, 509, 534, 537
8.2.5 Use information from a variety of consumer and public documents to explain a situation or decision and to solve a problem.	Students can use *Time Notebooks* feature. 96–97, 166–167, 318–319, 422–423, 532–533
8.2.9 Make reasonable statements and draw conclusions about a text, supporting them with accurate examples.	68, 140, 202, 266, 293, 364, 466, 468, 502, 521
Expository (Informational) Critique	
8.2.6 Evaluate the logic (inductive or deductive argument), internal consistency, and structural patterns of text.	68, 140, 202, 266, 364, 468, 502
Standard 3 **READING: Comprehension and Analysis of Literary Text** *Students read and respond to grade-level-appropriate historically or culturally significant works of literature, such as the selections in the **Indiana Reading List** (www.doe.state.in.us/standards/readinglist.html), which illustrate the quality and complexity of the materials to be read by students. At Grade 8, students read a wide variety of fiction, such as classic and contemporary literature, historical fiction, fantasy, science fiction, mysteries, adventures, folklore, mythology, poetry, short stories, dramas, and other genres.*	
Structural Features of Literature	
8.3.1 Determine and articulate the relationship between the purposes and characteristics of different forms of poetry (including ballads, lyrics, couplets, epics, elegies, odes, and sonnets).	69, 377, 399
Analysis of Grade-Level-Appropriate Literary Text	
8.3.2 Evaluate the structural elements of the plot, such as subplots, parallel episodes, and climax; the plot's development; and the way in which conflicts are (or are not) addressed and resolved.	71, 131, 311, 405, 489

ELA Academic Standards	Student Edition Pages
8.3.3 Compare and contrast the motivations and reactions of literary characters from different historical eras confronting either similar situations and conflicts or similar hypothetical situations.	71, 311, 405, 489
8.3.4 Analyze the importance of the setting to the mood, tone, or meaning of the text.	71, 131, 489
8.3.6 Identify significant literary devices, such as metaphor, symbolism, dialect or quotations, and irony, which define a writer's style and use those elements to interpret the work.	71, 131, 311, 405, 489
Literary Criticism	
8.3.7 Analyze a work of literature, showing how it reflects the heritage, traditions, attitudes, and beliefs of its author.	70–71, 130–131, 310–311, 404–405, 488–489
Standard 4 **WRITING: Processes and Features** *Students discuss, list, and graphically organize writing ideas. They write clear, coherent, and focused essays. Students progress through the stages of the writing process and proofread, edit, and revise writing.*	
Organization and Focus	
8.4.1 Discuss ideas for writing, keep a list or notebook of ideas, and use graphic organizers to plan writing.	9, 22, 25, 33, 41, 52, 61, 69, 75, 82, 95, 103, 107, 112, 115, 129, 137, 145, 159, 165, 173, 183, 193, 210, 213, 257, 263, 273, 285, 298, 309, 317, 326, 329, 347, 352, 363, 371, 382, 385, 393, 403, 415, 431, 438, 441, 451, 461, 466, 471, 487, 497, 515, 521, 527, 531, 540
8.4.2 Create compositions that have a clear message, a coherent thesis (a statement of position on the topic), and end with a clear and well-supported conclusion.	9, 47, 55, 85, 95, 107, 115, 142, 145, 178, 183, 201, 213, 223, 257, 273, 293, 298, 301, 329, 355, 385, 393, 438, 471, 487, 505, 531, 545
8.4.3 Support theses or conclusions with analogies (comparisons), paraphrases, quotations, opinions from experts, and similar devices.	15, 33, 41, 47, 52, 75, 85, 95, 103, 115, 125, 142, 159, 178, 183, 193, 201, 210, 213, 223, 257, 273, 279, 293, 301, 317, 326, 329, 355, 371, 385, 393, 403, 412, 421, 438, 461, 471, 487, 497, 505, 527, 531, 545

ELA Academic Standards	Student Edition Pages
8.4.10 Create an organizational structure that balances all aspects of the composition and uses effective transitions between sentences to unify important ideas.	15, 25, 33, 47, 55, 61, 69, 85, 95, 103, 107, 112, 115, 125, 137, 145, 165, 178, 183, 193, 210, 257, 263, 273, 279, 298, 309, 317, 347, 355, 363, 371, 377, 382, 393, 399, 403, 421, 431, 451, 461, 466, 471, 487, 497, 505, 512, 515, 531, 545
Evaluation and Revision	
8.4.7 Review, evaluate, and revise writing for meaning and clarity.	9, 15, 33, 75, 82, 85, 95, 103, 115, 125, 129, 137, 145, 165, 173, 178, 210, 257, 263, 270, 293, 298, 317, 326, 341, 352, 355, 371, 385, 403, 415, 431, 461, 471, 479, 515, 521, 540
8.4.11 Identify topics; ask and evaluate questions; and develop ideas leading to inquiry, investigation, and research.	15, 22, 25, 41, 47, 55, 69, 75, 82, 85, 95, 107, 112, 115, 125, 137, 142, 165, 173, 178, 183, 193, 201, 210, 257, 270, 279, 293, 298, 301, 309, 341, 347, 352, 363, 377, 382, 393, 415, 438, 451, 461, 466, 471, 487, 497, 505, 512, 521, 540, 545
8.4.8 Edit and proofread one's own writing, as well as that of others, using an editing checklist or set of rules, with specific examples of corrections of frequent errors.	9, 22, 25, 33, 41, 52, 55, 69, 75, 82, 85, 95, 107, 112, 115, 129, 137, 142, 145, 159, 165, 173, 178, 183, 201, 210, 257, 263, 270, 273, 285, 293, 298, 301, 317, 326, 329, 341, 352, 355, 363, 371, 382, 385, 393, 399, 412, 415, 421, 431, 441, 451, 455, 461, 471, 479, 497, 505, 512, 515, 521, 531, 545

ELA Academic Standards	Student Edition Pages
8.4.9 Revise writing for word choice; appropriate organization; consistent point of view; and transitions among paragraphs, passages, and ideas.	15, 22, 25, 33, 41, 47, 55, 61, 69, 75, 82, 85, 95, 103, 107, 125, 129, 137, 142, 145, 159, 165, 173, 193, 201, 210, 213, 257, 263, 270, 273, 279, 285, 293, 298, 317, 326, 329, 341, 355, 363, 371, 377, 393, 399, 403, 421, 431, 438, 441, 451, 466, 471, 479, 487, 497, 505, 512, 515, 521, 527, 531, 545

Standard 5

WRITING: Applications (Different Types of Writing and Their Characteristics)

At Grade 8, students continue to write narrative, expository (informational), persuasive, and descriptive essays (research reports of 700 to 1,000 words or more). Students are introduced to writing technical documents. Student writing demonstrates a command of Standard English and the research, organizational, and drafting strategies outlined in Standard 4—Writing Processes and Features. Writing demonstrates an awareness of the audience (intended reader) and purpose for writing.

In addition to producing the different writing forms introduced in earlier grades, such as letters, Grade 8 students use the writing strategies outlined in Standard 4—Writing Processes and Features to:

8.5.1 Write biographies, autobiographies, and short stories that: • tell about an incident, event, or situation, using well-chosen details. • reveal the significance of, or the writer's attitude about, the subject. • use narrative and descriptive strategies, including relevant dialogue, specific action, physical description, background description, and comparison or contrast of characters.	Students can write biographies after reading the *People in History* feature. 39, 80, 81, 102, 136, 164, 197, 267, 284, 322, 323, 346, 375, 392, 427, 437, 508, 509, 530
8.5.2 Write responses to literature that: • demonstrate careful reading and insight into interpretations. • connect response to the writer's techniques and to specific textual references. • make supported inferences about the effects of a literary work on its audience. • support statements with evidence from the text.	70–71, 130–131, 310–311, 404–405, 488–489
8.5.4 Write persuasive compositions that: • include a well-defined thesis that makes a clear and knowledgeable appeal. • present detailed evidence, examples, and reasoning to support effective arguments and emotional appeals. • provide details, reasons, and examples, arranging them effectively by anticipating and answering reader concerns and counterarguments.	15, 33, 41, 52, 75, 103, 125, 159, 193, 210, 263, 279, 317, 326, 347, 371, 403, 412, 421, 455, 461, 497, 521, 527
8.5.6 Write using precise word choices to make writing interesting and exact.	22, 25, 61, 82, 183, 213, 415, 466, 479, 512, 540

ELA Academic Standards	Student Edition Pages
8.5.7 Write for different purposes and to a specific audience or person, adjusting tone and style as necessary.	9, 15, 25, 33, 41, 47, 52, 55, 61, 69, 75, 85, 95, 103, 112, 115, 129, 137, 142, 159, 165, 173, 183, 193, 201, 213, 257, 263, 279, 285, 298, 301, 317, 329, 341, 352, 363, 377, 382, 385, 393, 412, 415, 421, 438, 441, 455, 466, 479, 487, 497, 512, 515, 521, 527, 531, 540

Standard 6
WRITING: English Language Conventions
Students write using Standard English conventions appropriate to this grade level.

Sentence Structure

8.6.1 Use correct and varied sentence types (simple, compound, complex, and compound-complex) and sentence openings to present a lively and effective personal style.	9, 22, 25, 33, 41, 47, 52, 61, 69, 75, 85, 95, 103, 107, 115, 129, 137, 142, 145, 159, 165, 173, 178, 183, 193, 210, 213, 257, 263, 270, 279, 285, 298, 309, 317, 326, 329, 347, 352, 355, 371, 377, 393, 399, 403, 415, 421, 431, 438, 441, 451, 455, 461, 471, 479, 487, 505, 512, 515, 521, 527, 540, 545
8.6.2 Identify and use parallelism (use consistent elements of grammar when compiling a list) in all writing to present items in a series and items juxtaposed for emphasis.	15, 33, 41, 52, 75, 103, 125, 159, 193, 210, 263, 279, 317, 326, 347, 371, 403, 412, 421, 455, 461, 497, 521, 527
8.6.3 Use subordination, coordination, noun phrases that function as adjectives (*These gestures—acts of friendship—were noticed but not appreciated.*), and other devices to indicate clearly the relationship between ideas.	9, 15, 22, 25, 41, 47, 52, 55, 61, 69, 75, 82, 85, 103, 107, 112, 115, 129, 137, 142, 159, 165, 173, 183, 193, 201, 213, 257, 263, 270, 279, 285, 298, 301, 309, 326, 329, 341, 347, 352, 355, 371, 377, 382, 385, 393, 399, 403, 412, 421, 431, 438, 451, 461, 466, 471, 479, 497, 505, 512, 515, 527, 531

ELA Academic Standards	Student Edition Pages
Grammar	
8.6.4 Edit written manuscripts to ensure that correct grammar is used.	9, 15, 22, 25, 47, 52, 55, 61, 69, 75, 95, 103, 112, 129, 137, 142, 145, 159, 165, 173, 178, 183, 193, 213, 257, 263, 279, 285, 298, 301, 326, 329, 341, 347, 355, 363, 371, 377, 385, 393, 399, 412, 415, 421, 431, 438, 451, 455, 461, 471, 479, 497, 512, 515, 521, 527, 540
Punctuation	
8.6.5 Use correct punctuation.	15, 22, 25, 33, 47, 52, 61, 69, 75, 82, 85, 95, 103, 107, 112, 115, 125, 137, 142, 145, 159, 165, 173, 178, 183, 201, 210, 257, 263, 273, 279, 293, 298, 301, 317, 326, 341, 347, 352, 355, 371, 377, 382, 385, 393, 399, 403, 412, 421, 438, 441, 455, 461, 466, 479, 487, 497, 505, 512, 521, 527, 540, 545
Capitalization	
8.6.6 Use correct capitalization.	9, 22, 25, 33, 41, 55, 61, 69, 75, 82, 85, 95, 103, 107, 125, 129, 137, 145, 159, 165, 173, 178, 183, 193, 201, 213, 257, 263, 270, 279, 285, 293, 298, 309, 317, 326, 329, 341, 347, 352, 355, 371, 377, 385, 393, 399, 403, 415, 421, 431, 441, 455, 461, 471, 479, 497, 512, 515, 521, 527, 531, 540, 545

ELA Academic Standards	Student Edition Pages
Spelling	
8.6.7 Use correct spelling conventions.	9, 15, 25, 33, 41, 47, 52, 55, 61, 69, 75, 82, 85, 103, 107, 112, 115, 125, 129, 137, 142, 145, 165, 173, 178, 193, 201, 210, 213, 263, 270, 273, 285, 293, 298, 301, 309, 326, 329, 341, 355, 363, 371, 377, 382, 393, 399, 412, 415, 421, 431, 438, 451, 461, 466, 479, 487, 497, 505, 515, 521, 527, 540
Standard 7 **LISTENING AND SPEAKING: Skills, Strategies, and Applications** *Students deliver focused, coherent presentations that convey ideas clearly and relate to the background and interests of the audience. They evaluate the content of oral communication. Students deliver well-organized formal presentations using traditional speech strategies, including narration, exposition, persuasion, and description. Students use the same Standard English conventions for oral speech that they use in their writing.*	
Organization and Delivery of Oral Communication	
8.7.2 Match the message, vocabulary, voice modulation (changes in tone), expression, and tone to the audience and purpose.	Students can present their writing. 9, 22, 25, 33, 41, 52, 55, 61, 69, 75, 82, 85, 95, 107, 112, 125, 129, 137, 142, 159, 165, 178, 183, 193, 201, 213, 257, 263, 273, 279, 285, 293, 298, 301, 317, 326, 329, 341, 347, 363, 371, 377, 382, 393, 399, 403, 421, 431, 438, 441, 451, 455, 461, 471, 479, 487, 497, 505, 512, 515, 521, 531, 545
8.7.3 Outline the organization of a speech, including an introduction; transitions, previews, and summaries; a logically developed body; and an effective conclusion.	Students can present their expository writing. 9, 47, 55, 85, 95, 107, 115, 142, 145, 178, 183, 201, 213, 223, 257, 273, 293, 298, 301, 329, 355, 385, 393, 438, 471, 487, 505, 531, 545

ELA Academic Standards	Student Edition Pages
8.7.4 **Use precise language, action verbs, sensory details, appropriate and colorful modifiers (***describing words, such as adverbs and adjectives***), and the active (***I recommend that you write drafts.***) rather than the passive voice (***The writing of drafts is recommended.***) in ways that enliven oral presentations.**	Students can present their descriptive writing. 22, 25, 61, 82, 183, 213, 415, 466, 479, 512, 540
8.7.5 **Use appropriate grammar, word choice, enunciation (clear speech), and pace (timing) during formal presentations.**	Students can present their compositions. 9, 15, 33, 41, 52, 55, 61, 69, 75, 95, 103, 115, 125, 129, 137, 145, 159, 165, 173, 193, 201, 210, 213, 257, 263, 279, 285, 293, 309, 317, 329, 341, 355, 363, 371, 377, 385, 393, 399, 412, 415, 421, 431, 441, 451, 455, 466, 479, 497, 505, 512, 515, 521, 527, 531, 545

Symbols of Indiana

State Flag

The Indiana flag, adopted in 1917, was the result of a statewide design competition. A flaming torch, representing liberty and enlightenment, is surrounded by 19 stars on a field of blue. The 13 stars in the outer circle represent the original 13 states of the United States. The five stars in the inner circle stand for the five states admitted to the Union prior to Indiana, while the largest star above the torch represents the state itself.

State Seal

With several previous designs, the official state seal was adopted by the Indiana General Assembly in 1963. The outer white border identifies the seal and the year—flanked by tulip tree leaves—that the first state constitution was enacted. The inner circle depicts a pioneer scene showing a woodsman, a bison, sycamore trees, the rolling hills of Indiana, and a beautiful sunset.

State Flower: Peony

The multicolored peony was chosen as the state flower of Indiana in 1957, replacing the zinnia. The peony, which blooms in late May and early June, appears in various shades of pink and red and also white. Grown widely across the state, the peony blossoms themselves are large and round and can appear in single or double blooms.

State Song: "On the Banks of the Wabash, Far Away"

The state song "On the Banks of the Wabash, Far Away," written by Indiana native Paul Dresser, was adopted by the state General Assembly in 1913. First published in 1897, the tune refers to Indianans' love of the land and of the Wabash River. The song's chorus states "Oh, the moonlight's fair tonight along the Wabash/From the fields there comes the breath of new mown hay/Through the sycamores the candle lights are gleaming/On the banks of the Wabash, far away."

State Bird: Cardinal

The popular cardinal was adopted as the state bird by the Indiana General Assembly in 1933. The male cardinal is easily recognizable because of his bright red color. The female cardinal is brown with red on her crest, wings, and tail. Indiana is home to the cardinal all year round, where they can be found nesting in thickets of brambles or low saplings.

State Tree: Tulip

The flowering tulip tree was adopted by the state General Assembly in 1931. Also known as the yellow poplar, this tall, stately tree grown statewide has distinctly shaped leaves that are featured on the state seal. The tree carries lovely yellow-green flowers in May or June, making it a popular addition to yards and parkways.

Indiana Counties

1. Lake
2. Porter
3. LaPorte
4. St. Joseph
5. Elkhart
6. Lagrange
7. Steuben
8. DeKalb
9. Noble
10. Kosciusko
11. Marshall
12. Starke
13. Jasper
14. Newton
15. Pulaski
16. Fulton
17. Whitley
18. Allen
19. Adams
20. Wells
21. Huntington
22. Wabash
23. Miami
24. Cass

25. White
26. Benton
27. Tippecanoe
28. Carroll
29. Howard
30. Grant
31. Blackford
32. Jay
33. Randolph
34. Delaware
35. Madison
36. Tipton
37. Clinton
38. Warren
39. Fountain
40. Montgomery
41. Boone
42. Hamilton
43. Henry
44. Wayne
45. Union
46. Fayette
47. Rush
48. Hancock

49. Marion
50. Hendricks
51. Putnam
52. Parke
53. Vermillion
54. Vigo
55. Clay
56. Owen
57. Morgan
58. Johnson
59. Shelby
60. Franklin
61. Decatur
62. Bartholomew
63. Brown
64. Monroe
65. Greene
66. Sullivan
67. Knox
68. Daviess
69. Martin
70. Lawrence
71. Jackson
72. Jennings

73. Ripley
74. Dearborn
75. Ohio
76. Switzerland
77. Jefferson
78. Scott
79. Washington
80. Orange
81. Dubois
82. Pike
83. Gibson
84. Posey
85. Vanderburgh
86. Warrick
87. Spencer
88. Perry
89. Crawford
90. Harrison
91. Floyd
92. Clark

0 50 kilometers
0 50 miles

Albers Equal Area projection

Indiana's People

Comparing the Population of Indiana and the United States

	Indiana	United States
Population, 2006	6,313,520	299,398,484
Population, percent change, 2000 to 2006	3.8%	6.4%
Persons under 18 years old	25.6%	24.8%
Persons 65 years old and over	12.4%	12.4%
Females	50.8%	50.7%
Males	49.2%	49.3%
Whites	88.6%	80.2%
African Americans	8.8%	12.8%
Persons of Hispanic or Latino origins	4.5%	14.4%
Native Americans	0.3%	0.2%
Asian Americans	1.2%	4.3%

Note: Data on race are from those reporting only one race.
Source: *American Community Survey*, U.S. Census Bureau.

Population 1900–2010

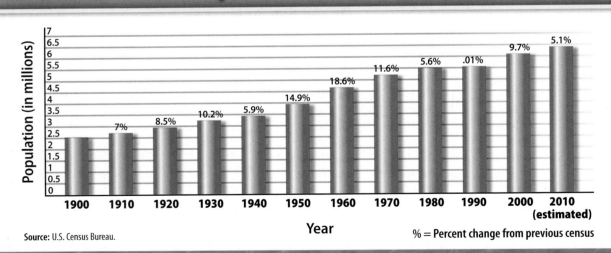

Source: U.S. Census Bureau.

% = Percent change from previous census

Indiana's Economy

Employment by Industry, 2006

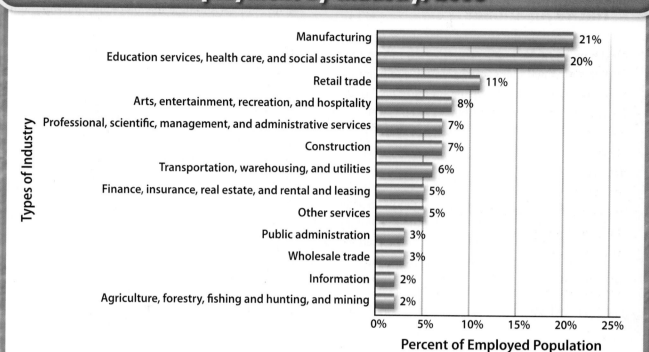

Types of Industry

Industry	Percent
Manufacturing	21%
Education services, health care, and social assistance	20%
Retail trade	11%
Arts, entertainment, recreation, and hospitality	8%
Professional, scientific, management, and administrative services	7%
Construction	7%
Transportation, warehousing, and utilities	6%
Finance, insurance, real estate, and rental and leasing	5%
Other services	5%
Public administration	3%
Wholesale trade	3%
Information	2%
Agriculture, forestry, fishing and hunting, and mining	2%

Percent of Employed Population Age 16 and Over

Source: American Community Survey, U.S. Census Bureau.

Indiana's Top 10 Leading Farm Products, 2006

Products	Value of receipts thousands $
Corn	1,851,472
Soybeans	1,519,780
Hogs	720,054
Dairy products	448,538
Cattle and calves	272,983
Turkeys	235,773
Chicken eggs	224,552
Greenhouse/nursery	169,700
Wheat	98,325
Hay	54,543

Source: U.S. Department of Agriculture.

Indiana's Employers by Number of Employees, 2004

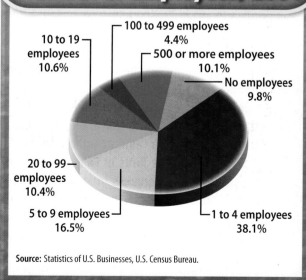

- 10 to 19 employees 10.6%
- 100 to 499 employees 4.4%
- 500 or more employees 10.1%
- No employees 9.8%
- 20 to 99 employees 10.4%
- 5 to 9 employees 16.5%
- 1 to 4 employees 38.1%

Source: Statistics of U.S. Businesses, U.S. Census Bureau.

A History of Indiana

Native Americans

The first people to settle Indiana probably came about 10,000 B.C. The term "B.C.," or before Christ, is used by historians to refer to the years before the birth of Jesus. The years after are "A.D." or *anno domini,* a Latin phrase meaning "in the year of the Lord." "B.C.E.," before common era, and "C.E.," common era, are often used instead of "B.C." and "A.D."

Beginning about 500 B.C., Native Americans known as Mound Builders lived in villages along the Ohio River in what is now southern Indiana. Here they built large earth mounds for their ceremonies. In the years following, other Native American groups, including the Miami, Delaware, and Shawnee, settled in the Indiana area.

Explorers, Traders, and Settlers

The first European explorer to reach Indiana was France's René-Robert Cavalier, Sieur de La Salle in 1679. He claimed the land for France and was followed by French fur traders who made contacts with the Native Americans. In 1763 France, defeated in war, gave up most of its North American lands to the British. Later, during the Revolutionary War, American officer George Rogers Clark defeated British forces in the Indiana area. In 1787 the war had ended and the new U.S. Congress passed the Northwest Ordinance. This law established the Northwest Territory that included present-day Indiana.

White settlers poured into the Northwest Territory, coming into conflict with Native Americans. In 1794 federal troops under General Anthony Wayne fought off Miami chief Little Turtle at Fallen Timbers in present-day Ohio. Congress then set up the Indiana Territory under General William Henry Harrison who later became a U.S. president. In 1811 Harrison defeated Shawnee chief Tecumseh at Tippecanoe. These victories ended the Native American attacks in the area, and opened more Indiana land to white settlers. Among these pioneers were Abraham Lincoln and his family from Kentucky.

Statehood

As more settlers arrived, Indiana Territory was split into several states. One of these states, Indiana, joined the Union in 1816. Meanwhile, Indiana farmers cleared forest land and raised corn, wheat, and livestock. New roads, canals, and railroads brought this farm produce to growing towns. Coal from Indiana mines provided fuel for factories that made machinery, clothes, and tools.

By 1850, Indiana residents had become known as "Hoosiers," a name which may have come from a pioneer greeting or from a description of workers. Like the rest of the nation, Hoosiers at this time were divided on the issue of slavery. However, when the Civil War broke out in 1861, Indiana sided with the North and sent about 200,000 men into battle for the Union cause.

An Industrial Economy

During the late 1800s, Indiana enjoyed an industrial boom. The discovery of natural gas and oil brought new companies that wanted to be near fuel sources. Standard Oil Company and the U.S. Steel Corporation both built large facilities along Indiana's Lake Michigan shoreline, making this area one of the nation's leading industrial centers.

During the early 1900s, many Hoosiers left their farms for jobs in city factories that made cars and machinery. Immigrants from eastern and southern Europe also found work in Indiana's industries. To demand better wages and working conditions, industrial workers joined labor unions. Indiana soon passed laws to shorten working hours, make factories safer, and set limits on child labor. Meanwhile, the new industrial society opened new educational and employment opportunities to Indiana women. Indianans such as Mary Wright Sewall, worked to gain women the right to vote as well as the right to control their money and property.

Economic downturns, such as the Great Depression, brought hardships to Indiana. The twentieth century's two world wars, however, boosted the economy of the state. Many social changes took place during wartime. For example, when the men went to war, Indiana women took over their jobs in the factories.

Modern Indiana

During the mid-1900s, machines increased farm production, while the number of farmers declined.

Most Hoosiers now lived and worked in cities, such as Indianapolis, Fort Wayne, Evansville, South Bend, and Gary. As in the rest of the nation, African Americans in Indiana called for equal rights. By the 1960s, more state laws protecting African American rights were passed.

Indiana went through great changes after the 1970s. At first, companies cut production and workers as a result of decreasing demand for factory-made goods. Beginning in the 1990s, however, conditions improved. Indiana businesses produced high-technology products, medications, vitamins, surgical supplies, aircraft engines, and transport vehicles. As the global economy expands in the 2000s, many Indiana products are increasingly sold in foreign countries.

Indiana's three major ports—at Portage, on Lake Michigan; and at Jeffersonville and Mt. Vernon on the Ohio River—contribute greatly to the state's economy. Over 70 million tons of waterborne cargo pass through Indiana each year.

REFERENCE ATLAS

NATIONAL GEOGRAPHIC

ATLAS KEY

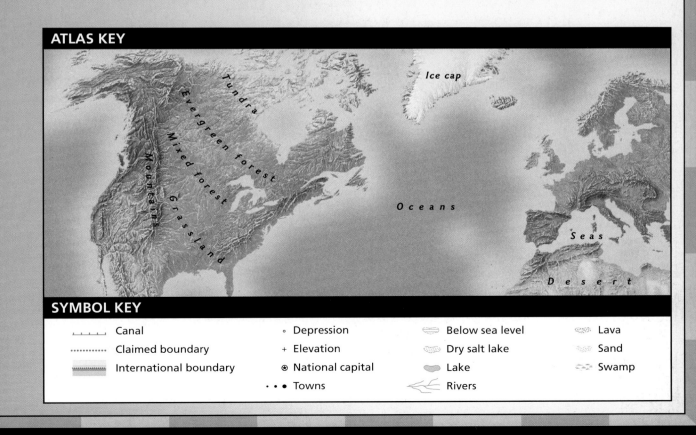

Tundra
Ice cap
Evergreen forest
Mixed forest
Mountains
Grassland
Oceans
Seas
Desert

SYMBOL KEY

⌊....⌋ Canal	○ Depression	🟰 Below sea level	🌊 Lava
.... Claimed boundary	+ Elevation	🟰 Dry salt lake	🟰 Sand
▓▓▓▓ International boundary	⊛ National capital	🟰 Lake	⌐⌐ Swamp
	• • ● Towns	≪ Rivers	

WORLD
POLITICAL

0 mi 2000
0 km 2000

WINKEL TRIPEL PROJECTION

NATIONAL
GEOGRAPHIC

ABBREVIATIONS

AUST.	AUSTRIA
B.&H.	BOSNIA & HERZEGOVINA
BELG.	BELGIUM
CROAT.	CROATIA
CZECH REP.	CZECH REPUBLIC
DEM. REP.	DEMOCRATIC
OF THE	REPUBLIC OF
CONGO	THE CONGO
EQ. GUINEA	EQUATORIAL GUINEA
EST.	ESTONIA
HUNG.	HUNGARY
LITH.	LITHUANIA
MACED.	MACEDONIA
MOLD.	MOLDOVA
NETH.	NETHERLANDS
SERB.	SERBIA
MONT.	MONTENEGRO
SLOV.	SLOVENIA
SWITZ.	SWITZERLAND
U.A.E.	UNITED ARAB EMIRATES

NORTH AMERICA
POLITICAL

0 mi   1000
0 km   1000

AZIMUTHAL EQUIDISTANT PROJECTION

NATIONAL GEOGRAPHIC

1. BAJA CALIFORNIA
2. BAJA CALIFORNIA SUR
3. SONORA
4. CHIHUAHUA
5. SINALOA
6. DURANGO
7. COAHUILA
8. NUEVO LEON
9. ZACATECAS
10. TAMAULIPAS
11. NAYARIT
12. AGUASCALIENTES
13. SAN LUIS POTOSI
14. JALISCO
15. GUANAJUATO
16. QUERETARO
17. HIDALGO
18. COLIMA
19. MICHOACAN
20. MEXICO
21. DISTRITO FEDERAL
22. TLAXCALA
23. MORELOS
24. PUEBLA
25. VERACRUZ
26. GUERRERO
27. OAXACA
28. TABASCO
29. CHIAPAS
30. CAMPECHE
31. QUINTANA ROO
32. YUCATAN

NORTH AMERICA
PHYSICAL

0 mi   1000
0 km   1000

AZIMUTHAL EQUIDISTANT PROJECTION

NATIONAL GEOGRAPHIC

ASIA

ARCTIC OCEAN

EUROPE

Chukchi Sea

Oodaaq Island

Lincoln Sea

Greenland Sea

Bering Sea

Point Barrow

North Magnetic Pole

Queen Elizabeth Islands

Ellesmere Island

GREENLAND

Gunnbjørn 12,139 ft 3,700 m

St. Lawrence Island

Seward Peninsula

Brooks Range

North Slope

Beaufort Sea

Melville Island

Hayes Peninsula

Nunivak Island

ALASKA

Mt. McKinley (Denali) 20,320 ft 6,194 m

Banks Island

Victoria Island

Prince of Wales I.

Devon I.

Somerset I.

Baffin Bay

Nuuk (Godthåb)

Bristol Bay

Kuskokwim

Alaska Range

Yukon

Mackenzie Mts.

Great Bear Lake

Boothia Peninsula

Melville Peninsula

Baffin Island

Davis Strait

Cape Farewell

Aleutian Range

Kenai Peninsula

Yukon Plateau

Foxe Basin

Kodiak I.

Gulf of Alaska 19,551 ft 5,959 m Mt. Logan

Coast Mountains

Mackenzie

Southampton Island

Hudson Strait

Ungava Bay

Labrador Sea

Alexander Archipelago

ROCKY

Great Slave Lake

CANADA

Queen Charlotte Islands

Peace

Slave

Athabasca

Hudson Bay

Belcher Islands

CANADIAN SHIELD

LABRADOR

PACIFIC

Vancouver Island

Fraser Plateau

Columbia Mts.

Lake Athabasca

Churchill

Nelson

James Bay

Island of Newfoundland

Avalon Peninsula

Olympic Peninsula

Columbia Plateau

Saskatchewan

Lake Winnipeg

Laurentian Mountains

Gaspé Pen.

Gulf of St. Lawrence

Cape Breton Island

Prince Edward Island

OCEAN

Cape Mendocino

Cascade Range

Snake

Missouri

Lake Superior

Ottawa

St. Lawrence

Nova Scotia

Bay of Fundy

Gulf of Maine

Cascade Range

Great Basin

Mt. Whitney 14,494 ft 4,418 m

MOUNTAINS

GREAT

Platte

Missouri

Lake Michigan

Lake Huron

L. Ontario

L. Erie

Washington

APPALACHIAN MOUNTAINS

Cape Cod

Long Island

ATLANTIC

Sierra Nevada

Colorado Plateau

Great Salt Lake

PLAINS

UNITED STATES

CENTRAL LOWLAND

Ohio

Chesapeake Bay

OCEAN

Death Valley -282 ft -86 m

Coast Ranges

Grand Canyon

High Plains

Arkansas

Ozark Plateau

Cape Hatteras

Bermuda Islands

Channel Islands

Sonoran Desert

California

Rio Grande

Red

Mississippi

COASTAL PLAIN

Florida

TROPIC OF CANCER

Baja California

Gulf of California

Sierra Madre Occidental

MEXICO

Gulf of Mexico

BAHAMAS

Florida Keys

Havana

CUBA

WEST

Virgin Islands

Guadeloupe

Orizaba 18,855 ft 5,747 m

Yucatan Peninsula

Cozumel Island

Cayman Islands

Greater Antilles

INDIES

Hispaniola

HAITI

DOMINICAN REPUBLIC

Puerto Rico

Martinique

Lesser Antilles

Mexico City

Sierra Madre Oriental

JAMAICA

Kingston

Caribbean Sea

Isthmus of Tehuantepec

BELIZE

Belmopan

Lesser Antilles

Trinidad

Gulf of Tehuantepec

GUATEMALA

Guatemala

San Salvador

EL SALVADOR

HONDURAS

Tegucigalpa

NICARAGUA

Managua

Lake Nicaragua

Isthmus of Panama

PANAMA

Panama

SOUTH AMERICA

COSTA RICA

San Jose

CENTRAL AMERICA

EQUATOR

1 130°W **2** 125°W 50°N **3** 120°W **4** 115°W **5** 110°W **6** 105°W **7** 100°W **8**

C · A · N

45°N

Cape Flattery
Mt. Olympus
7,965 ft
2,428 m
Seattle

Columbia

Missouri

C A S C A D E   R A N G E

C O L U M B I A

Blue Mts.

Clearwater Mts.

Bitterroot Range

R O C K Y

G R E A T

Black Hills

130°W
40°N

Cape Mendocino

Great Sandy Desert

P L A T E A U

Salmon River Mts.

Snake

Snake River Plain

Shoshone Falls

Absaroka Range

Bighorn Mts.

Wind River Range

Laramie Mts.

Missouri

N. Platte

Sand Hills

Platte

PACIFIC

S I E R R A   N E V A D A

Lake Tahoe

Central Valley

Great Salt Lake

G R E A T
B A S I N

Wasatch Range

Uinta Mts.

M O U N T A I N S

14,433 ft
4,399 m Mt. Elbert

Denver

35°N

OCEAN

San Francisco

Mt. Whitney
14,494 ft
4,418 m

Death Valley
-282 ft, -86 m

Lake Mead

Lake Powell

Colorado

San Juan Mts.

Sangre de Cristo Mts.

Arkansas

H i g h   P l a i n s

Point Conception

R A N G E S

Mojave Desert

Grand Canyon

Colorado Plateau

Red

Channel Islands

Salton Sea

Colorado

Sacramento Mts.

Llano Estacado

Dallas

San Diego

Los Angeles

Phoenix

Sonoran Desert

Rio Grande

Brazos

Edwards Plateau

30°N

125°W

120°W

115°W

Rio Grande

C O

Point Barrow

Beaufort Sea

ARCTIC OCEAN

Chukchi Sea

68°N

North Slope
Brooks Range

180°

RUSSIA

Bering Strait

ARCTIC CIRCLE

68°N

CANADA

110°W

25°N

Seward Pen.

St. Lawrence Island

A L A S K A

Yukon

Kuskokwim

Tanana

Alaska Range

Mt. McKinley (Denali)
20,320 ft, 6,194 m

172°W
60°N

Nunivak Island

Anchorage

60°N

M E X I C O

Bering Sea

Bristol Bay

Alaska Peninsula

Kodiak I.

Gulf of Alaska

Alexander Archipelago

105°W

52°N

TROPIC OF CANCER

100°W

ALASKA

0 mi   300
0 km   300

52°N

PACIFIC OCEAN

164°W **1** 156°W **2** 148°W **3** 140°W **4** 132°W **5** 105°W **6** 100°W **8**

UNITED STATES
PHYSICAL

0 mi   300
0 km   300

ALBERS CONIC EQUAL-AREA PROJECTION

NATIONAL GEOGRAPHIC

Lake of the Woods

Isle Royale
Lake Superior

Upper Peninsula

Minneapolis •

Mississippi

Milwaukee •

Lake Michigan

Lower Peninsula

Lake Huron

Chicago •

Detroit •
Lake Erie
• Cleveland

C E N T R A L
L O W L A N D

Pittsburgh •

• Indianapolis

Ohio

Wabash

St. Louis •

Flint Hills

Ozark Plateau

Boston Mts.
Memphis •

Ouachita Mts.

Tennessee

Mississippi

Cumberland

Appalachian Plateau
Cumberland Plateau
Allegheny Mts.

A P P A L A C H I A N   M O U N T A I N S

Blue Ridge

Mt. Mitchell
6,684 ft
2,037 m

Atlanta •

Savannah

Piedmont

Black Belt

Red

Lake Champlain

Adirondack Mts.

Green Mts.

White Mts.

Gulf of Maine

• Boston
Cape Cod

Connecticut

Hudson

Lake Ontario

Niagara Falls

Long Island

• New York City

• Philadelphia

Baltimore •
Delaware Bay
⊛ Washington

Chesapeake Bay

A T L A N T I C

O C E A N

Cape Hatteras

C O A S T A L

Houston •

New Orleans •

Mississippi River Delta

Jacksonville •

Cape Canaveral

Lake Okeechobee

The Everglades

• Miami

Gulf of Mexico

Florida Keys
Straits of Florida
TROPIC OF CANCER

CUBA

C A N A D A

N ↑

Hawaii inset

Niihau
Kauai
159°W
Oahu
Honolulu •
Molokai
156°W
Lanai
Kahoolawe
Maui — 21°N

Hawaii

Mauna Kea +
13,796 ft
4,205 m

P A C I F I C
O C E A N

PRINCIPAL HAWAIIAN ISLANDS

0 mi   100
0 km   100

90°W

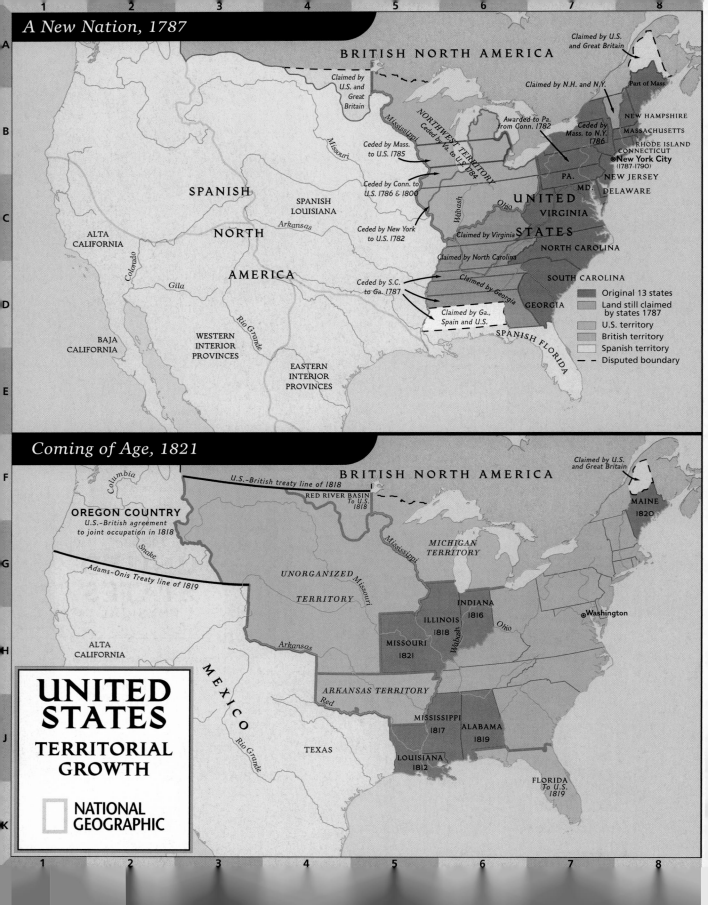

A New Nation, 1787

BRITISH NORTH AMERICA

Claimed by U.S. and Great Britain

Claimed by U.S. and Great Britain

Claimed by N.H. and N.Y.

Part of Mass.

NORTHWEST TERRITORY Ceded by Va. to U.S. 1784

Awarded to Pa. from Conn. 1782

Ceded by Mass. to U.S. 1785

Ceded by Mass. to N.Y. 1786

NEW HAMPSHIRE

MASSACHUSETTS

RHODE ISLAND
CONNECTICUT

New York City (1787-1790)

Ceded by Conn. to U.S. 1786 & 1800

Mississippi

Missouri

SPANISH

SPANISH LOUISIANA

Arkansas

Ceded by New York to U.S. 1782

PA.

Wabash

Ohio

NEW JERSEY

MD.

DELAWARE

NORTH

UNITED

VIRGINIA

STATES

ALTA
CALIFORNIA

Colorado

Gila

AMERICA

Claimed by Virginia

Claimed by North Carolina

NORTH CAROLINA

Ceded by S.C. to Ga. 1787

Claimed by Georgia

SOUTH CAROLINA

BAJA
CALIFORNIA

Rio Grande

WESTERN
INTERIOR
PROVINCES

EASTERN
INTERIOR
PROVINCES

Claimed by Ga., Spain and U.S.

GEORGIA

SPANISH FLORIDA

	Legend
	Original 13 states
	Land still claimed by states 1787
	U.S. territory
	British territory
	Spanish territory
- - -	Disputed boundary

Coming of Age, 1821

BRITISH NORTH AMERICA

Claimed by U.S. and Great Britain

Columbia

U.S.-British treaty line of 1818

RED RIVER BASIN
To U.S. 1818

MAINE
1820

OREGON COUNTRY
U.S.-British agreement to joint occupation in 1818

Snake

Adams-Onis Treaty line of 1819

UNORGANIZED

TERRITORY

Mississippi

Missouri

MICHIGAN
TERRITORY

INDIANA
1816

ILLINOIS
1818

Wabash

Ohio

Washington

ALTA
CALIFORNIA

MEXICO

MISSOURI
1821

Arkansas

ARKANSAS TERRITORY

Red

Rio Grande

TEXAS

MISSISSIPPI
1817

ALABAMA
1819

LOUISIANA
1812

FLORIDA
To U.S.
1819

UNITED STATES
TERRITORIAL GROWTH

NATIONAL GEOGRAPHIC

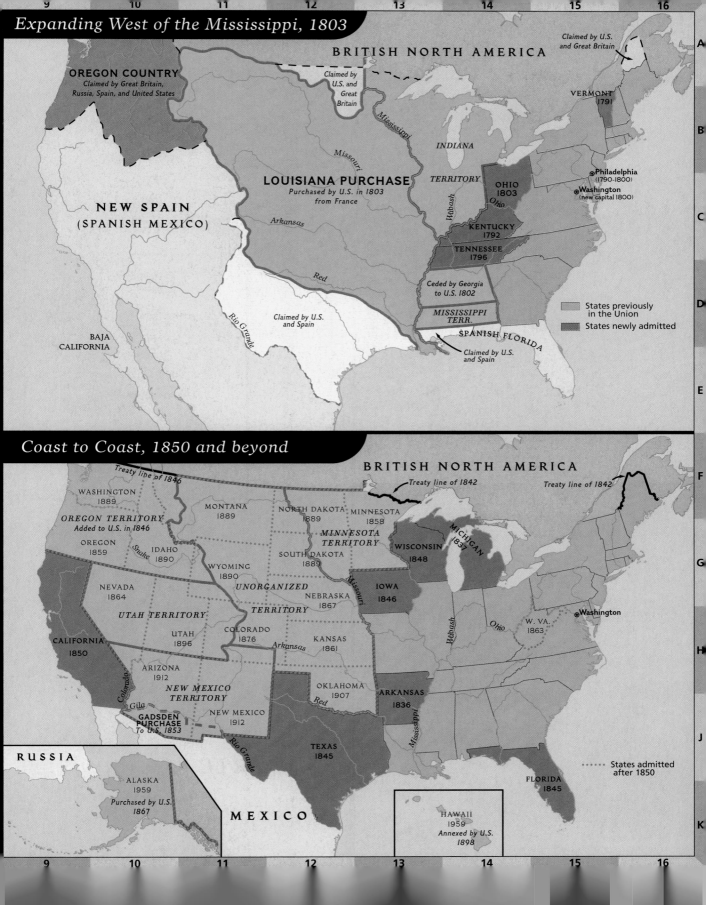

Expanding West of the Mississippi, 1803

BRITISH NORTH AMERICA

Claimed by U.S. and Great Britain

OREGON COUNTRY
Claimed by Great Britain, Russia, Spain, and United States

Claimed by U.S. and Great Britain

VERMONT 1791

NEW SPAIN (SPANISH MEXICO)

INDIANA TERRITORY

LOUISIANA PURCHASE
Purchased by U.S. in 1803 from France

Mississippi

Missouri

Arkansas

Red

Rio Grande

BAJA CALIFORNIA

Claimed by U.S. and Spain

OHIO 1803

Ohio

Wabash

KENTUCKY 1792

TENNESSEE 1796

Philadelphia (1790-1800)

Washington (new capital 1800)

Ceded by Georgia to U.S. 1802

MISSISSIPPI TERR.

SPANISH FLORIDA

Claimed by U.S. and Spain

States previously in the Union
States newly admitted

Coast to Coast, 1850 and beyond

Treaty line of 1846

BRITISH NORTH AMERICA

Treaty line of 1842

Treaty line of 1842

WASHINGTON 1889

OREGON TERRITORY
Added to U.S. in 1846

MONTANA 1889

NORTH DAKOTA 1889

MINNESOTA 1858

OREGON 1859

Snake

IDAHO 1890

MINNESOTA TERRITORY

WISCONSIN 1848

MICHIGAN 1837

NEVADA 1864

WYOMING 1890

SOUTH DAKOTA 1889

IOWA 1846

Missouri

UTAH TERRITORY

UNORGANIZED

NEBRASKA 1867

Wabash

Ohio

W. VA. 1863

Washington

CALIFORNIA 1850

UTAH 1896

COLORADO 1876

TERRITORY

KANSAS 1861

Arkansas

Colorado

ARIZONA 1912

NEW MEXICO TERRITORY

OKLAHOMA 1907

Red

ARKANSAS 1836

Mississippi

Gila

NEW MEXICO 1912

GADSDEN PURCHASE
To U.S. 1853

Rio Grande

TEXAS 1845

RUSSIA

ALASKA 1959
Purchased by U.S. 1867

MEXICO

States admitted after 1850

FLORIDA 1845

HAWAII 1959
Annexed by U.S. 1898

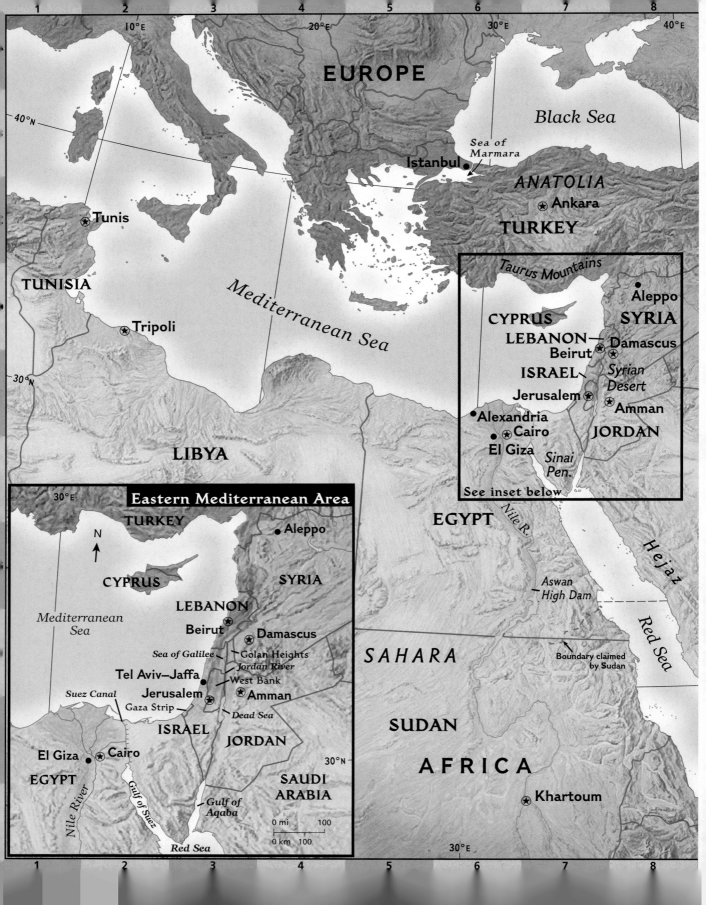

EUROPE

Black Sea

Sea of Marmara

Istanbul

ANATOLIA

⊛ Ankara

TURKEY

Taurus Mountains

CYPRUS

● Aleppo

SYRIA

LEBANON

Beirut ⊛ ⊛ Damascus

ISRAEL

Syrian Desert

Jerusalem ⊛

⊛ Amman

● Alexandria

● ⊛ Cairo

JORDAN

● El Giza

Sinai Pen.

See inset below

EGYPT

Nile R.

40°N

Mediterranean Sea

⊛ Tunis

TUNISIA

⊛ Tripoli

30°N

LIBYA

Hejaz

SAHARA

Red Sea

Aswan High Dam

Boundary claimed by Sudan

SUDAN

AFRICA

⊛ Khartoum

30°E

Eastern Mediterranean Area

30°E

N ↑

TURKEY

● Aleppo

CYPRUS

SYRIA

Mediterranean Sea

LEBANON

Beirut ⊛ ⊛ Damascus

Sea of Galilee — Golan Heights

Jordan River

Tel Aviv–Jaffa ● — West Bank

Jerusalem ⊛ ⊛ Amman

Suez Canal

Gaza Strip —

Dead Sea

ISRAEL

JORDAN

30°N

El Giza ● ⊛ Cairo

EGYPT

SAUDI ARABIA

Nile River

Gulf of Suez

Gulf of Aqaba

Red Sea

0 mi   100

0 km   100

MIDDLE EAST

PHYSICAL / POLITICAL

0 mi   500

0 km   500

AZIMUTHAL EQUIDISTANT PROJECTION

NATIONAL GEOGRAPHIC

United States Facts

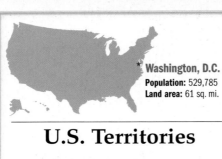

Washington, D.C.
Population: 529,785
Land area: 61 sq. mi.

U.S. Territories

Puerto Rico
Population: 3,987,837
Land area: 3,425 sq. mi.

Guam
Population: 180,692
Land area: 209 sq. mi.

U.S. Virgin Islands
Population: 107,560
Land area: 134 sq. mi.

American Samoa
Population: 57,066
Land area: 77 sq. mi.

The states are listed in the order they were admitted to the Union.

Population figures are based on the U.S. Bureau of the Census projections for July 2010. House of Representatives figures from the 2000 census are from the Clerk of the House of Representatives. States are not drawn to scale.

1 Delaware
Year Admitted: 1787
Population: 884,342
Land area: 1,955 sq. mi.
Representatives: 1
★ Dover

2 Pennsylvania
Year Admitted: 1787
Population: 12,584,487
Land area: 44,820 sq. mi.
Representatives: 19
Harrisburg ★

3 New Jersey
Year Admitted: 1787
Population: 9,018,231
Land area: 7,419 sq. mi.
Representatives: 13
Trenton ★

9 New Hampshire
Year Admitted: 1788
Population: 1,385,560
Land area: 8,969 sq. mi.
Representatives: 2
Concord ★

10 Virginia
Year Admitted: 1788
Population: 8,010,245
Land area: 39,598 sq. mi.
Representatives: 11
Richmond ★

11 New York
Year Admitted: 1788
Population: 19,443,672
Land area: 47,224 sq. mi.
Representatives: 29
★ Albany

17 Ohio
Year Admitted: 1803
Population: 11,576,181
Land area: 40,953 sq. mi.
Representatives: 18
★ Columbus

18 Louisiana
Year Admitted: 1812
Population: 4,612,679
Land area: 43,566 sq. mi.
Representatives: 7
★ Baton Rouge

19 Indiana
Year Admitted: 1816
Population: 6,392,139
Land area: 35,870 sq. mi.
Representatives: 9
Indianapolis ★

24 Missouri
Year Admitted: 1821
Population: 5,922,078
Land area: 68,898 sq. mi.
Representatives: 9
Jefferson City ★

25 Arkansas
Year Admitted: 1836
Population: 2,875,039
Land area: 52,075 sq. mi.
Representatives: 4
Little Rock ★

26 Michigan
Year Admitted: 1837
Population: 10,428,683
Land area: 56,809 sq. mi.
Representatives: 15
Lansing ★

27 Florida
Year Admitted: 1845
Population: 19,251,691
Land area: 53,997 sq. mi.
Representatives: 25
Tallahassee ★

28 Texas
Year Admitted: 1845
Population: 24,648,888
Land area: 261,914 sq. mi.
Representatives: 32
Austin ★

33 Oregon
Year Admitted: 1859
Population: 3,790,996
Land area: 96,003 sq. mi.
Representatives: 5
★ Salem

34 Kansas
Year Admitted: 1861
Population: 2,805,470
Land area: 81,823 sq. mi.
Representatives: 4
Topeka ★

35 West Virginia
Year Admitted: 1863
Population: 1,829,141
Land area: 24,087 sq. mi.
Representatives: 3
★ Charleston

36 Nevada
Year Admitted: 1864
Population: 2,690,531
Land area: 109,806 sq. mi.
Representatives: 3
★ Carson City

37 Nebraska
Year Admitted: 1867
Population: 1,768,997
Land area: 76,878 sq. mi.
Representatives: 3
Lincoln ★

42 Washington
Year Admitted: 1889
Population: 6,541,963
Land area: 66,582 sq. mi.
Representatives: 9
★ Olympia

43 Idaho
Year Admitted: 1890
Population: 1,517,291
Land area: 82,751 sq. mi.
Representatives: 2
★ Boise

44 Wyoming
Year Admitted: 1890
Population: 519,886
Land area: 97,105 sq. mi.
Representatives: 1
Cheyenne ★

45 Utah
Year Admitted: 1896
Population: 2,595,013
Land area: 82,168 sq. mi.
Representatives: 3
Salt Lake City ★

46 Oklahoma
Year Admitted: 1907
Population: 3,591,516
Land area: 68,679 sq. mi.
Representatives: 5
Oklahoma City ★

4 Georgia
Year Admitted: 1788
Population: 9,589,080
Land area: 57,919 sq. mi.
Representatives: 13

★ Atlanta

5 Connecticut
Year Admitted: 1788
Population: 3,577,490
Land area: 4,845 sq. mi.
Representatives: 5

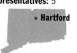
★ Hartford

6 Massachusetts
Year Admitted: 1788
Population: 6,649,441
Land area: 7,838 sq. mi.
Representatives: 10

Boston ★

7 Maryland
Year Admitted: 1788
Population: 5,904,970
Land area: 9,775 sq. mi.
Representatives: 8

Annapolis ★

8 South Carolina
Year Admitted: 1788
Population: 4,446,704
Land area: 30,111 sq. mi.
Representatives: 6

Columbia ★

12 North Carolina
Year Admitted: 1789
Population: 9,345,823
Land area: 48,718 sq. mi.
Representatives: 13

★ Raleigh

13 Rhode Island
Year Admitted: 1790
Population: 1,116,652
Land area: 1,045 sq. mi.
Representatives: 2

★ Providence

14 Vermont
Year Admitted: 1791
Population: 652,512
Land area: 9,249 sq. mi.
Representatives: 1

★ Montpelier

15 Kentucky
Year Admitted: 1792
Population: 4,265,117
Land area: 39,732 sq. mi.
Representatives: 6

Frankfort ★

16 Tennessee
Year Admitted: 1796
Population: 6,230,852
Land area: 41,220 sq. mi.
Representatives: 9

★ Nashville

20 Mississippi
Year Admitted: 1817
Population: 2,971,412
Land area: 46,914 sq. mi.
Representatives: 4

★ Jackson

21 Illinois
Year Admitted: 1818
Population: 12,916,894
Land area: 55,593 sq. mi.
Representatives: 19

★ Springfield

22 Alabama
Year Admitted: 1819
Population: 4,596,330
Land area: 50,750 sq. mi.
Representatives: 7

Montgomery
★

23 Maine
Year Admitted: 1820
Population: 1,357,134
Land area: 30,865 sq. mi.
Representatives: 2

★ Augusta

29 Iowa
Year Admitted: 1846
Population: 3,009,907
Land area: 55,875 sq. mi.
Representatives: 5

Des Moines
★

30 Wisconsin
Year Admitted: 1848
Population: 5,727,426
Land area: 54,314 sq. mi.
Representatives: 8

Madison
★

31 California
Year Admitted: 1850
Population: 38,067,134
Land area: 155,973 sq. mi.
Representatives: 53

★
Sacramento

32 Minnesota
Year Admitted: 1858
Population: 5,420,636
Land area: 79,617 sq. mi.
Representatives: 8

★
Saint Paul

38 Colorado
Year Admitted: 1876
Population: 4,831,554
Land area: 103,730 sq. mi.
Representatives: 7

Denver ★

39 North Dakota
Year Admitted: 1889
Population: 636,623
Land area: 68,994 sq. mi.
Representatives: 1

Bismarck
★

40 South Dakota
Year Admitted: 1889
Population: 786,399
Land area: 75,898 sq. mi.
Representatives: 1

Pierre
★

41 Montana
Year Admitted: 1889
Population: 968,598
Land area: 145,556 sq. mi.
Representatives: 1

★ Helena

47 New Mexico
Year Admitted: 1912
Population: 1,980,225
Land area: 121,365 sq. mi.
Representatives: 3

★
Santa Fe

48 Arizona
Year Admitted: 1912
Population: 6,637,381
Land area: 113,642 sq. mi.
Representatives: 8

Phoenix
★

49 Alaska
Year Admitted: 1959
Population: 694,109
Land area: 570,374 sq. mi.
Representatives: 1

Juneau ★

50 Hawaii
Year Admitted: 1959
Population: 1,340,674
Land area: 6,432 sq. mi.
Representatives: 2

Honolulu ★

Geography Skills Handbook

How Do I Study Geography?

Geographers have created these broad categories and standards as tools to help you understand the relationships among people, places, and environments.

- 🌐 5 Themes of Geography
- 🌐 6 Essential Elements
- 🌐 18 Geography Standards

5
Themes of Geography

1 Location

Location describes where something is. Absolute location describes a place's exact position on the Earth's surface. Relative location expresses where a place is in relation to another place.

2 Place

Place describes the physical and human characteristics that make a location unique.

3 Regions

Regions are areas that share common characteristics.

4 Movement

Movement explains how and why people and things move and are connected.

5 Human-Environment Interaction

Human-Environment Interaction describes the relationship between people and their environment.

6
Essential Elements

18
Geography Standards

I. The World in Spatial Terms
Geographers look to see where a place is located. Location acts as a starting point to answer "Where Is It?" The location of a place helps you orient yourself as to where you are.

1 How to use maps and other tools

2 How to use mental maps to organize information

3 How to analyze the spatial organization of people, places, and environments

II. Places and Regions
Place describes physical characteristics such as landforms, climate, and plant or animal life. It might also describe human characteristics, including language and way of life. Places can also be organized into regions. **Regions** are places united by one or more characteristics.

4 The physical and human characteristics of places

5 How people create regions to interpret Earth's complexity

6 How culture and experience influence people's perceptions of places and regions

III. Physical Systems
Geographers study how physical systems, such as hurricanes, volcanoes, and glaciers, shape the surface of the Earth. They also look at how plants and animals depend upon one another and their surroundings for their survival.

7 The physical processes that shape Earth's surface

8 The distribution of ecosystems on Earth's surface

9 The characteristics, distribution, and migration of human populations

IV. Human Systems
People shape the world in which they live. They settle in certain places but not in others. An ongoing theme in geography is the movement of people, ideas, and goods.

10 The complexity of Earth's cultural mosaics

11 The patterns and networks of economic interdependence

12 The patterns of human settlement

13 The forces of cooperation and conflict

14 How human actions modify the physical environment

V. Environment and Society
How does the relationship between people and their natural surroundings influence the way people live? Geographers study how people use the environment and how their actions affect the environment.

15 How physical systems affect human systems

16 The meaning, use, and distribution of resources

VI. The Uses of Geography
Knowledge of geography helps us understand the relationships among people, places, and environments over time. Applying geographic skills helps you understand the past and prepare for the future.

17 How to apply geography to interpret the past

18 How to apply geography to interpret the present and plan for the future

Globes and Maps

What Is a Globe? ▶

A **globe** is a round model of the Earth that shows its shape, lands, and directions as they truly relate to one another.

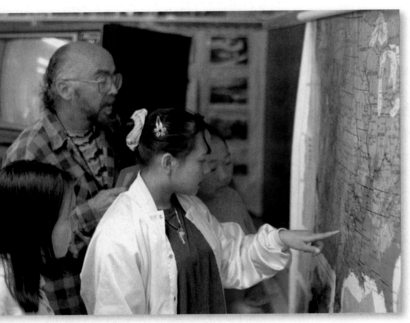

◀ What Is a Map?

A **map** is a flat drawing of all or part of the Earth's surface. Cartographers, or mapmakers, use mathematical formulas to transfer information from the round globe to a flat map.

Globes and Maps ▶

Globes and maps serve different purposes, and each has advantages and disadvantages.

	Advantages	Disadvantages
Globes	• Represent true land shape, distances, and directions	• Cannot show detailed information • Difficult to carry
Maps	• Show small areas in great detail • Display different types of information, such as population densities or natural resources • Transport easily	• Distort, or change, the accuracy of shapes and distances

Map Projections

When the Earth's surface is flattened on a map, big gaps open up. Mapmakers stretch parts of the Earth to show either the correct shapes of places or their correct sizes. Mapmakers have developed different projections, or ways of showing the Earth on a flat piece of paper. Below are different map projections.

Goode's Interrupted Equal-Area Projection ▼

A map with this projection shows continents close to their true shapes and sizes. This projection is helpful to compare land area among continents.

Robinson Projection ▼

The Robinson projection has minor distortions. Continents and oceans are close to their sizes and shapes, but the North and South Poles appear flattened.

Mercator Projection ▼

The Mercator projection shows land shapes fairly accurately but not size or distance. Areas that are located far from the Equator are quite distorted. The Mercator projection shows true directions, however, making it useful for sea travel.

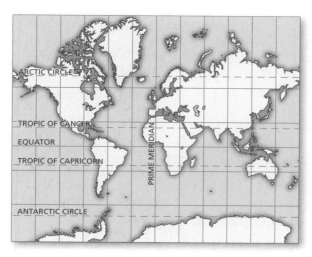

Winkel Tripel Projection ▼

This projection gives a good overall view of the continents' shapes and sizes. Land areas are not as distorted near the poles as they are in the Robinson projection.

Skills Practice

1 **Comparing and Contrasting** Explain the similarities and differences between globes and maps.

2 **Describing** Why do map projections distort some parts of the Earth?

Location

To locate places on Earth, geographers use a system of imaginary lines that crisscross the globe. These lines are called *latitude* and *longitude.*

Latitude ▶

- Lines of **latitude** are imaginary circles that run east to west around the globe. They are known as *parallels*. These parallels divide the globe into units called degrees.

- The **Equator** circles the middle of the Earth like a belt. It is located halfway between the North and South Poles. The Equator is 0° latitude.

- The letter *N* or *S* that follows the degree symbol tells you if the location is north or south of the Equator. The North Pole, for example, is 90°N (north) latitude, and the South Pole is 90°S (south) latitude.

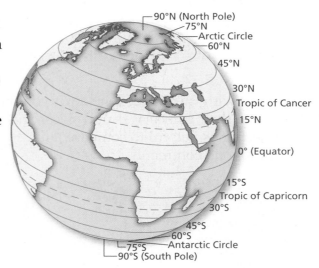

◀ Longitude

- Lines of **longitude,** also known as *meridians*, run from the North Pole to the South Pole. The **Prime Meridian** (also called the Meridian of Greenwich) is 0° longitude and runs through Greenwich, England.

- The letter *E* or *W* that follows the degree symbol tells you if the location is east or west of the Prime Meridian.

- On the opposite side of the Earth is the 180° meridian, also known as the International Date Line.

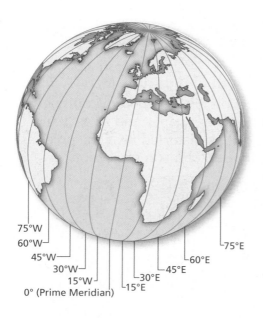

Absolute Location ▶

A place's exact location can be identified when you use both latitude and longitude. For example, Tokyo, Japan, is 36°N latitude and 140°E longitude.

Hemispheres

The Equator divides the Earth into Northern and Southern Hemispheres. Everything north of the Equator is in the Northern Hemisphere. Everything south of the Equator is in the Southern Hemisphere.

Northern Hemisphere   **Southern Hemisphere**

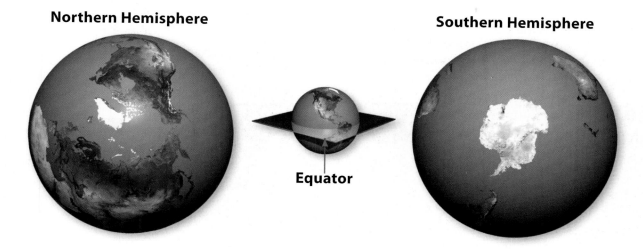

Equator

The Prime Meridian divides the Earth into Eastern and Western Hemispheres. Everything east of the Prime Meridian for 180 degrees is in the Eastern Hemisphere. Everything west of the Prime Meridian for 180 degrees is in the Western Hemisphere.

Western Hemisphere   **Eastern Hemisphere**

Prime Meridian

Skills Practice

1 Identifying What country is located at 30°S and 120°E?

2 Analyzing Visuals In which hemispheres is Europe located?

Parts of a Map

In addition to latitude and longitude, maps feature other important tools to help you interpret the information they contain.

Title
The title tells you what information the map is showing.

Cities
Cities are symbolized by a solid circle (●). This symbol is found in the key and on the map.

World War II in Europe and Africa

Boundary Lines
Boundary lines show the extent of an area's territory or political influence.

Compass Rose
The compass rose is a symbol that tells you where the cardinal directions—north, south, east, and west—are positioned.

Key
The key explains the symbols, colors, and lines on the map. The key is also called a *legend*.

Scale Bar
A measuring line, often called a scale bar, helps you figure distance on the map. The map scale shows the relationship between map measurements and actual distances on the Earth.

Capitals
Capitals are symbolized by a star (✪). This symbol is found in the key and on the map.

Map labels:
20°W, 10°W, 60°N, 0°, 20°E, 50°N

NORWAY, SWEDEN, FINLAND, Leningrad, ESTONIA, Moscow, North Sea, LATVIA, IRELAND, UNITED KINGDOM, DENMARK, LITHUANIA, Baltic Sea, SOVIET UNION, London, NETH., Berlin, Warsaw, Dunkirk, BELG., GERMANY, POLAND, Stalingrad, Paris, CZECH., FRANCE, SWITZ., Vienna, HUNGARY, ROMANIA, ITALY, YUGOSLAVIA, Black Sea, Rome, BULGARIA, Naples, ALBANIA, GREECE, TURKEY, Sicily, SYRIA, MOROCCO, Crete, LEBANON, ALGERIA, TUNISIA, Mediterranean Sea, PALESTINE, TRANS-JORDAN, El Alamein, Cairo, LIBYA, EGYPT, Red Sea, PORT.

Key:
- Major Axis powers
- Greatest extent of Axis control
- Allied or Ally-controlled
- Neutral nations

0 400 kilometers
0 400 miles
Lambert Azimuthal Equal-Area

Using Scale

All maps are drawn to a certain scale. The scale of a map is the size of the map compared to the size of the actual land surface. Thus, the scale of a map varies with the size of the area shown.

Small-Scale Maps ▼

A small-scale map like this shows a large land area but little detail.

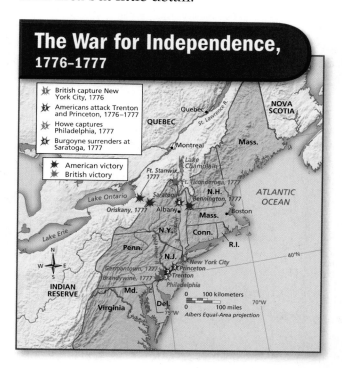

The War for Independence, 1776–1777

Large-Scale Maps ▼

A large-scale map like this shows a small land area with a great amount of detail.

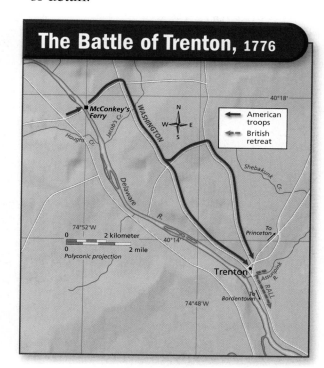

The Battle of Trenton, 1776

How Do I Use a Scale Bar?

A scale bar helps you determine actual distances that are represented on a map. First, measure the distance between two points on a map with a ruler. Then, check your measurement against the scale bar to find out how many kilometers or miles are represented by that length.

```
0    300 kilometers
0         300 miles
```

On the scale bar above, about ½ of an inch equals 300 miles. A little more than ½ of a centimeter is equal to 300 kilometers.

Skills Practice

1 **Defining** What is scale?

2 **Contrasting** What is the difference between a small-scale map and a large-scale map?

3 **Identifying** What are the four cardinal directions?

4 **Describing** Would you use a small-scale or a large-scale map to plan a car trip across the United States? Why?

Types of Maps

General Purpose Maps

Maps are amazingly useful tools. You can use them to show information and to make connections between seemingly unrelated topics. Geographers use many different types of maps. Maps that show a wide range of information about an area are called **general purpose maps.** Two of the most common general purpose maps are physical maps and political maps.

Physical Maps ▼

Physical maps call out landforms and water features. The map key explains what each color and symbol stands for.

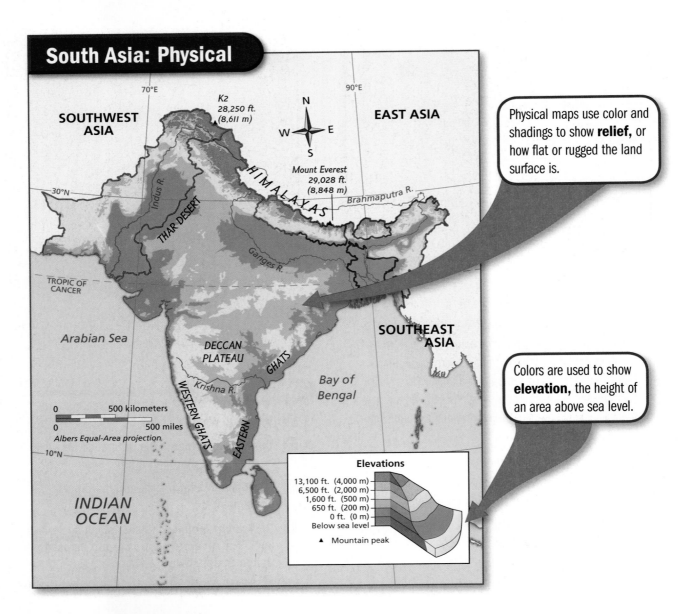

South Asia: Physical

SOUTHWEST ASIA

K2
28,250 ft.
(8,611 m)

EAST ASIA

Physical maps use color and shadings to show **relief,** or how flat or rugged the land surface is.

Mount Everest
29,028 ft.
(8,848 m)

HIMALAYAS

Indus R.

Brahmaputra R.

30°N

THAR DESERT

70°E

90°E

Ganges R.

TROPIC OF CANCER

Arabian Sea

DECCAN PLATEAU

GHATS

Krishna R.

WESTERN GHATS

EASTERN

Bay of Bengal

SOUTHEAST ASIA

Colors are used to show **elevation,** the height of an area above sea level.

0   500 kilometers
0   500 miles
Albers Equal-Area projection

10°N

INDIAN OCEAN

Elevations

13,100 ft. (4,000 m)
6,500 ft. (2,000 m)
1,600 ft. (500 m)
650 ft. (200 m)
0 ft. (0 m)
Below sea level

▲ Mountain peak

Political Maps ▼

Political maps show the names and political boundaries of states and countries, along with human-made features such as cities or transportation routes.

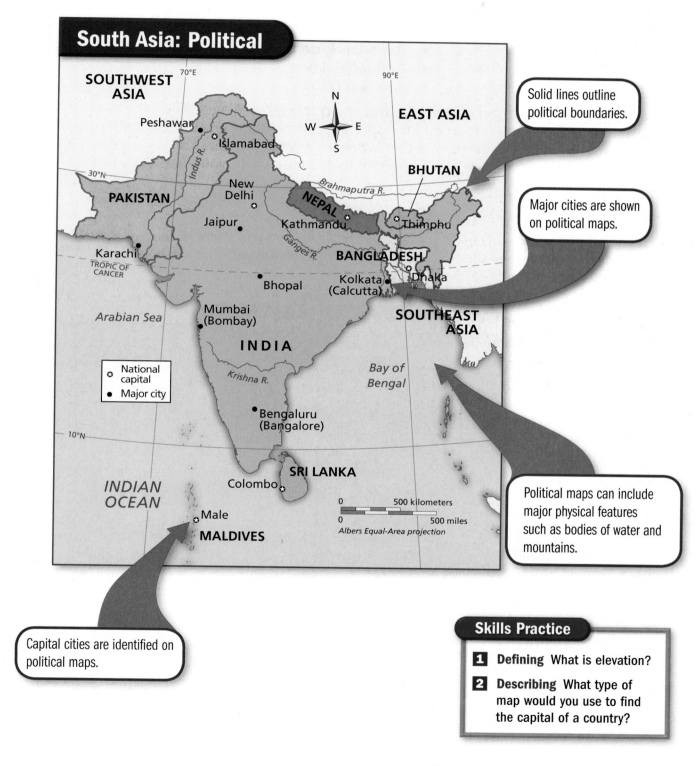

South Asia: Political

Solid lines outline political boundaries.

Major cities are shown on political maps.

Political maps can include major physical features such as bodies of water and mountains.

Capital cities are identified on political maps.

Skills Practice

1 Defining What is elevation?

2 Describing What type of map would you use to find the capital of a country?

Geography Skills Handbook   Ref 25

Types of Maps
Special Purpose Maps

Some maps are made to present specific types of information. These are called **thematic** or **special purpose maps.** These maps usually show specific topics in detail. Special purpose maps may include information about:

- climate
- historical expansion
- natural resources
- population density
- military battles
- election results

Look at some of the types of special purpose maps on these pages. The map's title is especially important for a special purpose map because it tells you the type of information that is being presented. Colors and symbols in the map key are also important tools to use when you read these types of maps.

Historical Maps ▼

Historical maps show events that occurred in a region over time. On the map below, you can see the extent of the United States in 1803 and what other parts of the continent were being explored.

Population Density Maps ▶

Population is not evenly spread across the usable land. Population density is the average number of people that live in a square mile or square kilometer. Population density maps use colors that are explained in a key to indicate how many people live in a given area.

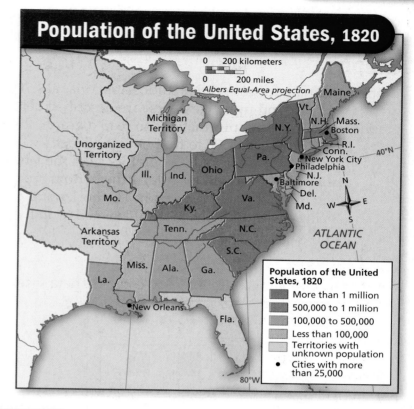

Population of the United States, 1820

0 — 200 kilometers
0 — 200 miles
Albers Equal-Area projection

Maine
Vt.
N.H.
Mass.
Boston
Michigan Territory
N.Y.
R.I.
Conn.
40°N
Unorganized Territory
Pa.
New York City
Philadelphia
N.J.
Baltimore
Del.
Ill.
Ind.
Ohio
Md.
Mo.
Va.
Ky.
ATLANTIC OCEAN
Arkansas Territory
Tenn.
N.C.
S.C.
Miss.
Ala.
Ga.
La.
New Orleans
Fla.
80°W

Population of the United States, 1820
- More than 1 million
- 500,000 to 1 million
- 100,000 to 500,000
- Less than 100,000
- Territories with unknown population
- • Cities with more than 25,000

The Battle of Gettysburg, Day 3

Gettysburg
General Lee
Seminary Ridge
Willoughby Run
Pitzer's Run
Pickett's Charge
Cemetery Hill
Culp's Hill
Rock
Cemetery Ridge
General Meade
Plum Run
Creek
Little Round Top
Big Round Top

— Confederate troops
— Union troops
← Confederate troop movements

0 — 1 kilometer
0 — 1 mile
Albers Equal-Area projection

◄ Military Maps

Military maps show the areas where battles occurred, troop movements, who controlled various sites, and who won the battles. Color-coded arrows and symbols shown in the key help you determine the sequence of events. It is also important to notice the geographical features near the battle site and how they could affect military strategy. On larger military maps, battle sites are often symbolized by a burst shell or a star.

Skills Practice

1 Identifying What type of special purpose map might show battles during World War II?

2 Contrasting What is the difference between a general purpose map and a special purpose map?

Graphs, Charts, and Diagrams

Graphs

Graphs present and summarize information visually. The types of graphs you will find in this textbook are described below. Each part of a graph provides useful information. To read a graph, follow these steps:

- Read the graph's title to find out its subject.
- To understand bar and line graphs, read the labels along the **axes**—the horizontal line along the bottom and the vertical line along the left side of the graph. The horizontal axis tells you what is being measured. The vertical axis tells you the unit of measurement being used.

Bar Graphs ▼

Bar graphs use bars or wide lines to compare data visually.

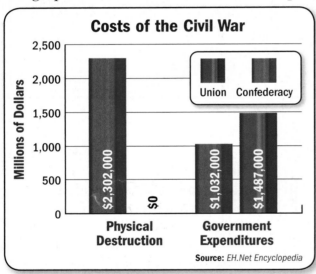

Costs of the Civil War

Source: *EH.Net Encyclopedia*

Circle Graphs ▼

You can use circle graphs when you want to show how the whole of something is divided into its parts. Because of their shape, circle graphs are often called *pie graphs*. Each slice represents a part or percentage of the whole pie. The complete circle represents a whole group—or 100 percent.

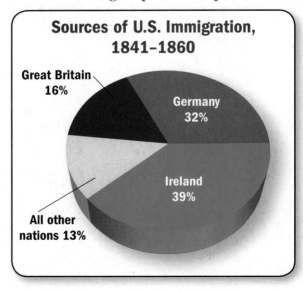

Sources of U.S. Immigration, 1841–1860

Great Britain 16%
Germany 32%
Ireland 39%
All other nations 13%

Line Graphs ▼

Line graphs help show changes over a period of time. The amounts being measured are plotted on the grid above each year and then are connected by a line.

Population of Virginia City, Nevada

*Estimate according to various Nevada historical sources.
Source: Nevada State Library and Archives, 2007

Charts

Charts present related facts and numbers in an organized way. One type of chart is a table. A table arranges data, especially numbers, in rows and columns for easy reference. Charts can also be used to summarize ideas or main points of broader topics. This allows you to review material and compare main ideas easily.

Army Salaries (monthly)

Rank	Civil War	World War II 1942	Vietnam War 1965	Iraq War 2007
Private	*$13	$50	$85	$1203 – 1543.20
Corporal	$14	$66	$210	$1699.50
Sergeant	$17	$78	$261	$1854 – 2339.10
Sergeant Major	$21	$138	$486	$4110

*Until 1864, African Americans in the Civil War were paid only $7.00 per month.

Source: *Bureau of Economic Analysis*; Princeton Review; www.militaryfactory.com

Diagrams

Diagrams are drawings that show steps in a process, point out the parts of an object, or explain how something works.

The USS *Maine*

1 **Torpedo tubes** are devices to launch torpedoes.
2 **Steam boilers** power the engines.
3 Munitions were stored in the **magazine**.
4 **Cowls** provided fresh air below deck.

Skills Practice

1 **Identifying** What percentage does the whole circle in a circle graph represent?

2 **Analyzing Information** What type of graph would best show the number of Republicans and Democrats in the U.S. House of Representatives?

Geographic Dictionary

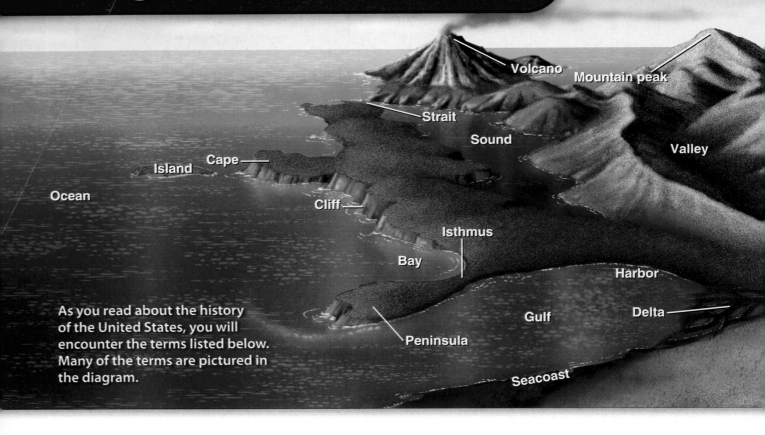

Volcano
Mountain peak
Strait
Sound
Valley
Island
Cape
Ocean
Cliff
Isthmus
Bay
Harbor
Peninsula
Gulf
Delta
Seacoast

As you read about the history of the United States, you will encounter the terms listed below. Many of the terms are pictured in the diagram.

absolute location exact location of a place on the Earth described by global coordinates

basin area of land drained by a given river and its branches; area of land surrounded by lands of higher elevations

bay part of a large body of water that extends into a shoreline, generally smaller than a gulf

canyon deep and narrow valley with steep walls

cape point of land that extends into a river, lake, or ocean

channel wide strait or waterway between two landmasses that lie close to each other; deep part of a river or other waterway

cliff steep, high wall of rock, earth, or ice

continent one of the seven large landmasses on the Earth

cultural feature characteristic that humans have created in a place, such as language, religion, housing, and settlement pattern

delta flat, low-lying land built up from soil carried downstream by a river and deposited at its mouth

divide stretch of high land that separates river systems

downstream direction in which a river or stream flows from its source to its mouth

elevation height of land above sea level

Equator imaginary line that runs around the Earth halfway between the North and South Poles; used as the starting point to measure degrees of north and south latitude

glacier large, thick body of slowly moving ice

gulf part of a large body of water that extends into a shoreline, generally larger and more deeply indented than a bay

harbor a sheltered place along a shoreline where ships can anchor safely

highland elevated land area such as a hill, mountain, or plateau

hill elevated land with sloping sides and rounded summit; generally smaller than a mountain

island land area, smaller than a continent, completely surrounded by water

isthmus narrow stretch of land connecting two larger land areas

lake a large inland body of water

latitude distance north or south of the Equator, measured in degrees

longitude distance east or west of the Prime Meridian, measured in degrees

lowland land, usually level, at a low elevation

map drawing of the Earth shown on a flat surface

meridian one of many lines on the global grid running from the North Pole to the South Pole; used to measure degrees of longitude

Mountain range

Source of river

Channel

Glacier

Highland

Lake

Plateau

Hills

Mouth of river

Canyon

Desert

River

Downstream   Upstream

Plain

Lowland

Basin

Tributary

mesa broad, flat-topped landform with steep sides; smaller than a plateau

mountain land with steep sides that rises sharply (1,000 feet or more) from surrounding land; generally larger and more rugged than a hill

mountain peak pointed top of a mountain

mountain range a series of connected mountains

mouth (of a river) place where a stream or river flows into a larger body of water

ocean one of the four major bodies of salt water that surround the continents

ocean current stream of either cold or warm water that moves in a definite direction through an ocean

parallel one of many lines on the global grid that circle the Earth north and south of the Equator; used to measure degrees of latitude

peninsula body of land jutting into a lake or ocean, surrounded on three sides by water

physical feature characteristic of a place occurring naturally, such as a landform, body of water, climate pattern, or resource

plain area of level land, usually at a low elevation and often covered with grasses

plateau large area of flat or rolling land at a high elevation, about 300 to 3,000 feet (90 to 900 m) high

Prime Meridian line of the global grid running from the North Pole to the South Pole at Greenwich, England; starting point for measuring degrees of east and west longitude

relief changes in elevation over a given area of land

river large natural stream of water that runs through land

sea large body of water completely surrounded by land

seacoast land lying next to a sea or ocean

sea level position on land level with surface of nearby ocean or sea

sound body of water between a coastline and one or more islands off the coast

source (of a river) place where a river or stream begins, often in highlands

strait narrow stretch of water joining two larger bodies of water

tributary small river or stream that flows into a larger river or stream; a branch of the river

upstream direction opposite the flow of a river; toward the source of a river or stream

valley area of low land between hills or mountains

volcano mountain created as ash or liquid rock erupts from inside the Earth

Unit 1

The Americas: Worlds Meet
Beginnings to 1770

Walnut carved Pilgrim bowl, 1608

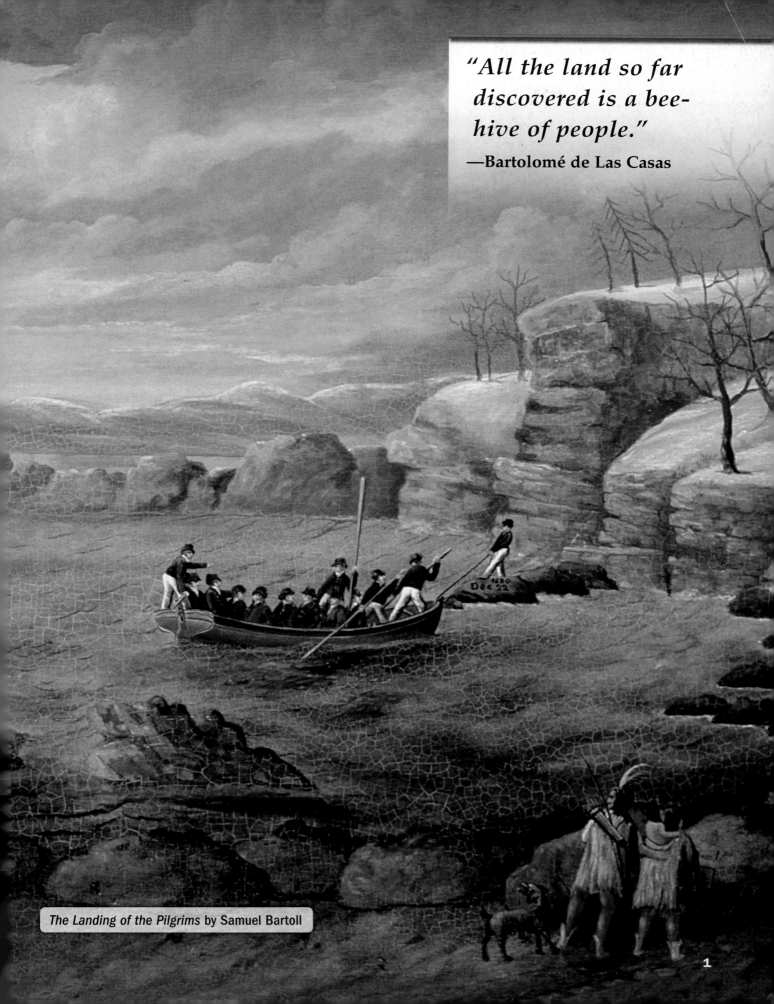

"All the land so far discovered is a bee-hive of people."
—Bartolomé de Las Casas

The Landing of the Pilgrims by Samuel Bartoll

Unit 1

Reading History

Identifying the Main Idea

Learn It!

Main ideas are the most important ideas in a paragraph, section, or chapter. Facts and examples that explain the main idea are the supporting details.

Main Idea
Maya traders transported goods along Mexico's coast.

Supporting Detail
The Maya traded many goods.

Supporting Detail
The traders visited a large area.

—from Chapter 1, p. 12

Maya traders also transported goods up and down Mexico's east coast. Their canoes carried jade statues, turquoise jewelry, cacao beans for making chocolate, and other goods to traders throughout a large area.

Practice It!

Read the paragraph and write the main idea and details on another sheet of paper.

—from Chapter 4, p. 89

Most people in New England lived in well-organized towns. The meetinghouse stood in the center of the town. This building was used for both church services and town meetings. The meetinghouse faced a piece of land called the *green* or *common*. Here cows grazed and the citizen army trained. Farmers lived in the town and worked in fields on its outskirts.

Main Idea
_____

Supporting Detail
_____
_____

Supporting Detail
_____
_____

Academic Vocabulary Preview

Listed below are the academic vocabulary words and their definitions that you will come across as you study Unit 1. Practice It! will help you study the words and definitions.

Academic Vocabulary	Definition	Practice It!
Chapter 1 The First Americans		
source (SAWRS) *p. 8*	to supply	**Identify** *the term from Chapter 1 that best completes the sentences.*
estimate (EHS · tuh · muht) *p. 9*	approximate number	**1.** Ancient civilizations created _____ systems for communication.
complex (KAHM · PLEHKS) *p. 11*	complicated; highly detailed	**2.** Scientific measures can provide an _____ on the age of artifacts.
link (LIHNK) *p. 13*	to join or connect	**3.** The Inca built paved roads to _____ outposts of their empire.
channel (CHA · nuhl) *p. 17*	a trench	
structure (STRUHK · chuhr) *p. 17*	a building	
Chapter 2 Exploring the Americas		
acquire (uh · KWYUHR) *p. 31*	to come into possession of	**Identify** *the term from Chapter 2 that best matches the underlined term or terms.*
impose (ihm · POHZ) *p. 32*	to establish or apply by authority	**4.** Some empires became wealthy after choosing to <u>establish</u> a tax on traded goods.
devote (dih · VOHT) *p. 39*	to give time, money, or effort to a cause	**5.** The <u>planet Earth</u> is divided into two hemispheres.
alter (AWL · tuhr) *p. 40*	to change	**6.** Europeans sailed to North America to <u>map</u> its coastline.
grant (GRANT) *p. 43*	special privilege	
found (FAUND) *p. 46*	to establish or set up	
globe (GLOHB) *p. 51*	the planet Earth	
chart (CHAHRT) *p. 51*	to map	
Chapter 3 Colonial America		
expand (ihk · SPAND) *p. 61*	to increase or grow	**Choose** *the word that best matches the meaning of each vocabulary term from Chapter 3 listed below.*
policy (PAH · luh · see) *p. 68*	a plan of action	**7. expand** **8. function**
ethnic (EHTH · nihk) *p. 74*	sharing a common culture	**a.** end **a.** operate
function (FUHNK · shuhn) *p. 75*	to operate	**b.** grow **b.** discuss
estate (ih · STAYT) *p. 77*	a piece of land	**c.** give **c.** provide
Chapter 4 Growth of the Thirteen Colonies		
rely (rih · LY) *p. 89*	to depend on	**Choose** *terms from Chapter 4 to complete the paragraph.*
principal (PRIHN · suh · puhl) *p. 93*	most important	Settlers in New England had to _____ on children to help grow food. In Southern Colonies, tobacco was a _____ crop. Farmers' _____ for success was greater in Southern Colonies due to a milder climate and rich soil.
successor (suhk · SEH · suhr) *p. 99*	one who follows another in order	
convert (kuhn · VUHRT) *p. 105*	to change religious beliefs	
design (dih · ZYN) *p. 106*	to plan	
prospect (PRAH · SPEHKT) *p. 110*	a chance for success	

The First Americans
Prehistory to 1492

Petroglyphs are carvings or inscriptions on rock. These petroglyphs in southern Utah were created by several cultures.

◄ Maya plaque

★ **c. 28,000 B.C.**
Asian hunters enter North America

★ **c. 1500 B.C.**
Olmec civilization develops in Mexico

★ **C. A.D. 700**
Maya Empire reaches its peak

C. A.D. 1000 ★
Leif Eriksson discovers Newfoundland

Americas

World

Prehistory

900

★ **c. 10,000 B.C.**
Last Ice Age ends

★ **c. 215 B.C.**
Great Wall of China built

Section 1: Migration to the Americas

Essential Question How did agriculture change the lives of early people?

Section 2: Cities and Empires

Essential Question How did the early civilizations of Mexico and Central America develop socially, politically, and economically?

Section 3: North American Peoples

Essential Question How was the way of life of the Native Americans of North America related to their environment?

History ONLINE
Chapter Overview Visit glencoe.com and click on **Chapter 1—Chapter Overviews** to preview chapter information.

Organizing Information
Make this Foldable to help organize what you learn about the first Americans.

Step 1 Fold a sheet of paper in half from side to side.

Step 2 Turn the paper and fold it into thirds. Cut the top layer only to make three equal tabs.

Step 3 Draw and label your Foldable as shown.

Reading and Writing On the front of the Foldable, diagram early migratory routes; label sites of the Mound Builders; show the empires of the Aztec, Inca, and other ancient civilizations; and include other visual information about the people of the Americas.

Aztec serpent ▶

▼ Anasazi mortar, A.D. 1200

★ **C. A.D. 1130**
Drought strikes Anasazi communities

C. A.D. 1300 ★
Hohokam civilization begins to decline

★ **A.D. 1325**
Aztec establish Tenochtitlán

★ **C. A.D. 1400**
Inca Empire begins to expand

1100

1300

1500

★ **A.D. 1095**
The Crusades begin

A.D. 1215 ★
England's King John signs Magna Carta

★ **A.D. 1312**
Mansa Mūsā begins rule of West African kingdom of Mali

★ **A.D. 1368**
Ming dynasty begins in China

Essential Question ◄

How did agriculture change the lives of early people?

Reading Guide

Content Vocabulary

archaeology *(p. 7)*   maize *(p. 9)*

artifact *(p. 7)*   carbon dating *(p. 9)*

nomad *(p. 8)*   culture *(p. 9)*

migration *(p. 8)*

Academic Vocabulary

source *(p. 8)*   estimate *(p. 9)*

Key People and Events

Ice Age *(p. 7)*

Reading Strategy

Taking Notes As you read, identify reasons early peoples migrated from place to place.

Reasons Early Peoples Migrated
1.
2.

American Diary

In 1974 at Meadowcroft, Pennsylvania, archaeologist James Adovasio and his team made an amazing discovery. Digging through soil and rock, they found fire pits, bones, shells, and stone tools. This evidence seemed to show that humans had been living there more than 14,000 years ago. For Adovasio, this "meant that people had been . . . in western Pennsylvania some four thousand years before any human being was supposed to have set foot anywhere in this hemisphere."

—*from* The First Americans

The Journey From Asia

Main Idea The first Americans were hunters and gatherers who came from Asia and spread throughout the Americas.

History and You Do you know if any prehistoric mammals, such as giant woolly mammoths or saber-toothed tigers, lived in your area? Read to find out why early peoples migrated to the Americas.

Recent archaeological finds such as those in Meadowcroft suggest that the first Americans arrived thousands of years ago, much earlier than once believed. By A.D. 1500, millions of Native Americans, belonging to more than 2,000 different groups, lived on the two continents of North America and South America.

When Europeans arrived in the Americas in the late 1400s, they found Native Americans living there. The Europeans wondered where these peoples had come from and how they happened to settle in the Americas. Some believed the Native Americans had come from Atlantis, an island that supposedly sank beneath the Atlantic Ocean.

Modern scientists are still trying to determine how the first people came to the Americas. Experts in **archaeology**, the study of ancient peoples, continue to piece together the story of the first Americans.

Archaeologists learn about the past from **artifacts**—the tools, weapons, baskets, and carvings of early peoples. Their discoveries show that many early peoples may have come across a land that later sank into the sea. This land was not the mythical Atlantis, however, but a strip of land called Beringia that once joined Asia and the Americas.

Crossing the Land Bridge

During its long history, Earth has gone through several ice ages. These are periods of extreme cold. Huge ice sheets, or glaciers, formed and covered much of Earth in the ice ages. The most recent **Ice Age** began 100,000 years ago and ended about 12,000 years ago. The lower sea level during this period exposed a strip of land that would have run from Siberia in northeastern Asia to what is now Alaska, the westernmost part of the Americas. That land bridge, Beringia, now lies under the Bering Strait.

If You Were There / Early Toolmakers

A Way to Survive As an early American, you moved from place to place in search of food and shelter. One of your most important advances was creating tools, which made hunting, gathering, building shelter, and making clothing much easier. You may have made tools from bone or antler. Most tools were made from stone. As technology advanced, you began making specific tools, such as food choppers, meat scrapers, and spear points.

Antler or bone tool found at Meadowcroft ▼

◄ Spear point from Meadowcroft

Early Americans left evidence of their culture at Meadowcroft Rockshelter, near Pittsburgh, Pennsylvania.

Critical Thinking

Making Inferences Why do you think you would have chosen stones to make tools?

Prehistoric Migrations to the Americas NATIONAL GEOGRAPHIC

◄ Prehistoric people may have come over the Bering Land Bridge. But they might also have arrived by boat, sailing along the eastern and western coasts of the Americas.

◄ Hunters learned to work together to bring down large animals.

Map Skills

Movement Along what major mountain ranges did the migration routes flow?

Searching for Hunting Grounds

The early Americans were **nomads,** people who moved from place to place. They ate grains and fruits but depended on hunting for much of their food. While on a hunt, they crossed Beringia into what is now Alaska and Canada.

The crossing of the land bridge was a **migration,** a movement of a large number of people into a new homeland. As the centuries passed, many people traveled from Asia either on foot across the land bridge or in boats. They spread out across the Americas, going as far east as the Atlantic Ocean and as far south as the tip of South America.

Hunting for Food

Native American legends tell of giant beasts that roamed Earth in ancient times. When the first Americans arrived from Asia, they did indeed find huge mammals. There were the saber-toothed tiger, the woolly mammoth, and the mastodon. The mammoth and mastodon resembled modern elephants in shape but had shaggy fur and long tusks.

Early Americans were skilled at hunting these beasts. Armed with spears, bands of hunters stalked herds of bison, mastodons, or mammoths and then charged at the animals, hurling their weapons. A single mammoth provided tons of meat, enough to feed a group of people for months. The hunters and their families used every part of the animal. They made the skin into clothing, carved the bones into weapons and tools, and may have used the long ribs to build shelters.

About 15,000 years ago, the Earth's temperatures began to rise. As the great glaciers melted and the oceans rose, Beringia was submerged again. The Americas were cut off from Asia. At the same time, the hunters of America faced a new challenge. The mammoths and other large animals began to die out, either from being overhunted or because of changes in the environment. Early Americans had to find other **sources,** or supplies, of food.

✔ **Reading Check** **Explaining** How do archaeologists learn about the past?

Settling Down

Main Idea Agriculture changed the way of life for early Americans.

History and You Think about the crops grown in your state or region. Read to find out about the foods that early Americans learned to grow.

• •

As the large animals disappeared, early Americans turned to other food sources. They hunted smaller game, caught fish, and gathered berries and grains. They also began to farm.

Planting Seeds and Farming

About 9,000 years ago, people living in what is now Mexico learned to plant and raise **maize,** an early form of corn. They also planted pumpkins, beans, and squash. Their harvests provided a steady, reliable source of food, so they no longer had to move from place to place. Farming also allowed people to spend time on activities other than finding food. This resulted in an improvement in the lives of early Americans.

Establishing Unique Cultures

Some early Americans remained nomadic hunters. Many others, however, knowing they would have a reliable food supply, began to settle down. Scientists have discovered villages that date from about 5,000 years ago. Using a method called **carbon dating,** scientists can measure the amount of radioactive carbon in an artifact made from bone or wood or another substance that was once alive. The amount of carbon provides an **estimate,** or approximate number, of the artifact's age.

The early Americans who settled down built permanent shelters from clay, stone, or wood. They made pottery and cloth. By studying and dating artifacts from these villages, scientists know that agriculture changed the lives of early Americans. These early Americans also developed common customs and beliefs. Over time, the groups of people living in the Americas developed their own **cultures,** or ways of life.

✔ **Reading Check** **Explaining** What is carbon dating? How does it work?

Section 1 Review

History ONLINE
Study Central™ To review this section, go to glencoe.com.

Vocabulary

1. Use each of these terms in a sentence that will help explain its meaning: archaeology, artifact, nomad, migration, source, maize, carbon dating, estimate, culture.

Main Ideas

2. **Explaining** How did early peoples arrive in the Americas?

3. **Describing** Describe the changes that early Americans underwent as the large animals disappeared.

Critical Thinking

4. **Determining Cause and Effect** How do you think the first Americans discovered that they could grow their own plants?

5. **Sequencing** Use a diagram like the one below to describe the sequence of events that resulted in the migration of nomads into North America from Asia.

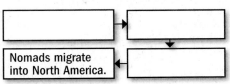

Nomads migrate into North America.

6. **Expository Writing** Write a short essay describing the elements of culture of the early Americans and the elements of culture for American society today.

Answer the
7. **Essential Question**
How did agriculture change the lives of early people?

Essential Question ◄

How did the early civilizations of Mexico and Central America develop socially, politically, and economically?

Reading Guide

Content Vocabulary

civilization (p. 11) Quechua (p. 15)
theocracy (p. 12) quipu (p. 15)
hieroglyphics (p. 12) terrace (p. 15)

Academic Vocabulary

complex (p. 11) link (p. 13)

Key People and Events

Olmec (p. 11)
Maya (p. 11)
Aztec (p. 13)
Inca (p. 14)

Reading Strategy

Taking Notes As you read, summarize the accomplishments of the Olmec, Maya, and Aztec.

Accomplishments
Olmec — Maya — Aztec

INDIANA ACADEMIC STANDARDS
United States History

8.4.1 Identify economic factors contributing to European exploration and colonization in North America, the American Revolution, and the drafting of the Constitution of the United States.

American Diary

Stories of "lost" cities led American explorer John Lloyd Stephens to southern Mexico in 1840. Stephens followed a steep mountain trail to a flat area covered with trees. Suddenly through openings in the trees, he "saw the front of a large building richly ornamented with . . . figures . . . curious and elegant." Stephens knew this palace had been built by a very advanced people.

—*from* Incidents of Travel in Central America Chiapas and Yucatán

The Maya built this great palace in the city of Palenque sometime during the A.D. 600s or 700s.

The Olmec, Maya, and Aztec

Main Idea The Olmec, Maya, and Aztec civilizations of Mexico and Central America flourished long before the arrival of Europeans.

History and You Do you use an electronic calendar to keep organized? Read to find out about the calendars and other accomplishments of early American civilizations.

. . . .

Stephens had come across the ruins of Palenque (puh•LEHNG•kay), an early Maya city. Although it was small, Palenque was an extraordinary place. Its structures, carved from the gray granite of the mountaintop, were wonders of design and craftsmanship.

Long before the Europeans arrived in the early 1500s, several great **civilizations,** or highly developed societies, arose in what is now Mexico and Central America. These civilizations built enormous cities in thick jungles and on mountaintops that were hard to reach. They also developed **complex,** or highly detailed, systems for writing, counting, and tracking time.

Among the largest and most advanced of these early civilizations were the Olmec, the Maya, and the Aztec. Each of these civilizations spread out over hundreds of miles, included millions of people, and thrived for several centuries.

The Olmec

The **Olmec** flourished between 1500 B.C. and 300 B.C. along the Gulf Coast of what are now Mexico, Guatemala, and Honduras. Olmec farmers produced enough food to sustain cities containing thousands of people. Olmec workers sculpted large stone monuments and built stone pavements and drainage systems. For reasons not fully understood, the Olmec civilization declined and then collapsed.

The Maya

The **Maya** built their civilization in the steamy rain forests of present-day Mexico, Guatemala, Honduras, and Belize. They planted maize, beans, sweet potatoes, and other vegetables to feed their large population, which may have reached 2 million people.

By the Numbers / Maya Mathematics

Number System The Maya used a system of dots and bars to represent their system of numbers. A dot represented a value of one, and a bar represented five. A shell-like figure stood for zero. To add two numbers together, the symbols for each number were combined to make a new single number.

5 + 6 = 11

Critical Thinking

Inferring What does a sophisticated counting system reveal about the interests of the Maya?

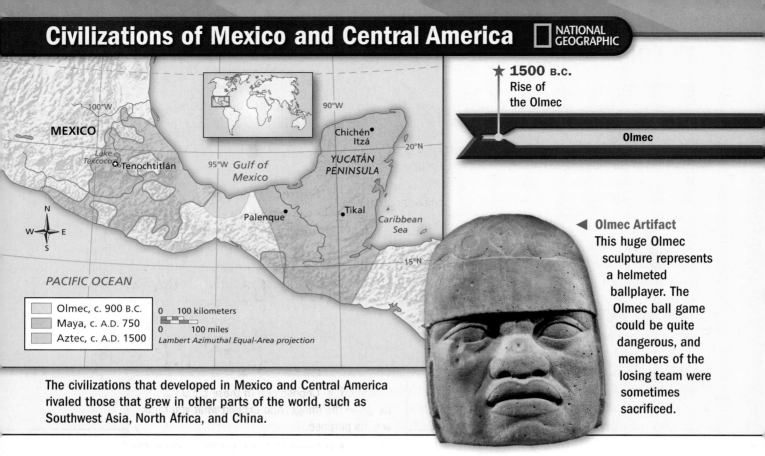

1500 B.C.
Rise of
the Olmec

Olmec

◀ **Olmec Artifact**
This huge Olmec sculpture represents a helmeted ballplayer. The Olmec ball game could be quite dangerous, and members of the losing team were sometimes sacrificed.

The civilizations that developed in Mexico and Central America rivaled those that grew in other parts of the world, such as Southwest Asia, North Africa, and China.

By A.D. 300, the Maya had built many large cities in the area. Each city had at least one stone pyramid. Some pyramids reached about 200 feet (61 m)—the height of a 20-story building. Steps ran up the pyramid sides to a temple on top.

The temples on top of the pyramids were religious and governmental centers. Here, priests performed rituals dedicated to the Maya gods. The Maya believed the gods controlled everything that happened on Earth. Because only priests knew the gods' wishes, the priests held great power in Maya society. Maya civilization was a **theocracy,** a society ruled by religious leaders.

Maya priests believed that the gods were visible in the stars, sun, and moon. They used their knowledge of astronomy to predict eclipses and to develop a 365-day calendar. Their desire to measure time increased their knowledge of mathematics. The Maya also developed a form of writing called **hieroglyphics.** Hieroglyphics uses symbols or pictures to represent things, ideas, and sounds.

Maya Transport and Trade

The Maya did not have wheeled vehicles or horses and carried goods overland on their backs. Maya traders traveled on a network of roads that were carved out of the jungle. Farmers brought maize and vegetables to outdoor markets in the cities and traded for cotton cloth, pottery, deer meat, and salt.

Maya traders also transported goods up and down Mexico's east coast. Their canoes carried jade statues, turquoise jewelry, cacao beans for making chocolate, and other goods to traders throughout a large area.

Decline of the Maya

Around A.D. 900, the Maya civilization in the lowlands began to decline. By 1100, the great cities were almost ghost towns. No one knows what caused the decline. Perhaps the soil became too exhausted by erosion and fire to produce enough food for the people.

History ONLINE
Student Web Activity Visit glencoe.com and complete the Chapter 1 Web Activity about the Maya.

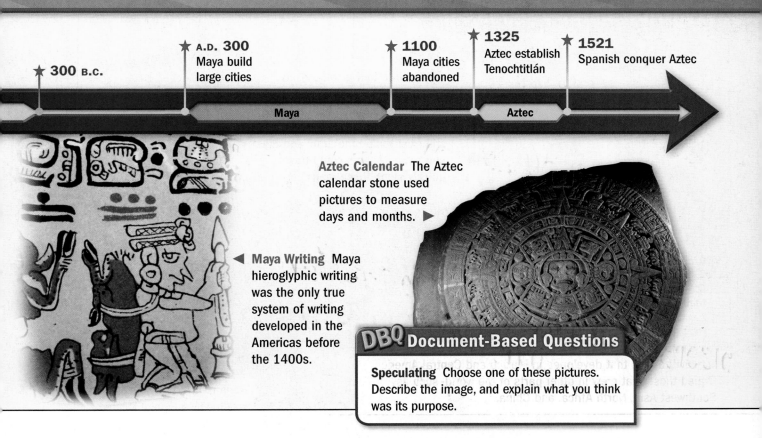

A.D. 300 Maya build large cities

300 B.C.

1100 Maya cities abandoned

1325 Aztec establish Tenochtitlán

1521 Spanish conquer Aztec

Maya

Aztec

Aztec Calendar The Aztec calendar stone used pictures to measure days and months. ▶

◀ **Maya Writing** Maya hieroglyphic writing was the only true system of writing developed in the Americas before the 1400s.

DBQ Document-Based Questions

Speculating Choose one of these pictures. Describe the image, and explain what you think was its purpose.

The Maya civilization collapsed, but descendants of the Maya still live in parts of Mexico and Central America today.

The Aztec

Centuries after the fall of the Maya, a group of hunters called the **Aztec** wandered through central Mexico, searching for a permanent home. In 1325 they came upon an island in Lake Texcoco (tehs•KOH•koh), today part of Mexico City. There the Aztec saw a sign: an eagle with a snake in its beak sitting on a cactus. According to Aztec legend, this sign from their god meant their journey had ended and that this island was to be their home.

Tenochtitlán

On this island emerged Tenochtitlán (tay•NAWCH•teet•LAHN), one of the greatest cities in the Americas. Its construction was a miracle of engineering and human labor. Directed by priests and nobles, workers toiled day and night. They pulled soil from the bottom of the lake to make causeways, or bridges

of earth, **linking**—or connecting—the island and the shore. They filled parts of the lake with earth so they could grow crops.

In time the Aztec capital expanded to the mainland around the lake. At its height Tenochtitlán was the largest city in the Americas and one of the largest in the world. Tenochtitlán was also a center of trade, attracting thousands of merchants to its outdoor marketplaces.

Aztec War and Religion

The Aztec civilization grew into a military empire. In the 1400s, the Aztec army marched through central and southern Mexico, conquering nearly all rival communities. Conquered people were forced to work as slaves in Aztec cities and villages.

Like the Maya, the Aztec organized their society around their religion. The Aztec believed that human sacrifices were necessary to keep the gods pleased and to ensure abundant harvests. They made sacrifices of thousands of prisoners of war.

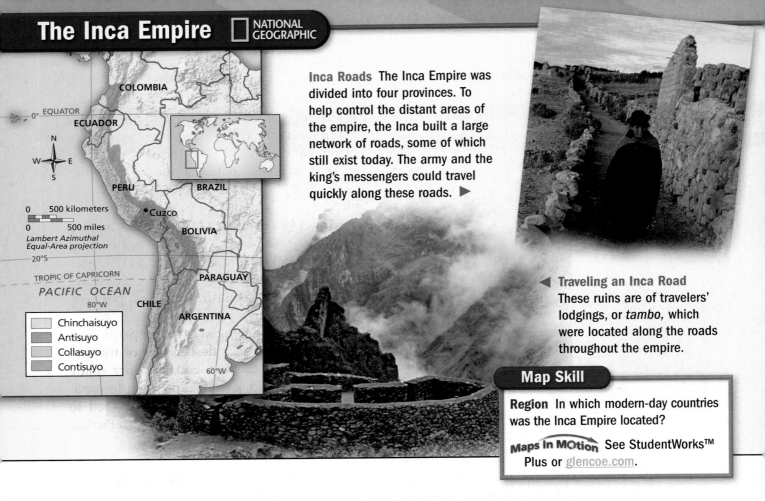

The Inca Empire

NATIONAL GEOGRAPHIC

Inca Roads The Inca Empire was divided into four provinces. To help control the distant areas of the empire, the Inca built a large network of roads, some of which still exist today. The army and the king's messengers could travel quickly along these roads. ▶

COLOMBIA
EQUATOR
ECUADOR
PERU
BRAZIL
Cuzco
0 500 kilometers
0 500 miles
Lambert Azimuthal Equal-Area projection
BOLIVIA
PACIFIC OCEAN
TROPIC OF CAPRICORN
PARAGUAY
80°W
CHILE
ARGENTINA
60°W

Chinchaisuyo
Antisuyo
Collasuyo
Contisuyo

◀ **Traveling an Inca Road**
These ruins are of travelers' lodgings, or *tambo*, which were located along the roads throughout the empire.

Map Skill

Region In which modern-day countries was the Inca Empire located?

Maps In Motion See StudentWorks™ Plus or glencoe.com.

A Great City Remembered

The first Europeans to see the Aztec capital were awed by its splendor. In 1519 Hernán Cortés led 550 Spanish soldiers into Tenochtitlán. Cortés wrote:

PRIMARY SOURCE

"There are forty towers at the least, all of stout construction and very lofty. . . . The workmanship both in wood and stone could not be bettered anywhere."
—Hernán Cortés, *Five Letters*

Bernal Díaz del Castillo, one of the soldiers, marveled at the "great stone towers and temples and buildings that rose straight up out of the water." Tenochtitlán, he explained, was a city of water. Some of the Spanish soldiers thought that Tenochtitlán was more magnificent than Rome and the other great European capitals of the time.

✔ Reading Check **Describing** Why was Tenochtitlán important?

The Inca

Main Idea The Inca in South America developed a well-organized empire with a structured society.

History and You How do you keep track of your school records? Read to learn about the Inca's record-keeping system.

• •

Another great American civilization developed in the western highlands of South America. The empire of the Inca was the largest of the early American civilizations.

Around 1200, the **Inca** people founded their capital city of Cuzco (KOOS•koh). In 1438 the Inca emperor named Pachacuti (PAH•chah•KOO•tee) came to the throne. Through conquest, Pachacuti and his son, Topa Inca, built a large empire. It stretched from north to south for more than 3,000 miles (4,828 km), from present-day Colombia to northern Argentina and Chile.

The Inca state was built on war, and the Inca army was powerful. All men between 25 and 50 years old could be drafted to serve in the army for up to five years. Their weapons included clubs, spears, and spiked copper balls on ropes. Using slings, Inca soldiers could throw stones 30 yards (27 m).

Residents of conquered areas who did not resist were allowed to participate in the growing empire's government. Those who resisted or rebelled were dealt with harshly. Many people preferred to accept the terms offered by the Inca rather than go to war with the powerful Inca armies.

Life in the Empire

At its height, the Inca Empire had a population of more than 9 million, including many conquered peoples. To control this large empire, the Inca built at least 10,000 miles (16,093 km) of stone-paved roads that ran over rugged mountains, across deserts, and through dense jungles. Rope bridges, made from grass, crossed deep canyons and rivers.

Runners carried messages to and from the emperor and linked, or connected, outposts of the empire to Cuzco. The Inca language, **Quechua** (KEH•chuh•wuh), became the official language for the entire empire.

Although the Inca did not have a system of writing, they developed a system of record keeping with string called **quipus** (KEE•poos). Using various lengths and colors of string knotted in special patterns, the quipus were used to record information about resources such as grain supplies.

To farm their mountainous lands, the Inca cut **terraces,** or broad platforms, into steep slopes. They built stone walls on the terraces to hold the soil and plants in place. Inca farmers grew maize, squash, tomatoes, peanuts, chili peppers, cotton, and potatoes.

All Inca land belonged to the emperor, who was believed to be a descendant of the sun god. To please the sun god, the Inca made magnificent gold jewelry and temple ornaments. The Inca also built cities devoted to religious ceremonies, including Machu Picchu, a site hidden high up in the Andes.

✔ **Reading Check** **Explaining** How did the Inca farm steep slopes?

Section 2 Review

History ONLINE
Study Central™ To review this section, go to glencoe.com.

Vocabulary

1. Write a short paragraph in which you use all of the following vocabulary terms: civilization, complex, theocracy, hieroglyphics, link, Quechua, quipu, terrace.

Main Ideas

2. Describing Describe the development of Tenochtitlán, and explain why the first Europeans to view the city were amazed by it.

3. Explaining How did the Inca build and govern their vast empire?

Critical Thinking

4. Making Inferences How does trade help enrich a civilization? Provide examples in your answer.

5. Categorizing Use a diagram like the one below to describe the role of religion in these early American civilizations.

6. Persuasive Writing Create a poster encouraging tourists to visit the ruins of an early American civilization. Use the images and text to describe the people and history of your chosen site.

Answer the
Essential Question

7. How did the early civilizations of Mexico and Central America develop socially, politically, and economically?

Essential Question ◄

How was the way of life of the Native Americans of North America related to their environment?

Reading Guide

Content Vocabulary

pueblo (p. 17)   clan (p. 22)
federation (p. 21)

Academic Vocabulary

channel (p. 17)   structure (p. 17)

Key People and Events

Mound Builders (p. 18)
Iroquois (p. 21)

Reading Strategy

Taking Notes As you read, identify the Native American peoples who lived in the different areas of North America.

West:

North:

Southwest:

Early North Americans

American Diary

In a Comanche story, Humpback, a powerful being, kept all of the buffalo for himself in a corral. Coyote, an animal known for his tricks, changed himself into a little dog and befriended Humpback's son. At night, Coyote slipped into the corral, barking loudly and stampeding the buffalo away. Humpback's son cried, "'Where is my little dog?' 'That was no dog,' Humpback said sadly. 'That was Coyote the Trickster. He has turned loose all our buffalo.'"

—*from* Dee Brown's Folktales of The Native American

Early Native Americans

Main Idea The Hohokam, the Anasazi, and the Mound Builders were among the most advanced of early North American civilizations.

History and You Has your area ever experienced a drought? How did the drought affect you? Read to learn how droughts may have caused the decline of a Native American civilization in the Southwest.

. . . .

The Comanche were only one of many Native American cultures that rose and flourished in North America long before Europeans arrived in the 1500s. Among the most advanced of these earliest Native American cultures were the Hohokam and Anasazi of the Southwest and the Mound Builders of the Ohio River valley.

The Hohokam

The dry, hot desert of what is now Arizona was home to the Hohokam people. They may have come from Mexico about 300 B.C. The Hohokam culture flourished from about A.D. 300 to 1300 in an area bordered by the Gila and Salt River valleys.

The Hohokam were experts at squeezing every drop of available water from the sun-baked soil. Their way of life depended on the irrigation **channels,** or trenches, they dug to carry river water into their fields. In addition to hundreds of miles of irrigation channels, the Hohokam left behind pottery, carved stone, and shells etched with acid. The shells came from trade with coastal peoples.

The Anasazi

The Anasazi (AH•nuh•SAH•zee) lived around the same time as the Hohokam, roughly A.D. 1 to 1300, in the area known as the Four Corners. (This is the meeting place of the states currently known as Utah, Colorado, Arizona, and New Mexico.) There they built great stone dwellings that the Spanish explorers later called **pueblos** (PWEH•blohs), or villages. Pueblo Bonito, one of the most spectacular of the Anasazi pueblos, can still be seen in New Mexico. The huge semicircular **structure,** or building, of stone and sun-dried earth resembles an apartment building. It is four stories high and has hundreds of rooms. Archaeologists have found traces of a complex road system linking Pueblo Bonito with other villages. This suggests that Pueblo Bonito was an important trade or religious center for the Anasazi people.

Primary Source / **Buffalo Robe**

For centuries, the Comanche and other Native American groups hunted herds of buffalo that used to wander on the Great Plains in what is now the central United States.

Using the Buffalo Sacred to the Native American peoples of the Plains, the buffalo provided many of the people's basic needs. Buffalo meat served as food, bones were made into tools and weapons, and skins were used to make shelters and clothing. Painted buffalo skins were often made into robes.

Critical Thinking

Explaining How do you think Native Americans such as the Comanche depended on the environment?

The Anasazi also built dwellings in the walls of steep cliffs. Cliff dwellings were easy to defend and offered protection from winter weather. Mesa Verde (MAY•suh VUHR•dee) in Colorado, one of the largest cliff dwellings, held several thousand inhabitants.

In about 1300 the Anasazi began leaving the pueblos and cliff dwellings to settle in smaller communities. Their large villages may have been abandoned because of droughts, long periods of little rainfall, during which their crops died.

The Mound Builders

The early cultures of Mexico and Central America appear to have influenced people living in lands to the north. In central North America, prehistoric Native Americans built thousands of mounds of earth that resembled the stone pyramids of the Maya and the Aztec. Some of the mounds contained burial chambers. Some were topped with temples, as in the Maya and Aztec cultures.

The mounds dotted the landscape from what is now known as Pennsylvania to the Mississippi River valley. Archaeologists think that the first mounds were built about 1000 B.C. They were not the work of a single group but of many different peoples, who are referred to as the **Mound Builders.**

Among the earliest Mound Builders were the Adena, hunters and gatherers who flourished in the Ohio Valley by 800 B.C. They were followed by the Hopewell people, who lived between 200 B.C. and A.D. 500. Farmers and traders, the Hopewell built huge burial mounds in the shapes of birds, bears, and snakes. Archaeologists have found freshwater pearls, shells, cloth, and copper in the mounds, indicating a widespread pattern of trade.

Cahokia

The largest settlement of the Mound Builders was Cahokia (kuh•HOH•kee•uh) in what is today Illinois. A people called the

Selected Sites of the Mound Builders   NATIONAL GEOGRAPHIC

Lake Superior

90°W   80°W

N
W   E
S

0   100 kilometers

0   100 miles

Lambert Azimuthal
Equal-Area projection

Lake Michigan   Lake Huron   Lake Ontario

Lake Erie

40°N

Cahokia

Missouri River   Ohio River   Serpent Mound

Kings Mounds

Spiro Mounds

Mississippi River

Moundville   ATLANTIC OCEAN

30°N

Adena site

Hopewell site

Mississippian site

Adena Culture The Great Serpent Mound in southern Ohio (below) is an example of the earthen mounds built by the Adena people. At nearly a quarter mile long, it is the largest serpent effigy mound in the United States. An effigy mound is one made in the shape of a living creature. ▼

Mississippians built Cahokia after A.D. 900. The city may have had 16,000 or more residents. The largest mound in Cahokia, the Monks Mound, rises nearly 100 feet (30 m).

Cahokia resembled the great cities of Mexico, even though it was nearly 2,000 miles (3,200 km) away. The great pyramid-shaped mound dominated the city. A temple crowned the summit. Perhaps priests studied the heavens from the temple, or the priest-ruler may have lived there. A legend of the Natchez people, descendants of the Mississippians, hints of a direct link to Mexico:

PRIMARY SOURCE

"Before we came into this land, we lived yonder under the sun; [the speaker pointed southwest toward Mexico]. . . . Our nation extended itself along the great water [the Gulf of Mexico], where the large river [the Mississippi] loses itself."

—Natchez legend

Reading Check **Explaining** How did the Mound Builders appear to be related to the Maya and Aztec cultures?

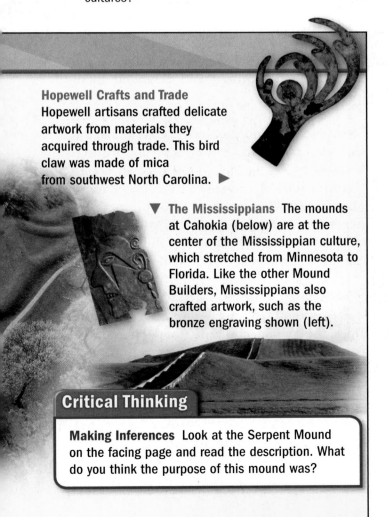

Hopewell Crafts and Trade
Hopewell artisans crafted delicate artwork from materials they acquired through trade. This bird claw was made of mica from southwest North Carolina. ▶

▼ **The Mississippians** The mounds at Cahokia (below) are at the center of the Mississippian culture, which stretched from Minnesota to Florida. Like the other Mound Builders, Mississippians also crafted artwork, such as the bronze engraving shown (left).

Critical Thinking

Making Inferences Look at the Serpent Mound on the facing page and read the description. What do you think the purpose of this mound was?

Other Native North Americans

Main Idea The early inhabitants of North America developed ways of life that were well suited to their environments.

History and You How has the climate in the area where you live affected the way that houses are built? Read to learn how Native Americans adapted to the climates of North America.

The civilizations of the Hohokam, the Anasazi, and the Mound Builders eventually faded away. A number of other Native American cultures arose to take their place. Around the time that Europeans began arriving, North America was home to many different societies.

Peoples of the North

The people who settled in the northernmost part of North America, in the lands around the Arctic Ocean, are called the Inuit. Some scientists think the Inuit were the last migrants to cross the land bridge that connected Asia with North America.

The Inuit had many skills that helped them survive in the cold Arctic climate. They may have brought some of these skills from Siberia, which was probably their original home. In the winter the Inuit built igloos, low-lying structures of snow blocks, which protected them from severe weather.

Their clothing of furs and sealskins was warm and waterproof. The Inuit were hunters and fishers. In the coastal waters, they pursued whales, seals, and walruses in small, skin-covered boats. On land they hunted caribou, large deerlike animals that lived in the far north. The Inuit made clothing from caribou skins and burned seal oil in lamps.

Peoples of the West

North America's West Coast had a mild climate and dependable food sources. These conditions created a favorable environment for many different groups.

Native American Cultures

NATIONAL GEOGRAPHIC

Arctic
Subarctic
Northwest Coast
Plateau
Great Basin
California
Southwest
Great Plains
Northeast Woodlands
Southeast

0   1,000 kilometers
0   1,000 miles
Lambert Azimuthal Equal-Area projection

INUIT
INUIT
TLINGIT
HAIDA
CHINOOK
YAKIMA
NEZ PERCE
BLACKFOOT
OJIBWA
SHOSHONE
DAKOTA
CHEYENNE OMAHA
PAWNEE
POMO
ANASAZI
UTE
NAVAJO
ZUÑI ACOMA
KIOWA
APACHE
OSAGE
COMANCHE
APACHE
CHICKASAW
CHOCTAW
CREEK
SAUK FOX
MIAMI
SHAWNEE
HURON
IROQUOIS
POWHATAN
CHEROKEE
WAMPANOAG
PEQUOT
NARRAGANSETT
IROQUOIS LEAGUE:
CAYUGA
MOHAWK
ONEIDA
ONONDAGA
SENECA

ROCKY MTNS.
SIERRA NEVADA
APPALACHIAN MTNS.
Great Lakes
Hudson Bay
PACIFIC OCEAN
ATLANTIC OCEAN
Gulf of Mexico
TROPIC OF CANCER

Differing Cultures Native American groups across North America developed their own unique ways of life. Styles of lodging and crafts varied from people to people.

The peoples of the northwestern coast, such as the Tlingit (TLIHNG•kuht), Haida, and Chinook, depended on the forest and the sea. They built wooden houses and made canoes, cloth, and baskets from tree bark. They fished for their main food, salmon, along the coast and in rivers such as the Columbia. They preserved the salmon by smoking it over fires.

Salmon was also important for the people of the plateau region, the area between the Cascade Mountains and the Rocky Mountains. The Nez Perce (NEHZ PUHRS) and Yakima peoples fished the rivers, hunted deer in forests, and gathered roots and berries. The Native Americans of the plateau region lived in earthen houses.

A great variety of cultures lived in what is now California. Along the northern coast, Native Americans fished for their food. In the more barren environment of the southern deserts, nomadic groups collected roots and

seeds. In the central valley of California, the Pomo gathered acorns and pounded them into flour.

In the Great Basin region, between the Sierra Nevada and the Rocky Mountains, the soil was too hard and rocky for farming. Peoples such as the Ute (YOOT) and Shoshone (shuh•SHOHN) traveled in search of food. They ate small game, pine nuts, juniper berries, roots, and some insects. The Great Basin peoples created temporary shelters from branches and reeds.

Peoples of the Southwest

Descendants of the Anasazi formed the Hopi, the Acoma, and the Zuni peoples of the Southwest. They built their homes from sun-dried mud bricks called adobe. They raised corn or maize as their basic food. They also grew beans, squash, melons, pumpkins, and fruit. Their trade network spread throughout the Southwest and into Mexico.

Southwest Pottery The peoples of the Southwest created beautiful pottery from the same clay with which they built their homes. Pots were used to store water and food. ▶

Buffalo Skin Bag The Native Americans of the Plains used the skins of the buffalo they hunted to make a number of everyday items. This buffalo skin bag shows a horse and rider. ▶

◀ **Longhouses** People of the East lived in bark-covered longhouses. Each building could shelter several families.

Northwest Artifact This ladle in the form of a bird was used by Native Americans in the Northwest at large parties called potlatches. Potlatches celebrated events such as births, deaths, and weddings. ▼

Map Skill

Region Identify some of the peoples who lived in the Great Plains region of North America.

 Maps In MOtion See StudentWorks™ Plus or glencoe.com.

In the 1500s, two new peoples settled in the region—the Apache and the Navajo. Unlike other peoples of the Southwest, these new groups were hunters and gatherers. They hunted deer and other game. In time, the Navajo settled in villages and built square houses called hogans. In addition to hunting, they began to grow maize and beans. They also began raising sheep in the 1600s.

Peoples of the Plains

The peoples of the Great Plains were nomadic. Their villages were temporary, lasting only for a growing season or two. When the people moved from place to place, they dragged their homes—cone-shaped skin tents called tepees—behind them. The men hunted antelope, deer, and buffalo. The women planted maize, squash, and beans.

When the Spanish brought horses to Mexico in the 1500s, some got loose and made their way north. Native Americans captured and tamed the wild horses. The Comanche, the Dakota, and other Plains peoples became skilled riders. They hunted and fought on horseback, using spears, bows and arrows, and clubs while riding.

Peoples of the East

The peoples who lived in the woodlands of eastern North America formed complex societies. The many Algonquian groups were linked by similar languages. The **Iroquois** (IHR•uh•KWAH) and Cherokee had formal law codes and formed **federations,** governments that linked different groups.

The Iroquois lived near Canada in what is now northern New York State. There were five Iroquois groups or nations: the Onondaga (AH•nuhn•DAW•guh), the Seneca, the Mohawk, the Oneida, and the Cayuga.

These groups often warred with each other. Finally, in the 1500s, these five groups established the Great Peace, an alliance that was joined in 1715 by the Tuscarora peoples. This alliance was called the Iroquois League.

The League created a constitution. At first the constitution was represented symbolically through art. Later, after the arrival of the Europeans, it was written down.

The Iroquois constitution established the Grand Council, a group of leaders who met regularly to settle disputes among the various peoples. Although Grand Council members were men, women played an important part in choosing delegates to the council. The different members of the Iroquois League were organized according to **clans,** or groups of related families. The women in each clan chose a clan mother. These clan mothers then chose the male members of the Grand Council.

The Iroquois constitution describes the Iroquois people's desire for peace:

PRIMARY SOURCE

"I am Dekanawidah and with the Five Nations' Confederate Lords I plant the Tree of Great Peace. . . . Roots have spread out from the Tree of the Great Peace, one to the north, one to the east, one to the south and one to the west."

—Dekanawidah, Iroquois Constitution

Peoples of the Southeast

The Southeast was also a woodlands area but with a warmer climate than the eastern woodlands. The Creek, Chickasaw, and Cherokee were among the region's Native American peoples.

The Creek lived in loosely knit farming communities in what is now Georgia and Alabama. There they grew corn, tobacco, squash, and other crops. The Chickasaw, most of whom lived farther west in what is now Mississippi, farmed the fertile river bottomlands. The Cherokee farmed in the mountains of Georgia and the Carolinas.

Wherever they lived in North America, the first Americans developed ways of life that were well suited to their environments. In the 1500s, however, the Native Americans would meet a new people with vastly different beliefs, cultures, and ways of life. These newcomers were the Europeans, and their arrival would change the Native Americans' world forever.

Reading Check Describing How did the peoples of the Great Plains use horses?

Section 3 Review

History ONLINE
Study Central™ To review this section, go to glencoe.com.

Vocabulary

1. Use each of these terms in a sentence that will help explain its meaning: channel, pueblo, structure, federation, clan.

Main Ideas

2. Describing Describe the cliff dwellings of the Anasazi and explain the advantages those dwellings offered.

3. Explaining What was the significance of the Iroquois League?

Critical Thinking

4. Making Connections What evidence suggests that the Mound Builders were influenced by other cultures?

5. Contrasting Use a diagram like the one below to show how the ways of life of Native American cultures differed by comparing their regions and forms of shelter.

Inuit	Hopi	Dakota
Region:	Region:	Region:
Shelter:	Shelter:	Shelter:

6. Descriptive Writing Choose one of the Native American peoples of North America and write two or three paragraphs describing a typical day in the life of a member of that group. Be sure to include details about the environment and the way of life of the group.

Answer the Essential Question

7. How was the way of life of the Native Americans of North America related to their environment?

Prehistoric tool ▶

Prehistoric Migration to the Americas
(beginning c. 28,000 B.C.)

Nomadic hunter-gatherers arrived over a land bridge from Siberia or by boat and migrated throughout North and South America.

Temperatures rose; ocean waters submerged the land bridge, and large animals died out. Populations grew as people hunted smaller animals and began farming.

Cities and Empires in Central and South America
(beginning c. 1500 B.C.)

Civilizations developed large cities and empires; systems for writing, time keeping, and counting; farming and manufacturing; engineering; far-ranging trade; and religion-based societies.

▲ Aztec serpent

| Olmec | Maya | Aztec | Inca |

Native American Civilizations in North America
(beginning c. A.D. 300)

North and West adapted to Arctic, forest, ocean, and desert life

Plains nomadic hunters and farmers skilled at riding horses

East woodland dwellers; Iroquois developed a federation and a constitution

Southwest adapted farming to desert conditions

Southeast hunted and farmed in the fertile valleys of the Appalachian Mountains

◀ Buffalo skin bag

STUDY TO GO Study anywhere, anytime! Download quizzes and flash cards to your PDA from glencoe.com.

INDIANA STATEWIDE TEST PRACTICE

TEST-TAKING TIP

Answer the questions you know first, and go back to those for which you need more time.

Reviewing Vocabulary

Directions: Choose the word or words that best completes the sentence.

1 **Early Americans were _____, people who moved from place to place.**

  A nomads
  B settlers
  C warriors
  D archaeologists

2 **Because the Maya civilization was a _____, the most powerful Maya were priests.**

  A culture
  B theocracy
  C democracy
  D federation

3 **The Anasazi built great stone dwellings that the Spanish explorers called _____.**

  A temples
  B teepees
  C pueblos
  D longhouses

4 **The Maya developed a form of writing called _____.**

  A artifacts
  B quipu
  C maize
  D hieroglyphics

Reviewing Main Ideas

Directions: Choose the best answer.

5 **Archaeologists believe that the Americas were first populated by people who**

  A sailed ships from Europe.
  B crossed into South America from Antarctica.
  C crossed a land bridge that connected northeastern Asia to what is now Alaska.
  D None of the above; evidence indicates that humans have always lived in the Americas.

6 **The most important agricultural product grown by the people of prehistoric America was probably**

  A wheat.
  B maize.
  C tobacco.
  D rice.

7 **The Creek, Chickasaw, and Cherokee peoples**

  A fished along North America's West Coast.
  B crossed Beringia into the Americas.
  C lived in farming communities throughout southeastern North America.
  D built thousands of mounds of earth, much like those of the Maya and the Aztec.

8 **Among the most advanced of the early civilizations of Mexico and Central America were the**

  A Apache and the Navajo.
  B Hohokam and the Anasazi.
  C Mound Builders, the Tlingit, and the Inuit.
  D Olmec, the Maya, and the Aztec.

GO ON

Critical Thinking

Directions: Choose the best answer.

9 **Which of these statements best describes the native groups of the Americas?**

   A They shared a common language.
   B They established one nation.
   C They had a primitive alphabet.
   D They created varied and distinct cultures.

Base your answers to questions 10 and 11 on the map below and your knowledge of Chapter 1.

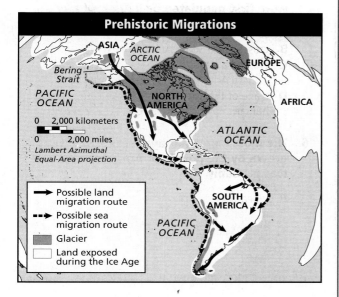

Prehistoric Migrations

0   2,000 kilometers
0   2,000 miles
Lambert Azimuthal Equal-Area projection

→ Possible land migration route
---→ Possible sea migration route
▨ Glacier
▢ Land exposed during the Ice Age

10 **The land bridge across the Bering Strait connected**

   A Asia and North America.
   B Central America and South America.
   C Europe and the Americas.
   D the Aztec and Inca Empires.

11 **Early Americans migrated**

   A across the Bering Strait alone.
   B by a number of different routes.
   C mainly from Southeast Asia.
   D mainly from southwestern Europe.

Constructed Response

Directions: Write a short response to each of the following questions. In your answer:

- *address all parts of the question*
- *use information from the chapter*
- *include facts, examples, and details relevant to the question*
- *use clear language*

12 **Why were some Native American groups more nomadic than others?**

13 **How did the Aztecs strengthen their power and expand their empire?**

14 **How did environment and food sources help shape Native American lifestyles in dry areas? In damp coastal areas? In mild climates?**

Base your answer to question 15 on the reading below and your knowledge of Chapter 1.

> We have obtained the consent of five nations. These are the Mohawks, the Oneidas, the Onondagas, the Cayugas, and the Senecas. Our desire is to form a compact for a union of our nations.
>
> —from The Constitution of the Five Nations

15 **Why might the five nations want to form a union?**

16 **Identify two Native American groups of the Plains and describe how they adapted to their environment.**

Need Extra Help?																
If You Missed Questions. . .	1	2	3	4	5	6	7	8	9	10	11	12	13	14	15	16
Go to Page. . .	8	12	17	12	7	9	22	12	23	7	8	8	13	17	21	21

Exploring the Americas
1400-1625

Henry Hudson landing in North America

◀ Inca noble

c. 1438 ★
The Inca leader
Pachacuti begins to
build an empire

1492 ★
Christopher
Columbus
reaches
America

★ 1497
John Cabot
sails to
Newfoundland

Americas

World

1400

1450

1500

1429 ★
Joan of Arc
defeats the
English at
Orléans

c. 1456
Johannes Gutenberg
uses movable metal
type in printing

★ c. 1500
Songhai
Empire rises
in Africa

Section 1: A Changing World

Essential Question What events and technological advances paved the way for European exploration?

Section 2: Early Exploration

Essential Question Why did Spain and Portugal want to find a sea route to Asia?

Section 3: Spain in America

Essential Question How did Spain's conquests affect the economic and social development of the Americas?

Section 4: Exploring North America

Essential Question Why did European nations establish colonies in North America?

History ONLINE
Chapter Overview Visit glencoe.com and click on **Chapter 2—Chapter Overviews** to preview chapter information.

FOLDABLES®
Study Organizer

Organizing Information
Make this Foldable to help you organize what you learn about the exploration of the Americas.

Step 1 Place three sheets of paper about 1 inch apart.

Step 2 Fold the paper to form five equal tabs.

Step 3 Staple the sheets and label each tab as shown.

Reading and Writing
As you read the chapter, list important people, places, and facts under the appropriate tabs of the Foldable.

Exploring the Americas
- *A Changing World*
- *Early Exploration*
- *Spain in America*
- *Exploring North America*

◄ Juan de Oñate

★ 1519
Cortés brings horses to North America

1598 ★
Juan de Oñate founds province of New Mexico

★ 1609
Henry Hudson explores the Hudson River area

1550   **1600**

★ 1517
Martin Luther promotes Church reform

★ 1522
Magellan's crew completes first voyage around the world

★ 1588
England defeats Spanish Armada

A Changing World

Essential Question ◄

What events and technological advances paved the way for European exploration?

Reading Guide

Content Vocabulary

classical *(p. 30)*   pilgrimage *(p. 33)*
technology *(p. 31)*   mosque *(p. 33)*
astrolabe *(p. 31)*   Quran *(p. 33)*

Academic Vocabulary

acquire *(p. 31)*   impose *(p. 32)*

Key People and Events

Crusades *(p. 29)*
Marco Polo *(p. 29)*
Renaissance *(p. 30)*
Mansa Mūsā *(p. 33)*

Reading Strategy

Taking Notes As you read, use a diagram like the one below to identify the advances in technology that paved the way for European voyages of exploration.

Technological
Advances

INDIANA ACADEMIC STANDARDS
United States History

8.4.1 Identify economic factors contributing to European exploration and colonization in North America, the American Revolution, and the drafting of the Constitution of the United States.

American Diary

In 1271 Marco Polo set off from Italy on a great journey to China. Polo crossed the Gobi, a desert area north of China, about which he wrote: "The length of this Desert is so great that 'tis said it would take a year and more to ride from one end of it to the other. And here, where its breadth is least [narrowest], it takes a month to cross it. 'Tis all composed of hills and valleys of sand, and not a thing to eat is to be found on it."

—*from* **The Travels of Marco Polo**

Camels still cross the vast deserts of Asia today.

New Ideas and Nations

Main Idea The Renaissance began in the Italian city-states and spread throughout Europe.

History and You What do you know about the ancient civilizations of Greece and Rome? Read to learn about the renewed interest in classical learning during the Renaissance.

. . . .

By the time Marco Polo returned from China, European interest in Asia had begun to grow. For centuries after the Roman Empire fell, the people of western Europe were isolated from the rest of the world. Dominated by the Catholic Church, their world was divided into a number of small kingdoms and city-states.

Meanwhile, the religion of Islam swept across the Middle East and Africa. European Christians feared losing access to the Holy Land—the birthplace of Christianity, in what is now Israel. In 1095 the Europeans launched the first of nine expeditions, known as the **Crusades,** to regain control of their holy sites from the Muslims.

The Crusades brought western Europeans into contact with the Middle East. Arab merchants sold spices, sugar, silk, and other goods from China and India to Europeans. As a result, European interest in Asia grew.

That interest grew even more after **Marco Polo** returned from China. In 1296 he began writing an account of his trip. He described Asia's marvels in his book *Travels,* which was widely read in Europe. Little did Marco Polo realize that 200 years later, *Travels* would inspire Christopher Columbus to sail in the opposite direction to reach the East.

The Growth of Trade

Merchants knew they could make a fortune selling goods from Asia. Wealthy Europeans clamored for spices from the East. They also wanted perfumes, silks, and precious stones.

Merchants first bought goods from Arab traders in the Middle East. These merchants then sent the goods overland by caravan to the Mediterranean Sea. From there the goods were sent by ship to Italian ports. The cities of Venice, Genoa, and Pisa prospered as centers of the growing trade. Arab merchants, however, charged high prices for their goods. Europeans began looking for a route to the East that bypassed the Arab merchants.

If **Y**ou Were **T**here / **A Young Explorer**

En Route Only 17 years old when his trip began, Marco Polo journeyed with his father and uncle, both Venetian merchants. If you were with them, you would have traveled on camels for more than three years. You also would have crossed almost 7,000 miles (11,265 km) of mountains and deserts before reaching your final destination: the fabled court of Kublai Khan (KOO-BLUH KAHN), the Mongol emperor of China.

Critical Thinking

Explaining How would you have traveled to China? How long would it have taken to reach your destination?

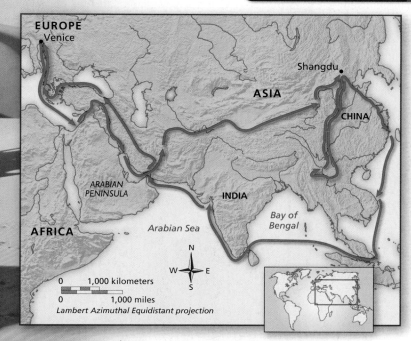

▲ Map of Marco Polo's journey to China

The Growth of Ideas

In the 1300s a powerful new spirit emerged in the Italian city-states and spread throughout Europe. Banking and the expansion of trade with Asia made Italian merchants wealthy. These citizens wanted to improve their knowledge of past civilizations and of the world. They studied the **classical**—ancient Greek and Roman—works with new interest. Taking a more experimental approach to science, many thinkers tested new and old theories and evaluated the results.

Many authors began to write about the individual and the universe. Artists studied the sculpture and architecture of the classical world. They particularly admired the harmony and balance in Greek art.

The Renaissance

This period of intellectual and artistic creativity was known as the **Renaissance** (REH•nuh•SAHNTS). The word means "rebirth" in French and refers to the renewed interest in classical Greek and Roman learning. The Renaissance spread throughout Europe over the next two centuries. It changed the way Europeans thought about themselves and the world. It also paved the way for an age of exploration and discovery.

Powerful Nations Emerge

During the Renaissance, merchants and bankers sought greater profits through foreign trade. They wanted to buy goods directly from the East. The development of nation-states in western Europe helped expand trade and interest in overseas exploration.

For years Europe was a patchwork of small states. By the 1400s, however, a new type of centralized state began to emerge in western Europe. Strong monarchs came to power in Spain, Portugal, England, and France. They began to establish national laws, courts, taxes, and armies to replace those of the local lords. These ambitious monarchs sought ways to increase trade and make their countries stronger and wealthier.

✔ **Reading Check** **Identifying** What goods did wealthy Europeans desire from the East?

LINKING PAST TO PRESENT   Navigation Tools

THEN "Land ho!" The tools that early explorers used to sail the uncharted seas were much different from the instruments used today. Early navigation tools such as the astrolabe could help determine a ship's approximate latitude by noting the locations of the stars.

NOW Today, navigation satellites do the work of an astrolabe—and much more. The NAVSTAR Global Positioning System (GPS) is a network of satellites launched by the United States. From space, the GPS can track the location of a ship or some other object on Earth within a few meters of its actual position.

Tropicus Capricorn̄

▼ Astrolabe

Technology's Impact

Main Idea Technology produced better means of navigation and paved the way for European voyages of exploration.

History and You Have you ridden in a vehicle with an onboard navigation system? Read to learn how the astrolabe and compass improved navigation in the 1400s.

. . . .

Advances in **technology**—the use of scientific knowledge for practical purposes—paved the way for European voyages of exploration. In the 1450s the introduction of the printing press made it much easier to print books. Now more people had access to books and to new information. Many Europeans read Marco Polo's *Travels* when it appeared in printed form in 1477.

Better Maps and Instruments

Most early maps were inaccurate because they were drawn from the often-mistaken impressions of traders and travelers. Little by

Hikers can use a handheld GPS receiver to stay on course in the wilderness. ▶

Critical Thinking

1. **Explaining** How have the tools used for navigation changed since the late 1400s?
2. **Analyzing** What major technological advancements have allowed improvements in navigation?

little, cartographers, or mapmakers, improved their skills. Using reports of explorers and information from Arab geographers, mapmakers made more accurate land and sea maps. These maps showed the directions of ocean currents. They also showed lines of latitude, which measured the distance north and south of the Equator.

Better instruments were developed for navigating the seas. Sailors could determine their latitude while at sea with an **astrolabe.** This instrument measured the positions of stars. Europeans also **acquired** the magnetic compass. A Chinese invention, the compass began to be widely used in Europe and the Middle East in the 1200s. The compass allowed sailors to determine their direction when they were far from land.

Better Ships

Advances in ship design allowed shipbuilders to build sailing vessels that were capable of long ocean voyages. The stern rudder and the triangular sail made it possible for ships to sail into the wind. Both of these new features came from the Arabs.

Then, in the late 1400s, the Portuguese developed the three-masted caravel. It was the first and most famous ship of the European age of exploration. The caravel sailed faster than earlier ships and carried more cargo and food supplies. It also could float in shallow water. This feature allowed sailors to explore inlets and to sail their ships up to the beach if they needed to make repairs. A Venetian sailor called the caravels "the best ships that sailed the seas."

By the mid-1400s, the Italian ports faced increased competition for foreign trade. As a result, a new era of exploration was launched. Powerful countries such as Portugal and Spain began searching for sea routes to Asia. Portugal began its explorations by sending ships down the west coast of Africa, an area Europeans had never visited before.

✔ **Reading Check** **Explaining** How did the caravel affect overseas exploration in the 1400s?

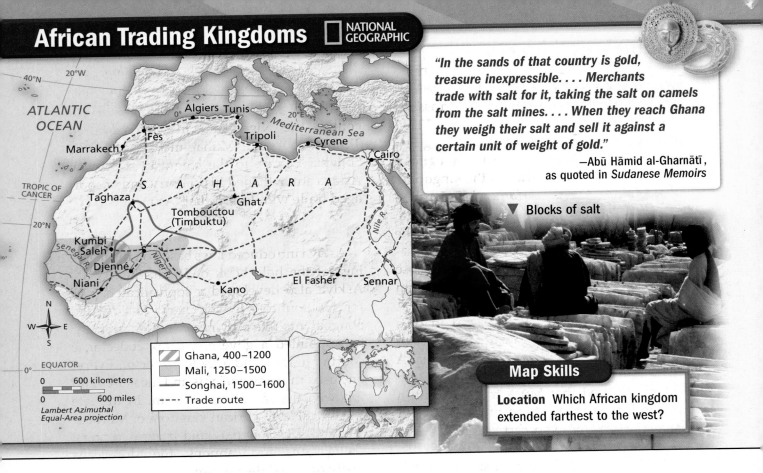

"In the sands of that country is gold, treasure inexpressible. . . . Merchants trade with salt for it, taking the salt on camels from the salt mines. . . . When they reach Ghana they weigh their salt and sell it against a certain unit of weight of gold."

—Abū Hāmid al-Gharnātī, as quoted in *Sudanese Memoirs*

▼ Blocks of salt

Ghana, 400–1200
Mali, 1250–1500
Songhai, 1500–1600
Trade route

Map Skills

Location Which African kingdom extended farthest to the west?

African Kingdoms

Main Idea Ghana, Mali, and Songhai were among the most powerful empires in Africa.

History and You What items are valued today because they are rare? Read to find out how rare items, such as salt, drove the economies of early African kingdoms.

. . . .

Powerful kingdoms flourished in Africa south of the Sahara between A.D. 400 and A.D. 1600. Africans mined gold, copper, and iron ore. Trade with Islamic societies in North Africa brought wealth as well as Islamic ideas and customs to the West African kingdoms.

City-states on the east coast of Africa also benefited from trade. Arab traders from the Middle East brought cotton, silk, and porcelain from India and China. They exchanged these goods for ivory and metals from the African interior.

The Portuguese sailed south along the western coast of Africa in the mid-1400s. They set up trading posts along the coastline. From these posts, they traded for gold and for enslaved people.

Ghana—A Trading Empire

Between A.D. 400 and A.D. 1100, a vast trading empire called Ghana emerged in West Africa. Well located between the salt mines of the Sahara and the gold mines to the south, Ghana prospered from the taxes **imposed,** or placed, on trade.

Caravans with gold, ivory, and slaves from Ghana crossed the Sahara to North Africa, where Muslim traders loaded caravans with salt, cloth, and brass and headed back to Ghana. Trading contacts led many West Africans to become Muslims.

In 1076 people from North Africa, called Almoravids, attacked Ghana and disrupted its trade routes. While Ghana fought the Almoravids, new trade routes and gold mines opened up to the east, bypassing Ghana. Ghana then began to decline, and new states emerged in the region.

Mali—A Powerful Kingdom

Mali, one of the new states, grew into a powerful kingdom. The people of Mali developed their own trade routes across the desert to North Africa. By the late 1200s, Mali's territory included the former kingdom of Ghana. The country was mainly agricultural, but gold mines enriched the kingdom.

Mali's greatest king, **Mansa Mūsā,** ruled from 1312 to 1337. He was described at the time as "the most powerful, the richest, the most fortunate, the most feared by his enemies, and the most able to do good to those around him." Mūsā made his kingdom famous.

In 1324 Mūsā, who was a Muslim, made a grand pilgrimage to the Muslim holy city of Makkah (Mecca) in western Saudi Arabia. A **pilgrimage** is a journey to a holy place. Arab writers reported that Mūsā traveled with a huge military escort. Ahead of him marched 500 royal servants who carried gold to distribute along the way.

Mūsā returned to Mali with an Arab architect who built great **mosques,** Muslim houses of worship, in the capital of Timbuktu. Under Mansa Mūsā, Timbuktu became an important center of Islamic art and learning.

The Songhai Empire

Some years later the Songhai (SAWNG•hy) people, who lived along the Niger River, rose up against Mali rule. They built a navy to control the Niger and in 1468 captured Timbuktu. Askìya Muhammad brought the Songhai Empire to the height of its power. Askìya strengthened his country and encouraged trade with Europe and Asia.

Plan of Government

Askìya introduced laws based on the teachings of the holy book of Islam, the **Quran.** Askìya also developed a sophisticated plan for his country's government. He divided Songhai into five provinces. To each province he appointed a governor, a tax collector, a court of judges, and a trade inspector. Everyone used the same weights and measures and followed the same legal system. In the late 1500s the North African kingdom of Morocco attacked the Songhai gold-trading centers. Using guns and cannons, the Moroccans easily defeated the empire.

✔ **Reading Check** **Explaining** What goods did African kingdoms use for trading? What did they trade for?

Section 1 Review

History ONLINE
Study Central™ To review this section, go to glencoe.com.

Vocabulary

1. Use each of these terms in a sentence that will help explain its meaning: classical, technology, astrolabe, acquire, impose, pilgrimage, mosque, Quran.

Main Ideas

2. **Identifying** Why did interest in trade with the East increase during the Renaissance?

3. **Describing** How were maps improved to help sailors?

4. **Discussing** How did Timbuktu, in Mali, become an Islamic cultural center?

Critical Thinking

5. **Organizing** Use a diagram like the following to show the exchange of goods and ideas between North Africa and Ghana.

North Africa → Ghana

6. **Persuasive Writing** Take on the role of Marco Polo. Write one paragraph for the back cover that will make readers want to buy your book, *Travels.*

Answer the
7. **Essential Question**
What events and technological advances paved the way for European exploration?

Essential Question ◄

Why did Spain and Portugal want to find a sea route to Asia?

Reading Guide

Content Vocabulary

saga *(p. 38)*   strait *(p. 41)*
line of demarcation   circumnavigate
  (p. 41)   *(p. 41)*

Academic Vocabulary

devote *(p. 39)*   alter *(p. 40)*

Key People and Events

Henry the Navigator *(p. 35)*
Bartholomeu Dias *(p. 36)*
Vasco da Gama *(p. 37)*
Christopher Columbus *(p. 38)*
Amerigo Vespucci *(p. 41)*
Ferdinand Magellan *(p. 41)*

Reading Strategy

Taking Notes As you read, use a diagram like the one below to identify the explorers discussed in this section who were sponsored by Portugal and Spain.

```
              Explorers
             /          \
  Sponsored by      Sponsored by
    Portugal            Spain
```

INDIANA ACADEMIC STANDARDS
United States History

8.4.1 Identify economic factors contributing to European exploration and colonization in North America, the American Revolution, and the drafting of the Constitution of the United States.

American Diary

In 1492 Christopher Columbus led 90 sailors on a voyage into the unknown. As the voyage dragged on, the sailors grew quarrelsome. Columbus wrote:
"I am told . . . that if I persist in going onward, the best course of action will be to throw me into the sea some night."
Then, on the morning of October 12, a cannon fired from the ship Pinta, indicating that land had been sighted. At dawn, Columbus left his ship, the Santa María, and went ashore.

—*from* The Log of Christopher Columbus

Christopher Columbus lands on the Caribbean island that he named San Salvador.

Seeking New Trade Routes

Main Idea Portugal took the lead in finding a sea route to India.

History and You What do you consider a long trip? A few hours on an airplane or a few days in a car? Read to learn about the long sea voyages that Portuguese ships made to find a sea route to India.

. . . .

Columbus believed he had arrived in the Indies—islands located southeast of China. Unfortunately, Columbus was wrong. The maps that Columbus and the first European explorers used did not include the Americas. They showed three continents—Europe, Asia, and Africa—merged in a gigantic landmass bordered by oceans. Some explorers thought that the Western (Atlantic) and Eastern (Pacific) Oceans ran together to form what they called the Ocean Sea. No one realized that another huge landmass was missing from the maps. They also did not realize that the oceans were as large as they are.

Columbus sailed for Spain, but Portugal was the first European power to explore the boundaries of the known world. Because Portugal lacked a Mediterranean port, it could not share in the trade between Asia and Europe. The country's rulers wanted to find a new route to China and India.

The Portuguese also hoped to find a more direct way to get West African gold. The gold traveled by caravan across the desert to North Africa and then by ship across the Mediterranean. Portuguese traders needed a better route.

Early Portuguese Voyages

Prince Henry of Portugal helped lay the groundwork for the era of exploration that was beginning. In about 1420, he set up a center for exploration at Sarges, on the southwestern tip of Portugal, "where endeth land and where beginneth sea."

Known as **Henry the Navigator,** the prince never intended to become an explorer himself. Instead, he planned the voyages and then analyzed the reports that his crews brought home. At Sarges, Prince Henry began his "school of navigation." There, astronomers, geographers, and mathematicians shared their knowledge with Portuguese sailors and shipbuilders. When each new voyage brought back new information, Henry's expert mapmakers updated the charts.

If You Were There / Ship's Boy on the *Santa María*

Life Aboard Ship Your day begins with prayers on deck. A single hot meal for the day is prepared over an open fire in the deck's sandbox. Your meal usually consists of salted meat or fresh fish, with dried peas and cheese. As a ship's boy, your major job is letting the crew know when it is time to do their chores. You do so by turning the sandglass every half-hour and calling out, "One glass is gone, and now the second flows!" After eight turns of the glass, or four hours, a new boy comes on deck to call the time. When you are off duty, you sleep anywhere on the deck that you can find shelter.

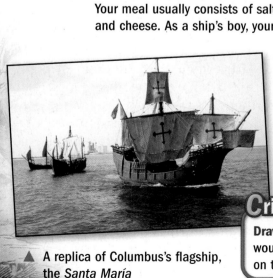

▲ A replica of Columbus's flagship, the *Santa María*

Critical Thinking

Drawing Conclusions What qualities would you need to be a crew member on the *Santa María*?

Early Portuguese Exploration

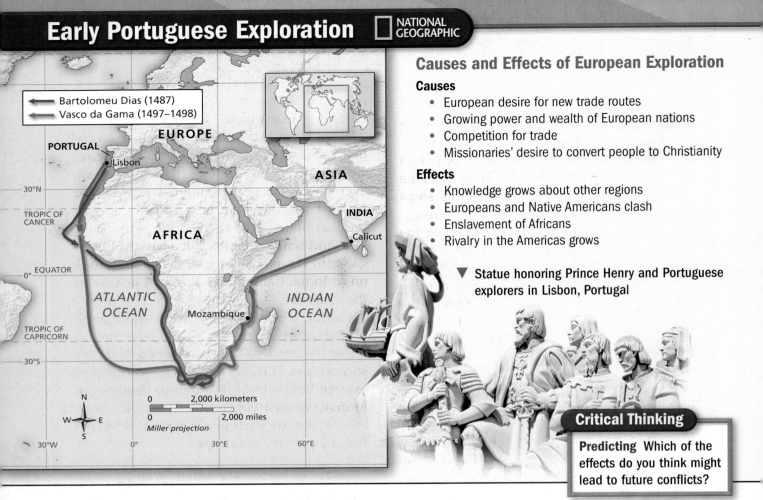

Bartolomeu Dias (1487)
Vasco da Gama (1497–1498)

EUROPE
PORTUGAL
Lisbon
30°N
TROPIC OF CANCER
AFRICA
ASIA
INDIA
Calicut
0° EQUATOR
ATLANTIC OCEAN
Mozambique
INDIAN OCEAN
TROPIC OF CAPRICORN
30°S

N
W E
S

0   2,000 kilometers
0   2,000 miles
Miller projection

30°W   0°   30°E   60°E

Causes and Effects of European Exploration

Causes
- European desire for new trade routes
- Growing power and wealth of European nations
- Competition for trade
- Missionaries' desire to convert people to Christianity

Effects
- Knowledge grows about other regions
- Europeans and Native Americans clash
- Enslavement of Africans
- Rivalry in the Americas grows

▼ Statue honoring Prince Henry and Portuguese explorers in Lisbon, Portugal

Critical Thinking

Predicting Which of the effects do you think might lead to future conflicts?

As Portuguese ships moved south along the coast of West Africa, they traded for gold and ivory and established a number of trading posts in the region. Because of its abundance of gold, the area came to be known as the Gold Coast. In the mid-1400s Portuguese traders began buying enslaved people there as well.

King John II of Portugal launched new efforts to realize the Portuguese dream of a trading empire in Asia. If the Portuguese could find a sea route around Africa, they could trade directly with India and China. In the 1480s the king urged Portuguese sea captains to explore farther south along the African coast.

Bartholomeu Dias

In 1487 King John sent **Bartholomeu Dias** to explore the southernmost part of Africa and from there to sail northeast into the Indian Ocean. Dias set out from Lisbon with two small caravels and a slower supply ship. The expedition was also assigned some of Portugal's best pilots. They sailed for days.

After passing the mouth of the Orange River in South Africa, Dias ran into a fierce storm that lasted nearly two weeks. The strong winds carried him southward, off course, and out of sight of land. When the winds finally died down, Dias steered east and then north until he found land again. Dias realized that he had sailed past the southernmost point of Africa, called a cape because it projects into the sea.

Dias charted a course back home. On the return journey, Dias passed the cape again. He wrote that he had been around the "Cape of Storms." On learning of Dias's discovery, King John renamed this southern tip of land.

History ONLINE
Student Web Activity Visit glencoe.com and complete the Chapter 2 Web Activity about Prince Henry the Navigator.

He called it the Cape of Good Hope. The king hoped that the passage around Africa might lead to a new route to India.

Vasco da Gama

The first Portuguese voyages to India were made years later. In July 1497, after much preparation, **Vasco da Gama** set out from Portugal with four ships. Da Gama did little coast hugging of Africa. Instead, his ships made a huge semicircular sweep through the Atlantic Ocean. At one point during the voyage, da Gama was closer to what is today Brazil than he was to Africa. It is said that da Gama made this unusual maneuver to reach currents that would help him round the Cape of Good Hope safely. During that huge sweep of the Atlantic, da Gama was out of sight of land for 96 days.

After rounding the Cape on November 22, da Gama visited cities along the coast of East Africa. Along the way, he met an Arab pilot who knew the Indian Ocean well. With the pilot's help, da Gama sailed on to India. He reached the port of Calicut in May 1498, completing the long-awaited eastern sea route to Asia.

The Portuguese Trading Empire

Events moved quickly after that. Less than six months after da Gama's return home, a fleet of 13 ships left Lisbon bound for the East. In command of this fleet was Pedro Álvares Cabral. With him were several captains, including Bartholomeu Dias. Cabral followed da Gama's route. His course, however, swung so wide around Africa that he reached Brazil, where he explored some of the coastline. Cabral claimed the land for his king and sent one of his ships back to Portugal with the good news while he continued on to India. Cabral gave Portugal a stake in the Americas.

Cabral returned home from India with cargoes of spices, porcelain, and other goods. Other Portuguese fleets repeated Cabral's success, and Portugal established its first permanent forts in India. Portuguese fleets began to make annual voyages to India. Their cargoes made the Portuguese capital of Lisbon the marketplace of Europe.

✔ **Reading Check** **Analyzing** What was the significance of the voyages of Dias and da Gama?

The Caravel

A Ship for Explorers Caravels ranged in length from 75 to 90 feet (23 to 27 m) and were suited for sailing along shallow coastlines. They were not, however, well suited for very long voyages, as they could not carry enough crew and supplies. Caravels were usually rigged with three or four masts, employing both square and triangular sails.

Critical Thinking

Explaining How did the caravel's lateen sails help sailors?

1 The triangular **lateen sail** caught wind that blew perpendicular to the ship, providing more maneuverability.

2 **Ballast stones** were placed in the hull of the ship to provide better balance.

3 A **bilge pump**, operating from the main deck, removed water from storage areas.

The Vikings in America The Vikings established a settlement that is now called L'Anse aux Meadows in Newfoundland. When Leif Eriksson and his crew arrived in North America, they were persuaded to stay by the lush meadows, thick forests, and streams filled with fish. A wandering crew member also discovered groves of wild grapes. When they departed for home, the Viking ships were full of timber, a rare item in Greenland, and grapes stored as wine or raisins.

Viking coins ▶

▼ Viking ship

"It is said, that their after-boat was filled with grapes. A cargo sufficient for the ship was cut, and when the spring came, they made their ship ready, and sailed away; and from its products Leif [Eriksson] gave the land a name, and called it Wineland [Vinland]. They sailed out to sea, and had fair winds until they sighted Greenland."

—from *Original Narratives of Early American History*

Viking bracelet ▶

Critical Thinking

Speculating Why do you think Leif Eriksson gave the land he found the name "Vinland"?

Columbus Crosses the Atlantic

Main Idea After Christopher Columbus reached the Americas, Spain and Portugal divided the world's unexplored regions.

History and You Do you like traveling to new places? Read to learn about the European exploration of the Americas.

. . . .

Christopher Columbus had a different plan for reaching Asia. He planned to get there by sailing west. Born in Genoa, Italy, in 1451, Columbus became a sailor for Portugal. He had traveled as far north as the Arctic Circle and as far south as the Gold Coast.

In the 1400s most educated people believed the world was round. A more difficult matter was determining its size. Columbus was among those who based their estimates of the Earth's size on the work of Ptolemy, an ancient Greek astronomer. Columbus believed Asia was about 2,760 miles (4,441 km) from

Europe—a voyage of about two months by ship. Ptolemy, however, underestimated the size of the world.

The Viking Voyages

Several centuries before Columbus, northern Europeans called Vikings had sailed to North America. In the A.D. 800s and 900s, Viking ships visited Iceland and Greenland and established settlements. According to Norse **sagas,** or traditional stories, a Viking sailor named Leif Eriksson explored a land west of Greenland about the year A.D. 1000. It was known as Vinland. Other Norse sagas describe failed attempts by the Vikings to settle in Vinland, which historians believe was North America. Archaeologists have found the remains of a Viking settlement in Newfoundland. No one is sure what other parts of North America the Vikings explored.

The Viking voyages to other lands were not well-known. Europeans did not "discover" the Americas until Columbus made his great voyage.

Spain Backs Columbus

For most of the 1400s, Spanish monarchs **devoted,** or committed, their energy to driving the Muslims out of Spain. The last Muslim kingdom in Spain fell in 1492. King Ferdinand and Queen Isabella of Spain could then focus on other goals. The Spanish were watching the seafaring and trading successes of neighboring Portugal with envy. They, too, wanted the riches of Asian trade.

Columbus needed a sponsor to finance his project of a westward voyage to Asia. He visited many European courts looking for support. After years of frustration, he finally found a sponsor in Spain.

Queen Isabella, a devout Catholic, was finally persuaded by her husband's minister of finance to support the expedition for two reasons. First, Columbus promised to bring Christianity to any lands he found. Second, if he found a way to Asia, Spain would become wealthy through the trade that would open up. The queen promised Columbus a share of any riches gained from lands he discovered on his way to Asia.

Columbus's First Voyage

On August 3, 1492, Columbus set out from Palos, Spain. He had two small ships, the *Niña* and the *Pinta,* and a larger one, the *Santa María.* Columbus served as captain of the *Santa María,* his flagship. The three ships carried about 90 sailors and a six-month supply of provisions. The small fleet stopped at the Canary Islands off the coast of West Africa for repairs and to stock up on supplies. Columbus then set out on the difficult voyage westward across unknown and mysterious stretches of the Atlantic Ocean.

The ships had good winds, but after a month at sea the sailors began to worry. Columbus, however, was determined.

People IN HISTORY

Isabella

Queen of Spain

Queen Isabella was a devout Catholic, and her beliefs were reflected in many aspects of her rule. She insisted that Columbus treat the Native Americans fairly and ordered Columbus to release several Native Americans that he brought back as slaves. Isabella truly hoped to Christianize the Native Americans. She decreed that because *"Indians . . . run away from the Christians . . . I order you . . . to compel the Indians to have dealings with the Christian settlers . . . to work on their buildings, to mine and collect gold . . . and to work on their farms and crop fields."*

Christopher Columbus

Italian Explorer

On his voyages, Columbus proved himself to be a great navigator and sailor. He believed he would discover great riches and new lands while exploring the Atlantic on the way to Asia. Before his first voyage, Columbus wrote: *"Your Highnesses commanded me . . . [to] go to . . . India, and for this accorded me great rewards and ennobled [praised] me so that from that time henceforth I might style myself 'Don' and be high admiral of the Ocean Sea and . . . Governor of the islands and continent which I should discover."*

CRITICAL Thinking

1. **Explaining** Based on the quotation, what were Columbus's goals for himself and his voyage?

2. **Analyzing** Which do you think was more important to Queen Isabella: converting the Native Americans to her religion or getting them to work? Explain your answer.

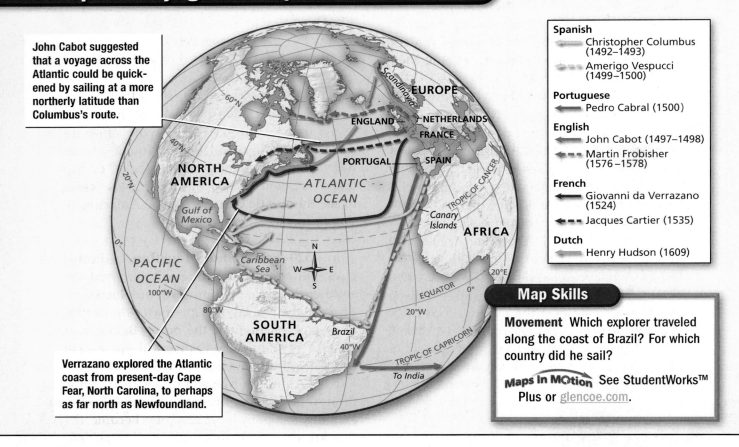

John Cabot suggested that a voyage across the Atlantic could be quickened by sailing at a more northerly latitude than Columbus's route.

Verrazano explored the Atlantic coast from present-day Cape Fear, North Carolina, to perhaps as far north as Newfoundland.

Spanish
Christopher Columbus (1492–1493)
Amerigo Vespucci (1499–1500)

Portuguese
Pedro Cabral (1500)

English
John Cabot (1497–1498)
Martin Frobisher (1576–1578)

French
Giovanni da Verrazano (1524)
Jacques Cartier (1535)

Dutch
Henry Hudson (1609)

Map Skills

Movement Which explorer traveled along the coast of Brazil? For which country did he sail?

Maps In Motion See StudentWorks™ Plus or glencoe.com.

He told the men, "I made this voyage to go to the Indies, and [I] shall continue until I find them, with God's help." To convince the crew that they had not traveled too far from home, Columbus **altered,** or changed, the distances in his ship's log.

"Tierra! Tierra!"

On October 12, 1492, at two o'clock in the morning, a lookout shouted, *"Tierra! Tierra!"*—"Land! Land!" He had spotted a small island, part of the group of islands now called the Bahamas. Columbus went ashore, claimed the island for Spain, and named it San Salvador. Although he did not know it, Columbus had reached the Americas.

Columbus explored the area for several months, convinced he had reached the East Indies, the islands off the coast of Asia. Today the Caribbean Islands are often referred to as the West Indies. Columbus called the local people Indians. He noted that they regarded the Europeans with wonder and often touched them to find out "if they were flesh and bones like themselves."

Columbus returned to Spain in triumph. Queen Isabella and King Ferdinand received him with great honor and agreed to finance his future voyages to the lands in the west. Columbus earned the title of Admiral of the Ocean Sea.

Columbus's Later Voyages

Columbus made three more voyages from Spain, in 1493, 1498, and 1502. He explored the Caribbean islands of Hispaniola (present-day Haiti and the Dominican Republic), Cuba, and Jamaica. He also sailed along the coasts of Central America and northern South America. He claimed the new lands for Spain and established settlements. Columbus also mapped the coastline of Central America.

Later explorations made it clear that Columbus had not reached Asia at all.

He had found a part of the globe that was unknown to Europeans, Asians, and Africans. In the following years, the Spanish explored most of the Caribbean region. In time their voyages led to the establishment of the Spanish Empire in the Americas.

Dividing the World

Both Spain and Portugal wanted to protect their claims, and they turned to Pope Alexander VI for help. In 1493 the pope drew a **line of demarcation,** an imaginary line running down the middle of the Atlantic from the North Pole to the South Pole. Spain was to control all lands to the west of the line; Portugal controlled all lands to the east of the line. Portugal, however, protested that the division favored Spain. As a result, in 1494 the two countries signed the Treaty of Tordesillas (TOHR•day•SEE•yuhs), an agreement to move the line farther west. The treaty divided the entire unexplored world between Spain and Portugal.

Exploring America

After Columbus, other voyagers explored the Americas. In 1502 **Amerigo Vespucci** sailed along South America's coast. Vespucci concluded that South America was a conti-

nent, not part of Asia. European geographers soon began calling the continent America, in honor of Amerigo Vespucci.

Another Spaniard, Vasco Núñez de Balboa (bal•BOH•uh), heard stories of the "great waters" beyond the mountains of Panama, in Central America. He hiked through steamy rain forests until he reached the opposite coast. There, in 1513, Balboa found a vast body of water, claiming it and the adjoining lands for Spain. Balboa was the first European to see the Pacific Ocean from the Americas.

Sailing Around the World

In 1520 **Ferdinand Magellan,** a Portuguese seaman sailing for Spain, reached the southernmost tip of South America. He sailed through the stormy waters of a **strait,** or narrow sea passage, into the ocean Balboa had seen. The waters were so peaceful—*pacifico* in Spanish—that Magellan named the ocean the Pacific. Although Magellan later died in the Philippine Islands, his crew continued west, arriving in Spain in 1522. They became the first known people to **circumnavigate,** or sail around, the world.

✓ **Reading Check** **Describing** Why did Spain finance Columbus's voyage?

Section 2 Review

History ONLINE
Study Central™ To review this section, go to glencoe.com.

Vocabulary

1. Using complete sentences, define the following terms: saga, devote, alter, line of demarcation, strait, circumnavigate.

Main Ideas

2. Identifying What route did the Portuguese explorers follow to get to Asia? Which explorer arrived first?

3. Describing How did Spain and Portugal divide up the entire unexplored world?

Critical Thinking

4. Analyzing How did Henry the Navigator further exploration?

5. Persuasive Writing Write a paragraph explaining why Americans might celebrate Eriksson Day rather than Columbus Day.

6. Sequencing Use a time line like the one below to show when the following explorers carried out their journeys: Columbus, Eriksson, Magellan, Balboa.

Answer the
7. Essential Question
Why did Spain and Portugal want to find a sea route to Asia?

Spain in America

Essential Question ◄

How did Spain's conquests affect the economic and social development of the Americas?

Reading Guide

Content Vocabulary

conquistador *(p. 43)*   encomienda *(p. 47)*

pueblo *(p. 46)*   plantation *(p. 47)*

mission *(p. 46)*

Academic Vocabulary

grant *(p. 43)*   found *(p. 46)*

Key People

Hernán Cortés *(p. 43)*

Montezuma *(p. 43)*

Francisco Pizarro *(p. 44)*

Atahualpa *(p. 44)*

Hernando de Soto *(p. 46)*

Reading Strategy

Taking Notes As you read, use a diagram like the one below to rank the social classes in the Spanish colonies.

Enslaved Africans

INDIANA ACADEMIC STANDARDS
United States History

8.4.1 Identify economic factors contributing to European exploration and colonization in North America, the American Revolution, and the drafting of the Constitution of the United States.

American Diary

In 1519 Hernán Cortés prepared to leave Cuba for Mexico with 11 ships carrying about 550 Spanish soldiers and 16 horses. Before setting off, Cortés said to his men: "I know in my heart that we shall take vast and wealthy lands, peoples such as have never before been seen. . . . If you do not abandon me, as I shall not abandon you, I shall make you in a very short time the richest of all men who have crossed the seas."

—*from* Cortés: The Life of the Conqueror by His Secretary

Cortés enters Tenochtitlán.

Explorers and Conquests

Main Idea Spanish explorers conquered Native American empires and found new lands.

History and You What would you look for as you hike along a nature trail? Read to learn what some Spanish explorers looked for as they traveled on foot through the Americas.

∙∙∙∙∙∙∙∙∙∙∙∙∙∙∙∙∙∙∙∙∙∙∙∙∙∙∙∙∙∙∙∙∙∙∙∙∙∙

Stories of gold, silver, and kingdoms wealthy beyond belief greeted the early Spanish explorers in the Americas. The reports led them far and wide in search of fabulous riches.

These explorers, known as **conquistadors** (kahn•KEES•tuh•dawrs), received **grants,** or special privileges, from the Spanish rulers. These grants gave them the right to explore and establish settlements in the Americas. In exchange, they agreed to give the Spanish crown one-fifth of any gold or other treasure discovered. This arrangement allowed Spanish rulers to launch expeditions with little risk. If a conquistador failed, he lost his own fortune. If he succeeded, both he and Spain gained wealth and glory.

Cortés Conquers the Aztec

When **Hernán Cortés** landed on the east coast of present-day Mexico in 1519, he was looking for gold and glory. He came with more than 500 soldiers, some horses, and a few cannons. Cortés soon learned about the great Aztec Empire and its capital of Tenochtitlán (tay•NAWCH•teet•LAHN).

The Aztec conquered many cities in Mexico to build their empire. These cities were forced to give crops, clothing, gold, and precious stones to the Aztec as tribute, or money paid for protection. Cortés formed alliances with a number of these conquered people against the Aztec. Then he marched into Tenochtitlán with his small army and his Native American allies.

The Aztec emperor, **Montezuma** (MAHN•tuh•ZOO•muh)—also spelled Moctezuma—welcomed Cortés and his soldiers and provided them with food and a fine palace. However, Cortés took advantage of the hospitality and made Montezuma his prisoner. The Aztec rebelled in the spring of 1520. During the fighting, which lasted for days, Montezuma was killed.

Primary Source / The Aztec and the Spanish

An Aztec View Hernán Cortés and his soldiers arrived on the Mexican coast in April 1519. The people of eastern Mexico felt fear and awe as they watched the soldiers. One Aztec later recalled:

"They came in battle array, as conquerors ... their spears glinted in the sun, and their pennons [banners] fluttered like bats. They made a loud clamor as they marched, for their coats of mail and their weapons clashed and rattled. ... They terrified everyone who saw them."

—from *The Broken Spears*

Critical Thinking

Comparing and Contrasting How do you think the Aztec's report differs from Cortés's speech?

Eventually, the Spanish were forced to leave Tenochtitlán. Cortés, however, was determined to retake the city. He waited until more Spanish troops arrived, and then he attacked and destroyed the Aztec capital in 1521. An Aztec poem describes the scene:

PRIMARY SOURCE

"Without roofs are the houses,
And red are their walls with blood.
· · · · · · · · · · · · · ·
Weep, my friends,
Know that with these disasters
We have lost our Mexican nation."

—from *Stolen Continents*

The Aztec Empire disintegrated, and Spain seized control of the region.

Pizarro Conquers the Inca

The conquistador **Francisco Pizarro** sailed down the Pacific coast of South America with about 180 Spanish soldiers. Pizarro had heard tales of the incredibly wealthy Inca Empire in what is now Peru. In 1532 Pizarro captured the Inca ruler, **Atahualpa** (AH•tah•WAHL•pah), and destroyed much of the Inca army.

The following year, the Spanish falsely accused Atahualpa of crimes and executed him. Without their leader, the Inca were not able to fight effectively. Pizarro soon gained control of most of the vast Inca Empire.

Why Spain Succeeded

The conquistadors' victories over the Aztec and Inca were quick and lasting. How could Cortés and Pizarro, with only their small armies, conquer such mighty empires?

First, the Spanish arrived with weapons—guns and cannons—and animals that the Aztec and Inca had never seen. The Spanish rode horses and had huge, ferocious dogs. To the Native Americans, the Spanish seemed almost like gods. Second, some Native Americans in the region disliked their Aztec overlords.

Spanish Explorers, 1513–1598

NATIONAL GEOGRAPHIC

- Ponce de León 1513
- Cabeza de Vaca 1528–1536
- De Soto 1539–1542
- Coronado 1540–1542
- Oñate 1598–1605
- Present-day boundaries

By the Numbers

American Wealth Sent to Spain

Value of gold and silver in millions of pesos

- 1503–05: 1
- 1536–40: 7
- 1576–80: 17.5
- 1616–20: 23

Source: *American Treasure and the Price of Revolution in Spain*

Map Skills

Movement Which conquistador explored areas along the southern half of the Mississippi River?

Maps In MOtion See StudentWorks™ Plus or glencoe.com.

Juan Ponce de León discovered Florida in 1513, while looking for the mythical Fountain of Youth. He was the first European to visit the site of St. Augustine.

The city of St. Augustine was founded by Pedro Menéndez de Avilés on September 8, 1565. ▼

"On Saturday, the 8th, the general landed with many banners spread, to the sound of trumpets and salutes of artillery. . . . The same day the general took formal possession of the country in the name of his Majesty."

—Francisco Lopez de Mendoza Grajales, The Founding of St. Augustine

◄ Spanish explorers built the Castillo San Marcos at St. Augustine between 1672 and 1695. They wanted to protect their holdings in Florida because of the growth of English settlements along the east coast of North America.

Critical Thinking

Explaining Why did the Spanish fortify St. Augustine?

These peoples assisted the conquistadors in overthrowing the Aztec. Finally, disease played an extremely large role in the Spanish conquest. With no immunity to European diseases, the Aztec and the Inca quickly fell victim to epidemics of smallpox and other diseases. This situation weakened their resistance to the invaders.

Spain in North America

Mexico and Peru were rich in silver and gold. Hoping to find similar wealth to the north, conquistadors explored the southeastern and southwestern parts of North America.

Juan Ponce de León made the first Spanish landing on the North American mainland, arriving on the east coast of present-day Florida in 1513. According to legend, Ponce de León hoped to find not only gold but also the legendary fountain of youth, "a spring of running water of such marvelous virtue" that drinking it "makes old men young again." Ponce de León's exploration led to the first Spanish settlement in what is now the United

States. In 1565, the Spanish built a fort at St. Augustine, Florida.

The Seven Cities of Cibola

Many other conquistadors searched for quick riches and several lost their lives trying. Álvar Núñez Cabeza de Vaca (cah•BAY•sah day VAH•cah) was part of a Spanish expedition to Florida in 1528.

After encountering troubles in Florida, the expedition, led by Pánfilo de Narváez, sailed south toward Mexico. However, in November 1528, three of the five boats were lost in a storm. The two boats that survived went aground on an island near what is now the state of Texas. Within a few months, only a handful of the Spaniards were still alive.

To survive among the Native Americans, de Vaca and an enslaved African named Estevanico became medicine men. Cabeza de Vaca later wrote that their method of healing was "to bless the sick, breathing on them," and to recite Latin prayers.

Native Americans in Slavery Mistreatment of the native peoples by the Spanish led the missionary Father Bartolomé de Las Casas to come to the native peoples' defense. His account led Spanish officials to prohibit the enslavement of local peoples.

"[T]he Spaniards still do nothing save tear the natives to shreds, murder them and inflict upon them untold misery, suffering and distress, tormenting, harrying and persecuting them mercilessly. . . . When the Spanish first journeyed there, the indigenous population of the island of Hispaniola stood at some three million; today only two hundred survive."

—Bartolomé de Las Casas,
A Short Account of the Destruction of the Indies

"[O]ne of the most important things in which the Audiencias [courts] are to serve us is in taking very especial care of the good treatment of the Indians and preservation of them. . . . We have ordered provision to be made that from henceforward the Indians in no way be made slaves."

—from *Colonialism*

DBQ Document-Based Questions

Analyzing According to Las Casas, what effect did Spanish treatment have on the Native American population?

In 1533 the Spaniards set off on a long trip across the Southwest. Reaching Mexico in 1536, Cabeza de Vaca related tales about seven cities of gold.

Inspired by these stories, **Hernando de Soto** led an expedition to the west. For three years they wandered throughout the present-day southeastern United States, seizing food and supplies from Native Americans. In 1541 De Soto crossed the Mississippi River. After reaching what is today Oklahoma, de Soto died of fever.

Francisco Vásquez de Coronado also wanted to find the "Seven Cities of Cibola." Traveling through northern Mexico and present-day Arizona and New Mexico, his expedition reached a Zuni settlement in 1540. They realized at once that there was no gold. Members of the expedition traveled west to the Colorado River and east into what is now Kansas. They found nothing but "windswept plains" and strange "shaggy cows" (buffalo).

✓ **Reading Check** **Analyzing** How were Spaniards able to defeat Native American empires?

Spanish Rule

Main Idea As the Spanish settled their colonies in the Americas, a strict social class structure formed.

History and You Have you ever visited or seen pictures of old Spanish missions in the American Southwest? Read to learn how the Spanish settled the Americas.

. . . .

Spanish law called for three kinds of settlements in the Americas—pueblos, missions, and presidios. **Pueblos,** or towns, were established as centers of trade. **Missions** were religious communities that usually included a small town, surrounding farmland, and a church. A presidio, or fort, was usually built near a mission.

The Spanish sent Juan de Oñate (day ohn•YAH•tay) from Mexico to gain control over frontier lands to the north and to convert the inhabitants to Christianity. In 1598 Oñate **founded,** or established, the province of New Mexico and introduced cattle and horses to the Pueblo people there.

Social Classes

A class system developed in Spain's empire. At the top were people who were born in Spain, called *peninsulares*. The *peninsulares* owned the land, served in the Catholic Church, and ran the local government. Below them were the creoles, people who were born in the Americas to Spanish parents. Lower in order were the mestizos (meh•STEE•zohs), people with Spanish and Native American parents. Still lower were the Native Americans, most of whom lived in great poverty. At the bottom were enslaved Africans.

In the 1500s, the Spanish government granted conquistadors who settled in the Americas an *encomienda*, the right to demand taxes or labor from Native Americans living on the land. This system turned the Native Americans into slaves. Grueling labor took its toll. Many Native Americans died from malnutrition and disease.

A Spanish priest, Bartolomé de Las Casas, condemned the cruel treatment of the Native Americans. He pleaded for laws to protect them. Las Casas claimed that millions had died because the Spanish "made gold their ultimate aim, seeking to load themselves with riches in the shortest possible time."

Las Casas's reports influenced the Spanish government to pass the New Laws in 1542. These laws forbade making slaves of Native Americans. Although not always enforced, these laws did correct the worst abuses.

The Plantation System

Some Spanish settlers made large profits by exporting crops and raw materials to Spain. In the West Indies, the main exports were tobacco and sugarcane. To raise these crops, the Spanish developed the plantation system. A **plantation** is a large farm.

The Spanish used Native Americans to work their plantations. Las Casas suggested replacing them with enslaved Africans— a suggestion he bitterly regretted later. He thought the Africans could endure the labor better than the Native Americans. As a result, thousands of Africans from West Africa were brought to the Americas. The Africans who survived the brutal ocean voyage were sold to plantation owners. By the late 1500s, plantation slave labor was an essential part of the economy of the colonies.

Reading Check **Identifying** Whom did Las Casas try to protect?

History ONLINE
Study Central™ To review this section, go to glencoe.com.

Section 3 Review

Vocabulary

1. Write sentences or short paragraphs in which you define the following terms: conquistador, grant, pueblo, mission, found, *encomienda*, plantation.

Main Ideas

2. **Explaining** What were the first adventurers to explore North America looking for?

3. **Discussing** How did slavery begin in the Americas?

Critical Thinking

4. **Analyzing** Why were some Native Americans willing to form alliances with Cortés?

5. **Categorizing** Use a diagram like the one below to identify the explorers who went to each region.

Mexico or Peru

Florida or the Southwest

6. **Expository Writing** Write a short essay describing the Spanish exploration and settlement of the Americas.

Answer the
7. **Essential Question**
How did Spain's conquests affect the economic and social development of the Americas?

Exploring North America

Why did European nations establish colonies in North America?

Reading Guide

Content Vocabulary
mercantilism (p. 50)

Northwest Passage (p. 51)

Columbian Exchange (p. 51)

coureur de bois (p. 52)

Academic Vocabulary
globe (p. 51)   chart (p. 51)

Key People and Events
Martin Luther (p. 49)

Protestant Reformation (p. 49)

John Calvin (p. 49)

John Cabot (p. 51)

Jacques Cartier (p. 51)

Henry Hudson (p. 51)

Reading Strategy
Taking Notes As you read, use a diagram like the one below to list the explorers who tried to find the Northwest Passage.

Search for the Northwest Passage

INDIANA ACADEMIC STANDARDS
United States History

8.1.2 Explain the struggle of the British, French, Spanish, and Dutch to gain control of North America during settlement and colonization.

8.4.2 Illustrate elements of the three types of economic systems, using cases from United States history.

8.4.9 Explain and evaluate examples of domestic and international interdependence throughout United States history.

American Diary

In 1639 a French nun named Marie of the Incarnation arrived in Quebec, New France's first colony. To convert Native Americans, she learned their languages and wrote religious books in those languages. In a letter, she wrote:

"You will perhaps laugh that at the age of fifty years I am beginning to study a new tongue [language], but one must undertake all things for the service of God and the salvation of one's neighbour."

—*from the book* Word From New France

Sister Marie and other French nuns arrive in Quebec.

A Divided Church

Main Idea Protestantism became a powerful religious force in Europe during the 1600s.

History and You What motivates people to demand changes? Read to find out why Christianity changed in the 1500s.

• •

The desire to spread Christianity was a major reason that Europeans explored and settled North America. The earlier explorers and settlers were Roman Catholics. As overseas exploration was advancing in the 1500s, a religious upheaval in Europe was sparking religious divisions.

In 1517 **Martin Luther,** a German priest, nailed a list of complaints about the Catholic Church on a local church door. Luther declared that the Bible was the only true guide for Christians. He rejected many Church practices—even the authority of the pope—because they were not mentioned in the Bible. Luther also believed that faith rather than good deeds was the way to salvation.

Within a few years, Luther had many followers who broke away from Catholicism to begin their own Christian churches. Luther's protests were the start of a great religious and historical movement known as the **Protestant Reformation.**

Protestantism Spreads in Europe

From Germany, Luther's ideas spread rapidly. **John Calvin,** a French religious thinker who lived in Geneva, Switzerland, also broke away from the Catholic Church. Like Luther, Calvin rejected the idea that good works alone would ensure a person's salvation and believed in the all-powerful nature of God.

Calvinists spread their faith to other people. Missionaries were sent from Geneva to all parts of Europe. Calvinism was established in France, the Netherlands, Scotland, and central and eastern Europe.

In England, King Henry VIII also left the Catholic Church, but not for strictly religious reasons. Pope Clement VII refused Henry's request to declare his first marriage invalid. In 1534 the English Parliament, working with the king, denied the authority of the pope and recognized the king as the head of the new Church of England.

Primary Source / **Fur Trader Among the Native Americans**

The Peacemaker Born in France, Jean Nicollet arrived in Quebec in 1618 at the age of 19. He became a fur trader and set out to learn Native American languages. For two years he lived among the Algonquins, *"always accompanying [them] on their expeditions and travels."* In about 1622 he succeeded in making peace between the Algonquins and the Iroquois. Eventually, Nicollet settled among the Nipissings, *"having his cabin apart, doing his own fishing and trading,"* but taking part in their frequent councils.

—from *The American Geologist*

▲ French fur trader Jean Nicollet and Native Americans participate in a peacemaking ceremony.

Critical Thinking

Comparing and Contrasting Do you think Nicollet's actions toward Native Americans were like or unlike the actions of other Europeans in North America? Explain.

Henry's daughter, Queen Elizabeth I, continued his religious reforms. England became firmly established as a Protestant nation.

Religious Rivalries in the Americas

The religious divisions between Catholics and Protestants in Europe also crossed the Atlantic. Spanish and French Catholics worked to spread their faith to the Native Americans. The Spanish settled in the southwestern and southeastern regions of North America, and the French settled in the northeast.

Dutch and English Protestants established colonies in lands along the Atlantic coast between the French and the Spanish settlements. Some of the English settlements were founded by Protestants who wanted to practice their beliefs in peace.

✔ **Reading Check** **Explaining** What role did religion play in the exploration of North America?

Economic Rivalry

Main Idea European nations competed to establish colonies in the Americas.

History and You Do you know if land in some parts of your neighborhood is more valuable than in other parts? Read to learn what the Dutch paid for Manhattan Island.

....

Religion was only one of the factors that pushed European nations across the Atlantic Ocean. The promise of great wealth was equally strong, especially as other Europeans watched Spain acquire gold and other riches from its colonies.

According to the economic theory of **mercantilism,** which was popular at the time, a nation's power is based on its wealth. Rulers tried to increase their nation's total wealth by acquiring gold and silver and by developing a continuing trade with other regions.

The Columbian Exchange NATIONAL GEOGRAPHIC

Crops, Food, Disease

Colonists, Animals, Plants, Disease

Enslaved People

ATLANTIC OCEAN

THE AMERICAS

EUROPE

AFRICA

ARCTIC CIRCLE

TROPIC OF CANCER

EQUATOR

Europeans brought wheat, grapes, and livestock to the Americas. Europeans also introduced diseases to which the Native Americans were not immune.

corn, potatoes, tomatoes, squashes, beans, peppers, peanuts, pecans, cocoa beans, vanilla beans, wild rice, cotton, tobacco, turkeys, hummingbirds, rattlesnakes, gray squirrels, guinea pigs

wheat, oats, barley, Asian rice, sugarcane, lettuce, onions, olives, grapes, peaches, oranges, lemons, coffee, soybeans, dandelions, roses, daisies, cows, horses, goats, sheep, pigs, chickens, sparrows, mice, rats, honeybees, smallpox, influenza, measles, malaria

Many foods associated with European cooking originated in the Americas. Ireland came to depend on the potato as a staple crop, while tomatoes form the basis of many Italian dishes.

Mercantilism provided great opportunities for individual merchants to make money. It also increased rivalry between nations.

Several countries in Europe competed for overseas territory that could produce wealth. They wanted to acquire colonies in the Americas that could provide valuable resources, such as gold and silver, or raw materials. The colonies also would serve as a place to sell European products.

The Columbian Exchange

The voyages of Columbus and other European explorers brought together two parts of the globe that previously had no contact: the continents of Europe, Asia, and Africa in one hemisphere and the Americas in the other. These contacts led to an exchange of plants, animals, and diseases that greatly altered life on both sides of the Atlantic Ocean. Scholars refer to this transfer as the **Columbian Exchange.**

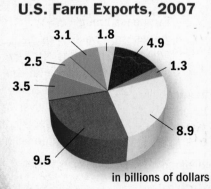

European Products in the United States

Food products introduced from Europe to the Americas are today a significant part of U.S. agriculture. The United States now exports many of these products to other countries, including Europe.

U.S. Farm Exports, 2007

3.1   1.8
2.5   4.9
3.5   1.3
           8.9
9.5

in billions of dollars

- ■ Wheat
- ■ Rice
- ■ Corn
- ■ Soybean
- ■ Others
- ■ Pork
- ■ Poultry and products
- ■ Dairy products

Source: U.S. Department of Agriculture estimates

Critical Thinking

Identifying Which of the agricultural exports in the chart above originated in the Americas? What percentage of exports did that product represent in 2007?

A Northwest Passage

The Treaty of Tordesillas had divided the Americas between Spain and Portugal. It did not allow for claims by other nations. England, France, and the Netherlands ignored the treaty. During the 1500s and early 1600s, these countries sent explorers to **chart,** or map, the coast of North America and, later, establish trade and colonies. Because the voyage to Asia—either around the southern tip of Africa or around South America—was long and difficult, they hoped to discover a **Northwest Passage** to Asia, a direct water route through the Americas.

In 1497 England sent **John Cabot,** an Italian, to look for a northern route to Asia. Cabot probably landed on the coast of present-day Newfoundland. England used Cabot's voyage as the basis for its claims to North America.

In 1524 France hired an Italian, Giovanni da Verrazano, to look for a northern sea route. Verrazano explored the coast of North America from present-day Nova Scotia down to the Carolinas.

In 1535, French explorer **Jacques Cartier** (KAR•tyay) sailed up the St. Lawrence River, hoping it would lead to the Pacific. From a mountain next to a Huron village on the river, Cartier wrote, "one sees a very great distance." He named the peak Mont-Royal, which means "royal mountain." This is the site of the city now called Montreal. Cartier heard stories about gold, but he found neither gold nor a sea route to Asia.

Hudson's Discoveries

The Netherlands, too, wanted to find a passage through the Americas. The Dutch nation hired **Henry Hudson,** an English sailor, to explore. In 1609 he discovered the river that now bears his name. In his ship, the *Half Moon,* Hudson sailed north on the Hudson River as far as the site of present-day Albany. Deciding that he had not found a passage to India, he turned back. The following year Hudson tried again, this time sent by England.

On this voyage, Hudson and his crew discovered the huge bay that today bears his name. Thinking he had reached the Pacific, Hudson spent months looking for an outlet. His unhappy crew, however, rebelled. Hudson, his son, and a few sailors were set adrift in a small boat—and never seen again.

French Trading Posts

France showed little interest in building an empire in the Americas. Its rulers focused on political and religious conflicts at home. The French saw North America as an opportunity to make profits from fishing and fur trading rather than as a place to settle.

Furs were popular in Europe. Traders made large profits from beaver pelts acquired in North America from Native Americans. In 1608 a French fur-trading company sent Samuel de Champlain to found a settlement in Quebec in what is now Canada. Champlain made several trips to the region and discovered Lake Champlain. He described the beautiful scenery and abundant wildlife, as well as the Native Americans he met there.

From Quebec, the French moved into other parts of Canada, where they built trading posts to collect furs gathered by Native Americans and French trappers. The trappers were called **coureurs de bois** (ku•RUHR duh BWAH), meaning "runners of the woods."

Dutch Settlements

After Hudson's voyage, the Dutch began to explore North America. Eager for world trade, the Netherlands had a large fleet of trading ships that sailed all over the world. In 1621 the Dutch West India Company set up a colony, New Netherland, in North America. There they settled at Fort Orange (later Albany) on the Hudson River and on Burlington Island in New Jersey. They also set up Fort Nassau near what is today Philadelphia.

The center of the new colony was New Amsterdam, located on the tip of Manhattan Island, where the Hudson River enters New York Harbor. In 1626 Governor Peter Minuit paid the Manhates people 60 Dutch guilders (about $24) in goods—cloth, axes, and hoes—for the island, which is today New York City.

✔ **Reading Check** **Analyzing** How did mercantilism create rivalries between European nations?

Section 4 Review

History ONLINE
Study Central™ To review this section, go to glencoe.com.

Vocabulary

1. Explain the significance of each of the following terms by using it in a sentence: mercantilism, globe, Columbian Exchange, chart, Northwest Passage, coureur de bois.

Main Ideas

2. **Explaining** What was the Protestant Reformation?

3. **Discussing** How did France's goals in North America differ from those of other European nations?

Critical Thinking

4. **Comparing and Contrasting** Discuss how Martin Luther's beliefs differed from those of Roman Catholics of his time.

5. **Diagramming** Use a diagram like the one below to identify the resources that moved between the two hemispheres in the Columbian Exchange.

The Americas ↔ Europe, Asia, and Africa

6. **Persuasive Writing** Write a speech that Henry Hudson might have given to his crew when they rebelled and threatened to kill him.

Answer the
7. **Essential Question**
Why did European nations establish colonies in North America?

Visual Summary

Motive for Exploration	Result

The Renaissance sparks an age of European exploration and discovery.

Technological advances in navigation and ship design allow long sea voyages.

European nations seek direct trade routes to Asia in order to bypass Arab traders.

Explorers sail to the Americas and along western Africa to India. West African gold and slave trade develops.

Queen Isabella of Spain ▶

Nation-states in Europe compete for power based on wealth.

Spain funds settlements in the Americas. Cortés defeats the Aztec, and Pizzaro conquers the Inca.

Portugal, Spain, England, France, and the Netherlands explore North America and set up colonies to provide raw materials, markets, and trade goods.

City of St. Augustine ▼

Catholics and Protestants clash after the Protestant Reformation.

Colonies in the Americas are established as bases for missionary work or areas where people can practice their religion freely.

 STUDY TO GO Study anywhere, anytime! Download quizzes and flash cards to your PDA from glencoe.com.

INDIANA STATEWIDE TEST PRACTICE

Reviewing Vocabulary

Directions: Choose the word or words that best completes the sentence.

1 New forms of _____, the use of scientific knowledge for practical purposes, aided European explorers.

  A technology
  B pilgrimages
  C classical works
  D sagas

2 Magellan's crew became the first known people to _____, or sail around, the world.

  A sponsor
  B circumnavigate
  C mission
  D pilgrimage

3 Spanish explorers, known as _____, received special grants to explore and establish settlements in the Americas.

  A pueblos
  B sagas
  C *encomiendas*
  D conquistadors

4 The economic theory of _____ stated that a nation's power was based on its wealth.

  A *encomienda*
  B reformation
  C mercantilism
  D exchange

Reviewing Main Ideas

Directions: Choose the best answer.

5 Why did Europeans seek trade routes to the East that bypassed Arab merchants?

  A European rulers forbade trading with non-Christians.
  B Arab merchants charged high prices for their goods.
  C Arab merchants offered inferior goods.
  D Arabs refused to trade with Europeans.

6 The Portuguese took the lead in exploring the boundaries of the known world because

  A they were the best sailors in the world.
  B their invention of the compass gave them an advantage in navigation.
  C lack of a Mediterranean port prevented Portugal from joining in the profitable trade between Asia and Europe.
  D they wanted to convert the entire world to Christianity.

7 In the West Indies, the Spanish developed the plantation system to

  A grow sugarcane and tobacco for export.
  B teach Native Americans European ways.
  C mine for gold and other precious metals.
  D protect the colonies from invaders.

8 Why was France most interested in North America?

  A as a place to settle
  B to enslave Native Americans
  C as a settlement for France's prisoners
  D to make profits from fishing and fur trading

GO ON

History ONLINE

For additional test practice, use **Self-Check Quizzes**—Chapter 2 at glencoe.com.

Critical Thinking

Directions: Choose the best answer.

9 **The Portuguese sought a sea route around Africa so they could**

   A trade directly with India and China.
   B sail quickly to the Americas.
   C carry out trade with Arab merchants.
   D open up trade with the eastern parts of Europe.

Base your answers to questions 10 and 11 on the map below and your knowledge of Chapter 2.

Religions of Western Europe

Catholic
Calvinist
Church of England
Lutheran

0   400 kilometers
0   400 miles
Lambert Azimuthal Equal-Area projection

10 **What was the major religion of the German States?**

   A Catholic
   B Calvinist
   C Church of England
   D Lutheran

11 **Why was the Lutheran religion centered in the German States?**

   A The German States had never been Catholic.
   B Martin Luther was a German theologist.
   C The German king founded the Lutheran religion.
   D The Reformation did not affect the German States.

Constructed Response

Directions: Write a short response to each of the following questions. In your answer:

- *address all parts of the question*
- *use information from the chapter*
- *include facts, examples, and details relevant to the question*
- *use clear language*

12 **Give one reason why relatively few Spanish soldiers were able to defeat the mighty Aztec and Inca Empires.**

13 **Describe one type of Spanish settlement in the Americas.**

Base your answer to question 14 on the reading below and your knowledge of Chapter 2.

> The ordinary means therefore to increase our wealth and treasure is by Forraign Trade, wherein wee must ever observe this rule; to sell more to strangers yearly than wee consume of theirs in value.
>
> —from Thomas Mun's *England's Treasure By Forraign Trade* (1664)

14 **How does this document state the central belief of mercantilism?**

15 **What was the Northwest Passage and why did explorers search for it?**

STOP

Need Extra Help?															
If you missed questions...	1	2	3	4	5	6	7	8	9	10	11	12	13	14	15
Go to page...	31	41	43	50	29	35	47	52	36	49	49	44	46	50	51

Chapter 3

Colonial America 1587-1770

William Penn meets with Native Americans in his colony of Pennsylvania.

1607 ★
English establish first permanent settlement at Jamestown

1612 ★
Tobacco planted in Virginia

1620 ★
Pilgrims land at Plymouth Rock

1630
Puritans begin settling Massachusetts Bay

Americas

World

1550

1600

1650

1585 ★
Hideyoshi becomes dictator of Japan

★ **1588**
England defeats Spanish Armada

★ **c. 1605**
Shakespeare writes *King Lear*

★ **1609**
Tea from China arrives in Europe

History ONLINE
Chapter Overview Visit glencoe.com
and click on **Chapter 3—Chapter
Overviews** to preview chapter information.

Section 1: Early English Settlements

Essential Question Why did the English settle in North America?

Section 2: New England Colonies

Essential Question Why did the Separatists and Puritans leave England and settle in North America?

Section 3: Middle Colonies

Essential Question How did the Middle Colonies develop?

Section 4: Southern Colonies

Essential Question How and why did the Southern Colonies grow?

FOLDABLES
Study Organizer

Summarizing Information

Make this Foldable to help you summarize what you learn about the early American colonies.

Step 1 Fold a sheet of notebook paper into thirds.

Step 2 Label the three sections as shown.

Reading and Writing As you read the chapter, take notes about the important people and events in the American colonies under the correct headings.

New England Colonies

Middle Colonies

Southern Colonies

◀ Mission church, San Diego, California

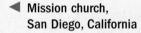

1697 ★
Spanish destroy last remains of Maya civilization in Yucatán

★ **1675**
King Philip's War begins

★ **1718**
French establish port of New Orleans

1769 ★
Mission of San Diego founded

1700

1750

★ **1670**
Alafin Ajagbo founds Oyo empire in Nigeria

★ **1685**
All Chinese ports open to foreign trade

★ **1702**
England and France go to war

★ **1740**
Frederick the Great introduces freedom of press in Prussia

Early English Settlements

Essential Question ◄

Why did the English settle in North America?

Reading Guide

Content Vocabulary

charter (p. 60)

joint-stock company (p. 60)

headright (p. 61)

burgesses (p. 61)

Academic Vocabulary

expand (p. 61)

Key People and Events

Sir Francis Drake (p. 59)

Sir Walter Raleigh (p. 59)

Captain John Smith (p. 61)

Pocahontas (p. 61)

House of Burgesses (p. 61)

Reading Strategy

Taking Notes As you read, use a diagram like the one below to list the hardships faced by the Jamestown settlers.

Hardships for Jamestown Settlers

INDIANA ACADEMIC STANDARDS
United States History

8.4.1 Identify economic factors contributing to European exploration and colonization in North America, the American Revolution, and the drafting of the Constitution of the United States.

American Diary

Captain John Smith, a leader of England's Jamestown colony, told an amazing tale of his capture by Native Americans. According to Smith, the Native Americans were prepared "to beat out his brains." Just then, Pocahontas, the 11-year-old daughter of Chief Powhatan, "got his head in her arms, and laid her own upon his to save him from death." The gesture moved the chief to spare Smith's life.

—from The Generall Historie of Virginia

England in America

Main Idea After defeating the Spanish Armada, England became more interested in establishing colonies in North America.

History and You Do you like reading mystery novels? Read to learn about the disappearance of the English colonists on Roanoke Island.

. . . .

The story of Smith and Pocahontas, whether true or not, comes from the earliest period of English settlement in America. Compared to the Spanish, who were their economic rivals, the English were slow to seek colonies.

The Spanish Armada

Trading rivalry and religious differences had been pushing England and Spain toward war for years. King Philip II, the powerful ruler of Spain, wanted to put a Catholic ruler on the throne of England. He did not consider Queen Elizabeth, a Protestant, the rightful ruler of England.

Also, English adventurers, such as **Sir Francis Drake,** had attacked Spanish ships and ports. Philip thought that Elizabeth should punish Drake for his raids. Instead, she honored Drake with knighthood. Philip

sent the Spanish Armada, Spain's fleet of warships, to conquer England, but it failed completely. Although war between England and Spain continued until 1604, the defeat of the armada marked the end of Spanish control of the seas. The way was clear for England to start colonies in North America.

The Lost Colony of Roanoke

The English had made several attempts to establish a base in North America. Sir Humphrey Gilbert claimed Newfoundland for Queen Elizabeth in 1583. However, before he could find a place for a colony, Gilbert died at sea.

The following year, Queen Elizabeth gave **Sir Walter Raleigh** the right to claim land in North America. Raleigh sent an expedition to find a good place to settle. His scouts made an enthusiastic report of Roanoke Island, off the coast of present-day North Carolina.

The first settlers, 100 men, had a difficult winter on the island and returned to England. In 1587 Raleigh then sent 91 men, 17 women, and 9 children to Roanoke. John White, artist and mapmaker, led the group. Shortly after arriving on the island, White's daughter gave birth. Virginia Dare was the first English child born in North America.

Ships arrive at Jamestown, Virginia.

Time Line — Early English Settlements

Settling America Most of the early English settlements were founded by private investors who asked the English monarch for charters, or documents, that granted the right to establish colonies in America. Later, England's government placed direct controls on the American colonies.

★ **1590** Settlers at Roanoke vanish

★ **1583** Sir Humphrey Gilbert claims New-foundland for Queen Elizabeth

★ **1607** Colonists settle at Jamestown

Critical Thinking

Theorizing Why do you think people in England invested in the founding of colonies in America?

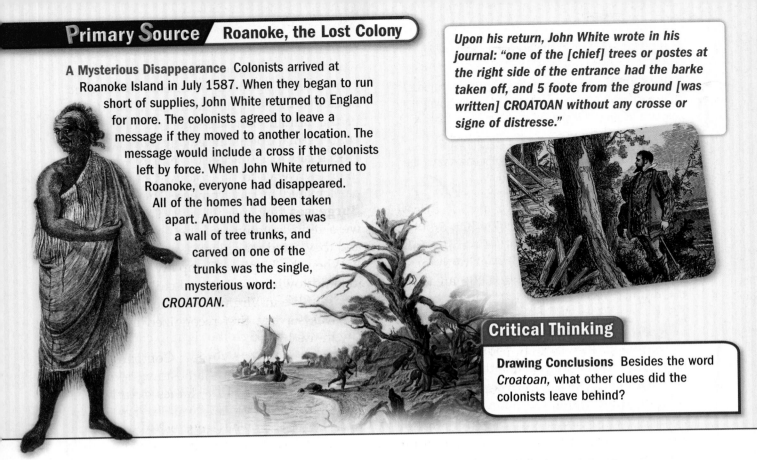

A Mysterious Disappearance Colonists arrived at Roanoke Island in July 1587. When they began to run short of supplies, John White returned to England for more. The colonists agreed to leave a message if they moved to another location. The message would include a cross if the colonists left by force. When John White returned to Roanoke, everyone had disappeared. All of the homes had been taken apart. Around the homes was a wall of tree trunks, and carved on one of the trunks was the single, mysterious word: *CROATOAN*.

Upon his return, John White wrote in his journal: "one of the [chief] trees or postes at the right side of the entrance had the barke taken off, and 5 foote from the ground [was written] CROATOAN without any crosse or signe of distresse."

Critical Thinking

Drawing Conclusions Besides the word *Croatoan*, what other clues did the colonists leave behind?

White explored the area and drew pictures of what he saw. In a book illustrated by White, another colonist described the Native American towns the settlers encountered:

PRIMARY SOURCE

"Their towns are small . . . a village may contain but ten or twelve houses—some . . . as many as twenty."
—from *A Brief and True Report of the New Found Land of Virginia*

Nine days after his granddaughter's birth, White returned to England for supplies. Although he had hoped to be back within a few months, the war with Spain delayed his return for nearly three years. When he returned to Roanoke, White found it deserted. Finding the word *Croatoan* carved on a gatepost, White believed the colonists had gone to Croatoan Island, about 50 miles to the south. Bad weather kept White from investigating, or examining further. The Roanoke colonists were never seen again.

Reading Check **Explaining** Why were England and Spain at war in the late 1500s?

Jamestown Settlement

Main Idea The first permanent English settlement in North America was at Jamestown.

History and You What obstacles would you have to overcome to create a home in the wilderness? Read to learn about the hardships of the Jamestown settlers.

For a time, the failure of the Roanoke colony discouraged others from planning English colonies in North America. However, the idea emerged again in 1606. Several groups of merchants sought **charters,** documents granting the right to organize settlements in an area, from King James I.

The Virginia Company

One group of merchants, the Virginia Company of London, received a charter. The Virginia Company was a **joint-stock company.** Investors bought stock, or part ownership, in the company in return for a share of its future profits. Settlers in America were to search for gold and establish trade in fish and furs.

In December 1606, the company sent 144 settlers in three ships to build a new colony in North America. In April 1607, the ships entered Chesapeake Bay and then sailed up a river flowing into the bay. The colonists named the river the James and their new settlement Jamestown to honor their king.

Jamestown Survives

The colonists faced hardships of disease and hunger. The colony survived its first two years because of 27-year-old **Captain John Smith,** an experienced explorer. Smith forced the settlers to work, explored the area, and sought corn from the local Native Americans led by Chief Powhatan. When John Smith returned to England, Jamestown lacked a strong leader. The winter of 1609–1610 became known as "the starving time." Fighting also broke out with the Native Americans.

The Virginia colonists finally discovered a way to make money for the investors by growing a type of tobacco using seeds from the West Indies. Soon planters all along the James River were raising tobacco.

The colony of Virginia began to prosper. Relations with the Native Americans improved after a colonist, John Rolfe, married **Pocahontas,** the daughter of Chief Powhatan. Land ownership was **expanded** when the Virginia Company gave a **headright,** or land grant, of 50 acres to settlers who paid their own way to the colony. Colonists also participated in government. The **House of Burgesses** first met in 1619. The **burgesses** were representatives of the colony's towns, and they could make local laws for the colony.

When the Virginia Company sent women to Jamestown, marriage and children became a part of life in Virginia. Another part of that life was slavery, first recognized in Virginia law in the 1660s.

By the 1620s, the Virginia Company faced financial troubles with Jamestown returning little profit. In 1624 King James canceled the company's charter and made Jamestown England's first royal colony in America.

Reading Check **Analyzing** Why was the House of Burgesses important?

Section 1 Review

History ONLINE
Study Central™ To review this section, go to glencoe.com.

Vocabulary

1. Use each of the following terms in a paragraph about the Jamestown settlement: charter, joint-stock company, expand, headright, burgesses.

Main Ideas

2. **Making Connections** Why was the defeat of the Spanish Armada important to England's quest for overseas colonies?

3. **Explaining** How did the Jamestown settlement survive the first two years?

Critical Thinking

4. **Making Inferences** Why do you think the king of England let a group of merchants try to establish a colony in North America?

5. **Organizing** Use a diagram like the one below to describe three attempts by the English to establish colonies in North America and the results.

Attempts to Colonize

Results

6. **Descriptive Writing** Imagine that you are a Native American who witnessed the arrival of the Jamestown colonists. Describe your first impression of these people in a report to Chief Powhatan.

Answer the
7. **Essential Question**
Why did the English settle in North America?

Jamestown

On May 14, 1607, English colonists began work on a settlement near the James River. They built a triangular fort of upright logs, about an acre in size, in just 19 days. Made of a storehouse, a church, and a number of houses, the fort was near water deep enough for ships to anchor. It also was in a secure place, where enemy ships could not fire directly into the fort. Relations with the local Native Americans were often difficult, although at times the colonists were able to trade copper and iron goods for badly needed food.

How Did Geography Affect Jamestown?

The Jamestown settlers faced the hardships of an unfamiliar climate—colder winters and warmer, humid summers. They also discovered that they had built their fort beside the dirtiest part of the James River. River water was drinkable only part of the year; in the summer, it turned salty and slimy. By autumn, disease, salt poisoning, and starvation had killed almost half the colonists.

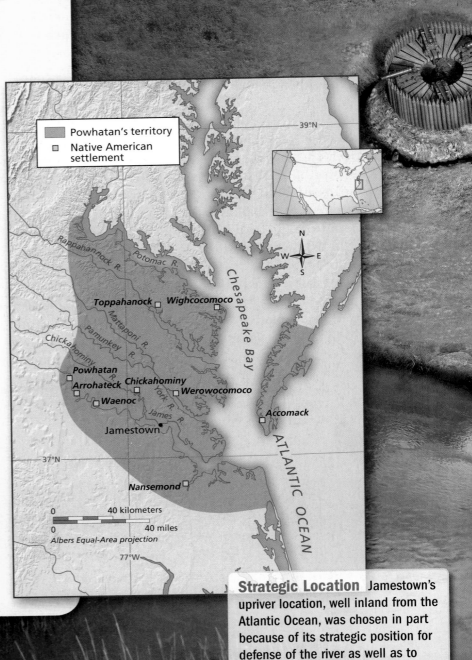

Powhatan's territory
Native American settlement

39°N

Rappahannock R.
Potomac R.
Chesapeake Bay

Toppahanock   Wighcocomoco

Mattaponi R.
Pamunkey R.
Chickahominy

Powhatan
Arrohateck   Chickahominy
Waenoc   Werowocomoco
York R.
James R.
Accomack

Jamestown

37°N

ATLANTIC OCEAN

Nansemond

0   40 kilometers
0   40 miles
Albers Equal-Area projection

77°W

Strategic Location Jamestown's upriver location, well inland from the Atlantic Ocean, was chosen in part because of its strategic position for defense of the river as well as to hide from Spanish ships that might be in the area.

Jamestown was built on a swampy, uninhabited site along the James River, which brought salty water from the ocean in the summer.

Jamestown Fort, 1607 The walls along the land sides were each 100 yards (91 meters) long. The wall along the river was 140 yards (128 meters) long.

The Scope of Suffering

Master George Percy was 27 years old when he helped establish the Jamestown Colony in 1607. He was one of the 38 aristocrats in the expedition and later served twice as the colony's governor before he returned to England.

"There were never Englishmen left in a foreign country in such misery as we were in this new-discovered Virginia."

Analyzing Geography

1. **Location** Why did the colonists choose Jamestown as their settlement site?
2. **Analyzing** In what ways was the fort's location a poor choice?

New England Colonies

Essential Question

Why did the Separatists and Puritans leave England and settle in North America?

Reading Guide

Content Vocabulary

dissent (p. 65)
Puritan (p. 65)
Separatist (p. 65)
Pilgrim (p. 65)
Mayflower Compact (p. 66)
Fundamental Orders of Connecticut (p. 68)

Academic Vocabulary

policy (p. 68)

Key People and Events

William Bradford (p. 66)
Squanto (p. 66)
John Winthrop (p. 67)
Roger Williams (p. 68)

Reading Strategy

Taking Notes As you read, use a diagram like the one below to list the colonies that the Separatists and Puritans formed in North America.

Colonies in North America
→ Separatist
→ Puritan

INDIANA ACADEMIC STANDARDS
United States History

8.1.1 Identify major Native American Indian groups of eastern North America and describe early conflict and cooperation with European settlers and the influence the two cultures had on each other.

8.3.1 Read maps to interpret symbols and determine the land forms and human features that represent physical and cultural characteristics of areas in the United States.

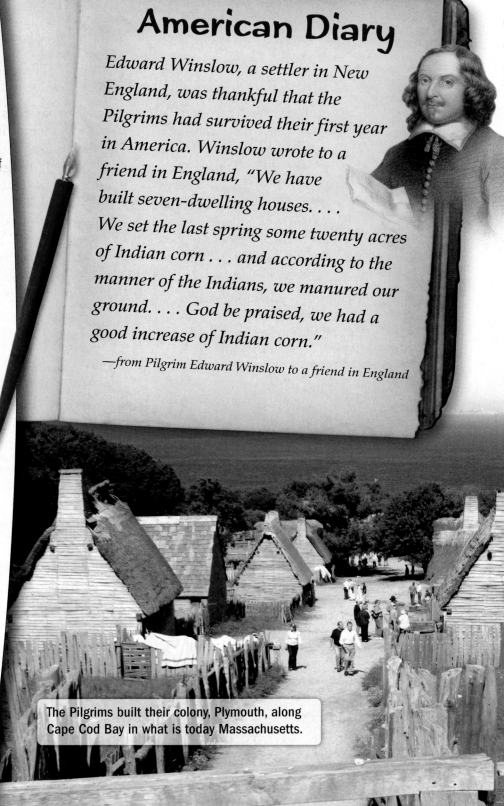

American Diary

Edward Winslow, a settler in New England, was thankful that the Pilgrims had survived their first year in America. Winslow wrote to a friend in England, "We have built seven-dwelling houses. . . . We set the last spring some twenty acres of Indian corn . . . and according to the manner of the Indians, we manured our ground. . . . God be praised, we had a good increase of Indian corn."

—from Pilgrim Edward Winslow to a friend in England

The Pilgrims built their colony, Plymouth, along Cape Cod Bay in what is today Massachusetts.

Religious Freedom

Main Idea To practice their religion more freely, a group of Separatists established the Plymouth colony in North America.

History and You Have you and a friend ever disagreed so much on an issue that you considered ending your friendship? Read about the reason why the Pilgrims settled in Plymouth.

. . . .

Unlike the Jamestown settlers, the next wave of colonists arrived in search of religious freedom. England had been a Protestant country since 1534, when King Henry VIII broke away from the Roman Catholic Church and formed the Anglican Church. Not everyone in England was happy with the new church, however. Many people **dissented**; that is, they disagreed with the beliefs or practices of the Anglicans. English Catholics, for example, still considered the pope the head of the church. They were often persecuted, or treated harshly, for that reason.

Some Protestants wanted to change, or reform, the Anglican Church. Others wanted to break away from it altogether. The Protestants who wanted to reform the Anglican Church were called **Puritans.** Those who wanted to leave and set up their own churches were known as **Separatists.**

The Separatists were persecuted in England, and some fled to the Netherlands. Though they found religious freedom there, the Separatists had difficulty finding work. They also worried that their children were losing their religious values and their English way of life.

The Pilgrims' Journey

Some Separatists in the Netherlands made an arrangement with the Virginia Company. The Separatists could settle in Virginia and practice their religion freely. In return they would give the company a share of any profits they made.

The Separatists considered themselves **Pilgrims** because their journey had a religious purpose. Only 35 of the 102 passengers who boarded the *Mayflower* in September 1620 were Pilgrims. The others were called "strangers." They were common people—servants, craftspeople, and poor farmers—who hoped to find a better life in America. Because Pilgrim beliefs shaped life in the Plymouth colony, however, all the early settlers are usually called Pilgrims.

If You Were There / A Teenage Pilgrim Girl

Creating a Home As a teenage Pilgrim girl, you help your mother cook, keep house, do laundry, and raise the younger children. When the men and boys eat their meals, you stand quietly behind the table. At a church gathering, you cannot talk, and you must keep your head covered with a bonnet when in public. You are taught to read, but not to write. Your clothes are usually a full skirt, an apron, and an upper garment with long sleeves—much like your mother wears.

Critical Thinking

Making Connections How does the life of a Pilgrim teenager compare to your life today?

The Mayflower Compact

The *Mayflower's* passengers planned to settle in the Virginia colony. The first land they sighted was Cape Cod, well north of their target. It was November, and winter was fast approaching. The colonists decided to drop anchor in Cape Cod Bay. They went ashore on a cold, bleak day in December at a place called Plymouth. **William Bradford,** their leader and historian, reported that "all things stared upon them with a weather-beaten face."

Plymouth was outside the territory of the Virginia Company and its laws. Before going ashore, the Pilgrims drew up a formal document, the **Mayflower Compact.** The compact pledged their loyalty to England. It also declared their intention of forming "a civil body politic, for our better ordering and preservation." The signers also promised to obey the laws passed "for the general good of the colony." The Mayflower Compact was a necessary step in the development of representative government in the new American colonies.

Help From the Native Americans

During their first winter in America, almost half the Pilgrims died of malnutrition, disease, and cold. In the spring, two Native Americans, **Squanto** and Samoset, befriended the colonists.

Squanto and Samoset showed the Pilgrims how to grow corn, beans, and pumpkins and where to hunt and fish. Without their help, the Pilgrims might not have survived. Squanto and Samoset also helped the Pilgrims make peace with the Wampanoag people who lived in the area. Massasoit, a Wampanoag leader, signed a treaty with the Pilgrims in March 1621. The two groups lived in harmony.

Reading Check Analyzing What was the significance of the Mayflower Compact?

The *Mayflower*

The *Mayflower*
In September 1620, 102 passengers set off on the *Mayflower* on the journey across the Atlantic. The 2,750-mile trip took more than two months. In early November, the *Mayflower* reached the shores of America.

New Settlements

Main Idea To escape religious persecution in England, thousands of Puritans migrated to North America and set up new colonies.

History and You How would you react if someone set up camp in your backyard? Read about the conflict between Native Americans and the settlers in New England.

. . . .

In 1625 Charles I became the king of England. Charles objected to the Puritans' calls for reform in the Anglican Church. Persecution of Puritans within the country increased again. As a result, some Puritans wanted to leave England.

In 1629 a group of Puritans formed the Massachusetts Bay Company. They received a royal charter to establish a colony north of Plymouth. This was the Puritans' chance to create a new society in America—a society based on the Bible.

The company chose **John Winthrop** to be the colony's governor. In 1630 Winthrop led about 900 men, women, and children to Massachusetts Bay. Most of them settled in a place they called Boston.

Growth and Government

During the 1630s, more than 15,000 Puritans journeyed to Massachusetts to escape religious persecution and economic hard times in England. This movement of people became known as the Great Migration.

At first John Winthrop and his assistants made the colony's laws. They were chosen by the General Court, which was made up of the colony's stockholders. In 1634 settlers demanded a larger role, or part, in the government. The General Court became an elected assembly. Adult male church members were allowed to vote for the governor and for their town's representatives to the General Court. In later years they also had to own property to vote.

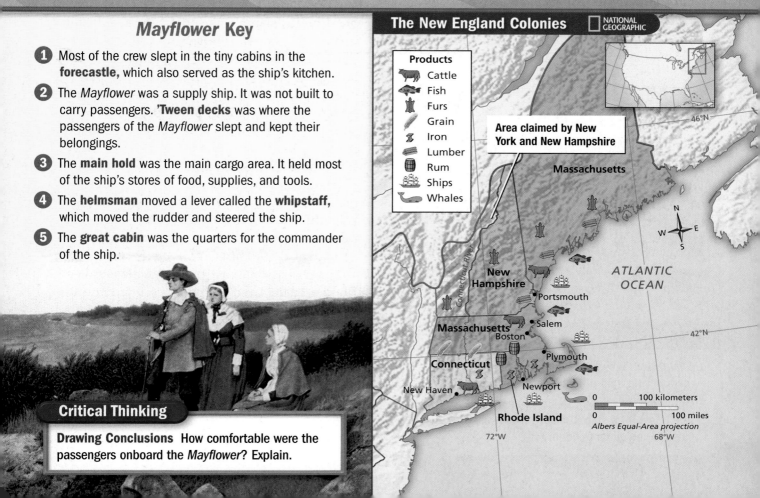

Mayflower Key

1. Most of the crew slept in the tiny cabins in the **forecastle,** which also served as the ship's kitchen.

2. The *Mayflower* was a supply ship. It was not built to carry passengers. **'Tween decks** was where the passengers of the *Mayflower* slept and kept their belongings.

3. The **main hold** was the main cargo area. It held most of the ship's stores of food, supplies, and tools.

4. The **helmsman** moved a lever called the **whipstaff,** which moved the rudder and steered the ship.

5. The **great cabin** was the quarters for the commander of the ship.

Critical Thinking

Drawing Conclusions How comfortable were the passengers onboard the *Mayflower*? Explain.

The New England Colonies — NATIONAL GEOGRAPHIC

Products
- Cattle
- Fish
- Furs
- Grain
- Iron
- Lumber
- Rum
- Ships
- Whales

Area claimed by New York and New Hampshire

Massachusetts

New Hampshire

Connecticut River

Portsmouth

ATLANTIC OCEAN

Salem

Massachusetts
Boston

Connecticut

Plymouth

New Haven

Newport

Rhode Island

ATLANTIC OCEAN

46°N

42°N

72°W

68°W

0   100 kilometers
0   100 miles
Albers Equal-Area projection

Should government be based on religion?

John Winthrop, a founder of the Massachusetts Bay Colony, believed that the colony should be governed on religious principles. Others, such as Roger Williams, disagreed and were banished from Massachusetts.

YES JOHN WINTHROP

It is yourselves who have called us to this office, and, being called by you, we have our authority from God. . . . If you stand for your natural corrupt liberties . . . you will not endure the least weight of authority . . . but if you will be satisfied to enjoy such civil and lawful liberties, such as Christ allows you, then will you quietly and cheerfully submit unto that authority which is set over you . . . for your good.
—from "'Little Speech' on Liberty"

ROGER WILLIAMS NO

I . . . only propose this case; There goes many a ship to sea, with many hundred souls in one ship, [which] is a true picture of a commonwealth. . . . It hath fallen out some times, that both Papists [Catholics] and Protestants, Jews and Turks, may be embarked in one ship; upon which supposal, I affirm . . . that none of the Papists, Protestants, Jews, or Turks, be forced to come to the ship's prayers or worship, or compelled from their own particular prayers or worship.
—from a letter to the town of Providence

DBQ Document-Based Questions

1. **Evaluating** How might Winthrop view people who held different religious views?
2. **Analyzing** Why might Williams have used the image of a ship at sea to make his case for religious freedom?

The Puritans came to America to put their religious beliefs into practice. They had little toleration for different beliefs, however. They criticized or persecuted people of other faiths. This lack of toleration led people to form new colonies in neighboring areas.

Connecticut and Rhode Island

The fertile Connecticut River valley, south of Massachusetts, was better for farming than was the stony soil around Boston. In the 1630s colonists began to settle in this area.

One such colonist, Massachusetts minister Thomas Hooker, grew dissatisfied with the way that Winthrop and other Puritan leaders ran the Massachusetts colony. In 1636 Hooker led his congregation through the wilderness to Connecticut where he founded the town of Hartford. Three years later Hartford and two other towns, Windsor and Wethersfield, formed a colony. They adopted a plan of government called the **Fundamental Orders of Connecticut.** This was the first written constitution in America. It described the organization of representative government in detail.

Good land drew colonists to Connecticut, but Rhode Island was settled by a minister named **Roger Williams** and other colonists who were forced out of Massachusetts. Williams felt that people should not be persecuted for their religious practices and that government should not force people to worship in a certain way. Williams also believed it was wrong for settlers to take land away from the Native Americans.

His ideas caused Massachusetts leaders to banish him in 1635. Williams took refuge with the Narraganset people. They later sold him land, where he founded the town of Providence. Williams received a charter in 1644 for a colony east of Connecticut called Rhode Island and Providence Plantations. With its **policy**—plan of action—of religious toleration, Rhode Island became a safe place for dissenters. It was the first place in America where people of all faiths could worship freely.

Others followed Williams's example, including John Wheelwright, who, in 1638, led a group of dissidents from Massachusetts to the north. They founded the town of Exeter in New Hampshire. Other Puritans settled Hampton the same year. New Hampshire became an independent colony in 1679.

Conflict With Native Americans

Native Americans traded furs for settlers' goods such as iron pots, blankets, and guns. In Virginia the colonists encountered the many tribes of the Powhatan confederacy. In New England the settlers met the Wampanoags, Narragansets, and other groups.

Conflicts arose, however. Usually settlers moved onto Native American lands without permission or payment. Throughout the colonial period, English settlers and Native Americans competed fiercely for the land.

In 1636 war broke out. Two traders were killed in Pequot territory, and Massachusetts sent troops to punish the Pequot. A Pequot attack then killed nine people in Connecticut. In May 1637, troops from Connecticut burned the main Pequot village, killing hundreds.

History ONLINE
Student Web Activity Visit glencoe.com and complete the Chapter 3 Web Activity about King Philip's War.

In 1675 New England went to war against the Wampanoag people and their allies. Metacomet, the Wampanoag chief, was known to settlers as King Philip. He wanted to stop the settlers from moving onto Native American lands. Metacomet tried to form a federation of local peoples, and many New England groups joined with him. The war began after settlers executed three Wampanoags for murder. Metacomet's forces then attacked towns across the region, killing hundreds of people.

The settlers and their Native American allies fought back. King Philip's War, as the conflict was called, ended in defeat for the Wampanoag and their allies. The war destroyed the power of the Native Americans in New England. The colonists were now free to expand their settlements.

Reading Check **Identifying** Which colony let people of all faiths worship freely?

Section 2 Review

History ONLINE
Study Central™ To review this section, go to glencoe.com.

Vocabulary

1. Use each of these terms in a sentence that will help explain its meaning: dissent, Puritan, Separatist, Pilgrim, Mayflower Compact, Fundamental Orders of Connecticut, policy.

Main Ideas

2. Explaining Why did the Pilgrims settle in Cape Cod instead of Virginia?

3. Discussing What was the significance of King Philip's War?

Critical Thinking

4. Comparing What did the Mayflower Compact and the Fundamental Orders of Connecticut have in common?

5. Determining Cause and Effect Use a diagram like the one below to describe the ways in which interactions with Native Americans helped Plymouth colony survive.

The colonists interact with Native Americans

6. Creative Writing Create a song that the Pilgrims might have sung as they crossed the Atlantic on the *Mayflower*. Write the lyrics from what you know about why the Pilgrims sailed to North America.

Answer the
7. Essential Question
Why did the Separatists and Puritans leave England and settle in North America?

Meet the Author

Elizabeth George Speare (1908–1994) based her novel *The Witch of Blackbird Pond* on events in Wethersfield, Connecticut, her home for 20 years. Speare's research into the town's history resulted in the diverse and rich characters at the center of this tale.

Building Background

Elizabeth George Speare used her native New England as the backdrop for many novels. In *The Witch of Blackbird Pond,* Kit leaves her home in Barbados to live with her aunt and uncle in Connecticut. There she befriends a Quaker woman accused of practicing witchcraft. Many authors use plot as the basis of their stories; however, the characters drive the plot in this tale. As you read this excerpt, pay attention to how one character responds to another.

Vocabulary

fatigue tiredness

consternation fear

hysterical very emotional

consorting keeping company

slander speak ill of

THE WITCH OF BLACKBIRD POND

Elizabeth George Speare

Kit busied herself to prepare a meal which none of them could eat. With fingers so heavy from **fatigue** and fear that she could scarcely force them to move, she cleared the table and put away the untouched food. She wondered if ever again she would escape from the sound of that dreadful breathing. Her own lungs ached with every sighing breath that Mercy drew.

Then without warning a new fear came rushing in upon her. From without the house there was an approaching sound of stamping feet and murmuring voices, gathering volume in the roadway outside. There was a crashing knock on the outer door. The three women's eyes met in **consternation.** Matthew

Wood reached the door in one stride and flung it open.

"How dare you?" he demanded in low-voiced anger. "Know you not there is illness here?"

"Aye, we know right enough," a voice replied.

"There's illness everywhere. We need your help to put a stop to it."

"What do you want?"

"We want you to come along with us. We're going for the witch." . . .

The voices sounded **hysterical.** "We should have run her out long ago."

"Time and again she's been seen **consorting** with the devil down in that meadow!"

"Now she's put a curse on our children. God knows how many more will be dead before morning!" . . .

"You'd better come with us, Matthew. Your own daughter's like to die. You can't deny it."

"I'll have naught to do with it," said Matthew firmly. "I'll hold with no witch hunt."

"You'd better hold with it!" the woman's voice shrilled suddenly. "You'd better look to the witch in your own household!"

"Ask that high and mighty niece of yours where she spends her time!" another woman shouted from the darkness. "Ask her what she knows about your Mercy's sickness!"

The weariness dropped suddenly from Matthew Wood. With his shoulders thrown back he seemed to tower in the doorway.

"Begone from my house!" he roared, his caution drowned in anger. "How dare you speak the name of a good, God-fearing girl? Any man who **slanders** one of my family has me to reckon with!"

There was a silence. "No harm meant," a man's voice said uneasily. " 'Tis only woman's talk."

"If you won't come there's plenty more in the town who will," said another. "What are we wasting our time for?"

The voices receded down the pathway, rising again in the darkness beyond. Matthew bolted the door and turned back to the dumfounded women.

"Did they wake her?" he asked dully.

"No," sighed Rachel. "Even that could not disturb her, poor child."

For a moment, there was no sound but that tortured breathing. Kit had risen to her feet and stood clinging to the table's edge. Now the new fear that was stifling her broke from her lips in an anguished whisper.

"What will they do to her?"

Her aunt looked up in alarm. Matthew's black brows drew together darkly. "What concern is that of yours?"

"I know her!" she cried. "She's just a poor helpless old woman! Oh, please tell me! Will they harm her?"

"This is Connecticut," answered Matthew sternly. "They will abide by the law. They will bring her to trial, I suppose. If she can prove herself innocent she is safe enough."

Analyzing Literature

1. **Respond**
   (a) How would you describe the tone of this passage?
   (b) What words and phrases evoke this tone?

2. **Interpret and Analyze** How do Matthew's emotions change throughout the passage?

3. **Evaluate and Predict**
   (a) What can you conclude about Matthew after reading this passage?
   (b) Based on Matthew's final comment, what action do you think the townspeople will take?

Middle Colonies

How did the Middle Colonies develop?

Reading Guide

Content Vocabulary

patroon *(p. 73)*

proprietary colony *(p. 74)*

pacifist *(p. 75)*

Academic Vocabulary

ethnic *(p. 74)*   function *(p. 75)*

Key People

Duke of York *(p. 74)*

William Penn *(p. 75)*

Quakers *(p. 75)*

Reading Strategy

Taking Notes As you read, use a diagram like the one below to show how the New York and Pennsylvania colonies split to form the four Middle Colonies under British rule.

```
New York ───┬─── [        ]
            └─── [        ]

Pennsylvania ──┬── [        ]
               └── [        ]
```

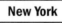

INDIANA ACADEMIC STANDARDS
United States History

8.1.2 Explain the struggle of the British, French, Spanish, and Dutch to gain control of North America during settlement and colonization.

8.3.1 Read maps to interpret symbols and determine the landforms and human features that represent physical and cultural characteristics of areas in the United States.

8.4.1 Identify economic factors contributing to European exploration and colonization in North America, the American Revolution, and the drafting of the Constitution of the United States.

American Diary

In August 1664, strong English forces demanded the surrender of the Dutch colony of New Netherland. Peter Stuyvesant, the colony's governor, at first flatly refused to surrender. Leading citizens pleaded with Stuyvesant to avoid "the absolute ruin and destruction of about fifteen hundred innocent souls." Reluctantly Stuyvesant surrendered on September 8. The colony became New York.

—*quoted in* A New World

Citizens persuade Governor Peter Stuyvesant not to open fire on the British.

England and the Colonies

Main Idea After seizing the Dutch colony of New Netherland, the English renamed the colony New York and formed the New Jersey colony.

History and You Have you ever won a prize and then shared it with your friends? Read how the English seized the New Netherland colony and then formed the New Jersey colony.

· ·

In England, the Puritans who controlled Parliament struggled for power against King Charles I. In 1642 a civil war began. Led by Oliver Cromwell, a Puritan, the Parliamentary forces defeated the king. Many Puritans from New England returned to England to join in this struggle.

Charles I was beheaded in 1649 on charges of treason. A new government was established with Cromwell as Protector. After Cromwell died in 1658, Parliament restored the monarchy but with new limitations. When Charles II became king in 1660, his reign was known as the Restoration.

In 1660 England had two clusters of colonies in what is now the United States. In the north were Massachusetts, New Hampshire, Connecticut, and Rhode Island. Maryland and Virginia were in the south. Between the two groups of English colonies were lands that the Dutch controlled.

The main settlement of the New Netherland colony was New Amsterdam, located on Manhattan Island. Blessed with a good seaport, New Amsterdam became a center of shipping to and from the Americas.

The Dutch West India Company wanted to increase the number of settlers in its colony. It offered large estates to anyone who could bring at least 50 settlers to work the land. The landowners who acquired these estates were called **patroons.** The patroons ruled like kings. They had their own courts and laws. Settlers owed the patroons labor and a share of their crops.

England Takes Over

New Netherland had an excellent harbor and a thriving river trade. The English wanted to acquire this valuable Dutch colony. In 1664 the English sent a fleet to attack New Amsterdam. At that time Peter Stuyvesant was governor of the colony. He was unprepared for a battle and surrendered the colony to the English forces.

Primary Source / New Netherland

Colonial Dutch Crafts By the mid-1600s, New Netherland had a growing population and a prosperous economy. Immigrant artisans from the Netherlands and other parts of Europe settled in the Dutch colony. They produced outstanding furniture, silverware, and other household items, such as this finely crafted silver bowl.

Two-handed silver bowl ▶

Critical Thinking

Drawing Conclusions Why do you think New Netherland, later New York, was a valuable colony?

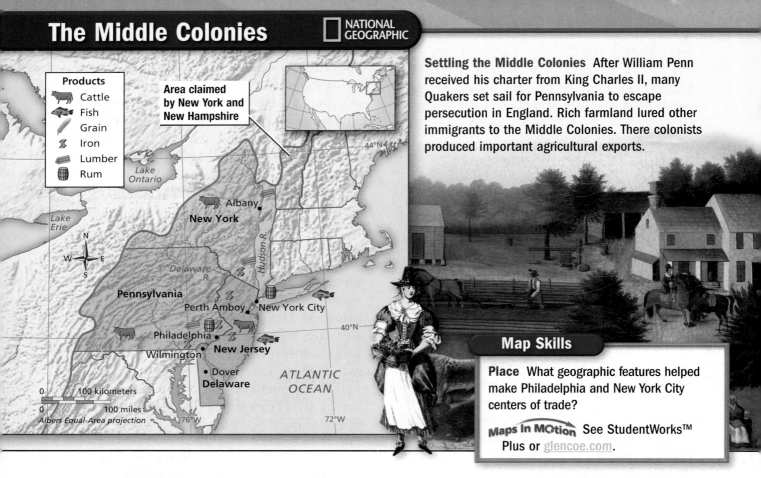

The Middle Colonies

NATIONAL GEOGRAPHIC

Products
- Cattle
- Fish
- Grain
- Iron
- Lumber
- Rum

Area claimed by New York and New Hampshire

Lake Ontario

Lake Erie

44°N

Albany
New York

Hudson R.

Delaware R.

Pennsylvania

Perth Amboy • New York City

40°N

Philadelphia

Wilmington • **New Jersey**

• Dover
Delaware

ATLANTIC OCEAN

N W E S

0   100 kilometers
0   100 miles
Albers Equal-Area projection

76°W   72°W

Settling the Middle Colonies After William Penn received his charter from King Charles II, many Quakers set sail for Pennsylvania to escape persecution in England. Rich farmland lured other immigrants to the Middle Colonies. There colonists produced important agricultural exports.

Map Skills

Place What geographic features helped make Philadelphia and New York City centers of trade?

Maps In MOtion See StudentWorks™ Plus or glencoe.com.

King Charles II gave the colony to his brother, the **Duke of York,** who renamed it New York. New York was a **proprietary colony,** a colony in which the owner, or proprietor, owned all the land and controlled the government. It differed from the New England colonies, where voters elected the governor and an assembly. Not until 1691 did the English government allow citizens of New York to elect their legislature.

New York continued to prosper under English control. It had a diverse population made up of Dutch, German, Swedish, and Native American people. Also among the population were Brazilian Jews, the first Jews to settle in North America.

In 1664 New York had about 8,000 inhabitants. That population also included at least 300 enslaved Africans. By 1683 the colony's population swelled to about 12,000 people. New York City, which was called New Amsterdam when it was controlled by the Dutch, was one of the fastest-growing locations in the colony.

New Jersey

The Duke of York gave the southern part of his colony, between the Hudson and Delaware Rivers, to Lord John Berkeley and Sir George Carteret. The proprietors named their colony New Jersey after the island of Jersey in the English Channel, where Carteret was born. To attract settlers, they offered large tracts of land and also promised freedom of religion, trial by jury, and a representative assembly. The assembly would make local laws and set tax rates.

Like New York, New Jersey was a place of **ethnic** and religious diversity. New Jersey had no natural harbors, so it did not develop a major port or city like New York, and New Jersey's proprietors made few profits. Both proprietors eventually sold their shares in the colony. By 1702 New Jersey had returned to the king, becoming a royal colony. However, the colonists continued to make local laws.

Reading Check **Explaining** Why did no major port develop in New Jersey?

Pennsylvania

Main Idea William Penn founded the colony of Pennsylvania and designed the city of Philadelphia.

History and You If given a choice, would you take land or money for a debt someone owed you? Read to learn how William Penn acquired Pennsylvania.

· ·

In 1681, **William Penn,** a wealthy English Quaker, received land as payment for a debt that King Charles II owed to Penn's father. The king gave Penn a tract of land in America stretching inland from the Delaware River. The new colony, named Pennsylvania, was nearly as large as England.

William Penn saw Pennsylvania as a "holy experiment," a chance to put his Quaker ideals into practice. The **Quakers,** or Society of Friends, believed that everyone was equal. People could follow their own "inner light" to salvation. They did not need clergy to guide them. Quakers were also **pacifists,** or people who refuse to use force or to fight in wars. They were considered a threat in England and were persecuted.

In 1682 Penn sailed to America to supervise the building of Philadelphia, the "city of brotherly love." Penn designed the city himself and wrote Pennsylvania's first constitution. Penn believed that the land belonged to the Native Americans and that settlers should pay for it. He negotiated several treaties with local Native Americans.

Penn advertised the colony throughout Europe. By 1683 more than 3,000 English, Welsh, Irish, Dutch, and German settlers had arrived. In 1701, in the Charter of Liberties, Penn granted colonists the right to elect representatives to the legislature.

Swedes had settled southern Pennsylvania before the Dutch and then the English took over the area. The Charter of Privileges allowed these lower counties to form their own legislature. The counties then **functioned,** or operated, as a separate colony known as Delaware under Pennsylvania's governor.

Reading Check **Inferring** What was William Penn's primary purpose for founding the colony of Pennsylvania?

Section 3 Review

History ONLINE
Study Central™ To review this section, go to glencoe.com.

Vocabulary

1. Define each of the following vocabulary terms and use each in a sentence: patroon, proprietary colony, ethnic, pacifist, function.

Main Ideas

2. **Describing** How were the colonies of New York and New Jersey governed?

3. **Summarizing** Describe three beliefs of the Quakers.

Critical Thinking

4. **Making Connections** Why do you think the Church of England might consider the Quakers a threat?

5. **Contrasting** Re-create the diagram below and describe how settlers in Pennsylvania and New England differed in the way they acquired land from Native Americans.

```
        Land Acquired From
         Native Americans
          /            \
  New England      Pennsylvania
   settlers          settlers
```

6. **Persuasive Writing** Take on the role of William Penn. Write an advertisement to persuade settlers to come to Pennsylvania. Include details about the Pennsylvania colony that people would find attractive.

Answer the
7. **Essential Question**
How did the Middle Colonies develop?

Essential Question ◄

How and why did the Southern Colonies grow?

Reading Guide

Content Vocabulary
indentured servant *(p. 77)*

tenant farmer *(p. 81)*

constitution *(p. 79)*

mission *(p. 82)*

debtor *(p. 80)*

Academic Vocabulary
estate *(p. 77)*

Key People and Events
Sir George Calvert, Lord Baltimore *(p.77)*

Nathaniel Bacon *(p. 78)*

James Oglethorpe *(p. 80)*

Louis Joliet *(p. 81)*

Jacques Marquette *(p. 81)*

René-Robert Cavelier, Sieur de La Salle *(p. 81)*

Reading Strategy
Taking Notes As you read, use a chart like the one below to identify the types of workers who came to the South and their reasons for coming.

Workers	Why They Came
indentured servants	

INDIANA ACADEMIC STANDARDS
United States History

8.1.2 Explain the struggle of the British, French, Spanish, and Dutch to gain control of North America during settlement and colonization.

8.3.1 Read maps to interpret symbols and determine the landforms and human features that represent physical and cultural characteristics of areas in the United States.

American Diary

Anthony Johnson was one of the first Africans in colonial Virginia. Arriving in 1621, Johnson worked on a tobacco plantation along the James River. He and his wife, Mary, eventually bought their way out of bondage. They acquired their own land and raised livestock. After Johnson's death, however, a Virginia court ruled that because he was an African "and by consequence an alien [foreigner]," the land rightly belonged to the British Crown.

—*quoted in* Africans in America

A Virginia plantation owner oversees the packing of tobacco leaves to be shipped to England.

Maryland and Virginia

Main Idea While Maryland grew and dealt with Protestant-Catholic conflicts, Virginia settlers continued to push westward.

History and You Can you build a house wherever you want? Read about how Virginia settlers responded to restrictions placed on where they could live.

. . . .

Former enslaved Africans such as Anthony Johnson rarely owned land in colonial America. White males controlled most property, especially plantations which became important to the economic growth of the Southern Colonies. As the number of plantations grew, the need for workers increased.

Not all people came to work in the colonies of their own free will. English criminals and prisoners of war were shipped to the colonies. They could earn their release by working for a period of time—usually seven years. African rulers sold their prisoners of war to European slave traders, who took the enslaved prisoners to the colonies. Many people also came to the colonies as **indentured servants.** To pay for their passage to America, they agreed to work without pay for a certain length of time.

Establishing Maryland

Maryland arose from the dream of **Sir George Calvert, Lord Baltimore.** Calvert wanted a safe place for his fellow Catholics who were being persecuted in England. King Charles I gave Calvert a proprietary colony north of Virginia. However, Calvert died before receiving the grant. His son, Cecilius, inherited the colony and named it Maryland. Cecilius sent two of his brothers to run the colony. They reached America in 1634.

Cecilius gave large **estates,** or pieces of land, to English aristocrats. He also granted land to other settlers. As the number of plantations grew and more workers were needed, the colony imported indentured servants and enslaved Africans.

For years the Calvert and Penn families argued over the boundary between Maryland and Pennsylvania. In the 1760s, they hired Charles Mason and Jeremiah Dixon to map the boundary and lay a line of stones bearing the Penn and Calvert crests—the Mason-Dixon line.

By the Numbers / **Slavery in Colonial America**

North and South Slavery was important to the economy of many of the American colonies. Most enslaved Africans lived in the Southern Colonies, where many worked on plantations, or large farms. The Northern Colonies had a smaller number of enslaved people but also profited from the international trade in Africans.

Enslaved People in the Colonies, 1650–1710

Year	North	South	Total
1650	880	720	1,600
1670	1,125	3,410	4,535
1690	3,340	13,389	16,729
1710	8,303	36,563	44,866

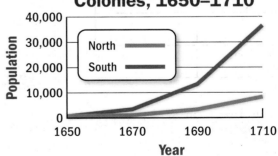

Enslaved People in the Colonies, 1650–1710

Population / Year
North
South

Source: The Gilder Lehrman Institute of American History

Critical Thinking

Speculating Why do you think more enslaved people lived in the Southern Colonies than in the Northern Colonies?

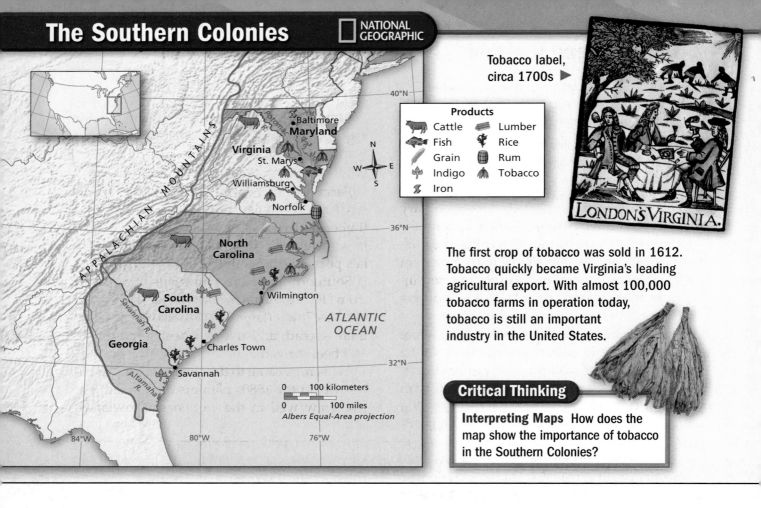

The Southern Colonies

NATIONAL GEOGRAPHIC

Products
- Cattle
- Fish
- Grain
- Indigo
- Iron
- Lumber
- Rice
- Rum
- Tobacco

Tobacco label, circa 1700s ▶

LONDON'S VIRGINIA.

The first crop of tobacco was sold in 1612. Tobacco quickly became Virginia's leading agricultural export. With almost 100,000 tobacco farms in operation today, tobacco is still an important industry in the United States.

Critical Thinking

Interpreting Maps How does the map show the importance of tobacco in the Southern Colonies?

Another conflict was harder to resolve. The Calverts had welcomed Protestants as well as Catholics in Maryland. Protestant settlers outnumbered Catholics. To protect the Catholics, the Act of Toleration was passed in 1649. The act granted Protestants and Catholics the right to worship freely. However, tensions continued. In 1692 the Protestant-controlled assembly made the Anglican Church the official church in Maryland. Catholics then faced the same restrictions as they had in England.

Bacon's Rebellion in Virginia

While other colonies were being founded, Virginia continued to grow. Settlers moved west and settled Native American lands. In the 1640s, to avoid conflicts, Virginia governor William Berkeley made a pledge to Native Americans. In exchange for a large piece of land, he agreed to keep settlers from pushing farther into their territory.

Nathaniel Bacon, a young planter in western Virginia, opposed the colonial government because it was dominated, or controlled, by easterners. Many westerners also resented Berkeley's pledge to stay out of Native American territory. Some settled in the forbidden areas. They then blamed the government for not protecting them.

In 1676 Bacon led attacks on Native American villages. His army also marched to Jamestown and drove Berkeley into exile. Only Bacon's sudden death kept him from governing Virginia. England then recalled Berkeley and sent troops to restore order.

Bacon's Rebellion showed that settlers would not be limited to the coast. The colonial government formed a militia to control Native Americans and opened up more land for settlement.

Reading Check **Analyzing** Why did Bacon oppose the colonial government?

The Carolinas and Georgia

Main Idea The Carolinas and Georgia developed into major Southern Colonies.

History and You Do you believe that people who are in debt should be given a fresh start in life? Read to learn the reasons why Georgia was created.

. . . .

In 1663 King Charles II created a proprietary colony south of Virginia called Carolina—Latin for "Charles's land." The king gave the colony to eight nobles who had helped him regain his throne. The proprietors set up estates and sold or rented land to settlers brought from England.

John Locke, an English philosopher, wrote a **constitution,** or plan of government, for the colony that covered topics such as land divisions and social ranking. Concerned with principles and rights, Locke argued that

"every man has a property in his own person. . . . The labour of his body, and the work of his hands . . . are properly his."

Carolina, however, did not develop as planned. It split into northern and southern Carolina, creating two colonies.

Northern and Southern Carolina

Farmers from inland Virginia settled northern Carolina. They grew tobacco and sold timber and tar. The northern Carolina coast lacked a good harbor, so farmers used Virginia's ports to conduct their trade.

Southern Carolina, however, prospered from fertile farmland and the harbor at Charles Town (later Charleston). Settlements there spread, and trade in deerskin, lumber, and beef thrived.

Two crops came to dominate Carolina agriculture. In the 1680s planters discovered that rice grew well in the wet coastal lowlands.

Founding the Thirteen Colonies

	Colony	1st Permanent Settlement	Reasons Founded	Founders or Leaders
New England Colonies	Massachusetts Plymouth Mass. Bay Colony	1620 1630	Religious freedom Religious freedom	John Carver, William Bradford John Winthrop
	New Hampshire	c. 1620	Profit from trade and fishing	Ferdinando Gorges, John Mason
	Rhode Island	1636	Religious freedom	Roger Williams
	Connecticut	1635	Profit from fur trade, farming; religious and political freedom	Thomas Hooker
Middle Colonies	New York	1624	Expand trade	Dutch settlers
	Delaware	1638	Expand trade	Swedish settlers
	New Jersey	1638	Profit from selling land	John Berkeley, George Carteret
	Pennsylvania	1682	Profit from selling land; religious freedom	William Penn
Southern Colonies	Virginia	1607	Expand trade	John Smith
	Maryland	1634	To sell land; religious freedom	Cecil Calvert
	North Carolina	c. 1660s	Profit from trade and selling land	Group of eight aristocrats
	South Carolina	1670	Profit from trade and selling land	Group of eight aristocrats
	Georgia	1733	Religious freedom; protection against Spanish Florida; safe home for debtors	James Oglethorpe

Chart Skills

Sequencing Which colony was the first to be settled? Which was the last?

Charts in Motion See StudentWorks™ Plus or glencoe.com.

Growing rice required much labor, so the demand for slave labor rose. Another important crop, indigo, was developed in the 1740s by a young Englishwoman named Eliza Lucas. Indigo, a blue flowering plant, was used to dye textiles.

By the early 1700s, Carolina's settlers wanted political power. In 1719 settlers in southern Carolina seized control from its proprietors. In 1729 Carolina became two royal colonies—North Carolina and South Carolina.

Georgia

Georgia, founded in 1733, was the last British colony set up in America. **James Oglethorpe** received a charter for a colony where debtors and poor people could make a fresh start. In Britain, debtors—those who were not able to repay debts—were imprisoned.

British officials also had hoped that Georgia, located north of Spanish Florida, would protect the other colonies from Britain's enemy, Spain. Oglethorpe and the first group of settlers built the forts and town of Savannah as a barrier against Spanish expansion.

Georgia did not develop as Oglethorpe planned. Few debtors settled there. Instead, hundreds of poor people came from Britain. Religious refugees from Central Europe and a small group of Jews also arrived.

Many settlers complained about Oglethorpe's rules, especially the limits on landholding and the bans on slave labor and rum. A frustrated Oglethorpe finally agreed to their demands. Disappointed with the colony's slow growth, he gave up and turned Georgia back over to the king in 1751.

By that time, the British had been in eastern North America for almost 150 years. They had lined the Atlantic coast with colonies.

Reading Check **Explaining** Why was Georgia founded?

People IN HISTORY

Anne Hutchinson

Dissenter banished from Massachusetts Bay Colony

Hutchinson held meetings in her home in Boston to discuss and give her views on recent sermons. Puritan leaders charged her with *"dishonoring"* the commonwealth. In her trial, she defended herself by arguing, *"there lyes a clear rule in Titus [book in the Christian Bible New Testament], that the elder women should instruct the younger."* She was convicted and banished in 1637.

Margaret Brent

Landowner in Maryland

Brent, one of Maryland's largest landowners and most powerful citizens, requested a vote in the Maryland Assembly on January 21, 1648. When her request was denied because she was a woman, the Assembly noted in its minutes that, *"the s[ai]d Mrs Brent protested ag[ain]st all proceedings in this . . . Assembly, unlesse shee may . . . have [a] vote."* Brent was so angry that she moved to Virginia, where she spent the rest of her life.

The French and Spanish in North America

Main Idea The French and the Spanish expanded their lands in North America.

History and You What might it be like to explore a large, unknown river that runs for hundreds of miles? Read to learn about the French explorers who traveled along the Mississippi River.

• •

The British were not the only Europeans colonizing North America. Elsewhere on the continent, the Spanish and the French built settlements of their own.

The French founded Quebec in 1608. At first they had little interest in large-scale settlement in North America. They were mainly concerned with fishing and trapping animals for their fur. French trappers and missionaries went far into the interior of North America. Forts and trading posts were built to protect their profitable trade.

In 1663 New France became a royal colony. King Louis XIV limited the privileges of the fur companies. He appointed a royal governor who supported new explorations.

Down the Mississippi River

In the 1670s, two Frenchmen—a fur trader, **Louis Joliet,** and a priest, **Jacques Marquette**—explored the Mississippi River by canoe. Joliet and Marquette hoped to find gold, silver, or other precious metals. They were also looking for a water passage to the Pacific Ocean. When they realized that the Mississippi flowed south into the Gulf of Mexico rather than west into the Pacific, they turned around and headed back upriver.

A few years later, **René-Robert Cavelier, Sieur de La Salle,** followed the Mississippi River all the way to the Gulf of Mexico. La Salle claimed the region for France, calling it Louisiana in honor of King Louis XIV. In 1718 the French governor founded the port of New Orleans. Later, French explorers and missionaries traveled west to the Rocky Mountains and southwest to the Rio Grande.

Growth of New France

French settlement in North America advanced slowly. New France was made up of estates along the St. Lawrence River. Estate holders received land in return for bringing settlers. Known as **tenant farmers,** the settlers paid their lord an annual rent and worked for him for a fixed number of days each year.

The French had better relations with the Native Americans than did other Europeans. French trappers and missionaries traveled deep into Indian lands. They lived among the Native American peoples, learned their languages, and respected their ways.

Although the missionaries had come to convert Native Americans to Catholicism, they did not try to change their customs. Most importantly, the French colony grew so slowly that Native Americans were not pushed off their lands.

Eliza Lucas Pinckney

Successful plantation manager in South Carolina

Lucas managed her father's three plantations in South Carolina and experimented with many crops. She marketed the colony's first crop of indigo, used to make blue dye. Lucas was proud of her work, writing, *"I am making a large plantation of Oaks which I look upon as my own property, whether my father gives me the land or not."*

CRITICAL Thinking

1. **Synthesizing** How did these three women challenge traditional views of women's roles?

2. **Analyzing** What evidence do you see in each of the quotes that the women's activities were not entirely accepted at that time?

Spanish Interests

In the early 1600s, England, France, and the Netherlands began colonizing North America. The Spanish, however, still controlled most of Mexico, the Caribbean, and Central and South America. They also expanded into the western and southern parts of the present-day United States.

Spain wanted to keep the other European powers from threatening its empire in America. To protect their claims, the Spanish sent soldiers, missionaries, and settlers north into present-day New Mexico. In 1609 or 1610, the Spanish founded Santa Fe. They also went to what is now Arizona in the late 1600s. When France claimed land around the Mississippi River, the Spanish moved into what is now Texas. Spain wanted to control the area between the French territory and Mexico. In the early 1700s, Spain built San Antonio and other military posts in Texas.

Spanish priests built a string of missions along the Pacific coast. **Missions** are religious settlements established to convert people to a faith. The missions helped the Spanish claim California. The Spanish did more than convert local Native Americans to Christianity.

Spanish missionaries and soldiers also brought them to the missions—often by force—to labor in fields and workshops.

In 1769 Junípero Serra, a Franciscan monk, founded a mission at San Diego. Over the next 15 years, Father Serra set up other missions in California along a route called *El Camino Real* (The Royal Highway). These missions later became cities, such as Los Angeles and Monterey. Serra traveled on foot to supervise the missions. Serra also supported Native Americans' rights by working to prevent Spanish soldiers from mistreating them.

European Conflicts

Rivalries between European nations carried over into the Americas. In North America, France and Britain were expanding their settlements. Both nations fought several wars in the early 1700s. When the two countries warred in Europe, fighting often erupted between their colonies in North America. In the late 1700s, wars in Europe would greatly shape events in America.

✓ **Reading Check** **Explaining** Why did Spain establish missions in California?

History ONLINE

Study Central™ To review this section, go to glencoe.com.

Section 4 Review

Vocabulary

1. Use each of these terms in a sentence that will help explain its meaning: indentured servant, estate, constitution, debtor, tenant farmer, mission.

Main Ideas

2. **Describing** How did Maryland deal with tensions between Protestant and Catholic settlers?

3. **Identifying** Who was John Locke, and what did he do for Carolina?

4. **Explaining** Why were the French slow to settle in North America?

Critical Thinking

5. **Analyzing** Why did demand for enslaved workers increase as the Southern Colonies grew?

6. **Determining Cause and Effect** Use a diagram like the one below to describe the causes and effects of Bacon's Rebellion.

7. **Descriptive Writing** Suppose you are a member of La Salle's expedition. Write an entry in your journal that describes your experiences along the Mississippi River for one day. Include things that you experienced through each of your five senses: sight, sound, taste, touch, and smell.

Answer the
Essential Question
8. How and why did the Southern Colonies grow?

Colonies

- Early settlements: Roanoke, Jamestown
- New England Colonies: Massachusetts, Rhode Island, Connecticut, New Hampshire
- Middle Colonies: New York, Pennsylvania, New Jersey, Delaware

◀ Plymouth Colony

- Southern Colonies: Maryland, Virginia, North Carolina, South Carolina, Georgia
- French colonies: New France
- Spanish colonies

Reasons Settled

- Claim and protect land in North America
- Profit from resources and trade
- Seek religious freedom and escape persecution
- Start a society based on the Bible (Puritans)
- Provide a safe haven for people of all religions
- Spread Christianity to Native Americans
- Seek political freedom and representative government
- Escape economic hard times

▼ Pilgrim women

Relations With Native Americans

- Trade and exchange of skills
- Learn Native American languages and customs (French)
- Often did not pay for land or honor treaties (British)
- Hostilities and fighting common

▲ Pocahontas

Types of Government

- Representative
- Proprietary
- Royal governor

Status of Slavery

- Permitted by law (originally banned in Georgia)
- Increasingly important to colonies as farms and plantations grew

◀ William Penn meets with Native Americans.

STUDY TO GO Study anywhere, anytime! Download quizzes and flash cards to your PDA from glencoe.com.

INDIANA STATEWIDE TEST PRACTICE

TEST-TAKING TIP

As you read each question, be sure to look for main ideas. A main idea repeated in an answer choice may be a clue that it is the right answer.

Reviewing Vocabulary

Directions: Choose the word or words that best completes the sentence.

1 **The Virginia Company gave a _____, or land grant, to colonists who paid their own travel expenses.**

  A charter
  B compact
  C headright
  D policy

2 **Protestants who wanted to leave the Anglican Church and set up their own churches were known as _____.**

  A Puritans
  B Separatists
  C Catholics
  D Turks

3 **In a _____, the owner owned all land and controlled the government.**

  A proprietary colony
  B royal colony
  C charter colony
  D joint-stock company

4 **A _____ was a plan of government for a colony.**

  A congress
  B monarch
  C constitution
  D charter

Reviewing Main Ideas

Directions: Choose the best answer.

5 **The end of Spain's control of the seas was a result of**

  A the harsh rule of King Philip II of Spain.
  B the discovery of gold in Mexico.
  C England's defeat of the Armada.
  D the founding of Jamestown.

6 **Roger Williams clashed with Massachusetts Puritans because**

  A he converted to Roman Catholicism.
  B he did not support religious persecution.
  C he wanted Native American land.
  D his views were considered too intolerant.

7 **The English wanted New Netherland because**

  A it had a fine harbor and river trade.
  B they wanted to liberate colonists.
  C they fought the Dutch in 1649.
  D the Dutch blocked English trade.

8 **Missions were set up along North America's Pacific coast by the**

  A English.
  B French.
  C Spanish.
  D Dutch.

GO ON

Critical Thinking

Directions: Choose the best answer.

9 **Which best describes how the French differed from other Europeans in colonizing North America?**

  A French missionaries wanted to spread Catholicism.
  B The French colonies alone set up representative government.
  C The French enjoyed better relations with Native Americans.
  D French officials promoted large-scale settlements in North America.

Base your answer to question 10 on the map below and your knowledge of Chapter 3.

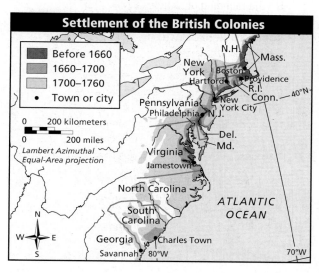

Settlement of the British Colonies

Before 1660
1660–1700
1700–1760
• Town or city

0   200 kilometers
0   200 miles
Lambert Azimuthal Equal-Area projection

N.H.
Mass.
New York   Boston
Hartford   Providence
R.I.
Conn.   40°N
New York City
Pennsylvania
Philadelphia   N.J.
Del.
Md.
Virginia
Jamestown

North Carolina
ATLANTIC OCEAN
South Carolina
Georgia   Charles Town
Savannah   80°W   70°W

10 **Based on the map, which colonies were most heavily settled before 1660?**

  A Georgia and South Carolina
  B Virginia and New York
  C Pennsylvania and New Jersey
  D Virginia and Massachusetts

Constructed Response

Directions: Write a short response to each of the following questions. In your answer:

  • *address all parts of the question*
  • *use information from the chapter*
  • *include facts, examples, and details relevant to the question*
  • *use clear language*

11 **Identify one major European/Native American leader in the colonies and explain how that individual aided in the European settlement and colonization of North America.**

12 **Identify the English colonies in North America and state the reasons for their founding.**

13 **Explain how the arrival of Europeans in North America affected both Native American and European cultures.**

Base your answer to question 14 on the reading below and your knowledge of Chapter 3.

> What will it availe [get] you to take . . . by force [what] you many quickly have by love, or to destroy them that provide you food. What can you get by [war], when we can hide our provisions [food supplies] and fly to the woods? Whereby you must famish [starve] by wronging us your friends.

Source: John Smith, *The Generall Historie of Virginia*

14 **Based on this quote made in 1608 by Powhatan to Captain John Smith, why did Powhatan believe that English settlers should establish peaceful relations with his people?**

STOP

Need Extra Help?														
If you missed question. . .	1	2	3	4	5	6	7	8	9	10	11	12	13	14
Go to page. . .	61	65	74	79	59	68	73	82	81	79	58	79	83	61

Growth of the Thirteen Colonies 1607-1770

Colonial scene, 1701

◄ Iroquois mask

★ **1651**
First Navigation Act regulates colonial trade

★ **c. 1570**
Iroquois Confederacy forms

Americas

World

1550   **1600**   **1650**

Japanese samurai ►

1603 ★
Tokugawa Shogunate emerges in Japan

★ **1610**
Galileo observes planets and stars with telescope

★ **1644**
Qing Dynasty is established in China

Section 1: Life in the Colonies

Essential Question How did geography affect the economic development of the three colonial regions?

Section 2: Government, Religion, Culture

Essential Question In what ways was an American culture developing during the colonial period?

Section 3: France and Britain Clash

Essential Question Why did conflict arise in North America between France and Great Britain?

Section 4: The French and Indian War

Essential Question How did the outcome of the French and Indian War determine who controlled North America?

History ONLINE
Chapter Overview Visit glencoe.com and click on **Chapter 4—Chapter Overviews** to preview chapter information.

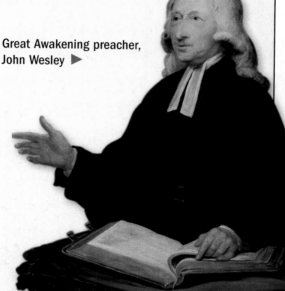

Great Awakening preacher, John Wesley ▶

FOLDABLES
Study Organizer

Organizing Information
Make this Foldable to help summarize what you learn about the growth of the colonies.

Step 1 Fold two sheets of paper in half and cut along the fold.

Step 2 Fold both sheets in half and then in half again.

Step 3 Cut tabs into three sheets so each sheet has its own tab. Leave the fourth sheet whole.

Step 4 Label your Foldable as shown.

Reading and Writing As you read the chapter, list facts about life in the colonies and the challenges colonists faced.

1676 Bacon's Rebellion

1689 ★ English Bill of Rights signed

English rulers William and Mary ▶

1700s Enslaved Africans brought to America

1700

1730 Emperor Yung Cheng reduces slavery in China

c. 1740 Great Awakening peaks

1754 French and Indian War begins

1750

1748 Montesquieu's The Spirit of Laws

1763 Proclamation of 1763

1765 Potato becomes most popular food in Europe

1767 Burma invades Siam

Life in the Colonies

Essential Question ◄

How did geography affect the economic development of the three colonial regions?

Reading Guide

Content Vocabulary

subsistence farming *(p. 89)*

triangular trade *(p. 90)*

Middle Passage *(p. 91)*

cash crop *(p. 92)*

surplus *(p. 93)*

Tidewater *(p. 94)*

backcountry *(p. 94)*

overseer *(p. 94)*

slave code *(p. 94)*

Academic Vocabulary

rely *(p. 89)*   principal *(p. 93)*

Key People and Events

Olaudah Equiano *(p. 91)*

Reading Strategy

Taking Notes As you read, use a diagram like the one below to describe the triangular trade route.

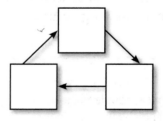

INDIANA ACADEMIC STANDARDS
United States History

8.1.10 Compare differences in ways of life in the northern and southern states, including the growth of towns and cities in the North and the growing dependence on slavery in the South.

8.3.6 Identify the agricultural regions of the United States and be able to give reasons for the type of land use and subsequent land development during different historical periods.

8.4.9 Explain and evaluate examples of domestic and international interdependence throughout United States history.

American Diary

In 1760 Englishman Andrew Burnaby traveled in the American colonies, observing daily life. He could not imagine that these colonies would ever unite for they were as different from one another as "fire and water," and each colony was jealous of the other. "In short, such is the difference of character, of manners, of religion, of interest, of the different colonies, that I think, . . . were they left to themselves, there would soon be a civil war, from one end of the continent to the other."

—*from* Travels Through the Middle Settlements in North America

Philadelphia, Pennsylvania, was one of the major seaports in colonial America.

The New England Colonies

Main Idea The economies of the New England Colonies focused on shipbuilding, fishing, and trade.

History and You Do people in your community manufacture products that are sold to other countries? Read to learn about how the economies of New England developed.

. . . .

Although Burnaby believed the colonies would never unite, they continued to grow. The number of people living in the colonies rose from about 250,000 in 1700 to approximately 2.5 million by the mid-1770s. The population of African Americans increased at an even faster rate—from about 28,000 to more than 500,000.

Immigration was important to this growth. Between 1607 and 1775, almost a million people—an estimated 690,000 Europeans and 278,000 Africans—came to the colonies. By 1775, about 2,500 Jewish immigrants lived in the colonies. Most people lived in the cities of New York, Philadelphia, Charles Town, Savannah, and Newport, where they were allowed to worship as they pleased.

There was another reason for the growing population. Colonial women tended to marry early and have large families. In addition, America—especially New England—turned out to be a very healthy place to live.

Most people in New England lived in well-organized towns. The meetinghouse stood in the center of the town. This building was used for both church services and town meetings. The meetinghouse faced a piece of land called the *green* or *common*. Here cows grazed and the citizen army trained. Farmers lived in the town and worked in fields on its outskirts.

Farming was the main economic activity in all of the colonies. New England farms were smaller than those farther south. Long winters and thin, rocky soil made large-scale farming difficult. Farmers in New England practiced **subsistence farming.** This means that they generally produced just enough to meet their families' needs, with little left over to sell or exchange. Most Northern farmers **relied,** or depended, on their children for labor. Everyone in the family worked—spinning yarn, preserving fruit, milking cows, fencing in fields, and sowing and harvesting grain.

Commerce in New England

New England also had a large number of small businesses. Some people used the water-power from the streams on their land to run mills for grinding grain or sawing lumber.

Primary Source | **Travel in Colonial America**

On the Road In colonial America, people traveled by land in a stagecoach, on horseback, or on foot. There were only a few roads, and they were unpaved and bumpy. Philip Mackenzie, a young colonial traveler, described a typical trip from Philadelphia to New York: "The Stage Wagon leaves Philadelphia Monday morning at Eight o'clock and [reaches] New York Tuesday afternoon late. We spent the Night at some Inn on the Road."
—from "Young Mackenzie Sees the World" in *The Way Our People Lived: An Intimate American History*

Critical Thinking

Making Connections How do you think geographic distance affected the unity of the American colonies?

American Whaling English colonists observed Native Americans hunting whales along the coast and took up the practice themselves. In the 1600s, whalers hunted right whales for their oil and bone. When the number of right whales began to decline in the early 1700s, the whalers started using ships to hunt the more profitable sperm whales that lived in the deep water.

Abundant wood from New England's forests allowed Americans to build excellent whaling vessels. ▶

◄ Whale oil lamps

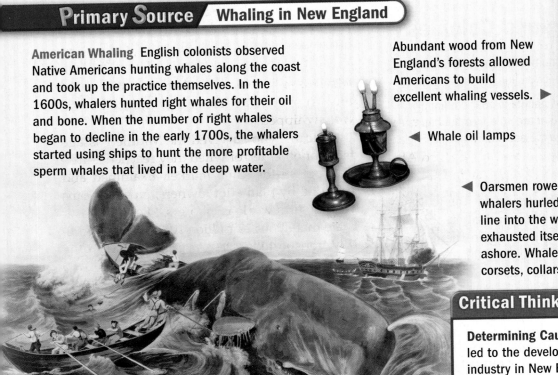

◄ Oarsmen rowed boats within range, and whalers hurled harpoons with an attached line into the whale. Once the animal exhausted itself, it was killed and towed ashore. Whale bone was used to make corsets, collars, and other products.

Critical Thinking

Determining Cause and Effect What factors led to the development of a large whaling industry in New England?

Women made cloth, garments, candles, and soap for their families. They sometimes made enough of these products to sell or trade. Large towns attracted skilled craftspeople. These people were blacksmiths, shoemakers, furniture makers, gunsmiths, metalsmiths, and printers.

Shipbuilding was an important industry in New England. The lumber for building ships came from the nearby forests. Lumber was transported down rivers to the shipyards in coastal towns.

The region also relied on fishing. New Englanders fished for many types of seafood: cod, halibut, crabs, oysters, and lobsters. Some New Englanders ventured far out to sea to hunt whales for oil and whalebone.

Colonial Trade

Northern coastal cities were the center of the shipping trade. They linked the Northern Colonies with the Southern Colonies. They also linked America to other parts of the world. New England ships sailed south along the Atlantic coast. They traded with the colo-nies and with islands in the West Indies. Ships also traveled across the Atlantic Ocean, carrying fish, furs, and fruit to trade for man-ufactured goods in both England and Europe.

These colonial merchant ships followed many different trading routes. Some went directly to England and back. Others followed routes that came to be called the **triangular trade** because the routes formed a triangle.

On one leg of the route, ships brought sugar and molasses from the West Indies to New England. In New England, the molasses would be made into rum. Next, the rum and other goods were shipped to West Africa and traded for enslaved Africans.

Slavery was widely practiced throughout West Africa. Many West African kingdoms enslaved those they defeated in war. Some of the enslaved people were then sold to Arab slave traders. Others were forced to work in gold mines or farm fields. With the arrival of the Europeans, enslaved Africans also began to be shipped to America in exchange for goods.

The Middle Passage

For enslaved Africans, the voyage to America usually began with a march to a European fort on the West African coast. Tied together with ropes around their necks and hands, they were traded to Europeans, branded, and forced aboard a ship.

The cruelty continued when enslaved Africans were shipped to the West Indies. This part of the voyage was known as the **Middle Passage. Olaudah Equiano,** a young African, was forced onto a ship to America. He later described the journey:

PRIMARY SOURCE

"We were all put under deck. . . . The closeness . . . the heat . . . added to the number in the ship, which was so crowded that each had scarcely room to turn himself, almost suffocated us. . . . The shrieks . . . the groans of the dying, rendered [made] the whole a scene of horror."

—from *The Interesting Narrative and Other Writings*

Chained together for more than a month, prisoners such as Equiano could hardly sit or stand. They were given little food or water. Africans who died or became sick were thrown overboard. Those who refused to eat were whipped.

Africans who survived the Middle Passage faced another terror when they reached American ports—the slave market. Examined and prodded by plantation owners, most Africans were sold to work as laborers. Historians estimate that about 12 million Africans were forcibly transported to the Americas between the late 1400s and mid-1800s.

With its part in the triangular trade and its shipbuilding and fishing industries, New England flourished. Its population grew, and towns and cities developed.

✔ **Reading Check** **Explaining** Where was the shipping center in America, and where did its trade extend?

Economics & History

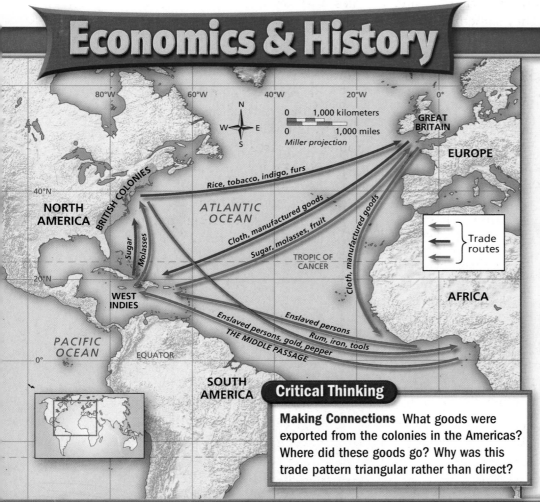

Triangular Trade During the colonial era, the desire for enslaved Africans to work plantations in the Americas led to a changed pattern of trade. Trade among Britain, Africa, and the American colonies formed a triangle. The trade in enslaved people formed one leg of the triangle—the terrible Middle Passage. Merchants sold British manufactured goods in Africa, bought enslaved Africans, and carried them to the West Indies to work on plantations. Plantation products, such as sugar, went to Europe, completing the triangle.

Critical Thinking

Making Connections What goods were exported from the colonies in the Americas? Where did these goods go? Why was this trade pattern triangular rather than direct?

The Middle Colonies

Main Idea The economies of the Middle Colonies depended on the sale of cash crops, such as wheat and corn.

History and You Have you ever visited a farm? What types of crops or animals were raised there? Read to learn about the effects farming had on the Middle Colonies.

· ·

With more fertile soil and a milder climate than New England's, the farms in the Middle Colonies produced bigger harvests. In New York and Pennsylvania, farmers grew large quantities of wheat and other **cash crops.** These crops were used by the farmers' families, but they also were sold in colonial markets and overseas.

Farmers sent cargoes of wheat and livestock to New York City and Philadelphia for shipment. These cities became busy ports. By the 1760s New York City, with 18,000 people, and Philadelphia, with 24,000 people, were the largest cities in the American colonies.

Industries of the Middle Colonies

Like the New England Colonies, the Middle Colonies also had industries. Some were home-based crafts such as carpentry and flour making. Others were larger businesses, such as lumbering, mining, and small-scale manufacturing. One iron mill in northern New Jersey employed several hundred workers. Many of these workers were from Germany. Other, smaller ironworks operated in New Jersey and Pennsylvania.

German Immigrants

Nearly 100,000 German immigrants came to America in the colonial era. Most settled in Pennsylvania. They successfully farmed the land using European agricultural methods.

The Germans, Dutch, Swedish, and other non-English immigrants gave the Middle Colonies a cultural diversity, or variety, not found in New England. This diversity created a tolerance for the many cultural differences.

Reading Check **Explaining** What are cash crops?

Primary Source | The African Slave Trade

A Terrible Trade The transatlantic slave trade began in the 1500s when colonists needed a large labor force to work in their mines and plantations. West African slave traders sold captives acquired through wars and raids. Between 1520 and 1860, nearly 12 million Africans were enslaved. Many did not survive the march to the coastal trading sites or the voyage across the Atlantic. Between 9 and 10 million people faced a life of slavery in the Americas.

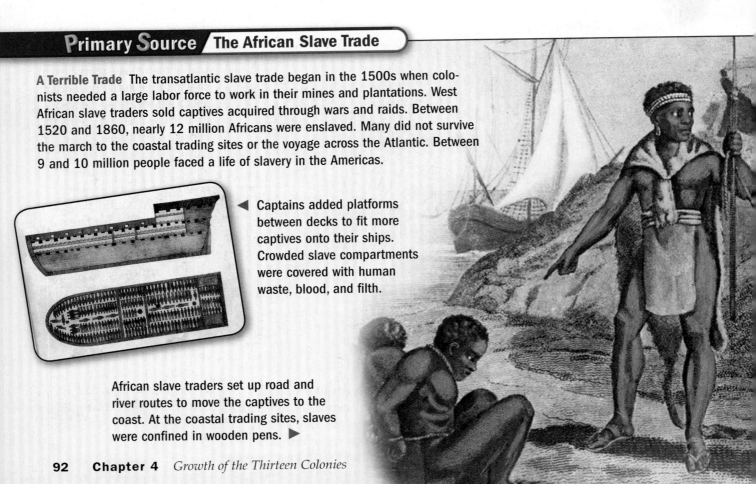

◄ Captains added platforms between decks to fit more captives onto their ships. Crowded slave compartments were covered with human waste, blood, and filth.

African slave traders set up road and river routes to move the captives to the coast. At the coastal trading sites, slaves were confined in wooden pens. ▶

The Southern Colonies and Slavery

Main Idea Slavery played a role in the economic success of the Southern Colonies.

History and You Think about the types of resources that are needed to manage a large farm. Read to learn about how the economies of the Southern Colonies developed as a result of the physical features of the land and enslaved Africans.

. . . .

Rich soil and a warm climate made the Southern Colonies well suited to certain kinds of farming. Southern farmers could cultivate large areas of land and produce harvests of cash crops. Most settlers in the Southern Colonies made their living from farming, and little commerce or industry developed. For the most part, London merchants rather than local merchants managed Southern trade.

Tobacco and Rice

Tobacco was the **principal,** or most important, cash crop of Maryland and Virginia.

Most tobacco was sold in Europe, where the demand for it was strong. Growing tobacco and preparing it for sale required a good deal of labor. At first, planters used indentured servants to work in the fields. When indentured servants became scarce and expensive, Southern planters began using enslaved Africans instead.

Slaveholders with large farms grew wealthy from their tobacco crop. Sometimes, however, a **surplus,** or extra amounts, of tobacco on the market caused prices to fall. As a result, the growers' profits also fell. In time, some tobacco planters switched to growing other crops, such as corn and wheat.

The main cash crop in South Carolina and Georgia was rice. In low-lying areas along the coast, planters built dams to create rice fields, called paddies. These fields were flooded when the rice was young and drained when the rice was ready to harvest. Work in the rice paddies was extremely strenuous. It involved standing knee-deep in the mud all day with no protection from the blazing sun or biting insects.

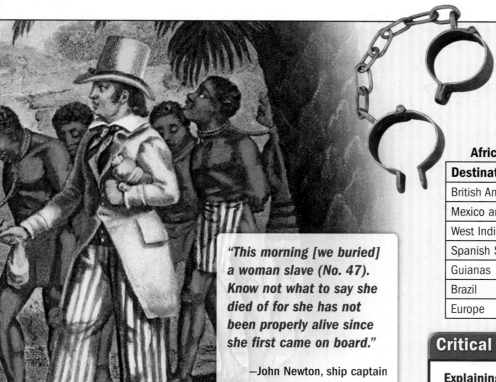

"This morning [we buried] a woman slave (No. 47). Know not what to say she died of for she has not been properly alive since she first came on board."

—John Newton, ship captain

◀ During the voyage, slaves were chained together in pairs—right leg to left leg. Crew members used whips and iron collars to punish the captives.

African Slave Trade 1450–1870

Destination	Total
British America/United States	427,000
Mexico and Central America	224,000
West Indies	4,040,000
Spanish South America	522,000
Guianas	531,000
Brazil	3,647,000
Europe	175,000

Critical Thinking

Explaining What did enslaved Africans experience on the journey from their homes to the Americas?

Plantations—Large and Small Owners of small plantations—those of a few hundred acres—usually owned fewer than 50 slaves. Wealthy planters, in contrast, typically required 200 or more slaves to work their vast estates, which covered several thousand acres.

◄ Plantations often included a Big House, where the owner and his family lived, as well as slaves' cabins, stables, livestock pens, gardens, a kitchen, a sick house, and workshops for blacksmiths, weavers, and tanners.

"I rose at 5 o'clock this morning and . . . ate milk for breakfast. I said my prayers. Jenny and Eugene [two house slaves] were whipped. I danced my dance [physical exercises]. I read law in the morning and Italian in the afternoon. . . . I walked about the plantation."

—Virginia plantation owner, 1709

▼ Most slaves worked in the fields from dawn to sunset. The landowner or a hired worker supervised the enslaved Africans.

Critical Thinking

Theorizing What problems do you think a Southern plantation owner commonly faced in the 1700s?

Because rice harvesting required so much strenuous work, rice growers relied on slave labor. Rice proved to be an even more profitable crop than tobacco. As rice became popular in Europe, its price rose steadily. By the 1750s, South Carolina and Georgia had the fastest-growing economies in the colonies.

Tidewater and Backcountry

Most of the large Southern plantations were located in the **Tidewater,** a region of flat, low-lying plains along the seacoast. Plantations, or large farms, were often located on rivers so crops could be shipped to market by boat.

Each plantation was a self-contained community with fields stretching out around a cluster of buildings. The planter's wife supervised the main house and the household servants. A plantation included slave cabins, barns, and stables, as well as buildings that were used for carpenter and blacksmith shops, storerooms, and kitchens. A large plantation might also have its own chapel and school.

West of the Tidewater lay a region of hills and forests climbing up toward the Appalachian Mountains. This region was known as the **backcountry** and was settled in part by hardy newcomers to the colonies. The backcountry settlers grew corn and tobacco on small farms. They usually worked alone or with their families. Some of these families had one or two enslaved Africans to help them with their work.

In the Southern Colonies, the independent small farmers of the backcountry greatly outnumbered the large plantation owners. The plantation owners, however, were much wealthier and had more influence. They controlled the economic and political life of the region.

Slavery

Most enslaved Africans lived on plantations. Some did housework, but most worked in the fields and often suffered great cruelty. The large plantation owners hired **overseers,** or bosses, to keep the enslaved Africans working hard.

In 1705, the colony of Virginia created a **slave code.** These were strict rules that governed the behavior and punishment of enslaved Africans and helped define the relationship between enslaved people and free people. Many other colonies soon followed with their own slave codes.

Some codes did not allow slaves to leave the plantation without the slaveholder's written permission. Some made it illegal to teach enslaved people to read or write. Many of the codes made it illegal for enslaved people to move about freely or assemble in large groups. The codes usually allowed slaves to be whipped for minor offenses and hanged or burned to death for serious crimes. Slaves who ran away were punished severely when caught.

African Traditions

Enslaved Africans had strong family ties. Often, however, their families were torn apart when a slaveholder sold family members to other slaveholders. Slaves turned to their African roots as a source of strength. They developed a culture that drew on the languages, customs, and traditions of their homelands in West Africa.

Some enslaved Africans learned trades such as carpentry, blacksmithing, or weaving. Skilled workers could sometimes set up shops, sharing their profits with the slaveholders. Some slaves were able to buy their freedom and joined the small population of free African Americans.

Criticism of Slavery

The majority of white Southerners were not slaveholders. Slavery, however, played an important role in the economic success of the Southern Colonies. That success came to be built on the idea that one human being could own another. Some colonists did not believe in slavery. There was less support for slavery in the Northern Colonies. For example, many Puritans refused to own enslaved people. In Pennsylvania, Quakers and Mennonites condemned slavery. Eventually the debate over slavery would erupt in a bloody war, setting the North against the South.

Reading Check **Describing** What was the purpose of slave codes?

History ONLINE
Study Central™ To review this section, go to glencoe.com.

Section 1 Review

Vocabulary

1. Define the following terms by using each one in a sentence: subsistence farming, rely, triangular trade, Middle Passage, cash crop, principal, surplus, Tidewater, backcountry, overseer, slave code.

Main Ideas

2. Discussing How did the coastal location of the New England colonies affect their prosperity?

3. Explaining Why were the Middle Colonies able to grow large quantities of crops?

4. Identifying How did cash crops affect the development of slavery?

Critical Thinking

5. Comparing and Contrasting Use a Venn diagram like the one below to compare and contrast characteristics of the Tidewater and the backcountry in Southern Colonies.

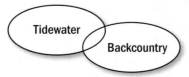

Tidewater   Backcountry

6. Expository Writing As a New England farmer, write a letter to relatives in Europe describing your family's daily life.

Answer the
7. Essential Question
How did geography affect the economic development of the three colonial regions?

What were people's lives like in the past?

These two pages will give you some clues to everyday life in the United States as you step back in time with TIME Notebook.

American Notes

FROM PRINCE TO ENSLAVEMENT TO LANDOWNER

In the 1700s, a formerly enslaved African, **VENTURE SMITH***, wrote about his life in a book titled* A Narrative of the Life and Adventures of Venture. *Here is an excerpt of his story.*

"I was born in Dukandarra, in Guinea [in Africa], about the year 1729.... My father's name was Saungm Furro, Prince of the tribe of Dukandarra."

At 6, Venture Smith was kidnapped by an enemy tribe and later sold to the crew of a slave ship. He wrote, "I was bought on board by one Robert Mumford ... for four gallons of rum, and a piece of calico, and called Venture, on account of his having purchased me with his own private venture [property]. Thus I came by my name. All the slaves that were bought for that vessel's cargo were two hundred and sixty."

NORTH WIND PICTURE ARCHIVES / ALAMY

Venture was brought to Connecticut—where he was sold several times. When he was about 35 he was able to purchase his freedom for "seventy-one pounds, two shillings." He earned this money doing odd jobs, such as "cleaning ... minks, raising potatoes and carrots, and by fishing in the night."

After years of more work—including sailing on a whaler—he was able to buy the freedom of his wife and children. In his book, Venture wrote, "My freedom is a privilege which nothing else can equal. Notwithstanding all the losses I have suffered ... by the injustice of knaves. ... I am now possessed of more than one hundred acres of land, and three habitable dwelling houses."

BOOM!

Bustling sea trade helped the populations of these port towns grow by leaps and bounds.

	1710	1730	1760
Boston	9,000	13,000	15,600
New York	5,700	8,600	18,000
Philadelphia	6,500	11,500	23,750
Charleston	3,000	4,500	8,000

BOSTON HARBOR IN 1750

MARY EVANS PICTURE LIBRARY / ALAMY

MANNERS

Oh, Behave!

George Washington, sometime before the age of 16, copied by hand a list of rules from a book called *Rules of Civility & Decent Behaviour in Company and Conversation: a Book of Etiquette.* It contains over 100 different things NOT to do in polite society. We have listed four of these tips below . . . and for fun we have added a fake. Can you spot the phony rule?

— Every action done in company ought to be with some sign of respect to those that are present.

— When in company, put not your radio on too loudly as it might congest the ears of others with noise.

— In the presence of others, sing not to yourself with a humming noise, nor drum with your fingers or feet.

— If you cough, sneeze, sigh, or yawn, do it not loud but privately; and speak not in your yawning, but put your handkerchief or hand before your face and turn aside.

— When you sit down, keep your feet firm and even, without putting one on the other or crossing them.

Answer: **The second item is the fake—the radio had not been invented yet!**

NORTH WIND PICTURE ARCHIVES / ALAMY

COLONIAL GAMES

Play Quoits

Do you feel left out of the fun when all your friends play quoits—the hot game of the 1700s? Just remember that quoits is a lot like horseshoes— only in this game you toss rings made of rope. Here is how to play one version:

JACK CAREY / ALAMY

1) Put two sets of four stakes in the ground—the sets should be 18 feet apart.

2) Standing next to one set, take turns with another player tossing two rings at the other set, while trying to loop them around the stakes.

3) Scoring:
   a. 2 points if your two rings land closer to a stake than either of your opponent's.
   b. 4 points if your ring goes around a stake—this is a "ringer."
   c. 3 points if your "ringer" lands on top of your opponent's ring.

4) Once a loop touches the ground, it's "dead." Even if it bounces up over a stake, it does not count.

5) After tossing their rings from one set, players start a new round by tossing from the other set.

6) The first player to score 21 points wins.

NUMBERS

UNITED STATES AT THE TIME

25 Percent of enslaved people who did not survive crossing the Atlantic from Africa to the Americas

0 Number of American political cartoons before Benjamin Franklin's first one appeared in the *Pennsylvania Gazette* in 1754; Franklin wanted the colonies to join together to defend themselves against a threat by the French and Native Americans

JOIN, or DIE.

CORBIS

3 to 10 About the number of years indentured servants had to work in the 1700s to pay back the person who paid for their passage to the Americas

2 Number of tines, or points, on that new thing called the fork, which has just appeared on a table near you; talk is there will soon be three or four tines

CRITICAL THINKING

Comparing and Contrasting How are George Washington's etiquette rules similar to and different from today's rules of good manners?

Hypothesizing Does sea trade today affect cities in the same way it did in the 1700s? Explain your answer.

Government, Religion, Culture

Essential Question ◄
In what ways was an American culture developing during the colonial period?

Reading Guide

Content Vocabulary
export (p. 99)
import (p. 99)
charter colony (p. 101)
proprietary colony (p. 101)
royal colony (p. 101)

Academic Vocabulary
successor (p. 99)

Key People and Events
Glorious Revolution (p. 99)
Navigation Acts (p. 100)
Great Awakening (p. 102)
Enlightenment (p. 103)

Reading Strategy
Taking Notes As you read, use a diagram like the one below to explain how the Great Awakening and the Enlightenment affected the colonists.

| Great Awakening | ⇒ | |
| Enlightenment | ⇒ | |

INDIANA ACADEMIC STANDARDS
United States History

8.1.9 Describe the influence of important individuals on social and political developments of the time such as the Independence movement and the framing of the Constitution.

8.2.1 Identify and explain essential ideas of constitutional government, which are expressed in the founding documents of the United States, including the Virginia Declaration of Rights, the Declaration of Independence, the Virginia Statute for Religious Freedom, the Massachusetts Constitution of 1780, the Northwest Ordinance, the 1787 U.S. Constitution, the Bill of Rights, the Federalist and Anti-Federalist Papers, *Common Sense*, Washington's Farewell Address (1796), and Jefferson's First Inaugural Address (1801).

American Diary

At 16 years old, Eliza Lucas Pinckney took over the family plantation when her father went to war. In 1741 she recorded: "Wrote to Mr. Murray to send down a boat load of white oak [strips], bacon and salted beef. . . . Sent up at the same time a barrel [of] salt." Eliza's major achievement, however, was finding a better way to make blue dye from the indigo plant. Used in military uniforms, the dye was in high demand. Eliza's success turned indigo into a very profitable crop.

—from the Journal of Eliza Lucas Pinckney

Drayton Hall, located near Charleston, South Carolina, was a rice plantation.

English Colonial Rule

Main Idea Although the American colonies developed some self-government, the British still set many laws, especially those concerning trade.

History and You How would you react if you were forced to buy clothes from only one store? Read to learn about the trade restrictions that England placed on its colonies.

. . . .

In her writings and activities, Eliza Lucas Pinckney celebrated a new American spirit. This spirit signaled that Americans were beginning to view themselves differently from the way Great Britain viewed them.

Trouble was brewing in England—and in the colonies—during the mid-1600s. England's monarchy was restored with Charles II on the throne. Many people, however, were not satisfied with his rule. James II, Charles's **successor**—the next king—attempted to take back the powers Parliament won during the English Civil War. He also tried to tighten royal control over the colonies.

In 1688 Parliament took action. It forced out James and placed his daughter Mary and her Dutch husband, William of Orange, on the throne. This change demonstrated the power of the elected representatives over the monarch. This period came to be known as the **Glorious Revolution.**

William and Mary signed an English Bill of Rights in 1689 guaranteeing certain basic rights to all citizens. This document became an important part of the heritage of English law that the American colonists shared. Some hundred years later, it inspired the people who created the American Bill of Rights.

England viewed its North American colonies as an economic resource. The colonies provided England with raw materials such as lumber. English manufacturers used these materials to produce finished goods, which they then sold to the colonists. This process followed an economic theory called mercantilism. As you learned earlier, this theory states that as a nation's trade grows, its gold reserves increase. The nation then becomes more powerful. To make money from its trade, England had to **export,** or sell abroad, more goods than it **imported,** or bought from foreign markets.

To ensure that only England benefited from trade with the colonies, Parliament passed several laws between 1651 and 1673.

If You Were There / Plantation Life

The Planter's Family As the son or daughter of a plantation owner, you enjoy great wealth and privilege. Your father serves in the colonial government, perhaps as a member of the royal governor's council. Your mother hosts elegant parties. If you are a planter's son, you are receiving the education of a British gentleman and learning business skills to run the plantation. If you are a daughter, you study art and music and are becoming skilled in managing a plantation household. Your home is decorated with the most fashionable furnishings imported from Britain.

Critical Thinking

Drawing Conclusions Do you think Eliza Lucas Pinckney's responsibilities were typical of a woman of the 1700s? Explain.

These **Navigation Acts** directed the trade between England and the colonies. Colonial merchants who had goods to send to England could not use foreign ships—even if those ships offered cheaper rates. The Navigation Acts also prevented the colonists from sending certain products, such as sugar or tobacco, outside the area that made up England's empire.

The colonists at first accepted the trade laws because they were guaranteed a place to sell their raw materials. Later, the colonists came to resent British restrictions. Merchants wanted to make their own manufactured goods and sell their products where they could get higher prices. Some colonists ignored these laws and began smuggling, or trading illegally, with other nations. Controls on trade would later cause even more conflict between the American colonies and England.

Reading Check **Identifying** What country strictly controlled shipping and trade with the colonies and why?

Colonial Government

Main Idea As the colonies grew, they developed some self-government.

History and You Does your school have a student council to represent students? Read to learn how colonists were represented in colonial governments.

The English colonists brought with them ideas about government and a respect for education that had been developing in England for centuries. By the 1600s, the English people had won political liberties, such as trial by jury, that were largely unknown elsewhere. At the heart of the English system were two principles of government—limited government and representative government. These two principles greatly influenced the development of the United States.

When the colonists reached North America, they believed that government was not all-powerful. This idea was already an accepted part of the English system of government.

Primary Source / Colonial Printing and Education

An Educated Population Literacy rates were generally high in New England and the Middle Colonies. Education in the South was limited primarily to the wealthy. By the 1700s, many printed materials were available throughout the colonies. Colonists' ability to read and express ideas in print would play a major role in the later struggle for independence.

◀ The first printing press in the colonies was set up in Cambridge, Massachusetts, in 1639. By the mid-1700s, presses were found throughout the colonies.

Newspapers started appearing in colonial cities in the first half of the 1700s. ▶

Massachusetts schoolmasters used *The New England Primer* to teach generations of students how to read and write. ▶

In Adam's Fall
We Sinned all.

Thy Life to Mend
This Book Attend.

The Cat doth play
And after slay.

A Dog will bite
A Thief at night.

An Eagles flight
Is out of sight.

The Idle Fool
Is whipt at School.

It first appeared in the Magna Carta, or the Great Charter. The Magna Carta was signed by King John on June 15, 1215.

The Magna Carta established the principle of limited government. This means that the power of the king, or government, is limited. This document also provided for protection against unjust punishment. It protected against the loss of life, liberty, and property.

As the colonies grew, their town meetings developed into small governments, responsible for making local laws. By the 1760s, there were three types of colonies in America—charter colonies, proprietary colonies, and royal colonies.

Charter Colonies

Connecticut and Rhode Island were **charter colonies.** Settlers were given a charter, or a grant of rights and privileges, to establish charter colonies. These colonists elected their own governors and the members of the legislature. Great Britain had the right to approve the governor, but the governor could not veto the acts of the legislature.

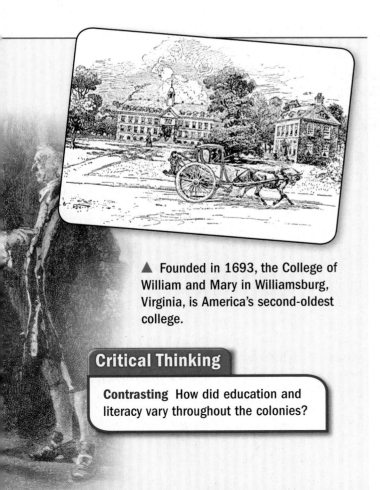

▲ Founded in 1693, the College of William and Mary in Williamsburg, Virginia, is America's second-oldest college.

Critical Thinking

Contrasting How did education and literacy vary throughout the colonies?

History ONLINE

Student Web Activity Visit glencoe.com and complete the Chapter 4 Web Activity about the Magna Carta.

Proprietary Colonies

The **proprietary colonies** of Delaware, Maryland, and Pennsylvania were ruled by proprietors. Proprietors were individuals or groups to whom Britain granted land. They were generally free to rule as they wished. Proprietors appointed the governor and members of the upper house of the legislature. The colonists elected the lower house.

Royal Colonies

By the 1760s, Georgia, Massachusetts, New Hampshire, New Jersey, New York, North Carolina, South Carolina, and Virginia were **royal colonies.** Britain directly ruled all royal colonies. In each, the king appointed a governor and council, known as the upper house, and the colonists elected an assembly called the lower house. The governor and the members of the council usually did what the British leaders told them to do. However, this often led to conflict with the colonists in the assembly. Most conflicts occurred when officials tried to enforce tax laws and trade restrictions.

Voting Rights

Colonial legislatures gave only some people a voice in government. Generally, white men who owned property had the right to vote. Most women, indentured servants, landless poor, and African Americans could not vote. In spite of these limits, the proportion of people involved in government was higher in the colonies, estimated at 80 to 90 percent, than anywhere in Europe. This strong participation in government gave Americans training that was valuable when the colonies became independent.

Reading Check **Drawing Inferences** How did the Magna Carta influence governments in the colonies?

People IN HISTORY

Benjamin Franklin
American Scientist and Revolutionary Leader

Although he was born in a poor family, Ben Franklin made a fortune as a printer in Philadelphia. By the age of 42, Franklin was one of the richest men in the colonies. He chose to retire from active business and become a "gentleman." He began to pursue "philosophical studies and amusements." He was especially curious about electricity, and his experiments made him famous. He wrote in his autobiography: *"What gave my book the more sudden and general celebrity, was the success of one of its proposed experiments, . . . drawing lightning from the clouds. . . . After [the experiments] were performed before the king and court, all the curious of Paris flocked to see them."*

CRITICAL Thinking

1. **Identifying** What does Franklin's autobiography tell you about the lives of gentlemen in the colonies?
2. **Analyzing** Why do you think Franklin's experiments with electricity made him famous?

An Emerging Culture

Main Idea An American culture, influenced by religion and education, began to develop in the colonies.

History and You What items or activities do you consider part of American culture? Grilled hamburgers? Playing baseball? Read to find out how the colonists began forming a culture that was different from European cultures.

From the 1720s through the 1740s, a religious revival called the **Great Awakening** swept through the colonies. In New England and the Middle Colonies, ministers called for "a new birth," a return to the strong faith of earlier days. One popular preacher was Jonathan Edwards of Massachusetts. People thought his sermons were powerful and convincing.

The English preacher George Whitefield started religious revivals beginning in 1739. Whitefield inspired worshipers throughout the colonies. The Great Awakening led to the formation of many new churches.

Family Roles

People adapted their traditions to the new conditions of life in America. Religion, education, and the arts contributed to a new American culture. The family, however, formed the basic foundation of colonial society.

Men were the formal heads of the households and represented the family in the community. Men worked in the fields and built barns, houses, and fences. Sons could work as indentured servants for local farmers. Young men also could be apprentices, or assistants, to workers who taught them a trade.

Women ran their households and cared for children. Many worked in the fields with their husbands. Married women were under their husbands' authority and had few rights. Young unmarried women might work for wealthy families as maids or cooks. Widows might work as teachers, nurses, or seamstresses. Widows and women who never married could run businesses and own property, but they could not vote.

Education

Most colonists valued education. Parents often taught their children to read and write at home. In New England and Pennsylvania, in particular, people set up schools to make sure everyone could read and study the Bible. In 1647 the Massachusetts Puritans passed a public education law. Each community with 50 or more homes was required to have a school.

By 1750, New England had a high level of literacy with about 85 percent of the men and about half of the women able to read. Many learned from *The New England Primer,* which combined lessons in good conduct with reading and writing.

Widows or unmarried women ran many colonial schools. Quakers and other religious groups in the Middle Colonies ran others. In towns and cities, craftspeople set up night schools for their apprentices.

The colonies' early colleges were founded to train ministers. The first was Harvard College, established in 1636 by the Puritans in Cambridge, Massachusetts. Anglicans founded William and Mary College in Virginia in 1693.

The Enlightenment

By the middle of the 1700s, many educated colonists were influenced by the **Enlightenment.** This movement began in Europe and was based upon the idea that knowledge, reason, and science could improve society. In the colonies, the Enlightenment increased interest in science. People observed nature, staged experiments, and published their findings. The best-known American scientist was Benjamin Franklin.

Freedom of the Press

In 1735 John Peter Zenger of the *New York Weekly Journal* faced charges of libel. He had printed a critical report about the royal governor of New York. Andrew Hamilton argued that free speech was a basic right of English people. He defended Zenger by asking the jury to base its decision on whether Zenger's article was true, not whether it was offensive. The jury found Zenger not guilty. Today the case is regarded as an important step in the development of a free press in America.

✓ **Reading Check** **Analyzing** In what ways did the Great Awakening influence culture in the colonies?

Section 2 Review

History ONLINE
Study Central™ To review this section, go to glencoe.com.

Vocabulary

1. Define each of the following terms and use it in a sentence: successor, export, import, charter colony, proprietary colony, royal colony.

Main Ideas

2. Explaining How did the Navigation Acts affect colonial trade?

3. Illustrating Discuss how people in the charter colonies participated in government.

4. Identifying What was taught from *The New England Primer?*

Critical Thinking

5. Summarizing Use a diagram like the one below to identify and describe the three types of colonies in America.

```
        Types of
        Colonies
       /    |    \
   [   ] [   ] [   ]
```

6. Persuasive Writing Write a short speech that Andrew Hamilton might have used to defend John Peter Zenger.

Answer the
7. Essential Question
In what ways was an American culture developing during the colonial period?

France and Britain Clash

Essential Question ◄

Why did conflict arise in North America between France and Great Britain?

Reading Guide

Content Vocabulary
Iroquois Confederacy (p. 105)   militia (p. 107)

Academic Vocabulary
convert (p. 105)   design (p. 106)

Key People and Events
George Washington (p. 106)
Albany Plan of Union (p. 107)

Reading Strategy
Taking Notes As you read, use a diagram like the one below to summarize why, in general, Native Americans had better relations with the French than with the British.

Native Americans

Relations With the British	Relations With the French

INDIANA ACADEMIC STANDARDS
United States History

8.1.1 Identify major Native American Indian groups of eastern North America and describe early conflict and cooperation with European settlers and the influence the two cultures had on each other.

8.1.2 Explain the struggle of the British, French, Spanish, and Dutch to gain control of North America during settlement and colonization.

8.1.3 Identify and explain the conditions, causes, consequences, and significance of the French and Indian War (1754–1763), and the resistance and rebellion against British imperial rule by the thirteen colonies in North America (1761–1775).

American Diary

In 1754 a small force of colonial soldiers, led by a young George Washington, fought the French in what is today western Pennsylvania. Washington later stated that the French "kept up a constant . . . fire upon us; which was returned [until] . . . the most tremendous rain . . . filled our trenches with Water, [and] Wet . . . the Ammunition . . . in a small temporary [post] . . . called Fort Necessity . . . and left us nothing but a few . . . Bayonets for defence."

—quoted in **An Eyewitness History: The Colonial Era**

George Washington's colonial troops surrendering to the French outside Fort Necessity

British-French Rivalry

Main Idea Rivalry between Great Britain and France led to a war for control of North America.

History and You Is it sometimes difficult to stay out of a conflict when people around you are arguing? Read to learn how Native Americans became involved in the conflict between the British and French.

· ·

As a young military officer, George Washington fought with British forces against the French. Both forces wanted control of lands west of the Appalachian Mountains. During the 1700s, Britain and France were two of the strongest powers in Europe. They competed for wealth and empire in different parts of the world. This rivalry caused bitter feelings between British and French colonists in North America.

This bitterness increased when British interests turned to the Ohio River valley. The French regarded this territory as their own. They did not want British colonists sharing in their profitable fur trade.

In the 1740s hostility between the two forces grew. British fur traders built a fort at a place called Pickawillany. Acting quickly, the French attacked Pickawillany and drove the British traders out of Ohio. French troops also began raiding towns in Maine and New York. In response, some New Englanders captured the important French fortress at Louisbourg on Cape Breton Island, north of Nova Scotia. Much to the disgust of the New Englanders, Britain returned Louisbourg to France.

Native Americans Take Sides

The French and British both knew that assistance from Native Americans could help them win control of North America. The French had an advantage over the British because they had many Native American allies.

Unlike the British, the French were interested mainly in fur trading. They did not want to take over Native American land. Also, French trappers and fur traders often married Native American women and followed their customs. French missionaries **converted**—changed the religious beliefs of—many Native Americans to Catholicism. For these reasons, Native Americans often helped the French and raided British settlements.

The Iroquois Confederacy

The most powerful group of Native Americans in the East was the **Iroquois Confederacy,** based in the New York area.

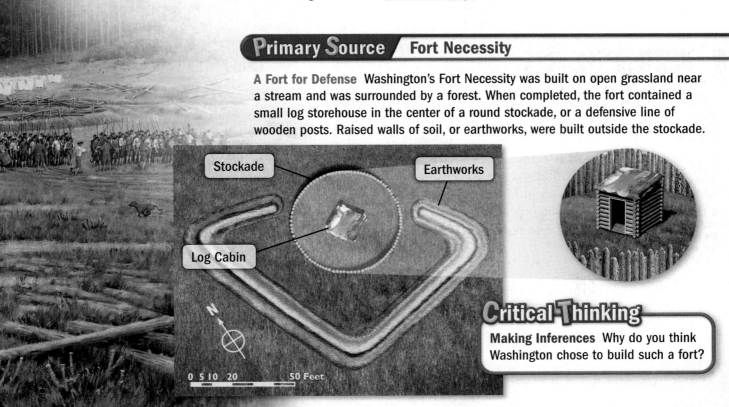

Primary Source / Fort Necessity

A Fort for Defense Washington's Fort Necessity was built on open grassland near a stream and was surrounded by a forest. When completed, the fort contained a small log storehouse in the center of a round stockade, or a defensive line of wooden posts. Raised walls of soil, or earthworks, were built outside the stockade.

Stockade

Earthworks

Log Cabin

N

0 5 10 20   50 Feet

Critical Thinking

Making Inferences Why do you think Washington chose to build such a fort?

America's first political cartoon, drawn by Benjamin Franklin in 1754, promoted his Albany Plan of Union. It reflects a popular superstition that a dead snake would come back to life if the pieces were placed next to each other. Each section represents a colony. The New England colonies are combined as one section.

1. **Identifying** The abbreviation *NE* stands for "New England." What colonies do the other sections represent?

2. **Interpreting** What warning does Franklin's cartoon convey about the approaching war with France?

The confederacy initially included five nations—the Mohawk, Seneca, Cayuga, Onondaga, and Oneida. Other groups of Native Americans later joined or were conquered by the Iroquois. After the Tuscarora joined in 1722, the English referred to the confederacy as the Six Nations.

The Iroquois managed to remain independent by trading with both the British and the French. By skillfully playing the British and French against each other, the Iroquois dominated the Great Lakes area.

By the mid-1700s, however, the Iroquois came under greater pressure as the British moved into the Ohio Valley. Eventually, the leaders of the confederacy gave certain trading rights to the British and reluctantly became their allies. By taking this step, the Iroquois upset the balance of power between the French and British that had been so difficult to establish.

✓ **Reading Check** **Explaining** Why did hostilities between the French and British increase during the early 1740s?

American Colonists Take Action

Main Idea The American colonists prepared to defend themselves against the French and their Native American allies.

History and You Has anyone ever tried to take something that was yours? How did you react? Read to learn how the colonists responded to the growing conflict between France and Great Britain.

A group of Virginians had plans for settling the Ohio Valley. In the fall of 1753, Governor Robert Dinwiddie of Virginia sent a surveyor named **George Washington** into the Ohio country. Washington was 21 years old. His mission was to tell the French that they were trespassing on land that Great Britain claimed. He was to demand that they leave.

Washington delivered the message, but it did no good. "The French told me," Washington said later, "that it was their absolute **design**, or plan, to take possession of the Ohio, and by God they would do it."

Washington's First Command

In the spring of 1754, Dinwiddie made Washington a lieutenant colonel. He then sent Washington back to the Ohio country with a **militia**—a group of civilians trained to fight in emergencies—of 150 men. The militia had instructions to build a fort where the Allegheny and Monongahela Rivers meet to form the Ohio River—the site of present-day Pittsburgh. Washington and his troops arrived to find the French already building Fort Duquesne (doo•KAYN) on that spot.

Washington established a small post nearby, called Fort Necessity. Although greatly outnumbered, the troops of the inexperienced Washington attacked a French force. The French quickly forced Washington's soldiers to surrender. The British soldiers were later released, and they returned to Virginia. Washington's published account of the ordeal made him famous throughout the colonies and Europe. Washington had been defeated at Fort Necessity. The colonists, however, regarded him as a hero who struck the first blow against the French.

The Albany Plan of Union

Meanwhile, representatives from several colonies met in Albany, New York, in June 1754 to discuss the threat of war. They wanted to find a way to defend themselves against the French. They also hoped to persuade the Iroquois to support the British.

The representatives adopted Benjamin Franklin's **Albany Plan of Union** for a united colonial government. Franklin's plan called for "one general government" for eleven of the American colonies. Not a single colonial assembly, however, approved the plan. No colony was willing to give up any of its power. Disappointed, Franklin wrote: "Everybody cries, a Union is necessary; but when they come to the manner and form of the union, [they] are perfectly distracted."

The Albany meeting failed to unite the colonists in fighting the French. Soon, a full-scale war—the French and Indian War— erupted.

Reading Check **Describing** Describe Washington's expeditions into French territory.

Section 3 Review

History ONLINE

Study Central™ To review this section, go to glencoe.com.

Vocabulary

1. Define each of the following terms by using it in a complete sentence: convert, Iroquois Confederacy, design, militia.

Main Ideas

2. Explaining How did the Iroquois remain independent from both the British and the French? How did that change?

3. Identifying What happened as a result of Washington's defeat at Fort Necessity?

Critical Thinking

4. Analyzing Why did Benjamin Franklin propose the Albany Plan of Union?

5. Determining Cause and Effect Use a diagram like the one below to identify the causes of the increasing rivalry between the French and the British in North America.

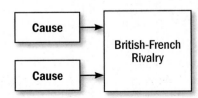

| Cause | → | British-French Rivalry |
| Cause | → | |

6. Creative Writing Write a short newspaper article describing the battle at Fort Necessity.

7. Answer the Essential Question Why did conflict arise in North America between France and Great Britain?

The French and Indian War

Essential Question

How did the outcome of the French and Indian War determine who controlled North America?

Reading Guide

Content Vocabulary

alliance (p. 109)   speculator (p. 112)

Academic Vocabulary

prospect (p. 110)

Key People and Events

General Edward Braddock (p. 109)

Seven Years' War (p. 110)

William Pitt (p. 110)

Jeffrey Amherst (p. 111)

James Wolfe (p. 111)

Treaty of Paris (p. 111)

Pontiac's War (p. 112)

Proclamation of 1763 (p. 112)

Reading Strategy

Taking Notes As you read, use a diagram like the one below to list the lands that France lost when the Treaty of Paris of 1763 was signed.

French Lands → To Britain, To Spain

INDIANA ACADEMIC STANDARDS
United States History

8.1.1 Identify major Native American Indian groups of eastern North America and describe early conflict and cooperation with European settlers and the influence the two cultures had on each other.

8.1.3 Identify and explain the conditions, causes, consequences, and significance of the French and Indian War (1754–1763), and the resistance and rebellion against British imperial rule by the thirteen colonies in North America (1761–1775).

American Diary

Commanded by General James Wolfe, about 1,800 British troops landed "on the North Shore [of Quebec] . . . an Hour before Day Break." To get in position to attack, the soldiers had to climb a steep cliff. Scrambling up the slope, the British soldiers ran into "a little Firing" from French guards. They continued to climb until they "gained the top of the [cliff]." By the time the sun rose over Quebec, British and French soldiers were prepared to battle on the Plains of Abraham outside the city.

—from a letter by General George Townshend

In 1759 British troops climbed steep cliffs in order to attack the French stronghold of Quebec.

The British Take Action

Main Idea William Pitt helped turn the tide of the French and Indian War to the colonists' favor.

History and You Has a friend ever given you advice that you wished you had followed? Read to learn why one British general was defeated because of his failure to accept advice.

• •

The Battle of Quebec, fought in 1759, was a deciding moment in the conflict between Britain and France. That conflict was known as the French and Indian War. This war raged in North America through the late 1750s and early 1760s. The French and Indian War was part of a larger struggle between the British and the French. That struggle involved, or included, control of world trade and power on the seas.

In 1754 the governor of Massachusetts made an announcement to the colonial assembly. He told them that the French were on the way to "making themselves masters of this Continent."

The French were building well-armed forts throughout the Great Lakes region and the Ohio River valley. Their network of **alliances,** or unions, with Native Americans allowed the French to control large areas of land, stretching from the St. Lawrence River in Canada all the way south to New Orleans. The French and their Native American allies seemed to be winning control of the American frontier. The final showdown was about to begin.

During the early stages of the French and Indian War, the British colonists fought the French and the Native Americans with little help from Britain. In 1754, however, the government in London decided to intervene in the conflict. It was alarmed by the new forts the French were building and by Washington's defeat at Fort Necessity. In the fall of 1754, Great Britain appointed **General Edward Braddock** commander in chief of the British forces in America. Braddock's mission was to drive the French forces from the Ohio Valley region.

Braddock Marches to Duquesne

In June 1755, Braddock started out from Virginia with about 1,400 red-coated British soldiers and a smaller force of blue-coated colonial militia. George Washington served as an aide to Braddock during the campaign.

Primary Source / Two Heroes: Wolfe and Montcalm

Known as outstanding commanders, both the British General Wolfe and the French General Montcalm lost their lives in the Battle of Quebec. During the fighting, Wolfe was shot in the chest and was "carried off wounded to the rear of the front line." He reportedly heard cries of "they [the French] run." Told that the French lines had broken, Wolfe died peacefully, satisfied that the British had won. Montcalm also was wounded in battle. As he lay in bed, Montcalm asked how long he had to live. When told "about a dozen hours," the French general said, "So much the better. . . . I am happy I shall not live to see the surrender of Quebec."

—from *Historical Journal of the Campaigns in North America*

General James Wolfe ▼

◄ Marquis de Montcalm

Critical Thinking

Making Generalizations Why are Wolfe and Montcalm considered heroes? What qualities do you think make a person a hero?

On the march to Fort Duquesne, Washington reported that Braddock:

"[halted] to level every mole hill, and to erect bridges over every brook, by which means we were four days in getting twelve miles."

—from *Life of Washington*

Washington told Braddock that his army's style of marching was not well suited to fighting on the frontier. Lined up in columns and rows wearing bright-colored uniforms, the troops became easy targets. Braddock ignored Washington's advice.

Native Americans and French troops ambushed the British on July 9. The British were confused and frightened. They could not even see their attackers, who were hidden in the forest and shooting at them from behind trees. Braddock was killed. Defeated, the British lost nearly 1,000 men. Washington led the survivors back to Virginia.

Britain Declares War on France

The fighting in America helped start a new war in Europe. This war was known as the **Seven Years' War.** After arranging an alliance with Prussia, Britain declared war on France in 1756. Prussia fought France and its allies in Europe. Britain fought France in the Caribbean, India, and North America.

Early in the war, French troops captured several British forts, and their Native American allies began raiding frontier farms from New York to Pennsylvania. They killed settlers, burned farmhouses and crops, and drove many families back toward the coast. French forces from Canada captured British forts at Lake Ontario and at Lake George.

Pitt Takes Charge

Great Britain's **prospects,** or chances for success, in America improved after **William Pitt** came to power. Pitt served as secretary of state and then as prime minister of Great Britain and was a great military planner.

The French and Indian War, 1754–1763   NATIONAL GEOGRAPHIC

Legend:
- British territory
- French territory
- Disputed territory
- British troop movements
- French troop movements
- British victory
- French victory
- City
- Fort

0   200 kilometers
0   200 miles
Albers Equal-Area projection

70°W   60°W

NEW FRANCE

Gulf of St. Lawrence

ACADIA

Ft. Beauséjour

Ft. Saint John

Louisbourg

Wolfe & Saunders

Wolfe & Saunders

Quebec

Montreal

Halifax

Amherst & Boscawen

Lake Champlain

Ft. Crown Point

Ft. Ticonderoga

Ft. William Henry

Ft. Frontenac

Ft. Niagara

Ft. Oswego

Lake Huron

Lake Ontario

Lake Erie

Hudson R.

Boston

New York City

Allegheny R.

Ft. Duquesne

Ft. Necessity

Braddock

Washington

Alexandria

Monongahela R.

ATLANTIC OCEAN

50°N

80°W

40°N

A War for North America During the French and Indian War, Great Britain and France each fought for control of the North American continent. Native American leaders, who had long played the European rivals against each other, were forced to choose sides.

To avoid arguments from the colonists about the cost of the war, Pitt decided that Great Britain would pay for the war supplies—no matter the cost. Pitt ran up an enormous debt. After the war the British raised the colonists' taxes to help pay this debt. Pitt had only delayed the moment when the colonists had to pay their share of the bill.

Pitt wanted more than just a clear path to the Western territories. He also intended to conquer French Canada. He sent British troops to North America under commanders **Jeffrey Amherst** and **James Wolfe.** In 1758 a British assault recaptured the fortress at Louisbourg. That same year a group of New Englanders, led by British officers, captured Fort Frontenac at Lake Ontario. Still another British force took Fort Duquesne in Pennsylvania, which was renamed Fort Pitt.

✓ **Reading Check** **Describing** Why was William Pitt successful at managing the war for Britain?

"*[Swords] and hatchets playing on every quarter with much . . . blood but our New Hampshire forces being fresh & courageous and the Enemy tired and much discouraged with the Defeat they met with, retreated and made their escape toward a Creek. . . . The day after ye battle three Frenchmen were taken up by the Guard of Fort Lymon who upon examination declared that their Army was entirely [defeated].*"
—Colonist Robert Moses, diary entry, 1755

◀ Mohawk chief Joseph Brant was an important British ally.

Map Skills

Region Which country controlled the territory around the Great Lakes?

Maps In MOtion See StudentWorks™ Plus or glencoe.com.

The Fall of New France

Main Idea The fall of Quebec and Montreal ended the French and Indian War in North America.

History and You What factors lead to success or failure in battle? Read to learn how the British defeated the French in the French and Indian War.
· ·

The British had so many victories in 1759 that people said the church bells of London wore thin with joyous ringing. The greatest victory of the war, though, took place in the heart of New France.

The Battle of Quebec

Quebec was the capital of New France and was located on top of a cliff overlooking the St. Lawrence River. Quebec was thought to be impossible to attack. In September 1759, British general James Wolfe's scouts spotted a poorly guarded path along the back of the cliff. During the night, Wolfe's soldiers overwhelmed the French guards and scrambled up the path. The British troops then surprised and defeated the French army on a field called the Plains of Abraham.

The Treaty of Paris

The fall of Quebec and General Amherst's capture of Montreal the following year brought an end to the fighting in North America. The **Treaty of Paris** of 1763 forced France to give Canada and most of its lands east of the Mississippi River to Great Britain. Great Britain also received Florida from France's ally, Spain. Spain acquired French lands west of the Mississippi River—the Louisiana Territory—as well as the port of New Orleans.

The Treaty of Paris marked the end of France as a power in North America. The continent was now divided between Great Britain and Spain.

✓ **Reading Check** **Determining Cause and Effect** What happened to France's territory as a result of its defeat in the war?

Trouble on the Frontier

Main Idea Continued conflict between Native Americans and British settlers led to the Proclamation of 1763.

History and You How would you feel if a CD you ordered and paid for never arrived? Read to learn why some land investors were furious about the Proclamation of 1763.

. . . .

The French loss dealt a blow to the Native Americans of the Ohio River valley. They had lost their French allies and trading partners. The British raised the prices of their goods and, unlike the French, refused to pay the Native Americans for the use of their land. Worst of all, more British settlers began moving west onto Native American lands.

Pontiac's War

Pontiac, chief of an Ottawa village near Detroit, regarded British settlers as a threat to his people's way of life. Just as Benjamin Franklin tried to bring the colonies together with his Albany Plan, Pontiac wanted Native American groups to unite to fight the British.

In the spring of 1763, Pontiac gathered forces and captured the British fort at Detroit and other British outposts. That summer, Native Americans killed settlers along the Pennsylvania and Virginia frontiers during **Pontiac's War.** The war finally ended in August 1765 after the British defeated Pontiac's allies. Pontiac signed a peace treaty, and the British pardoned him.

The Proclamation of 1763

To prevent more fighting, Britain called a halt to the settlers' westward expansion. The **Proclamation of 1763** set the Appalachian Mountains as the temporary western boundary for the colonies. The proclamation especially angered those who owned shares in land companies. These **speculators,** or investors, had already bought land west of the mountains. They were furious that Britain ignored their land claims. More conflicts would soon arise between Britain and the colonists.

✓ Reading Check **Examining** Why were some colonists angered by the Proclamation of 1763?

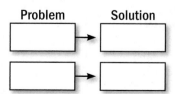

Section 4 Review

History ONLINE
Study Central™ To review this section, go to glencoe.com.

Vocabulary

1. Using complete sentences, define the following terms: alliance, prospect, speculator.

Main Ideas

2. **Identifying** Before Pitt took charge, what advantages did the French have in North America?

3. **Summarizing** What effect did the Treaty of Paris have on France?

4. **Discussing** Why did Pontiac want the Native Americans to join forces?

Critical Thinking

5. **Identifying Problems and Solutions** Use a chart like the one below to list the problems of General Braddock's army. List actions he could have taken that might have brought about France's defeat.

Problem	Solution

6. **Creative Writing** Write a conversation between two French fur trappers that describes how they might have felt about the Treaty of Paris.

Answer the
7. **Essential Question**
How did the outcome of the French and Indian War determine who controlled North America?

Main Idea	Supporting Details
Geography affects the economic development of the American colonies.	• Regional geographic characteristics lead to: - subsistence farming and commerce in New England, - an economy based on cash crops and industry in the Middle Colonies, and - a farming economy dependent on slavery in the South.
A distinctly American culture begins to develop during the colonial period.	• Americans embrace religion, education, science and the arts, the family, and freedom of the press.
American ideas about government have their beginnings in both British law and colonial government.	• The colonists are inspired by the English Bill of Rights and by the English ideals of limited government and representative government.
Native Americans generally have better relations with French settlers than British settlers.	• The British want the support of Native Americans in fighting the French but seize Native American land without paying them for it. • The French receive more Native American help because they trade with them and do not try to take their land.
Worldwide competition between Britain and France for wealth and land leads to conflict in North America.	• Both Britain and France want control of North American resources. • Conflicts over fur trading in the Ohio River valley eventually lead to the French and Indian War.
The French and Indian War shifts the balance of power in North America.	• The Treaty of Paris divides North America between Britain and Spain. • Conflicts build between the settlers and the Native Americans, as well as between the colonists and Britain.

▲ Powder horn from the French and Indian War

◀ New England whalers

STUDY TO GO Study anywhere, anytime! Download quizzes and flash cards to your PDA from glencoe.com.

INDIANA STATEWIDE TEST PRACTICE

TEST-TAKING TIP

> Be sure to read each question carefully to identify any key words that may help you to either choose the correct answer or eliminate incorrect answer choices.

Reviewing Vocabulary

Directions: Choose the word or words that best completes the sentence.

1 The voyage of enslaved people to the Americas was known as the _____.

 A Columbian Exchange
 B Middle Passage
 C triangular trade
 D Tidewater

2 To make money from trade, England had to _____, or sell abroad, more goods.

 A export
 B import
 C manufacture
 D sanction

3 A _____ is a group of civilians trained to fight in emergencies.

 A guard
 B sentinel
 C battalion
 D militia

4 Before 1763, _____, or investors, bought land west of the Appalachian Mountains.

 A brokers
 B regiments
 C speculators
 D proprietors

Reviewing Main Ideas

Directions: Choose the best answer.

5 Most German immigrants settled in

 A Massachusetts.
 B Pennsylvania.
 C Virginia.
 D New York.

6 Great Britain *directly* ruled

 A charter colonies.
 B proprietary colonies.
 C royal colonies.
 D all of the above

7 The Albany Plan of Union was not approved by the colonies because

 A it called for colonial independence.
 B it united colonists with the French.
 C it diminished a united colonial government.
 D colonies opposed giving up any powers.

8 How did the British victory over the French affect Native Americans in the Ohio River valley?

 A It helped them because the British paid for the use of Native American lands.
 B It hurt them because the French settled their lands.
 C It hurt them because they lost French allies and trading partners.
 D It helped them because the British lowered the prices of their goods.

GO ON ▶

History ONLINE

For additional test practice, use **Self-Check Quizzes**—Chapter 4 at glencoe.com.

Critical Thinking

Directions: Choose the best answer.

Base your answer to question 9 on the map below and your knowledge of Chapter 4.

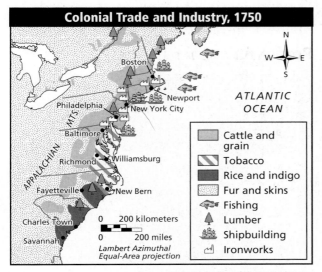

Colonial Trade and Industry, 1750

Boston
Newport
Philadelphia
New York City
Baltimore
Richmond · Williamsburg
Fayetteville · New Bern
Charles Town
Savannah

ATLANTIC OCEAN

APPALACHIAN MTS.

N
W — E
S

	Cattle and grain
	Tobacco
	Rice and indigo
	Fur and skins
	Fishing
	Lumber
	Shipbuilding
	Ironworks

0   200 kilometers
0   200 miles
Lambert Azimuthal Equal-Area projection

Source: *Historical Atlas of the United States*

9 Based on the map, which of the following was a major economic difference between New England and the Southern Colonies?

   A New England was a lumber producer, but the South was not.
   B Rice was grown in the South, but not in New England.
   C Grain and cattle were raised in New England, but not in the South.
   D Indigo was grown in New England, but not in the South.

10 All of the following developments of the French and Indian War would later affect relations between Britain and its American colonies EXCEPT

   A the use of lands west of the Appalachians.
   B the payment of Britain's huge war debt.
   C the settlement of the Louisiana Territory.
   D conflict with Native Americans.

Constructed Response

Directions: Write a short response to each of the following questions. In your answer:

- *address all parts of the question*
- *use information from the chapter*
- *include facts, examples, and details relevant to the question*
- *use clear language*

11 List the changes resulting from the Treaty of Paris of 1763 and discuss their significance.

Base your answer to question 12 on the reading below and your knowledge of Chapter 4.

> I will fear GOD, and honour the KING.
> I will honour my Father & Mother
> I will Obey my superiors.
> I will submit to my Elders.
> I will Love my Friends.
> I will forgive my Enemies, and pray to God for them.

Source: *The New England Primer*

12 Based on this excerpt, "The Dutiful Child's Promises" taken from the 1727 edition of *The New England Primer,* identify two traits that reflect the culture of colonial America.

Base your answer to question 13 on the reading below and your knowledge of Chapter 4.

> It is proposed that humble application be made for an act of Parliament of Great Britain, by virtue of which one general government may be formed in America, including all the said colonies, within and under which government each colony may retain its present constitution.

Source: The Albany Plan of Union

13 Based on this document, what was the Albany Plan proposing? How would it have affected colonial constitutions?

Need Extra Help?													
If you missed questions. . .	1	2	3	4	5	6	7	8	9	10	11	12	13
Go to page. . .	91	99	107	112	92	101	107	112	93	112	111	102	107

Unit 2

Creating a Nation
1763–1790

Seven-dollar bill, U.S., 1776

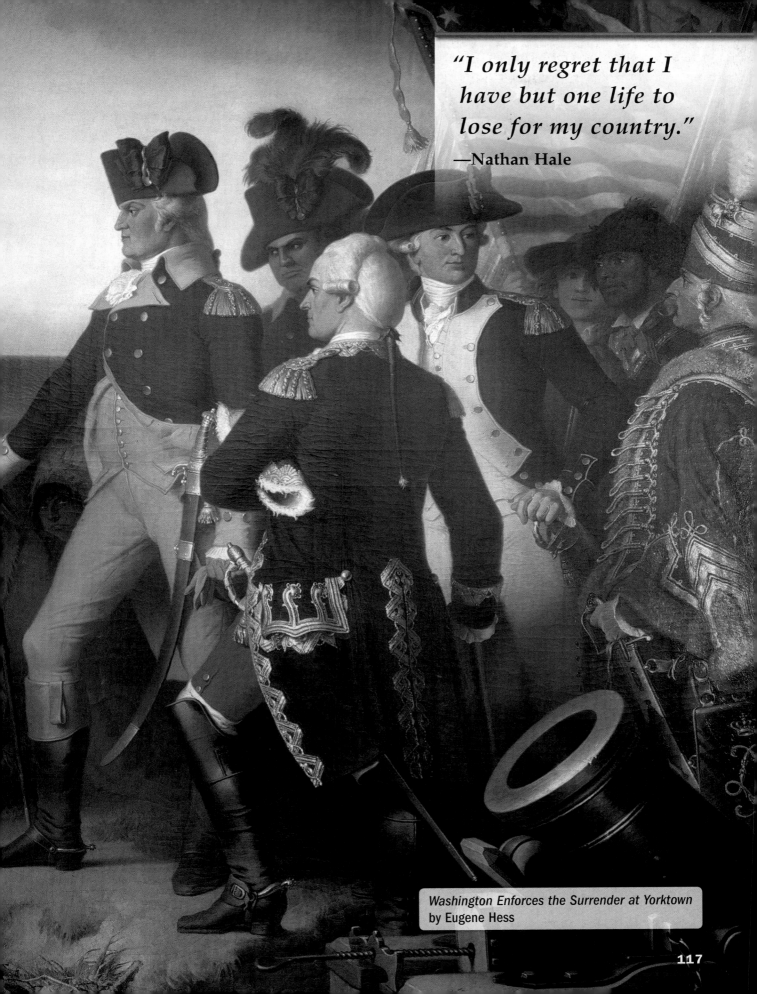

"I only regret that I have but one life to lose for my country."
—Nathan Hale

Washington Enforces the Surrender at Yorktown by Eugene Hess

Making Connections

Learn It!

When you make connections while reading, you connect the text with information you already know. This knowledge may be in math, science, geography, or any other subject area. You can also connect the text to personal experience.

Connect to Your Knowledge
What do you know about the Fourth of July?

1. The Fourth of July is the U.S. holiday celebrating the country's independence.
2. The Fourth of July is also known as Independence Day.
3. The term *freedom* also means "independence."

—*from Chapter 6, p. 153*
The Liberty Bell was rung every Fourth of July and for many public events until a crack appeared in about 1846. Today, the Liberty Bell is a symbol of freedom in the United States and throughout the world.

Practice It!

Read the paragraph below. On another sheet of paper, write three facts from your own knowledge that connect to the text.

—*from Chapter 6, p. 164*
To pay for the war, the Congress and the states printed hundreds of millions of dollars' worth of paper money. The bills quickly lost their value, though. The amount of bills in circulation grew faster than the supply of gold and silver backing them. This led to **inflation,** which means that it took more and more money to buy the same amount of goods. The Congress stopped issuing the paper money because no one would use it.

Connect to Your Knowledge
What do you know about inflation and paying higher prices for the same items?

1. _____
_____
_____

2. _____
_____
_____

3. _____
_____
_____

Academic Vocabulary Preview

Listed below are the academic vocabulary words and their definitions that you will come across as you study Unit 2. Practice It! will help you study the words and definitions.

Academic Vocabulary	Definition	Practice It!
Chapter 5 The Spirit of Independence		
prohibit (proh · HIH · buht) *p. 123*	to stop; disallow	**Identify** *the term from Chapter 5 that best completes the sentences.*
violate (VY · uh · LAYT) *p. 124*	to disturb or disregard	1. The British created a proclamation to _____ colonists from western settlement.
occupy (AH · kyuh · PY) *p. 127*	to control	
encounter (ihn · KOWN · tuhr) *p. 127*	an unexpected meeting	2. During wartime, enemy soldiers some-times _____ homes and cities.
approach (uh · PROHCH) *p. 135*	to move toward	
volunteer (VAH · luhn · TIHR) *p. 136*	to willingly step forward	3. Many soldiers _____ to serve in their country's military.
debate (dih · BAYT) *p. 141*	a discussion of opposing opinions	
status (STA · tus) *p. 142*	a rank or position	
Chapter 6 The American Revolution		
transfer (TRANS · FUHR) *p. 155*	to move from one place to another	**Choose** *the word that best matches the meaning of each vocabulary term from chapter 6 listed below.*
previous (PREE · vee · uhs) *p. 155*	earlier; coming before	
aid (AYD) *p. 161*	to help	4. **transfer** 6. **pursue**
issue (IH · shoo) *p. 165*	a point or matter of discussion	**a.** to move **a.** to continue
impact (IHM · PAKT) *p. 171*	an effect	**b.** to retain **b.** to retreat
sustain (suh · STAYN) *p. 173*	to suffer	**c.** to command **c.** to neglect
strategy (STRA · tuh · jee) *p. 175*	a plan of action	5. **issue** 7. **strategy**
pursue (puhr · SOO) *p. 177*	to continue	**a.** a story **a.** a game
		b. a paper **b.** a plan
		c. a matter **c.** a work
Chapter 7 A More Perfect Union		
abandon (uh · BAN · duhn) *p. 189*	to give up	**Choose** *terms from Chapter 7 to complete the paragraph.*
clause (KLAWZ) *p. 191*	a condition added to a document	A legal document may have a _____ that adds a condition to the document's terms. Leaders may hold a _____ to create legal documents. At these times, leaders may vote to _____ a docu-ment if they want it changed.
convention (kuhn · VEHN · shuhn) *p. 198*	a formal meeting	
amend (uh · MEHND) *p. 199*	to alter; improve	
tradition (truh · DIH · shuhn) *p. 205*	cultural beliefs and practices	
reside (rih · ZYD) *p. 208*	to exist or live within	

Chapter 5

The Spirit of Independence
1763-1776

Colonial militia members, known as minutemen, left their homes on short notice to fight the British.

British tax stamp ▶

★ **1763**
Treaty of Paris signed

★ **1765**
Colonists protest Stamp Act

★ **1770**
British troops clash with civilians in Boston Massacre

United States

World

1763   **1766**   **1769**

★ **1764**
Mozart writes first symphony at age eight

★ **1770**
Industrial Revolution begins in England

Section 1: Taxation Without Representation

Essential Question Following the French and Indian War, how did the British government anger the American colonists?

Section 2: Building Colonial Unity

Essential Question How did colonists react to British policies?

Section 3: A Call to Arms

Essential Question What brought about the clash between American colonists and British soldiers at Lexington and Concord?

Section 4: Moving Toward Independence

Essential Question Why did the American colonies choose to declare independence?

History ONLINE
Chapter Overview Visit glencoe.com and click on **Chapter 5—Chapter Overviews** to preview chapter information.

FOLDABLES
Study Organizer

Organizing Information

Make this four-tab Foldable to help you learn about the events that led to the American Revolution.

Step 1 Fold the top and bottom of a piece of paper into the middle.

Step 2 Fold the paper in half from side to side.

Step 3 Open and cut along the inside fold lines to form four tabs.

Step 4 Label the tabs as shown.

Reading and Writing

As you read the chapter, take notes about each section under the appropriate head. Use your Foldable to help you write a summary for each section.

Taxation Without Representation	Building Colonial Unity
A Call to Arms	Moving Toward Independence

Liberty Bell ▶

Statue of Minuteman, Concord, MA ▶

▲ Tea leaves from the Boston Tea Party

★ **1773** Patriots carry out Boston Tea Party

★ **1774** First Continental Congress meets

★ **1775** Battles fought at Lexington and Concord

1772

1775

★ **1772** Poland partitioned among Russia, Prussia, and Austria

★ **1774** Louis XVI becomes king of France

◀ Chair owned by Louis XVI

Taxation Without Representation

Essential Question ◄

Following the French and Indian War, how did the British government anger the American colonists?

Reading Guide

Content Vocabulary

revenue (p. 123)

writs of assistance (p. 123)

resolution (p. 125)

effigy (p. 125)

boycott (p. 125)

nonimportation (p. 125)

repeal (p. 125)

Academic Vocabulary

prohibit (p. 123)

violate (p. 124)

Key People and Events

Stamp Act (p. 124)

Patrick Henry (p. 125)

Samuel Adams (p. 125)

Reading Strategy

Taking Notes As you read, identify British policies that affected the colonists. Then describe the colonists' view of each policy.

British Policy	Colonists' View
→	
→	
→	

INDIANA ACADEMIC STANDARDS
United States History

8.1.3 Identify and explain the conditions, causes, consequences, and significance of the French and Indian War (1754–1763), and the resistance and rebellion against British imperial rule by the thirteen colonies in North America (1761–1775).

8.4.1 Identify economic factors contributing to European exploration and colonization in North America, the American Revolution, and the drafting of the Constitution of the United States.

American Diary

In London, Benjamin Franklin stated the American view on British taxes: "They will oppose it to the last. They do not consider it as at all necessary for you to raise money . . . by your taxes. . . . America has been greatly misrepresented . . . [as] refusing to bear any part of [the war's] expense. The Colonies . . . paid and clothed near 25,000 men during the last war, a number equal to [that of] Britain."

—in an interview before the House of Commons, 1766

A SET of PLANS and FORTS in AMERICA. Reduced from Actual Surveys 1765

Relations With Britain

Main Idea After the French and Indian War, Great Britain passed laws to protect British interests in the colonies.

History and You How do you feel when someone treats you unfairly? Read to learn how the colonists felt about British laws that affected them.

. . . .

With victory in the French and Indian War, the British gained control of a vast territory in North America. However, they faced the challenge of protecting their interests in the colonies and new territory. With the Proclamation of 1763, the British government set up new provinces. The proclamation also **prohibited,** or prevented, colonists from moving west of the Appalachian Mountains.

Limiting western settlement provided several advantages for Britain. It allowed the British government to control westward movement and to avoid conflict with Native Americans. Also, keeping colonists near the East Coast ensured a market for British goods in the coastal cities, where trade flourished.

Finally, closing western settlement allowed Britain to control the fur trade in the frontier. Britain planned to station 10,000 troops in the colonies to protect these interests.

Britain needed new **revenue,** or incoming money, to pay troop expenses. Also, the French and Indian War left Britain with a huge debt. The king and Parliament believed that the colonists should pay part of the cost, so they issued new taxes on the colonies and began to enforce existing taxes more strictly.

Britain's Trade Laws

In 1763 George Grenville, prime minister of Britain, decided to act against smuggling. When the colonists smuggled goods to avoid taxes, Britain lost revenue.

Grenville knew that American juries often found smugglers innocent. He convinced Parliament to pass a law allowing smugglers to be sent to vice-admiralty courts, which were run by officers and did not have juries. In 1767 Parliament authorized **writs of assistance.** These legal documents allowed customs officers to enter any location to search for smuggled goods.

The Sugar Act

In 1764 Parliament passed the Sugar Act. This act lowered the tax on imported molasses. Grenville hoped the lower tax would convince colonists to pay the tax instead of smuggling. The act also let officers seize goods from smugglers without going to court.

During the colonial period, the British built a number of forts throughout their American colonies.

By the Numbers / Pounds and Shillings

Britain's Per-Capita War Debt, 1765

Share of the debt per person:	
Britain:	£ £ £ £ £ £ £ £ £ £ £ £ £ £ £ £ £ £
Colonies:	S S S S S S S S S S S S S S S S

£ = 1 British pound   S = 1 British shilling

1 Pound (£) = 20 Shillings

Source: Don Cook. *The Long Fuse: How England Lost the American Colonies, 1760–1785.*

Britain's National Debt At the end of the French and Indian War, Great Britain's national debt soared to more than £140 million. British citizens paid far more on the debt per person than their counterparts in the colonies.

Critical Thinking

Analyzing How much more per-capita debt did residents of Britain have compared to residents of the colonies?

Map legend:
- Thirteen Colonies
- Other British Territory
- Spanish Territory
- - - - Proclamation Line of 1763

Map labels: Hudson's Bay Company, Louisiana Territory, Ohio River, Mississippi River, APPALACHIAN MOUNTAINS, ATLANTIC OCEAN, Gulf of Mexico, Florida, 40°N, 30°N, 80°W, 70°W

0 200 kilometers
0 200 miles
Lambert Azimuthal Equal-Area projection

"I can never look upon that Proclamation in any other light . . . than as a temporary expedient [solution] to quiet the Minds of the Indians and must fall . . . when those Indians are consenting to our Occupying the Lands."

—George Washington, 1767

Provisions of the Proclamation of 1763

- Created governments for the new North American territories won from France as a result of the French and Indian War
- Sought to prevent future conflicts with Native Americans
- Protected Native Americans by reserving the British Crown's right to enter into all land negotiations with them
- Forbade settlement of lands west of the Proclamation line
- Required settlers who had already moved west of the Proclamation line to move east of it
- Stated that the Native Americans were to govern the Proclamation territory under their own laws

Critical Thinking

Analyzing How did the Proclamation of 1763 attempt to protect Native American rights and lands?

The Sugar Act and the new laws to control smuggling angered colonists. They believed these British actions violated, or interfered with, their rights as English citizens. Writs of assistance violated their right to be secure in their homes. Vice-admiralty courts violated their right to a jury trial. Also, in vice-admiralty courts, defendants had to prove their innocence. This contradicted a British law stating "innocent until proved guilty."

These measures alarmed the colonists. James Otis, a lawyer in Boston, argued:

PRIMARY SOURCE

"No parts of [England's colonies] . . . can be taxed without their consent . . . every part has a right to be represented."

—from The Rights of the British Colonies

Reading Check **Explaining** Why did George Grenville want smugglers sent to vice-admiralty courts?

New Taxes

Main Idea As the British government passed new tax laws, resistance by the colonists grew.

History and You Suppose everyone in your community refused to buy from a certain store. How would this decision affect the store? Read to learn how boycotts by the colonists affected British merchants.

In 1765 Parliament passed the **Stamp Act.** This law placed a tax on almost all printed material, including newspapers, wills, and playing cards. All printed material had to have a stamp. British officials applied the stamp after the tax was paid.

Opposition to the Stamp Act centered on two points. Parliament had interfered in colonial affairs by taxing the colonies directly. In addition, it taxed the colonists without their consent.

Protesting the Stamp Act

A member of the Virginia House of Burgesses, **Patrick Henry,** persuaded the burgesses to take action against the Stamp Act. The Virginia assembly passed a **resolution**—a formal expression of opinion—declaring it had "the only and sole exclusive right and power to lay taxes" on its citizens.

In Boston **Samuel Adams** helped start an organization called the Sons of Liberty to protest the Stamp Act. People in other cities also organized the Sons of Liberty groups. Protesters burned **effigies**—rag figures—representing tax collectors and destroyed houses belonging to royal officials.

In October delegates from nine colonies met in New York at the Stamp Act Congress. They drafted a petition to the king and Parliament declaring that the colonies could not be taxed except by their own assemblies.

In colonial cities, people refused to use the stamps. They urged merchants to **boycott**—refuse to buy—British and European goods in protest. Thousands of merchants signed **nonimportation** agreements—pledges not to buy or use goods imported from Britain. As the boycott spread, British merchants lost so much business that they begged Parliament

to **repeal,** or cancel, the Stamp Act. In March 1766, Parliament repealed the law. However, on the same day, it passed the Declaratory Act. This law stated that Parliament had the right to tax and make decisions for the British colonies "in all cases."

The Townshend Acts

In 1767 Parliament passed a set of laws that came to be known as the Townshend Acts. British leaders knew from the Stamp Act that the colonists would resist internal taxes—those paid inside the colonies. As a result, the new taxes would apply only to imported goods such as glass, tea, and paper, with the tax being paid at the port of entry.

By this time, *any* British taxes angered the colonists. They believed that only their own representatives had the right to tax them. The colonists organized another boycott.

Throughout the colonies, women formed groups, sometimes called the Daughters of Liberty. They urged Americans to wear homemade fabrics and produce other goods they needed rather than buy British goods.

✔ **Reading Check** **Describing** How did the Sons of Liberty attempt to influence British policy?

Section 1 Review

History ONLINE
Study Central™ To review this section, go to glencoe.com.

Vocabulary

1. Use each of these terms in a sentence that will help explain its meaning: prohibit, revenue, writs of assistance, violate, resolution, effigy, boycott, nonimportation, repeal.

Main Ideas

2. **Specifying** What advantages did the British gain by limiting westward settlement?

3. **Explaining** Why did some colonists smuggle goods?

4. **Identifying** Opposition to the Stamp Act centered on what two main points?

Critical Thinking

5. **Contrasting** How did the British and the colonists differ on the issue of taxes?

6. **Determining Cause and Effect** Describe the responses of the colonists to the Stamp Act and the result. Use a diagram like the one below.

Stamp Act → Responses → Result

7. **Persuasive Writing** Write a letter to the editor of a colonial newspaper. Your goal is to try to persuade fellow colonists to boycott British goods.

Answer the Essential Question

8. Following the French and Indian War, how did the British government anger the American colonists?

Essential Question ◄
: How did the colonists
: react to British policies?

Reading Guide

Content Vocabulary
propaganda *(p. 127)*
committee of correspondence *(p. 128)*

Academic Vocabulary
occupy *(p. 127)*   encounter *(p. 127)*

Key People and Events
Crispus Attucks *(p. 127)*
Boston Massacre *(p. 127)*
Tea Act *(p. 128)*
Boston Tea Party *(p. 129)*
George III *(p. 129)*
Coercive Acts *(p. 129)*

Reading Strategy
Taking Notes As you read, take
notes on how the Intolerable Acts
affected the colonists.

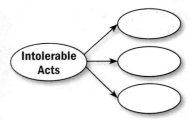

Intolerable Acts

INDIANA ACADEMIC STANDARDS
United States History

8.1.3 Identify and explain the conditions,
causes, consequences, and significance of
the French and Indian War (1754–1763), and
the resistance and rebellion against British
imperial rule by the thirteen colonies in
North America (1761–1775).

8.1.28 Recognize historical perspective and
evaluate alternative courses of action by
describing the historical context in which
events unfolded and by avoiding evaluation of
the past solely in terms of present-day norms.

8.1.29 Differentiate between facts and historical interpretations recognizing that the
historian's narrative reflects his or her judgment about the significance of particular
facts.

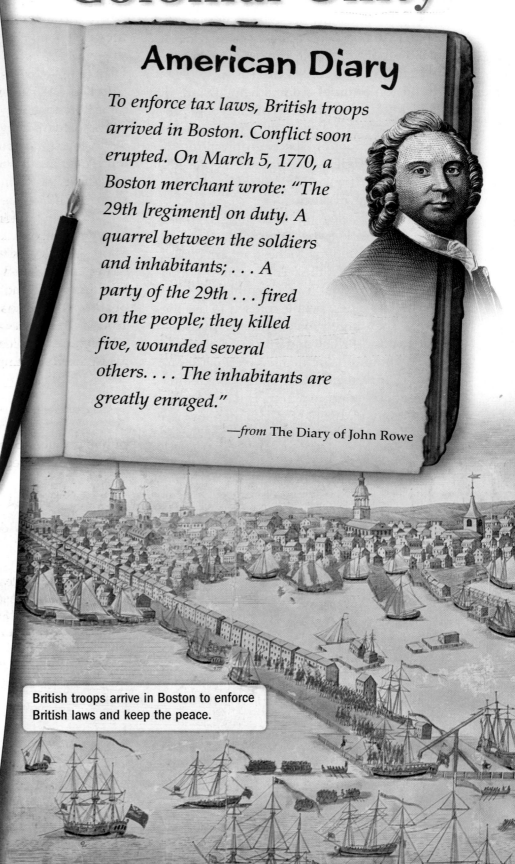

American Diary

To enforce tax laws, British troops
arrived in Boston. Conflict soon
erupted. On March 5, 1770, a
Boston merchant wrote: "The
29th [regiment] on duty. A
quarrel between the soldiers
and inhabitants; . . . A
party of the 29th . . . fired
on the people; they killed
five, wounded several
others. . . . The inhabitants are
greatly enraged."

—*from* The Diary of John Rowe

British troops arrive in Boston to enforce
British laws and keep the peace.

Trouble in Boston

Main Idea A violent clash between townspeople and British soldiers in Boston intensified anti-British feeling in the colonies.

History and You When someone taunts you, how do you react? Read to learn how British soldiers responded to the jeers of Bostonians.

By 1768, protests by the colonists were making British colonial officials nervous. They sent word to Britain that the colonies were on the brink of rebellion. Parliament sent troops to Boston. As angry Bostonians jeered, the "redcoats" set up camp in the center of the city.

Many colonists felt that the British had pushed them too far. First the British had passed laws that violated colonial rights. They also had sent an army to **occupy,** or control, colonial cities.

To make matters worse, the soldiers in Boston acted rudely and sometimes even violently toward the colonists. Mostly poor men, the redcoats earned little pay. Some stole goods from local shops or scuffled with boys who taunted them in the streets. The soldiers also competed off-hours for jobs that Bostonians wanted.

The Boston Massacre

On March 5, 1770, a fight broke out between Bostonians and the soldiers. While some British officers tried to calm the crowd, one man shouted, "We did not send for you. We will not have you here. We'll get rid of you, we'll drive you away!"

The angry townspeople moved toward the customhouse, where British taxes were collected, picking up sticks, stones, and clubs. As the crowd approached, the sentry panicked and called for help. The crowd threw sticks and stones at the soldiers. "Fire, you bloodybacks, you lobsters," the crowd screamed. "You dare not fire."

After one soldier was knocked down, the nervous redcoats did fire, killing five colonists. One Bostonian cried: "Are the inhabitants to be knocked down in the streets? Are they to be murdered . . . ?" Among the dead was **Crispus Attucks,** a dockworker who was part African, part Native American. The colonists called the tragic **encounter,** or unexpected meeting, the **Boston Massacre.**

The Word Spreads

Colonial leaders used the killings as **propaganda**—information made to influence public opinion. Samuel Adams put up posters that described the "Boston Massacre."

Primary Source / **Protesting the Boston Massacre**

AMERICANS!
BEAR IN REMEMBRANCE
The HORRID MASSACRE!
Perpetrated in King-ftreet, Boston,
New-England.
On the Evening of March the Fifth, 1770.
When FIVE of your fellow countrymen,
GRAY, MAVERICK, CALDWELL, ATTUCKS,
and CARR,
Lay wallowing in their Gore!
Being bafely, and moft inhumanly
MURDERED!
And SIX other...

Colonial Propaganda The event described by John Rowe became known as the Boston Massacre. People used that event to rally opposition to the British presence in Boston. This poster recalling the Boston Massacre was printed more than two years later.

Critical Thinking
Analyzing How does this poster indicate bias?

May 1773
Parliament passes the Tea Act.

November 30, 1773
Citizens of Boston vote to prevent three shiploads of tea from being unloaded.

December 16, 1773
Boston Tea Party: Boston citizens disguised as Native Americans board the ships and empty the tea into Boston Harbor.

March 31, 1774
George III and Parliament respond by closing Boston's port.

◀ Tea from the Boston Tea Party

"Fellow countrymen, we cannot afford to give a single inch! If we retreat now, everything we have done becomes useless!"
—Samuel Adams, December 1773

Critical Thinking

Speculating Why do you think the colonists disguised themselves as Native Americans to carry out the Boston Tea Party?

His posters showed a slaughter of innocent Americans by bloodthirsty redcoats. An engraving by Paul Revere showed British troops firing on an orderly crowd.

The Boston Massacre led many colonists to call for stronger boycotts on British goods. Aware of the opposition to its policies, Parliament repealed all the Townshend Acts taxes except the one on tea. The colonists ended their boycotts, except on tea. Trade with Britain resumed.

Some colonial leaders, however, continued to call for resistance to British rule. In 1772 Samuel Adams revived the Boston **committee of correspondence,** an organization used in earlier protests. Soon committees throughout the colonies were airing their grievances against Great Britain.

✓ **Reading Check** **Explaining** How did the colonists use the Boston Massacre to their advantage?

A Crisis Over Tea

Main Idea New British laws restricting colonial rights further enraged the colonists.

History and You If you destroyed someone else's property, would you expect to be punished for your actions? Read to find out about the consequences of the Boston Tea Party.

. . . .

In 1773 the British East India Company faced ruin. To save the company, Parliament passed the **Tea Act.** This law allowed the company a virtual monopoly, or sole control, of the trade for tea in America. The act let the company sell tea directly to shopkeepers and bypass colonial merchants who normally distributed the tea.

Colonial merchants called for a new boycott. Colonists vowed to stop the East India Company's ships from unloading.

The Daughters of Liberty issued a pamphlet declaring that rather than part with freedom, "we'll part with our tea."

The Boston Tea Party

Despite warnings of a brewing crisis, the East India Company shipped tea to a number of colonial cities. The colonists forced the ships sent to New York and Philadelphia to turn back. Three tea ships arrived in Boston Harbor in late 1773. The royal governor refused to let the ships leave and ordered them to be unloaded. The Boston Sons of Liberty acted swiftly. On December 16, a group of men disguised as Mohawks boarded the ships at midnight. They threw 342 chests of tea overboard, an event that became known as the **Boston Tea Party.**

Word of this act of defiance spread. Colonists gathered to celebrate. Yet no one spoke of challenging British rule. Most colonists saw themselves as British citizens.

The Intolerable Acts

When news of the Boston Tea Party reached London, King **George III** realized that Britain was losing control of the colonies. He declared, "We must master them or totally leave them alone." The British government responded by passing the **Coercive Acts** in 1774. These harsh laws were intended to punish the people of Massachusetts for their resistance to British law.

The Coercive Acts closed Boston Harbor until the Massachusetts colonists paid for the ruined tea. This action prevented the arrival of food and other supplies that normally came by ship. Worse, the laws took away certain rights. For example, the laws banned most town meetings in New England.

The Coercive Acts also forced Bostonians to shelter soldiers in their own homes. Parliament planned to isolate Boston with these acts. Instead the other colonies sent food and clothing to support Boston. The colonists held that the Coercive Acts violated their rights as English citizens. These rights included no quartering of troops in private homes and no standing army in peacetime.

Parliament then passed the Quebec Act. This law set up a government for Quebec. It also gave Quebec the area west of the Appalachians and north of the Ohio River. This provision ignored colonial claims to the area. The colonists expressed their feelings in *their* name for the new laws—the Intolerable Acts.

✔ **Reading Check** **Describing** How did the British react to the Boston Tea Party?

Section 2 Review

History ONLINE
Study Central™ To review this section, go to glencoe.com.

Vocabulary

1. Write a short paragraph in which you use all of the following vocabulary terms: occupy, encounter, propaganda, committee of correspondence.

Main Ideas

2. **Describing** Describe the events leading up to and following the Boston Massacre.

3. **Explaining** How did the Tea Act give an unfair advantage to the British East India Company?

Critical Thinking

4. **Evaluating** How did Samuel Adams and Paul Revere try to sway public opinion about the Boston Massacre?

5. **Organizing** Use a diagram like the one below to identify events and policies that led to rising tensions in the 1770s.

Rising Tensions

6. **Creative Writing** Write an account of the Boston Massacre from the point of view of a British soldier involved in the event.

Answer the
Essential Question

7. How did the colonists react to British policies?

America's LITERATURE

Meet the Author

Barry Denenberg (1946–) has said that the American Revolution is often presented to young people as a distant event. In writing *The Journal of William Thomas Emerson: A Revolutionary War Patriot*, Denenberg wanted to "bring the revolution to life by showing how it affected ordinary people and how they affected it."

Vocabulary

crown king

trampled crush

cowering crouching

feeble weak

soot ash

Building Background

In *The Journal of William Thomas Emerson: A Revolutionary War Patriot*, Barry Denenberg depicts life in Boston in the months leading up to the American Revolution as told by Will, a young orphan boy. Will works for Mr. Wilson, a tavern owner and member of the Committee, a group of colonists who oppose the British. As you read this excerpt, think about the actions of the Committee toward ordinary citizens and their effect on the political climate at the time.

THE JOURNAL OF WILLIAM THOMAS EMERSON: A REVOLUTIONARY WAR PATRIOT

Barry Denenberg

The Fitch Sisters and the Committee

Mrs. Thompson is still angry about the Fitch sisters, who have a shop on Milk Street. She never raises her voice like that.

"It's just like them to think they could bring in British goods and get away with it. You can count on the Fitch sisters to be concerned only about themselves, even in times like these. Imagine, claiming they are just trying to keep a roof over their heads and food on the table. Isn't that all any of us are doing?"

The Fitch sisters say that if they didn't have British goods to sell they would find themselves poor in no time. But Mrs. Thompson says they're only making it harder on themselves by defending their actions and they should just admit their mistake. . . .

"They ought to get the same treatment as Mr. Carlisle," Mrs. Thompson said.

Henry told me all about Mr. Carlisle. We saw him one day walking down King Street dressed in lace and ruffles. Henry said he has long been suspected of being loyal to the **crown** and one night he finally got what he deserved. Some of the men from town marched out to his house. Mr. Carlisle is very rich, Henry said, "Almost as rich as Mr. Dudley. Mr. Carlisle's house was one of the grandest in Boston."

As soon as the crowd arrived they **trampled** the lawn, hacked down the trees, and overran the gate that surrounds the house. They smashed the big front doors with axes and then poured into the house, where they tore up the floorboards, ripped the curtains from the windows and, after finding Mr. Carlisle's portrait, tore the eyes out.

They dragged his finely carved furniture outside and smashed it to bits, ran off with his carpets and drank his wine cellar dry.

They found Mr. Carlisle **cowering** upstairs, trying to hide behind his bed curtains. They pulled him out despite his **feeble** efforts to hold on to the bedpost and then took his feather bed and threw it out the window. A ladder was put up and Mr. Carlisle was lowered to those waiting below.

Once they had him outside, they stripped off his nightclothes, smeared him with hot tar and covered him with the insides of the feather bed.

When the house caught fire someone wanted to call for the firemen, but the crowd shouted him down, yelling, "LET IT BURN, LET IT BURN," and so they did. The flames, Henry said, could be seen for miles by dawn. . . .

Most of the men pulled nightcaps over their heads or darkened their faces with chimney **soot** so they wouldn't be recognized. Some were armed with sticks and clubs and Henry said that Mr. Carlisle was lucky not to have suffered even greater injury to his person than to his pride.

Of course, Mrs. Thompson didn't say any of this to me. I overheard it when she was talking to Mr. Wilson right before he went into the regular Tuesday night meeting with the Committee.

That's why I stay put on Tuesday nights. I never go anywhere. They meet late, after the tavern closes, in the small room next to the big barroom. As soon as I hear them all coming in I just lie there quietly on my cot and listen. . . .

Analyzing Literature

1. **Respond** If asked to take sides in Mr. Carlisle's situation, which side would you take and why?

2. **Recall and Interpret**
   (a) Who tarred and feathered Mr. Carlisle? How do you know?
   (b) Why do you think the Committee acted so drastically?

3. **Evaluate**
   (a) What do you think will happen to the Fitch sisters?
   (b) Do you think the author does a good job in bringing the American Revolution to life for readers? Explain your answer.

Essential Question

What brought about the clash between American colonists and British soldiers at Lexington and Concord?

Reading Guide

Content Vocabulary

militia *(p. 133)*   Loyalist *(p. 137)*

minutemen *(p. 134)*   Patriot *(p. 137)*

Academic Vocabulary

approach *(p. 135)*   volunteer *(p. 136)*

Key People and Events

Continental Congress *(p. 133)*

John Adams *(p. 133)*

John Jay *(p. 133)*

Richard Henry Lee *(p. 133)*

George Washington *(p. 133)*

Paul Revere *(p. 135)*

Reading Strategy

Taking Notes As you read, list three key actions of the Continental Congress. Use a diagram like the one below.

Continental Congress

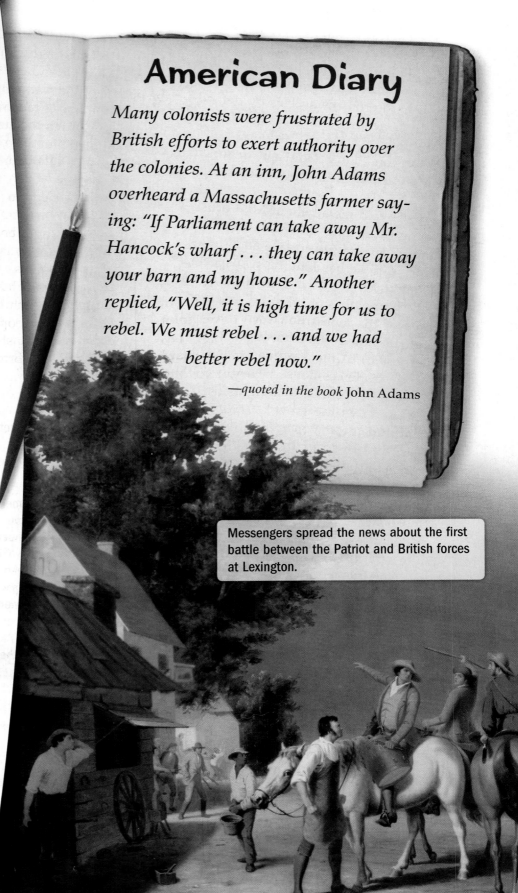

American Diary

Many colonists were frustrated by British efforts to exert authority over the colonies. At an inn, John Adams overheard a Massachusetts farmer saying: "If Parliament can take away Mr. Hancock's wharf . . . they can take away your barn and my house." Another replied, "Well, it is high time for us to rebel. We must rebel . . . and we had better rebel now."

—quoted in the book John Adams

Messengers spread the news about the first battle between the Patriot and British forces at Lexington.

The Continental Congress

Main Idea Colonial leaders met in Philadelphia to discuss their opposition to British policy.

History and You Have you ever worked with a group to accomplish a shared goal? Read to learn about the common goal that united the Continental Congress.

· ·

In September 1774, 55 delegates from all the colonies except Georgia arrived in Philadelphia. They had come to establish a political body to represent American interests and challenge British control. They called the new organization the **Continental Congress.**

Delegates to the Congress

Political leaders from across the colonies attended the Congress. Massachusetts sent fiery Samuel Adams and his cousin **John Adams,** a lawyer. New York sent **John Jay,** another lawyer. From Virginia came **Richard Henry Lee** and Patrick Henry, two outspoken defenders of colonial rights, as well as **George Washington.** Patrick Henry summed up the meaning of the gathering:

PRIMARY SOURCE

"The distinctions between Virginians, Pennsylvanians, New Yorkers, and New Englanders, are no more. I am not a Virginian, but an American."

—Patrick Henry, at the Continental Congress

Decisions of the Congress

The delegates drafted a statement of grievances calling for the repeal of 13 acts of Parliament. They believed these laws violated the "laws of nature, the principles of the English constitution, and the several charters" of the colonies. The delegates voted to boycott British trade. No British goods could be brought in or used in the colonies. No colonial goods could be sold to Britain.

The Congress also decided to endorse the Suffolk Resolves, so named because they were prepared by the people of Suffolk County, Massachusetts. These resolutions called on the people of the county to arm themselves against the British. The people responded by forming **militias**—groups of citizen soldiers.

✔ **Reading Check** **Explaining** What was the purpose of the Continental Congress?

If You Were There / Militias in the Colonies

Citizen Soldiers Even before the American Revolution, the American colonists had a long tradition of serving in the military. If you were a member of a militia, you were an important part of the defense of your town. You trained and drilled with the other soldiers. You practiced musket and cannon drills. You were required to provide your own weapons—usually a musket—and ammunition. As the break between Great Britain and the American colonies grew, town governments also supplied their militias. The chart to the left shows arms purchased by the town of Salem, Massachusetts.

Purchases authorized by Salem Provincial Congress, October 1774	
20 tons grape- and round shot, from 3 to 24 lb. @ £15	£300
10 tons bomb shells @ £20	£200
5 tons lead balls @ £33	£165
1,000 barrels of powder @ £8	£8,000
5,000 arms and bayonets @ £2	£10,000
And 75,000 flints	£100

Critical Thinking

Speculating What advantages would local militias have against British soldiers?

The First Battles

Main Idea America's fight for independence began when British troops clashed with minutemen at Lexington and Concord.

History and You Why would the element of surprise be a valuable weapon during a war? Read to learn how the minutemen used the element of surprise to their advantage.

. . . .

Colonists expected that if fighting against the British broke out, it would begin in New England. Militia companies in Massachusetts held frequent training sessions, made bullets, and stockpiled rifles and muskets. Some companies, known as **minutemen,** boasted they would be ready to fight on a minute's notice. In the winter of 1774–1775, a British officer stationed in Boston noted in his diary:

PRIMARY SOURCE

"The people are evidently making every preparation for resistance. They are taking every means to provide themselves with Arms."

—from *Diary of Frederick Mackenzie*

Britain Sends Troops

The British also prepared for conflict. King George announced to Parliament that the New England Colonies were "in a state of rebellion" and said that "blows must decide" who would control America. By April 1775, several thousand British soldiers were in and around Boston, with many more on the way. Their general, Thomas Gage, had instructions to take away the weapons of the Massachusetts militia and arrest the leaders.

Gage learned that the militia was storing arms and ammunition at Concord, a town about 20 miles (32 km) northwest of Boston. He ordered 700 troops under Lieutenant Colonel Francis Smith to march "to Concord, where you will seize and destroy all the artillery and ammunition you can find."

Alerting the Colonists

On the night of April 18, 1775, Dr. Joseph Warren walked the streets of Boston looking for any unusual activity by the British army. He saw a regiment form ranks in Boston Common and begin to march out of the city.

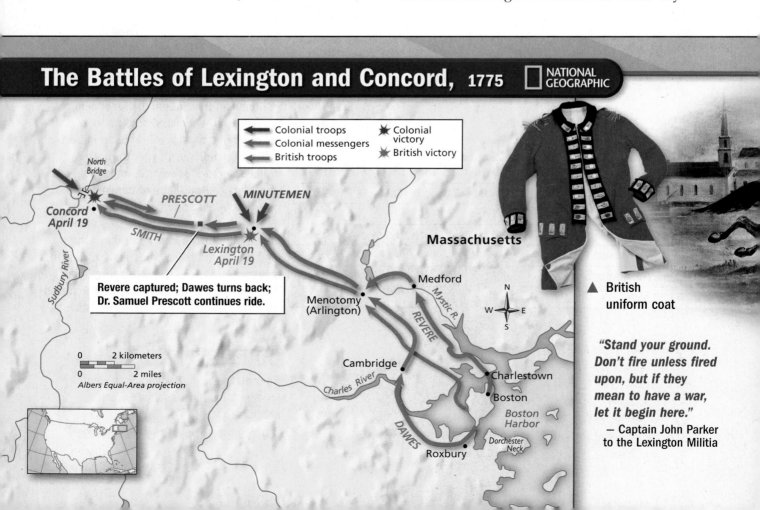

The Battles of Lexington and Concord, 1775 NATIONAL GEOGRAPHIC

Colonial troops
Colonial messengers
British troops

Colonial victory
British victory

North Bridge

Concord April 19

PRESCOTT

MINUTEMEN

SMITH

Lexington April 19

Revere captured; Dawes turns back; Dr. Samuel Prescott continues ride.

Menotomy (Arlington)

Medford

Mystic R.

REVERE

Massachusetts

Sudbury River

0   2 kilometers
0   2 miles
Albers Equal-Area projection

Cambridge

Charles River

DAWES

Charlestown

Boston

Boston Harbor

Dorchester Neck

Roxbury

▲ British uniform coat

"Stand your ground. Don't fire unless fired upon, but if they mean to have a war, let it begin here."
— Captain John Parker to the Lexington Militia

Warren rushed to alert **Paul Revere** and William Dawes, members of the Sons of Liberty. Revere and Dawes rode to Lexington, a town east of Concord, to warn Samuel Adams and John Hancock that the British were coming. Revere galloped across the moonlit countryside, shouting, "The regulars are out!" to people along the way. Upon hearing the news, Adams exclaimed, "What a glorious morning this is!" Adams was ready to fight for independence.

Lexington and Concord

At dawn the redcoats **approached,** or moved closer to, Lexington. There they discovered about 70 minutemen who had been alerted by Revere and Dawes. Led by Captain John Parker, the minutemen stood on the town common with muskets in hand. A minuteman reported:

PRIMARY SOURCE

"There suddenly appeared a number of the king's troops . . . the foremost of which cried, 'Throw down your arms, ye villains, ye rebels!'"

—from *The Military Journals of Two Private Soldiers*

A shot was fired, and then both sides let loose an exchange of bullets. When the fighting ended, eight minutemen lay dead. The British troops continued their march to Concord. When they arrived, they found that most of the militia's gunpowder had already been removed. They destroyed the remaining supplies. At Concord's North Bridge, waiting minutemen turned back the British.

Messengers on horseback had spread word of the British movements. All along the road from Concord to Boston, farmers, blacksmiths, and clerks hid behind trees and stone fences. As the British marched down the road, the militia fired. By the time the redcoats reached Boston, at least 174 were wounded and 73 were dead.

Looking back, the poet Ralph Waldo Emerson wrote in "The Concord Hymn" that the Americans at Lexington and Concord had fired the "shot heard 'round the world." The battle for independence had begun.

Reading Check **Explaining** How were the colonists preparing for war with Britain?

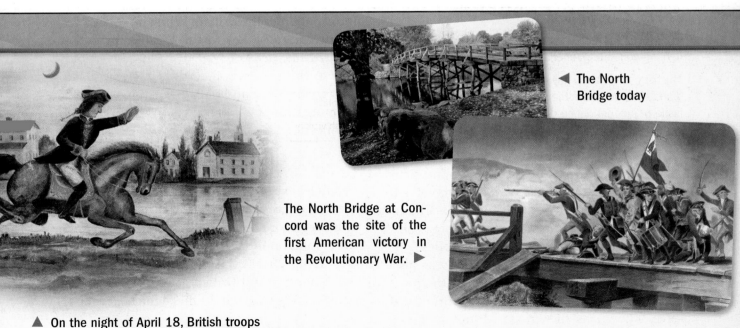

◄ The North Bridge today

The North Bridge at Concord was the site of the first American victory in the Revolutionary War. ►

▲ On the night of April 18, British troops secretly set out from Boston to Concord. Messengers, including Paul Revere (above), were sent to spread the alarm. When the British reached Lexington, Patriot minutemen were waiting.

Critical Thinking

Analyzing What happened after British forces reached Lexington?

Maps In MOtion See StudentWorks™ Plus or glencoe.com.

People IN HISTORY

Patrick Henry
Lawyer and Revolutionary

Henry was one of the first members of the Virginia House of Burgesses to argue for independence from Britain. In a debate over whether the state should form a militia, he vowed, *"Give me liberty or give me death!"*

Samuel Adams
Patriot Leader in Boston

Adams argued that Massachusetts should be independent from Britain long before anyone else did. After the Townshend Acts were passed, he wrote that it was *"irreconcilable to . . . common sense and reason, that a British house of commons, should have a right . . . to give and grant the property of the Colonists."*

CRITICAL Thinking

1. **Synthesizing** What did Patrick Henry and Samuel Adams have in common?
2. **Analyzing** What do you think Patrick Henry meant when he said, "Give me liberty or give me death!"?

More Military Action

Main Idea As colonial militias formed and the fighting continued, American loyalties were split.

History and You Have you ever taken sides in a dispute between two friends? Read to learn how the issue of independence divided Americans.

Shortly after Lexington and Concord, Benedict Arnold, a captain in the Connecticut militia, was authorized to raise a force of 400 men to seize Fort Ticonderoga on Lake Champlain. Ticonderoga was not only strategically located but also rich in military supplies.

Arnold learned that Ethan Allen was also mounting an expedition in Vermont to attack the fort. Arnold joined his militia with Allen's force, known as the Green Mountain Boys. Together they caught the British by surprise. Fort Ticonderoga surrendered on May 10, 1775.

Later during the war, Arnold sold military information to the British. When he conspired to surrender the key fort of West Point to the British, his treason was discovered. Arnold fled to British-controlled New York City. He was given command of British troops and led raids against the Americans in Virginia and Connecticut.

Building Forces

After Lexington and Concord, the committees of correspondence sent out calls for **volunteers,** or helpers, to join the militias. Soon the colonial militia assembled around Boston was about 20,000 strong. For several weeks, the American and British armies waited nervously to see who would make the next move.

History ONLINE
Student Web Activity Visit glencoe.com and complete the Chapter 5 Web Activity about Benedict Arnold.

The Battle of Bunker Hill

On June 16, 1775, about 1,200 militiamen under the command of Colonel William Prescott set up fortifications at Bunker Hill and nearby Breed's Hill, across the harbor from Boston.

The British decided to drive the Americans from their strategic locations overlooking the city. The next day the redcoats assembled at the bottom of Breed's Hill. Bayonets drawn, they charged up the hill. With his forces low on ammunition, Colonel Prescott reportedly shouted the order, "Don't fire until you see the whites of their eyes." The Americans opened fire, forcing the British to retreat. The redcoats charged two more times, receiving furious fire. In the end the Americans ran out of gunpowder and had to withdraw.

The British won the Battle of Bunker Hill but suffered heavy losses—more than 1,000 dead and wounded. As one British officer wrote in his diary, "A dear bought victory, another such would have ruined us." The British had learned that defeating the Americans on the battlefield would not be quick or easy.

Choosing Sides

As American colonists heard about these battles, they faced a major decision. Should they join the rebels or remain loyal to Great Britain? Those who chose to stay with Britain, the **Loyalists,** did not consider unfair taxes and regulations good reasons for rebellion. Some Loyalists lived in relative isolation and had not been part of the wave of discontent that turned many Americans against Britain. Still others expected Britain to win the war and wanted to gain favor with the British.

The **Patriots,** on the other hand, were colonists who supported the war for independence. They believed that British rule had become unbearable. The Patriots were determined to fight the British until American independence was won.

The American Revolution was not just a war between the Americans and the British. It was also a civil war among colonists—Patriots against Loyalists.

Reading Check **Analyzing** What did the British learn from the Battle of Bunker Hill?

Section 3 Review

History ONLINE
Study Central™ To review this section, go to glencoe.com.

Vocabulary

1. Define each of the following terms and use them in a paragraph: militia, minutemen, approach, volunteer, Loyalist, Patriot.

Main Ideas

2. Explaining How did endorsement of the Suffolk Resolves by the Continental Congress push the colonies closer to war?

3. Describing What tactics did the colonists use against the British troops on their march back from Concord to Boston?

Critical Thinking

4. Interpreting Reread Patrick Henry's quote about the Continental Congress. What change was occurring in the way the colonists saw themselves?

5. Comparing and Contrasting Use a diagram like the one below to show the similarities and differences between Patriots and Loyalists.

Loyalists — Both — Patriots

6. Creative Writing Write a one-act play in which ordinary people in a small town react to the news of the Battle of Lexington. Remember that not all colonists wanted independence from Britain.

Answer the
7. Essential Question
What brought about the clash between American colonists and British soldiers at Lexington and Concord?

Essential Question ◄

Why did the American colonies choose to declare independence?

Reading Guide

Content Vocabulary

petition *(p. 140)*   preamble *(p. 142)*

Academic Vocabulary

debate *(p. 141)*   status *(p. 142)*

Key People and Events

Second Continental Congress *(p. 139)*

Continental Army *(p. 139)*

Olive Branch Petition *(p. 140)*

Thomas Paine *(p. 140)*

Common Sense *(p. 140)*

Declaration of Independence *(p. 141)*

Reading Strategy

Taking Notes As you read, describe the parts of the Declaration of Independence. Use a diagram like the one below.

Declaration of Independence

Part 1:

↓

Part 2:

↓

Part 3:

↓

Part 4:

INDIANA ACADEMIC STANDARDS
United States History

8.1.4 Identify fundamental ideas in the Declaration of Independence (1776) and analyze the causes and effects of the Revolutionary War (1775–1783), including enactment of the Articles of Confederation and the Treaty of Paris.

8.1.9 Describe the influence of important individuals on social and political developments of the time such as the Independence movement and the framing of the

American Diary

Colonists debated the wisdom of pursuing peace or declaring independence from Britain. Thomas Paine wrote: "I have heard it asserted by some, that as America has flourished under her former connection with Great Britain, the same connection is necessary towards her future happiness. . . . Nothing can be more [false]. . . . We may as well assert that because a child has thrived upon milk, that it is never to have meat. . . . A government of our own is our natural right."

—*from* Common Sense

The Declaration of Independence is presented to the Second Continental Congress.

Colonial Leaders Emerge

Main Idea When the Second Continental Congress met for the first time, many leaders were not yet ready to call for independence.

History and You Do newspapers, books, or television news programs affect your opinion on important issues? Read to learn how a pamphlet by Thomas Paine influenced colonial opinion.

. . . .

On May 10, 1775, the **Second Continental Congress** assembled for the first time. However, many delegates were not yet prepared to break away from Great Britain. It would be another year before John Adams would ask Thomas Jefferson to write the Declaration of Independence.

The delegates to the Second Continental Congress included some of the greatest political leaders in America. Among those attending were John and Samuel Adams, Patrick Henry, Richard Henry Lee, and George Washington—all delegates to the First Continental Congress held in 1774. Several distinguished new delegates came as well.

Benjamin Franklin, one of the most respected men in the colonies, had been an influential member of the Pennsylvania legislature. In 1765, during the Stamp Act crisis, he represented the colonies in London and helped secure the repeal of the act.

John Hancock of Massachusetts was a wealthy merchant. He funded many Patriot groups, including the Sons of Liberty. The delegates chose Hancock as president of the Second Continental Congress.

Thomas Jefferson, only 32, had already earned a reputation as a brilliant thinker and writer. He served in the Virginia legislature.

The Second Continental Congress began to govern the colonies. It authorized the printing of money and set up a post office with Franklin in charge. It established committees to communicate with Native Americans and with other countries. Most important, the Congress created the **Continental Army** to fight against Britain in a more organized way than the colonial militias could. On John Adams's recommendation, the Congress unanimously chose George Washington to be the army's commander.

Primary Source / Creating the Declaration

Adams and Jefferson By June 1776, the Second Continental Congress was ready to separate from Britain. John Adams, Benjamin Franklin, Thomas Jefferson, Robert Livingston, and Roger Sherman formed the committee to draft a statement. Adams asked Jefferson to write the document because "he was so prompt, frank, explicit, and decisive upon committees and in conversation." Jefferson was reluctant, but Adams persuaded him, saying: "Reason first—You are a Virginian, and a Virginian ought to appear at the head of this business. Reason second—I am obnoxious, suspected, and unpopular. You are very much otherwise. Reason third—you can write ten times better than I can."

—from *The Writings of Thomas Jefferson*

◀ Early draft of the Declaration of Independence

Critical Thinking

Explaining What were Adams's reasons for wanting Jefferson to draft the Declaration of Independence?

Independence: Yes or No?

Many Americans were uncertain whether independence was the correct course for the colonies. After Americans and British troops had fought, however, other colonists felt strongly that independence should be their goal.

In 1776 Thomas Paine made an impassioned appeal for independence in his pamphlet *Common Sense:*

THOMAS PAINE

YES

"Every thing that is right or natural pleads for separation. The blood of the slain, the weeping voice of nature cries, 'tis time to part.'"

Other Americans did not want to break away from Britain. Colonists who felt a strong sense of loyalty to the king were called Loyalists. They believed British law should be upheld.

Loyalist Charles Inglis argued against going to war with Britain, saying:

CHARLES INGLIS

NO

"Ruthless war, with all its aggravated horrors, will ravage our once happy land—our seacoasts and ports will be ruined, and our ships taken. Torrents of blood will be spilt, and thousands reduced to beggary and wretchedness."

DBQ Document-Based Questions

1. **Analyzing** What is Paine's argument in favor of independence?
2. **Identifying** What did Inglis believe would result from war with Britain?

After Washington left to take charge of the forces in Boston, the delegates offered Britain one last chance to avoid war. The Congress sent a **petition,** or formal request, to George III. Called the **Olive Branch Petition,** it assured the king of the colonists' desire for peace and asked him to protect the colonists' rights. George III refused to receive the Olive Branch Petition. Instead he prepared for war, hiring more than 30,000 German troops to fight beside British troops.

The Colonies Take the Offensive

Meanwhile the Congress learned that British troops in what is now Canada were planning to invade New York. The Americans decided to strike first. Marching north from Fort Ticonderoga, a Patriot force captured Montreal. An American attack on Quebec led by Benedict Arnold failed, however.

Washington reached Boston in July 1775, a few weeks after the Battle of Bunker Hill. While he found the size of the militia growing every day, Washington realized that the members lacked discipline, organization, and leadership. He began the hard work of shaping these armed civilians into an army.

By March 1776, Washington judged the Continental Army ready to fight. He positioned the army in a semicircle around Boston and gave the order for its cannons to bombard the British forces. The redcoats, under Sir William Howe, hurriedly withdrew from the city. On March 17, Washington led his jubilant troops into Boston. The British troops sailed to Halifax, Nova Scotia.

Moving Toward Independence

In early 1776, support for the position of absolute independence was growing. In January 1776, **Thomas Paine** published a pamphlet called ***Common Sense.*** In bold language, Paine called for complete independence. *Common Sense* greatly influenced opinion throughout the colonies.

Reading Check **Explaining** What was the significance of the Olive Branch Petition?

The Colonies Declare Independence

Main Idea The Declaration of Independence announced the birth of a new nation, committing Americans to a struggle for independence.

History and You How do you celebrate the Fourth of July? Read to learn how Americans celebrated at the reading of the Declaration of Independence.

. . . .

At the Second Continental Congress in Philadelphia, the meeting hall was filled with spirited discussion, or **debate:** Should the colonies declare themselves an independent nation or stay under British rule? Virginia's Richard Henry Lee proposed a bold resolution:

PRIMARY SOURCE

"That these United Colonies are, and of right ought to be, free and independent States . . . and that all political connection between them and the State of Great Britain is, and ought to be, totally dissolved."

—Richard Henry Lee, resolution for independence

The Debate Over Independence

Congress debated Lee's resolution. Some delegates thought the colonies were not ready to form a separate nation. Others argued that war had already begun. Still others feared Britain's power to crush the rebellion.

As they debated, the Congress chose a committee to draft a **Declaration of Independence.** Jefferson was selected to write the declaration. Jefferson drew some ideas from English philosopher John Locke in his arguments for freedom. Locke wrote that people were born with certain natural rights to life, liberty, and property; that people formed governments to protect these rights; and that a government interfering with these rights might rightfully be overthrown.

On July 2, 1776, the Congress finally voted on Lee's resolution for independence. Twelve colonies voted for it. New York did not vote but later announced its support. Congress then took up Jefferson's draft of the Declaration of Independence, which they approved with some changes on July 4, 1776.

Primary Source | Independence Day

"The Second Day of July 1776, will be the most memorable [day], in the History of America. . . . It ought to be solemnized with Pomp and Parade, with Shews [shows], Games, Sports, Guns, Bells, Bonfires and Illuminations from one End of this Continent to the other from this Time forward forever more."
— John Adams, in a letter to his wife Abigail

The committee assigned ▶ to draft the Declaration: Benjamin Franklin, Thomas Jefferson, and John Adams

Advertisement for railroad transportation to Fourth of July celebration, 1876 ▶

◀ A Fourth of July celebration in New York in the early 1800s

A Day to Celebrate John Adams expected the Second Continental Congress's vote for independence on July 2, 1776, to be celebrated as a great national holiday. Instead, it was the date of the adoption of the Declaration of Independence that has come to be celebrated as Independence Day.

Critical Thinking

Analyzing How has Independence Day come to be celebrated?

John Hancock was the first to sign. Hancock remarked that he wrote his name large enough for King George to read it without his glasses. Eventually 56 delegates signed the paper announcing the birth of the United States.

Copies of the Declaration went out to the newly declared states. Washington had it read to his troops on July 9. In Worcester, Massachusetts, the reading of the Declaration of Independence was followed by "repeated [cheers], firing of musketry and cannon, bonfires, and other demonstrations of joy."

The Declaration of Independence

The Declaration has four major sections. It includes a **preamble,** or introduction, which states that people who wish to form a new country should explain their reasons for doing so. The next sections list the rights the colonists believed they should have and their complaints against Britain. The final section proclaims the existence of the new nation.

The Declaration of Independence states what Jefferson and many Americans thought were universal principles. It begins by describing traditional English rights:

PRIMARY SOURCE

"We hold these truths to be self-evident, that all men are created equal, that they are endowed by their Creator with certain unalienable Rights, that among these are Life, Liberty, and the pursuit of Happiness."

—Thomas Jefferson, *Declaration of Independence*

The Declaration states that government exists to protect these rights. If it does not, "it is the Right of the People to alter or to abolish it and to institute new Government." The Declaration goes on to list grievances against the king and Parliament. These include "cutting off our trade with all parts of the world" and "imposing taxes on us without our consent." Americans had "Petitioned for Redress" of these grievances. These petitions, however, were ignored or rejected by Britain.

The Declaration ends by announcing America's new **status,** or position. Now pledging "to each other our Lives, our Fortunes, and our sacred Honor," the Americans declared themselves a new nation.

Reading Check **Summarizing** According to John Locke, what is the purpose of government?

Section 4 Review

History ONLINE
Study Central™ To review this section, go to glencoe.com.

Vocabulary

1. Use each of these terms in a sentence that will help explain its meaning: petition, debate, preamble, status.

Main Ideas

2. **Explaining** What actions did the Second Continental Congress take to begin governing the colonies?

3. **Summarizing** What grievances against King George III were included in the Declaration of Independence?

Critical Thinking

4. **Interpreting** Reread the Primary Source quote from the Declaration of Independence above. Rewrite this quote in your own words, and explain its significance.

5. **Organizing Information** Using a diagram like the one below, describe each leader's role in the movement toward independence.

Leader	Role
Benjamin Franklin →	
John Hancock →	
Thomas Jefferson →	
George Washington →	

6. **Expository Writing** Prepare a help-wanted ad to locate a person who is qualified to write the Declaration of Independence. Describe the responsibilities of the job as well as the experience and character traits needed.

7. 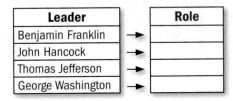 **Answer the Essential Question** Why did the American colonies choose to declare independence?

To help pay for the French and Indian War, Great Britain passed new laws and imposed new taxes on the American colonies.

The Boston Tea Party ▼

The colonists responded to the new laws by organizing boycotts and other protests. Tensions rose with the Boston Massacre and the Boston Tea Party.

▲ British uniform coat

The Continental Congress, a political body formed by representatives from the colonies, met for the first time and drafted a list of grievances with British policy.

Liberty Bell ▼

Fighting broke out between British troops and colonial militia at Lexington and Concord.

▲ Fighting at Concord's North Bridge

While the fighting continued, the Second Continental Congress approved the Declaration of Independence on July 4, 1776.

STUDY TO GO Study anywhere, anytime! Download quizzes and flash cards to your PDA from glencoe.com.

INDIANA STATEWIDE TEST PRACTICE

Reviewing Vocabulary

Directions: Choose the word or words that best completes the sentence.

1 To protest the Stamp Act, colonists _____ British and European goods.

A occupied
B boycotted
C purchased
D taxed

2 Organizations called _____ aired grievances against Great Britain.

A parliaments
B smugglers
C minutemen
D committees of correspondence

3 Colonists who supported the king and Great Britain were called _____.

A Loyalists
B Patriots
C militia
D minutemen

4 The introduction to the Declaration of Independence is called the _____.

A petition
B debate
C preamble
D resolution

Reviewing Main Ideas

Directions: Choose the best answer.

5 The writs of assistance authorized by the 1767 Parliament

A prevented colonists from trading with other nations besides England.
B taxed the colonists without their consent.
C allowed customs officers to search any location for smuggled goods.
D violated a colonist's right to a jury trial.

6 The Coercive Acts

A closed Boston Harbor to penalize colonists following the Boston Tea Party.
B gave Quebec the area west of the Appalachians and north of the Ohio River.
C lowered the tax on imported molasses.
D placed a tax on almost all printed material sold in the colonies.

7 The preamble to the Declaration of Independence

A lists colonists' complaints against Britain.
B lists the rights the colonists believed they should have.
C proclaims the existence of the new nation.
D states the reasons why the people wish to form a new country.

GO ON

History ONLINE

For additional test practice, use **Self-Check Quizzes**—Chapter 5 at glencoe.com.

Critical Thinking

Directions: Choose the best answer.

8 **All of the following are reasons the British government issued the Proclamation of 1763 EXCEPT**

   A to control the fur trade.
   B to allow colonists to settle in the West.
   C to avoid conflict with Native Americans.
   D to create governments for the new territories.

Base your answer to question 9 on the political cartoon below and your knowledge of Chapter 5.

Source: The Art Archive

9 **In this cartoon, colonists are pouring tea down the throat of a tax collector. The colonists are showing anger because**

   A Britain had promised not to tax tea.
   B British tea is not as good as colonial tea.
   C British tea taxes were too high.
   D British taxes on stamps were too high.

Constructed Response

Directions: Write a short response to each of the following questions. In your answer:

- *address all parts of the question*
- *use information from the chapter*
- *include facts, examples, and details relevant to the question*
- *use clear language*

10 **State how the Proclamation of 1763 affected the colonists.**

11 **State the primary reason American colonists opposed direct taxes placed on them by the British.**

Base your answer to question 12 on the reading below and your knowledge of Chapter 5.

> I agree, that 'two supreme and independent authorities cannot exist in the same state,' any more than two supreme beings in one universe; And, therefore, I contend, that our provincial legislatures are the only supreme authorities in our colonies.

Source: John Adams, "Novanglus"

12 **Based on the document, cite one reason Adams supported American independence from Britain.**

13 **How did the tradition of self-government play a role in the colonists' decision to declare independence?**

Need Extra Help?													
If you missed questions. . .	1	2	3	4	5	6	7	8	9	10	11	12	13
Go to page. . .	125	128	137	142	123	129	142	123	128	123	124	141	139

The Declaration of Independence

In Congress, July 4, 1776. The unanimous Declaration of the thirteen United States of America,

Words spelled as originally written.

What It Means

The Preamble The Declaration of Independence has four parts. The Preamble explains why the Continental Congress drew up the Declaration.

impel: force

What It Means

Natural Rights The second part, the Declaration of Natural Rights, lists the rights of the citizens. It goes on to explain that, in a republic, people form a government to protect their rights.

endowed: provided

usurpations: unjust uses of power

despotism: unlimited power

What It Means

List of Grievances The third part of the Declaration lists the colonists' complaints against the British government. Notice that King George III is singled out for blame.

[Preamble]

When in the Course of human events, it becomes necessary for one people to dissolve the political bands which have connected them with another, and to assume among the powers of the earth, the separate and equal station to which the Laws of Nature and of Nature's God entitle them, a decent respect to the opinions of mankind requires that they should declare the causes which **impel** them to the separation.

[Declaration of Natural Rights]

We hold these truths to be self-evident, that all men are created equal, that they are **endowed** by their Creator with certain unalienable Rights, that among these are Life, Liberty, and the pursuit of Happiness.

That to secure these rights, Governments are instituted among Men, deriving their just powers from the consent of the governed,

That whenever any Form of Government becomes destructive of these ends, it is the Right of the People to alter or to abolish it, and to institute new Government, laying its foundation on such principles and organizing its powers in such form, as to them shall seem most likely to effect their Safety and Happiness. Prudence, indeed, will dictate that Governments long established should not be changed for light and transient causes; and accordingly all experience hath shewn, that mankind are more disposed to suffer, while evils are sufferable, than to right themselves by abolishing the forms to which they are accustomed. But when a long train of abuses and **usurpations,** pursuing invariably the same Object evinces a design to reduce them under absolute **Despotism,** it is their right, it is their duty, to throw off such Government, and to provide new Guards for their future security.

[List of Grievances]

Such has been the patient sufferance of these Colonies; and such is now the necessity which constrains them to alter their former Systems of Government. The history of the present King of Great Britain is a history of repeated injuries and usurpations, all having in direct object the establishment of an absolute Tyranny over these States. To prove this, let Facts be submitted to a candid world.

He has refused his Assent to Laws, the most wholesome and necessary for the public good.

He has forbidden his Governors to pass Laws of immediate and pressing importance, unless suspended in their operation till his Assent should be obtained; and when so suspended, he has utterly neglected to attend to them.

He has refused to pass other Laws for the accommodation of large districts of people, unless those people would **relinquish** the right of Representation in the Legislature, a right **inestimable** to them and formidable to tyrants only.

He has called together legislative bodies at places unusual, uncomfortable, and distant from the depository of their public Records, for the sole purpose of fatiguing them into compliance with his measures.

He has dissolved Representative Houses repeatedly, for opposing with manly firmness his invasions on the rights of the people.

He has refused for a long time, after such dissolutions, to cause others to be elected; whereby the Legislative Powers, incapable of **Annihilation,** have returned to the People at large for their exercise; the State remaining in the mean time exposed to all the dangers of invasion from without, and **convulsions** within.

He has endeavoured to prevent the population of these States; for that purpose obstructing the Laws for **Naturalization of Foreigners;** refusing to pass others to encourage their migrations hither, and raising the conditions of new Appropriations of Lands.

He has obstructed the Administration of Justice, by refusing his Assent to Laws for establishing Judiciary powers.

He has made Judges dependent on his Will alone, for the **tenure** of their offices, and the amount and payment of their salaries.

He has erected a multitude of New Offices, and sent hither swarms of Officers to harass our people, and eat out their substance.

He has kept among us, in times of peace, Standing Armies without the Consent of our legislatures.

He has affected to render the Military independent of and superior to the Civil power.

He has combined with others to subject us to a jurisdiction foreign to our constitution, and unacknowledged by our laws; giving his Assent to their Acts of pretended Legislation:

relinquish: give up
inestimable: priceless

annihilation: destruction

convulsions: violent disturbances

Naturalization of Foreigners: process by which foreign-born persons become citizens

tenure: term

quartering: lodging

For **Quartering** large bodies of armed troops among us:

For protecting them, by a mock Trial, from punishment for any Murders which they should commit on the Inhabitants of these States:

For cutting off our Trade with all parts of the world:

For imposing Taxes on us without our Consent:

For depriving us in many cases, of the benefits of Trial by Jury:

For transporting us beyond Seas to be tried for pretended offences:

render: make

For abolishing the free System of English Laws in a neighbouring Province, establishing therein an Arbitrary government, and enlarging its Boundaries so as to **render** it at once an example and fit instrument for introducing the same absolute rule into these Colonies:

For taking away our Charters, abolishing our most valuable Laws, and altering fundamentally the Forms of our Governments:

For suspending our own Legislatures, and declaring themselves invested with power to legislate for us in all cases whatsoever.

abdicated: given up

He has **abdicated** Government here, by declaring us out of his Protection and waging War against us.

He has plundered our seas, ravaged our Coasts, burnt our towns, and destroyed the lives of our people.

He is at this time transporting large Armies of foreign Mercenaries to compleat the works of death, desolation and tyranny,

perfidy: violation of trust

already begun with circumstances of Cruelty & **perfidy** scarcely paralleled in the most barbarous ages, and totally unworthy the Head of a civilized nation.

He has constrained our fellow Citizens taken Captive on the high Seas to bear Arms against their Country, to become the executioners of their friends and Brethren, or to fall themselves by their Hands.

insurrections: rebellions

He has excited domestic **insurrections** amongst us, and has endeavoured to bring on the inhabitants of our frontiers, the merciless Indian Savages, whose known rule of warfare, is an undistinguished destruction of all ages, sexes and conditions.

petitioned for redress: asked formally for a correction of wrongs

In every stage of these Oppressions We have **Petitioned for Redress** in the most humble terms: Our repeated Petitions have been answered only by repeated injury. A Prince whose character is thus marked by every act which may define a Tyrant, is unfit to be the ruler of a free People.

Nor have We been wanting in attentions to our Brittish brethren. We have warned them from time to time of attempts by

unwarrantable jurisdiction: unjustified authority

their legislature to extend an **unwarrantable jurisdiction** over us. We have reminded them of the circumstances of our emigration and settlement here. We have appealed to their native justice and magnanimity, and we have conjured them by the ties of our common kindred to disavow these usurpations, which, would inevitably interrupt our connections and correspondence.

They too have been deaf to the voice of justice and of **consanguinity.** We must, therefore, acquiesce in the necessity, which denounces our Separation, and hold them, as we hold the rest of mankind, Enemies in War, in Peace Friends.

[Resolution of Independence by the United States]

We, therefore, the Representatives of the united States of America, in General Congress, Assembled, appealing to the Supreme Judge of the world for the **rectitude** of our intentions, do, in the Name, and by Authority of the good People of these Colonies, solemnly publish and declare, That these United Colonies are, and of Right ought to be Free and Independent States; that they are Absolved from all Allegiance to the British Crown, and that all political connection between them and the State of Great Britain, is and ought to be totally dissolved; and that as Free and Independent States, they have full Power to levy War, conclude Peace, contract Alliances, establish Commerce, and to do all other Acts and Things which Independent States may of right do. And for the support of this Declaration, with a firm reliance on the protection of divine Providence, we mutually pledge to each other our Lives, our Fortunes and our sacred Honor.

consanguinity: originating from the same ancestor

What It Means

Resolution of Independence The final section declares that the colonies are "Free and Independent States" with the full power to make war, to form alliances, and to trade with other countries.

rectitude: rightness

John Hancock
    President from
    Massachusetts

Georgia
Button Gwinnett
Lyman Hall
George Walton

North Carolina
William Hooper
Joseph Hewes
John Penn

South Carolina
Edward Rutledge
Thomas Heyward, Jr.
Thomas Lynch, Jr.
Arthur Middleton

Maryland
Samuel Chase
William Paca
Thomas Stone
Charles Carroll
    of Carrollton

Virginia
George Wythe
Richard Henry Lee
Thomas Jefferson
Benjamin Harrison
Thomas Nelson, Jr.
Francis Lightfoot Lee
Carter Braxton

Pennsylvania
Robert Morris
Benjamin Rush
Benjamin Franklin
John Morton
George Clymer
James Smith
George Taylor
James Wilson
George Ross

Delaware
Caesar Rodney
George Read
Thomas McKean

New York
William Floyd
Philip Livingston
Francis Lewis
Lewis Morris

New Jersey
Richard Stockton
John Witherspoon
Francis Hopkinson
John Hart
Abraham Clark

New Hampshire
Josiah Bartlett
William Whipple
Matthew Thornton

Massachusetts
Samuel Adams
John Adams
Robert Treat Paine
Elbridge Gerry

Rhode Island
Stephen Hopkins
William Ellery

Connecticut
Roger Sherman
Samuel Huntington
William Williams
Oliver Wolcott

What It Means

Signers of the Declaration The signers, as representatives of the American people, declared the colonies independent from Great Britain. Most members signed the document on August 2, 1776.

The Declaration of Independence **149**

The American Revolution
1776–1783

American soldiers in battle

★ **1776**
Declaration of Independence written

★ **1777**
Battle of Saratoga

★ **1778**
Act of Congress prohibits import of slaves into U.S.

Americas

World

1774

1776

1778

1774 ★
Joseph Priestley discovers oxygen

★ **1775**
England hires German mercenaries for war in North America

★ **1776**
Adam Smith's *Wealth of Nations* published

Section 1: The Early Years

Essential Question What challenges did the American revolutionaries face at the start of the war?

Section 2: The War Continues

Essential Question How did the United States gain allies and aid during the Revolutionary War?

Section 3: The War Moves West and South

Essential Question How did fighting in the West and South affect the course of the Revolutionary War?

Section 4: The War Is Won

Essential Question How did the Battle of Yorktown lead to American independence?

History ONLINE
Chapter Overview Visit glencoe.com and click on **Chapter 6—Chapter Overviews** to preview chapter information.

FOLDABLES
Study Organizer

Summarizing Information

Make this Foldable to help you summarize what you learn about the Revolutionary War.

Step 1 Begin with a 11" x 17" piece of paper.

Step 2 Fold the sides of the paper into the middle to make a shutter fold.

Step 3 Label the tabs as shown.

Reading and Writing

As you read the chapter, list important battles, people, and other facts under the correct tabs.

British Victories, Leaders, and Allies | Patriot Victories, Leaders, and Allies

◀ Continental infantryman

1780
British forces capture Charles Town, South Carolina

1781
British surrender at Yorktown

1782
Spain completes conquest of Florida

1783
Treaty of Paris

1780

1782

1779
Spain declares war on Britain

1780
Britain declares war on Holland

1783
Famine in Japan

Essential Question ◄

What challenges did the American revolutionaries face at the start of the war?

Reading Guide

Content Vocabulary

mercenary *(p. 155)*   recruit *(p. 155)*

Academic Vocabulary

transfer *(p. 155)*   previous *(p. 155)*

Key People and Events

Hessian *(p. 155)*

Molly Pitcher *(p. 155)*

General William Howe *(p. 156)*

Nathan Hale *(p. 156)*

Lemuel Hayes *(p. 157)*

Peter Salem *(p. 157)*

Benedict Arnold *(p. 159)*

General Horatio Gates *(p. 159)*

Reading Strategy

Taking Notes As you read, use a diagram like the one below to list the Patriot defeats and victories during the early years of the American Revolution.

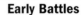

```
          Early Battles
         /            \
   Defeats            Victories
```

INDIANA ACADEMIC STANDARDS
United States History

8.1.4 Identify fundamental ideas in the Declaration of Independence (1776) and analyze the causes and effects of the Revolutionary War (1775–1783), including enactment of the Articles of Confederation and the Treaty of Paris.

8.3.1 Read maps to interpret symbols and determine the landforms and human features that represent physical and cultural characteristics of areas in the United States.

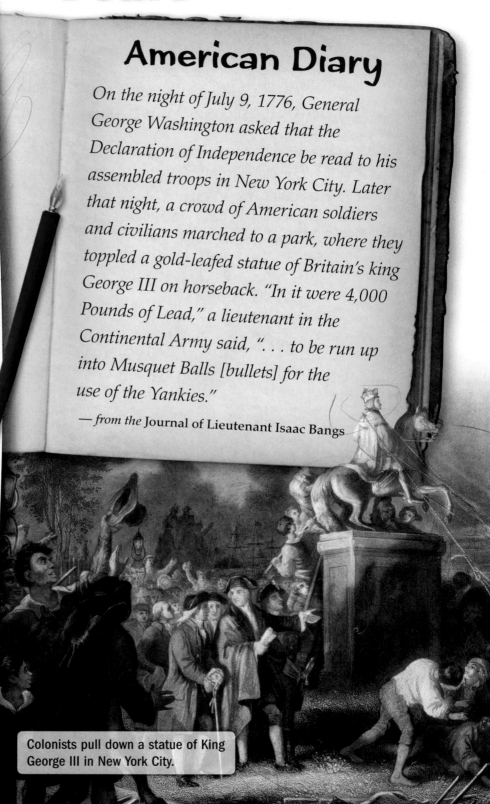

American Diary

On the night of July 9, 1776, General George Washington asked that the Declaration of Independence be read to his assembled troops in New York City. Later that night, a crowd of American soldiers and civilians marched to a park, where they toppled a gold-leafed statue of Britain's king George III on horseback. "In it were 4,000 Pounds of Lead," a lieutenant in the Continental Army said, ". . . to be run up into Musquet Balls [bullets] for the use of the Yankies."

—*from the* Journal of Lieutenant Isaac Bangs

Colonists pull down a statue of King George III in New York City.

The Opposing Sides

Main Idea The British and American forces each had advantages and disadvantages during the war for American independence.

History and You What qualities should a leader have? Read to learn how George Washington's leadership qualities were an advantage for the Patriots.

. . . .

As the toppling of the king's statue demonstrated, tensions between the colonies and Great Britain had reached a critical point after years of disagreement and negotiation. After the colonies declared independence from Britain in July 1776, the war for freedom was unavoidable.

Both sides expected the war for independence to be short. The British planned to crush the rebellion by force. Most of the Patriots—Americans who supported independence—believed the British would give up after losing one or two major battles. Few Patriots believed John Adams when he predicted in April 1776: "We shall have a long . . . and bloody war to go through."

At first glance the British had an overwhelming advantage in the war. They had the strongest navy in the world. They also had an experienced, well-trained army and the wealth of a worldwide empire. Great Britain also had a much larger population than the United States. More than 8 million people resided in Britain, compared with only 2.5 million in the United States.

The colonists suffered serious disadvantages. They lacked a regular army and a strong navy. American soldiers also lacked experience. Weapons and ammunition were in short supply. Many Patriots belonged to militia groups—local forces. However, they were volunteer soldiers who fought for short periods of time before returning home.

The Patriots faced another obstacle. Not all Americans supported the struggle for independence. Some people were neutral, taking neither side in the conflict. The Quakers, for example, would not participate in the war because they opposed all armed conflict. Still other Americans remained loyal to Britain.

The Loyalists

Those Americans who remained loyal to Britain and opposed the war for independence were called Loyalists or Tories. At least one American in five were thought to be Loyalists—perhaps as many as one in three. Some people changed sides during the war,

Primary Source / The Liberty Bell

Symbol of Freedom "Get us a good bell," wrote Isaac Norris, a Pennsylvania political leader to an aide in London in 1751. Arriving in 1752, the Liberty Bell was hung in the Pennsylvania State House (now Independence Hall). Its most famous ringing, on July 8, 1776, announced the first public reading of the Declaration of Independence. The Liberty Bell was rung every Fourth of July and for many public events until a crack appeared in about 1846. Today, the Liberty Bell is a symbol of freedom in the United States and throughout the world.

Critical Thinking

Speculating Why do you think symbols, such as statues, flags, and bells, are important to the people of a country?

THEN In 1776 women could not officially join the army. Yet their contributions proved critical to the war effort. Some women spied on British soldiers while others traveled with the troops, serving as cooks, seamstresses, and nurses. A few women even disguised themselves as men in order to become soldiers.

◀ Female Continental soldier

Colonist Lydia Darrah spied on the British and passed information to the Continental Army. ▶

depending on which army was closer. Loyalist support varied from region to region throughout the war. In general, it was strongest in the Carolinas and Georgia and weakest in New England.

Loyalists supported Britain for different reasons. Some people remained loyal because they were members of the Anglican Church, headed by the British king. Others depended on the British for their jobs. Some Loyalists feared the disorder that might break out from challenging the established government. Others simply could not understand what all the commotion was about and why the colonies wanted independence. No other country, one Loyalist complained, "faced a rebellion arising from such trivial causes."

Friends and families were divided over their loyalty to Britain. For example, William Franklin, son of Patriot Benjamin Franklin, was a Loyalist who had served as a royal governor. As one Connecticut man observed:

PRIMARY SOURCE

"Neighbor [was] . . . against neighbor, father against son and son against father, and he that would not thrust his own blade through his brother's heart was called an infamous villain."

—from *Less Than Glory*, by Norman Gelb

African Americans in the War

Some African Americans also sided with the Loyalists. At the start of the war, the British appealed to enslaved Africans to join them. Lord Dunmore, the royal governor of Virginia, announced that enslaved people who fought on the British side would be freed. Many men answered his call. Eventually some of them ended up free in Canada. Others settled in the British colony of Sierra Leone in Africa.

Patriot Advantages

The Americans held some advantages. They were fighting on their own ground and fought with great determination to protect

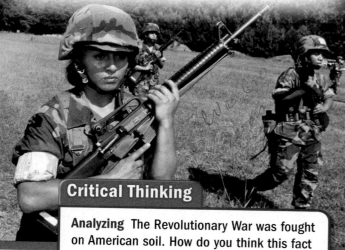

NOW Today, women play a critical role in the U.S. military. By the mid-1990s, Congress had opened nearly all military jobs to women, including combat roles. Today, about one in every seven soldiers on active duty is a woman, and many women hold leadership positions throughout the armed forces.

Critical Thinking

Analyzing The Revolutionary War was fought on American soil. How do you think this fact influenced the role of women in the war?

it. The British, however, had to wage war in a faraway land. They were forced to ship soldiers and supplies thousands of miles across the Atlantic.

Another advantage for the Americans was the type of soldiers fighting for the British. The British relied on **mercenaries**—hired soldiers—to fight for them. The Americans called the mercenaries **Hessians,** after the region in Germany from where most of them came. The Patriots were fighting for the freedom of their own land. They believed they had a much greater stake in winning the war than the hired soldiers did, who were fighting for money. This belief gave the Americans an edge over the Hessians in battle.

The Americans' greatest advantage was probably their leader, George Washington. Few could match him for courage, honesty, and determination. The war might have taken a different turn without Washington.

Raising an Army

The Americans placed great value on liberty and personal freedom for citizens. After throwing off the rule of the British Parliament, they were unwilling to **transfer**—or move—power to their own Continental Congress. In some ways the American Revolution was really 13 separate wars, with each state pursuing its own interests. As a result, the Congress experienced difficulty enlisting soldiers and raising money to fight the war.

The militia played an essential role in the Patriots' forces. However, the Americans also needed well-trained soldiers who could fight anywhere in the colonies. The Congress established the Continental Army but depended on the states to **recruit,** or enlist, soldiers.

At first, soldiers signed up for one year of army service. General Washington appealed for longer terms. "If we ever hope for success," he said, "we must have men enlisted for the whole term of the war." Eventually the Continental Congress offered enlistments for three years or for the length of the war. Most soldiers, however, still signed up for only one year.

It was also difficult to recruit officers. The best officers in the Continental Army were veterans of **previous,** or earlier, wars or young men who were recruited from the ranks.

Women also fought with the Patriot forces. Margaret Corbin of Pennsylvania went with her husband when he joined the Continental Army. After he died in battle, she took his place. Mary Ludwig Hays McCauley also joined her husband in battle. The soldiers called her "Moll of the Pitcher," or **Molly Pitcher,** because she carried water pitchers to the soldiers. As a teenager, Deborah Sampson of Massachusetts watched her brothers and their friends go off to war. She then disguised herself as a boy and enlisted.

✓ Reading Check **Summarizing** What disadvantages did the Patriots face?

Patriot Defeats and Victories

Main Idea After suffering defeat at the Battle of Long Island, the Americans rallied and won victories at Trenton and Princeton.

History and You Do you think a single victory can help a struggling sports team with a losing record? Read to learn how American troops rallied following a crushing defeat by the British.

. . . .

Most of the early battles in the war involved few troops. At Bunker Hill, for example, about 2,200 British soldiers fought 1,200 Americans. The British had not yet won a decisive victory over the Patriots, however. They realized they would need more troops to end the war quickly.

During the summer of 1776, Britain sent 32,000 troops across the Atlantic to New York. The British commander, **General William Howe,** hoped the sheer size of his army would convince the Patriots to give up. He was soon disappointed.

Defeat on Long Island

Although Washington and the Patriots had fewer than 20,000 troops, they were determined to fight. In late August the two sides clashed in the Battle of Long Island. Outnumbered and outmaneuvered, the Continental Army suffered a serious defeat at the hands of the British forces.

One Patriot, **Nathan Hale,** proved himself a hero at Long Island. A teacher from Connecticut, Hale volunteered to spy on British troops. He disguised himself as a Dutch schoolteacher. The British discovered his true identity, however, and hanged him. According to tradition, just before his hanging Hale said, "I only regret that I have but one life to lose for my country."

Although the Americans showed bravery, they ran short of supplies for the army. In the autumn of 1776, a British officer wrote that many of the Patriot soldiers killed on Long Island had not been wearing shoes, socks, or jackets. "They are also in great want of blankets," he said, predicting that the rebels would suffer during the winter.

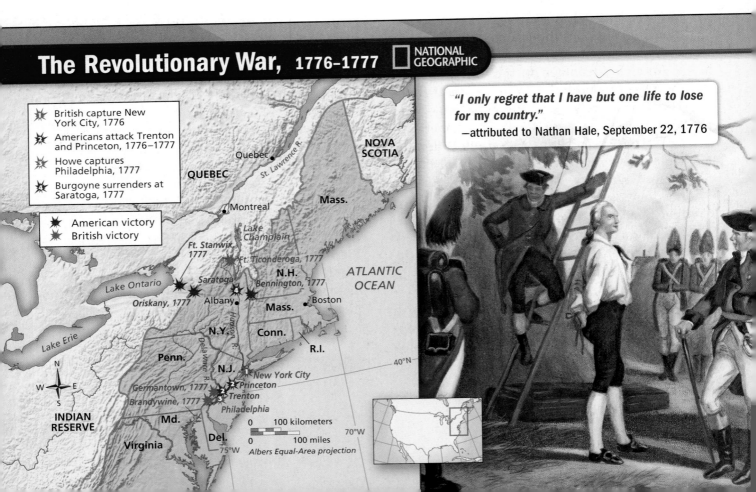

The Revolutionary War, 1776–1777
NATIONAL GEOGRAPHIC

✳✳ British capture New York City, 1776
✳✳ Americans attack Trenton and Princeton, 1776–1777
✳✳ Howe captures Philadelphia, 1777
✳✳ Burgoyne surrenders at Saratoga, 1777

✳ American victory
✳ British victory

Quebec
QUEBEC
St. Lawrence R.
Montreal
Lake Champlain
Ft. Stanwix 1777
Ft. Ticonderoga, 1777
Lake Ontario
Saratoga
N.H.
Bennington, 1777
Oriskany, 1777
Albany
Mass.
Boston
NOVA SCOTIA
Mass.
ATLANTIC OCEAN
Lake Erie
Hudson R.
N.Y.
Conn.
R.I.
Penn.
Delaware R.
N.J.
Princeton
New York City
Germantown, 1777
Trenton
Brandywine, 1777
Philadelphia
INDIAN RESERVE
Md.
Del.
Virginia

N W E S

0   100 kilometers
0   100 miles
Albers Equal-Area projection

40°N
70°W
75°W

"*I only regret that I have but one life to lose for my country.*"
—attributed to Nathan Hale, September 22, 1776

After the defeat on Long Island, Washington retreated to Manhattan. With the British in pursuit, the Continental Army retreated across New Jersey into Pennsylvania.

A Low Point

In the winter of 1776–1777, the Patriots' cause was near collapse. The size of the Continental Army had dwindled. Some soldiers completed their terms of service and went home. Other soldiers ran away.

Washington wrote his brother that if new soldiers were not recruited soon, "I think the game is pretty near up." Still, he could not believe that the fight for liberty would truly fail.

Washington pleaded with the Continental Congress for more troops. He even asked that the Congress allow free African Americans to enlist. Early in the war, however, the Southern states had persuaded the Congress not to allow African Americans in the Continental Army. Many white people in the South felt uncomfortable about giving guns to African Americans and allowing them to serve as

soldiers. In those Southern states that had large enslaved populations, the whites feared revolts.

African Americans Join the Fight

As the need for soldiers grew, some states ignored the ban and enlisted African Americans. Rhode Island raised an all–African American regiment in 1778. By the war's end, every state except South Carolina enlisted African Americans to fight.

Historians estimate that as many as 5,000 African Americans joined the Patriots. Among them were **Lemuel Hayes** and **Peter Salem,** who fought at Concord. African Americans fought because they believed in the Patriot cause or they needed the money. Some were enslaved Africans who had run away from slaveholders and fought to earn their freedom.

American Victories in New Jersey

The British settled in New York for the winter, leaving some troops in Princeton and Trenton, New Jersey. Washington saw a chance to catch the British off guard.

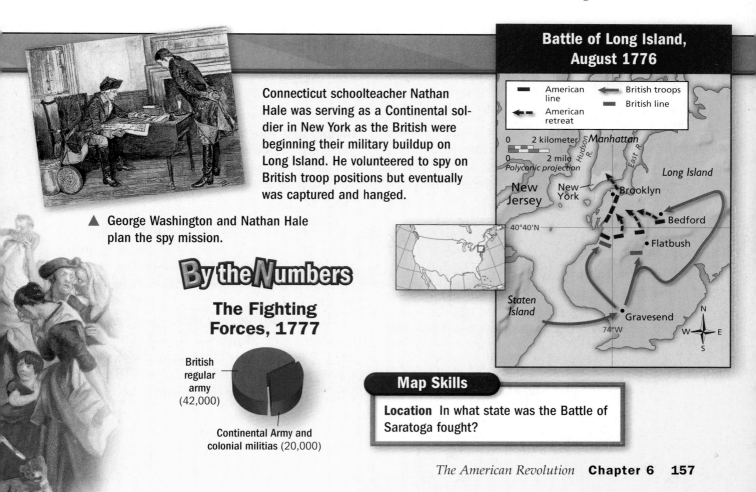

Connecticut schoolteacher Nathan Hale was serving as a Continental soldier in New York as the British were beginning their military buildup on Long Island. He volunteered to spy on British troop positions but eventually was captured and hanged.

▲ George Washington and Nathan Hale plan the spy mission.

By the Numbers

The Fighting Forces, 1777

British regular army (42,000)

Continental Army and colonial militias (20,000)

Battle of Long Island, August 1776

- American line
- American retreat
- British troops
- British line

0   2 kilometer
0   2 mile
Polyconic projection

Manhattan
New Jersey
New York
Brooklyn
Long Island
Bedford
Flatbush
Staten Island
Gravesend
Hudson R.
East R.
40°40'N
74°W
N S E W

Map Skills

Location In what state was the Battle of Saratoga fought?

The Battle of Trenton, 1776

NATIONAL GEOGRAPHIC

McConkey's Ferry

WASHINGTON

Jacob's Cr.

Houghs Cr.

Delaware R.

40°18'

Shebakunk Cr.

74°52'W

0   2 kilometer
0   2 mile
Polyconic projection

74°48'W

40°14'

To Princeton

Trenton

Assunpink R.

RALL

To Bordentown

American troops
British retreat

Washington's leadership at the Battle of Trenton led to an important victory for the Patriots:

✔ Washington's troops gained confidence.

✔ The Continental Army won badly needed supplies.

✔ New enlistments and reenlistments rose.

"Our Men pushed on with such rapidity, that they soon carried four pieces of Cannon out of Six, Surrounded the Enemy, and obliged 30 Officers and 886 privates to lay down their Arms without firing a Shot. Our loss was only two Officers and two or three privates wounded. The Enemy had between 20 and 30 killed."

—George Washington,
Letter, December 28, 1776

Map Skills

Movement In which direction did Washington's troops travel to attack the British at Trenton?

Washington was stationed in Pennsylvania across the Delaware River from the British camp in New Jersey. On Christmas night 1776, Washington and 2,400 troops crossed the icy river and surprised the enemy at Trenton the next day. The British sent reinforcements under Lord Charles Cornwallis, but Washington evaded those forces. Washington then marched to Princeton, where his army drove away the British. One British observer wrote:

PRIMARY SOURCE

"A few days ago, [the Americans] had given up the cause for lost. Their late successes have turned the scale and now they are all liberty-mad again."

—Nicholas Cresswell, quoted in *George Washington's War*

✔ **Reading Check** **Explaining** Why was the winter of 1776–1777 significant?

A British Plan for Victory

Main Idea The British plan to separate New England from the Middle Colonies was foiled at the Battle of Saratoga.

History and You Do you like to play chess or other games in which you outmaneuver your opponent? Read how the Americans outmaneuvered a British army and won a stunning victory.

• •

The British worked out a battle plan for 1777. They would take Albany, New York, and gain control of the Hudson River. This would separate New England from the Middle Colonies.

The plan involved a three-pronged attack. General John Burgoyne would lead nearly 8,000 troops south from Canada. A second force, under Lieutenant Colonel Barry St. Leger, would move east from Lake Ontario.

A third group, under General Howe, would move north from New York City. The three British forces would meet at Albany and destroy the Patriot troops.

The British Capture Philadelphia

Howe won battles in September 1777 at Brandywine and Paoli, near Philadelphia. Then Howe's troops captured Philadelphia, forcing the Continental Congress to flee. In early October, Washington attacked the British at nearby Germantown but had to withdraw. Howe decided to spend the winter in Philadelphia instead of going to Albany.

Patriots Slow the British

Meanwhile, problems delayed the British from taking Albany. In August, American soldiers halted St. Leger's advance at Fort Stanwix, New York. Led by **Benedict Arnold,** the Americans forced the British to retreat.

General Burgoyne's army was not making much progress toward Albany either. In July he captured Fort Ticonderoga, but trouble followed. Because he enjoyed good food and fine clothes, Burgoyne traveled with 30 wagons of luxury goods. This baggage, along with the trees downed by the Americans to block the British, slowed Burgoyne's journey.

Burgoyne needed supplies. He sent 800 troops and Native Americans to capture the American supply base at Bennington, Vermont. A local militia group, the Green Mountain Boys, attacked and defeated them. Desperate for supplies, Burgoyne retreated in October to Saratoga, New York.

The Battle of Saratoga

Burgoyne faced serious trouble at Saratoga. The British forces he expected did not arrive. The Americans had stopped St. Leger's army at Fort Stanwix, and Howe's forces were still in Philadelphia. In addition, American troops under the command of **General Horatio Gates** blocked Burgoyne's path to the south. Burgoyne found himself surrounded by a larger army. Burgoyne made a desperate attack on October 7. The Americans held firm.

On October 17, 1777, General Burgoyne surrendered. The British plan had failed. General Howe resigned as commander of the British troops in America. He was replaced by General Henry Clinton.

✔ **Reading Check** **Analyzing** Why was the Battle of Saratoga a turning point in the war?

History ONLINE
Study Central™ To review this section, go to glencoe.com.

Section 1 Review

Vocabulary

1. Use the terms mercenary, transfer, recruit, and previous in separate sentences that explain their meanings.

Main Ideas

2. Discussing What disadvantages did British forces face in the American Revolution?

3. Explaining Why were African Americans at first banned from serving in the Continental Army?

4. Analyzing What difficulties did General Burgoyne face at the Battle of Saratoga?

Critical Thinking

5. Analyzing Use a diagram like the one below to explain why the Loyalists supported Britain.

Loyalists

6. Persuasive Writing As a colonist, write a letter to the editor of your local newspaper. Point out the colonies' strengths and why you think you will win the war for independence.

Answer the
7. Essential Question
What challenges did the American revolutionaries face at the start of the war?

The War Continues

How did the United States gain allies and aid during the Revolutionary War?

Reading Guide

Content Vocabulary

desert *(p. 162)*   inflation *(p. 164)*

Academic Vocabulary

aid *(p. 161)*   issue *(p. 165)*

Key People and Events

Bernardo de Gálvez *(p. 161)*

Marquis de Lafayette *(p. 163)*

Friedrich von Steuben *(p. 163)*

Juan de Miralles *(p. 163)*

Judith Sargeant Murray *(p. 165)*

Abigail Adams *(p. 165)*

Reading Strategy

Taking Notes As you read, use a diagram like the one below to determine what aid the Patriots received during the American Revolution.

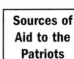

Sources of Aid to the Patriots

INDIANA ACADEMIC STANDARDS
United States History

8.1.4 Identify fundamental ideas in the Declaration of Independence (1776) and analyze the causes and effects of the Revolutionary War (1775–1783), including enactment of the Articles of Confederation and the Treaty of Paris.

8.1.9 Describe the influence of important individuals on social and political developments of the time such as the Independence movement and the framing of the Constitution.

American Diary

The Continental Congress sent Jonathan Austin of Boston to France to deliver the news of the American victory at Saratoga. Benjamin Franklin was already in France trying to get that country to help the Americans fight against the British. As soon as Austin arrived, Franklin nervously inquired, "Sir, is Philadelphia taken?" Austin answered, "Yes sir. . . . But sir, I have greater news than that. General Burgoyne and his whole army are prisoners of war!"

—*quoted in* Liberty! The American Revolution

Benjamin Franklin arrives at the Court of the French king, Louis XVI.

Gaining Allies

Main Idea Even with aid from other nations and individuals, the Patriots had difficulty financing their war for independence.

History and You Have you ever had to ask friends for help when you could not complete a task? Was the task easier to complete? Read about how the Americans sought help during their fight for independence.

. . . .

Like Ben Franklin, many Americans were excited by news of the victory at Saratoga in October 1777. Even more, Saratoga marked a turning point in the war. The European nations, especially France, realized that the Americans might actually win their war against Great Britain.

Now was the time for the Americans to seek support from Great Britain's rivals. By late 1777, Benjamin Franklin had been in Paris for a year. He was trying to get the French to support the Americans' fight for independence. With his skill and charm, Franklin gained many friends for the United States. The French had given the Americans money secretly, but they had not fully committed to an alliance.

France

News of the American victory at Saratoga caused a shift in France's policy. Realizing that the Americans had a chance of defeating Britain, the French openly announced support for the United States. In February 1778, the French and the Americans worked out a trade agreement and an alliance. France declared war on Britain and sent money, equipment, and troops to **aid,** or help, the American Patriots.

Spain

Other European nations also helped the American cause. They did so mostly because they hated the British. Although Spain did not recognize American independence until after the Revolution, Spain declared war on Britain in 1779. The Spanish governor of Louisiana, **Bernardo de Gálvez** (GAHL•ves), raised an army. Gálvez's soldiers forced British troops from Baton Rouge and Natchez. Then the army captured British forts at Mobile in 1780 and Pensacola in 1781. Gálvez's campaign through hundreds of miles of wilderness diverted British troops from other fronts of the war.

Primary Source / Franklin Memorabilia

The World's First Celebrity While serving as America's first ambassador to France, Benjamin Franklin was greatly admired by the country's nobles and thinkers. After all, he was a man of great charm and many talents—philosopher, writer, printer, scientist, inventor, politician, and diplomat. Much like a singer or movie star today, Franklin became so popular in America and Europe that his likeness appeared on many items—medallions, rings, watches, and small boxes. Fashionable ladies even adopted a hairstyle that resembled the famous fur cap that Franklin wore.

Critical Thinking

Making Connections How do you think Franklin used his personality and talents to benefit the American cause? Would you consider him a celebrity? Are there any celebrities today who are like Franklin? Explain.

Winter at Valley Forge

Word of the French-American alliance did not reach the United States until the spring of 1778. Meanwhile, British general Howe and his forces spent the winter in comfort in Philadelphia. Washington set up camp at Valley Forge, about 20 miles (32 km) to the west of the British. Washington and his troops endured a winter of terrible suffering. They lacked decent food, clothing, shelter, and medicine. Washington's greatest challenge at Valley Forge was keeping the Continental Army together.

Because it was difficult to get supplies delivered due to snowstorms and damaged roads, the Continental Army built huts and gathered supplies from the countryside. Several volunteers—including Washington's wife, Martha—made clothes for the troops and cared for the sick. Washington declared that no army had ever suffered "such uncommon hardships" with such "patience and fortitude."

Joseph Martin, a young private from Connecticut, spent the winter at Valley Forge.

"We had a hard duty to perform," he wrote years later, "and little or no strength to perform it with." Most of the men lacked blankets, shoes, and shirts. Martin made a pair of rough moccasins for himself out of a scrap of cowhide, which hurt his feet.

PRIMARY SOURCE

"The only alternative I had, was to endure this inconvenience or to go barefoot, as hundreds of my companions had to, till they might be tracked by their blood upon the rough frozen ground."
—Joseph Martin, in *A Narrative of a Revolutionary Soldier*

Not surprisingly, many men **deserted,** or left without permission, while the Continental Army was camped at Valley Forge. Some officers resigned. The army seemed to be falling apart.

Yet with strong determination, the Continental Army survived the winter. Conditions gradually improved and new soldiers joined the ranks in the spring. "The army grows stronger every day," one officer wrote. "There is a spirit of discipline among the troops that is better than numbers."

Primary Source | A Turning Point at Valley Forge

Winter Soldiers For the Continental Army, the winter of 1777 at Valley Forge was terrible. Soldiers suffered through a lack of food and clothing, and many became ill and died. By March, better weather had arrived along with a trickle of food and supplies. By April, Baron von Steuben was turning the troops into a fighting force.

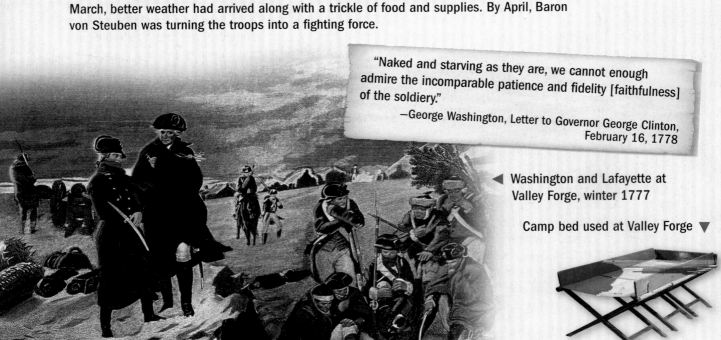

"Naked and starving as they are, we cannot enough admire the incomparable patience and fidelity [faithfulness] of the soldiery."
—George Washington, Letter to Governor George Clinton, February 16, 1778

◀ Washington and Lafayette at Valley Forge, winter 1777

Camp bed used at Valley Forge ▼

In April 1778, Washington told his troops of the Patriots' alliance with France. Everyone's spirits rose at the thought of help from overseas. The Continental Army celebrated with a religious service and a parade.

Help From Overseas

Among the leaders at Valley Forge was a French noble, the **Marquis de Lafayette** (LAH•fee•EHT). Lafayette was filled with enthusiasm for the ideas expressed in the Declaration of Independence and he rushed to join the battle for freedom. Lafayette wrote: "The future of America is closely bound up with the future of all mankind."

Upon his arrival in Philadelphia, Lafayette offered his services to General Washington. Lafayette became a trusted aide to Washington.

Other Europeans also volunteered to work for the Patriot cause. Two Poles—Thaddeus Kościusko (kawsh•CHUSH•koh), an engineer, and Casimir Pulaski, a cavalry officer—contributed to the American efforts. Promoted to general, Pulaski died in 1779, fighting for the Continental Army.

Friedrich von Steuben (STOO•buhn), a former army officer from Prussia, also came to help Washington. Von Steuben drilled the Patriot troops at Valley Forge, teaching them military discipline. He spoke little English, so he used aides to translate drills and a training manual that he wrote. Von Steuben turned the ragged Continental Army into a more effective fighting force.

Juan de Miralles (mee•RAH•yays) arrived in Philadelphia in 1778 as a representative of Spain. At his urging, Spain, Cuba, and Mexico sent financial aid to the colonies. Miralles befriended many Patriot leaders and loaned money to the cause.

Other Europeans who had recently moved to the United States also joined the Patriot cause. In fact, almost two-thirds of soldiers in the Pennsylvania regiments were foreign-born.

Even with the help of foreign nations like France and Spain, the Patriots would find it difficult to defeat the British. The Continental Army still needed large amounts of money to continue to fight the war.

Valley Forge today ▲

Baron von Steuben drills American recruits at Valley Forge, 1778. ▶

The Continental Army received important help from Europeans. Friedrich von Steuben was a Prussian officer who arrived at Valley Forge on February 23, 1778. Von Steuben began by training a "model company" of 100 chosen men. Each company commander was responsible for training the men in his company, including new recruits.

Critical Thinking

Describing What happened at Valley Forge to change the course of the war?

People IN HISTORY

Molly Pitcher

Heroine at the Battle of Monmouth Court House

Molly Pitcher may have done more than carry water to American soldiers at the Battle of Monmouth Court House in New Jersey on June 28, 1778. According to legend, when her husband collapsed from the heat, she heroically took his place in battle. On February 21, 1822, Pennsylvania recognized Molly Pitcher's service to the nation by granting her an annual pension of $40.

Abigail Adams

Wife of John Adams, delegate to the Continental Congress

Abigail Adams famously argued for women's rights in a letter to her husband, telling him, "If [particular] care and attention is not paid to the Ladies we are determined to [start] a [rebellion], and will not hold ourselves bound by any Laws in which we have no voice, or Representation."

CRITICAL Thinking

1. **Analyzing** Why do you think Molly Pitcher became a legendary heroine?
2. **Evaluating** Both Molly Pitcher and Abigail Adams challenged traditional women's roles. Why do you think their actions were accepted by society at that time?

Money Problems

Getting money to finance the war was a major problem. The Continental Congress had no power to raise money through taxes. Although the Congress received some money from the states and from foreign countries, much more was needed to finance the war.

To pay for the war, the Congress and the states printed hundreds of millions of dollars' worth of paper money. The bills quickly lost their value, though. The amount of bills in circulation grew faster than the supply of gold and silver backing them. This led to **inflation,** which means that it took more and more money to buy the same amount of goods. The Congress stopped issuing the paper money because no one would use it. However, the Americans had no other way to finance their fight for independence.

✓ **Reading Check** **Describing** How did Lafayette help the Patriot cause?

Life on the Home Front

Main Idea The ideals of liberty and freedom that inspired the American Revolution carried through to the issues of women's interests and slavery.

History and You Have you ever taken on more duties at home when another person was away? Read how women's roles changed during the American Revolution.

The war changed the lives of all Americans, even those who stayed at home. Thousands of men were away in military service, so many women took charge of their families. Other women ran their husbands' or their own businesses.

Changing Attitudes

The ideals of liberty and freedom inspired the American Revolution. These same ideals also caused some women to question their place and treatment in American society.

In an essay on education, **Judith Sargeant Murray** of Massachusetts argued that women's minds are as good as men's. Girls, therefore, should get as good an education as boys. Most girls received little schooling, so this was a radical idea.

Abigail Adams also stood up for women's interests. She wrote to her husband, John Adams, a member of Congress:

PRIMARY SOURCE

"I can not say that I think you [are] very generous to the Ladies, for whilst you are proclaiming peace and good will to Men, Emancipating all Nations, you insist upon retaining an absolute power over Wives."
—from *Adams Family Papers*

Hopes for Equality

The Revolutionary War ideals of freedom and liberty inspired some white Americans to question slavery. As early as the Stamp Act crisis, religious groups and other groups had voted to condemn slavery.

In 1778 Governor William Livingston of New Jersey asked the legislature to free all enslaved people in the state. He said slavery was "utterly inconsistent with the principles of Christianity and humanity." African Americans made similar arguments. In New Hampshire enslaved people asked the legislature for their freedom "so that the name of *slave* may not be heard in a land gloriously contending for the sweets of freedom."

From the start of the war, African Americans fought for the American cause and hoped the Revolution would help end slavery. Vermont, New Hampshire, Massachusetts, and Pennsylvania attempted to abolish slavery in their states. The **issue,** or matter, of slavery would remain unsettled for many years, however.

Treatment of Loyalists

During the war, thousands of Loyalists fought on the side of the British. Some Loyalists spied and informed on the Patriots. Many Loyalists, however, fled the colonies.

Loyalists who remained in the United States faced difficult times. Their neighbors often shunned them. Some became victims of mob violence. Loyalists who actively helped the British could be arrested and tried as traitors. Patriots executed a few Loyalists, but such measures were unusual.

✔ **Reading Check** **Describing** How were Loyalists treated by the Patriots during the war?

Section 2 Review

History ONLINE
Study Central™ To review this section, go to glencoe.com.

Vocabulary

1. Write a paragraph that explains how the following terms relate to the war for independence: aid, desert, inflation, issue.

Main Ideas

2. **Explaining** Why did the Patriots find it hard to finance the war for independence?

3. **Discussing** How did the war for independence affect slavery in the United States?

Critical Thinking

4. **Determining Cause and Effect** Use a diagram like the one below to identify the effects of the Revolutionary War on women who remained at home.

Effects of the War on Women

5. **Creative Writing** Write a paragraph in which you describe what Martha Washington might have experienced when she helped the soldiers during the winter at Valley Forge.

6. **Answer the Essential Question** How did the United States gain allies and aid during the Revolutionary War?

TIME NOTEBOOK

What were people's lives like in the past?

These two pages will give you some clues to everyday life in the United States as you step back in time with TIME Notebook.

American Voices

ONE TEEN'S WRITINGS FROM THE "WINTER OF DEATH"

At 15, **JOSEPH PLUMB MARTIN** *signed up with the Continental Army. At first, Martin was sure of his decision. But the fierce winter and lack of food and supplies at Valley Forge in 1778 shook his confidence. Here is what Martin wrote about during that long winter that killed over 2,000 soldiers.*

"We were absolutely literally starved. I do solemnly declare that I did not put a morsel of victuals [food] into my mouth for four days and as many nights, except a little black birch bark which I gnawed off a stick of wood, if that can be called victuals. I saw several of the men roast their old shoes and eat them, and I was afterwards informed . . . that some of the officers killed and ate a favorite little dog that belonged to one of them. If this is not 'suffering' I request to be informed what can pass under the name."

EXHAUSTED AND HUNGRY SOLDIERS AT VALLEY FORGE, 1778

STOCK MONTAGE, INC. / GETTY IMAGES

Fan-tastic

Do you like to gossip at parties but are afraid others are listening? Then this "secret language" is for you. Just grab a fan and start gabbing!

ACTION	WHAT IT MEANS
Open fan and wave it in front of your face.	"I'm jealous."
Close fan and strike it against your palm.	"I'm angry."
Open fan and wave it very slowly.	"I think you're interesting."
Close the fan and place one end against your lips.	"I don't want to talk."
Open fan and quickly wave it.	"I'm concerned."

COLONIAL GAMES
Nine Man Morris Scores a Ten!

What are all the colonial kids playing?
It is that entertaining game **Nine Man Morris**.

1. Get nine copper coins, nine silver coins, and a friend to play with you.

2. Make a drawing like the one shown on a piece of paper.

3. Give yourself the copper coins and your friend the silver ones.

4. Take turns placing your coins on the dots in the drawing.

5. Be the first to line up three of your coins in a row.

6. Capture one of the other player's coins when you get three in a row.

7. Keep playing until one player is down to two coins. The other player wins!

MILESTONES

EVENTS AND PEOPLE OF THE TIME

AMAZED. In 1771 world-famous composer Amadeus Mozart upon hearing the glass armonica, which was just invented by Benjamin Franklin. This musical instrument touches different spinning glasses to make music. It is similar to rubbing the rim of a glass to make a sound. Rumor has it that Mozart might someday compose music for Franklin's invention.

THE GLASS ARMONICA

PROHIBITED. Slavery, by the New England Quakers at their yearly meeting in 1770. The first colonial American group to do so, the Quakers have declared the enslavement of others to be wrong.

TRAINED. American soldiers at Valley Forge in 1778 by German aristocrat, Baron von Steuben, who speaks very little English. Hired by George Washington to get his soldiers in shape, Von Steuben ranted, screamed, and yelled at the troops—while an aide translated. But his raving paid off. He taught the soldiers to load rifles correctly and fight in formation. By the end of the long winter, the Americans were a more unified fighting force.

NUMBERS

UNITED STATES AT THE TIME

342 Number of crates—which held thousands of pounds of tea—dumped into Boston Harbor by angry Patriots who dressed as Native Americans on December 16, 1773

6 Days it takes to travel between Boston and New York in 1772 by stagecoach. Each day, travelers spend 18 hours on the bumpy roads and, each night, sleep in their clothes at inns

350 About the number of miles ridden in 6 days (a record time) by Israel Bissell, 23, in 1775, warning colonists, "To arms, to arms, the war has begun!"; the day after Paul Revere's more famous 20-mile ride

10,000 The approximate number of enslaved persons who earned their freedom by fighting against the British

40 Number of newspapers in the colonies during the American Revolution—six of which are published by women

CRITICAL THINKING

Explaining What does King George III mean when he says "blows must decide"? (See Verbatim)

Analyzing Primary Sources What was Joseph Martin's mood at Valley Forge in 1778? Do you think modern-day troops in war face similar issues? Explain your answer.

The War Moves West and South

Essential Question ◄

How did fighting in the West and South affect the course of the Revolutionary War?

Reading Guide

Content Vocabulary

blockade *(p. 170)*

privateer *(p. 170)*

guerrilla warfare *(p. 172)*

Academic Vocabulary

impact *(p. 171)*   sustain *(p. 173)*

Key People and Events

Joseph Brant *(p. 169)*

George Rogers Clark *(p. 169)*

John Paul Jones *(p. 170)*

Battle of Moore's Creek *(p. 171)*

General Charles Cornwallis *(p. 171)*

Francis Marion *(p. 172)*

Nathanael Greene *(p. 173)*

Reading Strategy

Taking Notes As you read, use a diagram like the one below to analyze how the Americans responded to the British naval blockade.

```
Response to
British Naval  ⟨ ☐
Blockade         ☐
```

INDIANA ACADEMIC STANDARDS
United States History

8.1.4 Identify fundamental ideas in the Declaration of Independence (1776) and analyze the causes and effects of the Revolutionary War (1775–1783), including enactment of the Articles of Confederation and the Treaty of Paris.

American Diary

A brave Mohawk war chief, Joseph Brant, blended Native American and British ways. Brant, however, spoke strongly on behalf of his people. On a 1776 visit to London, he said the Mohawks have "[shown] their zeal and loyalty to the . . . King; yet they have been very badly treated by his people. . . . Indeed, it is very hard when we have let the King's subjects have so much of our lands . . . [and] they should want to cheat us."

—Joseph Brant, speech, March 14, 1776

Loyalists and their Native American allies attack an American settlement in Pennsylvania's Wyoming Valley in the summer of 1778.

War in the West

Main Idea The British, along with their Native American allies, led attacks against settlers in the West.

History and You Do you have a nickname? If so, how did you get it? Read to learn the nickname of Henry Hamilton, the British commander at Detroit.

· ·

The concerns of Mohawk chief **Joseph Brant** and other Native Americans about their lands became entangled in the events of the American Revolution. As a result, several important battles involving Native Americans took place along the western frontier. Some Native Americans helped the Patriots, but more sided with the British. For them, the British seemed less of a threat than the Americans.

The British and Native Americans

West of the Appalachian Mountains, the British and their Native American allies raided American settlements. Joseph Brant led a number of brutal attacks in southwestern New York and northern Pennsylvania.

Henry Hamilton, British commander at Detroit, was called the "hair buyer." He earned this nickname because he paid Native Americans for settlers' scalps.

Victory at Vincennes

George Rogers Clark, a lieutenant colonel in the Virginia militia, set out to end the British attacks on western settlers. In July 1778, Clark and 175 soldiers sailed west down the Ohio River. After a march of about 120 miles (193 km), the Patriots seized the British post at Kaskaskia (ka•SKAS•kee•uh) in present-day Illinois. They then captured the British town of Vincennes (vihn•SEHNZ) in present-day Indiana.

British troops under Henry Hamilton's command recaptured Vincennes that December. Clark vowed to get it back. In February 1779, Clark and his troops led a surprise attack against the British and forced Hamilton to surrender. George Rogers Clark's victory at Vincennes strengthened the American position in the West.

✓ **Reading Check** **Summarizing** Describe events in the Revolutionary War in the west.

Time Line / **Native Americans in the Revolution**

The War on the Frontier At the time of the American Revolution, about 200,000 Native Americans lived along the western frontier. Their loyalties were divided between the British and the Americans.

★ **1776** Loyalist Cherokee attack North Carolina Patriots

★ **1782** Americans force peace on the Mohawk

★ **1775** Mohawk pledge neutrality

★ **1777** Mohawk turn to the British; defeated Cherokee lose land to Americans

▲ Native American war club

Critical Thinking

Hypothesizing Why do you think many Native Americans supported the British rather than the Americans?

Glory at Sea

Main Idea The American navy and American privateers had some successes against the powerful British navy.

History and You Besides George Washington, what other heroes of the American Revolution do you know? Read to learn about John Paul Jones, who became a naval hero during the Revolutionary War.

. . . .

As fighting continued on the western frontier, other battles raged at sea. Great Britain's powerful navy kept the ships of the Patriots and of their allies from entering or leaving American harbors. This **blockade** prevented supplies and reinforcements from reaching the Continental Army.

Privateers

To break the blockade, the Second Continental Congress ordered construction of 13 American warships. Only two of these ships, however, sailed to sea. Several were quickly captured by the British. The American navy was too weak to operate effectively.

The Congress authorized approximately 2,000 ships to sail as **privateers.** These were privately owned merchant ships with weapons. Finding crews for these ships was not difficult. Privateering was a profitable trade. Privateers captured more British ships at sea than the American navy.

John Paul Jones

A daring American naval officer, **John Paul Jones,** raided British ports. Near the coast of Great Britain in September 1779, Jones's ship, *Bonhomme Richard,* met the British warship *Serapis* escorting a fleet of merchant ships. The *Bonhomme Richard* and the *Serapis* fought for hours. The British captain asked whether Jones wished to surrender. Jones is said to have answered, "I have not yet begun to fight."

In the end, the *Serapis* surrendered, but the *Bonhomme Richard* sank not long after the battle. Still, his victory made John Paul Jones a naval hero to the American Patriots.

✔ **Reading Check** **Describing** How did privateers contribute to the American war effort?

Primary Source | **John Paul Jones**

The warships *Bonhomme Richard* and *Serapis*

"*I wish to have no Connection with any Ship that does not Sail fast, for I intend to go in harm's way.*"
—Captain John Paul Jones, Letter, 1778

Cannons like this one were used on the *Bonhomme Richard.* ▼

Critical Thinking
Analyzing Why did John Paul Jones want a fast ship?

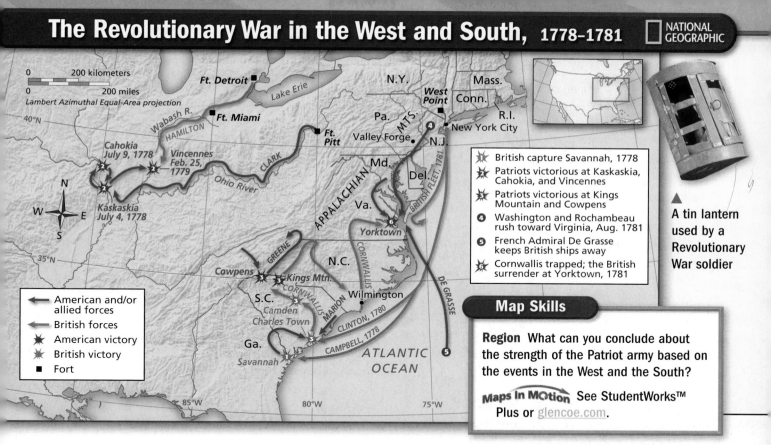

The Revolutionary War in the West and South, 1778–1781

0   200 kilometers
0   200 miles
Lambert Azimuthal Equal-Area projection

- British capture Savannah, 1778
- Patriots victorious at Kaskaskia, Cahokia, and Vincennes
- Patriots victorious at Kings Mountain and Cowpens
- ④ Washington and Rochambeau rush toward Virginia, Aug. 1781
- ⑤ French Admiral De Grasse keeps British ships away
- Cornwallis trapped; the British surrender at Yorktown, 1781

A tin lantern used by a Revolutionary War soldier

← American and/or allied forces
← British forces
✸ American victory
✸ British victory
■ Fort

Map Skills

Region What can you conclude about the strength of the Patriot army based on the events in the West and the South?

Maps In Motion See StudentWorks™ Plus or glencoe.com.

Struggles in the South

Main Idea Great Britain hoped that a strong campaign in the South would help the war.

History and You Has a strategy ever helped your team score a victory or helped you to do better on a test? Read to find out about American and British strategies in the South.

In the war's early years, the Americans won several battles in the South. In 1776 they crushed Loyalists at the **Battle of Moore's Creek,** near Wilmington, North Carolina. They also saved Charles Town, South Carolina, from the British. Although a small battle, its **impact,** or effect, was great.

By 1778 the British realized that bringing the American colonies back into the empire would not be easy. As a result, they changed their strategy and planned a hard-hitting offensive to finish the war.

The British concentrated their efforts in the South, where there were many Loyalists. They hoped to use British sea power and the support of the Loyalists to win decisive victories in the Southern states. Initially the strategy worked.

British Victories

In late 1778, General Henry Clinton sent 3,500 British troops from New York to take Savannah, Georgia. The British occupied the coastal city and overran most of the state.

In early 1780, Clinton himself headed south with a large army to attack the port of Charles Town, South Carolina. Charles Town surrendered in May, and the British took thousands of prisoners. It marked the worst American defeat of the war.

Clinton returned to New York, leaving **General Charles Cornwallis** in command of British forces in the South. The Continental Congress sent forces under General Horatio Gates to face Cornwallis. The two armies met at Camden, South Carolina, in August 1780. Although the British won, Cornwallis soon found that he could not control the area he had conquered. He and his troops faced a new kind of warfare.

This British cartoon was drawn in 1779, before the American Revolution ended. It shows a rider being thrown off of a horse.

1. **Analyzing** What evidence in the cartoon suggests that Britain was harsh toward the colonies?

2. **Drawing Conclusions** What outcome of the war does the cartoonist predict?

A. America B. Great Britain
C. Revolutionary War soldier

THE HORSE AMERICA THROWS HIS MASTER.

Guerrilla Warfare

The British received less help than they had expected from Loyalists in Southern states. Instead, as British troops moved through the countryside, small forces of Patriots attacked them. These bands of soldiers appeared suddenly, struck their blows, and then disappeared. This hit-and-run technique of **guerrilla warfare** caught the British off guard.

One successful guerrilla leader, **Francis Marion,** operated out of the swamps of eastern South Carolina. Known as the Swamp Fox, Marion was quick and smart. One British colonel grumbled that "the devil himself" could not catch Marion.

Help From Spain

When Bernardo de Gálvez became governor of Louisiana, Spain was neutral. That did not stop Gálvez from helping the colonists. He loaned thousands of dollars to the Americans and opened the port of New Orleans to free trade. Gálvez also had tons of supplies and ammunition shipped up the Mississippi River to American troops in the Northwest Territory. With this help, George Rogers Clark captured the key posts of Kaskaskia, Cahokia, and Vincennes.

In the summer of 1779, Spain declared war on Britain. Gálvez raised an army of Spanish soldiers along with Creoles, Native Americans, and African Americans and marched on British posts along the lower Mississippi. He captured Baton Rouge, Natchez, Mobile, and Pensacola. Gálvez's victories opened supply lines for military goods from Spain, France, Cuba, and Mexico.

According to historian Buchanan Parker Thomson, Gálvez had given:

PRIMARY SOURCE

". . . the most vital aid contributed by any one man to the struggling American colonies. In winning this triumphant victory over the last great British outpost, he had not only served his King to the limit of his strength, but had made to the United States the most important gift an ally could offer: the security of their southeastern and western frontiers."

—from *Spain: Forgotten Ally of the American Revolution*

Patriot Victories

After their victory at Camden, South Carolina, the British moved northward through the Carolinas in September 1780. At Kings Mountain, a British officer and more than 1,000 Loyalists defended an outpost against Patriot attack. The Patriots forced the British to retreat. The victory brought new support for independence from Southerners. They wanted to see an end to the war that was destroying their homes and farms.

In October 1780, **Nathanael Greene** replaced Gates as commander of the Continental forces in the South. Rather than lead an all-out attack on Cornwallis's forces, Greene split his army in two. In January 1781 one section of the army, led by General Daniel Morgan, defeated the British at Cowpens, South Carolina. Another section joined Marion's guerrilla raids.

Greene reunited his forces in March to meet Cornwallis's army at Guilford Courthouse, in present-day Greensboro, North Carolina. Greene's army was forced to retreat, but the British **sustained,** or suffered, great losses in the process. General Cornwallis abandoned the Carolina campaign.

History ONLINE

Student Web Activity Visit glencoe.com and complete the Chapter 6 Web Activity about the Revolutionary War in the South.

British Retreat

Cornwallis realized that the British had to act quickly to win the war. More French troops were on their way to America, and the Patriots still held Virginia. Troops and supplies were still moving south. In April 1781, Cornwallis marched north to Virginia. His troops carried out raids throughout the state. They nearly captured Governor Thomas Jefferson and the Virginia legislature in June. Jefferson fled on horseback, just ahead of the advancing British troops.

General Washington sent Lafayette and General Anthony Wayne south to fight Cornwallis. Meanwhile, Cornwallis set up camp at Yorktown, which was located on the Virginia coast. There he awaited further orders from Clinton in New York. The battle for the South was entering its final phase.

Reading Check **Evaluating** What effect did the Patriot victory at Kings Mountain produce?

Section 3 Review

History ONLINE

Study Central™ To review this section, go to glencoe.com.

Vocabulary

1. Define each of the following terms, and use it in a sentence: blockade, privateer, impact, guerrilla warfare, sustain.

Main Ideas

2. Stating Which side did more Native Americans take in the war for independence and why?

3. Discussing Why did the Americans need to break the British naval blockade?

4. Explaining How did Spain help to undermine Great Britain's Southern strategy?

Critical Thinking

5. Creative Writing Write a short play based on John Paul Jones and the battle between the *Bonhomme Richard* and the *Serapis.*

6. Determining Cause and Effect Use a diagram like the one below to show why the British lost control in the South.

British Defeats in the South

Answer the Essential Question

7. How did fighting in the West and South affect the course of the Revolutionary War?

The War Is Won

Essential Question ◀

How did the Battle of Yorktown lead to American independence?

Reading Guide

Content Vocabulary

ratify *(p. 177)*   ambush *(p. 178)*

Academic Vocabulary

strategy *(p. 175)*   pursue *(p. 177)*

Key People and Events

Comte de Rochambeau *(p. 175)*

François de Grasse *(p. 175)*

Battle of Yorktown *(p. 176)*

Benjamin Franklin *(p. 177)*

John Adams *(p. 177)*

John Jay *(p. 177)*

Treaty of Paris *(p. 177)*

Reading Strategy

Taking Notes As you read, use a diagram like the one below to list the forces that met Cornwallis at Yorktown.

INDIANA ACADEMIC STANDARDS
United States History

8.1.4 Identify fundamental ideas in the Declaration of Independence (1776) and analyze the causes and effects of the Revolutionary War (1775–1783), including enactment of the Articles of Confederation and the Treaty of Paris.

8.1.9 Describe the influence of important individuals on social and political developments of the time such as the Independence movement and the framing of the Constitution.

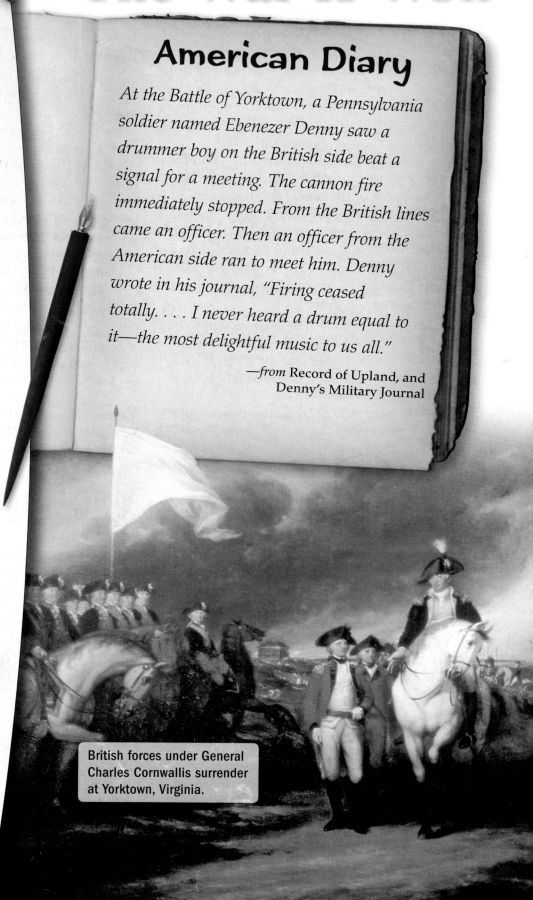

American Diary

At the Battle of Yorktown, a Pennsylvania soldier named Ebenezer Denny saw a drummer boy on the British side beat a signal for a meeting. The cannon fire immediately stopped. From the British lines came an officer. Then an officer from the American side ran to meet him. Denny wrote in his journal, "Firing ceased totally. . . . I never heard a drum equal to it—the most delightful music to us all."

—*from* Record of Upland, and Denny's Military Journal

British forces under General Charles Cornwallis surrender at Yorktown, Virginia.

Victory at Yorktown

Main Idea Washington's complicated battle plan led to the important American victory at Yorktown.

History and You How important is planning to the successful outcome of a project? Read to learn how Washington's planning helped the Americans win an important victory.

. . . .

Denny was proud to witness the steps leading to the British surrender at Yorktown. The buildup to this great event began a few months earlier. At that time, the Revolutionary War was at a critical point and both armies sought a victory. General Washington made plans to attack the British at Yorktown, Virginia, rather than in New York City. The Patriots hoped for help from the French.

In July 1780, French warships appeared off Newport, Rhode Island. The ships carried the promised French aid: soldiers commanded by **Comte de Rochambeau** (ROH•SHAM•BOH). Unfortunately, the British fleet arrived soon afterward and trapped the French ships in Newport.

In the autumn of 1780, Washington camped north of New York City. He waited for a second fleet of French ships. He also kept a close eye on the British army based in New York that General Clinton commanded. Washington planned to attack Clinton's army as soon as the second French fleet arrived. He had to wait a year to put this plan into action. The French fleet did not set sail for America until the summer of 1781.

Change in Plans

Washington followed the reports of the fighting in the South during 1780 and 1781. He knew that Cornwallis's troops were camped in Yorktown, Virginia, and that Lafayette was keeping them bottled up on the Yorktown peninsula. He also learned that Admiral **François de Grasse,** the French naval commander, was heading toward Chesapeake Bay instead of New York. Washington quickly changed his plans. He would advance on the British at Yorktown rather than at New York City.

Washington kept his new **strategy,** or plan of action, secret. He wanted Clinton to think the Patriots still planned to attack the British in New York. This, he hoped, would keep Clinton from sending aid to Cornwallis. Meanwhile, in July Rochambeau had marched his troops from Newport to join Washington.

Primary Source / Revolutionary Music

"Yankee Doodle" The song "Yankee Doodle" was played at the Yorktown surrender ceremony to annoy the British. British forces first sang "Yankee Doodle" to poke fun at what they considered the awkward ways of the Americans. The song tells the story of a poorly dressed Yankee "doodle," or simple person. The Americans, however, quickly made "Yankee Doodle" their own. They created new verses that made fun of the British and praised the Continental Army and its commander, George Washington.

Critical Thinking

Interpreting Do you think songs and other forms of music are important in fighting a war? Explain.

Washington and Rochambeau then rushed south with their armies. The secrecy was so strict that most soldiers did not know where they were going. One soldier wrote, "We do not know the object of our march, and are in perfect ignorance whether we are going against New York, or . . . Virginia."

Washington's troops marched 200 miles (322 km) in 15 days. General Clinton in New York did not detect the forces heading south toward Virginia. Three groups—Lafayette's troops, Washington's and Rochambeau's American-French army, and de Grasse's French fleet—would meet at Yorktown.

The Siege of Yorktown

Washington's plan worked perfectly. The British were thoroughly confused. By the end of September, 14,000 American and French troops had trapped Cornwallis's 8,000 British and Hessian troops at Yorktown. Meanwhile, de Grasse's fleet kept Cornwallis from escaping by sea. General Clinton and the rest of the British army waited in New York. They were unable to help Cornwallis.

Cornwallis's Defeat

On October 9, the Americans and French began a tremendous bombardment. One Hessian soldier wrote in his diary, "One saw men lying everywhere . . . whose heads, arms, and legs had been shot off."

British supplies began running low. Many soldiers were wounded or sick. On October 14, Washington's aide, Alexander Hamilton, led an attack that captured key British defenses. Cornwallis realized the hopelessness of his situation. On October 19 he surrendered his troops. The Patriots had won the **Battle of Yorktown.** They took nearly 8,000 British prisoners and captured more than 200 guns.

As the British marched between rows of French and American troops to hand over their weapons, a French band played "Yankee Doodle." A British band responded with a children's tune, "The World Turned Upside Down." Indeed it had.

Reading Check **Explaining** Why did Washington advance on Yorktown?

Chance & Error in History

What If Washington Had Stepped Down?

Throughout the Revolutionary War, Washington succeeded in holding his army together, despite many difficulties. He had to deal with low morale among soldiers who lived on poor rations and received low pay. The Continental Congress often interfered with his military operations. During the gloomy winter at Valley Forge, some congressmen and army officers plotted to replace Washington as commander in chief.

Washington as president ▶

From Soldier to Leader

Washington was commissioned a lieutenant colonel in 1754 in the French and Indian War. An excellent soldier, he was made brigadier general and was a major factor in Britain's defeat of the French.

Wilderness fighting had made Washington a trained military man. This training helped prepare him for his greatest military challenge—leading the American revolutionary forces.

"The fate of unborn millions will now depend, under God, on the courage and conduct of this army."

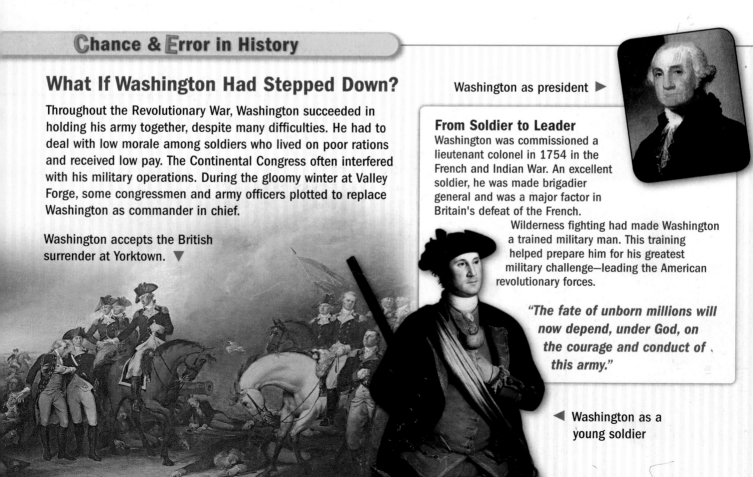

Washington accepts the British surrender at Yorktown. ▼

◀ Washington as a young soldier

Independence

Main Idea The Patriots' spirit and resolve helped them win independence.

History and You What sort of influence do you think America's fight for independence had on the rest of the world? Read to find out how American ideals affected the world.

The fighting did not end with Cornwallis's surrender at Yorktown. The British still held Savannah, Charles Town, and New York. A few more clashes took place on land and sea. The victory at Yorktown, however, convinced the British that the war was too costly to **pursue,** or continue.

The two sides sent delegates to Paris to work out a treaty. **Benjamin Franklin, John Adams,** and **John Jay** represented the United States. The American Congress **ratified,** or approved, the preliminary treaty in April 1783. The final **Treaty of Paris** was signed on September 3, 1783. By that time Britain had also made peace with France and Spain.

The Treaty of Paris was a triumph for the Americans. Great Britain recognized the United States as an independent nation. The British promised to withdraw all their troops from American territory. They also agreed to give Americans the right to fish in the waters off the coast of Canada.

The United States, in turn, agreed that British merchants could collect debts that Americans owed them. The treaty also stated that the Congress would advise the states to return to Loyalists the properties taken from them.

The Newburgh Conspiracy

Washington headquartered his strong army in Newburgh, New York, after the British surrendered. The Congress refused to fund the soldiers' pensions and failed to provide them with other pay. The soldiers' anger mounted. In disgust, some officers circulated a letter in March 1783. If their demands were not met, the letter said, the army should use force against Congress.

Washington realized that this threat of revolt was dangerous. The new nation could be destroyed. He persuaded the angry soldiers to be patient. Then Washington urged the Congress to meet their just demands. Washington's leadership ended the threat to the new nation. The Congress soon acted on the demands.

Washington Resigns

British troops left New York City in late November 1783. The war had truly ended. Washington could at last give up his command. On December 4, Washington said farewell to his troops. Three weeks later he formally resigned at a meeting of the Second Continental Congress. Washington said, "Having now finished the work assigned me I retire . . . and take my leave of all the employments of public life."

Washington returned home to Mount Vernon, Virginia, in time for Christmas. There he planned to remain and live quietly with his family.

Dr. Benjamin Rush ▶

Dr. Benjamin Rush, one of Washington's critics, served as surgeon general in the Continental Army. In a letter to John Adams, Rush compared Washington unfavorably to the hero of Saratoga, Horatio Gates.

"I have heard several officers who have served under General Gates compare his army to a well regulated family. . . . [They] have compared General Washington's imitation of an army to an unformed mob."

Critical Thinking

Analyzing What pressures did Washington face as a leader? Why do you think he did not quit?

Why the Americans Won

How did the Americans manage to win the Revolutionary War? How did they defeat Britain, the world's greatest power?

The Americans had several advantages in the war. First, they fought on their own land while the British had to bring troops and supplies from thousands of miles away. The siege of Yorktown showed how much the British depended on the sea. When their ships were blocked, the British troops had no support. Also, the Americans knew the local terrain and where to lay an **ambush**—a surprise attack. The British, in contrast, had much difficulty controlling the American countryside once they occupied the cities.

Second, help from other nations contributed to the American victory. The French supplied soldiers, ships, and loans. The Spanish gave aid when they attacked the British in the Mississippi Valley and along the Gulf of Mexico.

Perhaps most important, the American Revolution was a people's movement. Its outcome depended not on any one battle or event but on the determination and spirit of all Patriots. As Washington remarked about the patriotic crowds, "Here is an army they [the British] will never conquer."

Influence of the American Revolution

In 1776 the American colonists began a revolution. They made clear the principles of freedom and the rights outlined in the Declaration of Independence. These ideas bounded back across the Atlantic to influence the French Revolution. French rebels in 1789 fought in defense of "Liberty, Equality, and Fraternity." The French upheld these principles: "Men are born and remain free and equal in rights."

In 1791 the ideals of the American and French Revolutions traveled across the Caribbean and the Atlantic to the French colony of Saint Domingue. Inspired by talk of freedom, enslaved Africans took up arms. Led by Toussaint-Louverture, they shook off French rule. In 1804 Saint Domingue—present-day Haiti—became the second nation in the Americas to achieve independence from colonial rule. "We have asserted our rights," declared the revolutionaries. "We swear never to yield them to any power on earth."

Reading Check **Explaining** Why did Washington take action to end the Newburgh Conspiracy?

Section 4 Review

History ONLINE
Study Central™ To review this section, go to glencoe.com.

Vocabulary

1. Using complete sentences, define the following terms: strategy, pursue, ratify, ambush.

Main Ideas

2. Summarizing What role did the French play in the Patriot victory at Yorktown?

3. Explaining Why were the Americans successful in their fight for independence?

Critical Thinking

4. Categorizing Use a diagram like the one below to show what the United States and Great Britain agreed to in the Treaty of Paris.

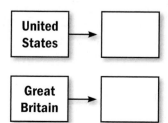

5. Expository Writing Write a paragraph comparing Washington's original plans to attack the British with his new secret strategy.

Answer the
6. Essential Question

How did the Battle of Yorktown lead to American independence?

Chapter 6

Visual Summary

The American Revolution

The Continental Army suffered setbacks in the early years of the Revolutionary War.

The colonists lacked a regular army and a strong navy. Money, weapons, and ammunition were in short supply.

Although the Americans were brave, military defeats and a dwindling army nearly ended the Patriots' cause.

The Battle of Saratoga (1777), however, was a key victory for the Continental Army because it stopped Britain's plan to separate New England from the Middle Colonies.

▲ Valley Forge

▼ The surrender at Yorktown

After the victory at Saratoga, France and Spain sent money, equipment, and troops to help the cause of the American Patriots.

The Patriots won battles in the West, the South, and at sea.

A new style of fighting used by the Patriots, guerrilla warfare, surprised the British, especially in the South.

Strategic, secret plans allowed the Americans to win the Battle of Yorktown in Virginia, capturing a large British army and essentially ending the war.

◀ Soldier's tin lantern

In the Treaty of Paris (1783), Great Britain recognized the United States as an independent nation, ending the Revolutionary War.

◀ Female Continental soldier

STUDY TO GO Study anywhere, anytime! Download quizzes and flash cards to your PDA from glencoe.com.

Battle of Yorktown

British general Charles Cornwallis moved into the Tidewater region of Virginia in the spring of 1781. He was ordered to provide a protected harbor for the British fleet in the lower Chesapeake Bay. He selected a spot near the city of Yorktown, Virginia, whose deep-water harbor on the York River seemed perfect. Cornwallis spent most of the summer fortifying Yorktown and Gloucester Point across the York River.

How Did Geography Affect the Battle of Yorktown?

Although Yorktown seemed a good choice, the city's location would make it impossible to defend. In September the French navy seized Chesapeake Bay. With the bay in French hands, Cornwallis was unable to get supplies or reinforcements coming by sea. By the end of September, nearly 18,000 American and French soldiers had gathered on the outskirts of Yorktown, while about 8,000 British soldiers occupied the town and Gloucester Point. Cornwallis was surrounded, his back to the York River. He soon surrendered and the Revolutionary War was all but over.

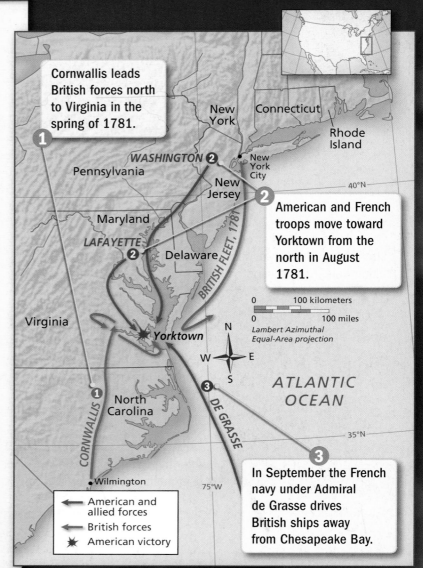

1 Cornwallis leads British forces north to Virginia in the spring of 1781.

2 American and French troops move toward Yorktown from the north in August 1781.

3 In September the French navy under Admiral de Grasse drives British ships away from Chesapeake Bay.

Map labels: New York, Connecticut, Rhode Island, WASHINGTON, Pennsylvania, New York City, New Jersey, Maryland, LAFAYETTE, Delaware, BRITISH FLEET, 1781, Virginia, Yorktown, North Carolina, CORNWALLIS, DE GRASSE, ATLANTIC OCEAN, Wilmington, 40°N, 35°N, 75°W

0 ___ 100 kilometers
0 ___ 100 miles
Lambert Azimuthal Equal-Area projection

← American and allied forces
← British forces
✳ American victory

March to Victory Washington, de Grasse, and Rochambeau led their forces to Yorktown.

George Washington—American general and commander of the Continental Army. Forces under Washington. Lafayette also moved toward Yorktown from the north.

François de Grasse—French admiral whose 28 ships took control of Chesapeake Bay; 3,000 soldiers aboard those ships landed at Yorktown

Rochambeau—French general whose troops joined Washington's Continental Army in its march toward Yorktown

The Yorktown Campaign

0   1 kilometer
0   1 mile
Polyconic projection

Realizing he was both outmanned and outgunned, Cornwallis sent for help. Before the reinforcements arrived, Cornwallis was forced to surrender his army on October 19.

The mortar barrel was elevated on a flat, wooden bed to launch bombs behind enemy lines.

York River

Gloucester

Swamp

Cornwallis
8,000

Yorktown

Rochambeau
9,000

French lines

American lines

Mill Pond

Field of British Surrender

General Lincoln

Lafayette's Headquarters

Washington's Headquarters

General Steuben

General Lafayette
8,000

N
W   E
S

Legend:
- British troops
- British defensive lines
- American and French attacks October 6–15
- American troops
- French troops
- French fleet
- French and American artillery

The *Ville de Paris* was the flagship of Admiral de Grasse during his operations in Virginia waters in the autumn of 1781. Reported to be the largest warship of its time, the *Ville de Paris* boasted 110 guns on 3 gun decks.

◀ On October 14–15, Americans and French stormed the small British forts (called redoubts) to the south of Yorktown.

Analyzing Geography

1. **Movement** From which direction did de Grasse's ships travel to Yorktown?

2. **Place** Why did Cornwallis choose Yorktown as the British base of operations? Why did this decision leave his forces vulnerable?

INDIANA STATEWIDE TEST PRACTICE

Reviewing Vocabulary

Directions: Choose the word or words that best completes the sentence.

1 **The Continental Army depended on the states to _____, or enlist, soldiers.**

A draft
B inaugurate
C impress
D recruit

2 **_____ means that it takes more and more money to buy the same amount of goods.**

A Inflation
B Deflation
C Depression
D Recession

3 **The British navy imposed a _____ that kept the ships of Patriots from entering or leaving American ports.**

A tariff
B sanction
C blockade
D mercenary

4 **Congress _____ the preliminary treaty of Paris in April 1783.**

A ignored
B ratified
C vetoed
D annulled

Reviewing Main Ideas

Directions: Choose the best answer.

5 **After crossing the Delaware River, Washington's surprise attack**

A was the Revolutionary War's last battle.
B boosted the morale of the Patriots.
C was followed by calls for his resignation.
D succeeded but caused many casualties.

6 **Americans had problems getting enough money to finance the war because**

A Congress did not have taxing powers.
B the states opposed the war.
C other countries would not help the Patriots.
D the British closed all colonial banks.

7 **In the South, Patriots used a hit-and-run battle technique known as**

A privateering.
B quartering.
C guerrilla warfare.
D blockading.

8 **Which of the following was one of the terms of the Treaty of Paris of 1783?**

A Britain recognized U.S. independence.
B British merchants agreed not to collect U.S. debts.
C Britain and the United States formed a naval alliance.
D Loyalists would be punished for their actions.

GO ON

History ONLINE

For additional test practice, use **Self-Check Quizzes**—Chapter 6 at glencoe.com.

Critical Thinking

Directions: Choose the best answer.

9 **Which of the following statements best describes France's role in the American Revolution?**

  A The French opposed the American revolt, fearing its effects on their monarchy.
  B France formed an alliance with the Americans supplying military help.
  C France gave moral support but refused military help to the Americans.
  D France and Britain together fought against the Americans.

Base your answer to question 10 on the map below and your knowledge of Chapter 6.

Patriot and Loyalist Strongholds

10 **Based on the map, where were Loyalist settlements the strongest?**

  A Virginia and Pennsylvania
  B the Carolinas
  C Massachusetts and Connecticut
  D Pennsylvania and New Jersey

Constructed Response

Directions: Write a short response to each of the following questions. In your answer:

  • *address all parts of the question*
  • *use information from the chapter*
  • *include facts, examples, and details relevant to the question*
  • *use clear language*

11 **Describe the role of African Americans in the Revolutionary War.**

12 **Discuss American battle strengths and weaknesses at the outset of the American Revolution.**

Base your answer to question 13 on the reading below and your knowledge of Chapter 6.

> Here is an army they [the British] will never conquer.
>
> —George Washington

13 **What did George Washington mean when he made this statement about the Patriot cause?**

14 **Identify one foreign figure who was involved in the American Revolution and explain how that individual aided the Patriot cause.**

 STOP

Need Extra Help?														
If You Missed Questions. . .	1	2	3	4	5	6	7	8	9	10	11	12	13	14
Go to Page. . .	155	164	170	177	158	164	172	177	161	153	154	155	178	163

A More Perfect Union 1777–1790

Delegates to the Constitutional Convention, 1787

U.S. Events

World Events

1776 ——— 1779 ——— 1782

★ 1777
Articles of
Confederation
written

1781 ★
Robert Morris
serves as superin-
tendent of finance
for the U.S.

★ 1783
Treaty of
Paris

1778 ★
France goes
to war
against
Britain

1780 ★
League of
Armed
Neutrality
is formed

1782 ★
Rama I starts new
dynasty in Siam

Palace, Bangkok,
Thailand (Siam) ▶

Section 1: The Articles of Confederation

Essential Question How effective was government under the Articles of Confederation?

Section 2: Convention and Compromise

Essential Question Why is the Constitution a document of compromises?

Section 3: A New Plan of Government

Essential Question What ideas and features are found in the United States Constitution?

History ONLINE
Chapter Overview Visit glencoe.com and click on **Chapter 7—Chapter Overviews** to preview chapter information.

FOLDABLES
Study Organizer

Organizing Information

Make this Foldable to help you organize what you learn about the differences between the Articles of Confederation and the Constitution.

Step 1 Fold an 11" x 17" piece of paper lengthwise to create three equal sections.

Step 2 Then fold it into four equal columns.

Step 3 Label your Foldable as shown.

Chapter 7: A More Perfect Union	Purpose	Description	Effectiveness
Articles of Confederation			
Constitution			

Reading and Writing As you read, describe each document by identifying its purpose and features, and evaluate how effective it was for governing.

E PLURIBUS UNUM

U.S. gold coin ▲

1784 Russians establish colony on Kodiak Island, Alaska

1785 First hot air balloon crosses English Channel

1785

1787
- Shays's Rebellion is suppressed
- U.S. introduces dollar currency
- Northwest Ordinance is passed

1788 U.S. Constitution is ratified

1788

1788 British establish penal colony in Australia

1789 French Revolution begins

1790 Philadelphia becomes federal capital of the U.S.

1791

◄ Guillotine

The Articles of Confederation

Reading Guide

Content Vocabulary

constitution *(p. 187)* petition *(p. 190)*

bicameral *(p. 187)* ordinance *(p. 190)*

republic *(p. 188)* depreciate *(p. 191)*

Academic Vocabulary

abandon *(p. 189)* clause *(p. 191)*

Key People and Events

Articles of Confederation *(p. 188)*

John Adams *(p. 193)*

Reading Strategy

Taking Notes As you read, use a diagram like the one below to identify the powers of the national government under the Articles of Confederation.

Powers of National Government

INDIANA ACADEMIC STANDARDS
United States History

8.1.5 Identify and explain key events leading to the creation of a strong union among the thirteen original states and in the establishment of the United States as a federal republic.

8.4.7 Trace the development of different kinds of money used in the United States and explain how money helps make saving easier.

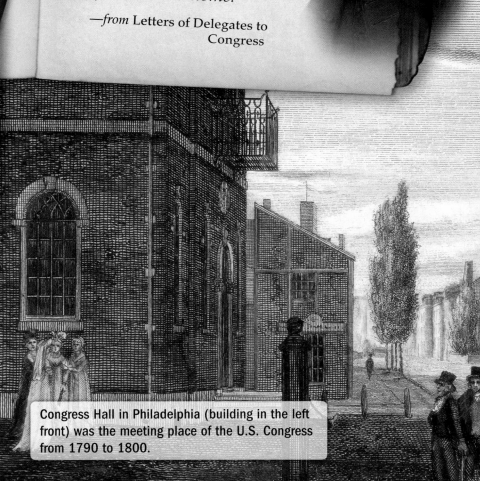

American Diary

As British forces approached Philadelphia on September 19, 1777, John Adams and members of the Second Continental Congress fled to York, Pennsylvania. Adams wrote to his wife: "War has no Charms for me. If I live much longer in Banishment I shall scarcely know my own Children. Tell my little ones, that if they will be very good, Pappa will come home."

—from Letters of Delegates to Congress

Congress Hall in Philadelphia (building in the left front) was the meeting place of the U.S. Congress from 1790 to 1800.

From Independent States to a Republic

Main Idea The Articles of Confederation created a weak central government and strong state governments.

History and You How hard is it to get a group of friends to agree on what type of movie to watch or game to play? Read about what was necessary for the new Congress to pass a law.

• •

It was important for the Second Continental Congress to create a plan for government that would satisfy the needs of all 13 states. The states were united against the British, but would they be able to work together and still maintain their independence? How would each state's government be organized? After rejecting British rule, the states' first task was to establish their own political institutions.

State Constitutions

In May 1776, the Continental Congress asked the states to organize their governments. Each state moved quickly to adopt a state **constitution,** or plan of government. By the end of 1776, eight states had drafted constitutions. New York and Georgia followed in 1777 and Massachusetts in 1780. Connecticut and Rhode Island kept their colonial charters as state constitutions.

Their experience with British rule made Americans cautious about placing too much power in the hands of a single ruler. For that reason, the states adopted constitutions that limited the power of the governor. Pennsylvania even replaced the office of governor with an elected council of 12 members.

Limiting Power

States also divided government functions between the governor (or Pennsylvania's council) and the legislature. Most states established two-house, or **bicameral,** legislatures to divide the power even further.

The writers of the constitutions not only wanted to prevent abuses of power in the states, but they also wanted to keep power in the hands of the people. State legislators were popularly elected, and elections were frequent. In most states, only white males who were at least 21 years old could vote. These citizens also had to own a certain amount of property or pay a certain amount of taxes. Some states allowed free African American males to vote.

When and Where | Capitals of the United States

Capital Cities of the United States

City	Length of Time as U.S. Capital
Philadelphia, Pennsylvania	May 10, 1775 to December 12, 1776
Baltimore, Maryland	December 20, 1776 to February 27, 1777
Philadelphia, Pennsylvania	March 4, 1777 to September 18, 1777
Lancaster, Pennsylvania	September 27, 1777 (one day)
York, Pennsylvania	September 30, 1777 to June 27, 1778
Philadelphia, Pennsylvania	July 2, 1778 to June 21, 1781
Princeton, New Jersey	June 30, 1783 to November 4, 1783
Annapolis, Maryland	November 26, 1783 to August 19, 1784
Trenton, New Jersey	November 1, 1784 to December 24, 1784
New York City, New York	January 11, 1785 to August 12, 1790
Philadelphia, Pennsylvania	December 6, 1790 to May 14, 1800
Washington, D.C.	November 17, 1800 to present

Nine different cities have served as capitals, or seats of government, of the United States.

Critical Thinking

Making Inferences Why do you think the United States had numerous capital cities between 1775 and 1800? Do you think it is important for a country to have a permanent location for its seat of government? Explain.

Richard Henry Lee of Virginia moved on June 7, 1776, that

"*a plan of confederation be prepared and transmitted to the respective colonies, for their consideration and approbation [approval].*"

ARTICLES
OF
Confederation
AND
Perpetual Union
BETWEEN THE
STATES
OF
NEW-HAMPSHIRE, MASSACHUSETTS-BAY, RHODE-

Writing the Articles Even though he opposed independence, John Dickinson was asked to chair the committee to draft the Articles of Confederation because of his knowledge of government institutions.

★ **1781** March 1 Articles of Confederation ratified

★ **1783** March 10 Troops demand back pay from Congress, threaten to mutiny

★ **1786** September 14 Annapolis Convention to reform regulation of commerce

★ **1787** May 17 Constitutional Convention convenes in Philadelphia

★ **1783** November 2 Continental Army officially disbanded

★ **1785** July 6 Congress approves a currency system based on the dollar

★ **1787** February 21 Congress calls convention to amend Articles of Confederation

State constitutions generally restricted the powers of the governors, which made the legislatures the most powerful branch of government. The state legislatures struggled to make taxes more fair, but disagreements arose. New challenges emerged as dependent colonies became self-governing states.

Forming a Republic

Americans agreed that their country should be a **republic,** a government in which citizens rule through elected representatives. They could not agree, however, on the organization and powers of their new republic. At first, most Americans favored a weak central government. They assumed the states would be like small, independent countries—similar to the way the colonies had been organized. The states would act independently on most issues, working together through a central government only to wage war and handle relations with other nations.

Planning a New Government

In 1776 the Second Continental Congress appointed a committee to draw up a plan for a new government. After much debate, the Congress adopted the **Articles of Confederation** in November 1777. The Articles, America's first constitution, provided for a new central government under which the states kept most of their power. For the states, the Articles of Confederation were "a firm league of friendship" in which each state retained "its sovereignty, freedom and independence." Under the Articles of Confederation, Congress had the authority to conduct foreign affairs, maintain armed forces, borrow money, and issue currency.

Congress, however, did not have the power to regulate trade, force citizens to join the army, or impose taxes. If Congress needed to raise money or troops, it had to ask the state legislatures—but they were not required to contribute.

Weaknesses of the Articles of Confederation

- Congress had no authority to raise money by collecting taxes
- Congress had no control over foreign trade
- Congress could not force states to carry out its laws
- All 13 states had to agree to any amendments, making it nearly impossible to correct problems

A Common Currency The national currency had little value. States issued their own money, and values varied from state to state.

According to George Washington, the Articles of Confederation were *"little more than the shadow without the substance."*

Regulating Trade Under the Articles of Confederation, the federal government did not have the authority to regulate commerce. In 1784 Congress wanted to take control of commerce for 15 years. The states, however, refused because they were afraid that Congress would then have too much power.

Critical Thinking

Predicting What economic problems might develop if a country uses different types of currency?

In addition, the government lacked a chief executive. The Confederation government carried on much of its business, such as selling western lands, through congressional committees.

The Articles of Confederation were not wholly supported by the states. Under the new plan, each state had one vote, regardless of its population, and all states had to approve the Articles and any amendments. States with large populations, however, believed they should have more votes. The states were also divided by whether or not they claimed land in the West. Maryland refused to approve the Articles until New York, Virginia, and other states **abandoned,** or gave up, land claims west of the Appalachian Mountains. Finally the states settled their differences. With Maryland's ratification, all 13 states approved the Articles. On March 1, 1781, the Confederation formally became the government of the United States of America.

The Confederation Government

The years between 1781 and 1789 were a critical period for the young American republic. The Articles of Confederation did not provide a government strong enough to handle the problems facing the United States. The Congress had limited authority. It could not pass a law unless 9 states voted in favor of it. Any attempt to change the Articles required the consent of all 13 states. This made it difficult for the Congress to pass laws when there was any opposition. Despite its weaknesses, the Confederation made some important achievements. Under the Confederation government, Americans won their independence from Britain and expanded the country's foreign trade. The Confederation also aided with settling and governing the nation's western territories.

Reading Check **Specifying** How many votes did each state have in the new Congress?

New Land Policies

Main Idea As people moved west, the country needed a process for new states joining the Union.

History and You Do you have to meet certain requirements to join some clubs or organizations? Read to learn the requirements for territories to become states.

· ·

At the beginning of the Revolutionary War, only a few thousand settlers lived west of the Appalachian Mountains. By the 1790s, the number was approaching 120,000. These western settlers hoped to organize their lands as states and join the Union. The Articles of Confederation, however, did not contain a provision for adding new states. Congress realized that it had to extend its national authority over the frontier. During the 1780s, all of the states except Georgia gave up their claims to lands west of the Appalachians. The central government took control of these lands. In 1784 Congress divided the western territory into self-governing districts. When the number of people in a district reached the population of the smallest existing state, that district could **petition,** or apply to, Congress for statehood.

The Ordinance of 1785

In 1785 the Confederation Congress passed an **ordinance,** or law, that established a procedure for surveying and selling the western lands north of the Ohio River. The new law divided this massive territory into townships 6 miles long (9.7 km) and 6 miles wide (9.7 km). These townships were to be further divided into 36 sections of 640 acres (259 ha) each that would be sold at public auction for at least a dollar an acre. Land speculators viewed the law as an opportunity to accumulate large tracts of land cheaply. Concerned about lawless people moving into western lands, Richard Henry Lee, the president of the Congress, urged that "the rights of property be clearly defined" by the government. The Congress drafted another ordinance to protect the interests of hardworking settlers.

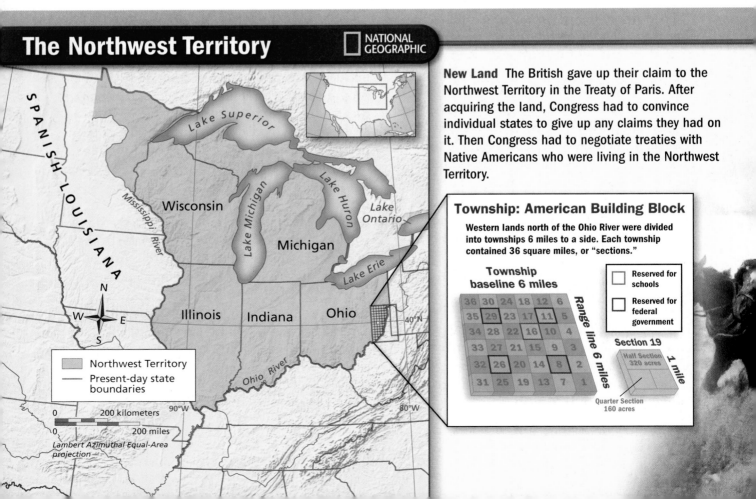

The Northwest Territory

NATIONAL GEOGRAPHIC

New Land The British gave up their claim to the Northwest Territory in the Treaty of Paris. After acquiring the land, Congress had to convince individual states to give up any claims they had on it. Then Congress had to negotiate treaties with Native Americans who were living in the Northwest Territory.

Township: American Building Block

Western lands north of the Ohio River were divided into townships 6 miles to a side. Each township contained 36 square miles, or "sections."

Township baseline 6 miles

Range line 6 miles

36	30	24	18	12	6
35	29	23	17	11	5
34	28	22	16	10	4
33	27	21	15	9	3
32	26	20	14	8	2
31	25	19	13	7	1

☐ Reserved for schools

☐ Reserved for federal government

Section 19

Half Section 320 acres

1 mile

Quarter Section 160 acres

SPANISH LOUISIANA

Lake Superior

Wisconsin

Lake Michigan

Lake Huron

Michigan

Lake Ontario

Lake Erie

Mississippi River

Illinois

Indiana

Ohio

40°N

Ohio River

☐ Northwest Territory

— Present-day state boundaries

0   200 kilometers

0   200 miles

90°W   80°W

Lambert Azimuthal Equal-Area projection

The Northwest Ordinance

The Northwest Ordinance, passed in 1787, created a single Northwest Territory out of the lands north of the Ohio River and east of the Mississippi River. The lands were to be divided into three to five smaller territories. When the population of a territory reached 60,000, the people could petition for statehood. Each new state would have the same rights and privileges as the original 13 states. The Northwest Ordinance included a bill of rights for the settlers, guaranteeing freedom of religion and trial by jury. It also stated, "There shall be neither slavery nor involuntary servitude in said territory." This **clause,** or condition added to a document, marked the first attempt to stop the spread of slavery in the United States. The Ordinance of 1785 and the Northwest Ordinance opened the way for settlement of the Northwest Territory in a stable and orderly manner.

Reading Check **Explaining** What rule did the Northwest Ordinance have about slavery?

Trouble on Two Fronts

Main Idea Financial problems and disputes with Britain and Spain revealed serious weaknesses of the Confederation government.

History and You Imagine paying ten times the normal price for a gallon of milk or a loaf of bread. Read about the economic problems of the late 1700s.

. . . .

The Confederation government did not have enough power to deal with the country's financial problems and issues with other nations.

Financial Problems

By 1781, the money printed during the Revolutionary War **depreciated,** or fell in value, so far that it was almost worthless. Unable to collect taxes, the Continental Congress and the states printed their own paper money. No gold or silver backed up these bills, so they had no real value.

Paying Debts The government needed money to pay off the debt from the Revolutionary War. Much of the new territory's land was sold at auction to raise money to pay off that debt. The government did not have enough money to pay the Revolutionary War veterans' salaries. Instead, it gave veterans land in the Northwest Territory. ▼

▲ **New Settlements** Land speculators also bought large tracts of land in the Northwest Territory to sell to settlers for a profit. A group of land speculators built Campus Martius when they arrived in the Northwest Territory. Campus Martius served as a fort until the town of Marietta, in present-day Ohio, was established.

Critical Thinking

Analyzing How did settlers benefit from the Northwest Ordinance of 1787?

Economics & History

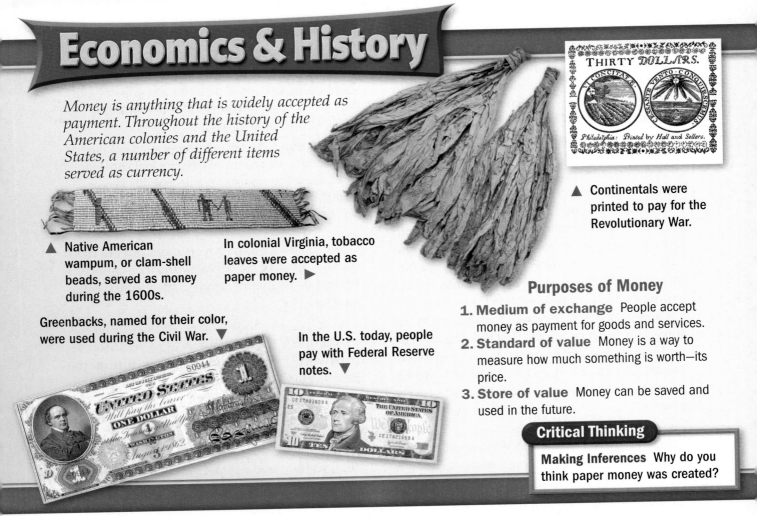

Money is anything that is widely accepted as payment. Throughout the history of the American colonies and the United States, a number of different items served as currency.

▲ Native American wampum, or clam-shell beads, served as money during the 1600s.

In colonial Virginia, tobacco leaves were accepted as paper money. ▶

Greenbacks, named for their color, were used during the Civil War. ▼

In the U.S. today, people pay with Federal Reserve notes. ▼

▲ Continentals were printed to pay for the Revolutionary War.

THIRTY DOLLARS.
Philadelphia: Printed by Hall and Sellers.

Purposes of Money

1. **Medium of exchange** People accept money as payment for goods and services.
2. **Standard of value** Money is a way to measure how much something is worth—its price.
3. **Store of value** Money can be saved and used in the future.

Critical Thinking

Making Inferences Why do you think paper money was created?

As more Continental dollars, or "Continentals," flowed into circulation, people realized that Congress could not redeem these bills for gold or silver. The public lost confidence in the money, and the value of the bills plummeted. Between 1779 and 1781, the number of Continental dollars required to buy one Spanish silver dollar rose from 40 to 146. "Not worth a Continental" became a common saying. At the same time, the price of food and other goods soared. In Boston and some other areas, high prices led to food riots.

The war for independence left the Continental Congress with a large debt. Congress had borrowed money from American citizens and foreign governments during the war. It still owed the Revolutionary soldiers their pay for their military service. Lacking the power to tax, the Confederation could not pay its debts. The Continental Congress requested funds from the states, but they were not required to contribute. The amount that was collected from the states amounted to only a small portion of the total money needed to pay off the debt.

Robert Morris's Import Tax

In 1781, faced with a total collapse of the country's finances, Congress created a department of finance led by Philadelphia merchant Robert Morris. While serving in Congress, Morris had proposed a 5 percent tax on imported goods to help pay the national debt. The plan required that the Articles of Confederation be changed to give Congress the power to levy the tax. Although 12 states approved the plan, Rhode Island's opposition killed it. A second effort in 1783 also failed to win unanimous approval by the states, and the financial crisis continued to worsen.

Problems With Britain

The weaknesses of the new American government became more evident as the United States encountered problems with other countries. In the Treaty of Paris of 1783, Britain promised to withdraw from the lands east of the Mississippi River. British troops, however, continued to occupy several strategic forts in the Great Lakes region.

British trade policy caused other problems. American merchants complained that the British were keeping Americans out of the West Indies and other profitable British markets. In 1785 Congress sent **John Adams** to London to discuss these difficulties. The British, however, were not willing to talk. They pointed to the failure of the United States to honor *its* promises made in the Treaty of Paris. The British claimed that Americans had agreed to pay Loyalists for the property taken from them during the Revolutionary War. The Congress had, in fact, recommended that the states pay the Loyalists. However, the states refused, and Congress could not require them to pay.

Problems With Spain

If American relations with Great Britain were poor, affairs with Spain were worse. Spain, which controlled Florida as well as lands west of the Mississippi River, was anxious to stop American expansion into its territory. As a result, Spain closed the lower Mississippi River to American shipping in 1784. Western settlers no longer had access to the Mississippi River, which they used for trade.

In 1786 American diplomats reached an agreement with Spain. Representatives from the Southern states, however, blocked the agreement because it did not include the right to use the Mississippi River. The weakness of the Confederation and its inability to deal with problems worried many leaders, including George Washington. Americans began to agree that the country needed a stronger government.

 Reading Check **Analyzing** Why did Spain close the lower Mississippi River to American shipping in 1784?

Section 1 Review

History ONLINE
Study Central™ To review this section, go to glencoe.com.

Vocabulary

1. Define each of the following terms in a sentence: constitution, bicameral, republic, abandon, petition, ordinance, clause, depreciate.

Main Ideas

2. **Explaining** Why did most states limit the power of their governors and divide the legislature into two bodies?

3. **Specifying** According to the Northwest Ordinance, when might the people of a territory petition for statehood?

4. **Explaining** Why did the Continental Congress have difficulty raising money?

Critical Thinking

5. **Predicting** How do you think the Northwest Ordinance would affect Native Americans?

6. **Analyzing** Use a graphic organizer like the one below to summarize the strengths and weaknesses of the Confederation government.

7. **Persuasive Writing** You are a delegate to the Second Continental Congress. Congress is debating whether to allow the central government to impose taxes. Take a stand on this issue, and write a short essay defending your position. Give specific reasons for your opinion.

Answer the
8. **Essential Question**
How effective was government under the Articles of Confederation?

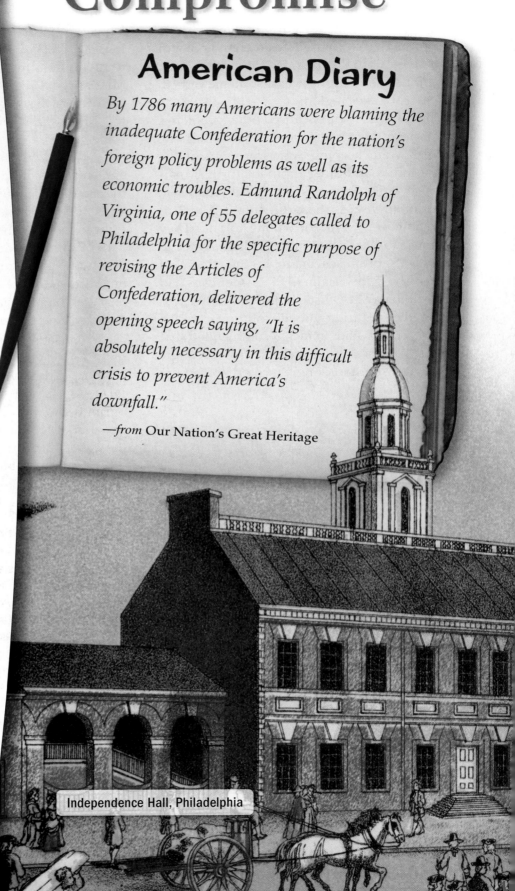

Essential Question ◄

Why is the Constitution a document of compromises?

Reading Guide

Content Vocabulary

depression *(p. 195)*   proportional *(p. 199)*
manumission *(p. 197)*   compromise *(p. 200)*

Academic Vocabulary

convention *(p. 198)*   amend *(p. 199)*

Key People and Events

Shays's Rebellion *(p. 196)*
James Madison *(p. 197)*
Alexander Hamilton *(p. 197)*
Virginia Plan *(p. 199)*
New Jersey Plan *(p. 199)*
Great Compromise *(p. 200)*
Three-Fifths Compromise *(p. 201)*

Reading Strategy

Taking Notes As you read, use a graphic organizer like the one below to take notes about each individual's plan for creating a new government.

Leader	Role
Edmund Randolph	
James Madison	
Roger Sherman	
Gouverneur Morris	

INDIANA ACADEMIC STANDARDS
United States History

8.1.5 Identify and explain key events leading to the creation of a strong union among the thirteen original states and in the establishment of the United States as a federal republic.

8.1.9 Describe the influence of important individuals on social and political developments of the time such as the Independence movement and the framing of the Constitution.

American Diary

By 1786 many Americans were blaming the inadequate Confederation for the nation's foreign policy problems as well as its economic troubles. Edmund Randolph of Virginia, one of 55 delegates called to Philadelphia for the specific purpose of revising the Articles of Confederation, delivered the opening speech saying, "It is absolutely necessary in this difficult crisis to prevent America's downfall."

—*from* **Our Nation's Great Heritage**

Independence Hall, Philadelphia

A Call for Change

Main Idea The government under the Articles of Confederation faced many problems.

History and You You make a plan, but the plan is not working—what do you do? Read to learn about the issues that challenged the government.

● ●

Many Americans called for the Articles of Confederation to be changed. They believed that the Confederation government was too weak to deal with the nation's problems. Those problems, however, were very difficult to solve. After the Revolutionary War, the United States experienced a **depression,** a period when economic activity slows and unemployment increases. Southern plantations were damaged during the war, and rice exports dropped sharply. Trade also decreased when the British closed the profitable West Indies market to American merchants. The little money that the government did have went to pay foreign debts, resulting in a serious currency shortage.

Shays's Rebellion

American farmers suffered because they could not sell their goods. They had trouble paying the money requested by the states to meet Revolutionary War debts. As a result state officials seized farmers' lands to pay their debts and threw many farmers in jail. Grumblings of protest soon grew into revolt. Resentment grew especially strong in Massachusetts. Farmers viewed the new government as just another form of tyranny. They wanted the government to issue paper money and make new policies to relieve debtors. In a petition to state officials, a number of farmers proclaimed:

PRIMARY SOURCE

"Surely your honours are not strangers to the distresses [problems] of the people but . . . know that many of our good inhabitants are now confined in [jail] for debt and taxes."
—"Petition from the Town of Greenwich, Massachusetts"

In 1786 angry farmers lashed out. Led by Daniel Shays, a former Continental Army captain, they forced courts in western Massachusetts to close so judges could not take away farmers' lands.

In January 1787, Shays led more than 1,000 farmers toward the federal arsenal in Springfield, Massachusetts, in search of guns and ammunition. The state militia ordered the advancing farmers to halt and then fired over their heads, but the farmers did not stop.

By the Numbers / Framers of the Constitution

Lawyers
31

Merchants
8

Politicians
4

Others
12

· Judges
· Physicians
· Planters
· Philosopher
· Professor
· Surveyor

Source: *Fifty-Five Fathers: The Story of the Constitutional Convention*

Occupations of the Framers Edmund Randolph was a lawyer and a graduate of William and Mary College. Although he did not sign the United States Constitution, he had much in common with his fellow delegates at the Federal Convention of 1787. Of the 55 men designing and debating the Constitution, nearly half were college educated and almost two-thirds practiced law.

Critical Thinking

Evaluating Do you think it is important for government leaders to have a college education? Why or why not?

Farmers Rebel in Massachusetts In 1787 Daniel Shays and rebellious farmers clashed with the state militia at the federal arsenal at Springfield.

"Rebellion [against a king] may be pardoned, or lightly punished, but the man who dares to rebel against the laws of a republic ought to suffer death."

—Samuel Adams

◄ The federal arsenal at Springfield was used to store weapons and ammunition.

Shays and his followers attack the arsenal. ►

"What country can preserve its liberties if their rulers are not warned from time to time that their people preserve the spirit of resistance?"

—Thomas Jefferson, in a letter to William S. Smith, November 13, 1787

Critical Thinking

Evaluating In your opinion, is Jefferson or Adams correct in his thinking? Justify your answer.

The militia fired again, killing four farmers. Shays and his followers scattered, and the uprising was over. **Shays's Rebellion** frightened many Americans. They worried that the government could not control unrest and prevent violence. On hearing of the rebellion, George Washington wondered whether "mankind, when left to themselves, are unfit for their own government." Thomas Jefferson, minister to France at the time, had a different view. "A little rebellion, now and then," he wrote, "is a good thing."

The Issue of Slavery

The Revolutionary War brought attention to the contradiction between the American battle for liberty and the practice of slavery. Between 1776 and 1786, 11 states—all except South Carolina and Georgia—outlawed or heavily taxed the importation of enslaved people.

Although slavery was not a major source of labor in the North, it existed and was legal in all the Northern states. Many individuals and groups began to work to end the institution of slavery in America. In 1774 Quakers in Pennsylvania organized the first American antislavery society. Six years later Pennsylvania passed a law that provided for the gradual freeing of enslaved people. Between 1783 and 1804, Connecticut, Rhode Island, New York, and New Jersey passed laws that gradually ended slavery.

Still, free African Americans faced discrimination. They were barred from many public places, and few states gave free African Americans the right to vote. The children of most free blacks had to attend separate schools. Free African Americans established their own institutions—churches, schools, and mutual-aid societies—to seek social and economic opportunities.

The states south of Pennsylvania clung to the institution of slavery. The plantation system was built on slavery, and many Southerners feared that their economy could not survive without it.

History ONLINE

Student Web Activity Visit glencoe.com and complete the Chapter 7 Web Activity about Shays's Rebellion.

Nonetheless, an increasing number of slaveholders began freeing the enslaved people that they held after the war. Virginia passed a law that encouraged **manumission,** the freeing of individual enslaved persons, and the state's population of free African Americans grew.

The abolition of slavery in the North divided the new country on the critical issue of whether people should be allowed to keep other human beings in bondage. This division came at the time when many American leaders decided that the Articles of Confederation needed to be strengthened. In the summer of 1787, when state representatives assembled to plan a new government, they compromised on this issue. It would take a civil war to settle the slavery question.

✔ **Reading Check** Explaining How did the North and South differ on slavery?

The Constitutional Convention

Main Idea National leaders reshape the government.

History and You When your family or group of friends faces a problem, does everyone agree to a solution right away? Read about how certain political views changed the United States government.

T he American Revolution led to a union of 13 states, but it had not yet created a nation. Some leaders were satisfied with a system of independent state governments that resembled the old colonial governments. Others supported a strong national government. They demanded a reform of the Articles of Confederation. Two Americans who were active in the movement for change were **James Madison,** a Virginia planter, and **Alexander Hamilton,** a New York lawyer.

People IN HISTORY

George Washington
Presiding Officer of the Constitutional Convention

George Washington did not want to attend the Constitutional Convention, but he did because he worried that the nation would not survive under the weak Articles of Confederation. The delegates unanimously chose him as the presiding officer, or leader, of the Convention. Washington said very little during the debates but became one of the Constitution's strongest supporters. He argued that later generations could make any changes necessary: *"I think the people . . . can, as they will have the aid of experience on their side, decide . . . on the . . . amendments [which] shall be found necessary, . . . I do not conceive that we are more inspired—have more [wisdom]—or possess more virtue than those who will come after us."*

CRITICAL Thinking

1. **Evaluating** How did Washington contribute to the success of the Constitutional Convention?

2. **Analyzing** Why did Washington support the Constitution's ratification?

In September 1786, Hamilton proposed calling a **convention,** or meeting, in Philadelphia to discuss trade issues. He also suggested that this convention consider what possible changes were needed to make "the Constitution of the Federal Government adequate to the exigencies [needs] of the Union."

At first, George Washington was not enthusiastic about the movement to revise the Articles of Confederation. When Washington heard about Shays's Rebellion, however, he changed his mind. After Washington agreed to attend the Philadelphia convention, the meeting took on greater significance. The Philadelphia meeting began in May 1787 and continued through one of the hottest summers on record. The 55 delegates included planters, merchants, lawyers, physicians, generals, governors, and a college president. Three of the delegates were under 30 years of age, and one, Benjamin Franklin, was over 80. Many were well educated. At a time when only one white man in 1,000 went to college, 26 of the delegates had college degrees. Other groups, such as Native Americans, African Americans, and women, were not considered part of the political process, so they were not represented at the convention.

The presence of George Washington and Benjamin Franklin ensured that many people would trust the Convention's work. Two Philadelphians also played key roles. James Wilson often read Franklin's speeches and did important work on the details of the Constitution. Gouverneur Morris, a powerful speaker and writer, wrote the final draft of the Constitution. James Madison was a keen supporter of a strong national government. Madison's careful notes documented the Convention's work. Madison is often called the "Father of the Constitution" because he was the author of the basic plan of government that the Convention adopted.

Organization

The delegates chose George Washington to preside over the meetings. The delegates also decided that each state would have one vote on all questions. A simple majority vote of those states present would make decisions.

Primary Source / **Signing of the Constitution**

"The Constitution is not an instrument for the government to restrain the people, it is an instrument for the people to restrain the government."
—Patrick Henry

Of the original 55 Convention delegates, only 39 signed the Constitution on September 17, 1787.

No meetings could be held unless delegates from at least 7 of the 13 states were present. Sessions were not open to the public, which allowed the delegates to talk freely.

The Virginia Plan

The Convention opened with a surprise from the Virginia delegation. Edmund Randolph proposed the creation of a strong national government. He introduced the **Virginia Plan,** which was largely the work of James Madison. The plan called for a two-house legislature, a chief executive chosen by the legislature, and a court system. The members of the lower house of the legislature would be elected by the people. The members of the upper house would be chosen by the lower house. In both houses the number of representatives would be **proportional,** or corresponding in size, to the population of each state. This would give Virginia many more delegates than Delaware, the state with the smallest population.

Delegates from Delaware, New Jersey, and other small states immediately objected. They preferred the Confederation system in which all states were represented equally. Delegates who were unhappy with the Virginia Plan rallied around William Paterson of New Jersey. On June 15, he presented an alternative plan. This plan revised the Articles of Confederation, which was all the Convention was empowered to do.

The New Jersey Plan

Paterson's **New Jersey Plan** kept the Confederation's one-house legislature, with one vote for each state. Congress, however, could set taxes and regulate trade—powers it did not have under the Articles of Confederation. Congress would elect a weak executive branch consisting of more than one person. Paterson argued that the Convention should not deprive the smaller states of the equality they had under the Articles. Thus, his plan was designed simply to **amend,** or improve, the Articles.

Reading Check **Making Connections** How did Shays's Rebellion influence the Constitutional Convention?

1. Washington, George, Va.
2. Franklin, Benjamin, Pa.
3. Madison, James, Va.
4. Hamilton, Alexander, N.Y.
5. Morris, Gouverneur, Pa.
6. Morris, Robert, Pa.
7. Wilson, James, Pa.
8. Pinckney, Charles C., S.C.
9. Pinckney, Charles, S.C.
10. Rutledge, John, S.C.
11. Butler, Pierce, S.C.
12. Sherman, Roger, Conn.
13. Johnson, William Samuel, Conn.
14. McHenry, James, Md.
15. Read, George, Del.
16. Bassett, Richard, Del.
17. Spaight, Richard Dobbs, N.C.
18. Blount, William, N.C.
19. Williamson, Hugh, N.C.
20. Jenifer, Daniel, Md.
21. King, Rufus, Mass.
22. Gorham, Nathaniel, Mass.
23. Dayton, Jonathan, N.J.
24. Carroll, Daniel, Md.
25. Few, William, Ga.
26. Baldwin, Abraham, Ga.
27. Langdon, John, N.H.
28. Gilman, Nicholas, N.H.
29. Livingston, William, N.J.
30. Paterson, William, N.J.
31. Mifflin, Thomas, Pa.
32. Clymer, George, Pa.
33. FitzSimons, Thomas, Pa.
34. Ingersoll, Jared, Pa.
35. Bedford, Gunning, Jr., Del.
36. Brearley, David, N.J.
37. Dickinson, John, Del.
38. Blair, John, Va.
39. Broom, Jacob, Del.
40. Jackson, William (Secretary)

◄ Washington led the delegates in the signing of the Constitution.

Critical Thinking

Interpreting How does the Constitution limit the power of the government?

Both Plans

- Were federal systems with three branches—legislative, executive, and judicial
- Gave the federal government more powers than it had under the Articles of Confederation

Virginia Plan

Legislative Branch
- Powerful legislature
- Two houses, with membership proportional to state's population
- Lower house elected by the people
- Upper house elected by lower house

Executive Branch
- Chosen by legislature
- Limited power
- Could veto legislation, subject to override

Judicial Branch
- Would serve for life
- Could veto legislation, subject to override

▲ Edmund Randolph proposed the Virginia Plan.

New Jersey Plan

Legislative Branch
- One house with equal representation from all states
- Legislature could collect taxes from states

Executive Branch
- Chosen by Congress
- Would serve a single term
- Subject to recall on request of state governors

Judicial Branch
- Appointed by executive branch
- Would serve for life

▲ William Paterson proposed the New Jersey Plan.

Critical Thinking

Making Inferences Which form of government would be favored by states with large populations? Why?

Compromise Wins Out

Main Idea A new Constitution is adopted.

History and You To resolve differences of opinion in a group, do you discuss options until you reach an agreement? Read how delegates reached a compromise on important issues.

The delegates had to decide whether to simply revise the Articles of Confederation or write a constitution for a new national government. On June 19, the states voted to work toward a national government based on the Virginia Plan, but they still had to resolve the thorny issue of representation that divided the large and small states.

The Great Compromise

The Convention appointed a committee to resolve their disagreements. Roger Sherman of Connecticut suggested what came to be known as the **Great Compromise.** A compromise is an agreement between two or more sides in which each side gives up some of what it wants. Sherman proposed a two-house legislature. In the lower house—the House of Representatives—the number of seats for each state would vary based on the state's population. In the upper house—the Senate—each state would have two members.

The Three-Fifths Compromise

The delegates also compromised on how to count enslaved people. Southern states wanted to include enslaved people in their population counts to gain delegates in the House of Representatives. Northern states objected because enslaved people were legally considered property. Some Northern delegates argued that enslaved people, as property, should be counted for the purpose of taxation but not representation. Neither side, however, considered giving enslaved people the right to vote.

The committee's solution, known as the **Three-Fifths Compromise,** was to count each enslaved person as three-fifths of a free person for determining both taxation and representation. In other words, every five enslaved persons would equal three free persons. The delegates voted to approve the Three-Fifths Compromise.

Slave Trade

Northern states banned slave trade within their borders and wanted to prohibit it nationwide. Southern states considered slavery and the slave trade essential to their economies. To keep the Southern states in the nation, Northerners agreed that the Congress could not interfere with the slave trade until 1808.

Bill of Rights

George Mason of Virginia proposed a bill of rights to be included in the Constitution. Some delegates worried that without a bill of rights the new national government might abuse its power. However, most delegates believed that the Constitution, with its carefully defined list of government powers, provided adequate protection of individual rights. Mason's proposal was defeated.

Approving the Constitution

The committees finished their work in late summer. On September 17, 1787, the delegates assembled in Philadelphia to sign the document. Three delegates refused to sign— Elbridge Gerry of Massachusetts, and Edmund Randolph and George Mason of Virginia. Gerry and Mason would not sign without a bill of rights. The approved draft of the Constitution was then sent to the states for consideration. The approval process for the Articles of Confederation required a unanimous vote of all the states. The new Constitution, however, required 9 of the 13 states to approve it. After that, the new government would come into existence.

✓ **Reading Check** **Analyzing** Who refused to sign the Constitution? Why?

Section 2 Review

History ONLINE
Study Central™ To review this section, go to glencoe.com.

Vocabulary

1. Define each of the following terms, and use it in a sentence: depression, manumission, convention, proportional, amend, compromise.

Main Ideas

2. **Specifying** What did the farmers in Shays's Rebellion want?

3. **Explaining** Why did New Jersey's delegates object to the Virginia Plan?

4. **Identifying** What key issues had to be resolved to create a Constitution that most states would accept?

Critical Thinking

5. **Contrasting** Use a chart like the one below to describe the differences between the Virginia and New Jersey Plans concerning the legislature, representation, and the executive branch.

	Virginia Plan	New Jersey Plan
Legislature		
Representation		
Executive Branch		

6. **Analyzing** Why do you think representation was such a thorny issue?

7. **Expository Writing** You have been asked to write a short announcement to inform your community about the Great Compromise. Summarize the key points of the agreement. Include any other details you think are important.

Answer the
Essential Question

8. Why is the Constitution a document of compromises?

George Mason ▶

Independence Hall in 2007, Philadelphia, Pennsylvania

Should the Constitution Be Ratified: Yes or No?

Building Background

After the delegates in Philadelphia wrote the U.S. Constitution, it had to be approved by the American people. Delegates in each state met at special conventions to decide whether to accept or reject the Constitution. The Constitution would only become the new plan of government of the United States if nine of the 13 states ratified, or approved, it.

People who opposed the Constitution were called Antifederalists. Antifederalists feared a strong national government. They were afraid that a strong central government would take away the rights of citizens. Federalists, however, supported the Constitution. They believed that the Constitution would give the national government power to manage the problems facing the United States. At the same time, the Federalists argued, the Constitution would protect the rights of the individual.

NO

PATRICK HENRY

I look upon that paper [the Constitution] as the most fatal plan that could possibly be conceived[1] to enslave a free people.

GEORGE MASON

There is no declaration of rights, and the laws of the general government being paramount[2] to the laws and constitutions of the several States, the declarations of rights in the separate States are no security.

---

[1] **conceived** formed

[2] **paramount** of higher authority

YES

JAMES WILSON

I am satisfied that any thing nearer to perfection could not have been accomplished. If there are errors, it should be remembered, that the seeds of reformation³ are sown in the work itself, and the concurrence⁴ of two thirds of the congress may at any time introduce alterations and amendments. . . . I am bold to assert, that it is the BEST FORM OF GOVERNMENT WHICH HAS EVER BEEN OFFERED TO THE WORLD.

ALEXANDER HAMILTON

There is an idea . . . that a vigorous Executive is inconsistent with the genius of republican government. . . .

[However,] a feeble Executive implies a feeble execution⁵ of the government. A feeble execution is but another phrase for a bad execution; and a government ill executed, whatever it may be in theory, must be, in practice, a bad government.

---

³ **reformation** change
⁴ **concurrence** agreement
⁵ **execution** plan

▼ James Wilson

The Assembly Room where the U.S. Constitution was signed

DBQ Document-Based Questions

1. **Identifying** According to Wilson, how can the Constitution be changed?

2. **Drawing Conclusions** Why do you think Henry believed that the Constitution would "enslave a free people"?

3. **Analyzing** One of George Mason's objections to the Constitution was that it had no bill of rights. Do you think he objected to it for other reasons? Explain your answer.

4. **Evaluating** Which person do you think argued the most persuasively? Why? Write a paragraph that explains your opinion.

Essential Question ◀

What ideas and features are found in the United States Constitution?

Reading Guide

Content Vocabulary

federalism (p. 206)

legislative branch (p. 207)

executive branch (p. 207)

Electoral College (p. 207)

judicial branch (p. 208)

checks and balances (p. 208)

amendment (p. 210)

Academic Vocabulary

tradition (p. 205)   reside (p. 208)

Key People

John Locke (p. 206)

Baron de Montesquieu (p. 206)

Reading Strategy

Taking Notes As you read, use a chart like the one below to identify ways in which each branch of the federal government can check, or limit, the power of the other branches.

Branch	Example
Executive	
Legislative	
Judicial	

INDIANA ACADEMIC STANDARDS
United States History

8.2.1 Identify and explain essential ideas of constitutional government, which are expressed in the founding documents of the United States, including the Virginia Declaration of Rights, the Declaration of Independence, the Virginia Statute for Religious Freedom, the Massachusetts Constitution of 1780, the Northwest Ordinance, the 1787 U.S. Constitution, the Bill of Rights, the Federalist and Anti-Federalist Papers, *Common Sense,* Washington's Farewell Address (1796), and Jefferson's First Inaugural Address (1801).

American Diary

As Benjamin Franklin was leaving the last session of the Constitutional Congress, a woman asked, "Well Doctor, what have we got: a republic or a monarchy?" Franklin answered, "A republic, if you can keep it." He meant that in order to maintain a republic—a system of government in which the people elect representatives to exercise power for them—citizens must take an active role.

—quoted in the "Papers of Dr. James McHenry, 1787"

The U.S. Constitution on display at the National Archives, Washington, D.C.

Roots of the Constitution

Main Idea As the Framers wrote the Constitution, they borrowed ideas from other political systems and philosophers of the Enlightenment.

History and You Has a person influenced you to do better in school or participate in an activity that helps others? Read to learn about the ideas and thinkers who helped shape the Constitution.

After four long and difficult months, Franklin and the other delegates had produced a new constitution. The document provided the framework for a strong central government for the United States. Although a uniquely American document, the Constitution has roots in many other civilizations. The delegates studied and discussed the history of political thought at length—starting with ancient Greece—so that their new government could avoid the mistakes of the past. Many ideas found in the Constitution came from the study of European political institutions and political writers. British ideas and institutions influenced the delegates.

The Framers who shaped the document were familiar with the parliamentary system of Britain, and many had participated in the colonial assemblies or their state assemblies. They valued the individual rights guaranteed by the British judicial system. Although the Americans broke away from Britain, they respected many British **traditions,** or cultural beliefs and practices.

European Influences

The English Magna Carta (1215) placed limits on the power of the monarch. England's lawmaking body, Parliament, emerged, or became known, as a force that the monarch had to depend on to pay for wars and to finance the royal government. Like Parliament, the colonial assemblies controlled their colonies' funds. For that reason the assemblies had some control over colonial governors. The English Bill of Rights of 1689 provided another model for Americans. Many Americans felt that the Constitution also needed a bill of rights. The Framers of the Constitution believed in the ideas about the nature of people and government promoted by European writers of the Enlightenment. The Enlightenment was a movement of the 1700s that promoted knowledge, reason, and science as a means of improving society.

By the Numbers / The Delegates Talk

Speeches—Long and Short Except for two short breaks, the delegates met six days a week from May to September 1787. Although they met for only five to six hours each day, the heat, the debating, and the sitting often made it feel longer. During the Convention, many delegates gave speeches to share their ideas and knowledge about government. Some delegates gave more speeches than others.

Delegate	Number of Speeches
Gouverneur Morris	173
James Wilson	168
James Madison	161
George Washington	1

Gouverneur Morris ▶

Critical Thinking

Making Generalizations Do you think talking a lot convinces people to listen to you more? Explain.

James Madison and other architects of the Constitution were familiar with the work of **John Locke** and **Baron de Montesquieu** (mahn·tuhs·KYOO), two philosophers of the Enlightenment.

Locke, an English philosopher, believed that all people have natural rights. These natural rights include the rights to life, liberty, and property. In his *Two Treatises of Civil Government* (1690), he wrote that government is based on an agreement, or contract, between the people and the ruler. Many Americans interpreted natural rights to mean the rights of Englishmen defined in the Magna Carta and the English Bill of Rights. The Framers viewed the Constitution as a contract between the American people and their government. The contract protected the people's natural rights by limiting the government's power. In *The Spirit of Laws* (1748), the French writer Montesquieu declared that the powers of government should be separated and balanced against each other. This separation would prevent any single person or group from gaining too much power. The powers of government should also be clearly defined and limited to prevent abuse. Following the ideas of Montesquieu, the Framers of the Constitution carefully specified and divided the powers of government.

The Federal System

The Constitution created a federal system of government that divided powers between the national, or federal, government and the states. In the Articles of Confederation, the states held most powers. Under the Constitution, the states gave up some powers to the federal government and kept others. **Federalism,** or sharing power between the federal and state governments, is one of the distinctive features of the United States government. Under the Constitution, the federal government gained broad powers to tax, regulate trade, control the currency, raise an army, and declare war. It could also pass laws that were "necessary and proper" for carrying out its responsibilities. This power allowed Congress to make laws as needed to deal with new situations.

LINKING PAST to PRESENT The United States Flag

THEN On June 14, 1777, Congress resolved that "the flag of the United States be thirteen stripes, alternate red and white; that the union be thirteen stars, white in a blue field representing a new constellation." Congress, however, did not specify how to arrange the stars. As a result, some flags had stars arranged in a circle, whereas other flags had the stars aligned.

◀ American flag, 1795–1818, had 15 stars and 15 stripes. In 1818 Congress set the number of stripes at 13.

◀ A legend claims that Betsy Ross made the first American flag, but no historical evidence supports this claim.

The Constitution, however, left important powers in the hands of the states. The states had the power to regulate trade within their borders. They also could establish local governments and schools and set marriage and divorce laws.

The Constitution also allows for power to be shared between the federal and state governments. Both federal and state governments have the power to tax and administer criminal justice.

The Supreme Law of the Land

The Constitution and the laws that Congress passed were to be "the supreme law of the land." No state could make laws or take actions that went against the Constitution. Any dispute between the federal government and the states was to be settled by the federal courts on the basis of the Constitution. Under the new federal system, the Constitution became the final and supreme authority.

Reading Check Describing What is the principle of federalism?

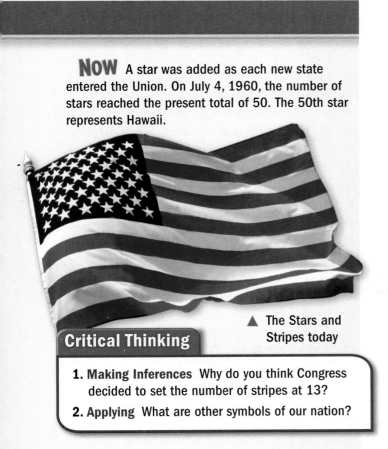

NOW A star was added as each new state entered the Union. On July 4, 1960, the number of stars reached the present total of 50. The 50th star represents Hawaii.

▲ The Stars and Stripes today

Critical Thinking

1. **Making Inferences** Why do you think Congress decided to set the number of stripes at 13?
2. **Applying** What are other symbols of our nation?

The New Government

Main Idea The Constitution divides and limits power among three branches of government.

History and You Do you think government leaders should be limited to what they can or cannot do? Read about the division of powers and responsibilities of government.

• •

Montesquieu's idea of a division of powers led the Framers to divide the federal government into three branches—legislative, executive, and judicial. The first three articles, or parts, of the Constitution describe each branch's powers and responsibilities.

Branches of Government

Article I of the Constitution establishes Congress as the **legislative branch,** or lawmaking branch, of the government. Congress is composed of the House of Representatives and the Senate. As a result of the Great Compromise between large and small states, each state's representation in the House is proportional to its population. Representation in the Senate is equal—two senators for each state. The powers of Congress include collecting taxes, coining money, and regulating trade. Congress also can declare war and "raise and support armies." Finally, it makes all laws needed to fulfill its functions as stated in the Constitution. Memories of King George III's rule made some delegates reluctant to establish a powerful executive, or ruler. Others believed that the Articles of Confederation failed, in part, because it lacked an executive branch. They argued that a strong executive would limit the power of Congress.

Article II of the Constitution established the **executive branch,** headed by the president, to carry out the nation's laws and policies. The president serves as commander in chief of the armed forces and conducts relations with foreign countries. The president and a vice president are elected by a special group called the **Electoral College,** made of presidential electors.

This cartoon was published in 1788, as the state conventions were voting to ratify the new Constitution.

1. **Interpreting** What do the pillars represent?

2. **Synthesizing** What is the significance of the ninth pillar?

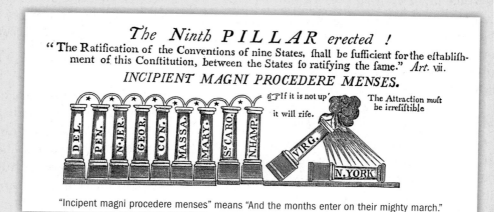

The Ninth PILLAR erected !

" The Ratification of the Conventions of nine States, fhall be fufficient for the eftablifh-ment of this Conftitution, between the States fo ratifying the fame." *Art.* vii.

INCIPIENT MAGNI PROCEDERE MENSES.

If it is not up it will rife.

The Attraction muft be irrefiftible

"Incipent magni procedere menses" means "And the months enter on their mighty march."

Each state's voters select electors to cast their votes for the president and vice president. Every state has the same number of electors as it has senators and representatives in Congress. The president and vice president serve a four-year term.

Article III deals with the **judicial branch,** or court system. The nation's judicial power **resides,** or exists, in "one supreme Court" and any other lower federal courts that Congress might establish. The Supreme Court and the federal courts hear cases involving the Constitution, laws passed by Congress, and disputes between states.

System of Checks and Balances

The Framers built in a system of **checks and balances.** Each branch has ways to check, or limit, the power of the others so that no single branch can dominate the government. Both the House and the Senate must pass a bill for it to become law. The president can check Congress by vetoing, or rejecting, the bill. Congress can check the president by overriding, or voting down, the veto. To override a veto, two-thirds of the members of both houses must vote for the bill.

The system of checks and balances also applies to the Supreme Court. The president appoints Supreme Court justices, and the Senate must approve the appointments. Over time, the Court has become a check on Congress and the president by ruling on the constitutionality of laws and presidential acts. This system has kept a balance of power among the branches and has limited abuses.

National Citizens

The Constitution created citizens who choose their officials—directly or indirectly. Officials answer to the people rather than to the states. The new government pledged to protect the personal freedoms of its citizens. Americans showed the world that it was possible for a people to change its form of government through discussion and choice—rather than through chaos, force, or war. The world watched the new nation to see if its experiment in self-government really would work.

Reading Check **Explaining** What is the purpose of the first three articles of the Constitution?

Debate and Adoption

Main Idea After a much heated debate, the states ratified the Constitution.

History and You How do some people influence a group's decisions more than others? Read how influential leaders helped ratify the Constitution.

. . . .

The delegates produced the Constitution, but before it could go into effect, nine states had to ratify, or approve, it. A great debate then took place throughout the country. In newspapers, at meetings, and in ordinary conversations, Americans discussed the arguments for and against the new Constitution.

Federalists and Antifederalists

Supporters of the new Constitution were called Federalists. Federalists enjoyed the support of two of the most respected men in America—George Washington and Benjamin Franklin. Gifted political thinkers James Madison, Alexander Hamilton, and John Jay also backed the Constitution. Madison, Hamilton, and Jay wrote a series of essays explaining and defending the Constitution. These essays appeared in newspapers around the country. Called the Federalist Papers, they were later published as a book and sent to delegates at state conventions. Jefferson called the essays "the best commentary on the principles of government which was ever written."

People who opposed the Constitution were called Antifederalists. Antifederalists responded to the Federalists by writing their own essays, now known as the Antifederalist Papers. Their main argument was that the strong national government created by the Constitution would take away the liberties Americans had fought for in the war against Great Britain. The government would ignore the will of the states and the people and favor the wealthy few over the common people.

Antifederalists favored local government that was controlled more closely by the people. A central government, they feared, would be made of a small group of individuals.

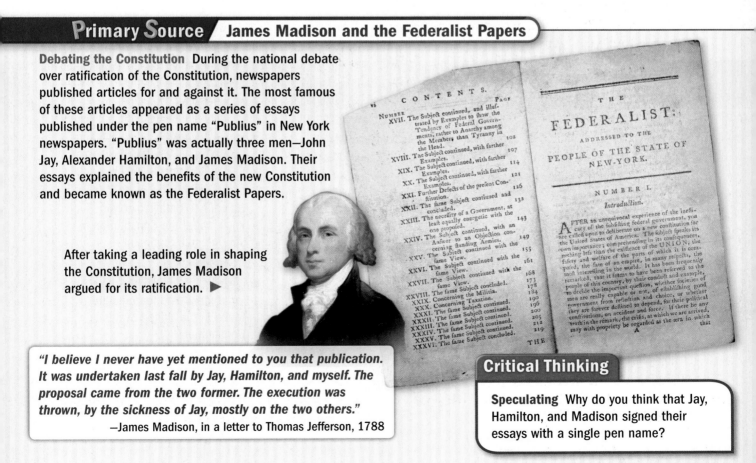

Primary Source / James Madison and the Federalist Papers

Debating the Constitution During the national debate over ratification of the Constitution, newspapers published articles for and against it. The most famous of these articles appeared as a series of essays published under the pen name "Publius" in New York newspapers. "Publius" was actually three men—John Jay, Alexander Hamilton, and James Madison. Their essays explained the benefits of the new Constitution and became known as the Federalist Papers.

After taking a leading role in shaping the Constitution, James Madison argued for its ratification. ▶

"I believe I never have yet mentioned to you that publication. It was undertaken last fall by Jay, Hamilton, and myself. The proposal came from the two former. The execution was thrown, by the sickness of Jay, mostly on the two others."
—James Madison, in a letter to Thomas Jefferson, 1788

Critical Thinking

Speculating Why do you think that Jay, Hamilton, and Madison signed their essays with a single pen name?

They agreed with Patrick Henry, who warned that the Constitution was "incompatible with [contrary to] the genius of republicanism."

Protecting Rights

Perhaps the strongest criticism of the Constitution was that it lacked a bill of rights to protect individual freedoms. Several state conventions announced that they would not ratify it without the addition of a bill of rights. Mercy Otis Warren expressed the problem:

PRIMARY SOURCE

"We have struggled for liberty & made costly sacrifices . . . and there are still many among us who [value liberty] too much to relinquish . . . the rights of man for the Dignity of Government."
—from a letter to Catherine Graham

The Federalists feared disorder without a strong central government. Antifederalists worried about the oppression that might result if power was concentrated in a central government.

Adopting the Constitution

On December 7, 1787, Delaware became the first state to approve the Constitution. By June 21, 1788, the ninth state—New Hampshire—ratified it. In theory, that meant the new government could go into effect. However, without the support of the two largest states—New York and Virginia—the future of the new government was bleak.

In Virginia, Patrick Henry charged that the Constitution did not sufficiently limit the power of the central government. Still, Virginia ratified the Constitution after being assured that it would include a bill of rights amendment. An **amendment** is something added to a document. The Bill of Rights would be added in 1791. In July 1788, New York finally ratified the Constitution, followed by North Carolina in November 1789 and Rhode Island in May 1790. The nation celebrated its new government.

Reading Check **Explaining** Why was it important that New York and Virginia ratify the Constitution?

Section 3 Review

History ONLINE
Study Central™ To review this section, go to glencoe.com.

Vocabulary

1. Use each of these terms in a sentence that will help explain its meaning: tradition, federalism, legislative branch, executive branch, Electoral College, judicial branch, reside, checks and balances, amendment.

Main Ideas

2. **Identifying** What features of the Constitution developed from the ideas of Baron de Montesquieu?

3. **Explaining** Why does the Constitution divide power among branches of government?

4. **Specifying** Why did Virginia eventually ratify the Constitution?

Critical Thinking

5. **Interpreting** If a state law conflicts with a federal law, which law will prevail? How do you know?

6. **Identifying Central Issues** Use a diagram like the one below to summarize the Antifederalist arguments against the Constitution.

7. **Persuasive Writing** Take the role of James Madison. Write an essay for the Federalist Papers, urging ratification of the Constitution. Use details that you know about the Constitution to support your argument.

Answer the
8. **Essential Question**
What ideas and features are found in the United States Constitution?

Visual Summary

The first constitution of the United States was the Articles of Confederation. The United States Constitution, ratified in 1788, replaced the Articles of Confederation and has served as the plan for government ever since.

Articles of Confederation	United States Constitution
Established a weak central government and strong state governments	Created a federal system that divided powers between the national government and state governments
"a firm league of friendship" in which each state retained its "sovereignty, freedom and independence"	"the supreme law of the land"
Congress could: • conduct foreign affairs • maintain armed forces • borrow money • issue currency	Congress can: • issue taxes • regulate trade • control currency • raise an army • declare war • pass laws that are "necessary and proper" to carry out its responsibilities
Congress could not: • regulate trade • force citizens to join the army • impose taxes	States can: • regulate trade within their borders • establish local government schools • set marriage and divorce laws
No chief executive; rule by congressional committees	Three branches of government: • legislative (makes the laws) • executive (carries out the laws) • judicial (interprets the laws) Includes a system of checks and balances so that no branch becomes more powerful than another
One state, one vote	Congress includes: • House of Representatives—number of representatives for each state based on the state's population • Senate—two senators per state
An agreement was needed by 9 of the 13 states to approve a law.	Both the House of Representatives and the Senate must approve a bill for it to become law. The president may approve or veto the bill.

◀ Independence Hall, Philadelphia, Pennsylvania

STUDY TO GO

Study anywhere, anytime! Download quizzes and flash cards to your PDA from glencoe.com.

Reviewing Vocabulary

Directions: Choose the word or words that best completes the sentence.

1 A(n) _____ is a form of government in which citizens rule through elected representatives.

  A ordinance
  B republic
  C petition
  D compromise

2 An agreement in which each side gives up some of what it wants is a(n) _____.

  A convention
  B amendment
  C compromise
  D manumission

3 A system of government in which powers are shared between the national and state governments is referred to as _____.

  A federalism
  B manumission
  C legislative
  D electoral

4 The _____ is composed of the House of Representatives and the Senate.

  A executive branch
  B judicial branch
  C Electoral College
  D legislative branch

Reviewing Main Ideas

Directions: Choose the best answer.

5 Under the Articles of Confederation, Congress did not have the authority to

  A conduct foreign affairs.
  B maintain armed forces.
  C borrow money.
  D force citizens to join the army.

6 Shays's Rebellion erupted when

  A New England merchants refused to pay income taxes.
  B the state of Delaware issued more paper currency.
  C Massachusetts officials seized farmers' lands to pay their debts.
  D the Northwest Ordinance set aside funds for public schools.

7 The Framers of the Constitution wanted to protect people's natural rights, an idea reflected in the work of

  A English philosopher John Locke.
  B French writer Baron de Montesquieu.
  C King George III.
  D Daniel Shays of Massachusetts.

8 In the debate over the ratification of the Constitution, the Federalists most feared

  A too much control from government.
  B the establishment of a state religion.
  C disorder without a strong federal government.
  D a national sales tax.

GO ON

History ONLINE

For additional test practice, use **Self-Check Quizzes**—Chapter 7 at glencoe.com.

Critical Thinking

Directions: Choose the best answer.

9 **Why was the Great Compromise necessary for the creation of the Constitution?**

A It solved the problem of counting enslaved people for representation and taxation.

B It addressed the major disagreement between the large and the small states.

C It suggested a bill of rights to protect individuals' rights.

D It eliminated the slave trade immediately.

Base your answers to questions 10 and 11 on the political cartoon below and your knowledge of Chapter 7.

The Ninth PILLAR erected !

" The Ratification of the Conventions of nine States, fhall be fufficient for the eftablifhment of this Conftitution, between the States fo ratifying the fame." *Art.* vii.

INCIPIENT MAGNI PROCEDERE MENSES.

☞If it is not up it will rife.

The Attraction muft be irrefiftible

Source: The Granger Collection

10 **According to the cartoon, which two states had not yet ratified the Constitution?**

A Delaware and Pennsylvania

B New Hampshire and New Jersey

C Massachusetts and Maryland

D Virginia and New York

11 **Why was the lack of support of these two states a concern for the new government?**

A They were the two largest states.

B Both states disapproved of a bill of rights.

C All 13 states needed to ratify the Constitution for it to go into effect.

D Both states threatened to form separate countries without changes to the Constitution.

Constructed Response

Directions: Write a short response to each of the following questions. In your answer:

- *address all parts of the question*
- *use information from the chapter*
- *include facts, examples, and details relevant to the question*
- *use clear language*

12 **Describe a weakness of the Articles of Confederation.**

13 **Why did the smaller states oppose the Virginia Plan?**

Base your answer to question 14 on the reading below and your knowledge of Chapter 7.

> That [the Constitution] will meet the full and entire [approval] of every state is not perhaps to be expected; but each will doubtless consider, that had her interest been alone consulted, the consequences might have been particularly disagreeable or injurious to others.
>
> —George Washington

14 **Which criticism of the Constitution does Washington address and how does he respond?**

15 **Why did the Framers build a system of checks and balances into the new government?**

STOP

Need Extra Help?															
If you missed questions. . .	1	2	3	4	5	6	7	8	9	10	11	12	13	14	15
Go to page. . .	188	200	206	207	188	195	206	210	200	210	210	189	199	209	208

Constitution Handbook

For more than 200 years, the Constitution has provided the framework for the United States government and has helped preserve the basic rights of American citizens. It is the highest authority in the nation and the basic law of the United States. It is also a symbol of our nation, representing our system of government and our basic ideals, such as liberty and freedom.

Essential Question ◄

Why is citizen participation essential to the preservation of the U.S. political system?

Reading Guide

Content Vocabulary

Preamble (p. 215)

popular sovereignty (p. 215)

republicanism (p. 215)

federalism (p. 216)

enumerated powers (p. 216)

reserved powers (p. 216)

concurrent powers (p. 216)

amend (p. 218)

implied powers (p. 219)

Academic Vocabulary

involve (p. 221)   diminish (p. 223)

Reading Strategy

Taking Notes As you read, use a diagram like the one below to identify the seven major principles on which the Constitution is based.

Federalism

Major Principles

The Constitution

Main Idea The Constitution sets forth the basic principles of government.

History and You What principles do you live by? Read to learn how the basic principles of the Constitution assure the rights of the people.

. . . .

The **Preamble,** or introduction, to the Constitution reflects the basic idea of American government—the right of the people to govern themselves. It also lists six goals for the United States government:

PRIMARY SOURCE

"to form a more perfect Union, establish Justice, insure domestic Tranquility [peace], provide for the common defence, promote the general Welfare, and secure the Blessings of Liberty to ourselves and our Posterity [descendents]."

—United States Constitution

Major Principles

The principles outlined in the Constitution were the Framers' solution to the problems of a representative government. The Constitution rests on seven major principles: (1) popular sovereignty, (2) republicanism, (3) limited government, (4) federalism, (5) separation of powers, (6) checks and balances, and (7) individual rights.

Popular Sovereignty The Declaration of Independence states that governments derive their powers from "the consent of the governed." The opening words of the Constitution, "We the People," reinforce this idea of **popular sovereignty**—or "authority of the people."

Republicanism Under **republicanism,** voters hold sovereign power. The people elect representatives and give them the responsibility to make laws and conduct government. For most Americans today, the terms *republic* and *representative democracy* mean the same thing: a system of limited government in which the people are the ultimate source of governmental power.

Limited Government The Framers saw both benefits and risks in creating a powerful national government. They agreed that the nation needed strong central authority but feared misuse of power. They wanted to prevent the government from using its power to give one group special advantages or to deprive another group of its rights. By creating a limited government, they made certain the government would have only those powers granted by the people.

Article I of the Constitution states the powers that the government has and the powers that it does not have. Other limits on government appear in the Bill of Rights, which guarantees certain rights and liberties to the people.

Limited government can be described as the "rule of law." No person or group of people is above the law. Government officials must obey the law.

Federalism When the states banded together under the Constitution, they gave up some independence. States could no longer print their own money or tax items imported from other states. Nevertheless, each state governed itself much as it had in the past.

This system, in which the power to govern is shared between the national government and the states, is called the federal system, or **federalism.** Our federal system allows the people of each state to deal with their needs in their own way. At the same time, it lets the states act together to deal with matters that affect all Americans.

The Constitution defines three types of government powers. **Enumerated powers** belong only to the federal government. These include the power to coin money, regulate interstate and foreign trade, maintain the armed forces, and create federal courts (Article I, Section 8).

The second kind of powers are those retained by the states, known as **reserved powers.** They include such rights as the power to establish schools, pass marriage and divorce laws, and regulate trade within a state. Although reserved powers are not listed specifically in the Constitution, the Tenth Amendment says that all powers not specifically granted to the federal government "are reserved to the States."

The third set of powers defined by the Constitution are **concurrent powers**—powers shared by the state and federal governments. Among these powers are the right to raise taxes, borrow money, provide for public welfare, and administer criminal justice.

When conflicts arise between state law and federal law, the Constitution declares that the Constitution is "the supreme Law of the Land." Conflicts between state law and federal law must be settled in a federal court.

Separation of Powers To prevent any single group or institution in government from gaining too much authority, the Framers divided the federal government into three branches: legislative, executive, and judicial. Each branch has its own functions and powers. The legislative branch, Congress, makes the laws. The executive branch, headed by the president, carries out the laws. The judicial branch, consisting of the Supreme Court and other federal courts, interprets and applies the laws.

Checks and Balances As an additional safeguard, the Framers established a system of checks and balances in which each branch of government can check, or limit, the power of the other branches. This system helps maintain a balance in the power of the three branches. For example, Congress can pass a

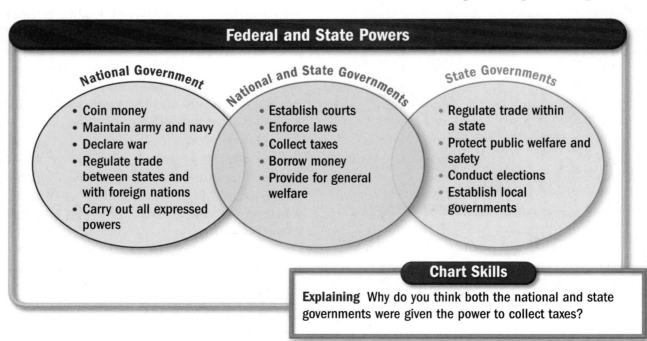

Federal and State Powers

National Government
- Coin money
- Maintain army and navy
- Declare war
- Regulate trade between states and with foreign nations
- Carry out all expressed powers

National and State Governments
- Establish courts
- Enforce laws
- Collect taxes
- Borrow money
- Provide for general welfare

State Governments
- Regulate trade within a state
- Protect public welfare and safety
- Conduct elections
- Establish local governments

Chart Skills

Explaining Why do you think both the national and state governments were given the power to collect taxes?

A System of Checks and Balances

Can impeach president;
Can override veto;
Can reject appointments;
Can refuse to approve treaties

Can impeach judges;
Can reject appointment
of judges

UNITED STATES
CONGRESS

Can veto
legislation

Can declare
acts of legislature
unconstitutional

LEGISLATIVE BRANCH

Can appoint judges

EXECUTIVE BRANCH

Can declare presidential
actions unconstitutional

JUDICIAL BRANCH

Critical Thinking

1. **Describing** How can the judicial branch check the power of the executive branch?
2. **Describing** How can the executive branch check the power of the judicial branch?

law. Then the president can reject the law by vetoing it. However, Congress can override, or reverse, the president's veto if two-thirds of the members of both houses vote again to approve the law.

Over the years, the Supreme Court has acquired the power to determine the meaning of the Constitution and to declare that a law or a government policy goes against the Constitution. In doing so, the Court provides a check on the powers of Congress and the president. Judicial decisions—those made by the courts—can be overruled by amending the Constitution. The president and the Senate provide a check on the judicial branch through their power to appoint and approve federal judges. Congress can also change a law so that it no longer conflicts with the Constitution, or it can amend the Constitution. The Fourteenth Amendment, passed by Congress in 1866, overturned the Supreme Court's rul-

ing in the *Dred Scott* decision, which had ruled that enslaved African Americans were not citizens.

Individual Rights The Bill of Rights became part of the U.S. Constitution in 1791. These first 10 consitutional amendments protect basic liberties and rights that you may have taken for granted—including freedom of speech, freedom of the press, freedom of assembly, freedom of religion, and the right to a trial by jury.

The 17 amendments that follow the Bill of Rights expand the rights of Americans and adjust certain provisions of the Constitution. Included among them are amendments that abolish slavery, define citizenship, guarantee the right to vote to all citizens aged 18 years and older, authorize an income tax, establish the direct election of senators, and set a two-term limit on the presidency.

Many people have come to the United States in search of religious freedom. The principle of religious freedom became rooted in early America as people of different religions learned to live and work together.

In 1777 Thomas Jefferson wrote a resolution on religious freedom that was adopted by the Virginia State legislature in 1786. ▶

The Virginia Statute for Religious Freedom
"No man shall be compelled to frequent or support any religious worship, place, or ministry whatsoever, nor shall be enforced, restrained, molested, or [burdened] in his body or goods, nor shall otherwise suffer on account of his religious opinions or belief; but that all men shall be free to profess, and by argument to maintain, their opinion in matters of religion, and that the same shall in no [way] diminish enlarge, or affect their civil capacities."

—from Thomas Jefferson, "The Virginia Statute for Religious Freedom"

Freedom of religion became one of the principles upon which the United States was founded. In 1791 the First Amendment to the Constitution barred the federal government from establishing a religion or from adopting any law limiting religious freedom.

Critical Thinking

Explaining Why do you think Americans regard religious freedom as an important principle?

A Living Constitution

Two years after the Constitutional Convention, Benjamin Franklin wrote, "Our Constitution is in actual operation; everything appears to promise that it will last; but in this world nothing is certain but death and taxes."

Despite Franklin's uncertainty about the Constitution's future, it is still very much alive today. The Constitution has survived because the Framers wrote a document that the nation could alter and adapt to meet changing needs. The result is a flexible document that can be interpreted in different ways in keeping with the conditions of a particular time. The Constitution's flexibility allows the government to deal with matters the Framers never anticipated—such as regulating nuclear power plants or developing a space program. In addition, the Constitution contains a provision for **amending**—changing or adding to—the document.

Amending the Constitution The Framers intentionally made the amendment process difficult to discourage minor or frequent changes. Although thousands of amendments—changes to the Constitution—have been proposed since 1788, only 27 of them have actually become part of the Constitution.

An amendment can be proposed in two ways: by the vote of two-thirds of both houses of Congress or by two-thirds of the state legislatures asking for a special convention on the amendment. The second method has never been used. Ratification of an amendment requires approval by three-fourths of the states. States ratify amendments by the approval of state legislatures or by special state conventions.

Only the Twenty-first Amendment—which repealed the Eighteenth Amendment, banning the sale of alcoholic beverages—was ratified by state conventions. Voters in each state chose the delegates to the special conventions.

Interpreting the Constitution The Constitution includes two provisions that give Congress the power to act as needed to meet changing conditions. The first of these provisions is what is known as the "elastic clause" (Article I, Section 8). It directs Congress to "make all Laws which shall be necessary and proper" for executing all the powers of government. Congress has interpreted this clause to mean that it has certain

implied powers, powers not specifically defined in the Constitution. Over the years, Congress has drawn on its implied powers to pass laws to deal with the needs of society.

The second provision used to expand congressional authority, the "commerce clause" (Article I, Section 8), gives Congress the power to "regulate Commerce with foreign Nations, and among the several States." Congress has used this clause to expand its powers into a number of areas, such as regulation of the airline industry, radio and television, and nuclear energy.

The process of amending the Constitution and applying its principles in new areas helps keep our government functioning well. In 1974 Barbara Jordan, an African American member of Congress and a constitutional scholar, spoke about her faith in the constitutional process:

PRIMARY SOURCE

"Through the process of amendment, interpretation, and court decision I have finally been included in 'We, the people.' . . . My faith in the Constitution is whole; it is complete; it is total.

—from her speech before the House, July 25, 1974

Reading Check **Explaining** What are reserved powers?

The Federal Government

Main Idea The U.S. federal government has three branches: the legislative branch, the executive branch, and the judicial branch.

History and You Have you ever written to a representative, senator, president, or chief justice? Read to learn about the duties of officials in the different branches of the federal government.
. . . .

The Constitution explains how our federal, or national, government is set up and how it works. The federal government is divided among the three branches: legislative, executive, and judicial.

The Legislative Branch

Congress, the legislative branch, makes laws, imposes taxes, and declares war. It has two parts—the House of Representatives and the Senate. The House of Representatives has 435 voting members and 5 nonvoting delegates from the District of Columbia, Puerto Rico, Guam, American Samoa, and the Virgin Islands. The number of representatives from each state is determined by the state's population. Representatives, who must be at least 25 years old, serve two-year terms.

Women in Congress

Jeannette Rankin
First woman in U.S. Congress (1917)

Firsts Patsy Mink of Hawaii, elected in 1964, became the first Asian American woman and the first woman of color in the U.S. Congress. In 1968 Shirley Chisholm of Brooklyn, New York, was the first African American woman elected to Congress. The first Latino woman elected to Congress was Ileana Ros-Lehtinen of Florida. She was elected in 1988.

Nancy Pelosi
First woman Speaker of the U.S. House (2007) ▶

Critical Thinking

Making Generalizations Does democracy require participation in government by all groups? Explain.

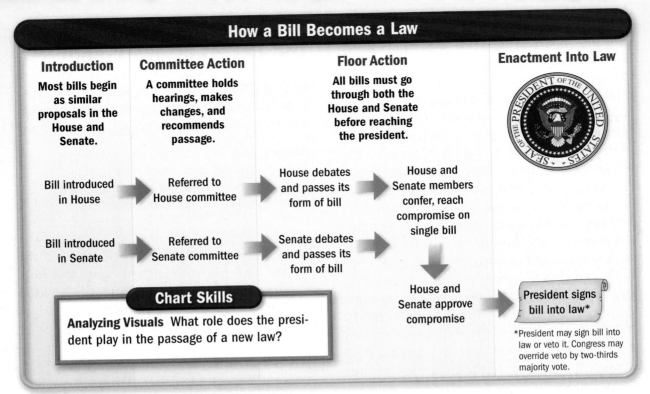

How a Bill Becomes a Law

Introduction

Most bills begin as similar proposals in the House and Senate.

Committee Action

A committee holds hearings, makes changes, and recommends passage.

Floor Action

All bills must go through both the House and Senate before reaching the president.

Enactment Into Law

Bill introduced in House → Referred to House committee → House debates and passes its form of bill → House and Senate members confer, reach compromise on single bill

Bill introduced in Senate → Referred to Senate committee → Senate debates and passes its form of bill →

House and Senate approve compromise → President signs bill into law*

*President may sign bill into law or veto it. Congress may override veto by two-thirds majority vote.

Chart Skills

Analyzing Visuals What role does the president play in the passage of a new law?

The Senate has 100 senators, 2 from each state. Senators, who must be at least 30 years old, serve six-year terms. One-third of Senate seats come up for election every 2 years.

The Role of Congress Congress makes the nation's laws and controls government spending. All tax and spending bills begin in the House of Representatives and are approved in both the House and the Senate before the president signs them into law.

Congress also keeps a check on the actions of the executive branch. The House can impeach, or bring charges against, any federal official suspected of wrongdoing. Officials found guilty may be removed from office. The Senate also holds certain special powers. It can ratify treaties and approve presidential appointments of federal officials.

The Executive Branch

The executive branch carries out the laws passed by Congress. It includes the president, the vice president, and various offices, departments, and agencies.

The President The president carries out the nation's laws with the help of many executive offices, departments, and agencies. As head of the executive branch, the president has the following roles, each with specific powers and duties:

- **Chief Diplomat:** directs foreign policy, appoints ambassadors, and negotiates treaties with other nations.

- **Commander in Chief:** uses the military in crises at home and abroad with congressional approval or declaration of war.

- **Head of State:** representative of all Americans; receives foreign dignitaries; bestows honors on Americans.

- **Legislative Leader:** proposes laws to Congress; sets goals for legislation and working to see that they are passed. In the annual State of the Union address, the president presents goals for legislation. The vice president also serves in the Legislative branch as the President of the Senate.

Cabinet and Vice President The secretaries, or heads, of departments form the cabinet, a group that helps the president set government policy. Members of the cabinet advise the president on issues related to their departments. The Constitution gives the vice president no duties aside from presiding over the Senate. It is the president who determines what the vice president will do, such as working with Congress or making trips abroad.

The Judicial Branch

The Constitution calls for a Supreme Court and the creation of lower courts as Congress wishes. In 1789 Congress passed a Judiciary Act, which added a series of district courts to the federal court system. Appeals, or circuit courts, were added in 1891 to ease the workload of the Supreme Court.

Lower Federal Courts The duties of the lower federal courts are the following:

- **District Courts:** handle civil and criminal cases that come under federal authority; 91 district courts, with at least 1 in every state.

- **Appeals Courts:** review disctrict court decisions; overturn a verdict of the district court or order a retrial; 14 appeals courts in the United States.

The Supreme Court The Supreme Court stands at the top of the American legal system. It is one of the coequal branches of the national government, along with Congress and the president. The Supreme Court is comprised of nine justices: the chief justice of the United States and eight associate justices. Congress has the power to set this number and the power to change it.

The Constitution does not describe the duties of the justices, which have developed from laws and customs in response to national needs. The main duty of the justices is to hear and rule on cases. This duty **involves** them in three tasks: deciding which cases to hear from among thousands of appeals each year; deciding the case itself; and explaining the decision, called the Court's opinion.

The role of the judicial branch has grown as the powers implied in the Constitution have been put into practice. In the 1803 case *Marbury* v. *Madison,* Chief Justice John Marshall expanded Supreme Court powers by striking down an act of Congress. In that decision, the Court defined its right to determine whether a law violates the Constitution. Although not mentioned in the Constitution, this principle, known as judicial review, has become a major power of the judicial branch.

Reading Check **Describing** What is Congress's role in government spending?

The Supreme Court

◄ Seated left to right: Anthony Kennedy, John Paul Stevens, Chief Justice John G. Roberts, Jr., Antonin Scalia, David Souter. Standing left to right: Stephen Breyer, Clarence Thomas, Ruth Bader Ginsburg, Samuel Alito, Jr.

Critical Thinking

Describing Why do you think the number of justices is set an an uneven number?

Rights, Duties, and Responsibilities

Rights	Duties	Responsibilities
Security protection by government **Equality** equal treatment under the law **Liberty** rights guaranteed under the Constitution	• Obey the law • Pay taxes • Defend the nation • Serve in court • Attend school	• Be informed and vote • Participate in your community and government • Respect the rights and property of others • Respect different opinions and ways of life

Chart Skills

Contrasting How do duties differ from responsibilities?

Rights and Citizen Participation

Main Idea U.S. citizenship brings with it certain rights and responsibilities.

History and You Are you a good citizen? What are the rights and responsibilities of citizenship? Read to learn why American citizens have a responsibility to their community, the environment, and the law.

All American citizens have certain basic rights, but they also have specific responsibilities. Living in a democracy means that every citizen is partly responsible for how society is governed and for the actions the government takes on each citizen's behalf.

The Rights of American Citizens

The rights of Americans fall into three broad categories: the right to be protected from unfair government actions, to have equal treatment under the law, and to enjoy basic freedoms.

Due Process The Fifth Amendment states that no person shall "be deprived of life, liberty, or property, without due process of law." Due process of law means that the government must follow procedures established by law and guaranteed by the Constitution, treating all people according to these principles.

Equal Protection All Americans, regardless of race, religion, or political beliefs, have the right to be treated the same under the law.

The Fourteenth Amendment requires every state to grant its citizens "equal protection of the laws."

Basic Freedoms The basic freedoms involve the liberties outlined in the First Amendment—freedom of speech, freedom of religion, freedom of the press, freedom of assembly, and the right to petition. In a democratic society, power exists in the hands of the people. Therefore, its citizens must be able to exchange ideas freely.

Limits on Rights Our rights are not unlimited. The government can establish laws or rules to protect the health, safety, security, and moral standards of a community. Moreover, rights may be limited to prevent one person's rights from interfering with the rights of others. The restrictions of rights, however, must be reasonable and must apply to everyone equally.

Citizen Participation

A citizen is a person who owes loyalty to and is entitled to the protection of a state or nation. How do you become an American citizen? Generally, citizenship is granted to anyone born within the borders of the United States. Citizenship is also granted to anyone born outside of the United States if one parent is a U.S. citizen. A person of foreign birth can become a citizen through the process of naturalization. Before being admitted citizenship, applicants must be willing to give up any foreign allegiance and must promise to obey the Constitution and the laws of the United States.

As citizens of the United States, we are expected to carry out certain duties and responsibilities. Duties are things we are required to do by law. Responsibilities are things we should do. Fulfilling both our duties and our responsibilities helps ensure that we have a good government and that we continue to enjoy our rights.

Duties One of the duties of all Americans is to obey the law. Laws help keep order; protect the health, safety, and property of citizens; and make it possible for people to live together peacefully. If you believe a law needs to be changed, you can work through your elected representatives to improve it.

Americans also have a duty to pay taxes. The government uses tax money for purposes, such as defending the nation, providing health insurance for senior citizens, and building roads and bridges.

Another duty of citizens is to defend the nation. All males aged 18 and older must register with the government in case they are needed for military service.

The Constitution guarantees all Americans the right to a trial by a jury of their peers (equals). For this reason, citizens are often called to serve on juries after they become eligible at the age of 18. Having jurors on hand is necessary to guarantee the right to a fair and speedy trial.

Responsibilities Responsibilities are not as clear-cut as duties. Because responsibilities are voluntary, people are not arrested or punished if they do not fulfill these obligations. The quality of our lives **diminishes** if responsibilities are neglected.

Perhaps your most important responsibility as a citizen will be to vote when you reach the age of 18. Voting allows you to participate in government and guide its direction. When you vote for people in government, you will be exercising your right of self-government. If you disapprove of the job your representatives are doing, you can express your views to them or help elect other people in the next election.

✓ **Reading Check** **Summarizing** What is the difference between a duty and a responsibility?

Constitution Handbook Review

Vocabulary

1. Use each of these terms in a sentence: Preamble, popular sovereignty, republicanism, federalism, enumerated powers, reserved powers, concurrent powers, amend, implied powers, involve, diminish.

Main Ideas

2. **Making Connections** How are popular sovereignty and voting connected?

3. **Explaining** Are the rights of American citizens unlimited? Explain.

Critical Thinking

4. **Evaluating** What is the importance of federalism in the Constitution?

5. **Comparing** Re-create the chart below, and describe how each branch of government has power over another branch.

Branch	Power
Legislative	
Executive	
Judicial	

6. **Expository Writing** Write a short essay summarizing the major principles found in the Preamble.

Answer the
7. **Essential Question**
Why is citizen participation essential to the preservation of the U.S. political system?

The Constitution of the United States

The Constitution of the United States is truly a remarkable document. It was one of the first written constitutions in modern history. The entire text of the Constitution and its amendments follows. For easier study, those passages that have been set aside or changed by the adoption of amendments are printed in blue. Also included are explanatory notes that will help clarify the meaning of important ideas presented in the Constitution.

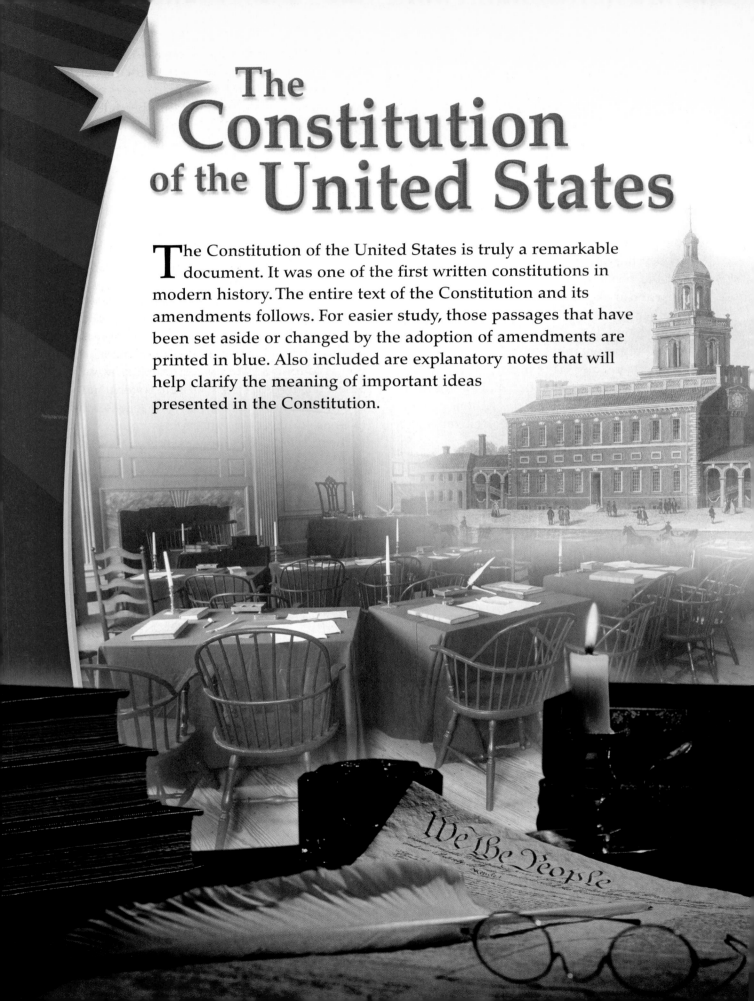

Preamble

We the People of the United States, in Order to form a more perfect Union, establish Justice, insure domestic Tranquility, provide for the common defence, promote the general Welfare, and secure the Blessings of Liberty to ourselves and our Posterity, do ordain and establish this **Constitution** for the United States of America.

Article I

Section 1

All legislative Powers herein granted shall be vested in a Congress of the United States, which shall consist of a Senate and House of Representatives.

Section 2

[1.] The House of Representatives shall be composed of Members chosen every second Year by the People of the several States, and the Electors in each State shall have the Qualifications requisite for Electors of the most numerous Branch of the State Legislature.

[2.] No Person shall be a Representative who shall not have attained the Age of twenty five Years, and been seven Years a Citizen of the United States, and who shall not, when elected, be an Inhabitant of that State in which he shall be chosen.

[3.] Representatives and direct Taxes shall be apportioned among the several States which may be included within this Union, according to their respective Numbers, which shall be determined by adding to the whole Number of free Persons, including those bound to Service for a Term of Years, and excluding Indians not taxed, three fifths of all other Persons. The actual **Enumeration** shall be made within three Years after the first Meeting of the Congress of the United States, and within every subsequent Term of ten Years, in such Manner as they shall by Law direct. The Number of Representatives shall not exceed one for every thirty Thousand, but each State shall have at Least one Representative; and until such enumeration shall be made, the State of New Hampshire shall be entitled to chuse three, Massachusetts eight, Rhode-Island and Providence Plantations one, Connecticut five, New-York six, New Jersey four, Pennsylvania eight, Delaware one, Maryland six, Virginia ten, North Carolina five, South Carolina five, and Georgia three.

[4.] When vacancies happen in the Representation from any State, the Executive Authority thereof shall issue Writs of Election to fill such Vacancies.

[5.] The House of Representatives shall chuse their Speaker and other Officers; and shall have the sole Power of **Impeachment.**

The **Preamble** introduces the Constitution and sets forth the general purposes for which the government was established. The Preamble also declares that the power of the government comes from the people.

The printed text of the document shows the spelling and punctuation of the parchment original.

What It Means

Article I. The Legislative Branch The Constitution contains seven divisions called articles. Each article covers a general topic. For example, Articles I, II, and III create the three branches of the national government—the legislative, executive, and judicial branches. Most of the articles are divided into sections.

What It Means

Representation The number of representatives from each state is based on the size of the state's population. Each state is entitled to at least one representative. *What are the qualifications for members of the House of Representatives?*

Vocabulary

preamble: introduction

constitution: principles and laws of a nation

enumeration: a census or population count

impeachment: the bringing of charges against an official

Electing Senators Originally, senators were chosen by the state legislators of their own states. The Seventeenth Amendment changed this so that senators are now elected by the people. There are 100 senators, 2 from each state. The vice president serves as president of the Senate.

▲ John Adams, the first vice president

Impeachment One of Congress's powers is the power to impeach—to accuse government officials of wrongdoing, put them on trial, and if necessary remove them from office. *Which body has the power to decide the official's guilt or innocence?*

Vocabulary

president pro tempore: the presiding officer of Senate who serves when the vice president is absent

indictment: the charging of a person with an offense

quorum: the minimum number of members that must be present to conduct sessions

adjourn: to suspend a session

emolument: salary

bill: the draft of a proposed law

revenue: income raised by government

Section 3

[1.] The Senate of the United States shall be composed of two Senators from each State, chosen by the Legislature thereof, for six Years; and each Senator shall have one Vote.

[2.] Immediately after they shall be assembled in Consequence of the first Election, they shall be divided as equally as may be into three Classes. The Seats of the Senators of the first Class shall be vacated at the Expiration of the second Year, of the second Class at the Expiration of the fourth Year, and of the third Class at the Expiration of the sixth Year, so that one third may be chosen every second Year; and if Vacancies happen by Resignation, or otherwise, during the Recess of the Legislature of any State, the Executive thereof may make temporary Appointments until the next Meeting of the Legislature, which shall then fill such Vacancies.

[3.] No Person shall be a Senator who shall not have attained to the Age of thirty Years, and been nine Years a Citizen of the United States, and who shall not, when elected, be an Inhabitant of that State for which he shall be chosen.

[4.] The Vice President of the United States shall be President of the Senate, but shall have no Vote, unless they be equally divided.

[5.] The Senate shall chuse their other Officers, and also a **President pro tempore,** in the Absence of the Vice President, or when he shall exercise the Office of the President of the United States.

[6.] The Senate shall have the sole Power to try all Impeachments. When sitting for that Purpose, they shall be on Oath or Affirmation. When the President of the United States is tried, the Chief Justice shall preside: And no Person shall be convicted without the Concurrence of two thirds of the Members present.

[7.] Judgment in Cases of Impeachment shall not extend further than to removal from Office, and disqualification to hold and enjoy any Office of honor, Trust or Profit under the United States: but the Party convicted shall nevertheless be liable and subject to **Indictment,** Trial, Judgment and Punishment, according to Law.

Section 4

[1.] The Times, Places and Manner of holding Elections for Senators and Representatives, shall be prescribed in each State by the Legislature thereof; but the Congress may at any time by Law make or alter such Regulations, except as to the Places of chusing Senators.

[2.] The Congress shall assemble at least once in every Year, and such Meeting shall be on the first Monday in December, unless they shall by Law appoint a different Day.

Section 5

[1.] Each House shall be the Judge of the Elections, Returns and Qualifications of its own Members, and a Majority of each shall constitute a **Quorum** to do Business; but a smaller Number may **adjourn** from day to day, and may be authorized to compel the Attendance of absent Members, in such Manner, and under such Penalties as each House may provide.

[2.] Each House may determine the Rules of its Proceedings, punish its Members for disorderly Behaviour, and, with the Concurrence of two thirds, expel a Member.

[3.] Each House shall keep a Journal of its Proceedings, and from time to time publish the same, excepting such Parts as may in their Judgment require Secrecy; and the Yeas and Nays of the Members of either House on any question shall, at the Desire of one fifth of those Present, be entered on the Journal.

[4.] Neither House, during the Session of Congress, shall, without the Consent of the other, adjourn for more than three days, nor to any other Place than that in which the two Houses shall be sitting.

Section 6

[1.] The Senators and Representatives shall receive a Compensation for their Services, to be ascertained by Law, and paid out of the Treasury of the United States. They shall in all Cases, except Treason, Felony and Breach of the Peace, be privileged from Arrest during their Attendance at the Session of their respective Houses, and in going to and returning from the same; and for any Speech or Debate in either House, they shall not be questioned in any other Place.

[2.] No Senator or Representative shall, during the Time for which he was elected, be appointed to any civil Office under the Authority of the United States, which shall have been created, or the **Emoluments** whereof shall have been encreased during such time; and no Person holding any Office under the United States, shall be a Member of either House during his Continuance in Office.

Section 7

[1.] All **Bills** for raising **Revenue** shall originate in the House of Representatives; but the Senate may propose or concur with Amendments as on other Bills,

[2.] Every Bill which shall have passed the House of Representatives and the Senate, shall, before it become a Law, be presented to the President of the United States: If he approve he shall sign it, but if not he shall return it, with his Objections to that House in which it shall have originated, who shall enter the Objections at large on their Journal, and proceed to reconsider it. If after such Reconsideration two thirds

▲ Congresswoman Nydia Velázquez represents New York's 12th District.

What It Means

Congressional Salaries To strengthen the federal government, the Founders set congressional salaries to be paid by the United States Treasury rather than by members' respective states. Originally, members were paid $6 per day. In 2006 all members of Congress received a base salary of $165,200.

What It Means

Where Tax Laws Begin All tax laws must originate in the House of Representatives. This ensures that the branch of Congress that is elected by the people every two years has the major role in determining taxes.

What It Means

How Bills Become Laws A bill may become a law only by passing both houses of Congress and by being signed by the president. The president can check Congress by rejecting—vetoing—its legislation. *How can Congress override the president's veto?*

of that House shall agree to pass the Bill, it shall be sent, together with the Objections, to the other House, by which it shall likewise be reconsidered, and if approved by two thirds of that House, it shall become a Law. But in all such Cases the Votes of both Houses shall be determined by yeas and Nays, and the Names of the Persons voting for and against the Bill shall be entered on the Journal of each House respectively. If any Bill shall not be returned by the President within ten Days (Sundays excepted) after it shall have been presented to him, the Same shall be a Law, in like Manner as if he had signed it, unless the Congress by their Adjournment prevent its Return, in which Case it shall not be a Law.

[3.] Every Order, **Resolution,** or Vote to which the Concurrence of the Senate and House of Representatives may be necessary (except on a question of Adjournment) shall be presented to the President of the United States; and before the Same shall take Effect, shall be approved by him, or being disapproved by him, shall be repassed by two thirds of the Senate and House of Representatives, according to the Rules and Limitations prescribed in the Case of a Bill.

Section 8

[1.] The Congress shall have the Power To lay and collect Taxes, Duties, **Imposts** and Excises, to pay the Debts and provide for the common Defence and general Welfare of the United States; but all Duties, Imposts and Excises shall be uniform throughout the United States;

[2.] To borrow Money on the credit of the United States;

[3.] To regulate Commerce with foreign Nations, and among the several States, and with the Indian Tribes;

[4.] To establish an uniform Rule of **Naturalization,** and uniform Laws on the subject of Bankruptcies throughout the United States;

[5.] To coin Money, regulate the Value thereof, and of foreign Coin, and fix the Standard of Weights and Measures;

[6.] To provide for the Punishment of counterfeiting the Securities and current Coin of the United States;

[7.] To establish Post Offices and post Roads;

[8.] To promote the Progress of Science and useful Arts, by securing for limited Times to Authors and Inventors the exclusive Right to their respective Writings and Discoveries;

[9.] To constitute **Tribunals** inferior to the supreme Court;

[10.] To define and punish Piracies and Felonies committed on the high Seas, and Offences against the Law of Nations;

[11.] To declare War, grant **Letters of Marque** and **Reprisal,** and make Rules concerning Captures on Land and Water;

[12.] To raise and support Armies, but no Appropriation of Money to that Use shall be for a longer Term than two Years;

[13.] To provide and maintain a Navy;

What It Means

Powers of Congress Expressed powers are those powers directly stated in the Constitution. Most of the expressed powers of Congress are listed in Article I, Section 8. These powers are also called enumerated powers because they are numbered 1–18. *Which clause gives Congress the power to declare war?*

▲ Civil War money

Vocabulary

resolution: legislature's formal expression of opinion

impost: tax

naturalization: procedure by which a citizen of a foreign nation becomes a citizen of the United States

tribunal: a court

letter of marque: authority given to a citizen to outfit an armed ship and use it to attack enemy ships in time of war

reprisal: taking by force property or territory belonging to another country or to its citizens

[14.] To make Rules for the Government and Regulation of the land and naval Forces;

[15.] To provide for calling forth the Militia to execute the Laws of the Union, suppress **Insurrections** and repel Invasions;

[16.] To provide for organizing, arming, and disciplining, the Militia, and for governing such Part of them as may be employed in the Service of the United States, reserving to the States respectively, the Appointment of the Officers, and the Authority of training the Militia according to the discipline prescribed by Congress;

[17.] To exercise exclusive Legislation in all Cases whatsoever, over such District (not exceeding ten Miles square) as may, by Cession of particular States, and the Acceptance of Congress, become the Seat of Government of the United States, and to exercise like Authority over all Places purchased by the Consent of the Legislature of the State in which the Same shall be, for the Erection of Forts, Magazines, Arsenals, dock-Yards, and other needful Buildings;—And

[18.] To make all Laws which shall be necessary and proper for carrying into Execution the foregoing Powers, and all other Powers vested by this Constitution in the Government of the United States, or in any Department or Officer thereof.

Section 9

[1.] The Migration or Importation of such Persons as any of the States now existing shall think proper to admit, shall not be prohibited by the Congress prior to the Year one thousand eight hundred and eight, but a Tax or **duty** may be imposed on such Importation, not exceeding ten dollars for each Person.

[2.] The Privilege of the Writ of Habeas Corpus shall not be suspended, unless when in Cases of Rebellion or Invasion the public Safety may require it.

[3.] No Bill of Attainder or ex post facto Law shall be passed.

[4.] No Capitation, or other direct, Tax shall be laid, unless in Proportion to the Census or enumeration herein before directed to be taken.

[5.] No Tax or Duty shall be laid on Articles exported from any State.

[6.] No Preference shall be given by any Regulation of Commerce or Revenue to the Ports of one State over those of another; nor shall Vessels bound to, or from, one State, be obliged to enter, clear, or pay Duties in another.

[7.] No Money shall be drawn from the Treasury, but in Consequence of **Appropriations** made by Law; and a regular Statement and Account of the Receipts and Expenditures of all public Money shall be published from time to time.

[8.] No Title of Nobility shall be granted by the United States: And no Person holding any Office of Profit or Trust under them, shall, without the Consent of the Congress, accept of any present, Emolument, Office, or Title, of any kind whatever, from any King, Prince, or foreign State.

What It Means

Elastic Clause The final enumerated power is often called the "elastic clause." This clause gives Congress the right to make all laws "necessary and proper" to carry out the powers expressed in the other clauses of **Article I.** It is called the elastic clause because it lets Congress "stretch" its powers to meet situations the Founders could never have anticipated.

What does the phrase **"necessary and proper"** in the elastic clause mean? Almost from the beginning, this phrase was a subject of dispute. The issue was whether a strict or a broad interpretation of the Constitution should be applied. The dispute was first addressed in 1819, in the case of *McCulloch* v. *Maryland*, when the Supreme Court ruled in favor of a broad interpretation.

What It Means

Habeas Corpus A writ of habeas corpus issued by a judge requires a law official to bring a prisoner to court and show cause for holding the prisoner. A bill of attainder is a bill that punished a person without a jury trial. An "ex post facto" law is one that makes an act a crime after the act has been committed. *What does the Constitution say about bills of attainder?*

Vocabulary

insurrection: rebellion

duty: tax

appropriations: funds set aside for a specific use

Limitations on the States Section 10 lists limits on the states. These restrictions were designed, in part, to prevent an overlapping in functions and authority with the federal government.

Section 10

[1.] No State shall enter into any Treaty, Alliance, or Confederation; grant Letters of Marque and Reprisal; coin Money; emit Bills of Credit; make any Thing but gold and silver Coin a Tender in Payment of Debts; pass any Bill of Attainder, ex post facto Law, or Law impairing the Obligation of Contracts, or grant any Title of Nobility.

[2.] No State shall, without the Consent of the Congress, lay any Imposts or Duties on Imports or Exports, except what may be absolutely necessary for executing its inspection Laws: and the net Produce of all Duties and Imposts, laid by any State on Imports or Exports, shall be for the Use of the Treasury of the United States; and all such Laws shall be subject to the Revision and Controul of the Congress.

[3.] No State shall, without the Consent of Congress, lay any Duty of Tonnage, keep Troops, or Ships of War in time of Peace, enter into any Agreement or Compact with another State, or with a foreign Power, or engage in War, unless actually invaded, or in such imminent Danger as will not admit of delay.

Article II

Article II. The Executive Branch Article II creates an executive branch to carry out laws passed by Congress. Article II lists the powers and duties of the presidency, describes qualifications for office and procedures for electing the president, and provides for a vice president.

Section 1

[1.] The executive Power shall be vested in a President of the United States of America. He shall hold his Office during the Term of four Years, and, together with the Vice President, chosen for the same Term, be elected, as follows:

[2.] Each State shall appoint, in such Manner as the Legislature thereof may direct, a Number of Electors, equal to the whole Number of Senators and Representatives to which the State may be entitled in the Congress: but no Senator or Representative, or Person holding an Office of Trust or Profit under the United States, shall be appointed an Elector.

[3.] The Electors shall meet in their respective States, and vote by Ballot for two Persons, of whom one at least shall not be an Inhabitant of the same State with themselves. And they shall make a List of all the Persons voted for, and of the Number of Votes for each; which List they shall sign and certify, and transmit sealed to the Seat of the Government of the United States, directed to the President of the Senate. The President of the Senate shall, in the Presence of the Senate and House of Representatives, open all the Certificates, and the Votes shall then be counted. The Person having the greatest Number of Votes shall be the President, if such Number be a Majority of the whole Number of Electors appointed; and if there be more than one who have such Majority, and have an equal Number of Votes, then the House of Representatives shall immediately chuse by Ballot one of them for President; and if no person have a Majority,

▲ **United States coins**

then from the five highest on the List the said House shall in like Manner chuse the President. But in chusing the President, the Votes shall be taken by States, the Representation from each State having one Vote; A quorum for this Purpose shall consist of a Member or Members from two thirds of the States, and a Majority of all the States shall be necessary to a Choice. In every Case, after the Choice of the President, the Person having the greatest Number of Votes of the Electors shall be the Vice President. But if there should remain two or more who have equal Votes, the Senate shall chuse from them by Ballot the Vice President.

[4.] The Congress may determine the Time of chusing the Electors, and the Day on which they shall give their Votes; which Day shall be the same throughout the United States.

[5.] No Person except a natural born Citizen, or a Citizen of the United States, at the time of the Adoption of this Constitution, shall be eligible to the Office of President; neither shall any Person be eligible to that Office who shall not have attained to the Age of thirty five Years, and been fourteen Years a Resident within the United States.

[6.] In Case of the Removal of the President from Office, or of his Death, Resignation, or Inability to discharge the Powers and Duties of the said Office, the Same shall devolve on the Vice President, and the Congress may by Law provide for the Case of Removal, Death, Resignation or Inability, both of the President and Vice President, declaring what Officer shall then act as President, and such Officer shall act accordingly, until the Disability be removed, or a President shall be elected.

[7.] The President shall, at stated Times, receive for his Services, a Compensation, which shall neither be increased nor diminished during the Period for which he shall have been elected, and he shall not receive within that Period any other Emolument from the United States, or any of them.

[8.] Before he enter on the Execution of his Office, he shall take the following Oath or Affirmation:—"I do solemnly swear (or affirm) that I will faithfully execute the Office of President of the United States, and will to the best of my Ability, preserve, protect and defend the Constitution of the United States."

Section 2

[1.] The President shall be Commander in Chief of the Army and Navy of the United States, and of the Militia of the several States, when called into the actual Service of the United States; he may require the Opinion, in writing, of the principal Officer in each of the executive Departments, upon any Subject relating to the Duties of their respective Offices, and he shall have Power to grant Reprieves and Pardons for Offences against the United States, except in Cases of Impeachment.

What It Means

Previous Elections The Twelfth Amendment, added in 1804, changed the method of electing the president stated in Article II, Section 3. The Twelfth Amendment requires that the electors cast separate ballots for president and vice president.

What It Means

Qualifications The president must be a citizen of the United States by birth, at least 35 years of age, and a resident of the United States for 14 years.

What It Means

Vacancies If the president dies, resigns, is removed from office by impeachment, or is unable to carry out the duties of the office, the vice president becomes president. The Twenty-fifth Amendment sets procedures for presidential succession.

What It Means

Salary Originally, the president's salary was $25,000 per year. The president's current salary is $400,000 plus a $50,000 nontaxable expense account per year. The president also receives living accommodations in two residences—the White House and Camp David.

What It Means

The Cabinet Mention of "the principal officer in each of the executive departments" is the only suggestion of the president's cabinet to be found in the Constitution. The cabinet is an advisory body, and its power depends on the president. Section 2, Clause 1, also makes the president—a civilian—the head of the armed services. This established the principle of civilian control of the military.

Presidential Powers An executive order is a command issued by a president to exercise a power which he or she has been given by the U.S. Constitution or by a federal statute. In times of emergency, presidents sometimes have used the executive order to override the Constitution of the United States and the Congress. During the Civil War, President Lincoln suspended many fundamental rights guaranteed in the Constitution and the Bill of Rights. He closed down newspapers that opposed his policies and imprisoned some who disagreed with him. Lincoln said that these actions were justified to preserve the Union.

Article III. The Judicial Branch The term "judicial" refers to courts. The Constitution set up only the Supreme Court but provided for the establishment of other federal courts. The judiciary of the United States has two different systems of courts. One system consists of the federal courts, whose powers derive from the Constitution and federal laws. The other includes the courts of each of the 50 states, whose powers derive from state constitutions and laws.

Statute Law Federal courts deal mostly with "statute law," or laws passed by Congress, treaties, and cases involving the Constitution itself.

[2.] He shall have Power, by and with the Advice and Consent of the Senate, to make Treaties, provided two thirds of the Senators present concur; and he shall nominate, and by and with the Advice and Consent of the Senate, shall appoint Ambassadors, other public Ministers and Consuls, Judges of the supreme Court, and all other Officers of the United States, whose Appointments are not herein otherwise provided for, and which shall be established by Law: but the Congress may by Law vest the Appointment of such inferior Officers, as they think proper, in the President alone, in the Courts of Law, or in the Heads of Departments.

[3.] The President shall have Power to fill up all Vacancies that may happen during the Recess of the Senate, by granting Commissions which shall expire at the End of their next Session.

Section 3

He shall from time to time give to the Congress Information of the State of the Union, and recommend to their Consideration such Measures as he shall judge necessary and expedient; he may, on extraordinary Occasions, convene both Houses, or either of them, and in Case of Disagreement between them, with Respect to the Time of Adjournment, he may adjourn them to such Time as he shall think proper; he shall receive Ambassadors and other public Ministers; he shall take Care that the Laws be faithfully executed, and shall Commission all the Officers of the United States.

Section 4

The President, Vice President and all civil Officers of the United States, shall be removed from Office on Impeachment for, and Conviction of, Treason, Bribery, or other high Crimes and Misdemeanors.

Article III

Section 1

The judicial Power of the United States shall be vested in one supreme Court, and in such inferior Courts as the Congress may from time to time ordain and establish. The Judges, both of the supreme and inferior Courts, shall hold their Offices during good Behaviour, and shall, at stated Times, receive for their Services a Compensation, which shall not be diminished during their Continuance in Office.

Section 2

[1.] The judicial Power shall extend to all Cases, in Law and Equity, arising under this Constitution, the Laws of the United States, and Treaties made, or which shall be made, under their Authority;—to all Cases affecting Ambassadors, other public Ministers and Consuls;—to all Cases of admiralty and maritime Jurisdiction;—to Controversies to which the United States shall be a Party;—to Controversies between two or more States;—between a State and Citizens of another State;—between Citizens of different States;—between Citizens of the same State claiming Lands under Grants of different States, and between a State, or the Citizens thereof, and foreign States, Citizens or Subjects.

[2.] In all Cases affecting Ambassadors, other public Ministers and Consuls, and those in which a State shall be Party, the supreme Court shall have **original Jurisdiction.** In all the other Cases before mentioned, the supreme Court shall have **appellate Jurisdiction,** both as to Law and Fact, with such Exceptions, and under such Regulations as the Congress shall make.

[3.] The Trial of all Crimes, except in Cases of Impeachment, shall be by Jury; and such Trial shall be held in the State where the said Crimes shall have been committed; but when not committed within any State, the Trial shall be at such Place or Places as the Congress may by Law have directed.

Section 3

[1.] **Treason** against the United States, shall consist only in levying War against them, or in adhering to their Enemies, giving them Aid and Comfort. No Person shall be convicted of Treason unless on the Testimony of two Witnesses to the same overt Act, or on Confession in open Court.

[2.] The Congress shall have Power to declare the Punishment of Treason, but no Attainder of Treason shall work Corruption of Blood, or Forfeiture except during the Life of the Person attainted.

Article IV

Section 1

Full Faith and Credit shall be given in each State to the public Acts, Records, and judicial Proceedings of every other State. And the Congress may by general Laws prescribe the Manner in which such Acts, Records and Proceedings shall be proved, and the Effect thereof.

Section 2

[1.] The Citizens of each State shall be entitled to all Privileges and Immunities of Citizens in the several States.

[2.] A Person charged in any State with Treason, Felony, or other Crime, who shall flee from Justice, and be found in another State, shall on Demand of the executive Authority of the State from which he fled, be delivered up, to be removed to the State having Jurisdiction of the Crime.

[3.] No Person held to Service of Labour in one State, under the Laws thereof, escaping into another, shall, in Consequence of any Law or Regulation therein, be discharged from such Service or Labour, but shall be delivered up on Claim of the Party to whom such Service or Labour may be due.

What It Means

The Supreme Court A court with "original jurisdiction" has the authority to be the first court to hear a case. The Supreme Court has "appellate jurisdiction" and mostly hears cases appealed from lower courts.

What It Means

Article IV. Relations Among the States Article IV explains the relationship of the states to one another and to the national government. This article requires each state to give citizens of other states the same rights as its own citizens, addresses admitting new states, and guarantees that the national government will protect the states.

Vocabulary

original jurisdiction: authority to be the first court to hear a case

appellate jurisdiction: authority to hear cases that have been appealed from lower courts

treason: violation of the allegiance owed by a person to his or her own country, for example, by aiding an enemy

Section 3

[1.] New States may be admitted by the Congress into this Union; but no new State shall be formed or erected within the Jurisdiction of any other State; nor any State be formed by the Junction of two or more States, or Parts of States, without the Consent of the Legislatures of the States concerned as well as of the Congress.

[2.] The Congress shall have Power to dispose of and make all needful Rules and Regulations respecting the Territory or other Property belonging to the United States; and nothing in this Constitution shall be so construed as to Prejudice any Claims of the United States, or of any particular State.

Section 4

The United States shall guarantee to every State in this Union a Republican Form of Government, and shall protect each of them against Invasion; and on Application of the Legislature, or of the Executive (when the Legislature cannot be convened), against domestic Violence.

Article V

The Congress, whenever two thirds of both Houses shall deem it necessary, shall propose **Amendments** to this Constitution, or, on the Application of the Legislatures of two thirds of the several States, shall call a Convention for proposing Amendments, which, in either Case, shall be valid to all Intents and Purposes, as Part of this Constitution, when ratified by the Legislatures of three fourths of the several States, or by Conventions in three fourths thereof, as the one or the other Mode of **Ratification** may be proposed by the Congress; Provided that no Amendment which may be made prior to the Year One thousand eight hundred and eight shall in any Manner affect the first and fourth Clauses in the Ninth Section of the first Article; and that no State, without its Consent, shall be deprived of its equal Suffrage in the Senate.

Article VI

[1.] All Debts contracted and Engagements entered into, before the Adoption of this Constitution, shall be as valid against the United States under this Constitution, as under the Confederation.

[2.] This Constitution, and the Laws of the United States which shall be made in Pursuance thereof; and all Treaties made, or which shall be made, under the Authority of the United States, shall be the supreme Law of the Land; and the Judges in every State shall be bound thereby, any Thing in the Constitution or Laws of any State to the Contrary notwithstanding.

[3.] The Senators and Representatives before mentioned, and the Members of the several State Legislatures, and all executive

---

What It Means

Republic Government can be classified in many different ways. The ancient Greek philosopher Aristotle classified government based on the question: Who governs? According to Aristotle, all governments belong to one of three major groups: (1) autocracy—rule by one person; (2) oligarchy—rule by a few persons; or (3) democracy—rule by many persons. A republic is a form of democracy in which the people elect representatives to make the laws and conduct government.

What It Means

Article VI. National Supremacy Article VI contains the "supremacy clause." This clause establishes that the Constitution, laws passed by Congress, and treaties of the United States "shall be the supreme Law of the Land." The "supremacy clause" recognized the Constitution and federal laws as supreme when in conflict with those of the states.

Vocabulary

amendment: a change to the Constitution
ratification: the process by which an amendment is approved

and judicial Officers, both of the United States and of the several States, shall be bound by Oath or Affirmation, to support this Constitution; but no religious Test shall ever be required as a Qualification to any Office or public Trust under the United States.

Article VII

The Ratification of the Conventions of nine States, shall be sufficient for the Establishment of this Constitution between the States so ratifying the Same.

Done in Convention by the Unanimous Consent of the States present the Seventeenth Day of September in the Year of our Lord one thousand seven hundred and Eighty seven and of the Independence of the United States of America the Twelfth. In witness whereof We have hereunto subscribed our Names,

What It Means

Article VII. Ratification Article VII addresses ratification and declares that the Constitution would take effect after it was ratified by nine states.

Signers

George Washington,
President and Deputy
from Virginia

New Hampshire
John Langdon
Nicholas Gilman

Massachusetts
Nathaniel Gorham
Rufus King

Connecticut
William Samuel Johnson
Roger Sherman

New York
Alexander Hamilton

New Jersey
William Livingston
David Brearley
William Paterson
Jonathan Dayton

Pennsylvania
Benjamin Franklin
Thomas Mifflin
Robert Morris
George Clymer
Thomas FitzSimons
Jared Ingersoll
James Wilson
Gouverneur Morris

Delaware
George Read
Gunning Bedford, Jr.
John Dickinson
Richard Bassett
Jacob Broom

Maryland
James McHenry
Daniel of
　St. Thomas Jenifer
Daniel Carroll

Virginia
John Blair
James Madison, Jr.

North Carolina
William Blount
Richard Dobbs Spaight
Hugh Williamson

South Carolina
John Rutledge
Charles Cotesworth
　Pinckney
Charles Pinckney
Pierce Butler

Georgia
William Few
Abraham Baldwin

Attest:
William Jackson, Secretary

The Amendments This part of the Constitution consists of amendments. The Constitution has been amended 27 times throughout the nation's history.

What It Means

The Bill of Rights The first 10 amendments are known as the Bill of Rights (1791). These amendments limit the powers of government. The First Amendment protects the civil liberties of individuals in the United States. The amendment freedoms are not absolute, however. They are limited by the rights of other individuals. *What freedoms does the First Amendment protect?*

Vocabulary

quarter: to provide living accommodations

warrant: a document that gives police particular rights or powers

probable cause: a reasonable basis to believe a person is linked to a crime

Amendment I

Congress shall make no law respecting an establishment of religion, or prohibiting the free exercise thereof; or abridging the freedom of speech, or of the press; or the right of the people peaceably to assemble, and to petition the Government for a redress of grievances.

Amendment II

A well regulated Militia, being necessary to the security of a free State, the right of the people to keep and bear Arms, shall not be infringed.

Amendment III

No Soldier shall, in time of peace be **quartered** in any house, without the consent of the Owner, nor in time of war, but in a manner to be prescribed by law.

Amendment IV

The right of the people to be secure in their persons, houses, papers, and effects, against unreasonable searches and seizures, shall not be violated, and no **Warrants** shall issue, but upon **probable cause,** supported by Oath or affirmation, and particularly describing the place to be searched, and the persons or things to be seized.

Amendment V

No person shall be held to answer for a capital, or otherwise infamous crime, unless on a presentment or indictment of a Grand Jury, except in cases arising in the land or naval forces, or in the Militia, when in actual service in time of War or public danger; nor shall any person be subject for the same offence to be twice put in jeopardy of life or limb; nor shall be compelled in any criminal case to be a witness against himself, nor be deprived of life, liberty, or property, without due process of law; nor shall private property be taken for public use, without just compensation.

Amendment VI

In all criminal prosecutions, the accused shall enjoy the right to a speedy and public trial, by an impartial jury of the State and district wherein the crime shall have been committed, which district shall have been previously ascertained by law, and to be informed of the nature and cause of the accusation; to be confronted with the witnesses against him; to have compulsory process for obtaining witnesses in his favor, and to have the Assistance of Counsel for his defence.

Amendment VII

In Suits at **common law,** where the value in controversy shall exceed twenty dollars, the right of trial by jury shall be preserved, and no fact tried by a jury, shall be otherwise re-examined in any Court of the United States, than according to the rules of common law.

Amendment VIII

Excessive **bail** shall not be required, nor excessive fines imposed, nor cruel and unusual punishments inflicted.

Amendment IX

The enumeration in the Constitution, of certain rights, shall not be construed to deny or disparage others retained by the people.

What It Means

Powers Reserved to the People This amendment prevents government from claiming that the only rights people have are those listed in the Bill of Rights.

Amendment X

The powers not delegated to the United States by the Constitution, nor prohibited by it to the States, are reserved to the States respectively, or to the people.

What It Means

Powers Reserved to the States The final amendment of the Bill of Rights protects the states and the people from an all-powerful federal government. It establishes that powers not given to the national government—or denied to the states—by the Constitution belong to the states or to the people.

Amendment XI

The Judicial power of the United States shall not be construed to extend to any suit in law or equity, commenced or prosecuted against one of the United States by Citizens of another State, or by Citizens or Subjects of any Foreign State.

What It Means

Suits Against States The Eleventh Amendment (1795) limits the jurisdiction of the federal courts. The Supreme Court had ruled that a federal court could try a lawsuit brought by citizens of South Carolina against the state of Georgia. This case, *Chisholm* v. *Georgia*, decided in 1793, raised a storm of protest, leading to passage of the Eleventh Amendment.

Amendment XII

The electors shall meet in their respective states and vote by ballot for President and Vice-President, one of whom, at least, shall not be an inhabitant of the same state with themselves; they shall name in their ballots the person voted for as President, and in distinct ballots the person voted for as Vice-President, and they shall make distinct lists of all persons voted for as President, and of all persons voted for as Vice-President, and of the number of votes for each, which lists they shall sign and certify, and transmit sealed to the seat of the government of the United States, directed to the President of the Senate;—The President of the Senate shall, in the presence of the Senate and House of Representatives, open all the certificates and the votes shall then be counted;—The person

Vocabulary

common law: law established by previous court decisions

bail: money that an accused person provides to the court as a guarantee that he or she will be present for a trial

Election of President and Vice President The Twelfth Amendment (1804) corrects a problem that had arisen in the method of electing the president and vice president. This amendment provides for the Electoral College to use separate ballots in voting for president and vice president. *If no candidate receives a majority of the electoral votes, who elects the president?*

Abolition of Slavery Amendments Thirteen (1865), Fourteen (1868), and Fifteen (1870) often are called the Civil War amendments because they grew out of that great conflict. The Thirteenth Amendment outlaws slavery.

Rights of Citizens The Fourteenth Amendment (1868) originally was intended to protect the legal rights of the freed slaves. Today it protects the rights of citizenship in general by prohibiting a state from depriving any person of life, liberty, or property without "due process of law." In addition, it states that all citizens have the right to equal protection of the law in all states.

Vocabulary

majority: more than half

devolve: to pass on

abridge: to reduce

having the greatest number of votes for President, shall be the President, if such number be a majority of the whole number of Electors appointed; and if no person have such majority, then from the persons having the highest numbers not exceeding three on the list of those voted for as President, the House of Representatives shall choose immediately, by ballot, the President. But in choosing the President, the votes shall be taken by states, the representation from each state having one vote; a quorum for this purpose shall consist of a member or members from two-thirds of the states, and a **majority** of all the states shall be necessary to a choice. And if the House of Representatives shall not choose a President whenever the right of choice shall **devolve** upon them, before the fourth day of March next following, then the Vice-President shall act as President, as in the case of the death or other constitutional disability of the President. The person having the greatest number of votes as Vice-President, shall be the Vice-President, if such number be a majority of the whole number of Electors appointed, and if no person have a majority, then from the two highest numbers on the list, the Senate shall choose the Vice-President; a quorum for the purpose shall consist of two-thirds of the whole number of Senators, and a majority of the whole number shall be necessary to a choice. But no person constitutionally ineligible to the office of President shall be eligible to that of Vice-President of the United States.

Amendment XIII

Section 1

Neither slavery nor involuntary servitude, except as a punishment for crime whereof the party shall have been duly convicted, shall exist within the United States, or any place subject to their jurisdiction.

Section 2

Congress shall have power to enforce this article by appropriate legislation.

Amendment XIV

Section 1

All persons born or naturalized in the United States, and subject to the jurisdiction thereof, are citizens of the United States and of the State wherein they reside. No State shall make or enforce any law which shall **abridge** the privileges or immunities of citizens of the United States; nor shall any State deprive any person of life, liberty, or property, without due process of law; nor deny to any person within its jurisdiction the equal protection of the laws.

Section 2

Representatives shall be apportioned among the several States according to their respective numbers, counting the whole number of persons in each State, excluding Indians not taxed. But when the right to vote at any election for the choice of electors for President and Vice-President of the United States, Representatives in Congress, the Executive and Judicial officers of a State, or the members of the Legislature thereof, is denied to any of the male inhabitants of such State, being twenty-one years of age, and citizens of the United States, or in any way abridged, except for participation in rebellion, or other crime, the basis of representation therein shall be reduced in the proportion which the number of such male citizens shall bear to the whole number of male citizens twenty-one years of age in such State.

Section 3

No person shall be a Senator or Representative in Congress, or elector of President and Vice-President, or hold any office, civil or military, under the United States, or under any State, who, having previously taken an oath, as a member of Congress, or as an officer of the United States, or as a member of any State legislature, or as an executive or judicial officer of any State, to support the Constitution of the United States, shall have engaged in **insurrection** or rebellion against the same, or given aid or comfort to the enemies thereof. But Congress may by a vote of two-thirds of each House, remove such disability.

Section 4

The validity of the public debt of the United States, authorized by law, including debts incurred for payment of pensions and bounties for service in suppressing insurrection or rebellion, shall not be questioned. But neither the United States nor any State shall assume or pay any debt or obligation incurred in aid of insurrection or rebellion against the United States, or any claim for the loss or **emancipation** of any slave; but all such debts, obligations and claims shall be held illegal and void.

Section 5

The Congress shall have power to enforce, by appropriate legislation, the provisions of this article.

What It Means

Representation in Congress This section reduced the number of members a state had in the House of Representatives if it denied its citizens the right to vote. Later civil rights laws and the Twenty-fourth Amendment guaranteed the vote to African Americans.

What It Means

Penalty for Engaging in Insurrection The leaders of the Confederacy were barred from state or federal offices unless Congress agreed to remove this ban. By the end of Reconstruction all but a few Confederate leaders were allowed to return to public life.

What It Means

Public Debt The public debt acquired by the federal government during the Civil War was valid and could not be questioned by the South. However, the debts of the Confederacy were declared to be illegal. *Could former slaveholders collect payment for the loss of their slaves?*

Vocabulary

insurrection: rebellion against the government

emancipation: freedom from slavery

Amendment XV

Section 1

The right of citizens of the United States to vote shall not be denied or abridged by the United States or by any State on account of race, color, or previous condition of servitude.

Section 2

The Congress shall have power to enforce this article by appropriate legislation.

Amendment XVI

The Congress shall have power to lay and collect taxes on incomes, from whatever source derived, without **apportionment** among the several States, and without regard to any census or enumeration.

Amendment XVII

Section 1

The Senate of the United States shall be composed of two Senators from each State, elected by the people thereof, for six years; and each Senator shall have one vote. The electors in each State shall have the qualifications requisite for electors of the most numerous branch of the State legislatures.

Section 2

When vacancies happen in the representation of any State in the Senate, the executive authority of such State shall issue writs of election to fill such vacancies: *Provided,* That the legislature of any State may empower the executive thereof to make temporary appointments until the people fill the vacancies by election as the legislature may direct.

Section 3

This amendment shall not be so construed as to affect the election or term of any Senator chosen before it becomes valid as part of the Constitution.

Amendment XVIII

Section 1

After one year from ratification of this article, the manufacture, sale, or transportation of intoxicating liquors within, the importation thereof into, or the exportation

Vocabulary

apportionment: the distribution of seats in the House based on population thereof from the United States and all territory subject to the jurisdiction thereof for beverage purposes is hereby prohibited.

Section 2

The Congress and the several States shall have concurrent power to enforce this article by appropriate legislation.

Section 3

This article shall be inoperative unless it shall have been ratified as an amendment to the Constitution by the legislatures of the several States, as provided in the Constitution, within seven years from the date of the submission hereof to the States by the Congress.

Amendment XIX

Section 1

The right of citizens of the United States to vote shall not be denied or abridged by the United States or by any State on account of sex.

Section 2

Congress shall have power by appropriate legislation to enforce the provisions of this article.

Amendment XX

Section 1

The terms of the President and Vice President shall end at noon on the 20th day of January, and the terms of the Senators and Representatives at noon on the 3d day of January, of the years in which such terms would have ended if this article had not been ratified; and the terms of their successors shall then begin.

Section 2

The Congress shall assemble at least once in every year, and such meeting shall begin at noon on the 3d day of January, unless they shall by law appoint a different day.

Section 3

If, at the time fixed for the beginning of the term of the President, the **President elect** shall have died, the Vice President elect shall become President. If a President shall not have been chosen before the time fixed for the beginning of his term, or if the President elect shall have failed to qualify, then the Vice President elect shall act as President until a President shall have qualified; and the Congress may by law

What It Means

Woman Suffrage The Nineteenth Amendment (1920) guaranteed women the right to vote. By then women had already won the vote in many state elections, but the amendment made their right to vote in all state and national elections constitutional.

What It Means

"Lame Duck" The Twentieth Amendment (1933) set new dates for Congress to begin its term and for the inauguration of the president and vice president. Under the original Constitution, elected officials who retired or who had been defeated remained in office for several months. For the outgoing president, this period ran from November until March. Such outgoing officials, referred to as "lame ducks," could accomplish little. *What date was fixed as Inauguration Day?*

Vocabulary

president elect: the individual who is elected president but has not yet begun serving his or her term provide for the case wherein neither a President elect nor a Vice President elect shall have qualified, declaring who shall then act as President, or the manner in which one who is to act shall be selected, and such person shall act accordingly until a President or Vice President shall have qualified.

Section 4

The Congress may by law provide for the case of the death of any of the persons from whom the House of Representatives may choose a President whenever the right of choice shall have devolved upon them, and for the case of the death of any of the persons from whom the Senate may choose a Vice President whenever the right of choice shall have devolved upon them.

Section 5

Sections 1 and 2 shall take effect on the 15th day of October following the ratification of this article.

Section 6

This article shall be inoperative unless it shall have been ratified as an amendment to the Constitution by the legislatures of three-fourths of the several States within seven years from the date of its submission.

Amendment XXI

Section 1

The eighteenth article of amendment to the Constitution of the United States is hereby repealed.

Section 2

The transportation or importation into any State, Territory, or Possession of the United States for delivery or use therein of intoxicating liquors, in violation of the laws thereof, is hereby prohibited.

Section 3

This article shall be inoperative unless it shall have been ratified as an amendment to the Constitution by conventions in the several States, as provided in the Constitution, within seven years from the date of the submission hereof to the States by the Congress.

Amendment XXII

Section 1

No person shall be elected to the office of the President more than twice, and no person who has held the office of

President, or acted as President, for more than two years of a term to which some other person was elected President shall be elected to the office of the President more than once. But this Article shall not apply to any person holding the office of President when this Article was proposed by the Congress, and shall not prevent any person who may be holding the office of President, or acting as President, during the term within which this Article becomes operative from holding the office of President or acting as President during the remainder of such term.

Section 2

This article shall be inoperative unless it shall have been ratified as an amendment to the Constitution by the legislatures of three-fourths of the several States within seven years from the date of its submission to the States by the Congress.

Amendment XXIII

Section 1

The **District** constituting the seat of Government of the United States shall appoint in such manner as the Congress may direct:

A number of electors of President and Vice President equal to the whole number of Senators and Representatives in Congress to which the District would be entitled if it were a State, but in no event more than the least populous State; they shall be in addition to those appointed by the States, but they shall be considered, for the purposes of the election of President and Vice President, to be electors appointed by a State; and they shall meet in the District and perform such duties as provided by the twelfth article of amendment.

Section 2

The Congress shall have power to enforce this article by appropriate legislation.

Amendment XXIV

Section 1

The right of citizens of the United States to vote in any primary or other election for President or Vice President, for electors for President or Vice President, or for Senator or Representative in Congress, shall not be denied or abridged by the United States or any State by reason of failure to pay any poll tax or other tax.

What It Means

Presidential Electors for the District of Columbia The Twenty-third Amendment (1961) allows citizens living in Washington, D.C., to vote for president and vice president, a right previously denied residents of the nation's capital. The District of Columbia now has three presidential electors, the number to which it would be entitled if it were a state.

What It Means

Abolition of Poll Tax The Twenty-fourth Amendment (1964) prohibits poll taxes in federal elections. Prior to the passage of this amendment, some states had used such taxes to keep low-income African Americans from voting. In 1966 the Supreme Court banned poll taxes in state elections as well.

Vocabulary

District: the site of the nation's capital, occupying an area between Maryland and Virginia

Presidential Disability and Succession The Twenty-fifth Amendment (1967) established a process for the vice president to take over leadership of the nation when a president is disabled. It also set procedures for filling a vacancy in the office of vice president.

This amendment was used in 1973, when Vice President Spiro Agnew resigned from office after being charged with accepting bribes. President Richard Nixon then appointed Gerald R. Ford as vice president in accordance with the provisions of the 25th Amendment. A year later, President Nixon resigned during the Watergate scandal and Ford became president. President Ford then had to fill the vice presidency, which he had left vacant upon assuming the presidency. He named Nelson A. Rockefeller as vice president. Thus, individuals who had not been elected held both the presidency and the vice presidency. *Whom does the president inform if he or she cannot carry out the duties of the office?*

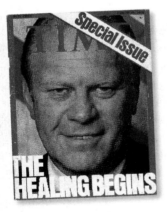

▲ President Gerald Ford

Vocabulary

vacancy: an office or position that is unfilled or unoccupied

Section 2

The Congress shall have power to enforce this article by appropriate legislation.

Amendment XXV

Section 1

In case of the removal of the President from office or of his death or resignation, the Vice President shall become President.

Section 2

Whenever there is a **vacancy** in the office of the Vice President, the President shall nominate a Vice President who shall take the office upon confirmation by a majority vote of both Houses of Congress.

Section 3

Whenever the President transmits to the President pro tempore of the Senate and the Speaker of the House of Representatives his written declaration that he is unable to discharge the powers and duties of his office, and until he transmits to them a written declaration to the contrary, such powers and duties shall be discharged by the Vice President as Acting President.

Section 4

Whenever the Vice President and a majority of either the principal officers of the executive departments or of such other body as Congress may by law provide, transmit to the President pro tempore of the Senate and the Speaker of the House of Representatives their written declaration that the President is unable to discharge the powers and duties of his office, the Vice President shall immediately assume the power and duties of the office of Acting President.

Thereafter, when the President transmits to the President pro tempore of the Senate and the Speaker of the House of Representatives his written declaration that no inability exists, he shall resume the powers and duties of his office unless the Vice President and a majority of either the principal officers of the executive department or of such other body as Congress may by law provide, transmit within four days to the President pro tempore of the Senate and the Speaker of the House of Representatives their written declaration that the President is unable to discharge the powers and duties of his office. Thereupon Congress shall decide the issue, assembling within forty-eight hours for that purpose if not in session. If the Congress, within twenty-one days after receipt of the latter written declaration, or, if Congress is not in session, within twenty-one days after Congress is required to assemble, determines by two-thirds vote of both Houses that the President is unable to discharge the powers and duties of his office, the Vice President shall continue to discharge the same as Acting President; otherwise, the President shall resume the power and duties of his office.

Amendment XXVI

Section 1

The right of citizens of the United States, who are eighteen years of age or older, to vote shall not be denied or abridged by the United States or by any State on account of age.

Section 2

The Congress shall have power to enforce this article by appropriate legislation.

Amendment XXVII

No law, varying the compensation for the services of Senators and Representatives, shall take effect, until an election of representatives shall have intervened.

What It Means

Eighteen-Year-Old Vote The Twenty-sixth Amendment (1971) guarantees the right to vote to all citizens 18 years of age and older.

What It Means

Restraint on Congressional Salaries The Twenty-seventh Amendment (1992) makes congressional pay raises effective during the term following their passage. James Madison offered the amendment in 1789, but it was never adopted. In 1982 Gregory Watson, then a student at the University of Texas, discovered the forgotten amendment while doing research for a school paper. Watson made the amendment's passage his crusade.

▼ Joint meeting of Congress

Unit 3

Launching the Republic
1789–1825

Original limestone marker along National Road, 1806

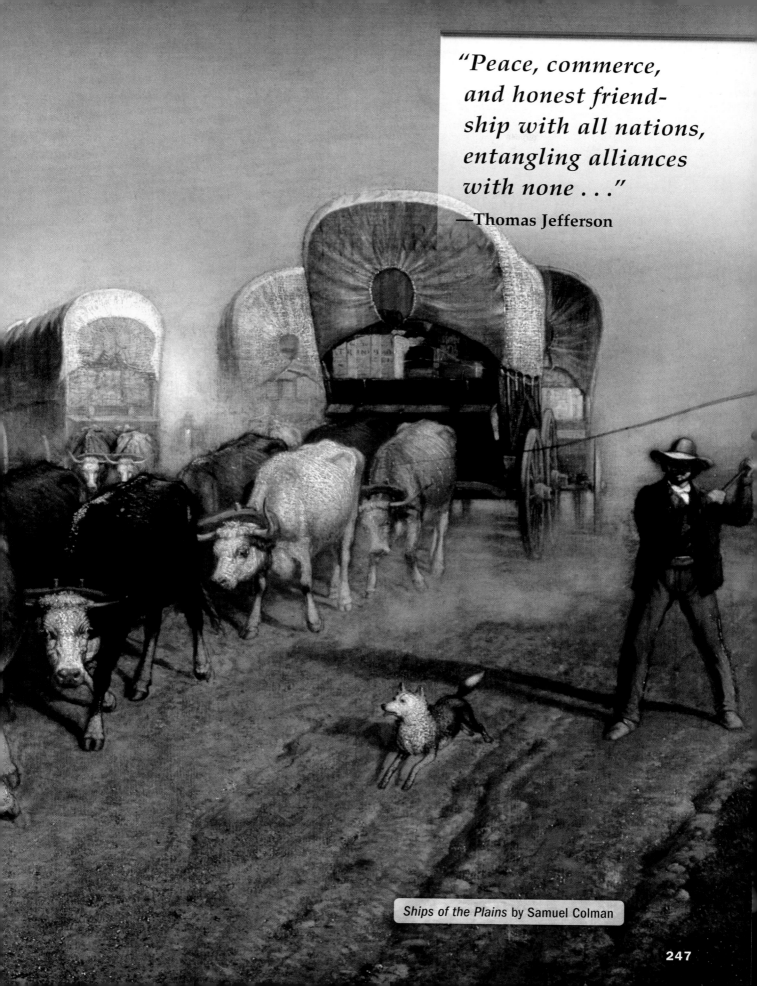

"*Peace, commerce, and honest friendship with all nations, entangling alliances with none . . .*"
—Thomas Jefferson

Ships of the Plains by Samuel Colman

Reading History

Summarizing Information

Learn It!

When you summarize information, you recount key points from the text. As you read to summarize, stop occasionally to answer the 5W questions in your own words: *Who? What? Where? When? Why?*

Who? Thomas Pinckney

What? Negotiated Pinckney's Treaty

Where? Spain

When? 1795

Why? To settle differences between the U.S. and Spain

—from Chapter 8, p. 263

Spanish leaders feared that the United States and Great Britain would work together against them in North America. Thomas Pinckney was sent to Spain to settle the differences between the United States and Spain. In 1795 **Pinckney's Treaty** gave the Americans free navigation of the Mississippi River and the right to trade at New Orleans.

Practice It!

Read the paragraphs and answer the 5W questions on another sheet of paper.

—from Chapter 10, p. 306

In 1793 **Eli Whitney** of Massachusetts invented the cotton gin. The **cotton gin** was a simple machine that quickly and efficiently removed the seeds from the cotton fiber.

Whitney also started using **interchangeable parts.** These were identical machine parts that could be put together quickly to make a complete product. These parts also made machine repair easier. Interchangeable parts allowed for the production of different kinds of goods on a large scale. This reduced the price of the goods.

Who? _____

What? _____

Where? _____

When? _____

Why? _____

Academic Vocabulary Preview

Listed below are the academic vocabulary words and their definitions that you will come across as you study Unit 3. Practice It! will help you study the words and definitions.

Academic Vocabulary	Definition	Practice It!
Chapter 8 The Federalist Era		
uniform (YOO · nuh · FAWRM) *p. 255*	identical; unchanging	**Identify** *the term from Chapter 8 that best completes the sentences.*
accumulate (uh · KYOO · muh · LAYT) *p. 256*	to collect; to gather together	1. Many citizens prefer a _____ system of law that is identical in each state.
challenge (CHA · luhnj) *p. 261*	to try to get or obtain	2. Avoiding foreign conflicts was a _____ to the new American government.
maintain (mayn · TAYN) *p. 261*	to keep; to uphold	
resolve (rih · ZAHLV) *p. 269*	to bring to an end	3. Governments often send delegates to help _____ disputes with other countries.
principle (PRIHN · suh · puhl) *p. 270*	a basic or fundamental reason, truth, or law	
Chapter 9 The Jefferson Era		
similar (SIH · muh · luhr) *p. 278*	having common qualities	**Identify** *the term from Chapter 9 that best matches the underlined term.*
conflict (KAHN · FLIHKT) *p. 279*	a disagreement	4. Thomas Jefferson surrounded himself with those with nearly the same views.
purchase (PUHR · chuhs) *p. 283*	something bought and paid for	5. The president of the United States has the power to make certain decisions.
authority (uh · THAHR · uh · tee) *p. 283*	power to decide; power over others	
react (ree · AKT) *p. 289*	to respond	6. The size of the United States doubled with the gain of the Louisiana Territory.
restriction (rih · STRIHK · shuhn) *p. 291*	a limit	
underestimate (UHN · duhr · EHS · tuh · MAYT) *p. 295*	to misjudge	
goal (GOHL) *p. 297*	an aim; a purpose	
Chapter 10 Growth and Expansion		
contribute (kuhn · TRIH · byuht) *p. 305*	to help to cause an event or situation	**Choose** *the word that best matches the meaning of each vocabulary term listed below.*
element (EH · luh · muhnt) *p. 307*	one part of a larger whole	7. **contribute** 9. **element**
reveal (rih · VEEL) *p. 313*	to show something that was hidden	a. help a. routine
region (REE · juhn) *p. 314*	a geographic area with similar features	b. convince b. part
intense (ihn · TEHNS) *p. 322*	exhibiting strong feeling	c. create c. whole

internal (ihn · TUHR · nuhl) *p. 322*	within a location such as a nation or state	8. **reveal** 10. **region**
		    a. show a. map
		    b. hide b. globe
		    c. order c. area

Chapter 8

The Federalist Era 1789–1800

Election scene, Detroit, early 1800s

GEORGE WASHINGTON

PRESIDENTS

U.S. Events

World Events

★ **1789**
- Washington becomes first president
- Judiciary Act passes

★ **1791**
Bill of Rights added to Constitution

1790

1792

★ **1789**
- Lavoisier's table of 33 elements published
- The French Revolution begins

★ **1792**
France declares war on Austria

Section 1: The First President

Essential Question What were the precedents that Washington established as the first president of the United States?

Section 2: Early Challenges

Essential Question What challenges did the United States face during Washington's administration?

Section 3: The First Political Parties

Essential Question How did the Federalist and Republican Parties form, and on what issues did they disagree?

History ONLINE
Chapter Overview Visit glencoe.com and click on **Chapter 8—Chapter Overviews** to preview chapter information.

FOLDABLES Study Organizer

Organizing Information
Make this Foldable to organize what you learn about early political parties.

Step 1 Fold a piece of 11" x 17" paper in half.

Step 2 Fold up the bottom edge two inches. Staple the outer edges of the flap to create pockets.

Step 3 Label each side as shown. Use the pockets to hold index cards or quarter sheets of paper.

Reading and Writing
As you read the chapter, list leaders and key ideas for the Federalist and Republican Parties.

◀ John Jay

★ **1794**
Whiskey Rebellion

★ **1795**
Nation's first chief justice, John Jay, retires from court

JOHN ADAMS

★ **1798**
• Alien and Sedition Acts pass
• XYZ affair

★ **1800**
Congress meets in Capitol for first time

1794

1796

1798

★ **1793**
The Louvre opens as public museum in Paris

★ **1794**
Slavery abolished in all French colonies

★ **1796**
Jenner develops smallpox vaccine

★ **1799**
Rosetta stone is discovered

Chapter 8   251

The First President

What were the precedents that Washington established as the first president of the United States?

Reading Guide

Content Vocabulary

precedent *(p. 253)*   bond *(p. 256)*
cabinet *(p. 253)*   unconstitutional *(p. 257)*
national debt *(p. 255)* tariff *(p. 257)*

Academic Vocabulary

uniform *(p. 255)*   accumulate *(p. 256)*

Key People and Events

Thomas Jefferson *(p. 253)*
Alexander Hamilton *(p. 253)*
John Jay *(p. 255)*
Bill of Rights *(p. 255)*

Reading Strategy

Taking Notes As you read, use a diagram like the one below to organize the departments and their secretaries under Washington's authority.

```
┌─────────────────────────────┐
│     Executive Branch of      │
│  Government Under Washington │
└─────────────────────────────┘
   ┌────┐   ┌────┐   ┌────┐
   │    │   │    │   │    │
   └────┘   └────┘   └────┘
```

INDIANA ACADEMIC STANDARDS
United States History

8.1.6 Identify the steps in the implementation of the federal government under the United States Constitution, including the First and Second Congresses of the United States (1789–1792).

8.1.9 Describe the influence of important individuals on social and political developments of the time such as the Independence movement and the framing of the Constitution.

8.4.8 Examine the development of the banking system in the United States.

American Diary

George Washington faced many challenges and had to make choices when he became the nation's first president. He understood that the destiny of the new nation was in the hands of the people. At his first inauguration, Washington said: "The preservation of the sacred fire of liberty and the destiny of the republican model of government are justly . . . staked on the experiment entrusted to the hands of the American people."

—from Washington's First Inaugural Address

President Washington

Main Idea President Washington and the new Congress had to make many decisions about the structure of the new government.

History and You If you were founding our nation's government, what do you think would be most important? Read about the choices that Washington and the new Congress had to make.

· ·

On April 30, 1789, George Washington took the oath of office as the first president of the United States under the federal Constitution. (Several presidents served under the Articles of Confederation.) John Adams became vice president.

Washington knew that the **precedents,** or traditions, he established would shape the future of the United States. "No slip will pass unnoticed," he said. With Congress, Washington would create departments within the executive branch, set up the court system, and add the Bill of Rights to the Constitution.

The First Congress

During the summer of 1789, Congress set up three departments and two offices in the executive branch of government. Washington chose prominent political figures to head them. The State Department, led by **Thomas Jefferson,** handled relations with other nations. The Department of the Treasury, led by **Alexander Hamilton,** handled financial matters. Henry Knox provided for the nation's defense as the secretary of the Department of War. To handle the government's legal affairs, Washington chose Edmund Randolph as attorney general. The office of postmaster general also was established.

The three department heads and the attorney general became known as the **cabinet.** However, Congress debated how much power the president should have over the cabinet. Senators were evenly divided in voting on the issue.

Vice President John Adams broke the tie. He voted to allow the president the authority to dismiss cabinet officers without Senate approval. This decision strengthened the president's position and it established his authority over the executive branch.

Judiciary Act of 1789

The first Congress also had to decide how to set up the nation's judicial system.

The first president takes the oath of office at Federal Hall in New York City.

Primary Source — **Customs and Traditions**

Washington's Precedents

In a letter to James Madison, Washington noted that the actions of the new government would be "the first of every thing, in our situation." Washington knew that what he did as the first president would set the standard for later presidents. Washington did set many precedents for the presidency, including:

✔ the Inaugural Address
✔ two terms in office
✔ creation of the cabinet
✔ foreign policy of neutrality

—*The Writings of George Washington*

▲ President Bush's Inaugural Address

Analyzing Why are precedents important?

Bill of Rights

Ratified December 15, 1791, the first 10 amendments to the U.S. Constitution state specific guarantees of individual freedoms. These rights and protections help Americans define the meaning of liberty. Examples are given below.

▲ The Bill of Rights

I Congress shall make no law respecting an establishment of religion, or prohibiting the free exercise thereof; or **abridging** the freedom of speech, or of the press; or the right of the people peaceably to assemble, and to petition the Government for a **redress** of grievances.

IV The right of the people to be secure in their persons, houses, papers, and effects, against unreasonable searches and seizures, shall not be violated, and no **Warrants** shall issue, but upon probable cause, supported by Oath or affirmation, and particularly describing the place to be searched, and the persons or things to be seized.

VI In all criminal prosecutions, the accused shall enjoy the right to a speedy and public trial, by an impartial jury of the State and district wherein the crime shall have been committed, which district shall have been previously ascertained by law, and to be informed of the nature and cause of the accusation; to be confronted with the witnesses against him; to have compulsory process for obtaining witnesses in his favor, and to have the Assistance of Counsel for his defence.

X The powers not delegated to the United States by the Constitution, nor prohibited by it to the States, are reserved to the States respectively, or to the people.

I: The First Amendment combines the five separate freedoms of religion, speech, press, assembly, and petition, or formally requesting changes of the government.

IV: The Fourth Amendment protects Americans against "unreasonable searches and seizures." No soldier, government agent, or police officer can search your home or take your property without probable, or a valid, cause.

VI: In the United States of America, the government cannot imprison people without announcing a charge, keep them imprisoned without a trial, hold a trial in secret, or stop them from seeing a lawyer.

X: This amendment is meant to prevent the federal government from abusing its power by going beyond what the Constitution allows.

VOCABULARY
abridging (uh·BRIHJ·ing): reducing
redress (rih·DREHS): fair adjustment
warrants (WAWR·uhnts): documents granting authorization

Critical Thinking

1. **Differentiating** How is freedom of speech different from freedom of the press?

2. **Making Connections** Following the terrorist attacks of September 11, 2001, many have called for increased police powers. Do you think the rights listed in the Fourth and Sixth Amendments should apply to Americans suspected of terrorism?

3. **Evaluating** Why do you think the Tenth Amendment is important?

Disagreements arose between those favoring a **uniform,** or standard, national legal system and those favoring state courts. The two groups reached a compromise in the Judiciary Act of 1789 with which Congress established a federal court system with 13 district courts and three circuit courts to serve the nation. State laws remained, but the federal courts had the power to reverse state decisions.

The Supreme Court would be the final authority on many issues. President Washington nominated **John Jay** to lead the Supreme Court as chief justice. The Senate approved Jay's nomination. With the Judiciary Act, Congress took the first steps toward creating a strong and independent national judiciary.

The Bill of Rights

Americans had long feared strong central governments. They fought a revolution to get rid of one and did not want to replace it with another. Many people insisted that the Constitution needed to include guarantees of civil liberties. Some states supported the Constitution on the condition that a bill of rights be added in the near future to guarantee personal liberties.

To fulfill promises to these states, James Madison introduced a set of amendments during the first session of Congress. Congress passed 12 amendments, and the states ratified 10 of them. In December 1791, these 10 amendments, the **Bill of Rights,** were added to the Constitution.

The Bill of Rights limits the powers of government. Its purpose is to protect the rights of individual liberty, such as freedom of speech, and the rights of persons accused of crimes, including trial by jury. With the Tenth Amendment, Madison hoped to use the states as an important line of defense against a too-powerful national government. (*See pages 236–237 for the Bill of Rights.*)

Reading Check **Identifying** What did the Judiciary Act do?

The New Country's Economy

Main Idea The new country's economy developed under the guidance of Alexander Hamilton.

History and You Have you ever borrowed money from a family member or one of your friends? By doing so, you acquired a debt and had to figure out how to pay it back. Hamilton faced a similar challenge with the nation's debt.

. . . .

President Washington rarely proposed laws and almost always approved the bills that Congress passed. The first president concentrated mainly on foreign affairs and military matters. Washington left the government's economic policies to his dynamic secretary of the treasury, Alexander Hamilton. When Washington appointed him to the position, Hamilton was only 34 years old. Yet he had bold plans and definite policies to deal with the country's finances.

The new nation faced serious financial problems. The **national debt**—the amount of money owed by the nation's government—was growing. Hamilton tried to find a way to improve the government's financial reputation and strengthen the nation at the same time.

Hamilton's Plan

Days after he took office, Hamilton was asked by the House of Representatives to prepare a plan for the "adequate support of public credit." This meant that the United States needed a way to borrow money for its government, its industrial development, and its commercial activity. How good the government's credit would be in the future depended on how well it could pay back the money it currently owed.

In 1790 Hamilton made his proposal. He said the new government should pay off the millions of dollars in debts owed by the Confederation government to other countries and to individual American citizens. The states fought for the nation's independence, Hamilton argued, so the national government should pay for the cost of their help.

Economics & History

Protective Tariffs *In the late 1700s, American industries lacked the experience to make goods efficiently. As a result, their production costs were higher than those of their foreign competitors. A protective tariff would raise the price of imported products, helping American companies compete.*

Hat made in Britain $7

Hat made in U.S. $6

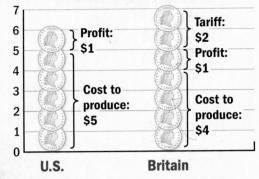

Breakdown of Cost

U.S.:
- Profit: $1
- Cost to produce: $5

Britain:
- Tariff: $2
- Profit: $1
- Cost to produce: $4

▲ A British-made hat would cost $5 in Britain. The same hat made in America is $6. With a $2 tariff, Americans pay $7 for the imported British hat but only $6 for the American-made hat.

Critical Thinking

1. **Drawing Conclusions** Which hat would sell more with the tariff? Why?
2. **Speculating** How might the issue of tariffs impact U.S. relations with Britain?

Hamilton also believed that federal payment of state debts would give the states a strong interest in the success of the national government.

Opposition to the Plan

Congress agreed to pay money owed to other nations. However, Hamilton's plan to pay off the debt to American citizens unleashed a storm of protest. When borrowing money during the American Revolution, the government issued **bonds.** These are paper notes promising to repay the money in a certain length of time. While waiting for the payment, many of the original bond owners—shopkeepers, farmers, and soldiers—sold the bonds for less than their value. They were purchased by speculators, people who risk money in order to make a larger profit. Hamilton proposed that these bonds be paid off at their original value.

Opponents believed that Hamilton's plan would make speculators rich. They said his plan was "established at the expense of national justice, gratitude, and humanity." The original bond owners also felt betrayed by the government. They lost money on their bonds while new bond owners profited.

Even stronger opposition came from the Southern states, which **accumulated,** or collected, much less debt than the Northern states. Southern states complained that they would have to pay more than their share under Hamilton's plan.

Compromise Results in a Capital

To win support for his plan, Hamilton worked out a compromise with Southern leaders. If they voted for his plan to pay off the state debts, he would, in return, support locating the new nation's capital in the South.

A special district would be laid out between Virginia and Maryland along the banks of the Potomac River. This district became Washington, D.C. While workers prepared the new city, the nation's capital was moved from New York to Philadelphia.

The Fight Over the Bank

To help build a strong national economy, Hamilton also asked Congress to create a national bank—the Bank of the United States. Both private investors and the national government would own the Bank's stock, or shares of ownership.

In 1792 only eight other banks existed in the nation, all of them established by the states. Madison and Jefferson opposed a national bank, believing it would benefit the wealthy. They also charged that the Bank was **unconstitutional**—or inconsistent with the Constitution. Hamilton agreed that the Constitution did not specifically say a bank could be created. However, he argued, Congress still had the power to do so. Washington agreed, and a national bank was created.

Tariffs and Taxes

Hamilton believed that agricultural America would benefit from more manufacturing. He proposed a **tariff**—a tax on imports—to protect new American industries from foreign competition. The South, having little industry, opposed such tariffs. Hamilton, however, won support in Congress for low tariffs, which raised money rather than protected industry.

Hamilton's plan also called for national taxes to help the government pay off the national debt. At Hamilton's request, Congress approved a variety of taxes, including one on whiskey distilled in the United States.

Hamilton also planned to give the national government new financial powers. Opponents, such as Jefferson and Madison, however, feared a strong national government run by the wealthy. Their vision of America was very different.

Reading Check **Summarizing** Summarize Hamilton's plan for building the nation's economy.

Section 1 Review

History ONLINE
Study Central™ To review this section, go to glencoe.com.

Vocabulary

1. Use each term in a sentence to help explain its meaning: precedent, cabinet, uniform, national debt, bond, accumulate, unconstitutional, tariff.

Main Ideas

2. **Discussing** How did the first Congress support President Washington in establishing the executive branch?

3. **Summarizing** Why did Madison and Jefferson disagree with Hamilton's proposal for a national bank? What was the outcome?

Critical Thinking

4. **Diagramming** Use a diagram like the one below to show the court system established by the Judiciary Act of 1789. List the two levels and explain their powers.

Level:
Power:

Level:
Power:

5. **Contrasting** Discuss the arguments of those in favor of and against Hamilton's plan to improve the economy.

6. **Expository Writing** Do you think the first Congress was right in giving the president the authority to dismiss cabinet members without the approval of the Senate? Write a paragraph explaining your point of view.

Answer the
7. **Essential Question**
What were the precedents that Washington established as the first president of the United States?

Choosing the Location of Washington, D.C.

Before 1790 the United States had no permanent capital city. Early Congresses met in various cities. A political compromise established the nation's capital along the Potomac River.

How Did Geography Affect the Early Development of Washington, D.C.?

The city's site was selected by George Washington. He may have chosen it for its natural scenery or his belief that the Potomac would become a great navigable waterway. Unfortunately, debris and silt were deposited in the shallow tidal areas around the developing city. Ships could not travel the length of the river. The stagnant water created unhealthy conditions and a rotten smell.

◄ French architect Pierre L'Enfant designed the plan for the city of Washington, D.C., in 1791.

▲ **Map of Washington, D.C., 1791** L'Enfant's basic plan included wide avenues and major streets radiating out from traffic circles. Modern Washington, D.C., still retains many of the elements of L'Enfant's plan.

◄ Mathematician and inventor Benjamin Banneker was hired in 1791 to help survey the land for the new national capital. In addition to his other talents, Banneker was also a farmer and a publisher of a well-known yearly almanac.

◄ **The City's Location**
Straddling the Potomac River, Washington, D.C., was laid out on land handed over to the federal government from both Maryland and Virginia. The Virginia land was given back to Virginia in 1846. Thus, all of the city's current area was originally part of Maryland.

Washington, D.C., is famous for its cherry blossoms. This scene shows blossoms along the Tidal Basin.

The Tidal Basin To help reduce the amount of stagnant water near the Potomac, an inlet called the Tidal Basin was created in the 1880s. The basin provides a means for draining the Washington Channel and flushing the channel with relatively clean water with each change of tide.

1. Washington Monument
2. Jefferson Memorial
3. Franklin Delano Roosevelt Memorial
4. White House

Washington, D.C., in 1801 The city was slowly rising from a marshy site on the Potomac River. The nation's capital had only two noteworthy buildings—the president's mansion (later called the White House) and the still-unfinished Capitol. Between them stretched about two miles of muddy streets. ▶

Analyzing Geography

1. **Human-Environment Interaction** One of the reasons that the site was chosen as the capital was that it was in the center of the country. What are the advantages of such a location?

2. **Location** How do you think the location of Washington, D.C., affected its early growth? Explain.

Early Challenges

Essential Question ◄····

What challenges did the United States face during Washington's administration?

Reading Guide

Content Vocabulary

neutrality (p. 262)

impressment (p. 263)

Academic Vocabulary

challenge (p. 261)   maintain (p. 261)

Key People and Events

Whiskey Rebellion (p. 261)

Battle of Fallen Timbers (p. 262)

Treaty of Greenville (p. 262)

Edmond Genêt (p. 263)

Jay's Treaty (p. 263)

Pinckney's Treaty (p. 263)

Reading Strategy

Taking Notes As you read, use a diagram like the one below to summarize how the treaties described in this section affected the United States.

Treaty	Effect
Treaty of Greenville →	
Jay's Treaty →	
Pinckney's Treaty →	

INDIANA ACADEMIC STANDARDS
United States History

8.1.1 Identify major Native American Indian groups of eastern North America and describe early conflict and cooperation with European settlers and the influence the two cultures had on each other.

8.1.6 Identify the steps in the implementation of the federal government under the United States Constitution, including the First and Second Congresses of the United States (1789–1792).

American Diary

In 1791 Congress passed a tax on the manufacture and sale of whiskey. Opposition to the tax was strong in western Pennsylvania. Farmers refused to pay and attacked tax collectors. The federal government took action against the Whiskey Rebellion. Alexander Hamilton believed that using force to stop the rebellion would: "do us a great deal of good and add to the solidity of every thing in this country."

—*from* American Politics in the Early Republic

President Washington reviews the troops before their march west to shut down the Whiskey Rebellion.

The Whiskey Rebellion and the West

Main Idea The new government was faced with challenges in Pennsylvania and on the frontier.

History and You Have you ever opposed a government action? Read to learn how the new government handled rebellious citizens.

The Whiskey Rebellion was only one **challenge,** or demanding situation, faced by the new government. Native Americans, aided by the British and Spanish, were resisting the American settlers' expansion westward. Britain and France were pressuring the United States to become more involved in their conflicts. President Washington stood firm by not involving the United States in foreign conflicts.

The Whiskey Rebellion

Washington was concerned about the growing resistance of western Pennsylvania farmers to the tax on whiskey. Their protest turned violent in July 1794. An armed mob attacked tax collectors and burned down buildings. This armed protest, called the **Whiskey Rebellion,** alarmed government leaders. Washington and his advisers decided to crush the challenge. This action sent messages that the government would use force when necessary to **maintain,** or keep, the social order.

Struggle Over the West

The new government also faced difficult problems in the West. Washington worried about European ambitions in the Northwest Territory. He signed treaties with the Native Americans, hoping to lessen the influence of the British and Spanish on them. American settlers ignored the treaties and moved onto lands promised to the Native Americans. Fighting broke out between the two groups.

Washington sent an army under General Arthur St. Clair to restore order in the Northwest Territory. In November 1791, St. Clair's forces were defeated by Little Turtle, chief of the Miami people. More than 600 American soldiers died in the battle by the Wabash River.

Many Americans believed an alliance with France would help them defeat the British, Spanish, and Native Americans in the West.

Primary Source | The Whiskey Rebellion

Thomas Jefferson accused Hamilton of orchestrating the rebellion: "an insurrection [rebellion] was announced & proclaimed & armed against, but could never be found."

▲ Rebels tar and feather a tax collector during the Whiskey Rebellion.

Critical Thinking

Explaining How did Alexander Hamilton want to respond to the rebellion?

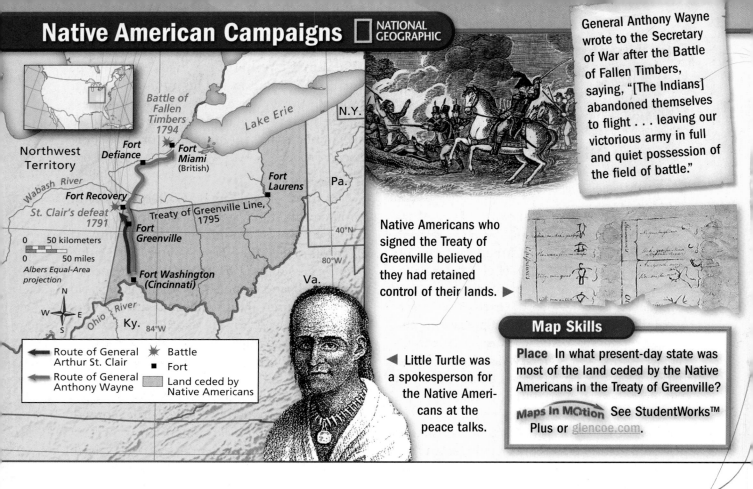

Native American Campaigns NATIONAL GEOGRAPHIC

Northwest Territory

Battle of Fallen Timbers 1794

Fort Defiance

Fort Miami (British)

Fort Laurens

Lake Erie

N.Y.

Pa.

Wabash River

Fort Recovery

St. Clair's defeat 1791

Treaty of Greenville Line, 1795

Fort Greenville

40°N

80°W

Fort Washington (Cincinnati)

Va.

0   50 kilometers
0   50 miles
Albers Equal-Area projection

Ohio River

Ky.   84°W

← Route of General Arthur St. Clair
← Route of General Anthony Wayne
✳ Battle
▪ Fort
▨ Land ceded by Native Americans

General Anthony Wayne wrote to the Secretary of War after the Battle of Fallen Timbers, saying, "[The Indians] abandoned themselves to flight . . . leaving our victorious army in full and quiet possession of the field of battle."

Native Americans who signed the Treaty of Greenville believed they had retained control of their lands. ▶

◀ Little Turtle was a spokesperson for the Native Americans at the peace talks.

Map Skills

Place In what present-day state was most of the land ceded by the Native Americans in the Treaty of Greenville?

Maps In Motion See StudentWorks™ Plus or glencoe.com.

The possibility of French involvement prompted Britain to take action in the West. In 1794 the British government urged Native Americans to destroy American settlements west of the Appalachians. The British also began building a new fort in Ohio.

The Native Americans demanded that all settlers north of the Ohio River leave the territory. Washington sent another army under Anthony Wayne, a former Revolutionary War general, to challenge their demands. In August 1794 his army defeated more than 1,000 Native Americans led by the Shawnee chief Blue Jacket at the **Battle of Fallen Timbers** (near present-day Toledo, Ohio). The Battle of Fallen Timbers crushed the Native Americans' hopes of keeping their land. In the **Treaty of Greenville** (1795), they agreed to surrender most of the land in what is now Ohio.

✔ **Reading Check** Analyzing Why did some Americans want to form an alliance with France?

Problems With Europe

Main Idea President Washington wanted the nation to remain neutral in foreign conflicts.

History and You Have you ever been in the middle of a disagreement between two friends? Read why Washington looked for middle ground in a war between Britain and France.

. . . .

Most Americans cheered the French Revolution of 1789 because of its similarity to America's own revolution. By 1793, however, the French Revolution turned bloody. Public opinion was now divided.

When Britain and France went to war in 1793, some Americans sympathized with France and others supported Britain. Washington hoped that the United States could maintain its **neutrality**—not taking sides in the conflict between France and Britain. As time passed, however, remaining neutral became more difficult.

Washington Proclaims Neutrality

The French tried to involve the United States in their conflict with Britain. They sent diplomat **Edmond Genêt** (zhuh•NAY) to recruit American volunteers to attack British ships. In response, President Washington issued a Proclamation of Neutrality, which prohibited American citizens from fighting in the war. It also barred French and British warships from American ports. The British captured American ships that traded with the French and forced the American crews into the British navy. This practice of **impressment** angered the Americans.

Washington sent John Jay, chief justice of the Supreme Court, to negotiate a peaceful solution with Britain. Few Americans approved of **Jay's Treaty.** In it, the British agreed to withdraw from American soil. However, the treaty did not deal with the issue of impressment or British interference with American trade. Washington found fault with the treaty but realized it would end the crisis. The Senate narrowly approved it after a fierce debate.

Treaty With Spain

Spanish leaders feared that the United States and Great Britain would work together against them in North America. Thomas Pinckney was sent to Spain to settle the differences between the United States and Spain. In 1795 **Pinckney's Treaty** gave the Americans free navigation of the Mississippi River and the right to trade at New Orleans.

Washington's Farewell

Washington decided not to seek a third term. In his Farewell Address, he attacked political parties and involvement in foreign affairs. He also urged his fellow citizens to:

PRIMARY SOURCE

"Observe good faith and justice toward all nations. . . .
. . . It is our true policy to steer clear of permanent alliances."

—from *The Annals of America*

These parting words influenced the nation's foreign policy for more than 100 years.

Reading Check **Explaining** What was the significance of Jay's Treaty?

Section 2 Review

History ONLINE
Study Central™ To review this section, go to glencoe.com.

Vocabulary

1. Write headlines for newspaper stories about the U.S. role in the Britain-France conflict. Use and show understanding of the terms: challenge, maintain, neutrality, impressment.

Main Ideas

2. **Identifying** What did Washington's actions in crushing the Whiskey Rebellion signify to the country?

3. **Discussing** How did the British challenge U.S. neutrality in the war between France and Britain?

Critical Thinking

4. **Comparing and Contrasting** Compare and contrast U.S. attitudes and actions toward the Native Americans and U.S. actions in foreign affairs.

5. **Determining Cause and Effect** Use a diagram like the one below to show the causes and the effect of the Battle of Fallen Timbers.

6. **Persuasive Writing** Imagine that you disagree with Washington's policy of neutrality in the war between France and Britain. Write a letter to the president to persuade him to side with France.

Answer the
Essential Question

7. What challenges did the United States face during Washington's administration?

Essential Question ◄

How did the Federalist and Republican Parties form, and on what issues did they disagree?

Reading Guide

Content Vocabulary

partisan *(p. 265)*   sedition *(p. 270)*

implied powers   nullify
  (p. 266)   *(p. 270)*

caucus *(p. 268)*   states' rights *(p. 270)*

alien *(p. 269)*

Academic Vocabulary

resolve *(p. 269)*   principle *(p. 270)*

Key People and Events

XYZ affair *(p. 269)*

Alien and Sedition Acts *(p. 270)*

Virginia and Kentucky Resolutions *(p. 270)*

Reading Strategy

Taking Notes As you read, create a diagram like the one below. Identify the differences between the Federalists and the Republicans on the role of the federal government.

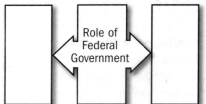

Federalists	Issue	Republicans
	Role of Federal Government	

INDIANA ACADEMIC STANDARDS
United States History

8.1.7 Describe the origin and development of political parties, the Federalists and the Democratic-Republicans, (1793–1801) and examine points of agreement and disagreement between these parties.

8.1.9 Describe the influence of important individuals on social and political developments of the time such as the Independence movement and the framing of the Constitution.

American Diary

Although many Americans hailed George Washington as a great leader, the president did not escape criticism. One critic was Ben Franklin's grandson, Benjamin Franklin Bache, a writer and publisher. Washington, Bache wrote, was "but a man, and certainly not a great man." Bache even criticized Washington's military leadership during the American Revolution, describing him as "ignorant of war both in theory and useful practice."

— *from* Remarks Occasioned by the Late Conduct of Mr. Washington

George and Martha Washington

Opposing Views

Main Idea By 1796, Americans began to take opposing sides on issues. Two political parties emerged from the debates.

History and You When you disagree with someone, do you voice your opinion? Read to learn what happened when conflict occurred between the supporters of Hamilton and Jefferson.

• •

President Washington's character and military record were admired by most Americans. However, harsh attacks on his policies and on his personality appeared from time to time in newspapers. One paper even called Washington "the scourge and the misfortune of his country."

Most attacks on Washington came from supporters of Thomas Jefferson. They were trying to discredit the policies of Washington and Hamilton by attacking the president. By 1796 Americans were beginning to divide into opposing groups and to form political parties.

At that time many Americans considered political parties harmful. Parties—or "factions," as they were called—were to be avoided as much as a strong central government. The nation's Founders did not even mention political parties when they wrote the Constitution.

Washington disapproved of political parties and warned that they would divide the nation. To others it seemed natural that people would disagree about issues. They also knew that people who hold similar views tend to band together.

In Washington's cabinet, Alexander Hamilton and Thomas Jefferson often took opposing sides on issues. They disagreed on economic policy and foreign relations. Nor could they agree on the power of the federal government or on interpretations of the Constitution. Even Washington was **partisan**—favoring one side of an issue. Although he believed he stood above politics, Washington usually supported Hamilton's positions.

Political Parties Emerge

In Congress and in the nation at large, similar differences existed. By the mid-1790s two distinct political parties formed.

Primary Source | **Political Cartoons**

Jefferson Criticized
Newspapers that supported Washington and Hamilton ridiculed Thomas Jefferson in print and in cartoons. In this cartoon, Jefferson is throwing the U.S. Constitution into a fire.

Critical Thinking

Making Inferences Cartoonists often use a symbol to stand for a larger idea. What does the eagle represent? What is the eagle trying to do?

Will Political Parties Harm the Nation?

In his Farewell Address, George Washington warned the nation that the development of political parties would lead to trouble. Thomas Jefferson believed that while the new parties had different opinions, they still had much in common.

YES GEORGE WASHINGTON

"The alternate domination of one faction [group] over another, sharpened by the spirit of revenge . . . is itself a frightful despotism [tyranny]. But this leads at length to a more formal and permanent despotism. The disorders and miseries which result gradually incline the minds of men to seek security . . . in the absolute power of an individual."

THOMAS JEFFERSON NO

"Every difference of opinion is not a difference of principle. . . . We are all Republicans, we are all Federalists. . . . Let us, then, with courage and confidence pursue our own Federal and Republican principles, our attachment to union and representative government."

DBQ Document-Based Questions

1. **Analyzing** Why did George Washington fear the emergence of political parties?

2. **Interpreting** What did Thomas Jefferson mean when he said, "We are all Republicans, we are all Federalists"?

The name *Federalist* was first used to describe someone who supported ratification of the Constitution. By the 1790s, the word meant the people who supported the policies of the Washington administration.

Generally, Federalists stood for a strong federal government. They admired Britain because of its stability and distrusted France because of the violent changes following the French Revolution. Federalist policies favored banking and shipping interests. Federalists received the strongest support in the Northeast, especially New England, and from wealthy plantation owners in the South.

Efforts to turn public opinion against Federalist policies began seriously in late 1791 when Philip Freneau (freh•NOH) began publishing the *National Gazette.* Jefferson, then secretary of state, helped the newspaper get started. Later he and Madison organized people who disagreed with Hamilton. They called their party the Republicans, or the Democratic-Republicans.

The Republicans wanted to limit the government's power. They feared that a strong federal government would endanger people's liberties. They supported the French and condemned what they regarded as the Washington administration's pro-British policies. Republican policies appealed to small farmers and urban workers, especially in the Middle Atlantic states and the South.

Views of the Constitution

One difference between Federalists and Republicans was the basis of government power. In Hamilton's view, the federal government had **implied powers.** These were powers that were not expressly forbidden in the Constitution.

Hamilton used the idea of implied powers to justify a national bank. He argued that the Constitution gave Congress the power to issue money and to regulate trade. A national bank would clearly help the government perform these responsibilities. Therefore, he reasoned, creating a bank was within the constitutional power of Congress.

Jefferson and Madison disagreed with Hamilton. They believed in a strict interpretation of the Constitution. They accepted the idea of implied powers but in a much more limited sense than Hamilton did. Jefferson and Madison believed that implied powers are those powers that are "absolutely necessary" to carry out the expressed powers.

The People's Role

The differences between Federalists and Republicans, however, went deeper than disagreements about the Constitution. The parties also disagreed about the role of ordinary citizens in government.

Federalists supported representative government, in which elected officials ruled in the people's name. Too much democracy, Federalists claimed, was dangerous to liberty. Therefore, they did not believe that it was wise to let the public become too involved in politics.

Hamilton said:

PRIMARY SOURCE

"The people are turbulent and changing; they seldom judge or determine right."

—from a speech at the Constitutional Convention

Public office, Federalists thought, should be held by honest and educated men of property who would protect the rights of all the nation's people. Ordinary people were too likely to be swayed by agitators.

In contrast, the Republicans feared a strong central government controlled by only a few people. They believed that democracy and liberty would be safe only if ordinary people participated fully in government. As Jefferson said in a letter:

PRIMARY SOURCE

"I am not among those who fear the people. They, and not the rich, are our dependence [what we depend on] for continued freedom."

—from *The Papers of Thomas Jefferson*

People IN HISTORY

Alexander Hamilton

Leader of the Federalist Party

Hamilton believed that the federal government could act as needed to govern the country well, even if those powers were not stated in the Constitution. He used this argument to defend the creation of a national bank. Specifically, he concluded that:

"It is the manifest [obvious] design and scope of the Constitution to vest in Congress all the powers requisite [needed] to the effectual administration of the finances of the United States."

Thomas Jefferson

Leader of the Republican Party

Jefferson believed all powers not clearly given to the federal government in the Constitution should be left to the states. He fought against the broad federal powers used by the Washington administration, arguing: "[B]y a compact ... [the states] constituted a General Government for special purposes,—delegated to that government certain definite powers, reserving, each State to itself, the ... right to their own self-government."

CRITICAL Thinking

1. **Contrasting** How did Jefferson and Hamilton differ in their views on the constitutional powers of the federal government?

2. **Defending** With which view do you agree more? Why?

In this British cartoon, Great Britain, on the hilltop, is greatly amused by French-American relations, while other European leaders look on.

1. **Analyzing** What appears to be in the French sack? What are the French trying to get the United States to do?

2. **Making Connections** Why is the character representing Great Britain greatly amused by the situation?

A. United States
B. French leaders
C. European leaders
D. Great Britain

PROPERTY PROTECTED, a la Françoise.

Washington tried to get his two advisers to work out their differences. Knowing that Jefferson was dissatisfied, Washington wrote to Jefferson:

PRIMARY SOURCE

"I . . . ardently wish that some line could be marked out by which both of you could walk."

—from *George Washington: Letters and Addresses*

Nevertheless, Jefferson resigned as secretary of state and soon after Hamilton resigned as secretary of the treasury. The rival groups and their points of view moved further apart.

The Election of 1796

In the presidential election of 1796, candidates sought office for the first time as members of rival political parties. To prepare for the election, the Federalists and the Republicans held meetings called **caucuses.** At the caucuses, members of Congress and other leaders chose their parties' candidates for office.

The Federalists nominated Vice President John Adams for president and Charles Pinckney for vice president. The Republicans put forth former secretary of state Jefferson for president and Aaron Burr for vice president. Adams and Jefferson, once good friends, became bitter rivals. The Federalists expected to easily carry the New England region. The Republicans' strength lay in the Southern states. Most of that region's votes went to Thomas Jefferson.

In the end, Adams received 71 electoral votes, winning the election. Jefferson finished second with 68 votes. Under the provisions of the Constitution at that time, the person with the second-highest number of electoral votes became vice president. Jefferson, therefore, became the new vice president. The administration that took office on March 4, 1797, had a Federalist president and a Republican vice president.

Reading Check **Explaining** How did members of opposing parties become president and vice president in the election of 1796?

President John Adams

Main Idea During his administration, President John Adams faced a dispute with France and the issue of states' rights at home.

History and You Do you think you should be free to say or write anything you want about the government? Read to find out why the Federalists passed laws restricting freedom of speech.

. . . .

John Adams spent most of his life in public service. One of Massachusetts's most active patriots, he later became ambassador to France and to Great Britain and served two terms as vice president under Washington.

The XYZ Affair

When Adams became president, he inherited the dispute with France. The French regarded the 1794 Jay's Treaty as an American attempt to help the British in their war with France. To punish the United States, the French seized American ships that carried cargo to Britain.

History ONLINE

Student Web Activity Visit glencoe.com and complete the Chapter 8 Web Activity about John Adams.

In the fall of 1797, Adams sent a delegation to Paris to try to **resolve**—bring to an end—the dispute. French foreign minister Charles de Talleyrand, however, refused to meet with the Americans. Instead, Talleyrand sent three agents who demanded a bribe and a loan for France from the Americans. "Not a sixpence," the Americans replied and sent a report of the incident to the United States. Adams was furious. He referred to the three French agents as X, Y, and Z. Adams urged Congress to prepare for war. The incident became known as the **XYZ affair.**

Alien and Sedition Acts

As public anger rose against France, Americans became more suspicious of **aliens**—immigrants living in the country who were not citizens. Many Europeans who came to the United States in the 1790s supported the ideals of the French Revolution.

The Alien and Sedition Acts

Naturalization Act
Required that aliens be residents for 14 years instead of 5 years before they became eligible for U.S. citizenship

Alien Acts
Allowed the president to imprison aliens and to send those he considered dangerous out of the country

Sedition Act
Made it a crime to speak, write, or publish "false, scandalous, and malicious" criticisms of the government

Why they were passed
The Federalist-controlled Congress wanted to:
- strengthen the federal government.
- silence Republican opposition.

Results
- Discouraged immigration and led some foreigners already in the country to leave
- Convicted 10 Republican newspaper editors who had criticized the Federalists in government

Reaction
- Opposition to Federalist party grows
- Led to movement to allow states to overturn federal laws

Some Americans questioned whether these aliens would remain loyal if the United States went to war with France.

Federalists responded with strict laws to protect the nation's security. In 1798 they passed a group of measures known as the **Alien and Sedition Acts. Sedition** refers to activities aimed at weakening the established government. The Alien Act allowed the president to imprison aliens, or send those considered dangerous out of the country.

Domestic and Foreign Affairs

In response to the Alien and Sedition Acts, Republicans looked to the states to preserve people's liberties by standing up to what they regarded as Federalist tyranny. Madison and Jefferson drafted documents of protest that the Virginia and Kentucky legislatures passed.

The **Virginia and Kentucky Resolutions** of 1798 and 1799 claimed that the Alien and Sedition Acts violated the Constitution. Therefore, they could not be put into action. The Kentucky Resolutions further suggested that states might **nullify**—legally overturn—federal laws considered unconstitutional.

The resolutions supported the **principle,** or basic idea, of **states' rights.** This principle stated that the powers of the federal government should be limited to those clearly assigned to it by the Constitution. The states should have all other powers not expressly forbidden to them. The issue of states' rights would remain an important issue.

To help themselves politically, the Federalists urged Adams to declare war on France. Adams, however, refused to rush to war. Instead, he appointed a new commission to seek peace with France.

In 1800 the French agreed to a treaty and stopped their attacks on American ships. The agreement with France was in the best interest of the United States. However, it hurt Adams's chance for reelection. Rather than applauding the agreement, Hamilton and his supporters now opposed their own president. The Federalists were split. Republican prospects for capturing the presidency were now greatly improved. The road was clear for Thomas Jefferson in the election of 1800.

✓ **Reading Check** **Summarizing** How did peace with France affect the Federalists?

Section 3 Review

History ONLINE
Study Central™ To review this section, go to glencoe.com.

Vocabulary

1. Write sentences to demonstrate your understanding of the following words. You may combine two or more words in a sentence: partisan, implied powers, caucus, resolve, alien, sedition, nullify, principle, states' rights.

Main Ideas

2. **Discussing** How did the Federalists and the Republicans view the role of ordinary people in government?

3. **Explaining** Why did some Americans feel threatened by the passage of the Alien and Sedition Acts?

Critical Thinking

4. **Comparing** How did Jefferson's views about the Constitution's implied powers differ from the views of Alexander Hamilton?

5. **Expository Writing** Write a paragraph explaining, in your own words, how Adams tried to avoid war with France.

6. **Making Connections** Use a diagram like the one below to summarize each event and explain how it influenced the next one.

XYZ Affair → Alien and Sedition Acts → Virginia and Kentucky Resolutions

Answer the
7. **Essential Question**
How did the Federalist and Republican Parties form, and on what issues did they disagree?

Visual Summary

Precedents Set by Washington Administration

| Separation of powers | Strong and independent national court system | Limits on government's powers (Bill of Rights) | Use of force to maintain social order | Neutrality in foreign affairs |

◄ Little Turtle

Challenges Faced by Washington and Adams Administrations

| Management of the national debt | Debate over national taxes and protective tariffs | Conflicts with Europeans and Native Americans in the West | Role of ordinary people in government | Pressure to end neutrality in British-French wars | States' rights versus the power of the federal government |

Viewpoints Held by New Political Parties

	Federalists	Republicans
Economic Policy	Protective tariffs; emphasis on manufacturing	Free trade; emphasis on agriculture
Foreign Relations	Support for Britain	Support for France
Role of the Federal Government	Strong federal government	Strong state governments
Interpretation of the Constitution	Loose interpretation; federal government has implied powers	Strict interpretation; federal government limits powers to those needed to carry out the Constitution
Role of People in Government	Rule by wealthy class	Rule by ordinary people

STUDY TO GO Study anywhere, anytime! Download quizzes and flash cards to your PDA from glencoe.com.

INDIANA STATEWIDE TEST PRACTICE

TEST-TAKING TIP

As you read the first part of a multiple-choice question, try to anticipate the answer before you look at the choices. If your answer is one of the choices, it is probably correct.

Reviewing Vocabulary

Directions: Choose the word or words that best completes the sentence.

1 To help President Washington govern, Congress created executive departments. The department heads became the president's _____.

A caucus
B congress
C cabinet
D partisans

2 A tax on imports is called a(n) _____.

A debt
B tariff
C implied power
D precedent

3 The United States tried to maintain its _____ and did not take sides in the war between France and Great Britain.

A states' rights
B impressment
C neutrality
D national legal system

4 _____ are those powers that are not expressly forbidden in the U.S. Constitution.

A Implied powers
B Expressed powers
C Popular sovereignty
D Checks and balances

Reviewing Main Ideas

Directions: Choose the best answer.

5 With the Judiciary Act of 1789, Congress

A placed state courts under federal courts.
B established a federal court system with 13 district courts.
C blocked state laws in favor of federal laws.
D named judges for all federal and state courts.

6 The Whiskey Rebellion was

A an armed uprising by farmers in Ohio.
B a violent slave rebellion in Virginia.
C a skirmish between U.S. soldiers and Ohio Native Americans.
D a protest by Pennsylvania farmers over a federal excise tax.

7 The Virginia and Kentucky Resolutions

A were drafted by Federalists opposing Republican uses of federal power.
B claimed that the Alien and Sedition Acts violated the Constitution.
C distributed land to settlers in Virginia and Kentucky.
D rejected the principle of states' rights.

GO ON

History ONLINE

For additional test practice, use **Self-Check Quizzes**—Chapter 8 at glencoe.com.

Critical Thinking

Directions: Choose the best answer.

Base your answer to question 8 on the political cartoon below and your knowledge of Chapter 8.

Source: CORBIS

8   This 1798 cartoon shows a fight between two members of the House of Representatives over the Sedition Act. What was the purpose of the Sedition Act?

A   protect states' rights
B   set immigration laws
C   control political opposition
D   nominate candidates for president

Base your answer to question 9 on the excerpt below and your knowledge of Chapter 8.

> I . . . warn you in the most solemn manner against the baneful [harmful] effects of the spirit of party generally.
>
> This spirit, unfortunately, is inseparable from our nature. . . . It exists under different shapes in all governments . . . but, in those of the popular form, it is seen in its greatest rankness, and is truly their worst enemy.
>
> —George Washington's Farewell Address

9   According to Washington, why do political parties exist?

A   They are a necessary part of government.
B   It is human nature for people to form political parties.
C   The Constitution states that the nation must have political parties.
D   Political parties are needed to protect democracy and liberty.

Constructed Response

Directions: Write a short response to each of the following questions. In your answer:

- *address all parts of the question*
- *use information from the chapter*
- *include facts, examples, and details relevant to the question*
- *use clear language*

10   Identify two precedents George Washington set as the first president.

11   Why was the Bill of Rights created?

Base your answer to question 12 on the excerpt below and your knowledge of Chapter 8.

> The powers not delegated to the United States by the Constitution, nor prohibited by it to the States, are reserved to the States respectively, or to the people.
>
> —Tenth Amendment to the U.S. Constitution

12   Which political party—Federalists or Republicans—do you think supported this amendment more? Explain.

STOP

Need Extra Help?												
If you missed questions. . .	1	2	3	4	5	6	7	8	9	10	11	12
Go to page. . .	253	257	262	266	253	261	270	269	263	253	255	255

Chapter 9

The Jefferson Era 1800-1816

Monticello, located in Charlottesville, Virginia, was the home of Thomas Jefferson.

PRESIDENTS

THOMAS JEFFERSON 1801–1809

JAMES MADISON 1809–1817

U.S. Events

★ **1801** Robert Fulton builds first submarine

★ **1803** Supreme Court establishes judicial review

★ **1804** Lewis and Clark begin expedition

★ **1804** Alexander Hamilton duels with Aaron Burr

World Events

1800

1805

Drawing of Fulton's submarine ▶

★ **1803** War begins again between France and Britain

★ **1804** Napoleon proclaims himself emperor of France

★ **1806** Holy Roman Empire officially ends

★ **1808** Extensive excavations begin at Pompeii

FOLDABLES®
Study Organizer

Organizing Information

Make this four-tab Foldable to help you learn about the events of the Jefferson era.

Step 1 Fold the sides of a piece of paper into the middle to make a shutter fold.

Step 2 Cut each tab at the midpoint to form four tabs.

Step 3 Label the tabs as shown.

Jefferson's Administration | The Louisiana Purchase
Growing Conflict | The War of 1812

Reading and Writing

As you read the chapter, take notes about each section under the appropriate head. Use your Foldable to help you write a summary for each section.

◄ The U.S. Capitol after it was burned by the British in 1814.

◄ Tecumseh

1811
Tecumseh joins British forces after the Battle of Tippecanoe

1812
U.S. declares war on Britain

1814 ★
British forces burn Washington, D.C.

★ **1815**
Battle of New Orleans

1810

1812

1816

★ **1809**
Ecuador wins independence from Spain

1812 ★
Napoleon invades Russia

1813 ★
Simón Bolívar becomes dictator of Venezuela

★ **1814**
Congress of Vienna meets

★ **1815**
Napoleon defeated at Waterloo

The Republicans Take Power

Essential Question ◄

In what ways did Thomas Jefferson and the Republicans limit the powers of the government?

Reading Guide

Content Vocabulary

laissez-faire *(p. 278)*

judicial review *(p. 279)*

customs duties *(p. 278)*

Academic Vocabulary

similar *(p. 278)*

conflict *(p. 279)*

Key People and Events

Thomas Jefferson *(p. 277)*

Aaron Burr *(p. 277)*

Judiciary Act of 1801 *(p. 279)*

Marbury v. Madison *(p. 279)*

Reading Strategy

Taking Notes As you read, use a diagram like the one below to identify how the Republicans reduced the role of government.

Reducing the Role of Government

INDIANA ACADEMIC STANDARDS
United States History

8.1.8 Evaluate the significance of the presidential and congressional election of 1800 and the transfer of political authority and power to the Democratic-Republican Party led by the new president, Thomas Jefferson (1801).

8.1.12 Explain the main issues, decisions, and consequences of landmark Supreme Court cases.

American Diary

For eight years, Thomas Jefferson opposed the Federalists and eventually won the presidency as a member of a new political party—the Democratic-Republicans. In his Inaugural Address, Jefferson tried to reach out to Federalists and bridge the gap that developed between the two parties. "We are all Republicans, we are all Federalists. . . . Let us, then, with courage and confidence pursue our own Federal and Republican principles, our attachment to union and representative government."

—from Jefferson's first Inaugural Address, 1801

The Capitol, Washington, D.C., 1800

The Election of 1800

Main Idea The election of 1800 showed that power could be peacefully transferred even when the political parties were in disagreement.

History and You Think about today's political campaigns. Are they based on emotional appeals or serious discussion of the issues? Read to find out how the presidential election campaign of 1800 was conducted.

· ·

The Federalist and Republican Parties fought a bitter election campaign in 1800. Federalists supported President Adams for a second term and Charles Pinckney for vice president. Republicans nominated **Thomas Jefferson** for president and **Aaron Burr** as his running mate.

The election campaign of 1800 differed greatly from campaigns of today. Neither Adams nor Jefferson traveled around the country to gather support. This would have been considered inappropriate. Instead, the candidates and their supporters began a letter-writing campaign. They sent hundreds of letters to leading citizens and newspapers to make their views public. Federalists accused Jefferson, who believed in freedom of religion, of being "godless." Republicans warned that the Federalists favored the wealthy and would bring back monarchy.

Election Deadlock

Jefferson and Burr each received 73 electoral votes. Because of the tie vote, the House of Representatives had to decide the election. At this time, the electors voted for each candidate individually. The candidate with the majority of votes became president. The candidate with the next-largest number of votes became vice president.

In the House, Federalists saw a chance to prevent the election of Jefferson. They supported Burr. For 35 ballots, the election remained tied. Finally, at Alexander Hamilton's urging, one Federalist decided not to vote for Burr. Jefferson became president, and Burr became vice president.

To prevent another tie between a presidential and vice-presidential candidate, Congress passed the Twelfth Amendment to the Constitution in 1803. Electors now had to vote for the president and vice president on separate ballots.

By the Numbers — Election Results, 1800

Boundary disputed by Britain and the U.S.

0 400 kilometers
0 400 miles
Albers Equal-Area projection

Presidential Candidate
- ☐ Jefferson (Democratic-Republican)
- ☐ Adams (Federalist)
- 3 Electoral votes

NH 6
VT 4
MA 16
NY 12
RI 4
PA 8 7
NJ 7
CT 9
Indiana Terr.
Terr. NW of Ohio R.
DE 3
VA 21
MD 3
KY 4
TN 3
NC 8 4
Terr. South of Ohio R.
SC 8
GA 4
Miss. Terr.

Critical Thinking

Speculating Do you think a person's political views will always match those of his or her political party?

Invention and Design Thomas Jefferson was a passionate inventor and architect. He invented a plow that was easy to use on hills, a machine to make macaroni, and a device to encode secret messages. Jefferson also designed his Monticello home and the Rotunda on the campus of the University of Virginia.

"One new idea leads to another, that to a third, and so on through a course of time until some one, with whom no one of these ideas was original, combines all together, and produces what is justly called a new invention."

—*The Writings of Thomas Jefferson*

▲ Jefferson employed other people's inventions at his Monticello home. He used a copying machine, known as a "polygraph," invented by John Isaac Hawkins. This machine used two pens to copy words at the same time, allowing the writer to create automatic duplicates of documents.

◄ Thomas Jefferson and Charles-Louis Clerisseau were the architects for Virginia's State Capitol in Richmond. Jefferson's design was inspired by first-century Roman architecture.

Critical Thinking

Drawing Conclusions What characteristics do you think a person should have in order to be a successful inventor?

Jefferson's Inauguration

Jefferson, dressed in everyday clothes, walked from his boardinghouse to the Senate to be sworn in as president. President Adams chose not to attend the ceremony.

In his Inaugural Address, Jefferson tried to bridge the gap between the political parties. Then he outlined some of his goals. They included "a wise and frugal government" and "the support of state governments in all their rights." Jefferson believed a large federal government threatened liberty. The states, he believed, could better protect freedom.

Jefferson believed in reducing the power and size of the government. These ideas were **similar** to the French philosophy known as **laissez-faire** (LEH•SAY FEHR). This phrase means "let people do as they choose."

✔ **Reading Check** **Describing** What does the Twelfth Amendment require?

Jefferson's Presidency

Main Idea Thomas Jefferson wanted to reduce the power of the federal government.

History and You How do you think government should balance individual liberty with national interests? Read about Jefferson's views.

Thomas Jefferson had strong ideas about how to make the United States a great nation. He surrounded himself with those who shared his views.

Cutting Costs

Jefferson and Albert Gallatin, secretary of the treasury, reduced the national debt. They scaled down military expenses. All federal internal taxes, including the whiskey tax, were repealed. Government funds would come only from **customs duties**—taxes on imported goods—and from the money raised from the sale of western lands. Jefferson also limited the number of federal government workers to a few hundred people.

Judiciary Act of 1801

Before Jefferson took office, the Federalists passed the **Judiciary Act of 1801.** This act set up regional courts for the United States with 16 judges and other judicial officials.

In his last days as president, John Adams made hundreds of appointments to these judicial positions with the approval of the Federalist-controlled Congress. Adams also asked John Marshall, secretary of state, to serve as chief justice. Thus, Adams shut Jefferson out of the appointment process and ensured Federalist control of the courts.

Adams and Marshall worked around the clock to process these judicial appointments. The appointments could not take effect, however, until the papers, also known as commissions, for these last-minute "midnight judges" were received. When Jefferson became president, a few of the commissions had not yet been delivered. He told his Secretary of State James Madison not to deliver them. One commission was to go to William Marbury.

Marbury v. Madison

To force the delivery of his commission, Marbury took his case directly to the Supreme Court. He claimed this court had jurisdiction. John Marshall wrote an opinion turning down Marbury's claim. He noted that the Constitution did not give the Court jurisdiction to decide Marbury's case.

In *Marbury v. Madison,* three principles of judicial review were established: (1) the Constitution is the supreme law; (2) the Constitution must be followed when there is a **conflict,** or disagreement, between it and any other law; and (3) the judicial branch must uphold the Constitution and nullify, or cancel, unconstitutional laws.

Marshall broadened federal power at the expense of the states. In *McCulloch* v. *Maryland* (1819), the Court held that Congress is allowed to do more than the Constitution expressly authorizes it to do. In *Gibbons* v. *Ogden* (1824), the Court held that federal law takes precedence over state law in interstate transportation.

Reading Check **Summarizing** Summarize the three principles of judicial review.

Section 1 Review

History ONLINE
Study Central™ To review this section, go to glencoe.com.

Vocabulary

1. Use the following terms in sentences that show you understand their meanings: similar, laissez-faire, customs duties, judicial review, conflict.

Main Ideas

2. **Discussing** How did President Jefferson's Inaugural Address reflect his beliefs about government?

3. **Explaining** Explain how the Federalists benefited from the Judiciary Act of 1801.

Critical Thinking

4. **Identifying Central Issues** Use a diagram like the one below to show how the powers of the Supreme Court and federal law were extended.

Case	Decision
Marbury v. *Madison*	
McCulloch v. *Maryland*	
Gibbons v. *Ogden*	

5. **Persuasive Writing** You are a supporter of Thomas Jefferson in the 1800 election. Write a letter to voters that will appear in all the newspapers in your state.

Answer the
6. **Essential Question**
In what ways did Thomas Jefferson and the Republicans limit the powers of the government?

Essential Question ◄

How did the Louisiana Purchase affect the nation's economy and politics?

Reading Guide

Content Vocabulary
Conestoga wagon *(p. 281)*
secede *(p. 285)*

Academic Vocabulary
purchase *(p. 283)*   authority *(p.283)*

Key People and Events
Napoleon Bonaparte *(p. 282)*
Meriwether Lewis *(p. 284)*
William Clark *(p. 284)*
Sacagawea *(p. 284)*
Zebulon Pike *(p. 285)*

Reading Strategy
Taking Notes As you read, use a diagram like the one below to describe the areas that Lewis and Clark and Zebulon Pike explored.

Explorer	Area Explored
Lewis and Clark ➡	
Zebulon Pike ➡	

INDIANA ACADEMIC STANDARDS
United States History

8.1.11 Explain the events leading up to and the significance of the Louisiana Purchase (1803) and the expedition of Lewis and Clark (1803–1806).

8.3.7 Using maps identify changes influenced by growth, economic development, and human migration in the eighteenth and nineteenth centuries.

American Diary

In this journal entry from May 5, 1805, Meriwether Lewis describes America's bounty along the trail: "Buffalo Elk and goats or Antelopes feeding in every direction; we kill whatever we wish, the buffalo furnish us with fine veal and fat beef, we also have venison and beaver tails when we wish them; the flesh of the Elk and goat are less esteemed, and certainly are inferior. We have not been able to take any fish for some time past. The country is as yesterday beautiful in the extreme."

—*from the journals of Lewis and Clark*

Lewis and Clark explore the lands west of the Mississippi River.

Western Territory

Main Idea As Americans moved west in the early 1800s, Spain and France made a secret agreement about land that affected American trade.

History and You If you have ever moved to a new city or state, what challenges did you face? How did you learn where grocery stores or your school were located? Read to learn about challenges that the pioneers experienced as they moved west.

• •

During the early 1800s, Americans moved west in search of land and adventure. Pioneers traveled over the mountains into Kentucky and Tennessee. Many also set out for the less settled areas of the Northwest Territory. Most of these pioneers were farmers. They made a long and exhausting journey over the Appalachian Mountains. Pioneers heading to the western lands had to trudge along crude, muddy roads or cut their way through dense forests.

Settlers loaded their household goods into **Conestoga wagons,** sturdy vehicles topped with white canvas. These westward-bound pioneers traveled with their two most valued possessions: rifles and axes. Rifles were carried for protection and for hunting animals for food. Axes helped the settlers cut through the dense forests so that their wagons could travel through them.

In 1800 the territory of the United States extended only as far west as the Mississippi River. The area to the west of the river was known as the Louisiana Territory. This region belonged to Spain. It was an enormous area of land, anchored to the south by the city of New Orleans and extending west to the Rocky Mountains. Its northern boundaries remained undefined.

Many of the pioneers established farms along rivers that fed into the upper Mississippi River. They used the river system to ship their crops to markets. The goods they sent downriver were unloaded in New Orleans. The goods were then loaded onto other ships and sent to markets on the East Coast. If the farmers did not have access to the Mississippi River, then there was no way to ship their goods.

Even though the Spanish controlled the region, they allowed the Americans to sail on the lower Mississippi and trade in New Orleans. For the western farmers, this agreement was vital to their economic survival.

Primary Source / The Journals

Exploring the West From 1804 to 1806, Meriwether Lewis and William Clark explored and mapped more than 7,000 miles (11,265 km) from St. Louis to the Pacific Ocean and back. During the journey, they met with many Native Americans and accumulated valuable information about the western frontier.

In addition to their travel supplies, the expedition also took along items that were used to trade or give as gifts to the Native Americans. These items included:

- 12 dozen pocket mirrors
- 144 small pairs of scissors
- 8 brass kettles
- 33 pounds (15 kg) of tiny beads of assorted colors

Critical Thinking

Speculating What challenges do you think the expedition might have faced?

Wagons to Go West Conestoga wagons were first built in the Conestoga Creek region of Lancaster, Pennsylvania. During the mid-1700s, these sturdy wagons transported settlers over the Appalachian Mountains. As people pushed even farther westward, Conestoga wagons could be seen rolling across the plains toward Oregon and California.

1 Six to eight draft horses or a dozen oxen pull the wagon. The driver rides or walks beside the animals.

2 The boat-shaped wagon's high front and back keep goods from falling out on steep mountain trails.

3 A **toolbox** attached to the side of the wagon holds spare parts for needed repairs.

4 A white canvas cloth stretches over the hoops, or **wagon bows.** This cover protects passengers and cargo from heat, rain, and snow.

5 Broad **wheels** help keep the heavy wagon from being mired in the mud.

The average Conestoga wagon was 21 feet (6 m) long and 11 feet (3 m) high. It could carry up to 12,000 pounds (5,443 kg) of cargo.

Critical Thinking

Listing List three things a family traveling by wagon will have to plan for.

The French Threat

In 1802, however, the Spanish suddenly changed their policy. They refused to allow American goods to move into or past New Orleans. President Jefferson confirmed that Spain and France had secretly agreed to transfer the Louisiana Territory to France.

Jefferson was alarmed. This agreement between Spain and France posed a serious diplomatic and economic threat to the United States. France's leader, **Napoleon Bonaparte,** had plans to create empires in Europe and the Americas. Jefferson believed French control would put American trade on the Mississippi River at risk. Jefferson authorized Robert Livingston, the new minister to France, to offer as much as $10 million for New Orleans and West Florida in order to gain control of the territory. Jefferson believed that France had gained Florida as well as Louisiana in its secret agreement with Spain.

Revolt in Santo Domingo

Napoleon saw Santo Domingo as an important Caribbean naval base from which he could control an American empire. Events in Santo Domingo, however, ended Napoleon's dream of a Western empire.

The ideas of the French Revolution inspired enslaved Africans and other laborers in Santo Domingo to revolt against the island's plantation owners. Toussaint-Louverture (TOO•SA LOO•vuhr•TYUR) led the rebels. After fierce fighting, the rebels won and declared the colony an independent republic. Toussaint-Louverture established a new government.

In 1802 Napoleon sent troops to regain control of Santo Domingo, but they were not successful. By 1804, the French were driven out of Santo Domingo. The country regained its original name of Haiti.

Reading Check **Explaining** Why did French control of the Louisiana Territory worry Jefferson?

The Nation Expands

Main Idea The Louisiana Purchase opened a vast area to exploration and settlement.

History and You Imagine you are preparing to lead an expedition to explore new lands. Who would you travel with? What would you like to research? Read about the exploration of the Louisiana Territory.

• •

Without Santo Domingo, Napoleon had little use for Louisiana. Napoleon, however, needed money to finance his plans for war against Britain. The French believed that it was time to sell the Louisiana Territory.

French foreign minister Charles de Talleyrand informed the American diplomats that the entire Louisiana Territory was for sale. Robert Livingston and James Monroe, who was Jefferson's new special representative, were taken completely by surprise. They were not authorized to accept such an offer. The deal, however, was too good to pass up. After a few days of negotiation, the parties agreed on a price of $15 million.

The new territory would provide cheap and abundant land for farmers for future generations and give the United States control of the Mississippi River. Jefferson worried, though, about whether the **purchase** was legal. The Constitution said nothing about acquiring new territory. By what **authority,** or power, could he justify the purchase? Livingston wrote from Paris. He urged Jefferson to accept the deal before Napoleon changed his mind. Jefferson decided the government's treaty-making powers allowed the purchase of the new territory. The Senate approved it in October 1803. The size of the United States doubled.

Lewis and Clark

Little was known about the newly acquired land west of the Mississippi. Even before the deal was complete, Jefferson had been making plans to learn more about the western territory. He persuaded Congress to sponsor an expedition to gather information about the new land. Jefferson was particularly interested in the expedition as a scientific venture.

Louisiana Purchase and Westward Expansion   NATIONAL GEOGRAPHIC

United States, 1803
Lewis and Clark
Lewis and Clark return
Pike
■ Fort

"The great objects in view . . . were to . . . acquire such geographical knowledge of the southwestern boundary of Louisiana as to enable our Government to enter into a definite arrangement for a line of demarcation between that territory and North Mexico."

—Lt. Zebulon Pike, 1806

▼ Zebulon Pike Expedition

Map Skills

Movement Why did the expedition travel so far north into the territory?

Maps In MOtion See StudentWorks™ Plus or glencoe.com.

People IN HISTORY

Sacagawea
Shoshone Interpreter

Sacagawea, the daughter of a Shoshone chief, was kidnapped by the Hidatsa when she was a young girl. Later, she was sold to a French Canadian fur trader who married her.

The couple brought along their infant son when they were hired as interpreters by Meriwether Lewis and William Clark for their expedition to the Pacific Ocean.

Sacagawea made herself invaluable. She negotiated the purchases of horses, found edible wild plants, and made moccasins and clothing. Clark wrote that her presence alone calmed fears among Native Americans:

William Clark's journal ▼

"The sight of This Indian woman . . . confirmed those people of our friendly intentions, as no woman ever accompanies a war party of Indians in this quarter [region]."

—from the journals of Lewis and Clark

CRITICAL Thinking

Theorizing What challenges might the expedition have faced without Sacagawea?

The expedition would document findings about the territory's plants and animals and recommend sites for future forts.

The expedition was also responsible for finding and mapping the fabled "Northwest Passage." In order to trade with Asia, Europeans had to sail around Africa. The route was time-consuming and costly, so European explorers searched, unsuccessfully, for a more direct route. Once the Americas were colonized, Americans and Europeans continued to sail around Africa or around the tip of South America in order to reach Asia. It became more important than ever to find a water route across North America.

To head the expedition, Jefferson chose **Meriwether Lewis,** his 28-year-old private secretary. During the Whiskey Rebellion, Lewis joined the militia and had been in the army since that time. The expedition's coleader was **William Clark.** Clark was 32 years old and a friend of Lewis's.

Both Lewis and Clark were well-informed amateur scientists. They both had conducted business with Native Americans. Together they assembled a crew of expert river men, gunsmiths, carpenters, scouts, and a cook. Two men of mixed Native American and French heritage served as interpreters. An African American named York was also a member of the group.

The expedition left St. Louis in the spring of 1804 and worked its way up the Missouri River. Lewis and Clark kept a journal and made notes on what they saw and did.

Along their journey, the members of the expedition encountered many Native American groups. One young Shoshone woman named **Sacagawea** (SA•kuh•juh•WEE•uh) joined their group as a guide. After 18 months and nearly 4,000 miles (6,437 km), Lewis and Clark reached the Pacific Ocean. They spent the winter there, and then both explorers headed back east along separate routes.

The expedition returned in September 1806. Lewis and Clark collected valuable information about people, plants, animals, and the geography of the West. Perhaps most important, their journey inspired people to move westward.

Pike's Expedition

Jefferson sent others to explore the wilderness in addition to Lewis and Clark. Lieutenant **Zebulon Pike** led two expeditions between 1805 and 1807. He traveled through the upper Mississippi River valley and into present-day Colorado. In Colorado he found a snowcapped mountain he called Grand Peak, known today as Pikes Peak. Americans learned about the Great Plains and Rocky Mountains from his travels. Pike also mapped part of the Rio Grande and traveled across northern Mexico and what is now southern Texas.

Federalists Plan to Secede

Many Federalists opposed the Louisiana Purchase. They feared that states created from the territory would be Republican and the Federalists would lose power. A group of Federalists in Massachusetts plotted to **secede,** or withdraw, from the Union. New England would become the "Northern Confederacy."

The plotters wanted their plan to be successful. They realized that the Northern Confederacy would have to include New York. The Massachusetts Federalists needed a powerful friend in that state who would support their plan. They turned to Aaron Burr. The Republicans cast aside Burr when he refused to withdraw from the 1800 election. The Federalists gave Burr their support when he ran for governor of New York in 1804.

Burr and Hamilton

Alexander Hamilton had never trusted Aaron Burr. Now Hamilton was concerned about rumors of secession. He heard that Burr had secretly agreed to lead New York out of the Union. Hamilton accused Burr of plotting treason. When Burr lost the election for governor, he blamed Hamilton and challenged him to a duel. In July 1804, the two men—armed with pistols—met in Weehawken, New Jersey. Hamilton hated dueling and pledged not to shoot at his rival. Burr, however, aimed to hit Hamilton and shot him. Hamilton was seriously wounded and died the next day. Burr fled to avoid arrest.

✓ **Reading Check** **Summarizing** Why did France sell the Louisiana Territory to the United States?

Section 2 Review

History ONLINE
Study Central™ To review this section, go to glencoe.com.

Vocabulary

1. Define each of the following terms: Conestoga wagon, purchase, authority, secede.

Main Ideas

2. Specifying How did the secret agreement between Spain and France affect American settlers?

3. Summarizing Discuss the reaction of the Federalists to the Louisiana Purchase.

Critical Thinking

4. Organizing Create a graphic organizer like the one below that lists the benefits of acquiring the Louisiana Territory.

5. Creative Writing You are the cook on the Lewis and Clark expedition. Write a one-paragraph diary entry that describes the crew and how you feel about the trip so far.

Answer the
6. Essential Question
How did the Louisiana Purchase affect the nation's economy and politics?

Essential Question ◄

What were the challenges to the nation's stability during the late 1700s and early 1800s?

Reading Guide

Content Vocabulary

tribute (p. 287)   embargo (p. 290)
neutral rights (p. 289)   nationalism (p. 293)
impressment (p. 289)

Academic Vocabulary

react (p. 289)   restriction (p. 291)

Key People and Events

Embargo Act (p. 290)
Nonintercourse Act (p. 290)
Tecumseh (p. 291)
Battle of Tippecanoe (p. 293)
Henry Clay (p. 293)
John Calhoun (p. 293)

Reading Strategy

Taking Notes As you read, create a chart like the one below, and describe the actions the United States took in each of the situations.

	Action Taken
Demand for Tribute	
Attacks on the *Chesapeake*	
Tecumseh's Confederation	

INDIANA ACADEMIC STANDARDS
United States History

8.1.13 Explain the causes and consequences of the War of 1812, including the Rush-Bagot Agreement (1818).

8.3.2 Identify and create maps showing the physical growth and development of the United States from settlement of the original thirteen colonies through Reconstruction (1877) including transportation routes used during the period.

American Diary

"We are now about to embark upon an expedition, which may terminate in our sudden deaths, our perpetual [eternal] slavery, or our immortal glory. The event is left for futurity [the future] to determine. The first quality of a good seaman, is, personal courage,—the second, obedience to orders,—the third, fortitude [strength] under sufferings; to these may be added, an ardent [passionate] love of country. I am confident you possess them all."

—Lt. Stephen Decatur to the crew of the USS Essex

Stephen Decatur and U.S. sailors attack a gunboat in Tripoli's harbor.

Americans on Foreign Seas

Main Idea Pirates made travel by sea dangerous and brought the United States into conflict with Tripoli.

History and You Think about the dangers at sea that sailors face. Read to learn about the challenges of those Americans who traded on the open seas in the early 1800s.

• •

Sea travel was dangerous in the early 1800s. Sailors fought deadly storms and were threatened by pirates. Many Americans, however, depended on trade with foreign nations and were forced to rely on traveling by ship.

In 1785 the *Empress of China* returned to New York from China with a highly prized cargo of tea and silk. The goods sold for a fabulous profit. Soon, ships from New York, Philadelphia, and New England sailed regularly to China and India, transporting furs and other goods. American merchant ships began sailing to South America, Africa, and lands along the Mediterranean Sea.

War between France and Britain in the mid-1790s gave an additional boost to American shipping. To avoid being captured or destroyed by the enemy, many French and British merchant ships remained at home. American shippers profited from the situation and increased their trade. By 1800, the United States had almost 1,000 merchant ships trading around the world.

Barbary Pirates

Sailing on foreign seas could be dangerous because of piracy. For example, pirates from the Barbary Coast states of North Africa—Morocco, Algiers, Tripoli, and Tunis—terrorized European ships that were sailing on the Mediterranean Sea. Pirates demanded **tribute,** or protection money, from their country's governments to let their ships pass safely. European countries routinely paid tribute so that their ships would be undisturbed. They believed that it was less expensive to pay the Barbary Coast pirates than it was to go to war with them.

War With Tripoli

The United States, too, had to pay tribute to the Barbary Coast states. The ruler of Tripoli, however, did not think it was enough. In 1801 he asked the United States for more money. When President Jefferson refused, Tripoli declared war on the United States.

Primary Source / **USS Constitution**

Still Serving In 1794 President George Washington authorized the construction of six warships, including the *Constitution,* to protect American merchant ships. Today, the USS *Constitution* is the oldest active ship serving in the United States Navy.

The USS *Constitution* in Boston Harbor ▶

Critical Thinking

Speculating Why do you think the newly created United States needed a navy?

Jefferson sent ships to blockade Tripoli. The Americans, though, could not defeat the pirates, and the conflict continued.

Pirates seized the United States warship *Philadelphia* in 1804. They towed the ship into Tripoli Harbor and threw the crew into jail. Stephen Decatur, a 25-year-old U.S. Navy captain, took action. He slipped into the heavily guarded harbor with a small raiding party. Decatur burned the captured ship to prevent the pirates from using it. A British admiral praised the deed as the "most bold and daring act of the age."

The war ended in June 1805. Tripoli agreed to stop demanding tribute, but the United States had to pay $60,000 for the prisoners to be released. It would not be until 1815, however, that American tribute payments ended completely.

Reading Check Explaining Why did Tripoli declare war on the United States?

Freedom of the Seas

Main Idea A war between Great Britain and France threatened the security of the United States, as well as American shipping and trade.

History and You What problems might develop when a country refuses to trade with other countries? What do you think happens to that country's industries and its standard of living? Read to find out what happened when Thomas Jefferson tried to stop trade to avoid getting drawn into a war.

• •

Thomas Jefferson was reelected in 1804, and his second term began with the nation at peace. Across the Atlantic Ocean, however, Great Britain and France were fighting a war that threatened to interfere with American trade. The United States ended the war with Tripoli in 1805. Now the United States was caught in the middle of a war between Great Britain and France.

Primary Source / The Barbary Wars

An Ongoing War The first Barbary War took place from 1801 to 1805. In 1805 Tripoli agreed to stop demanding tribute from the United States. Pirate raids, however, continued on American ships. After the War of 1812, Stephen Decatur and the United States Navy used military force to stop the raids and end tribute payments permanently.

The USS *Enterprise* defeated and captured the pirate vessel *Tripoli* in 1801. Seventy-five percent of the *Tripoli*'s crew was killed in the fighting, while there were no casualties on the *Enterprise*. ▼

Stephen Decatur and his crew attack one of Tripoli's gunboats. Decatur became a national hero as a result of his actions in the Barbary Wars. ▼

Commodore Edward Preble took command of the U.S. Mediterranean fleet in 1803. His leadership helped defeat Tripoli and end the war. ▶

Critical Thinking

Predicting How do you think European countries viewed the U.S. actions after the wars?

Economics & History

A nation's balance of trade is the difference between the value of a nation's exports and its imports. A nation has a trade surplus when it exports more than it imports. For example, if the United States exported $100 in cotton and imported $50 in tea, it would be experiencing a trade surplus, or positive balance of trade.

▼ New Orleans, 1841

Graph Skills

Applying In 1810 did the United States have a positive or negative balance of trade? Explain.

Graphs In Motion See StudentWorks™ Plus or glencoe.com.

Imports and Exports, 1800–1820

Nonintercourse Act
Embargo Act
2
Panic of 1819
War of 1812
1
3

Millions of $ — 180, 160, 140, 120, 100, 80, 60, 40, 20, 0

Year — 1800, 1805, 1810, 1815, 1820

1 Exports: goods sold **2 Imports:** goods purchased **3 Balance of trade:** difference between the value of a nation's exports and its imports

Source: *Historical Statistics of the United States*

Neutral Rights Violated

When Britain and France went to war in 1803, America had a prosperous trade with both countries. As long as the United States remained neutral, shippers could continue doing business. A nation not involved in a conflict had **neutral rights.** That is, it had the right to sail the seas and not take sides.

For two years, American shipping prospered. By 1805, however, Britain and France lost patience with American "neutrality." Britain blockaded the French coast and threatened to search all ships trading with France. France later announced that it would search and seize ships caught trading with Britain.

American Sailors Kidnapped

The British were in desperate need of sailors for their naval war. Many of their own sailors had deserted due to the terrible living conditions in the British Royal Navy. British naval ships began stopping American ships to search for suspected British deserters. The British then forced these deserters to return to the British navy. This practice of forcing people to serve in the navy was **impressment.** While some of those taken were deserters from the British navy, the British also impressed thousands of native-born and naturalized American citizens.

Attack on the *Chesapeake*

Often the British waited for American ships outside an American harbor where they boarded and searched them. This occurred in June 1807 off the coast of Virginia. The *Leopard*, a British warship, stopped the American vessel *Chesapeake*. The *Leopard's* captain demanded to search the American ship for British deserters, but the *Chesapeake's* captain refused. The British opened fire, crippling the *Chesapeake* and killing three crew members.

News of the attack spread. Americans **reacted** with an anti-British fury not seen since the Revolutionary War. Secretary of State James Madison responded to the news.

Jefferson's embargo policy had a disastrous effect on American trade, and it did not stop the British and French from seizing American ships.

1. **Interpreting** What are King George and Napoleon Bonaparte doing?

2. **Drawing Conclusions** Do you think this cartoon supports Jefferson's embargo policy? Why or why not?

A. King George of England

B. Thomas Jefferson

C. Napoleon Bonaparte of France

He called the attack an outrage. Many Americans demanded war against Britain. President Jefferson, though, sought a course of action other than war.

A Disastrous Trade Ban

Because Britain violated America's neutral rights, Jefferson banned some trade with Britain. The attack on the *Chesapeake* triggered even stronger measures.

In December 1807, Congress passed the **Embargo Act.** An **embargo** prohibits trade with another country. In addition to Britain, the act banned imports from and exports to *all* foreign countries. Jefferson wanted to prevent Americans from using other countries to trade with France and Britain indirectly. Jefferson and Madison wanted to avoid war, but they also wanted to hurt Britain by banning the trade of agricultural products.

The embargo of 1807 was a disaster. It wiped out all American commerce with other nations and was ineffective against Britain. The British simply turned to Latin America for agricultural goods. Congress then enacted the weaker **Nonintercourse Act.** This act prohibited trade only with Britain and France and their colonies, but it too was unpopular and unsuccessful.

Jefferson Leaves Office

Jefferson followed Washington's precedent by making it clear that he would not be a candidate for a third term. The Republicans chose James Madison as their candidate for president. The Federalists nominated Charles Pinckney and hoped that anger over the embargo would help them win. Pinckney carried most of New England, but the Federalist ticket gained little support from the other regions. Madison won the presidency with 122 electoral votes to Pinckney's 47 votes.

Reading Check **Summarizing** Why was the Embargo Act ineffective?

Student Web Activity Visit glencoe.com and complete the Web Activity about American trade issues in the early 1800s.

War Fever

Main Idea Trade issues with Britain and France and tensions between Native Americans and settlers challenged James Madison.

History and You Why do you think tension between different groups occurs? Read about the conflicts among the various groups during the early 1800s.

· ·

James Madison took office as president under unfavorable conditions. At home and abroad, the nation was involved in the embargo crisis. Meanwhile, Britain continued to halt American ships. Cries for war with Britain grew louder.

Closer to War

In 1810 Congress passed a law permitting direct trade with either France or Britain, depending on which country first lifted its trade **restrictions,** or limits, against America. Napoleon seized the opportunity and promised to end France's trade restrictions.

The French, however, continued to seize American ships, selling them and pocketing the proceeds. Americans were deeply divided. The nation was on the verge of war, but it was hard to decide whether the enemy was Britain or France. Madison believed that Britain was the bigger threat to the United States.

Frontier Conflicts

Madison also received news about problems in the West. Ohio became a state in 1803. White settlers wanted more land in the Ohio Valley. Native Americans already gave up many millions of acres. However, the settlers continued to move onto lands that were guaranteed to Native Americans by the treaty.

Tensions increased as some Native Americans renewed their contacts with British agents and fur traders in Canada.

Other Native Americans pursued a new strategy. **Tecumseh** (tuh•KUHM•suh), a powerful Shawnee chief, built a confederacy among Native American nations in the Northwest.

Territorial Expansion, 1800–1820 ☐ NATIONAL GEOGRAPHIC

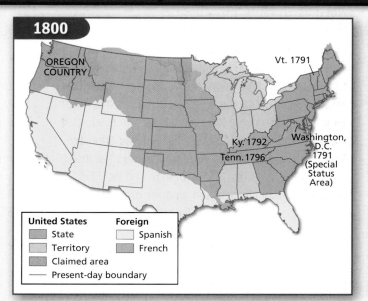

1800

OREGON COUNTRY

Vt. 1791

Ky. 1792

Tenn. 1796

Washington, D.C. 1791 (Special Status Area)

United States
State
Territory
Claimed area
— Present-day boundary

Foreign
Spanish
French

1820

British Treaty Line of 1818

Red River Basin 1818

Maine 1820

OREGON COUNTRY U.S.-British Occupation

LOUISIANA PURCHASE 1803

IL 1818   IN 1816   OH 1803

MO

Spanish Treaty Line of 1819

MS 1817   AL 1819

LA 1812

Florida Cession 1819

United States
State
Territory
Special status
Claimed area

Foreign
Spanish
— Present-day boundary

Map Skills

Place Describe the changes in French territory between 1800 and 1820.

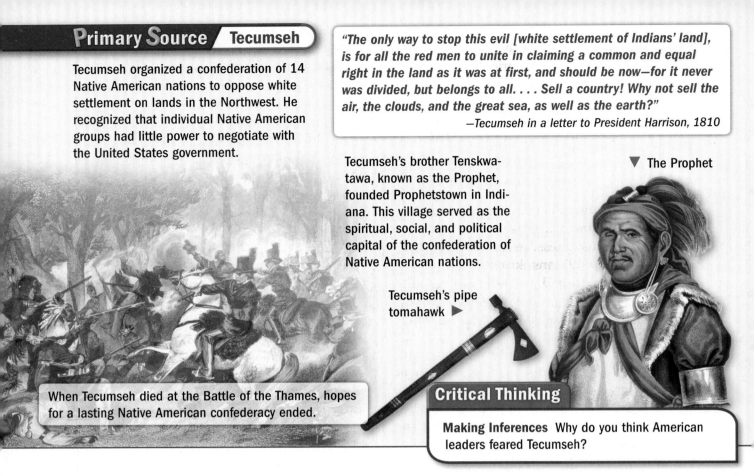

Tecumseh organized a confederation of 14 Native American nations to oppose white settlement on lands in the Northwest. He recognized that individual Native American groups had little power to negotiate with the United States government.

"The only way to stop this evil [white settlement of Indians' land], is for all the red men to unite in claiming a common and equal right in the land as it was at first, and should be now—for it never was divided, but belongs to all. . . . Sell a country! Why not sell the air, the clouds, and the great sea, as well as the earth?"

—Tecumseh in a letter to President Harrison, 1810

Tecumseh's brother Tenskwatawa, known as the Prophet, founded Prophetstown in Indiana. This village served as the spiritual, social, and political capital of the confederation of Native American nations.

▼ The Prophet

Tecumseh's pipe tomahawk ▶

When Tecumseh died at the Battle of the Thames, hopes for a lasting Native American confederacy ended.

Critical Thinking

Making Inferences Why do you think American leaders feared Tecumseh?

Tecumseh believed that a strong alliance—with the backing of the British in Canada—could halt white movement into Native American lands. A commanding speaker, Tecumseh had great political skills. He believed the U.S. government's treaties with separate Native American nations were worthless. "The Great Spirit gave this great island to his red children," he said. No one nation had the right to give it away.

Tecumseh had a powerful ally in his brother, Tenskwatawa, known as the Prophet. The Prophet urged Native Americans to return to their ancestors' customs. His message attracted a large following. The Prophet founded Prophetstown in northern Indiana, located near where the Tippecanoe and Wabash Rivers meet.

A Meeting With Harrison

William Henry Harrison, governor of the Indiana Territory, became alarmed by the growing power of the two Shawnee brothers.

He feared they would form an alliance with the British. Harrison warned Tecumseh in a letter that the United States had more warriors than all the Indian nations combined. Tecumseh replied to Harrison in person.

PRIMARY SOURCE

"Brother . . . Since the peace was made, you have killed some Shawnees, Delawares and Winnebagoes. . . . You have taken land from us and I do not see how we can remain at peace if you continue to do so. You try to force red people to do some injury. It is you that are pushing them on to some mischief. You endeavor [try] to make distinctions. You try to prevent the Indians from doing as they wish—to unite and let them consider their lands common property of the whole."

—from *Tecumseh, an Indian Moses*

The Battle of Tippecanoe

When Tecumseh went south to expand the confederacy, Harrison attacked Prophetstown on the Tippecanoe River. After more than two hours, the Prophet's forces fled in defeat.

The **Battle of Tippecanoe** was declared a glorious victory for the Americans. Harrison's victory, however, resulted in something the American people hoped to prevent. Tecumseh joined forces with the British, whom, settlers believed, had supplied his confederacy with guns.

War Hawks

In the meantime, President Madison faced demands for a more aggressive policy toward Britain. The most pressure came from a group of young Republicans known as the War Hawks. They wanted war with Britain. The leading War Hawks were Kentucky's **Henry Clay** and South Carolina's **John Calhoun.**

The War Hawks were mainly from the West and South. They supported increases in military spending and were driven by hunger for land. War Hawks from the West wanted the fertile forests of southern Canada, whereas Southerners desired Spanish Florida. The War Hawks also wanted to expand the nation's power. Their **nationalism**—or loyalty to their country—appealed to a renewed American patriotism.

Not everyone, however, wanted war. The Federalists in the Northeast remained strongly opposed to it.

Declaring War

By the spring of 1812, Madison knew that war with Britain was inevitable. In a message to Congress on June 1, he cited:

PRIMARY SOURCE

"Such is the spectacle of injuries and indignities which have been heaped on our country."
—from Madison's "War Message"

Madison asked for a declaration of war.

Meanwhile, the British had decided to end their policy of search and seizure of American ships. Unfortunately, it took much time for this news to travel across the Atlantic, and leaders in Washington, D.C., did not know about Britain's change in policy. Word of the policy change arrived too late. Once set in motion, the war machine could not be stopped.

 Reading Check **Summarizing** What factors led to the war with Britain?

Section 3 Review

History ONLINE
Study Central™ To review this section, go to glencoe.com.

Vocabulary

1. Define each of the following terms in a sentence: tribute, neutral rights, impressment, react, embargo, restriction, nationalism.

Main Ideas

2. **Discussing** How widespread was American trade by 1800? Include information about the types of goods that were traded.

3. **Explaining** Explain why U.S. security was threatened as a result of the war between Britain and France.

4. **Summarizing** How did conflict on the American frontier increase tensions between the United States and Britain?

Critical Thinking

5. **Drawing Conclusions** Use a diagram like the one below to identify how people from each region felt about going to war with Britain.

6. **Expository Writing** Take the role of William Henry Harrison. Write a letter to the president explaining why you plan to attack Prophetstown.

Answer the
7. **Essential Question**
What were the challenges to the nation's stability during the late 1700s and early 1800s?

The War of 1812

Essential Question

How did the United States benefit from its victory in the War of 1812?

Reading Guide

Content Vocabulary

frigate *(p. 296)*   privateer *(p. 296)*

Academic Vocabulary

underestimate *(p. 295)*

goal *(p. 297)*

Key People and Events

Andrew Jackson *(p. 296)*

Battle of Horseshoe Bend *(p. 296)*

Francis Scott Key *(p. 297)*

Treaty of Ghent *(p. 298)*

Battle of New Orleans *(p. 298)*

Reading Strategy

Taking Notes As you read, re-create the diagram below and describe each battle's outcome.

Battle		Outcome
Lake Erie	→	
Washington, D.C.	→	
New Orleans	→	

INDIANA ACADEMIC STANDARDS
United States History

8.1.13 Explain the causes and consequences of the War of 1812, including the Rush-Bagot Agreement (1818).

8.3.1 Read maps to interpret symbols and determine the landforms and human features that represent physical and cultural characteristics of areas in the United States.

American Diary

"When the detachment [small military unit], sent out to destroy Mr. Madison's house, entered his dining parlor, they found a dinner table spread. . . . You will readily imagine, that these preparations were beheld, by a party of hungry soldiers, with no indifferent eye. . . . They sat down to it, therefore, not indeed in the most orderly manner . . . and having satisfied their appetites . . . they finished by setting fire to the house which had so liberally entertained them."

—quoted from George Robert Gleig, a British soldier, in 1814

In August 1814, British troops burn Washington, D.C.

War Begins

Main Idea The United States was unprepared for war with Great Britain.

History and You Have you ever been unprepared for a quiz or a test? Read to learn how the United States was unprepared for the War of 1812.

. . . .

The War Hawks were confident that they would achieve a quick victory over the British. The Americans, however, were overall unprepared for war.

The regular army had fewer than 7,000 troops, and the states had between 50,000 and 100,000 poorly trained militia. Military commanders who were veterans of the American Revolution were too old for warfare. Support for the conflict was not unanimous, and some states opposed "Mr. Madison's War." In addition, the Americans **underestimated,** or misjudged, the strength of the British and their Native American allies.

The war began in July 1812. General William Hull led the American army from Detroit into Canada. Tecumseh and his warriors met Hull, who feared a massacre by the Native Americans. Hull surrendered Detroit to the British. General William Henry Harrison also made an unsuccessful attempt to invade Canada. Harrison decided that the Americans could make no headway into Canada as long as the British controlled Lake Erie.

Naval Battles

Oliver Hazard Perry, who commanded the Lake Erie naval forces, was ordered to seize the lake from the British. On September 10, 1813, Perry's ships defeated the British naval force. After the battle, Perry sent General Harrison the message "We have met the enemy and they are ours."

Lake Erie was now under American control. The British and their Native American allies tried to pull back from the Detroit area, but Harrison cut them off. In the Battle of the Thames on October 5, Tecumseh was killed.

The Americans also attacked the town of York (present-day Toronto), burning the parliament buildings. Even though Canada remained unconquered, the Americans had won some victories by the end of 1813.

Primary Source / Escape from Washington

Dolley Madison wrote her sister the day before British forces burned Washington, D.C.

"At this late hour, a wagon has been procured; I have had it filled with the . . . most valuable portable articles belonging to the house [White House].

I insist on waiting until the large picture of General Washington is secured. . . . And now, dear sister, I must leave this house. . . . When I shall again write to you, or where I shall be to-morrow, I cannot tell!!"

—Dolley Madison in a letter to her sister, 1814

Critical Thinking

Making Inferences Why do you think the British burned the White House?

▲ Dolley Madison, wife of President James Madison

The U.S. Navy had three of the fastest **frigates,** or warships, afloat. When the *Constitution* destroyed two British vessels within four months, Americans rejoiced. **Privateers,** armed private ships, also captured numerous British vessels, boosting American morale.

Setbacks for Native Americans

Before the Battle of the Thames, Tecumseh talked with the Creeks in the Mississippi Territory about a confederation. However, hopes for a confederation died with Tecumseh.

In March 1814, **Andrew Jackson** attacked the Creeks. Jackson's forces slaughtered more than 550 Creek people. Known as the **Battle of Horseshoe Bend,** the defeat forced the Creeks to give up most of their lands.

✔ **Reading Check** **Evaluating** Do you think the United States was prepared to wage war? Explain.

The British Offensive

Main Idea Americans were instilled with a sense of national pride after the Battle of New Orleans.

History and You When have you heard "The Star-Spangled Banner"? Read how the War of 1812 inspired the creation of the national anthem.

· ·

British fortunes improved in the spring of 1814. After winning the war against Napoleon, Britain was able to send more forces to America.

Attack on Washington, D.C.

The British sailed into Chesapeake Bay in August 1814. Their destination was Washington, D.C. On the outskirts of the capital, British troops quickly overpowered the American militia. They then marched into the city.

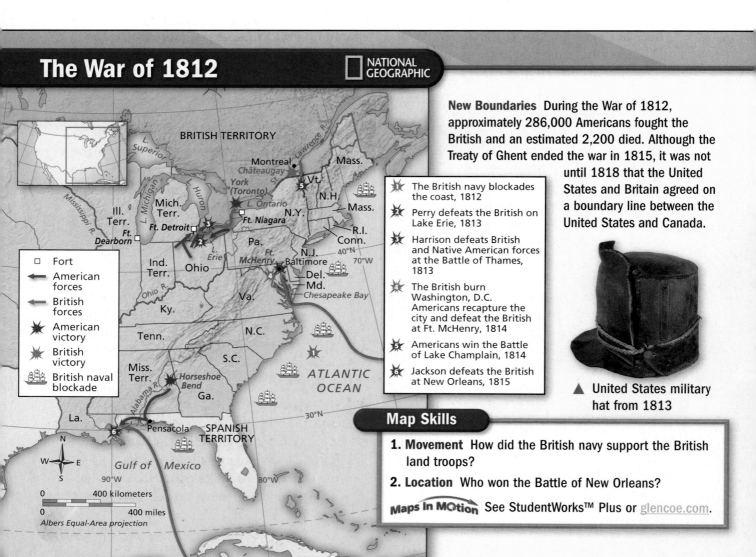

The War of 1812

NATIONAL GEOGRAPHIC

New Boundaries During the War of 1812, approximately 286,000 Americans fought the British and an estimated 2,200 died. Although the Treaty of Ghent ended the war in 1815, it was not until 1818 that the United States and Britain agreed on a boundary line between the United States and Canada.

1 The British navy blockades the coast, 1812

2 Perry defeats the British on Lake Erie, 1813

3 Harrison defeats British and Native American forces at the Battle of Thames, 1813

4 The British burn Washington, D.C. Americans recapture the city and defeat the British at Ft. McHenry, 1814

5 Americans win the Battle of Lake Champlain, 1814

6 Jackson defeats the British at New Orleans, 1815

▲ United States military hat from 1813

Map Skills

1. **Movement** How did the British navy support the British land troops?

2. **Location** Who won the Battle of New Orleans?

Maps In Motion See StudentWorks™ Plus or glencoe.com.

Fort
American forces
British forces
American victory
British victory
British naval blockade

The Battle of New Orleans

A Final Battle As a large British fleet approached New Orleans, the Americans prepared for battle. On January 8, 1815, the British attacked New Orleans. Andrew Jackson's force of about 7,000 troops hid behind cotton bales and concentrated their fire on the advancing British. Andrew Jackson's troops won the battle within half an hour.

There were 289 British killed during the battle compared to 71 Americans. The victory made Andrew Jackson a national hero. ▼

Jean Lafitte was a ▲ famous smuggler along the Gulf Coast. Hoping to gain a pardon for his illegal activities, he provided the Americans with information about British activities in the area.

◀ Andrew Jackson wears the uniform of a major general, his rank in the U.S. Army at the time of the Battle of New Orleans.

Critical Thinking

Speculating Why do you think people support presidential candidates who have had successful military careers?

"They proceeded, without a moment's delay, to burn and destroy everything in the most distant degree connected with the government," reported a British officer.

The Capitol and the president's mansion were among the buildings burned. Fortunately, a thunderstorm put out the fires before they could do more damage. August 24, 1814, was a low point for Americans.

Baltimore Holds Firm

To everyone's surprise, the British did not try to hold Washington, D.C. They left the city and sailed north to Baltimore. In mid-September, the people of Baltimore were ready for the attack and held firm against the British. A determined defense and fierce artillery fire from Fort McHenry in the harbor kept the British from entering the city.

Francis Scott Key, an attorney, watched the bombs burst over Fort McHenry during the night of September 13. The next morning he saw the American flag still flying over the fort. Deeply moved, Key wrote a poem that became known as "The Star-Spangled Banner." Congress designated "The Star-Spangled Banner" as the national anthem in 1931.

Defeat at Plattsburgh

Meanwhile, General Sir George Prevost led more than 10,000 British troops into New York from Canada. His **goal** was to capture Plattsburgh, a key city on the shore of Lake Champlain. The invasion was stopped when an American naval force on the lake defeated the British fleet in September 1814. Fearing the Americans would surround them, the British retreated into Canada.

After the Battle of Lake Champlain, the British decided the war in North America was too costly and unnecessary. They had defeated Napoleon in Europe. To keep fighting the United States would result in little gain and was not worth the effort.

The War Ends

American and British representatives signed a peace agreement in December 1814 in Ghent, Belgium. The **Treaty of Ghent** did not change any existing borders. Nothing was mentioned about the impressment of sailors. Even neutral rights became a dead issue because of Napoleon's defeat.

Before word of the treaty reached the United States, one final—and ferocious—battle occurred at New Orleans. British army troops moved toward New Orleans in December 1814. Andrew Jackson and his troops were waiting for them.

The British troops advanced on January 8, 1815. The redcoats were no match for Jackson's soldiers. Jackson's soldiers hid behind thick cotton bales. The bales absorbed the British bullets, while the British advancing in the open provided easy targets for American troops. In a short but gruesome battle, hundreds of British soldiers were killed. At the **Battle of New Orleans,** Americans achieved a decisive victory. Andrew Jackson became a hero, and his fame helped him win the presidency in 1828.

American Nationalism

New England Federalists opposed "Mr. Madison's War" from the start. These unhappy Federalists gathered in December 1814 at the Hartford Convention in Connecticut. A few favored secession, but most wanted to remain with the Union. To protect their interests, they made a list of proposed amendments to the Constitution.

In the triumph following the war, the Federalists' grievances seemed unpatriotic. The party lost the public's respect and was weakened. The War Hawks took over the leadership of the Republican Party and carried on the Federalist philosophy of a strong national government. They favored trade, western expansion, the energetic development of the economy, and a strong army and navy.

After the War of 1812, Americans felt a new sense of patriotism and a strong national identity. The young nation also gained new respect from other nations in the world.

Reading Check Identifying Cause and Effect What were the effects of the War of 1812?

Section 4 Review

History ONLINE
Study Central™ To review this section, go to glencoe.com.

Vocabulary

1. Define each of the following terms in a sentence: underestimate, frigate, privateer, goal.

Main Ideas

2. **Specifying** Why was the Battle of the Thames important for the United States in the War of 1812?

3. **Determining Cause and Effect** How did the outcome of the war affect the Federalist Party?

Critical Thinking

4. **Summarizing** Use a diagram like the one below to describe how the War Hawks influenced the Republican Party after the War of 1812.

Ideas Favored by War Hawks

5. **Making Connections** In what way did the writing of "The Star-Spangled Banner" represent the American spirit at the end of the War of 1812?

6. **Expository Writing** Take the role of an American who has witnessed the burning of Washington, D.C. Write a letter to your family out West describing your feelings about the British actions.

Answer the
7. **Essential Question** How did the United States benefit from its victory in the War of 1812?

Jefferson's Influence on Government

▲ Thomas Jefferson

- The federal government's size and power are reduced.
- The Constitution is the supreme law.
- The power of the Supreme Court and federal law are strengthened.

War of 1812

▲ Tecumseh

- War with Britain is fueled by nationalism and a desire for land.
- Tecumseh's death weakens both Native Americans and the British defense.
- The Federalists lose support after the U.S. victory.
- The United States gains worldwide respect.
- Patriotism grows.

▲ Conestoga wagon

Louisiana Purchase

- The U.S. purchases the Louisiana Territory from France for $15 million.
- The newly-acquired land doubles the size of the United States.
- The Mississippi River trade route is secured.
- Westward exploration and settlement increase.
- Some Federalists want to secede.

War with Tripoli ▶

Challenges to U.S. Stability

- Spain and France control Mississippi River trade and the Northwest Territory.
- Napoleon plans to build an American empire.
- War breaks out with Tripoli.
- France and Britain violate U.S. neutrality.
- A trade embargo creates political and economic problems.
- Frontier conflicts with the British and Native Americans continue.

STUDY TO GO Study anywhere, anytime! Download quizzes and flash cards to your PDA from glencoe.com.

INDIANA STATEWIDE TEST PRACTICE

Reviewing Vocabulary

Directions: Choose the word or words that best completes the sentence.

1 President Jefferson believed in reducing the power and size of the federal government, ideas which were similar to a philosophy called _____ .

   A nationalism
   B laissez-faire
   C restriction
   D judicial review

2 In the early 1800s, countries paid _____ so that their ships could sail on the Mediterranean Sea without being attacked.

   A frigates
   B tributes
   C customs duties
   D privateers

3 A(n) _____ prohibits trade with other countries.

   A embargo
   B tribute
   C customs duty
   D impressment

4 A common trait of the War Hawks was their _____, or loyalty to the United States.

   A tribute
   B authority
   C laissez-faire
   D nationalism

Reviewing Main Ideas

Directions: Choose the best answer.

5 Which of the following statements is a principle of judicial review?

   A The Constitution is the supreme law of the land.
   B State law takes precedence over federal law.
   C The Constitution should not be followed when it conflicts with any other law.
   D The legislative branch is responsible for upholding the Constitution.

6 Which factor influenced Napoleon's decision to sell the Louisiana Territory to the United States?

   A the movement of American settlers west
   B France's plans to wage war against Russia
   C the loss of the naval base at Santo Domingo
   D Spain's attack on French naval ships

7 Because the British desperately needed sailors for their naval war with France, they

   A recruited thousands of Barbary pirates.
   B increased their sailors' pay.
   C forced American citizens to serve in the British navy.
   D begged the United States to fight against France.

8 Which of the following was a setback for the British in the War of 1812?

   A the death of Tecumseh
   B the British victory over Napoleon
   C the burning of Washington, D.C.
   D the Hartford Convention

GO ON

Critical Thinking

Directions: Choose the best answer.

9 **When Britain and France went to war in 1803, how did the war impact Americans?**

A The French asked Jefferson to supply American troops to fight the British.

B Both countries respected U.S. neutral shipping rights.

C Both countries violated U.S. neutral shipping rights.

D Jefferson asked Congress to immediately declare war.

Base your answers to questions 10 and 11 on the map below and your knowledge of Chapter 9.

Election Results, 1800

Boundary disputed by Britain and the U.S.

Presidential Candidate
- Jefferson (Democratic-Republican)
- Adams (Federalist)
- **3** Electoral votes

Indiana Terr. · Terr. NW of Ohio R. · Terr. South of Ohio R. · Miss. Terr.

NH 6 · VT 4 · MA 16 · NY 12 · RI 4 · PA 8 · 7 · 5 · 5 · NJ 7 · CT 9 · DE 3 · VA 21 · KY 4 · MD · TN 3 · NC 8 · 4 · SC 8 · GA 4

10 **Which of the following states split its votes between the presidential candidates?**

A Virginia

B Georgia

C New York

D Pennsylvania

11 **Based on the map, which of the following generalizations is correct?**

A The Northeast was a strong Democratic-Republican area.

B The territories were strongly Federalist.

C The New England area supported the Federalist Party.

D The Federalists carried the western states.

Constructed Response

Directions: Write a short response to each of the following questions. In your answer:

- *address all parts of the question*
- *use information from the chapter*
- *include facts, examples, and details relevant to the question*
- *use clear language*

12 **What was the importance of the Supreme Court's decision in *Marbury* v. *Madison*?**

13 **How did the United States benefit from the Louisiana Purchase?**

14 **Who were the War Hawks and what did they support?**

15 **Were the causes of the War of 1812 resolved by the end of the war? Why or why not?**

STOP

Need Extra Help?															
If you missed questions...	1	2	3	4	5	6	7	8	9	10	11	12	13	14	15
Go to page...	278	287	290	293	279	283	289	297	289	277	277	279	283	293	298

Chapter 10

Growth and Expansion
1790–1825

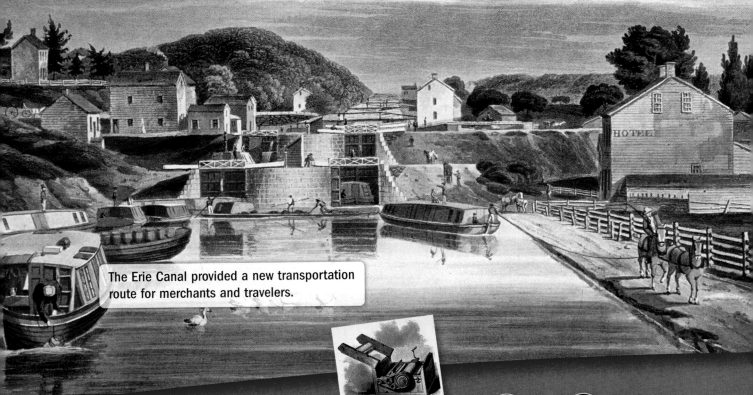

The Erie Canal provided a new transportation route for merchants and travelers.

GEORGE WASHINGTON

★ **1790**
Washington, D.C., founded

★ **1793**
Eli Whitney invents cotton gin

JOHN ADAMS

THOMAS JEFFERSON

1807 ★
Robert Fulton designs first practical steamboat

PRESIDENTS

U.S. Events

World Events

1790

1800

★ **1792**
Russia invades Poland

◁ Russian general's uniform

★ **1804**
Haiti claims independence from France

Section 1: Economic Growth
Essential Question What effects did the Industrial Revolution have on the U.S. economy?

Section 2: Westward Bound
Essential Question How did land and water transportation affect westward expansion?

Section 3: Unity and Sectionalism
Essential Question How were nation-building issues resolved in the early 1800s?

History ONLINE
Chapter Overview Visit glencoe.com and click on **Chapter 10—Chapter Overviews** to preview chapter information.

FOLDABLES
Study Organizer

Organizing Information
Make this Foldable to help organize what you learn about how transportation methods changed in the early 1800s.

Step 1 Place two sheets of paper on top of one another about one inch apart.

Step 2 Fold the papers to form four equal tabs.

Step 3 Staple the sheets, and label each tab as shown.

Reading and Writing As you read the chapter, list the inventors, inventions, and routes that changed transportation in the United States in the early 1800s.

This flag from Fort McHenry inspired Key to write "The Star-Spangled Banner." ▶

JAMES MADISON

1814 ★
Francis Scott Key writes poem that becomes national anthem

1813 ★
Jane Austen writes *Pride and Prejudice*

1815 ★
Napoleon defeated at Battle of Waterloo

JAMES MONROE

★ **1820**
Missouri Compromise passed

★ **1822**
Franz Liszt debuts as pianist in Vienna at age 11

JOHN Q. ADAMS

★ **1823**
Mexico becomes a republic

★ **1825**
Erie Canal completed

1810 ——————— **1820** ——————— **1830**

Essential Question ◀

What effects did the Industrial Revolution have on the U.S. economy?

Reading Guide

Content Vocabulary

cotton gin (p. 306)

capitalism (p. 307)

interchangeable parts (p. 306)

capital (p. 307)

patent (p. 306)

free enterprise (p. 307)

factory system (p. 306)

Academic Vocabulary

contribute (p. 305)

element (p. 307)

Key People and Events

Industrial Revolution (p. 305)

Eli Whitney (p. 306)

Reading Strategy

Taking Notes As you read, use a diagram like the one below to identify the major elements of the free enterprise system.

Free Enterprise System

INDIANA ACADEMIC STANDARDS
United States History

8.3.9 Analyze human and physical factors that have influenced migration and settlement patterns and relate them to the economic development of the United States.

8.4.3 Evaluate how the characteristics of a market economy have affected the economic and labor development of the United States.

8.4.5 Analyze contributions of entrepreneurs and inventors in the development of the United States economy.

American Diary

Lucy Larcom started working in the textile mills of Lowell, Massachusetts, at 11 years of age. She later recalled her life in the factory. "I had learned to do a spinner's work, and I obtained permission to tend some frames that stood directly in front of the river-windows with only them and the wall behind me, extending half the length of the mill,—and one young woman beside me. . . . I was, when with strangers, rather a reserved girl; so I kept myself occupied with the river, my work, and my thoughts."

—from A New England Girlhood

Winslow Homer painted young women heading to work in the mills.

The Growth of Industry

Main Idea New technology changed the way things were made.

History and You Do you know someone who works in a factory? What is his or her job like? Read to learn how new technology spurred the Industrial Revolution in New England.

. . . .

Lucy Larcom was one of the many young women who worked in the new industries that developed in the Northeast during the early 1800s. Since colonial times, most people lived and worked on farms. Thus, workers were in short supply for jobs outside of the home. To make up for this lack of workers, Americans developed tools that made their jobs easier and more efficient.

People working in their homes or in workshops made cloth and most other goods. Using hand tools, they made furniture, farm equipment, household items, and clothing.

In the mid-1700s, however, the way goods were made began to change. These changes appeared first in Great Britain. British inventors created machinery to perform some of the work involved in cloth making, such as spinning. Because these machines ran on waterpower, British cloth makers built textile mills along rivers and installed the new machines in these mills. People left their homes and farms to work in the mills and earn wages. This historic development is so important that it is known as the **Industrial Revolution.**

Industrial Revolution in New England

The Industrial Revolution took root in the United States around 1800. The changes appeared first in New England. The region's geography **contributed,** or added, to the development of the Industrial Revolution.

First, farming was difficult with New England's poor soil. Many people willingly gave up farming to find work elsewhere. Second, New England had rivers and streams to provide the waterpower needed to run the machines in the new factories. Third, New England was close to other resources, including coal and iron deposits in Pennsylvania. Fourth, the area had many ports. Raw materials like cotton, as well as finished goods like cloth, were shipped through these ports.

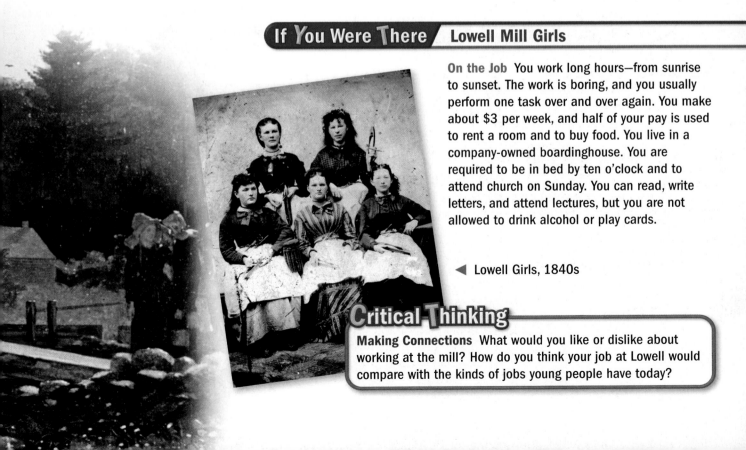

If You Were There / Lowell Mill Girls

On the Job You work long hours—from sunrise to sunset. The work is boring, and you usually perform one task over and over again. You make about $3 per week, and half of your pay is used to rent a room and to buy food. You live in a company-owned boardinghouse. You are required to be in bed by ten o'clock and to attend church on Sunday. You can read, write letters, and attend lectures, but you are not allowed to drink alcohol or play cards.

◄ Lowell Girls, 1840s

Critical Thinking

Making Connections What would you like or dislike about working at the mill? How do you think your job at Lowell would compare with the kinds of jobs young people have today?

New Technology

The invention of new machines and technology led to the Industrial Revolution. For example, the spinning jenny, the water frame—which spun thread—and the power loom—which wove the thread into cloth—allowed many steps in making cloth to be done by machine. These machines saved both time and money.

In 1793 **Eli Whitney** of Massachusetts invented the **cotton gin.** The cotton gin was a simple machine that quickly and efficiently removed the seeds from the cotton fiber.

Whitney also started using **interchangeable parts.** These were identical machine parts that could be put together quickly to make a complete product. These parts also made machine repair easier. Interchangeable parts allowed for the production of different kinds of goods on a large scale. This reduced the price of the goods.

Patents and Factories

In 1790 Congress passed a patent law to protect the rights of inventors. A **patent** gives an inventor the sole legal right to the invention and its profits for a certain period of time.

Although the British tried to keep their new industrial technology a secret, a few British workers brought their knowledge to the United States. One such worker was Samuel Slater. He memorized the design of the machines used in the British factory in which he worked.

Once in the United States, Slater took over the management of a cotton mill in Pawtucket, Rhode Island. There he duplicated the British machines that made cotton thread. Women working in their homes then wove the thread into cloth. Slater's mill marked an important step in the Industrial Revolution in the United States.

Francis Cabot Lowell improved on Slater's process in 1814. In Lowell's textile plant in Massachusetts, all the stages of cloth making were performed under one roof. Lowell began the **factory system,** where all manufacturing steps are brought together in one place to increase efficiency.

Growth of Industry New England was the perfect location for the Industrial Revolution to begin in the United States because its rushing rivers provided power to run the machinery. The industrial growth that began in New England spread to other areas of the country. By 1870, the nation's industrial cities were growing.

Slater Mill in Pawtucket, Rhode Island Because Britain prohibited the export of textile machinery, Slater had to design his factory and build the machines from memory. It was an immediate success. ▼

"If thou canst do this thing, I invite thee to come to Rhode Island, and have the credit of introducing cotton-manufacture into America."
—Moses Brown, in a letter to Samuel Slater in 1789

Growth of Industrial Cities NATIONAL GEOGRAPHIC

ATLANTIC OCEAN

0   200 kilometers
0   200 miles
Lambert Azimuthal Equal-Area projection

Free Enterprise

Industrial growth requires an economic system that allows competition to flourish with little government interference. **Capitalism** is the economic system of the United States. Under capitalism, individuals put their **capital,** or money, into a business, hoping that the business will be successful and make a profit.

Free enterprise is another term used to describe the American economy. In a free enterprise economy, people are free to buy, sell, and produce whatever they want. They can also work wherever they wish. The major **elements,** or parts, of free enterprise are competition, profit, private property, and economic freedom. Business owners have the freedom to produce the products that they think will sell the best and be the most profitable. In a free enterprise economy, buyers also compete to find the best products at the lowest prices.

✓ Reading Check **Describing** How did New England's physical geography support the growth of industries?

Agriculture Expands

Main Idea Agriculture expanded and remained the leading occupation of most Americans in the 1800s.

History and You Do any of your relatives own and work on a farm? Read to learn how agriculture expanded in the 1800s.

. . . .

Although many New Englanders went to work in factories during the first half of the 1800s, agriculture remained the country's leading economic activity. Most Americans still lived and worked on farms.

In the Northeast, farms were small and worked by families. Farmers in the Northeast usually marketed their produce locally. In the South, cotton production rose dramatically. The demand for cotton grew steadily with the development of the textile industries of New England and Europe.

History ONLINE
Student Web Activity Visit glencoe.com and complete the Chapter 10 Web Activity about the Industrial Revolution.

Textile Mill The Lowell factory system was designed to bring work and workers together. A typical Lowell textile mill in 1830 housed 4,500 spindles, 120 power looms, and more than 200 employees under one roof.

◄ A water frame was used to spin thread.

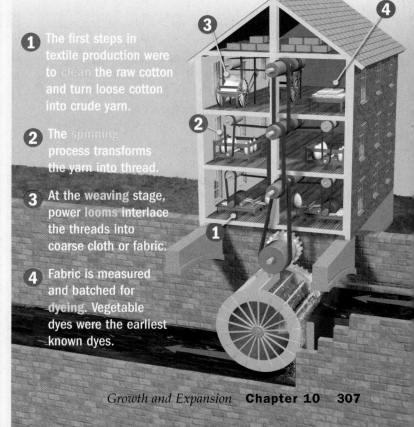

1 The first steps in textile production were to clean the raw cotton and turn loose cotton into crude yarn.

2 The spinning process transforms the yarn into thread.

3 At the weaving stage, power looms interlace the threads into coarse cloth or fabric.

4 Fabric is measured and batched for dyeing. Vegetable dyes were the earliest known dyes.

Critical Thinking

Determining Cause and Effect Did the increase of factories lead to better technology, or did better technology lead to more factories? Explain.

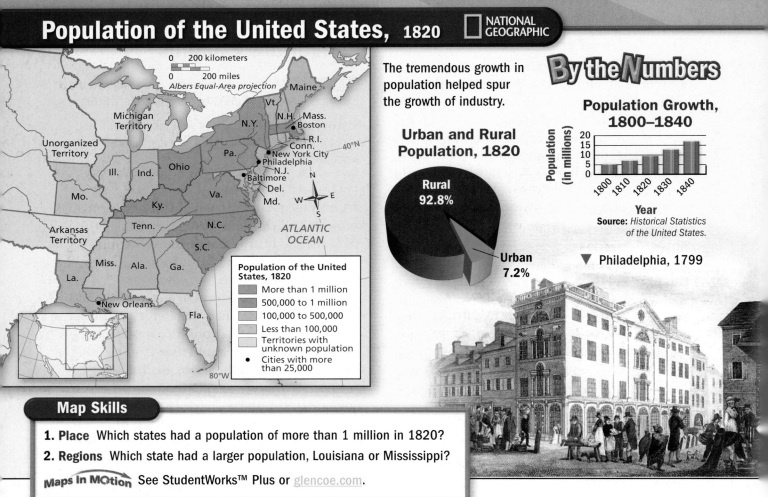

Population of the United States, 1820
NATIONAL GEOGRAPHIC

0   200 kilometers
0   200 miles
Albers Equal-Area projection

Population of the United States, 1820
- More than 1 million
- 500,000 to 1 million
- 100,000 to 500,000
- Less than 100,000
- Territories with unknown population
- • Cities with more than 25,000

The tremendous growth in population helped spur the growth of industry.

Urban and Rural Population, 1820

Rural 92.8%

Urban 7.2%

By the Numbers

Population Growth, 1800–1840

Population (in millions): 20, 15, 10, 5, 0

Year: 1800, 1810, 1820, 1830, 1840

Source: *Historical Statistics of the United States.*

▼ Philadelphia, 1799

Map Skills

1. **Place** Which states had a population of more than 1 million in 1820?
2. **Regions** Which state had a larger population, Louisiana or Mississippi?

Maps In Motion See StudentWorks™ Plus or glencoe.com.

Southern plantation owners used enslaved workers from Africa to plant, tend, and pick the cotton. The recently invented cotton gin encouraged the planters to raise even larger amounts of the crop. The new machine made it possible to clean cotton faster and more cheaply than could be done by hand. Between 1790 and 1820, cotton production soared from 3,000 bales produced per year to more than 300,000 bales produced per year in the South.

Agriculture also expanded in the West. Southern farmers seeking new land moved west to plant cotton. Western farmers in the region north of the Ohio River concentrated on raising pork and cash crops such as corn and wheat.

Reading Check **Contrasting** How was agriculture different in the Northeast than in the South?

Economic Independence

Main Idea The growth of factories and trade led to the development of corporations and cities.

History and You If you had your choice, would you prefer living in the city or in the country? Why? Read to learn about the growth of cities in the 1800s.

Small investors, such as shopkeepers, merchants, and farmers, financed most new businesses. These people invested their money in hopes of earning profits if the new businesses succeeded. Low taxes, minimum government regulations, and competition encouraged people to invest in new industries.

Corporations Develop

Large businesses called corporations began to develop rapidly in the 1830s when legal obstacles to their formation were removed.

The rise of these new corporations made it easier to sell stock—shares of ownership in a company—to finance improvement and development.

Cities Come of Age

The growth of factories and trade led to the growth of towns and cities. Many cities developed along rivers because factories could take advantage of the water power and ship goods to markets more easily. Older cities such as New York, Boston, and Baltimore also grew as centers of commerce and trade.

Along New York City's South Street, shipping piers extended for 3 miles (4.8 km). The value of merchandise shipped from these piers rose from $84 million in 1825 to $146 million in 1836. An English traveler wrote of the busy New York City waterfront:

PRIMARY SOURCE

"Every thought, word, look, and action of the multitude seemed to be absorbed by commerce."

—quoted in *The Growing Years*, by Margaret L. Coit

Moving westward, towns such as Pittsburgh, Cincinnati, and Louisville profited from their locations on major rivers. As farmers in the West shipped more of their products by water, these towns grew rapidly.

Cities and towns looked quite different from modern urban areas. Buildings were made of wood or brick. Streets and sidewalks were unpaved, and barnyard animals often roamed freely. There were no sewers to carry away waste and dirty water, so the danger of diseases such as cholera and yellow fever was very real. In 1793, for example, a yellow fever epidemic in Philadelphia killed thousands.

Fire posed another threat to cities. Sparks from a fireplace or chimney could easily ignite a wooden building and spread to others. Few towns or cities had organized fire companies, thus fires could be disastrous.

Cities and towns offered many opportunities, such as a variety of jobs to choose from and steady wages. As cities grew, libraries, museums, and shops were built, providing people with places to enjoy during their leisure time. For many, the jobs and attractions of city life outweighed any of the dangers.

Reading Check Analyzing Why were rivers important for the growth of cities?

Section 1 Review

History ONLINE
Study Central™ To review this section, go to glencoe.com.

Vocabulary

1. Define each term in a sentence: contribute, cotton gin, interchangeable parts, patent, factory system, capitalism, capital, free enterprise, element.

Main Ideas

2. **Summarizing** How did inventions like the cotton gin and interchangeable parts revolutionize the textile industry?

3. **Explaining** Why were Southern plantations able to increase their cotton production between 1790 and 1821?

4. **Specifying** What conditions encouraged people to invest in the new businesses?

Critical Thinking

5. **Determining Cause and Effect** Use a diagram like the one below to identify why the Industrial Revolution first began in New England.

Characteristics of New England

Industrial Revolution

6. **Personal Writing** It is 1830, and you have just moved to New York City. Write a letter to your friends back on the farm describing what your new life is like.

Answer the Essential Question

7. What effects did the Industrial Revolution have on the U.S. economy?

America's LITERATURE

Meet the Author

Laurie Halse Anderson (1961–) began researching *Fever 1793* after reading a newspaper article about an epidemic that killed 10 percent of the population of Federalist-era Philadelphia. During her studies, she examined the politics, food, religion, and medicine of the period. This information helped her create realistic details in the life of Mattie, the main character in the story.

Building Background

In *Fever 1793,* Laurie Halse Anderson tells the story of Mattie, a young girl living through the horrors of a yellow fever outbreak in Philadelphia. At the time, Philadelphia was the young country's largest city and capital. During the epidemic, the American government, along with many residents, fled the city. Throughout the novel, Anderson weaves historical facts with the fictional story. In the following scene, Mattie wanders the city alone after the death of her grandfather. While reading, pay attention to the actions that depict Mattie's personal strength and maturity.

Vocabulary

acquainted familiar

shift dress

tethered tied

exorbitant very high

thrive gain in health

quill feather shaft

pestilence contagious disease

Second Street in Philadelphia, 1790s ▶

FEVER 1793

Laurie Halse Anderson

My feet moved, taking me up one street and down the next. I didn't see another person for blocks, not even a grave digger or a physician. The sound of my shoes tapping across the cobblestones echoed down the street like a latecomer sneaking into church. I walked past the homes of people **acquainted** with my family. They were all deserted. My **shift** darkened with sweat. Surely I wasn't the only person left in Philadelphia?

* * *

When I came upon the open windows of the *Federal Gazette* office, it was a shock. A horse was **tethered** by the door. I stumbled through the door, eager for a friendly face.

"Can I help you?"

"It's me, Mr. Brown. William Cook's granddaughter."

The printer looked up from his desk. The dark circles under his eyes and lines of worry across his brow made him look as if he had aged years in the course of a month.

"What do you need, Matilda? I've no time for social calls today."

I hesitated. What could Mr. Brown do? I couldn't work a press; he couldn't bring Grandfather back from the grave.

"Please, Sir," I said. "I would like to place an advertisement in your newspaper. I'm searching for my mother. She's gone."

Mr. Brown pulled a stained kerchief out of his trouser pocket and rubbed it over his face and neck.

"Matilda, there is nothing I'd rather do than run an advertisement for your mother. But look about you." He spread his arms to take in the shop. "There is hardly any paper to be had for a hundred miles. The *Gazette* is the last paper being printed in the city, and I have to print on half-sheets. Five other newspapers have closed down. I wish I could flee myself."

He paused and looked out the window. I thought he had forgotten me.

"But I must stay. This paper is the only method of communication left in the city. I must print physicians' notices, orders from the mayor . . ."

"Mr. Brown? Sir?"

He took a deep breath and looked up.

"In the beginning of August, this was the largest city in the United States. Forty thousand people lived here. Near as I can tell," he pointed to the jumble of notes and letters on the desk before him, "more than half the city has fled, twenty thousand people."

"How many dead, Sir?"

"More than three thousand, enough to fill house after house, street after street."

I'm searching for my mother.
She's gone.

"I went to the market, but found no food," I said.

"Few farmers dare come into town. They charge **exorbitant** prices for their wares, and get whatever they ask," he said bitterly. "Those who don't die of the fever are beginning to starve. You've seen the rats?"

I nodded.

"The rats **thrive**. I should write that." He dipped a **quill** into the ink pot and scribbled a note. "The only creatures to benefit from this **pestilence** are the rats. Go home, Matilda, take my regards to your grandfather, but tell him he must lock all the doors and pray for frost."

I started to tell him what had happened, but a man burst through the door waving a letter and shouting. Mr. Brown shooed me from his shop with a wave of his hand. No matter. Telling him wouldn't bring Grandfather back, and it was clear he couldn't help me.

Analyzing Literature

1. **Respond and Connect**
   (a) How might Mattie feel at the beginning of the passage as she walks the streets alone?
   (b) How does Mattie feel as she encounters Mr. Brown?

2. **Recall and Interpret**
   (a) What is Mr. Brown's occupation?
   (b) Why is a newspaper important during this plague?

3. **Evaluate** What actions show Mattie's maturity during this crisis?

Westward Bound

Reading Guide

Content Vocabulary

census *(p. 313)*   canal *(p. 315)*
turnpike *(p. 313)*   lock *(p. 316)*

Academic Vocabulary

reveal *(p. 313)*   region *(p. 314)*

Key People

Robert Fulton *(p. 314)*
De Witt Clinton *(p. 315)*

Reading Strategy

Taking Notes As you read, use a time line like the one below to identify major developments in transportation during the early 1800s.

1800	1810	1820	1830

INDIANA ACADEMIC STANDARDS
United States History

8.3.2 Identify and create maps showing the physical growth and development of the United States from settlement of the original thirteen colonies through Reconstruction (1877) including transportation routes used during the period.

8.3.11 Identify ways people modified the physical environment as the United States developed and describe the impacts that resulted.

8.4.5 Analyze contributions of entrepreneurs and inventors in the development of the United States economy.

American Diary

In the early 1800s, pioneers wrote many letters that praised the qualities of the territory west of the Appalachians. One immigrant wrote about the land in Illinois: "[It has] the most fertile soil in the U[nited] States. . . . [In] general, the farmer has nothing to do, but fence in his fields: plough his ground and plant his crop. He may then expect, from an acre, from 50 to 100 bushels [of] corn; and from 10 to 50 of wheat; the quality of both which articles is superior to that of any I ever saw."

—quoted in Westward Expansion:
An Eyewitness History

Fort Dearborn, at the site of Chicago, Illinois, 1820

Moving West

Main Idea Transportation routes such as roads improved as settlers moved west, and steamboats greatly improved the transport of goods along rivers.

History and You Have you ever taken a trip to another state? How did you get there? Read to learn about the new network of roads that connected the country.

• •

Settlers poured into Illinois and other frontier areas west of the Appalachian Mountains during the 1800s. The typical frontier family moved from place to place as the line of settlement continued to push westward.

The first **census**—the official count of a population—of the United States in 1790 **revealed** a population of nearly 4 million. Most Americans at that time lived east of the Appalachian Mountains and within a few hundred miles of the Atlantic coast.

Within a few decades this pattern changed. The number of settlers heading west increased dramatically. In 1811 a Pennsylvania resident reported seeing 236 wagons filled with people and their possessions traveling on the road to Pittsburgh. A man in Newburgh, New York, counted 60 wagons rolling by in a single day. By 1820, just 30 years after the first census, the population of the United States had more than doubled to about 10 million people. Nearly 2 million of these people lived west of the Appalachians.

Traveling west was not easy. The 363-mile (584 km) trip from New York City to Buffalo could take as long as three weeks. A pioneer family moving west faced hardships and dangers along the way.

Roads and Turnpikes

The nation needed good inland roads for travel and for the shipment of goods. Private companies built many **turnpikes,** or toll roads. The fees travelers paid to use those roads helped finance their construction. Many of the roads had a base of crushed stone. The land was often muddy in some areas. To aid travel, companies built "corduroy roads." These roads consisted of logs laid side by side, like the ridges of corduroy cloth.

Ohio became a state in 1803. The new state asked the federal government to build a road to connect it with the East. In 1806 Congress approved funds for a national road to the West and five years later agreed on the route.

By the Numbers / Western Settlement

A Road to the West

New States Between 1800 and 1830, westward expansion increased the population in three new states—Ohio, Indiana, and Illinois.

Population in Ohio, Indiana, and Illinois

Year	Ohio	Indiana	Illinois
1800	42,159	2,632	2,458
1810	230,760	24,520	12,282
1820	581,434	147,178	55,211
1830	937,903	343,031	157,445

Source: *Historical Statistics of the United States.*

Critical Thinking

Synthesizing How do you think a region's physical geography influenced where people settled?

Construction of the road began in 1811 at the Potomac River in Cumberland, Maryland. However, work on the road stopped during the War of 1812. The first section, from Maryland to Wheeling, Virginia (now West Virginia), did not open until 1818. The route closely followed that of a military road built by George Washington in 1754. In later years, the national road reached Ohio and continued on to Vandalia, Illinois. Congress viewed the National Road as a military necessity, but it did not take on any other road-building projects.

River Travel

River travel had definite advantages over travel by wagon and horse. It was far more comfortable than traveling by roads, which were at that time often nothing more than wide, rough paths. Also, boats or river barges could carry far larger loads of farm products or other goods than a wagon.

River travel had two problems, however. The first was a result of the geography of the eastern part of the United States. Most major rivers in the **region** flowed in a north-south direction, not east to west, the direction in which most people and goods were headed. Second, traveling upstream by barge against the current was extremely difficult and slow.

Steam engines were already being used in the 1780s and 1790s to power boats in quiet waters. Inventor James Rumsey equipped a small boat on the Potomac River with a steam engine. John Fitch, another inventor, built a steamboat that navigated the Delaware River. Neither boat, however, had enough power to withstand the strong currents and winds found in and along large rivers or open bodies of water.

In 1802 Robert Livingston, a political and business leader, hired **Robert Fulton** to develop a steamboat with a powerful engine. Livingston wanted the steamboat to carry cargo and passengers up the Hudson River from New York City to Albany.

In 1807 Fulton had his steamboat, the *Clermont*, ready for a trial on the Hudson. A newly designed engine powered the boat. The *Clermont* made the 150-mile (241 km) trip

LINKING PAST TO PRESENT — Roads: Tying the Nation Together

THEN For a large part of the early 1800s, the National Road was the nation's busiest land route to the West. It stimulated trade, as well as settlement on the western frontier.

Major Roads Before the Civil War

Mohawk Turnpike

Chicago Turnpike

Pa.

Boston Post Rd.

Ill. Ind. Ohio Wheeling

Indianapolis Columbus 40°N

Vandalia National Road Baltimore

St. Louis Va. Md.

Wilderness Road Great Valley Rd. N

Cumberland Gap

W   E

S

35°N

Natchez Trace

Coastal Traffic

ATLANTIC OCEAN

0   200 kilometers

0   200 miles   30°N

Albers Equal-Area projection

80°W   75°W

In an 1879 interview, a man recalled the heyday of the National Road: "The wagons were so numerous that the leaders of one team [of horses] had their noses in the trough [feed box] at the end of the next wagon ahead."
—"The Old National Pike," *Harper's New Monthly Magazine*, November 1879

◄ The National Road was the nation's first federally funded highway. When completed in 1837, the gravel road extended from the Eastern Seaboard to Vandalia, Illinois.

Some roads in the East were rough corduroy roads. ►

from New York City to Albany in the unheard-of time of 32 hours. Using only sails, the trip would have taken four days.

About 140 feet (43 m) long and 14 feet (4 m) wide, the *Clermont* offered great comforts to its passengers. They could sit or stroll about on deck. At night they could relax in the sleeping compartments below deck. The engine was noisy, but its power provided a fairly smooth ride.

Steamboats ushered in a new age in river travel. They greatly improved the transport of goods and passengers along major inland rivers. Shipping goods became cheaper and faster. Regular steamboat service began along the Mississippi River, between New Orleans and Natchez, Mississippi, in 1812. Steamboats also contributed to the growth of other river cities like Cincinnati and St. Louis. By 1850, some 700 steamboats were carrying cargo and passengers within the United States.

✔ **Reading Check** **Identifying** What advantages did river travel offer?

Canals

Main Idea Business and government officials developed a plan to build a canal to link the eastern and western parts of the country.

History and You Have you ever worked long and hard to build something? Read to learn about the accomplishment of thousands of laborers who constructed the Erie Canal.

Steamboats were a great improvement in transportation, but their routes depended on the existing river system. Because most major rivers in the eastern United States flowed north to south, steamboats could not effectively tie together the eastern and western parts of the country.

Business and government officials led by **De Witt Clinton** in New York developed a plan to link New York City with the Great Lakes region. They would build a **canal**—an artificial waterway—across New York state. The canal would connect Albany on the Hudson River with Buffalo on Lake Erie.

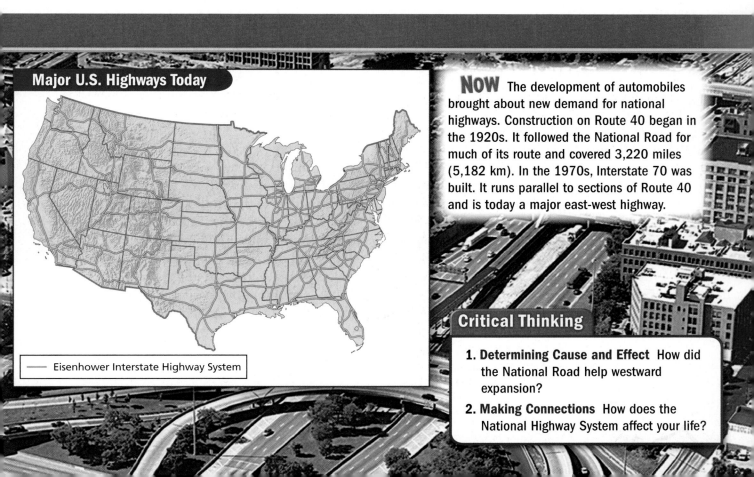

Major U.S. Highways Today

—— Eisenhower Interstate Highway System

NOW The development of automobiles brought about new demand for national highways. Construction on Route 40 began in the 1920s. It followed the National Road for much of its route and covered 3,220 miles (5,182 km). In the 1970s, Interstate 70 was built. It runs parallel to sections of Route 40 and is today a major east-west highway.

Critical Thinking

1. **Determining Cause and Effect** How did the National Road help westward expansion?

2. **Making Connections** How does the National Highway System affect your life?

Canals, 1820–1860

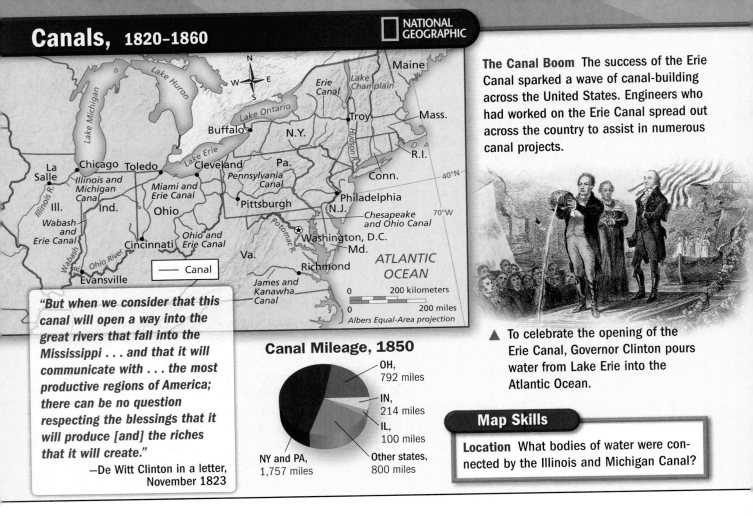

The Canal Boom The success of the Erie Canal sparked a wave of canal-building across the United States. Engineers who had worked on the Erie Canal spread out across the country to assist in numerous canal projects.

▲ To celebrate the opening of the Erie Canal, Governor Clinton pours water from Lake Erie into the Atlantic Ocean.

"But when we consider that this canal will open a way into the great rivers that fall into the Mississippi . . . and that it will communicate with . . . the most productive regions of America; there can be no question respecting the blessings that it will produce [and] the riches that it will create."
—De Witt Clinton in a letter, November 1823

Canal Mileage, 1850

- OH, 792 miles
- IN, 214 miles
- IL, 100 miles
- Other states, 800 miles
- NY and PA, 1,757 miles

Map Skills

Location What bodies of water were connected by the Illinois and Michigan Canal?

Building the Erie Canal

Thousands of laborers, many of them Irish immigrants, worked on the construction of the 363-mile (584 km) Erie Canal. Along the canal they built a series of **locks**—separate compartments in which water levels were raised or lowered. Locks provided a way to raise and lower boats at places canal levels changed.

Construction of the canal proved dangerous for workers. Diggers were buried when canal beds collapsed and others died in blasting accidents. The swamps in which they toiled led to disease among the workers.

After more than two years of construction, the Erie Canal opened on October 26, 1825. Clinton boarded a barge in Buffalo and traveled on the canal to Albany. From there he sailed down the Hudson River to New York City. As crowds cheered, the officials poured water from Lake Erie into the Atlantic Ocean.

Improving Canal Travel

In its early years, the Erie Canal did not allow steamboats. Their powerful engines could damage the canal's earthen embankments. Instead, teams of mules or horses hauled the boats and barges. A two-horse team pulled a 100-ton (91 t) barge about 24 miles (39 km) in one day. This was fast compared with travel by wagon. In the 1840s, the canal banks were reinforced to accommodate steam tugboats that could pull the barges.

The success of the Erie Canal led to an explosion in canal building. By 1850, the United States had more than 3,600 miles (5,794 km) of canals. Canals lowered the cost of shipping goods and brought prosperity to the towns along their routes. Perhaps most important, they linked regions of a growing country.

 Reading Check Finding the Main Idea Why were canals built?

Western Settlement

Main Idea Americans continued to move westward, settling near rivers so they could ship their goods to markets.

History and You Think about what your life might be like if you could not watch TV or use the computer. Read to learn about the lives of Western families in the early 1800s.

· ·

Americans moved westward in waves. The first wave began before the 1790s and led to the admission of four new states between 1791 and 1803—Vermont, Kentucky, Tennessee, and Ohio. A second wave of westward growth began between 1816 and 1821. Five new western states were created—Indiana, Illinois, Mississippi, Alabama, and Missouri.

The new states reflected the dramatic growth of the region west of the Appalachians. In 1800 only 387,000 white settlers lived west of the Appalachian Mountains. By 1820, that number had grown to more than 2.4 million people. Ohio, for example, had only 45,000 settlers in 1800. By 1820, it had 581,000 settlers.

Pioneer families tended to settle in communities along the great rivers, such as the Ohio and the Mississippi. They settled by rivers so they could ship their crops and other goods to markets. The canals, which crisscrossed the land in the 1820s and 1830s, allowed people to live farther away from the rivers.

People also often preferred to settle with others from their home communities. Indiana, for example, was settled mainly by people from Kentucky and Tennessee. Michigan's pioneers came mostly from the New England area.

Western families often gathered together for social events. Men took part in sports such as wrestling. Women met for quilting and sewing parties. Both men and women participated in cornhuskings. These were gatherings where farm families shared the work of stripping the outer layers from corn.

Life in the West did not include the conveniences of Eastern town life. However, the pioneers had not traveled to the West to live a pampered life. They wanted to make a new life for themselves and their families. America's population continued to spread westward in the years ahead.

✔ **Reading Check** **Describing** What was life like for families on the western frontier?

Section 2 Review

History ONLINE
Study Central™ To review this section, go to glencoe.com.

Vocabulary

1. Define the following terms by using each one in a sentence: census, reveal, turnpike, region, canal, lock.

Main Ideas

2. Discussing How were the improvements in westward travel financed in the early 1800s?

3. Identifying What were the benefits of canal travel?

4. Listing What determined where people would settle as they moved westward?

Critical Thinking

5. Analyzing Use a chart like the one below to describe why each item was important to the nation's growth.

	Significance
National Road	
Clermont	
Erie Canal	

6. Persuasive Writing Would you have preferred Eastern city life or life in a western settlement in 1820? Write a paragraph to persuade people to join you in one of the two places.

Answer the
7. Essential Question
How did land and water transportation affect westward expansion?

TIME NOTEBOOK

What were people's lives like in the past?

These two pages will give you some clues to everyday life in the United States as you step back in time with TIME Notebook.

BETTMANN / CORBIS

American Voices

FULL STEAM AHEAD!

ROBERT FULTON *might not have invented the steamboat, but he does believe in its potential to turn waterways into business routes and transform America's economic future. In 1807 he's ready for his trial run of the first commercial passenger steamboat. The boat is 150 feet (46 m) long and only 13 feet (4 m) wide and will travel from New York City to Albany—and back again. People are terrified the engines that power the ship's two paddle wheels will explode, so he has a tough time getting passengers onboard. In this letter, Fulton describes what happens just as the ship leaves the dock in New York City.*

ROBERT FULTON

NORTH WIND PICTURE ARCHIVES / ALAMY

"The moment arrived in which the word was to be given for the boat to move. My friends were in groups on the deck. There was anxiety mixed with fear among them. They were silent, sad, and weary. I read in their looks nothing but disaster, and almost repented of my efforts. The signal was given and the boat moved on a short distance and then stopped and became immovable. To the silence of the preceding moment, now succeeded murmurs of discontent, and agitations, and whispers and shrugs. I could hear distinctly repeated, 'I told you it was so; it is a foolish scheme: I wish we were well out of it.' . . . I went below and examined the machinery, and discovered that the cause was a slight maladjustment . . . The boat was again put in motion."

VERBATIM

WHAT PEOPLE ARE SAYING

❝ If Uncle Sam needs, I'll be glad to assist him. ❞

POLITICAL CARTOON IN 1813
that makes the first-known use of the term "Uncle Sam"

❝ The land is ours. No one has a right to remove us, because we were the first owners. ❞

TECUMSEH,
chief of the Shawnees, in 1810, in response to a message sent by President Madison

❝ Let us bind the republic together with a perfect system of roads and canals. Let us conquer space. ❞

CONGRESSMAN JOHN C. CALHOUN,
from South Carolina, in 1816

Sea Talk

The **U.S.S. CONSTITUTION,** *the world's largest warship with its 54 cannons, was instrumental in helping the United States win the War of 1812. Want to join its crew of 450? If so, you'll have to learn some sea terms. Here's a seafaring glossary.*

1. **KEEL OVER:** Putting a ship in for repair

2. **TACK:** The course or direction boats take into the wind

3. **LET THE CAT OUT OF THE BAG:** Sailors who do wrong are disciplined with a cat-o'-nine-tails whip that's kept in a red sack

4. **SHIPSHAPE:** Good condition

BETTMANN / CORBIS

First Things First

Someone's got to be first—see if you can match up each name with the correct description.

ILLUSTRATION WORKS / GETTY IMAGES

1. Thomas Hopkins Gallaudet
2. Thomas Jefferson
3. James Madison
4. James Madison Randolph
5. Frederick Graff

a. First president to wear pants instead of knee breeches.
b. First child born in the White House (1806)—his grandfather was Thomas Jefferson.
c. Founder of first school for advanced education of hearing-impaired students.
d. First president to shake hands instead of bowing when meeting people.
e. Engineer for Philadelphia Water Works who installed the country's first fire hydrant in 1801.

Answers: 1. c; 2. d; 3. a; 4. b; 5. e

NUMBERS

UNITED STATES AT THE TIME

$15 million Price the United States pays for the Louisiana Purchase in 1803

16 Number of states in the Union in 1800—that number will grow to 23 by 1820

17 Age of Sacagawea when she started guiding Lewis and Clark on their famous expedition

BETTMANN / CORBIS

18 Months it takes Lewis and Clark to reach the Pacific in 1805

19th Date in August 1812 that the U.S.S. *Constitution* earns its nickname "Old Ironsides" after defeating the British warship, *Guerriere*

MILESTONES

EVENTS AND PEOPLE OF THE TIME

BORROWED. The music from the English song "To Anacreon in Heaven" by Francis Scott Key for his new poem "The Star-Spangled Banner," which he wrote in 1814.

STARVED. Many Vermont farmers and their families as snow falls all summer in 1816—a year some call "eighteen hundred and froze-to-death." Some think the bizarre weather is caused by last year's volcanic eruption in the Dutch East Indies that sent dust and ash far up into the air where it blocked out the sun.

DUG. First shovel of dirt as work on the proposed 363-mile-long Erie Canal begins in 1817. Many are labeling it "The Big Ditch."

BITTEN. United States officials, by insects in 1800 as the country's government moves from Philadelphia to Washington, D.C.—a place many complain is a bug-infested swamp.

NORTH WIND PICTURE ARCHIVES / ALAMY

RESCUED. Treasures, such as the original Declaration of Independence and a famous portrait of George Washington, by First Lady Dolley Madison after the British set fire to the White House in 1814.

CRITICAL THINKING

Describing What was the atmosphere like on board Fulton's steamboat on its first voyage?

Theorizing Was Tecumseh, the chief of the Shawnees, ju in his response to President Madison's message? Expl answer.

Unity and Sectionalism

Essential Question ◄

How were nation-building issues resolved in the early 1800s?

Reading Guide

Content Vocabulary
sectionalism (p. 322)
state sovereignty (p. 322)
American System (p. 323)

Academic Vocabulary
intense (p. 322)   internal (p. 322)

Key People and Events
Missouri Compromise (p. 323)
McCulloch v. Maryland (p. 324)
Gibbons v. Ogden (p. 324)
Adams-Onís Treaty (p. 326)
Monroe Doctrine (p. 326)

Reading Strategy
Taking Notes As you read, create a diagram like the one below to list the three parts of Henry Clay's American System.

INDIANA ACADEMIC STANDARDS
United States History

8.1.12 Explain the main issues, decisions, and consequences of landmark Supreme Court cases.

8.1.14 Examine the international problem that led to the Monroe Doctrine (1823) and assess its consequences.

American Diary

"If we look to the history of other nations, ancient or modern, we find no example of a growth so rapid—so gigantic; of a people so prosperous and happy. In [thinking about] what we still have to perform, the heart of every citizen must expand with joy when he reflects how near our Government has approached to perfection."

—from James Monroe's Inaugural Address, March 1817

Philadelphia residents celebrate the Fourth of July in 1819.

The Era of Good Feelings

Main Idea After the War of 1812, a new spirit of nationalism spread throughout the United States.

History and You Do you believe your favorite sports team is better than any other team? Read on to find out about the national pride many Americans felt for their country.

● ●

The absence of major political divisions after the War of 1812 helped forge a sense of national unity. In the 1816 presidential election, James Monroe, the Republican candidate, faced almost no opposition. The Federalists, weakened by doubts of their loyalty during the War of 1812, barely existed as a national party. Monroe won the election by an overwhelming margin.

Although the Federalist Party had almost disappeared, many of its programs had gained popularity. Support grew for tariffs to protect industries and a national bank.

Political differences among citizens, however, seemed to fade. A Boston newspaper called these years the Era of Good Feelings. President James Monroe symbolized these good feelings. Monroe had been involved in national politics since the American Revolution. He wore breeches, or short pants, and powdered wigs—styles no longer in fashion at that time. With his sense of dignity, Monroe represented a united America, free of political strife.

Early in his term, Monroe toured the nation. No president since George Washington had done so. Monroe even paid for the trip using his own expenses and tried to travel without an official escort. Local officials everywhere greeted the president and celebrated his visit.

Monroe arrived in Boston, the former Federalist stronghold, in the summer of 1817. About 40,000 well-wishers cheered him. John Adams, the second president, invited Monroe to his home. Abigail Adams praised the new president's "unassuming manner."

Monroe did not think the demonstrations were meant for him personally. He wrote James Madison that they revealed a "desire in the body of the people to show their attachment to the union."

Two years later Monroe continued his tour throughout the country. He traveled as far south as Savannah and as far west as Detroit. In 1820 President Monroe won reelection, receiving all but one electoral vote.

Reading Check **Summarizing** Why did James Monroe appeal to people?

Primary Source / Celebrating Independence

Fourth of July Independence Day was first observed on July 8, 1776. On that day in Philadelphia, the Declaration of Independence was read in public for the first time. The next year, Philadelphia honored the nation's independence on July 4—the day the Declaration of Independence was adopted by the Continental Congress. People celebrated the occasion with bonfires, parades, and fireworks. In 1826 Thomas Jefferson wrote: "Let the annual return of this day forever refresh our recollections of [our] rights, and an undiminished devotion to them."

Critical Thinking

Making Connections How do people express patriotism for the United States today?

Sectionalism and the American System

Main Idea Regional differences brought an end to the Era of Good Feelings.

History and You Why do people support certain political leaders? Read about three influential spokespeople in Congress during the early 1800s.

· ·

Regional differences soon brought an end to the Era of Good Feelings. Most Americans felt a strong allegiance to the region where they lived. They thought of themselves as Westerners or Southerners or Northerners. This **sectionalism,** or loyalty to their region, grew more **intense** over national policies.

Most white Southerners, for example, supported slavery. They argued that states were given the right in the Constitution to govern themselves. Southerners believed the federal government and people in the North were interfering with a state's right to maintain the institution of slavery.

The different regions also disagreed strongly on the need for tariffs, a national bank, and **internal** improvements. Internal improvements were federal, state, and privately funded projects, such as canals and roads, to develop the nation's transportation system. Three regional spokespersons emerged in Congress.

John C. Calhoun

John C. Calhoun, a planter from South Carolina, had called for war with Great Britain in 1812. He remained a nationalist for some time after the war. Calhoun supported internal improvements, the development of industries, and a national bank. He believed that these programs would benefit the South.

In the 1820s, however, Calhoun's views began to change. He emerged as a chief supporter of **state sovereignty,** the idea that states have autonomous power, or the right to govern themselves. Calhoun became a strong opponent of national programs.

People IN HISTORY

John C. Calhoun
Politician from South Carolina

Calhoun was a fierce supporter of states' rights. He believed that if the federal government passed a law where it overstepped its authority over states, then people had the right to refuse to obey it. *"Let it never be forgotten that, where the majority rules without restriction, the minority is the subject."*

Daniel Webster
Politician from New England

Webster argued against the right of states to declare laws invalid. He stated, *"I say, the right of a state to annul [declare invalid] a law of Congress, cannot be maintained, but on the ground of the unalienable right of man to resist [the cruel use of power]; that is to say, upon the ground of revolution."*

Calhoun and other Southerners opposed high tariffs. Calhoun argued that tariffs raised the prices of manufactured goods that they could not make for themselves and that high tariffs protected inefficient manufacturers.

Daniel Webster

Daniel Webster was first elected to Congress in 1812 to represent his home state of New Hampshire. He later represented Massachusetts in both the House and the Senate. Webster at first supported free trade and the shipping interests of New England. In time Webster came to favor the Tariff of 1816, which protected American industries from foreign competition. He also supported other policies that he thought would strengthen the nation and help the North.

Webster gained fame as one of the greatest public speakers of his day. As a U.S. senator, he spoke eloquently in defense of the nation as a whole against sectional interests. In one of his most memorable speeches, Webster declared, "Liberty and Union, now and forever, one and inseparable!"

Henry Clay

Henry Clay of Kentucky was another leading War Hawk. He became speaker of the House of Representatives in 1811 and a leader who represented the interests of the Western states. He also served as a member of the delegation that negotiated the Treaty of Ghent, ending the War of 1812. Above all, Henry Clay became known as the national leader who tried to resolve sectional disputes.

The Missouri Compromise

Sectional tension reached new heights in 1820. The issue was whether to allow slavery in states when they joined the Union. The South wanted Missouri admitted as a slave state, whereas Northerners wanted it to be free of slavery. The issue was further complicated when Maine, still a part of Massachusetts, also applied for statehood.

Eventually Henry Clay helped work out a compromise that preserved the balance between North and South. The **Missouri Compromise,** reached in March 1820, provided for the admission of Missouri as a slave state and Maine as a free state. Slavery was banned in the rest of the Louisiana Territory north of the 36°30'N parallel.

Henry Clay believed his policies would benefit all sections of the nation. In an 1824 speech, he called his program the "American System." The **American System** included three parts: (1) a protective tariff, (2) a program of internal improvements, and (3) a national bank. Not everyone saw Clay's program in such positive terms. Many Southerners did not see the benefits of the tariff or internal improvements.

In the end, little of Clay's American System went into effect. Congress eventually adopted some internal improvements, but they were not on the scale Clay hoped for. Congress created a Second National Bank in 1816, but it remained controversial.

Henry Clay

Politician from Kentucky

Clay's ability to resolve arguments earned him the nickname "The Great Compromiser." He was a strong nationalist. In a speech on the Senate floor, he said: *"If the . . . sad event of the dissolution [breaking up] of this Union is to happen, that I shall not survive to behold the sad and heart-rending [distressing] spectacle."*

CRITICAL Thinking

1. **Comprehending** According to Webster, when might a state declare the federal government's laws invalid?
2. **Contrasting** Describe the differences in the three men's views about the power of government.
3. **Analyzing** How does Clay's statement reflect nationalist views?

A Compromise on Slavery Missouri's application for statehood sparked a national debate over the issue of slavery. Northern Congressional leaders sought to restrict the entry of Missouri as a slave state. Southern leaders retaliated by blocking Maine's application for statehood. The Missouri Compromise allowed for Missouri to be admitted as a slave state and Maine as a free state.

Map legend:
- Free state/territory
- Closed to slavery by the Missouri Compromise
- Slave state/territory
- Territory opened to slavery by the Missouri Compromise

"All know that permitting the slaves of the South to spread in the West . . . will dilute [weaken] the evil everywhere . . . getting finally rid of it."
—Thomas Jefferson in a letter, December 1820

"Freedom and slavery are the parties which stand this day before the senate, and upon its decision the empire of the one or the other will be established in the new state which we are about to admit into the Union."
—Senator Rufus King, February 1820

Map Skills

Location Was the Unorganized Territory open or closed to slavery?

Maps In MOtion See StudentWorks™ Plus or glencoe.com.

McCulloch v. Maryland

The Supreme Court also became involved in sectional and states' rights issues at this time. Its decisions strengthened the power of the national government. The state of Maryland imposed a tax on the Baltimore branch of the Second National Bank of the United States, a federal institution. The Bank refused to pay the state tax. The case, **McCulloch v. Maryland,** reached the Court in 1819.

Speaking for the Court, Chief Justice John Marshall ruled that Maryland had no right to tax the Bank. Marshall argued that the Constitution gave certain powers to the federal government, such as collecting taxes, borrowing money, and regulating commerce. Marshall claimed that the national bank helped the federal government carry out these powers.

Next, Marshall stated that the government could use any method that was necessary to carry out its powers, as long as it was not forbidden by the Constitution. Finally, Marshall claimed that a state government could not interfere with a federal agency that was using its constitutional powers in that state. The tax was interfering with the bank and its constitutional powers and was, thus, unconstitutional.

Gibbons v. Ogden

Another Supreme Court case, **Gibbons v. Ogden,** established that states could not enact legislation that would interfere with congressional power over interstate commerce. People who supported states' rights believed that the Court's decisions in these cases increased federal power at the expense of state power. Nationalists welcomed the rulings' support for federal power.

Reading Check Explaining Describe how the Supreme Court's decisions affected the power of the federal government.

Foreign Affairs

Main Idea The United States defined its role in the Americas with the Monroe Doctrine.

History and You Have you ever had to take a stand on an issue with a friend? Read about American foreign policies in the early 1800s.

. . . .

The War of 1812 heightened Americans' pride in their country. Americans also realized that the United States had to establish a new relationship with the "Old World."

Relations With Britain

In the 1817 Rush-Bagot Treaty, the United States and Britain agreed to limit the number of naval vessels on the Great Lakes and remove weapons located along the border of the United States and British Canada.

The Convention of 1818 set the boundary of the Louisiana Territory between the United States and Canada at the 49th parallel. The convention also created a secure and demilitarized border. In other words, each country agreed to maintain its border without armed forces. Through Secretary of State John Quincy Adams's efforts, Americans also gained the right to settle in the Oregon Country.

Relations With Spain

Spain owned East Florida and also claimed West Florida. The United States argued that West Florida was part of the Louisiana Purchase. In 1810 and 1812, Americans simply added parts of West Florida to Louisiana and Mississippi. Spain objected but took no action.

General Andrew Jackson was ordered to stop Seminole raids on America from Florida. In April 1818, Jackson invaded Spanish East Florida and seized two Spanish forts. Secretary of State Adams had not authorized Jackson's actions, but he did nothing about them.

Latin America and the Monroe Doctrine

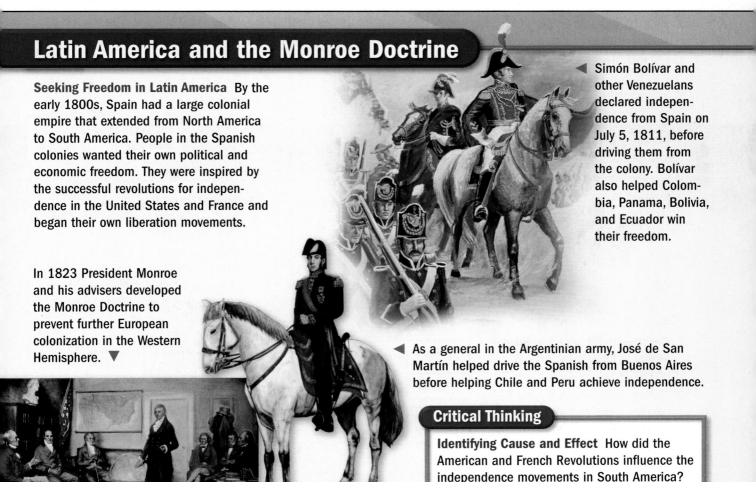

Seeking Freedom in Latin America By the early 1800s, Spain had a large colonial empire that extended from North America to South America. People in the Spanish colonies wanted their own political and economic freedom. They were inspired by the successful revolutions for independence in the United States and France and began their own liberation movements.

◄ Simón Bolívar and other Venezuelans declared independence from Spain on July 5, 1811, before driving them from the colony. Bolívar also helped Colombia, Panama, Bolivia, and Ecuador win their freedom.

In 1823 President Monroe and his advisers developed the Monroe Doctrine to prevent further European colonization in the Western Hemisphere. ▼

◄ As a general in the Argentinian army, José de San Martín helped drive the Spanish from Buenos Aires before helping Chile and Peru achieve independence.

Critical Thinking

Identifying Cause and Effect How did the American and French Revolutions influence the independence movements in South America?

Jackson's raid demonstrated American military strength. Secretary of State Adams believed that the Spanish did not want war and wanted to settle the dipute. His assumption was correct.

Adams-Onís Treaty and Mexico

With the **Adams-Onís Treaty** in 1819, the United States gained East Florida, and Spain also abandoned all claims to West Florida. In return the United States gave up its claims to Spanish Texas and agreed to border boundaries. As a result, the United States gained a territory in the Pacific Northwest.

Meanwhile Spain was losing power in its vast empire, especially in Mexico. In the fall of 1810 a priest, Miguel Hidalgo (ee•DAHL•goh), led a rebellion in Mexico. Hidalgo called for racial equality and the redistribution of land. The Spanish defeated the revolutionary forces and executed Hidalgo. In 1821 Mexico finally gained its independence.

Bolívar and San Martín

Simón Bolívar, also known as "the Liberator," led the independence movement that won freedom for the present-day countries of Venezuela, Colombia, Panama, Bolivia, and Ecuador. José de San Martín successfully achieved independence for Chile and Peru. By 1824, Spain lost control of most of South America.

The Monroe Doctrine

In 1822 the Quadruple Alliance—France, Austria, Russia, and Prussia—discussed a plan to help Spain regain its American holdings. The possibility of increased European involvement in North America led President Monroe to take action.

The president issued a statement, later known as the **Monroe Doctrine,** on December 2, 1823. The United States would not interfere with any existing European colonies in the Americas. However, North and South America "are henceforth not to be considered as subjects for future colonization by any European powers." The Monroe Doctrine became an important element in American foreign policy.

✔ **Reading Check** **Making Inferences** Why was the Monroe Doctrine issued?

Section 3 Review

History ONLINE
Study Central™ To review this section, go to glencoe.com.

Vocabulary

1. Define the following terms using complete sentences: sectionalism, intense, internal, state sovereignty, American System.

Main Ideas

2. **Describing** Describe the overall feeling in the U.S. after the War of 1812.

3. **Listing** What issues divided the country at the end of the Era of Good Feelings?

4. **Explaining** Why was the Monroe Doctrine issued?

Critical Thinking

5. **Organizing** Use a diagram like the one below to show the effects of the Missouri Compromise.

6. **Persuasive Writing** If you had been a congressperson at the time, do you think you would have supported the ideas of John C. Calhoun or Henry Clay? Write a paragraph explaining who you would support and why.

7. **Answer the Essential Question**

How were nation-building issues resolved in the early 1800s?

Growth and Expansion

The Economy Grows

- The Industrial Revolution and the factory system energize the U.S. economy.
- Free enterprise encourages economic growth.
- Agriculture expands in the South and West.
- Corporations emerge, and people invest in new industries.
- Towns and cities develop as a result of increased trade.

Westward Expansion Occurs

- Turnpikes are constructed to make it easier to travel and trade.
- Steamboats improve the transportation of goods and passengers along rivers.
- Canals are built to link the eastern and western parts of the U.S.
- America's population continues to move west.

▲ Corduroy road

Sectional Differences Emerge

- People living in different regions disagree about national policies.
- The issue of slavery continues to divide Southerners and Northerners.
- The Missouri Compromise attempts to resolve the issue of slavery in states being admitted in the Union.
- The Supreme Court supports federal power over states' rights.

▲ Slater Mill, Pawtucket, Rhode Island

The U.S. Defines Its Role With Europe

- Policy agreements are made peacefully with Britain.
- The U.S. acquires West and East Florida from Spain.
- Spain loses most of its colonies in South America as a result of independence movements.
- The U.S. issues the Monroe Doctrine to prevent the establishment of new European colonies in the Western Hemisphere.

▲ Water frame

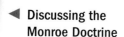

◄ Discussing the Monroe Doctrine

STUDY TO GO Study anywhere, anytime! Download quizzes and flash cards to your PDA from glencoe.com.

TEST-TAKING TIP

To answer vocabulary questions 1–4, first look at the terms listed as answers. See if you can mentally define each one. Then read the question to select the right answer.

Reviewing Vocabulary

Directions: Choose the word or words that best completes the sentence.

1 Francis Cabot Lowell began the _____, in which all manufacturing steps are brought together in one place.

  A free enterprise system
  B factory system
  C cottage system
  D American system

2 Officials in New York built a _____ to link New York City with the Great Lakes.

  A turnpike
  B corduroy road
  C canal
  D shipping line

3 The first _____ of the United States revealed that the country had a population of nearly 4 million in 1790.

  A poll tax
  B draft
  C census
  D patent

4 _____, or loyalty to a region, began to divide the United States after the Era of Good Feelings.

  A Sectionalism
  B Sovereignty
  C Fraternalism
  D Monarchism

Reviewing Main Ideas

Directions: Choose the best answer.

5 Which of the following is a major element of the free enterprise system?

  A Government controls most aspects of the national economy.
  B Business and government leaders create a national plan for producing goods.
  C All workers are required to join labor unions.
  D Competition among businesses operates with little government interference.

6 The invention of the cotton gin

  A encouraged farmers in the Northeast to plant cotton.
  B dramatically increased Southern cotton production.
  C had no impact on the demand for cotton.
  D encouraged plantation owners to free enslaved workers.

7 Pioneer families tended to settle in communities along major rivers

  A to gain greater protection from Native Americans.
  B to make it easier for them to travel east.
  C because they provided fresh drinking water.
  D so that they could more easily ship their crops to market.

8 In the mid-1800s, by whom were tariffs *least* likely to be supported?

  A Southern planters
  B Northeastern factory owners
  C Westerners living on the frontier
  D free African Americans living in the North

GO ON ➡

History ONLINE

For additional test practice, use **Self-Check Quizzes**—Chapter 10 at glencoe.com.

Critical Thinking

Directions: Choose the best answer.

Base your answer to question 9 on the reading below and your knowledge of Chapter 10.

> **Section 8.** *And be it further enacted,* that in all that territory ceded by France to the United States, under the name of Louisiana, . . . slavery . . . shall be, and is hereby forever prohibited.
>
> —from the Missouri Compromise

9   The issue addressed in this section of the Missouri Compromise was

A   poll taxes in the Louisiana Territory.
B   the spread of slavery.
C   voting rights in Louisiana.
D   workers' rights and labor unions in Louisiana.

Base your answer to question 10 on the map below and your knowledge of Chapter 10.

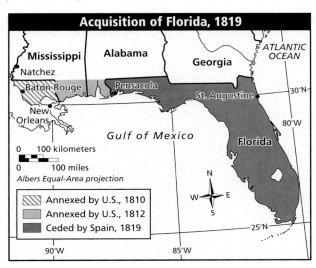

Acquisition of Florida, 1819

Mississippi
Alabama
Georgia
ATLANTIC OCEAN
Natchez
Baton Rouge
Pensacola
St. Augustine
New Orleans
30°N
80°W
Gulf of Mexico
Florida
0   100 kilometers
0   100 miles
Albers Equal-Area projection
25°N
90°W
85°W

Annexed by U.S., 1810
Annexed by U.S., 1812
Ceded by Spain, 1819

N W E S

10   Based on the map, which country ceded most of Florida to the United States in 1819?

A   Britain   C   Spain
B   France   D   Portugal

Constructed Response

Directions: Write a short response to each of the following questions. In your answer:

- *address all parts of the question*
- *use information from the chapter*
- *include facts, examples, and details relevant to the question*
- *use clear language*

11   Identify one of the technological advances of the early 1800s, and state its effect on American life.

Base your answer to question 12 on the reading below and your knowledge of Chapter 10.

> With the existing colonies . . . of any European power we . . . shall not interfere. But with the [Latin American] governments who have declared their independence . . . we could not view any [involvement] for the purpose of oppressing them . . . by any European power in any other light than as the [showing] of an unfriendly disposition toward the United States.
>
> —from James Monroe, Speech to Congress, December 1823

12   According to this excerpt, what are Monroe's views on the involvement of European powers in Latin America?

13   Identify two major parts of Henry Clay's American System. What were the system's results?

14   What did the Marshall Supreme Court interpret the Constitution to mean regarding the powers of the federal government?

STOP

Need Extra Help?														
If you missed questions. . .	1	2	3	4	5	6	7	8	9	10	11	12	13	14
Go to page. . .	306	315	313	322	307	308	317	323	323	329	306	326	323	324

Nationalism and Sectionalism
1820–1860

Child's sled from 1848

"We are the nation of human progress, and who will, what can, set limits to our onward march?"
—John L. O'Sullivan

Log cabin and farm site in Ohio, 1831

Reading History

Making Inferences

Learn It!

To comprehend some texts, you will need to make inferences. When you infer, you use clues from the text along with your own knowledge to figure out the author's meaning.

Question: Why do you think the Cherokees' journey west is called the Trail of Tears?

Inference Process

Text Clue:
Cherokee leaders were reluctant to relocate their people.

Text Clue:
Many Cherokee died on the journey.

Background Knowledge:
It is difficult to lose your home and experience the loss of family and friends.

—from Chapter 11, p. 346
Filled with sadness and anger, their leaders gave in, and the long march to the West began. . . . Around 2,000 Cherokee died in camps waiting for the move to begin. About another 2,000 died along the way from starvation, disease, and exposure to brutal weather.

Practice It!

Read the paragraph, and follow the inference process on another sheet of paper.

—from Chapter 13, p. 412
The South was behind other sections of the country in **literacy,** the number of people able to read and write. One reason . . . was the South's geography. The South had few people per square mile. Many families could not send their children great distances to attend school. In addition, many Southerners believed that education was a private matter, not a state function.

Question: How did the South's agricultural economy affect its children's education?

Inference Process

Text Clue:
_____

Text Clue:
_____

Background Knowledge:
_____

Academic Vocabulary Preview

Listed below are the academic vocabulary words and their definitions that you will come across as you study Unit 4. The activities in the Practice It! column will help you study the words and definitions.

Academic Vocabulary	Definition	Practice It!
Chapter 11 The Jackson Era		
select (suh · LEHKT) *p. 337*	to choose	**Choose** *terms from Chapter 11 to complete the paragraph.* The president of the United States is an elected member of the **1.** _____ government. In an election, if no presidential candidate receives a majority of electoral votes, members of the House of Representatives **2.** _____ the president. The House is an **3.** _____ of the U.S. legislative government.
participate (pahr · TIH · suh · PAYT) *p. 340*	to take part in	
federal (FEH · duh · ruhl) *p. 343*	the central governing authority	
survive (suhr · VYV) *p. 347*	to continue to live	
institution (IHN · stuh · TOO · shuhn) *p. 349*	an organization	
symbol (SIHM · buhl) *p. 352*	an object representing something else	
Chapter 12 Manifest Destiny		
access (AK · sehs) *p. 359*	the ability to get to	**Identify** *the term from Chapter 12 that best completes the sentence.* **4.** In the early 1800s, many Americans wanted _____ to the Pacific Ocean. **5.** Spain encouraged families to _____ a colony in Texas. **6.** Before earning statehood, California wrote a _____ that banned slavery.
establish (ihs · TA · blihsh) *p. 367*	to set up	
resource (REE · SOHRS) *p. 374*	an available source of wealth	
commence (kuh · MENTS) *p. 375*	to begin	
constitution (KAHNT · stuh · TOO · shuhn) *p. 380*	a list of fundamental laws to support a government	
incorporate (ihn · KAWR · puh · RAYT) *p. 382*	to include; to bring into	
Chapter 13 North and South		
innovation (IH · nuh · VAY · shuhn) *p. 389*	a new idea or method	**Identify** *the term from Chapter 13 that best matches the underlined word or phrase.* **7.** Canals and railways <u>changed</u> trade in the United States in the early 1800s. **8.** Many <u>towns</u> in the North did not allow enslaved people to attend school. **9.** Today, slavery is not <u>allowed by law</u> in the United States.
transform (trants · FAWRM) *p. 391*	to change	
community (kuh · MYOO · nuh · tee) *p. 396*	a group of people living in a particular place	
license (LY · suhnts) *p. 397*	to grant official authority	
consequence (KAHNT · suh · kwehnts) *p. 402*	a result	
legal (LEE · guhl) *p. 409*	permitted by law	
Chapter 14 The Age of Reform		
lecture (LEHK · chuhr) *p. 419*	a speech intended as a warning	**Choose** *the word that best matches the meaning of each vocabulary term listed below.* **10. lecture** **11. capable** a. praise a. able b. essay b. loud c. speech c. unable
route (ROOT) *p. 430*	a line of travel	
capable (KAY · puh · buhl) *p. 437*	having the necessary abilities	
ministry (MIH · nuh · stree) *p. 438*	religious services	

The Jackson Era 1824–1845

In the 1830s, many Native Americans were forced to move west along what became known as the Trail of Tears.

JAMES MONROE 1817–1825

★ **1823** Monroe Doctrine issued

JOHN Q. ADAMS 1825–1829

ANDREW JACKSON 1829–1837

1830 ★ Indian Removal Act

★ **1833** Force Bill passes

PRESIDENTS

U.S. Events

World Events

1820   **1825**   **1830**

★ **1822** Brazil gains independence from Portugal

1826 ★ French scientist Niépce produces first photograph

★ **1829** Louis Braille publishes reading system for the blind

Section 1: Jacksonian Democracy

Essential Question How did political beliefs and events shape Andrew Jackson's presidency?

Section 2: Conflicts Over Land

Essential Question How did Andrew Jackson's presidency affect Native Americans?

Section 3: Jackson and the Bank

Essential Question How do economic issues affect the president and presidential elections?

History ONLINE

Chapter Overview Visit <u>glencoe.com</u> and click on **Chapter 11—Chapter Overviews** to preview chapter information.

FOLDABLES®
Study Organizer

Organizing Information
Make this Foldable to organize what you learn about the Jackson era.

Step 1 Fold a sheet of paper into fourths from top to bottom.

Step 2 Fold the paper into thirds along the long axis. You have formed a table with three columns and four rows.

Step 3 Label the left column with the chapter number and the titles of the sections. Label column two "Problems." Label column three "Solutions."

Chapter 11	Problems	Solutions
Jackson Democracy		
Conflicts Over Land		
Jackson and the Bank		

Reading and Writing As you read, use your Foldable to write down the problems that arose during the Jackson era and attempts to solve these problems.

Abraham Lincoln, "The Rail Splitter" ▶

★ **1834** Abraham Lincoln elected to Illinois legislature

★ **1836** "Nature" by Ralph Waldo Emerson published in Boston

MARTIN VAN BUREN 1837–1841

★ **1838** Cherokee forced to move west

WILLIAM HENRY HARRISON 1841

JOHN TYLER 1841–1845

1835

Queen Victoria's Imperial State Crown ▶

★ **1837** Victoria becomes Queen of Great Britain

★ **1839** Scottish blacksmith, Kirkpatrick Macmillan, produces first bicycle

1840

1845

Jacksonian Democracy

Essential Question ◄

How did political beliefs and events shape Andrew Jackson's presidency?

Reading Guide

Content Vocabulary

majority (p. 337)
plurality (p. 337)
spoils system (p. 340)
caucus (p. 340)

nominating convention (p. 340)
tariff (p. 341)
nullify (p. 341)
secede (p. 341)

Academic Vocabulary

select (p. 337)
participate (p. 340)

Key People and Events

Andrew Jackson (p. 337)
John Quincy Adams (p. 337)
Nullification Act (p. 341)

Reading Strategy

Taking Notes As you read about the parties competing in the election of 1828, use a diagram like the one below to organize the information.

Party → Candidate → Views

INDIANA ACADEMIC STANDARDS
United States History

8.1.17 Identify the key ideas of Jacksonian democracy and explain their influence on political participation, political parties, and constitutional government.

8.1.18 Analyze different interests and points of view of individuals and groups involved in the abolitionist, feminist and social reform movements, and in sectional conflicts.

8.2.8 Explain ways that citizens can participate in political parties, campaigns, and elections.

American Diary

As a supporter of the "common man," Andrew Jackson lost the 1824 presidential election to John Quincy Adams. Because no candidate won an electoral vote majority, the election went to the House of Representatives, which elected Adams. Jackson's supporters, "the humble members of society—the farmers, mechanics and laborers," believed Jackson was cheated out of the presidency by a "corrupt bargain."

—*from* The White House Historical Association

Andrew Jackson's inauguration in 1828

Elections of 1824 and 1828

Main Idea John Quincy Adams and Andrew Jackson introduced new ways of campaigning in the presidential elections of 1824 and 1828.

History and You Think of the ways that presidential candidates campaign today. What methods do they use? Read to find out about the new ways of campaigning that John Quincy Adams and Andrew Jackson brought about.

. . . .

From 1816 to 1824, the United States had only one major political party, the Jeffersonian Republicans, or the Republican Party. In 1824, when James Monroe declined to run for a third term as president, four candidates from the party competed for the presidency. The views of the four candidates differed on the role of the federal government. Their views also differed because they represented different regions of the country.

The party nominated William H. Crawford, a former congressman from Georgia. The other three candidates were favorite sons—meaning they were backed by their home states rather than the national party. **Andrew Jackson** and Henry Clay came from the West. Clay, of Kentucky, was Speaker of the House of Representatives. Jackson, of Tennessee, was not a Washington politician, but he was a hero of the War of 1812. Raised in poverty, he claimed to speak for the Americans who had been left out of politics. **John Quincy Adams,** of Massachusetts, son of former president John Adams, was popular with merchants of the Northeast.

Striking a Bargain

In the election, Jackson received the largest number of popular votes. However, no candidate received a **majority,** or more than half, of the electoral votes. Jackson won a **plurality,** or the largest single share. According to the Twelfth Amendment of the Constitution, when no candidate receives a majority of electoral votes, the House of Representatives **selects,** or chooses, the president.

While the House was preparing to vote on the next president, Henry Clay met with John Quincy Adams. Clay agreed to use his influence as Speaker of the House to defeat Jackson. In return, Clay may have hoped to gain the position of secretary of state.

With Clay's help, Adams was elected president in the House. Adams quickly named Clay as secretary of state, traditionally the stepping-stone to the presidency. Jackson's followers accused the two men of making a "corrupt bargain" and stealing the election.

By the Numbers / Presidential Elections

Election of 1824

Candidate*	Electoral Votes	House Votes
John Q. Adams	84	13
Andrew Jackson	99	7
William H. Crawford	41	4
Henry Clay	37	-

Election of 1828

Candidate*	Electoral Votes
Andrew Jackson Democratic Republican	178
John Q. Adams National Republican	83

*All candidates represented the Democratic Republican Party.

Critical Thinking

Analyzing What major differences can you see between the results of the two elections?

The Adams Presidency

Adams and Clay denied any wrongdoing, and no evidence of a deal ever emerged. Still, the charge of a "corrupt bargain" cast a long shadow over Adams's presidency. A hard-working and intelligent man, Adams was determined to leave his mark on the presidency.

In his first message to Congress, Adams announced an ambitious program of legislation. In addition to improving roads and waterways, Adams urged that the government spend money to build a national university, set up astronomical observatories, and support scientific research.

Adams's proposals, however, horrified his opponents who desired a more limited role for the federal government. It would be wrong, they believed, to spend the taxpayers' money on such projects.

In the end, Congress granted the president funds for improving rivers, harbors, and roads, but this was far less than Adams wanted. The rejection of many of Adams's proposals set the stage for the president's defeat in his 1828 reelection attempt.

The Election of 1828

By 1828, the Republican Party had divided into two separate parties: the Democratic-Republicans, who supported Jackson, and the National Republicans, who supported Adams. Jackson's Democratic-Republicans, or Democrats, favored states' rights and mistrusted strong central government. Many Democrats were people from the frontier, immigrants, or workers in the big cities.

The National Republicans wanted a strong central government. They supported federal measures, such as road building and the Bank of the United States, that would shape the nation's economy. Many National Republicans were merchants or farmers.

During the campaign both parties resorted to mudslinging, or attempts to ruin their opponents' reputations with insults. The Democratic-Republicans accused Adams of betraying the people. They put out a handbill

Primary Source | The Campaign of 1828

Rachel Donelson Jackson ▲

Jackson Attacked The presidential campaign of 1828 was one of the dirtiest in American history. Supporters of President John Quincy Adams attacked Andrew Jackson in print. The so-called "coffin handbills" (below) criticized Jackson's execution of six soldiers for desertion during the War of 1812. The handbills backfired, either because they exaggerated too much or because most Americans approved of what Jackson did. In addition, Jackson's opponents accused his wife, Rachel Donelson Jackson, of bigamy. When Rachel died before the inauguration, Jackson blamed those who slandered her.

Some Account of some of the Bloody Deeds of GEN. JACKSON.

"Gentle reader, it is for you to say, whether this man, who carries a sword cane, and is willing to run it through the body of any one who may presume to stand in his way, is a fit person to be our President."

—from the "Coffin Handbill"

calling the election a contest "between an honest patriotism, on the one side, and an unholy, selfish ambition, on the other." The National Republicans fought back. They created a vicious campaign song to play up embarrassing incidents in Jackson's life. One involved Jackson's order in the War of 1812 to execute soldiers who deserted.

Mudslinging was not the only new tactic introduced in the 1828 campaign. Election slogans, rallies, buttons, and events such as barbecues also were used to stir up enthusiasm. All of these new features became a permanent part of American political life.

In the election of 1828, Jackson received most of the votes cast in the frontier states. He also received many votes in the South, where his support for states' rights was popular. John C. Calhoun of South Carolina, who had been Adams's vice president, switched parties to run with Jackson. Calhoun also supported states' rights. Jackson won the election in an overwhelming victory, or landslide.

✔ **Reading Check** **Identifying** What campaign practices of the 1828 election still are used today?

Philadelphia editor John Binns published several "coffin handbills" attacking Andrew Jackson. This cartoon shows Binns ⒜ struggling to carry a burden consisting of coffins for Secretary of State Henry Clay ⒝ and President John Quincy Adams ⒞. Adams is clinging to the presidential chair that he was soon to lose.

Critical Thinking

Interpreting What is the cartoonist trying to say about the coffin handbills?

Jackson as President

Main Idea Andrew Jackson made the American political system more democratic.

History and You What are the requirements for today's citizens to be eligible to vote? Read on to learn how President Jackson expanded voting rights to include a larger number of people.

• •

Andrew Jackson was everything most Americans admired—a patriot, a self-made man, and a war hero. Thousands of farmers and laborers arrived in Washington to hear Jackson's Inaugural Address. Later, a crowd attended the White House reception. They filled the elegant rooms, trampling carpets with muddy shoes and spilling food on chairs. They were there to shake the hand of the president who seemed just like them.

"Old Hickory"

Like many of his supporters, Andrew Jackson was born in a log cabin. During the War of 1812, he defeated the Creek Nation in the Battle of Horseshoe Bend and the British at the Battle of New Orleans. His troops called him "Old Hickory" because he was as tough as a hickory stick.

Small farmers, craftspeople, and others who felt left out of the expanding American economy loved Jackson. They felt that his rise from a log cabin to the White House demonstrated the American success story.

New Voters

President Andrew Jackson promised "equal protection and equal benefits" for all Americans—at least for all white American men. During his first term, a spirit of equality spread throughout American politics.

In the nation's early years, only men who owned property or paid taxes had suffrage, or the right to vote. By the 1820s, many states had loosened the property requirements. Democracy expanded as people who had not been allowed to vote became new voters.

In 1832 South Carolina called a state convention to declare the tariffs of 1828 and 1832 null and void. In addition, the state threatened to secede, or withdraw, from the Union if the federal government attempted to use force to collect those tariffs within its borders.

"It is hereby declared . . . that the . . . laws for the imposing of duties . . . on the importation of foreign commodities. . . are null, void, and no law, nor binding upon this State. . . .

Any act authorizing the employment of a military or naval force against the State of South Carolina, . . . [is] inconsistent with the . . . continuance of South Carolina in the Union."

—from the South Carolina Ordinance of Nullification

Vice President John C. Calhoun argued that any state had the authority to call a formal convention to declare null and void any federal law it considered unconstitutional. Tensions between Calhoun and President Jackson increased when Jackson sided with those opposing nullification.

The Nullification Proclamation declared that nullification was unconstitutional. It also stated that threatening to secede was an act of treason.

"I consider, then, the power to annul a law of the United States, assumed by one State, incompatible with the existence of the Union, . . . and destructive of the great object for which it was formed."

—President Andrew Jackson's proclamation from the nullification

President Andrew Jackson privately threatened to march an army into South Carolina to hang Calhoun. Instead, he issued a proclamation against nullification. Congress passed a bill to lower tariffs—along with a bill to enforce it.

Critical Thinking

Comparing and Contrasting How did each side in the nullification crisis defend its position?

For the first time, white male sharecroppers, factory workers, and others **participated,** or took part, in the political process. Women, however, could not vote, and African Americans and Native Americans had few rights of any kind.

Also, by 1828, 22 of the 24 states had changed their constitutions to allow the people, rather than the state legislatures, to choose presidential electors. This change further broadened democracy.

The Spoils System

Democrats wanted to open up government jobs to people from all walks of life. They argued that ordinary citizens could handle any government job. Many Democrats were disturbed that the federal government had become a bureaucracy, a system in which nonelected officials carry out laws.

President Jackson fired many federal workers and replaced them with his supporters. The fired employees protested.

They charged that Jackson was acting like a tyrant. Jackson responded that new federal employees would be good for democracy.

One Jackson supporter said: "To the victors belong the spoils." In other words, because the Jacksonians won the election, they had the right to the spoils, or the benefits of victory. The practice of replacing government employees with the winner's supporters is called the **spoils system.**

Electoral Changes

Jackson's supporters abandoned the unpopular **caucus** system, in which major candidates were chosen by members of Congress. The caucuses were replaced by **nominating conventions** in which delegates from the states chose the party's presidential candidate. This system allowed many people to participate in the selection of candidates.

Reading Check **Describing** What is a caucus system?

The Tariff Debate

Main Idea A fight over tariffs ignited a crisis on the question of states' rights versus the rights of the federal government.

History and You Can you ignore a school rule? Read how South Carolina rejected a federal law.

A **tariff** is a fee paid on imported goods. The high tariff on European manufactured goods pleased Northeastern factory owners. Tariffs made European goods more expensive, prompting American consumers to buy American-made goods. Southerners hated the tariff, because tariffs meant higher prices.

John C. Calhoun of South Carolina argued that a state had the right to **nullify,** or cancel, a federal law if it was considered to be against state interests. Because the states created the federal government, he argued, the states are the final authority. Daniel Webster disagreed, claiming that nullification would destroy the Union.

Nobody knew Jackson's views. At a dinner, however, Jackson spoke directly to Calhoun: "Our federal union . . . must be preserved!" Answering the challenge, Calhoun said, "The Union—next to our liberty, most dear." He meant that the Union must take second place to a state's liberty to overrule the Constitution if its interests were threatened.

In 1832 Congress enacted a lower tariff, but it did not cool the protest. South Carolina passed the **Nullification Act,** declaring it would not pay the "illegal" tariffs of 1828 and 1832. The state threatened to **secede,** or break away, from the Union if the U.S. federal government interfered.

To ease the crisis, Jackson backed a bill that would gradually lower the tariff. Jackson, however, had Congress pass the Force Bill, allowing him to use the military to enforce acts of Congress. South Carolina accepted the new tariff but nullified the Force Bill.

Reading Check **Explaining** How would Northeastern factory owners react to a high tariff?

Section 1 Review

History ONLINE
Study Central™ To review this section, go to glencoe.com.

Vocabulary

1. Define each of the following words by using it in a sentence: majority, plurality, select, participate, spoils system, caucus, nominating convention, tariff, nullify, secede.

Main Ideas

2. Specifying What key issue split the Republican Party in the 1828 presidential election?

3. Explaining Why did Andrew Jackson fire many government employees?

4. Summarizing Why was the issue of states' rights versus federal authority serious?

Critical Thinking

5. Making Inferences Why do you think Speaker of the House Henry Clay was willing to make the "corrupt bargain"?

6. Organizing Use a diagram like the one below to describe the changes that took place in the political system under Andrew Jackson.

7. Creative Writing Write three questions you would ask President Andrew Jackson if you interviewed him. Then write answers to the questions as you think Jackson might have responded.

Answer the
8. Essential Question
How did political beliefs and events shape Andrew Jackson's presidency?

Conflicts Over Land

Reading Guide

Content Vocabulary

relocate *(p. 343)*

guerrilla tactics *(p. 347)*

Academic Vocabulary

federal *(p. 343)*   survive *(p. 347)*

Key People and Events

Indian Removal Act *(p. 343)*

Indian Territory *(p. 344)*

General Winfield Scott *(p. 345)*

Trail of Tears *(p. 346)*

Black Hawk *(p. 346)*

Osceola *(p. 347)*

Reading Strategy

Taking Notes As you read, use a diagram like the one below to describe how each group of Native Americans resisted removal and the result.

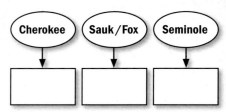

INDIANA ACADEMIC STANDARDS
United States History

8.1.24 Identify the influence of individuals on political and social events and movements such as the abolition movement, the Dred Scott case, women's rights, and Native American Indian removal.

American Diary

As they moved west in 1838 during a forced removal from their lands, the Cherokee were said to be on a "Trail of Tears." A legend developed that a Cherokee rose appeared along the road wherever a Cherokee tear landed. Poet Rick Brown described the event:

"As wagons, weighted, marked their way, from New Echota to where they close; where each tear fell, as some will tell, will be seen a Cherokee rose."

—quoted from "A Cherokee Rose"

The Seminole people of Florida fought against being forced to abandon their homes and way of life.

Moving Native Americans

Main Idea Thousands of Native Americans were forced to abandon their lands to white settlers and move West.

History and You How long have you lived in your community? How would you feel if you were forced to leave your home? Read how Native Americans reacted to their forced move.

· ·

While the nation had expanded westward by the 1830s, many Native Americans still lived in the eastern part of the country. The "Five Civilized Tribes"—the Cherokee, Creek, Seminole, Chickasaw, and Choctaw—lived in Georgia, Alabama, Mississippi, and Florida. These tribes had established farming societies with successful economies.

Because the area west of the Mississippi was dry and seemed unsuitable for farming, few white Americans lived there. Many settlers wanted the **federal**—or national—government to **relocate** Native Americans living in the Southeast to this area. They wanted to force the Native Americans to leave their land and move west.

President Andrew Jackson, a man of the frontier himself, supported the settlers' demand for Native American land. Jackson had fought the Creek and Seminole peoples in Georgia and Florida. In his Inaugural Address, he stated that he intended to move all Native Americans to the Great Plains.

Many Americans believed that the Great Plains was a wasteland that would never be settled. They thought that if they moved Native Americans to that region, the nation's conflict with them would be over.

Indian Removal Act

In 1830 President Jackson pushed the **Indian Removal Act** through Congress. The act allowed the federal government to pay Native Americans to move west.

Jackson then sent officials to make treaties with the Native Americans in the Southeast.

By the Numbers / Forced Migration

The Five Civilized Tribes east of the Mississippi were forced to migrate to Oklahoma under provision of Congress. Thousands died along the way.

Forced Migration, 1830–1840

Tribe	Number of people
Choctaw	~4,000
Creek	~15,000
Chickasaw	~5,000
Cherokee	~16,000
Seminole	~3,500

Number of people (0, 5,000, 10,000, 15,000, 20,000)

Critical Thinking

Analyzing What would be the advantage to white settlers if Congress forced Native Americans off their Eastern lands?

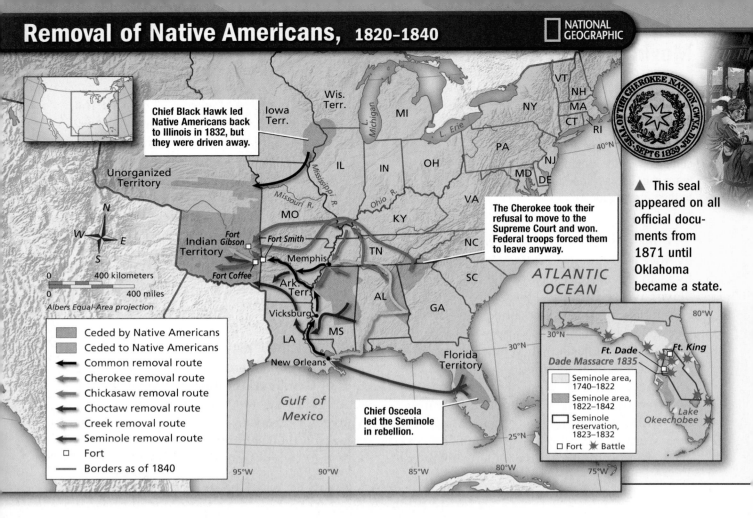

Chief Black Hawk led Native Americans back to Illinois in 1832, but they were driven away.

The Cherokee took their refusal to move to the Supreme Court and won. Federal troops forced them to leave anyway.

▲ This seal appeared on all official documents from 1871 until Oklahoma became a state.

Chief Osceola led the Seminole in rebellion.

Map legend:
- Ceded by Native Americans
- Ceded to Native Americans
- Common removal route
- Cherokee removal route
- Chickasaw removal route
- Choctaw removal route
- Creek removal route
- Seminole removal route
- □ Fort
- Borders as of 1840

400 kilometers
400 miles
Albers Equal-Area projection

- Seminole area, 1740–1822
- Seminole area, 1822–1842
- Seminole reservation, 1823–1832
- □ Fort ✳ Battle

Ft. Dade Ft. King
Dade Massacre 1835
Lake Okeechobee

Most Native American leaders felt forced to accept payment for their lands. In 1834 Congress created the **Indian Territory.** This was an area in present-day Oklahoma that was set aside for the relocation of Native Americans from the Southeast.

The Cherokee Nation

The Cherokee, however, refused to give up their land. In treaties of the 1790s, the federal government recognized the Cherokee in Georgia as a separate nation. Georgia, however, refused to recognize Cherokee laws. As pressure to leave mounted, the Cherokee appealed to the people of the United States:

History ONLINE

Student Web Activity Visit glencoe.com and complete the Web Activity about the struggles of Native Americans.

PRIMARY SOURCE

"We are aware, that some persons suppose it will be for our advantage to remove beyond the Mississippi. . . . Our people universally think otherwise. . . . We wish to remain on the land of our fathers."
—Cherokee appeal, 1830

When the government's position did not change, the Cherokee sued the state of Georgia. Eventually the Cherokee took their case to the Supreme Court. In *Worcester* v. *Georgia* (1832), Chief Justice John Marshall ruled that Georgia had no right to interfere with the Cherokee. Only the federal government had power in Cherokee matters.

President Jackson supported Georgia's efforts to remove the Cherokee. He declared that he would ignore the Supreme Court, saying, "John Marshall has made his decision, now let him enforce it."

◀ A Cherokee village in the Southeast

"My troops already occupy many positions in the country that you are to abandon, and thousands and thousands are approaching from every quarter, to render [make] resistance and escape alike hopeless. All those troops, regular and militia, are your friends. . . . Obey them when they tell you that you can remain no longer in this country."

—General Winfield Scott's address to the Cherokee Nation, 1838

▼ John Ross was elected chief of the Cherokee Nation in 1828 and held that post until his death in 1866. In the late 1830s, he led the fight against removal.

"A [false] Delegation, . . . proceeded to Washington City with this pretended treaty, and by false and fraudulent representations [replaced] . . . the legal and accredited Delegation of the Cherokee people, and obtained for this instrument, . . . the recognition of the United States Government. And now it is presented to us as a treaty, ratified by the Senate, and approved by the President."

—letter to the Senate and House of Representatives, 1836

◀ Wilma Mankiller, first female chief of the Cherokee, at a monument to John Ross on the Cherokee Reservation in Oklahoma, 2000

Critical Thinking

Making Inferences Do you think that General Scott wanted a peaceful solution to the government's disagreement with the Cherokee Nation? Why or why not?

Maps In Motion See StudentWorks™ Plus or glencoe.com.

The Trail of Tears

By 1835, the Cherokee were divided and feeling hopeless. That year, the federal government persuaded a small number—about 500—of Cherokee to sign The Treaty of New Echota, giving up their people's land. The treaty gave Jackson the legal document he needed to remove Native Americans. Approval of the treaty by the U.S. Senate sealed the fate of the Cherokee. Among the few who spoke out against approving the treaty were Daniel Webster and Henry Clay, but the treaty passed by a single vote.

Most of the 17,000 Cherokee, however, refused to honor the treaty. Cherokee Chief John Ross wrote a letter to the United States government. The letter explained that the Cherokee who had signed the treaty did not represent the Cherokee people. The letter asked the government not to enforce the treaty. This plea, however, did not soften the resolve of either President Jackson or the white settlers.

The Cherokee resisted the government's offer of western lands until 1838 when Jackson's successor, Martin Van Buren, began their removal. General John Wool resigned his command in protest. This delayed the action, but only temporarily. His replacement, **General Winfield Scott,** arrived at New Echota, the Cherokee capital, in May 1838. With 7,000 federal troops, General Scott and the U.S. Army began the invasion of the Cherokee Nation.

Scott threatened to use force if the Cherokee did not leave. He told them he had positioned troops all around the country so that resistance and escape were hopeless. The Cherokee knew that fighting would lead to their destruction.

People IN HISTORY

Black Hawk

Leader of a group of Sauk and Fox Native Americans

Black Hawk led 1,000 people, including old men, women, and children, back into Illinois in order to plant crops in their old tribal lands. He did not plan on an armed confrontation but believed that they still owned the land. *"We had never sold our country. We never received any annuities [payments] from our American father! And we are determined to hold on to our village!"*

Sequoyah

Developed the written alphabet for the Cherokee language

Sequoyah believed that Europeans had power because of their written language. He spent 12 years developing 86 symbols to represent all the syllables of the Cherokee language. A Cherokee poet, Alexander Lawrence Posey, wrote about the importance of Sequoyah's achievement: *"Thy name shall descend to every age. . . . The people's language cannot perish— nay."*

CRITICAL Thinking

1. **Analyzing** What did each Native American leader hope to accomplish?
2. **Evaluating** Which leader's actions had a better result? Why?

Filled with sadness and anger, the Cherokee leaders gave in, and the long march to the West began. One traveler from Maine witnessed seeing hundreds of Cherokee marching by:

PRIMARY SOURCE

"[The] aged . . . nearly ready to drop into the grave, were traveling with heavy burdens attached to the back—on the frozen ground . . . with no covering for the feet."

—from *The Trail of Tears*

Around 2,000 Cherokee died in camps waiting for the move to begin. About another 2,000 died along the way from starvation, disease, and exposure to brutal weather. Their forced journey west became known to the Cherokee people as the Trail Where They Cried. Historians call it the **Trail of Tears.**

✓ Reading Check **Explaining** What was the purpose of the Indian Removal Act?

Native American Resistance

Main Idea Some groups of Native Americans attempted to resist relocation. Most were taken from their lands by force.

History and You Think about how you might react if you were forced to do something that you thought was wrong. Would you attempt to resist? Read how some Native Americans responded to relocation.

In 1832 the Sauk chieftain, **Black Hawk,** led a group of Sauk and Fox people back to Illinois, their homeland. They wanted to recapture this area, which had been given up in a treaty. The Illinois state militia and federal troops responded with force, gathering nearly 4,500 soldiers. They chased the Fox and Sauk to the Mississippi River and slaughtered most of them as they tried to flee westward into present-day Iowa.

The Seminole people of Florida were the only Native Americans who successfully resisted their removal. Although they were pressured in the early 1830s to sign treaties giving up their land, the Seminole chief, **Osceola,** and some of his people refused to leave Florida. The Seminole decided to go to war against the United States instead.

In 1835 the Seminole joined forces with a group of African Americans who had run away to escape slavery. Together they attacked white settlements along the Florida coast. They used **guerrilla tactics,** making surprise attacks and then retreating back into the forests and swamps. In December 1835, the Seminole ambushed soldiers under the command of Major Francis Dade. Only a few of the 110 soldiers **survived,** or lived through, the attack. The Dade Massacre prompted a call for more troops to fight the Seminole.

By 1842, more than 1,500 Americans had died in the Seminole wars. The government gave up and allowed some Seminole to stay in Florida. Many, however, had died fighting. Many more were caught and forced to move west.

After 1842, only a few scattered groups of Native Americans lived east of the Mississippi. Most had been moved west. Native Americans had given up more than 100 million acres (40 million ha) of Eastern land to the federal government. In return, they received about $68 million and 32 million acres (13 million ha) in lands west of the Mississippi River. There they lived, organized by tribes, on reservations. Eventually, white settlements would extend into these areas as well.

The Five Civilized Tribes were relocated in the eastern half of present-day Oklahoma on lands claimed by several Plains groups, including the Osage, Comanche, and Kiowa. U.S. Army leaders got agreements from the Plains groups to let the Five Civilized Tribes live in peace. Settled in their new homes, the Five Civilized Tribes developed governments and built farms and schools. They also created a police force, the Lighthorsemen, to maintain safety in the area.

Reading Check **Analyzing** What was the significance of the Dade Massacre?

Section 2 Review

History ONLINE
Study Central™ To review this section, go to glencoe.com.

Vocabulary

1. Define each of the following terms and use the terms in a paragraph about conflicts over land: federal, relocate, guerrilla tactics, survive.

Main Ideas

2. Explaining Why did white settlers want the government to move Native Americans from the Southeast to the Great Plains?

3. Describing What were some of the features of the new Native American communities in the West?

Critical Thinking

4. Sequencing Identify the events that resulted in the eventual removal of the Cherokee from their land. Use a diagram like the one below.

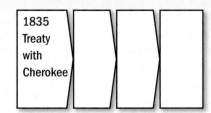

1835 Treaty with Cherokee

5. Contrasting Faced with removal from their lands, how did the response of the Seminole differ from that of the Cherokee?

6. Persuasive Writing Write a letter to Andrew Jackson discussing whether the Native Americans should be allowed to stay on their homelands.

Answer the Essential Question

7. How did Andrew Jackson's presidency affect Native Americans?

Reading Guide

Content Vocabulary

veto *(p. 349)*   laissez-faire *(p. 351)*

depression *(p. 350)*

Academic Vocabulary

institution *(p. 349)*   symbol *(p. 352)*

Key People and Events

Henry Clay *(p. 349)*

Daniel Webster *(p. 349)*

Martin Van Buren *(p. 349)*

William Henry Harrison *(p. 351)*

John Tyler *(p. 351)*

James Polk *(p. 352)*

Reading Strategy

Taking Notes As you read, use a diagram like the one below to identify the actions by Andrew Jackson that put the Bank of the United States out of business.

↓
| |
↓
| |
↓
Bank of United States Closes

INDIANA ACADEMIC STANDARDS
United States History

8.1.12 Explain the main issues, decisions, and consequences of landmark Supreme Court cases.

8.4.8 Examine the development of the banking system in the United States.

American Diary

President Jackson rested at the Hermitage, his home outside of Nashville, Tennessee, when he wanted to escape his critics in Washington. Many accused him of considering himself a "king," especially when he wanted to dissolve the national bank. To explain his actions Jackson declared the president must protect, "the liberties and rights of the people and the integrity of the Constitution against the Senate, or the House of Representatives, or both together."

—*from* The American Presidency

Andrew Jackson's home, the Hermitage

War Against the Bank

Main Idea President Jackson forced the National Bank to close, and economic problems split the Democratic Party.

History and You Do you have a bank account? What would happen to your money if an economic crisis occurred? Read to find out about the economic problems of the 1830s.

. . . .

For years, Jackson attacked the Bank of the United States as being an organization of wealthy Easterners that ordinary citizens could not control. The Bank of the United States was a powerful **institution,** or organization. It held the federal government's money and controlled much of the country's money supply. However, many western settlers, who borrowed money to run their farms, were unhappy with the Bank's strict lending policies. Although the Bank was chartered by Congress, it was run by private bankers rather than elected officials.

The Bank's president, Nicholas Biddle, represented everything Jackson disliked. Jackson prided himself on being a self-made man who started with nothing. Biddle, however, came from a wealthy Philadelphia family and had a good education, social status, and experience in financial matters.

The Bank as an Election Issue

In 1832 Jackson's opponents gave him the chance to take action against the Bank. Senators **Henry Clay** and **Daniel Webster,** friends of Biddle, planned to use the Bank to defeat Jackson in the 1832 presidential election. They persuaded Biddle to apply early for a new charter—a government permit to operate the Bank—even though the Bank's current charter did not expire until 1836.

Clay and Webster believed the Bank had popular support. They thought that an attempt by Jackson to veto the charter would lead to his defeat and allow Henry Clay to be elected president.

When the bill to renew the Bank's charter came to Jackson to sign, he was sick in bed. Jackson told his friend **Martin Van Buren,** "The bank . . . is trying to kill me. But I will kill it!" Jackson **vetoed,** or rejected, the bill. Jackson felt the Bank was unconstitutional despite the Supreme Court's decision to the contrary in *McCulloch* v. *Maryland* (1819).

Primary Source "King Andrew the First"

BORN TO COMMAND.

OF VETO MEMORY.

HAD I BEEN CONSULTED.

KING ANDREW THE FIRST.

◄ This political cartoon of Andrew Jackson shows him being a tyrant who was trampling on the rights of all Americans.

Critical Thinking

Interpreting What tells you the cartoonist is depicting Jackson as a dictatorial leader? What is Jackson seen walking on?

Primary Sources

INTERPRETING POLITICAL CARTOONS

President Andrew Jackson struck a fatal blow to the Bank of the United States when he ordered the withdrawal of all federal deposits from the Bank.

1. **Making Inferences** Are the members of Congress supporters or opponents of the Bank? How do you know?

2. **Interpreting** What meaning does the cartoonist convey with his portrayal of Major Jack Downing?

A. Bank of the United States B. members of Congress C. President Andrew Jackson D. Major Jack Downing, mythical character representing the average citizen

Jackson angrily stated his beliefs about the Bank to Congress:

PRIMARY SOURCE

"When the laws . . . make the rich richer and the potent more powerful, the humble members of society . . . who [lack] . . . the means of securing like favors to themselves, have a right to complain of the injustice of their government."

—Andrew Jackson, on vetoing the Bank's charter

The Election of 1832

The Bank did play a large part in the election of 1832. The strategy for gaining support for Clay as president, however, backfired. Most people supported Jackson's veto, and Jackson was reelected. Jackson decided on a plan to "kill" the Bank ahead of the 1836 schedule. He ordered the withdrawal of all government deposits from the Bank and placed the funds in smaller state banks. In 1836 he refused to sign a new charter for the Bank, and it closed.

The Panic of 1837

When Jackson decided not to run for a third term in 1836, the Democrats chose Martin Van Buren, Jackson's friend and vice president. Van Buren faced opposition from the Whigs, a new party that included former National Republicans and other anti-Jackson forces. The Whigs nominated three different candidates, each of whom had a following in a different part of the nation. Jackson's popularity and his personal support helped Van Buren win easily.

Soon after the election, the country entered a severe economic **depression,** a period in which business and employment fall to a very low level. The depression began with the Panic of 1837. Land values dropped, investments declined, and banks failed. Thousands of businesses closed. Many people lost their jobs. In the South, cotton prices fell to record lows. Farmers plunged into debt and lost their land. In the cities, many people could not afford food or rent.

President Van Buren believed in the principle of **laissez-faire**—that government should interfere as little as possible in the nation's economy. Van Buren persuaded Congress to establish an independent federal treasury in 1840. The government would no longer deposit its money in private banks as it had been doing during Jackson's presidency. Instead, the government would store its money in the federal treasury. The private banks had used government funds to back their banknotes. The new treasury system would keep banks from using government funds in this way and help prevent further bank crises.

Van Buren and his supporters hailed the new law as a "second declaration of independence." Members of Van Buren's own Democratic Party, however, along with the Whigs, criticized the act. The split in the Democratic Party gave the Whigs a chance to win the presidency in 1840.

✔ **Reading Check** **Explaining** What was the purpose of the new treasury system?

The Whigs Take Power

Main Idea After Harrison's death, Tyler took the presidency in a direction that went against the Whigs' goals, and the Whigs lost power.

History and You Do you think political ads portray candidates as they really are? Read to find out how the Whigs came to power.

· ·

The Democrats had been in control of the presidency for 12 years. With the country still in the depths of depression, though, the Whigs thought they had a chance to win the election in 1840.

The Log Cabin Campaign

The Whigs nominated **William Henry Harrison,** a hero of the War of 1812, to run against President Van Buren. **John Tyler,** a planter from Virginia, was Harrison's running mate. Because Harrison had gained national fame by defeating Tecumseh's followers in the Battle of Tippecanoe, the Whigs' campaign slogan was "Tippecanoe and Tyler Too."

Primary Source | Harrison's Log Cabin Campaign

A Baltimore journalist made fun of William Henry Harrison, writing, "Give him a barrel of hard cider, and . . . he will sit the remainder of his days in his log cabin by the side of the fire and study moral philosophy!" The Whigs turned the insult to their advantage by creating the log cabin campaign, which depicted Harrison as a man of the people.

Stunts and Songs Harrison supporters from Kentucky rolled a large paper ball from Kentucky to Baltimore in support of their candidate (below). This event inspired a campaign jingle. ▶

What has caused this great commotion, motion
Our country through?
It is the ball rolling on
For Tippecanoe and Tyler too
And with them we'll beat the little Van, Van, Van
Van is a used-up man!

Campaign Practices The Whigs used the symbol of the log cabin to present Harrison as a simple farmer. The party raised money to support their candidate by selling memorabilia, such as this china pitcher (above left).

Critical Thinking

Summarizing How did the log cabin insult backfire?

To win the election, Harrison had to gain the support of the laborers and farmers who had voted for Jackson. The Whigs adopted a log cabin as their **symbol,** or an object that represents something else. Political cartoons in newspapers showed Harrison, a wealthy man from Virginia, in front of a log cabin. The Whigs wanted to show that their candidate was a "man of the people."

The Whigs also ridiculed Van Buren as "King Martin," a wealthy snob who had spent the people's money on fancy furniture for the White House. The log cabin campaign seemed to work, and Harrison went on to defeat Van Buren by a wide margin. William Henry Harrison became the first Whig president.

Inauguration day, 1841, was bitterly cold. Harrison, however, insisted on delivering his speech without a hat or coat. He died of pneumonia 32 days later. Harrison served the shortest term of any American president. John Tyler of Virginia became the first vice president to gain the presidency because the elected president died in office.

Tyler's Presidency

Although Tyler had been elected vice president as a Whig, he had once been a Democrat. Whig party leaders had placed Tyler on the ticket with Harrison mainly to attract Southern voters. As president, Tyler vetoed several bills sponsored by Whigs in Congress, including a bill to recharter the Bank of the United States. His lack of party loyalty outraged many Whigs. Most of Tyler's cabinet resigned. Whig leaders in Congress expelled Tyler from the party.

It seemed that the Whigs could not agree on their party's goals. Increasingly, Whigs voted according to sectional ties—North, South, and West—not party ties. This division may explain why the Whig candidate, Henry Clay, lost the election of 1844 to Democratic candidate **James Polk.** After only four years, the Whigs were out of power again.

✔ **Reading Check** **Describing** How did the Whigs lose power in the election of 1844?

Section 3 Review

History ONLINE
Study Central™ To review this section, go to glencoe.com.

Vocabulary

1. Define each of the following terms and use each word in a sentence: institution, veto, depression, laissez-faire, symbol.

Main Ideas

2. Explaining Why did President Van Buren do little to solve the nation's economic problems?

3. Describing How did the log cabin campaign help Harrison win the election?

Critical Thinking

4. Interpreting Reread Andrew Jackson's quote about the National Bank. Based on his words, why did Jackson want to close the Bank of the United States?

5. Diagramming Use a diagram like the one below to describe Henry Clay's strategy to win the 1832 election. Explain the actual result.

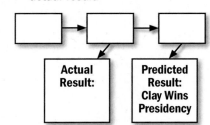

Actual Result:

Predicted Result: Clay Wins Presidency

6. Creative Writing Write a "catchy" campaign slogan for either Andrew Jackson or Henry Clay that would help the candidate win the 1832 presidential election.

Answer the
7. Essential Question
How do economic issues affect the president and presidential elections?

Visual Summary

Main Idea	Supporting Details
The Election of 1828 transformed American political campaigns.	• Mudslinging, election slogans, rallies, buttons, and campaign events were first practiced in 1828.
President Andrew Jackson made changes to the American political system.	• Jackson established the spoils system (replacing government employees with supporters of the winning candidate). • His supporters created nominating conventions to select presidential candidates.
President Jackson supported the demands of western settlers for Native American land.	• In 1830 Jackson pushed the Indian Removal Act through Congress. This law forced Native Americans to move west.
Some Native American groups resisted relocation.	• The Cherokee Nation sued to keep its land. However, after a few Cherokee signed a treaty in 1835, thousands were forced to move west on the "Trail of Tears." • The Seminole resisted removal by using guerrilla tactics to attack white settlements on the Florida coast.
President Jackson opposed the Bank of the United States.	• Jackson believed the national bank was undemocratic and unconstitutional. He vetoed a bill extending the bank's charter, eventually forcing it to close.

STUDY TO GO ▶ Study anywhere, anytime! Download quizzes and flash cards to your PDA from glencoe.com.

INDIANA STATEWIDE TEST PRACTICE

TEST-TAKING TIP

Pay attention to other test questions as you read. Sometimes the information in one question contains help for another.

Reviewing Vocabulary

Directions: Choose the word or words that best completes the sentence.

1 In the election of 1824, no candidate received a _____, or more than half, of the electoral votes.

A majority
B plurality
C quorum
D minority

2 President Andrew Jackson began the practice of rewarding people with government jobs on the basis of their political support. This is called the _____ system.

A caucus
B spoils
C federal
D laissez-faire

3 The federal government forced the Five Civilized Tribes to _____ to Oklahoma.

A apologize
B write
C relocate
D export

4 The idea that government should interfere as little as possible with the nation's economy is called _____.

A majority rule
B laissez-faire
C agrarianism
D checks and balances

Reviewing Main Ideas

Directions: Choose the best answer.

5 In the 1828 presidential election, Andrew Jackson's Democratic-Republican Party

A wanted a strong central government.
B supported setting up a national bank.
C favored states' rights.
D was dominated by merchants and farmers.

6 In *Worcester* v. *Georgia* (1832), Chief Justice John Marshall ruled that

A Georgia had no right to interfere with the Cherokee.
B the "spoils system" was unconstitutional.
C the federal government had no authority over Native Americans.
D states had to support a national bank.

7 Jackson attacked the Bank of the United States because

A it was being run by corrupt elected officials.
B it provided loans to all citizens.
C it financed foreign business deals that put Americans out of work.
D it was controlled by wealthy Easterners.

8 One reason the Whigs won the presidential election of 1840 was that

A they made a "corrupt bargain" with Henry Clay to steal the presidency.
B the Democrats split over Van Buren.
C they ended the Panic of 1837.
D they gained support from laborers and farmers rather than the wealthy elite.

GO ON ▶

Critical Thinking

Directions: Choose the best answer.

Base your answers to questions 9 and 10 on the image below and your knowledge of Chapter 11.

9 **Political parties use symbols to present their ideas and their candidates. Which party used the log cabin as a symbol for their candidate in 1840?**

A the Democratic party for Andrew Jackson
B the Whig party for William Henry Harrison
C the Republican party for Abraham Lincoln
D the Jacksonian party for Martin Van Buren

10 **The use of a log cabin as a political party symbol tells the voters that the party represents**

A eastern merchants.
B lumberjacks.
C new immigrants.
D the common man.

Constructed Response

Directions: Write a short response to each of the following questions. In your answer:

- *address all parts of the question*
- *use information from the chapter*
- *include facts, examples, and details relevant to the question*
- *use clear language*

11 **Identify two political changes that took place during the presidency of Andrew Jackson.**

Base your answer to question 12 on the reading below and your knowledge of Chapter 11.

> If anything be found in the national constitution . . . which ought not to be in it, the people know how to get rid of it. If any construction . . . [is] unacceptable to them so as to become practically a part of the constitution, they will amend it.

Source: *The Writings and Speeches of Daniel Webster*

12 **What did Webster say people should do with a federal law if they did not agree with it?**

13 **What was the Trail of Tears?**

14 **State two reasons President Jackson and others objected to the Second Bank of the United States.**

STOP

Need Extra Help?														
If you missed questions. . .	1	2	3	4	5	6	7	8	9	10	11	12	13	14
Go to page. . .	337	340	343	351	338	344	349	351	351	351	339	341	345	349

Chapter 12

Manifest Destiny 1818–1853

Traveling along the Oregon Trail

PRESIDENTS

JAMES MADISON 1809–1817

JAMES MONROE 1817–1825

JOHN Q. ADAMS 1825–1829

ANDREW JACKSON 1829–1837

1809 Elizabeth Ann Seton founds Sisters of Charity

1824 Russia surrenders land south of Alaska

1824 U.S. House elects John Q. Adams president

U.S. Events

1810

1820

1830

World Events

1821 Mexico declares independence from Spain

1826 First Burmese War ends

1830 France occupies Algeria

History ONLINE
Chapter Overview Visit glencoe.com
and click on **Chapter 12—Chapter
Overviews** to preview chapter information.

Section 1: The Oregon Country

Essential Question How did the belief in Manifest Destiny
influence western settlement?

Section 2: Independence for Texas

Essential Question Why did Texans fight for their independence
from Mexico?

Section 3: War With Mexico

Essential Question How did Mexican lands in the West become
part of the United States?

Section 4: California and Utah

Essential Question What factors affected the settlement of
California and Utah in the West?

FOLDABLES
Study Organizer

Organizing Information
Make this Foldable to help
organize what you learn about the expansion
of the United States.

Step 1 Fold four sheets
of paper in half from top
to bottom. Cut each paper
in half along the folds.

Step 2 Fold each piece
of paper in half from top to
bottom again.

Step 3 On each folded
paper, make a cut 1 inch
from the side on the top
flap.

Step 4 Place the folded
papers one on top of the
other, and staple the sections together.

Reading and Writing As you read, note
dates and events about new territories in
Oregon, Texas, New Mexico, California, and
Utah.

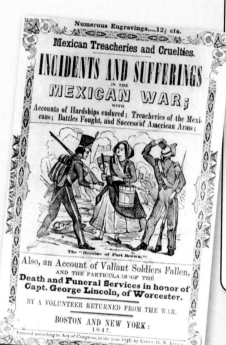

Numerous Engravings....12½ cts.

Mexican Treacheries and Cruelties.

INCIDENTS AND SUFFERINGS
IN THE
MEXICAN WAR;
WITH
Accounts of Hardships endured; Treacheries of the Mexi-
cans; Battles Fought, and Success of American Arms;

The "Heroine of Fort Brown."

Also, an Account of Valiant Soldiers Fallen,
AND THE PARTICULARS OF THE
**Death and Funeral Services in honor of
Capt. George Lincoln, of Worcester.**

BY A VOLUNTEER RETURNED FROM THE WAR.

BOSTON AND NEW YORK:
1847.

Entered according to Act of Congress, in the year 1847, by Lieut. G. N. Allen.

**MARTIN
VAN BUREN
1837–1841**

★ **1839**
Mutiny
occurs on
slave ship
Amistad

**WILLIAM
HENRY
HARRISON
1841**

**JOHN TYLER
1841–1845**

1845 ★
U.S.
annexes
Texas

★ **1846**
Congress
declares
war on
Mexico

**JAMES POLK
1845–1849**

**ZACHARY
TAYLOR
1849–1850**

1840

1850

1839 ★
Opium War
begins between
Britain and
China

◀ A man pulls
Chinese
women in a
rickshaw

★ **1842**
Treaty of
Nanking gives
Hong Kong to
Great Britain

★ **1846**
Neptune
discovered

Essential Question ◄

How did the belief in Manifest Destiny influence western settlement?

Reading Guide

Content Vocabulary

joint occupation (p. 359)

emigrant (p. 362)

mountain man (p. 360)

prairie schooner (p. 362)

rendezvous (p. 360)

Manifest Destiny (p. 363)

Academic Vocabulary

plus (p. 359)   access (p. 359)

Key People and Events

Adams-Onís Treaty (p. 359)

Oregon Trail (p. 362)

Henry Clay (p. 363)

Reading Strategy

Taking Notes As you read, list key events in a time line like the one below.

1819   1825   1836   1846

INDIANA ACADEMIC STANDARDS
United States History

8.1.15 Explain the concept of Manifest Destiny and describe its impact on westward expansion of the United States.

8.3.1 Read maps to interpret symbols and determine the landforms and human features that represent physical and cultural characteristics of areas in the United States.

8.3.5 Describe the importance of the major mountain ranges and the major river systems in the development of the United States.

American Diary

Families left everything familiar behind when they made the often uncomfortable and dangerous trip to the Western frontier. Martha Gay was a 13-year-old who, in 1851, left Springfield, Missouri, in a covered wagon. She later wrote about the experience of leaving loved ones and friends behind: "Farewell sermons were preached and prayers offered for our safety. . . . All places of business and the schools were closed . . . and everybody came to say goodbye to us."

—*from* One Woman's West

A mountain man gives advice to pioneers.

Rivalry in the Northwest

Main Idea Several nations claimed the Oregon Country, but many Americans wanted the land for its access to the Pacific Ocean.

History and You If you were deep in the wilderness and starving, what might you do to survive? Read to learn how pioneers survived as they traveled west.

• •

The Oregon Country was the huge area located between the Pacific Ocean and the Rocky Mountains north of California. It included all of what is now Oregon, Washington, and Idaho **plus** parts of Montana and Wyoming. The region also contained about half of what is now the Canadian province of British Columbia.

In the early 1800s, four nations claimed the vast, rugged land known as the Oregon Country. The United States based its claim on Robert Gray's discovery of the Columbia River in 1792 and on the Lewis and Clark expedition. Great Britain based its claim on British explorations of the Columbia River. Spain, which had also explored the Pacific coast in the late 1700s, controlled California to the south. Russia had settlements that extended south from Alaska into Oregon.

Adams-Onís Treaty

Many Americans wanted control of Oregon in order to **access,** or get to, the Pacific Ocean. In 1819 Secretary of State John Quincy Adams negotiated the **Adams-Onís Treaty** with Spain. The Spanish agreed to set the limits of their territory at what is now California's northern border and to give up all claims to Oregon. In 1824 Russia also gave up its claim to the land south of Alaska.

In 1818 Adams worked out an agreement with Britain for **joint occupation** of the area. This meant that people from both the United States and Great Britain could settle there. When Adams became president in 1825, he proposed that the two nations divide Oregon along the 49°N line of latitude. Britain refused, insisting on a larger share. Unable to resolve their dispute, the two countries agreed to extend the joint occupation. In the following years, thousands of Americans streamed into the Oregon Country.

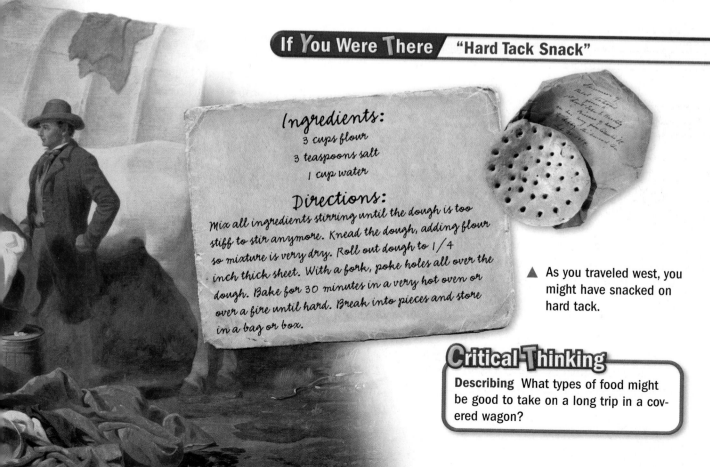

If You Were There / "Hard Tack Snack"

Ingredients:
3 cups flour
3 teaspoons salt
1 cup water

Directions:
Mix all ingredients stirring until the dough is too stiff to stir anymore. Knead the dough, adding flour so mixture is very dry. Roll out dough to 1/4 inch thick sheet. With a fork, poke holes all over the dough. Bake for 30 minutes in a very hot oven or over a fire until hard. Break into pieces and store in a bag or box.

▲ As you traveled west, you might have snacked on hard tack.

Critical Thinking

Describing What types of food might be good to take on a long trip in a covered wagon?

Life in the Mountains The lives of mountain men were difficult and unpredictable. Mountain men often faced the threat of starvation, dehydration, extreme heat, frigid cold, and deadly attacks by animals and hostile Native Americans.

> **"I defy the annals of chivalry to furnish the record of a life more wild and perilous than that of a Rocky Mountain trapper."**
> —Francis Parkman, *The Oregon Trail*

◄ Type of canteen used by mountain men ►

Map Skills

Location What rendezvous site was used most often?

Maps In MOtion See StudentWorks™ Plus or glencoe.com.

Mountain Men

The first Americans to reach the Oregon Country were not farmers but fur traders. They came to trap beaver, whose skins were in great demand in the eastern United States and in Europe. The British established several trading posts in the region, as did merchant John Jacob Astor of New York. In 1808 Astor organized the American Fur Company. It became the most powerful fur company in America. Astor traded on the East Coast, the Pacific Northwest, and China.

At first the merchants traded for furs that the Native Americans supplied. Gradually American adventurers joined the trade. These people, who spent most of their time in the Rocky Mountains, came to be known as **mountain men.** These tough, independent men made their living by trapping beaver. Many had Native American wives and adopted Native American ways. They lived in buffalo-skin lodges and dressed in fringed buckskin pants, moccasins, and beads.

Some mountain men worked for fur-trading companies; others worked for themselves. Throughout the spring and early summer, they hiked across the mountains, setting traps and then collecting the beaver pelts. As they did their work, the mountain men explored the mountains, valleys, and trails of the West. Jim Beckwourth, an African American from Virginia, explored Wyoming's Green River. Robert Stuart and Jedediah Smith found the South Pass, a broad break through the Rockies. South Pass later became the main route that settlers took to Oregon.

In late summer, mountain men gathered for a **rendezvous** (RAHN•dih•voo), or meeting. The annual rendezvous was the most important event of the year for mountain men. They met with the trading companies to exchange their "hairy banknotes"—beaver skins—for traps, guns, coffee, and other goods. They met old friends and exchanged news. They relaxed by competing in races and swapping stories about their most exciting adventures.

Mountain men had to be resourceful. They needed courage and intelligence in order to survive in the wilderness. For example, trapper Joe Meek told how, when faced with starvation, he once held his hands "in an anthill until they were covered with ants, then greedily licked them off." The mountain men took pride in joking about the dangers they faced.

Over time, the mountain men could no longer make a living by trapping because most of the beaver were killed. Some moved to Oregon and settled on farms. With their knowledge of the western lands though, several mountain men, such as Jim Bridger and Kit Carson, found work as guides. They led the parties of settlers now streaming west. Beginning in the 1830s, the mountain men carved out several east-to-west passages that played a vital role in western settlement. The most popular route was the Oregon Trail. Others included the California Trail and the Santa Fe Trail.

✓ **Reading Check** **Explain** Why did trading posts develop in the Oregon Country?

Oregon and Manifest Destiny

Main Idea Many people believed that God had given the entire continent to Americans and wanted them to settle western land.

History and You When you prepare to take a trip, what types of items do you pack? Read how pioneers made a 2,000-mile journey, carrying only what they would need in a covered wagon.

In the 1830s, Americans began traveling to the Oregon Country to settle. Economic troubles in the East and reports of Oregon's fertile land made the West look attractive.

The Whitman Mission

Among the first settlers of the Oregon Country were missionaries who wanted to bring Christianity to the Native Americans. Dr. Marcus Whitman and his wife, Narcissa, went to Oregon in 1836 and built a mission among the Cayuse people near the present site of Walla Walla, Washington.

Primary Source / The Whitman Mission

A Settlement in the Oregon Country In 1836 Dr. Marcus Whitman and his new bride, Narcissa, arrived at Waiilatpu, on the Walla Walla River in present-day Washington. The Whitmans built a mission to provide medical care and convert the Cayuse to Christianity. Narcissa's journals provide a vivid account of their experiences. Her initial optimism turned to frustration as the Cayuse resisted their efforts.

"They [the Cayuse] are an exceedingly proud . . . people, and keep us constantly . . . [practicing] patience and forbearance. . . . Notwithstanding all this, there are many redeeming qualities in them, else we should have been discouraged long ago. We are more and more encouraged the longer we stay among them."
—Narcissa Whitman, in a letter to her mother

▼ The Whitman Mission became a primary stopping point for settlers traveling along the Oregon Trail. In 1847 a measles epidemic broke out, killing many Cayuse children.

Critical Thinking

Drawing Conclusions Why would people traveling to the Oregon Country stop at the Whitman mission?

New settlers unknowingly brought measles to the mission. An epidemic killed many children of the Cayuse. Blaming the Whitmans for the sickness, the Cayuse attacked the mission in November 1847 and killed the Whitmans and 11 others. Despite this, the flood of settlers into Oregon continued.

The Oregon Trail

In the early 1840s, "Oregon fever" swept through the Mississippi Valley. The depression caused by the Panic of 1837 hit the region hard. People formed societies to gather information about Oregon and to plan and make the long trip. The "great migration" had begun. Tens of thousands of people made the trip. These pioneers were called **emigrants** because they left the United States to go to Oregon.

Before the difficult 2,000-mile (3,219-km) journey, these pioneers stuffed their canvas-covered wagons, called **prairie schooners,** with supplies. From a distance these wagons looked like schooners, or ships, at sea. Gathering in Independence or other towns in Missouri, they followed the **Oregon Trail** across the Great Plains, along the Platte River, and through the South Pass of the Rocky Mountains. After they crossed the mountains, they traveled north and west along the Snake and Columbia Rivers into the Oregon Country.

Oregon Country, 1846

NATIONAL GEOGRAPHIC

Settling the Northwest After the War of 1812, the United States and Britain agreed that settlers from both countries could live in the Oregon Country. Most of the British who lived in the region were trappers, while most of the Americans were farmers. The British Hudson's Bay Company maintained order.

Native Americans relied on the Columbia River for transportation, as well as a source of food. The river was also valuable to white settlers. ▼

"The buffalo will dwindle away, and the large wandering communities [of Native Americans] who depend on them . . . must be broken and scattered. . . . Within a few years the traveler may pass in tolerable security through their country. . . . Its danger and its charm will have disappeared."
—Francis Parkman, *The Oregon Trail*

◄ Most emigrants packed their wagons so full that they had to make the long trip on foot.

Map Skills

Location What geographic feature lies at about 41° N and 115° W?

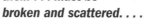 See StudentWorks™ Plus or glencoe.com.

Manifest Destiny

Since colonial times many Americans had believed their nation had a special role to fulfill. For years people thought the nation's mission should be to serve as a model of freedom and democracy. In the 1800s that vision changed. Many believed that the mission of the United States was to spread freedom by occupying the entire continent. In 1819 John Quincy Adams expressed what many Americans were thinking when he said expansion to the Pacific was as inevitable "as that the Mississippi should flow to the sea."

In the 1840s, New York newspaper editor John O'Sullivan expressed the idea of a national mission in more specific words. O'Sullivan declared it was America's "**Manifest Destiny** to overspread and to possess the whole of the continent which Providence has given us." O'Sullivan meant that the United States was clearly destined—set apart for a special purpose—by God to extend its boundaries all the way to the Pacific Ocean.

"Fifty-Four Forty or Fight"

Many Americans wanted the United States to own all of Oregon. In the 1844 presidential election, James K. Polk, the Democratic nominee, supported this demand. Democrats used the slogan "Fifty-Four Forty or Fight," referring to the line of latitude they believed should be the nation's northern border in Oregon.

Polk's Whig opponent, **Henry Clay,** did not take a strong position on the Oregon issue. Polk won the election because Whig support was not united behind Clay.

A firm believer in Manifest Destiny, Polk was focused on making Oregon part of the United States. Britain, however, would not accept a border at "Fifty-Four Forty." This would mean giving up its land claim entirely. In 1846 the two countries finally compromised. They set the border between American and British parts of Oregon at latitude 49°N.

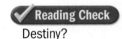 **Reading Check** **Defining** What is Manifest Destiny?

Section 1 Review

Vocabulary

1. Use each of these terms in a sentence that will help explain its meaning: plus, access, joint occupation, mountain man, rendezvous, emigrant, prairie schooner, Manifest Destiny.

Main Ideas

2. **Specifying** Which nations claimed the Oregon Country? How did John Quincy Adams help resolve the claims?

3. **Explaining** What was James K. Polk's campaign slogan in the 1844 election? What did the slogan mean?

Critical Thinking

4. **Analyzing** During the 1840s, many more Americans than British settled in the Oregon Country. How do you think this influenced negotiations over the territory?

5. **Summarizing** Create a diagram like the one below to list details about what life was like for a mountain man. Add more boxes to your diagram if necessary.

Life of a Mountain Man

6. **Creative Writing** Take the role of a pioneer about to travel to the Oregon Country. A friend asks why you are leaving. Write your answer in the voice of your character. Include details about who you are, your reasons for going, and your feelings about the journey ahead.

Answer the
7. **Essential Question**
How did the belief in Manifest Destiny influence western settlement?

Spanish mission in the Southwest

Was Manifest Destiny Justified?

Building Background

In 1845 a magazine editor named John L. O'Sullivan declared that it was the "manifest destiny" of Americans to expand westward to the Pacific Ocean. Many Americans believed in this concept of Manifest Destiny—the idea that God had given the continent to Americans and wanted them to settle western land. Manifest Destiny did have its opponents, however. Long-time public servant Albert Gallatin expressed his opposition to Manifest Destiny and to war with Mexico in an 1847 pamphlet *Peace with Mexico*.

NO

ALBERT GALLATIN

It is said, that the people of the United States have a hereditary superiority of race over the Mexicans, which gives them the right to subjugate[1] and keep in bondage the inferior nation. . . .

Is it compatible with the principle of Democracy, which rejects every hereditary claim of individuals, to admit a hereditary superiority of races? . . . Can you for a moment suppose, that a very doubtful descent from men, who lived one thousand years ago, has transmitted to you a superiority over your fellow-men? . . . At this time, the claim is but a pretext for covering and justifying unjust usurpation[2] and unbounded ambition. . . .

Among ourselves, the most ignorant, the most inferior, either in physical or mental faculties,[3] is recognized as having equal rights, and he has an equal vote with any one, however superior to him in all those respects. This is founded on the immutable[4] principle that no one man is born with the right of governing another man.

[1] **subjugate** conquer
[2] **usurpation** seizure
[3] **faculties** abilities
[4] **immutable** unchanging

YES

JOHN L. O'SULLIVAN

Texas is now ours. Already, before these words are written, her convention has undoubtedly ratified the acceptance, by her congress, of our proffered[5] invitation into the Union. . . . Her star and her stripe may already be said to have taken their place in the glorious blazon[6] of our common nationality. . . .

The next session of Congress will see the representatives of the new young state in their places in both our halls of national legislation, side by side with those of the old Thirteen. . . .

Other nations have undertaken to intrude themselves into [the question of Texas. They have come] between us and the proper parties to the case, in a spirit of hostile interference against us, for the avowed[7] object of thwarting[8] our policy and hampering our power, limiting our greatness and checking the fulfillment of our manifest destiny to overspread the continent allotted by Providence for the free development of our yearly multiplying millions.

---

5 **proffered** offered
6 **blazon** showy display

7 **avowed** declared openly
8 **thwarting** stopping

Texas celebrates entering the Union.

DBQ Document-Based Questions

1. **Summarizing** According to O'Sullivan, what was Manifest Destiny?

2. **Making Inferences** Why do you think O'Sullivan mentions Texas's future representation in Congress?

3. **Analyzing** What does Albert Gallatin think is the real motivation underlying the idea of Manifest Destiny?

4. **Evaluating** Imagine you could interview Gallatin and O'Sullivan. Write a list of three questions you could ask each man about his views on Manifest Destiny.

Independence for Texas

Reading Guide

Content Vocabulary

Tejano (p. 367)   decree (p. 368)
empresario (p. 367)   annex (p. 371)

Academic Vocabulary

establish (p. 367)   remove (p. 368)

Key People and Events

Stephen F. Austin (p. 367)
Antonio López de Santa Anna (p. 368)
Alamo (p. 369)
Sam Houston (p. 370)

Reading Strategy

Taking Notes Use a time line like the one below to list key events in Texas history.

1835   1836

Oct. | Mar. | May

Dec. | Feb. | Apr. | Sept.

INDIANA ACADEMIC STANDARDS
United States History

8.1.15 Explain the concept of Manifest Destiny and describe its impact on westward expansion of the United States.

8.1.29 Differentiate between facts and historical interpretations recognizing that the historian's narrative reflects his or her judgment about the significance of particular facts.

8.3.7 Using maps identify changes influenced by growth, economic development, and human migration in the eighteenth and nineteenth centuries.

American Diary

Thomas Jefferson Pilgrim was an immigrant who heard about opportunities in Texas. In New Orleans, he bought a ticket to Texas and a new life. "We were now on the Gulf. . . . Soon all on board were seasick except the crew and me and many wished that they had never started. . . . [After landing at Matagorda Bay] the others went eastward to the Brazos, I on foot and alone, made my way north to San Felipe, about 60 miles distant."

—from the diary of Thomas J. Pilgrim

Settlers lived on estates in southeast Texas.

A Clash of Cultures

Main Idea People from the United States and Mexico settled Texas.

History and You If someone from a different culture offered you a large amount of land on the condition that you adopt his or her language and customs, would you take it? Read to find out how settlers in Texas reacted to a similar situation.

• •

Conflict over Texas began in 1803, when the United States bought the Louisiana Territory from France. Americans claimed that the land in present-day Texas was part of the purchase. Spain protested. In the Adams-Onís Treaty, the United States agreed to drop its claim to the region.

Land Grants

At the time, few people lived in Texas. Most residents—about 3,000—were **Tejanos** (teh•HAH•nohs), or Mexicans who claimed Texas as their home. Native Americans, such as the Comanches, Apaches, and Kiowas, also lived in the area. Because the Spanish wanted to promote the growth of Texas, they offered vast tracts of land to people who agreed to bring families to settle there. The people who obtained these grants and recruited the settlers were called **empresarios.**

American Moses Austin received the first land grant in 1821. He died, however, before he could **establish,** or set up, his colony. Mexico won its independence from Spain in 1821. Austin's son, **Stephen F. Austin,** received permission from the new Mexican government to organize the colony. Austin recruited 300 American families to settle in Texas. Austin's success made him a leader among the American settlers.

From 1823 to 1825, Mexico passed laws offering new settlers land at extremely low prices. In return the colonists agreed to learn Spanish, become Mexican citizens, convert to Catholicism—the religion of Mexico—and obey Mexican law. Mexican leaders hoped to attract settlers from all over, but most settlers came from the United States.

Growing Tension

By 1830 Americans in Texas far outnumbered Mexicans. Further, these American colonists had not adopted Mexican ways. In the meantime, the United States had twice offered to buy Texas from Mexico.

Primary Source / Migration to Texas

Texas's Appeal By 1830 there were 4,000 members of Austin's colonies and approximately 16,000 Americans in Texas—four times the Mexican population. Inexpensive land drew many to Texas. The efforts of Mary Austin Holley, a cousin and close friend of Stephen F. Austin, also helped. Holley's books and letters provided information for settlers. Her descriptions of Texas as a land of "surpassing beauty . . . a *splendid* country— an enchanting spot" attracted many settlers.

Cost of Land in 1825	
Land in the U.S.	$1.25 per acre
Land in Texas	4¢ per acre

Critical Thinking

Predicting How do you think settlers made a living in Texas?

The Mexican government viewed the growing American influence in Texas with alarm. In 1830 the Mexican government issued a **decree,** or official order, that stopped all immigration from the United States. At the same time, the decree encouraged the immigration of Mexican and European families with generous land grants. Trade between Texas and the United States was discouraged by placing a tax on goods that were imported from the United States.

These new policies angered the Texans. The prosperity of many citizens depended on trade with the United States. Many had friends and relatives who wanted to come to Texas. In addition, those colonists who held slaves were uneasy about the Mexican government's plans to end slavery.

Attempt at Reconciliation

Some of the American settlers called for independence. Others hoped to stay within Mexico but on better terms. In 1833 General **Antonio López de Santa Anna** became president of Mexico. Stephen F. Austin traveled to Mexico City with the Texans' demands to **remove,** or take away, the ban on American settlers and to make Texas a separate state of Mexico.

Santa Anna agreed to the first request but refused the second. Austin sent a letter back to Texas, suggesting that plans for independence get underway. The Mexican government intercepted the letter and arrested Austin.

While Austin was in jail, Santa Anna named himself dictator and overthrew Mexico's constitution of 1824. Without a constitution to protect their rights, Texans felt betrayed. Santa Anna placed Texas under greater central control. This loss of local power dismayed many people. Even Austin, finally released from prison, now saw that dealing with Santa Anna was impossible. He concluded that war was unavoidable.

✔ **Reading Check** **Explaining** What role did empresarios play in colonization?

Chance & Error in History

What If the Defenders Had Abandoned the Alamo?

William Travis and almost 200 other defenders—mostly volunteers—were determined to hold the Alamo for a cause in which they believed. In February 1836, Travis wrote several unsuccessful letters, asking the people of Texas and the United States for help.

General Antonio López de Santa Anna, Mexico's president, hoped the fall of the Alamo would convince other Texans that it was useless to resist his armies. Instead, the heroism of those in the Alamo inspired Texans to carry on the struggle. "Remember the Alamo!" became the battle cry of the Texas army.

Travis's Appeal for Aid at the Alamo, February 24, 1836

To the People of Texas & all Americans in the world— Fellow citizens & compatriots—I am besieged, by a thousand or more of the Mexicans under Santa Anna— I have sustained a continual Bombardment & cannonade for 24 hours & have not lost a man. . . . I shall never surrender or retreat. Then, I call on you in the name of Liberty, of patriotism & everything dear to the American character, to come to our aid, with all dispatch. . . . If this call is neglected, I am determined to sustain myself as long as possible & die like a soldier who never forgets what is due to his own honor & that of his country—

Victory or Death
William Barret Travis
Lt. Col. comdt.

The Struggle for Independence

Main Idea Texans fought for their independence from Mexico.

History and You Did you know that Texas was once a nation? Read why Texas remained independent before it became a state.

· ·

During 1835 unrest among Texans sometimes erupted in open conflict. Santa Anna sent an army into Texas to punish the rebels. In October some Mexican troops tried to seize a cannon held by Texans at the town of Gonzales. The Texans taunted the Mexicans. They put a white flag on the cannon, bearing the words "Come and Take It." After a brief battle, the Texans drove back the Mexican troops. Texans consider this to be the first fight of the Texan Revolution.

The Texans called for volunteers. Many answered, including African Americans and Tejanos. In December 1835, the Texans freed San Antonio from a larger Mexican force.

Santa Anna's Letter Explaining the Attack
"[Travis's] responses were insulting, which made it imperative to assault the fort before it could be reinforced by Samuel Houston. . . . The obstinancy [stubbornness] of Travis and his soldiers was the cause of the death of the whole of them, for not one would surrender."

Critical Thinking

1. **Identifying Cause and Effect** What effect did the defeat of the Alamo have on the Texas independence movement?

2. **Speculating** What do you think might have happened to the independence movement had the defenders of the Alamo abandoned the fort?

Despite these victories, problems arose. Various groups argued over who would lead and what actions to take. In early 1836, when Texas should have been preparing to face Santa Anna, plans had stalled.

The Battle of the Alamo

Santa Anna marched north, furious at the loss of San Antonio. When his army reached San Antonio in late February 1836, it found a small Texan force barricaded inside a nearby mission called the **Alamo.**

Although the Texans had cannons, they lacked gunpowder. The Texans were at a further disadvantage because they had only about 180 soldiers to take on Santa Anna's army of several thousand. The Texans had brave leaders, however, including Davy Crockett and a tough Texan named Jim Bowie. The commander, William B. Travis, who was only 26 years old, was determined to hold his position at the Alamo. Travis managed to send messages through Mexican lines. Several messages appealed to the people of Texas and the United States for aid.

For 12 long days, through several attacks, the defenders of the Alamo kept Santa Anna's army at bay with rifle fire. On March 6, 1836, Mexican cannon fire smashed the Alamo's walls.

The Mexicans were too numerous to hold back. They entered the fortress, killing all the defenders, including Travis, Crockett, and Bowie. Only a few women and children and some servants survived to tell of the battle.

Although the defenders at the Alamo had been defeated, they had bought the Texans time to gather troops and supplies.

Texas Declares Its Independence

During the siege at the Alamo, Texan leaders were meeting at Washington-on-the-Brazos, where they were writing a new constitution. There, on March 2, 1836—four days before the fall of the Alamo—American settlers and Tejanos declared independence from Mexico. They then established the Republic of Texas.

Texas War for Independence, 1835–1836

NATIONAL GEOGRAPHIC

Legend:
- Mexican forces
- Mexican victory
- Texan forces
- Texan victory
- Austin's colony
- Disputed territory

UNITED STATES

Unorganized Terr.

Red R.

Arkansas

Brazos R.

REPUBLIC OF TEXAS

Boundary claimed by Mexico

Colorado R.

Louisiana

Washington-on-the-Brazos 1836

Alamo, March 6, 1836

San Jacinto April 21, 1836

HOUSTON

Boundary claimed by Texas

San Antonio Bexar, Dec. 10, 1835

Gonzales, Oct. 2, 1835

Brazoria

SANTA ANNA 1836

Goliad, March 20, 1836

Refugio, March 14, 1836

Nueces R.

URREA 1836

San Patricio Feb. 27, 1836

N W E S

28°N

0 200 kilometers
0 200 miles
Albers Equal-Area projection

Rio Grande

Gulf of Mexico

26°N

MEXICO

96°W 94°W

From Independence to Statehood Texas remained independent for several years. At first the United States refused to annex Texas. To pressure the United States, Texas threatened to form an alliance with Great Britain. The United States did not want the British near its southern border, and in 1845 Texas was admitted to the Union as a slave state.

The Republic of Texas had a three-branch government. Its first Congress met in 1837 at this house in present-day Houston. ▼

▲ Texas banknote, 1838

"In my judgment it would be far better for this Country that Texas should remain an independent State if this were possible."
—Senator James Buchanan

Map Skills

Location What battle was fought northeast of Brazoria?

Maps In MOtion See StudentWorks™ Plus or glencoe.com.

The Texas Declaration stated that the government of Santa Anna had violated the Mexican Constitution. It noted that the Texans' protests against these violations were met with force. The declaration proclaimed the following:

PRIMARY SOURCE

"The people of Texas, in solemn convention assembled, appealing to a candid world for the necessities of our condition, do hereby resolve and declare, that our political connection with the Mexican nation has forever ended, and that the people of Texas do now constitute a free, Sovereign, and independent republic."
—The Declaration of Independence of Texas

With Mexican troops in Texas, it was not possible to hold an election to ratify the constitution and vote for leaders. Texas leaders set up a temporary government.

The government named **Sam Houston** as commander in chief of the Texas forces. Houston wanted to prevent the Mexicans from overrunning other forts. He ordered the troops at Goliad to abandon their position. As they retreated, however, they came face to face with Mexican troops. After a fierce fight, several hundred Texans surrendered. On Santa Anna's orders, the Texans were executed. This action outraged Texans, who called it the "Goliad Massacre."

The Battle of San Jacinto

Houston gathered an army of about 900 at San Jacinto (SAN huh•SIHN•toh), near the site of present-day Houston. Santa Anna was camped nearby with an army of more than 1,300. On April 21, the Texans launched a surprise attack, shouting, "Remember the Alamo! Remember Goliad!" They killed more than 600 soldiers and captured about 700 more—including Santa Anna. On May 14, 1836, Santa Anna signed a treaty that recognized the independence of Texas.

The Lone Star Republic

In September 1836, Texans elected Sam Houston as their president. Mirabeau Lamar, who had fought at the Battle of San Jacinto, served as vice president. Houston sent a delegation to Washington, D.C., asking the United States to **annex,** or take control of, Texas.

Andrew Jackson, however, refused their request. An addition of another slave state would upset the balance of slave and free states in Congress. For the moment, Texas would remain an independent country.

The Road to Statehood

After winning independence, Texas still had difficulties with Mexico, and it faced a mounting debt. Many Texans wanted to join the United States. Southerners favored Texas annexation, but Northerners opposed admitting another slave state to the Union. President Martin Van Buren did not want to inflame the slavery issue or risk war with Mexico. He put off the question of annexing Texas. John Tyler, who became president in 1841, supported Texas annexation. The Senate, however, was still divided over the slavery issue and failed to ratify the annexation treaty.

The situation changed with the 1844 presidential campaign. Manifest Destiny was a popular idea at the time. The South wanted Texas. The North favored gaining all of Oregon. Candidate James K. Polk supported both actions. After Polk won, Congress passed a resolution to annex Texas. In 1845 Texas joined the Union.

Reading Check **Identifying** What was the role of Sam Houston in Texas history?

Section 2 Review

History ONLINE
Study Central™ To review this section, go to glencoe.com.

Vocabulary

1. Write a short paragraph in which you use all of the following vocabulary terms: Tejano, empresario, establish, decree, remove, annex.

Main Ideas

2. **Explaining** How did Stephen Austin try to resolve tensions with the Mexican government?

3. **Specifying** Why was the Battle of San Jacinto important?

Critical Thinking

4. **Contrasting** In a diagram like the one below, describe the Mexican government's expectations for the settlement of Texas. Describe how the actual settlement differed from these expectations and the result.

Expectation: → Actual: → Result:

5. **Synthesizing** How did the Texan defeats at the Alamo and Goliad affect Texans?

6. **Persuasive Writing** Take the role of Stephen Austin. Write what you would say to President Santa Anna to persuade him to agree to Texans' demand for independence.

Answer the Essential Question

7. Why did Texans fight for their independence from Mexico?

War With Mexico

How did Mexican lands in the West become part of the United States?

Reading Guide

Content Vocabulary
rancho (p. 374)

Californios (p. 376)

ranchero (p. 374)

cede (p. 377)

Academic Vocabulary
resource (p. 374)

commence (p. 375)

Key People and Events
Santa Fe Trail (p. 373)

John C. Frémont (p. 374)

Winfield Scott (p. 377)

Treaty of Guadalupe Hidalgo (p. 377)

Mexican Cession (p. 377)

Gadsden Purchase (p. 377)

Reading Strategy
Taking Notes As you read, describe the achievements of each individual in the chart below.

	Achievements
William Becknell	
John C. Frémont	
Winfield Scott	

INDIANA ACADEMIC STANDARDS
United States History

8.1.15 Explain the concept of Manifest Destiny and describe its impact on westward expansion of the United States.

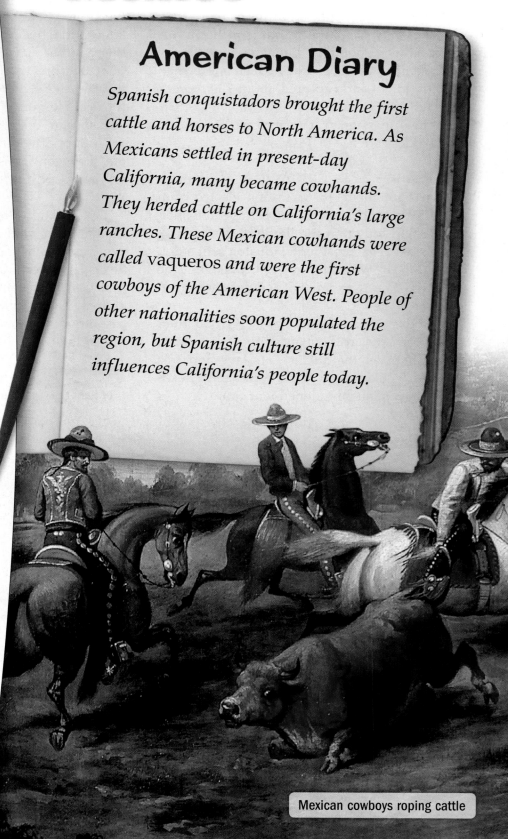

American Diary

Spanish conquistadors brought the first cattle and horses to North America. As Mexicans settled in present-day California, many became cowhands. They herded cattle on California's large ranches. These Mexican cowhands were called vaqueros and were the first cowboys of the American West. People of other nationalities soon populated the region, but Spanish culture still influences California's people today.

Mexican cowboys roping cattle

The New Mexico Territory

Main Idea The Santa Fe Trail was a busy trade route from Missouri to the large Mexican province of New Mexico.

History and You Can you imagine finding your way from Missouri to New Mexico without roads? Read how a trader established the Santa Fe Trail.

. . . .

In the early 1800s, New Mexico was the vast region between the Texas and California territories. It included all of present-day New Mexico, Arizona, Nevada, and Utah and parts of Colorado and Wyoming. Native Americans had lived in the area for thousands of years. Spanish conquistadors began exploring there in the late 1500s and made it part of Spain's colony of Mexico. In 1610 the Spanish founded the settlement of Santa Fe. Missionaries followed soon after.

When Mexico won its independence in 1821, it inherited New Mexico from Spain. The Spanish had tried to keep Americans away from Santa Fe, fearing that Americans would want to take over the area. The Mexican government, however, welcomed American traders. It hoped that the trade would boost the economy of the province.

William Becknell, the first American trader to reach Santa Fe, arrived in 1821 with a supply of goods. Becknell's route came to be known as the **Santa Fe Trail.** The trail started near Independence, Missouri, and crossed the prairies to the Arkansas River. It followed the river west toward the Rocky Mountains before turning south into New Mexico. The trail was mostly flat, and Becknell used wagons to transport his goods.

Other traders followed Becknell, and the Santa Fe Trail became a busy trade route. As trade with New Mexico increased, Americans began settling in the area. Many saw New Mexico as part of the Manifest Destiny of the United States.

Reading Check **Describing** Where did the Santa Fe Trail begin and end?

By the Numbers   Los Angeles in 1850

Types of Employment A census of Los Angeles County, California, was taken in 1850. Many people in Los Angeles were farmers, miners, merchants, watchmakers, blacksmiths, and physicians.

Los Angeles Population, 1850

Males 61%

Females 39%

Los Angeles Ages, 1850

People 40 and older 13%

People 39 and younger 87%

Source: 1850 Federal Census Los Angeles County, California

Critical Thinking

Analyzing Describe the characteristics of Los Angeles' population.

The Santa Fe Trail

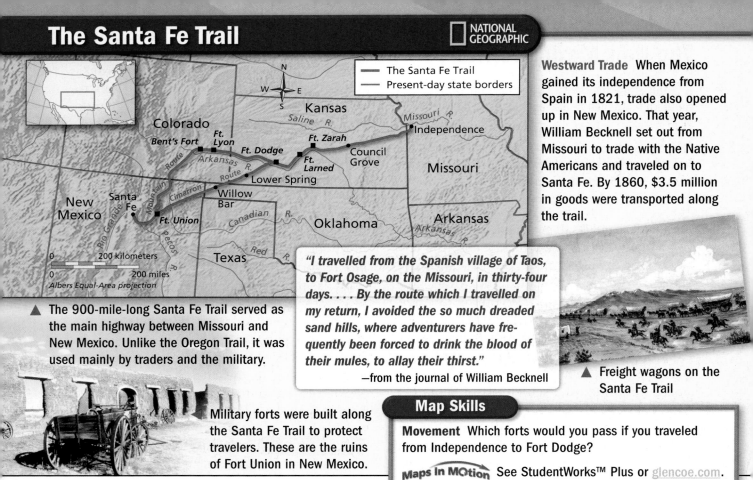

The Santa Fe Trail
Present-day state borders

The 900-mile-long Santa Fe Trail served as the main highway between Missouri and New Mexico. Unlike the Oregon Trail, it was used mainly by traders and the military.

"I travelled from the Spanish village of Taos, to Fort Osage, on the Missouri, in thirty-four days. . . . By the route which I travelled on my return, I avoided the so much dreaded sand hills, where adventurers have frequently been forced to drink the blood of their mules, to allay their thirst."
—from the journal of William Becknell

Military forts were built along the Santa Fe Trail to protect travelers. These are the ruins of Fort Union in New Mexico.

Westward Trade When Mexico gained its independence from Spain in 1821, trade also opened up in New Mexico. That year, William Becknell set out from Missouri to trade with the Native Americans and traveled on to Santa Fe. By 1860, $3.5 million in goods were transported along the trail.

Freight wagons on the Santa Fe Trail

Map Skills

Movement Which forts would you pass if you traveled from Independence to Fort Dodge?

Maps In Motion See StudentWorks™ Plus or glencoe.com.

California's Spanish Culture

Main Idea California was settled by Mexicans.

History and You Did you know that *Los Angeles* means "the angels" in Spanish? Read to learn about California's Spanish heritage.

Spanish explorers and missionaries from Mexico settled California in the 1700s. Captain Gaspar de Portolá and Father Junípero Serra built a chain of missions that eventually extended from San Diego to Sonoma.

The missions were used to convert Native Americans to Christianity. Native Americans also farmed the land and worked at weaving and other crafts. American mountain man Jedediah Smith described the missions as "large farming and grazing establishments."

After Mexico gained its independence from Spain in 1821, California became a state in the new Mexican nation. Mexican settlers bought available mission lands and set up huge estates called **ranchos.** Native Americans worked the land in return for food and shelter. **Rancheros**—ranch owners—treated Native Americans almost like slaves.

In the 1840s, more Americans reached California. **John C. Frémont,** an army officer, wrote of the region's mild climate and vast natural **resources.** Americans began to talk about adding California to the Union. They argued that the nation would then be safely bordered by the Pacific Ocean rather than by a foreign country. Shippers also hoped to build ports on the Pacific coast for trade with East Asia.

Reading Check Examining What was the purpose of the California missions?

History ONLINE
Student Web Activity Visit glencoe.com and complete the Chapter 12 Web Activity about California missions.

War With Mexico

Main Idea War broke out between the United States and Mexico.

History and You Think about how important California is to the United States. Read to find out how the United States acquired this land from Mexico.

. . . .

President Polk saw New Mexico and California as belonging to the United States. After Mexico refused to sell the lands, Polk plotted to gain them through war. Polk, however, wanted to provoke Mexico to strike first so that he could justify a war.

Relations between the two countries were strained. Mexico still claimed Texas as its own. The two nations also disagreed about the Texas-Mexico border. The United States insisted that the Rio Grande formed the border. Mexico claimed that the border lay along the Nueces (nu•AY•suhs) River, 150 miles (241 km) farther north.

Conflict Begins

Polk sent John Slidell to Mexico to propose a deal. Slidell was authorized to offer $30 million for California and New Mexico in return for Mexico's acceptance of the Rio Grande as the Texas boundary. In addition the United States would take over payment of Mexico's debts to American citizens. The Mexican government refused to discuss the offer and announced its intention to reclaim Texas for Mexico.

Polk ordered General Zachary Taylor to march his soldiers across the disputed borderland. On April 25, 1846, Mexican soldiers attacked Taylor's force. Taylor sent the report the president wanted to hear: "Hostilities may now be considered as **commenced** [begun]."

On May 11, the president told Congress that Mexico had "invaded our territory and shed American blood upon the American soil." Congress passed a declaration of war against Mexico.

People IN HISTORY

John C. Frémont

Western Explorer and Supporter of the Bear Flag Revolt

John C. Frémont was a mapmaker who led several western expeditions. He set out on his third expedition in 1845 when the United States was on the verge of a war with Mexico over the annexation of Texas. In June 1846, during the Bear Flag Revolt, he supported a small group of Americans who declared the area independent. They named it the Bear Flag Republic. Frémont later wrote that he saw their actions as *"movements with the view of establishing a settled and stable government, which may give security to their persons and property."*

CRITICAL Thinking

1. **Theorizing** Based on Frémont's quotation, how do you think the Mexican government treated California settlers?
2. **Speculating** Why do you think Frémont supported the revolt?

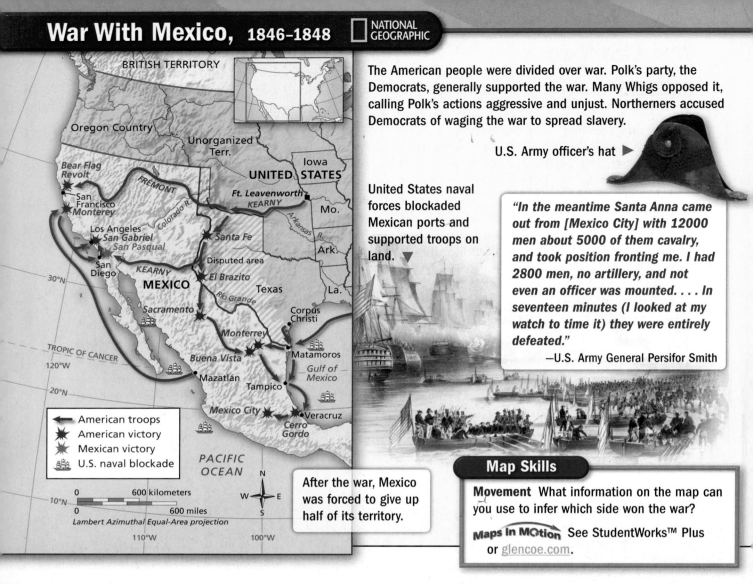

The American people were divided over war. Polk's party, the Democrats, generally supported the war. Many Whigs opposed it, calling Polk's actions aggressive and unjust. Northerners accused Democrats of waging the war to spread slavery.

U.S. Army officer's hat ▶

United States naval forces blockaded Mexican ports and supported troops on land. ▼

"In the meantime Santa Anna came out from [Mexico City] with 12000 men about 5000 of them cavalry, and took position fronting me. I had 2800 men, no artillery, and not even an officer was mounted. . . . In seventeen minutes (I looked at my watch to time it) they were entirely defeated."

—U.S. Army General Persifor Smith

After the war, Mexico was forced to give up half of its territory.

Map Skills

Movement What information on the map can you use to infer which side won the war?

Maps In Motion See StudentWorks™ Plus or glencoe.com.

Polk's War Plan

Polk's war plan had three parts. First, American troops would drive Mexican forces out of the disputed border region in Texas and secure the border. Second, the United States would seize New Mexico and California. Finally, American forces would take Mexico City, the capital of Mexico.

Zachary Taylor accomplished the first goal. By early 1847, his army had captured the towns of Matamoros, Monterrey, and Buena Vista. The Texas border was secure.

While Taylor made progress in northern Mexico, American forces also advanced farther west. General Stephen Watts Kearny led about 1,500 troops along the Santa Fe Trail from Fort Leavenworth to New Mexico. The Mexican governor fled, allowing the Americans to capture New Mexico's capital, Santa Fe, on August 18, 1846, without firing a shot. Kearny then led his army across the deserts toward California.

The Bear Flag Republic

In June 1846, a small group of Americans seized the town of Sonoma north of San Francisco and proclaimed the independent Republic of California. They called the new country the Bear Flag Republic.

John C. Frémont and mountain man Kit Carson also met in Sonoma. Frémont declared that he would conquer California. Many **Californios,** the Mexicans who lived in California, were outraged by his declaration.

They might have supported a revolt for local control, but they opposed what looked like an attempt to seize land.

In July 1846, a United States Navy force under Commodore John Sloat captured the ports of Monterey and San Francisco. Sloat declared California annexed to the United States. Sloat's fleet sailed for San Diego, carrying Frémont and Carson. The Americans captured San Diego and moved north to Los Angeles.

After Sloat's ships left, many Californios in San Diego rose up against the Americans who had taken over the city. General Kearny and his troops put down the revolt. By January 1847, California was fully controlled by the United States.

The Capture of Mexico City

President Polk gave the task of capturing Mexico City to General **Winfield Scott.** In March 1847, Scott's army landed near the Mexican port of Veracruz. The army captured Veracruz after a three-week siege and then fought its way some 300 miles to Mexico City. By mid-September 1847, the Americans had taken Mexico City. The Mexican government surrendered. It would also be forced to surrender half of its territory.

The United States Expands

The **Treaty of Guadalupe Hidalgo** (GWAH•duhl•oop hih•DAL•goh) was signed in February 1848. Mexico gave up Texas and agreed to the Rio Grande as the border between Texas and Mexico. In what was called the **Mexican Cession,** Mexico ceded, or gave, California and New Mexico to the United States for the price of $15 million.

In 1853 the United States paid Mexico $10 million for the **Gadsden Purchase,** a strip of land along the southern edge of present-day Arizona and New Mexico. With the Gadsden Purchase, the U.S. mainland reached its present size.

 Reading Check **Evaluating** Was President Polk's war plan successful? Explain.

Section 3 Review

History ONLINE
Study Central™ To review this section, go to glencoe.com.

Vocabulary

1. Define each of the following terms in a sentence: rancho, ranchero, resource, commence, Californios, cede.

Main Ideas

2. Specifying What was the original purpose of the Santa Fe Trail?

3. Explaining Why did Americans want to acquire California?

4. Identifying What issues existed between the United States and Mexico before they went to war?

Critical Thinking

5. Analyzing Describe how trade promoted United States territorial growth.

6. Organizing Use a diagram like the one below to describe each part of Polk's war plan and the goal he was trying to achieve.

Polk's War Plan

Goal

7. Creative Writing Write the words to a short national anthem for the Bear Flag Republic. Include details designed to evoke pride among the citizens of the country.

Answer the
8. Essential Question

How did Mexican lands in the West become part of the United States?

California and Utah

Essential Question ◄

What factors affected the settlement of California and Utah in the West?

Reading Guide

Content Vocabulary

forty-niner *(p. 379)*   vigilante *(p. 380)*
boomtown *(p. 379)*

Academic Vocabulary

constitution *(p. 380)*   incorporate *(p. 382)*

Key People and Events

Levi Strauss *(p. 380)*
Mormon *(p. 381)*
Joseph Smith *(p. 381)*
Brigham Young *(p. 382)*

Reading Strategy

Taking Notes As you read, take notes in a diagram like the one below. Describe what a person or group did and what their roles were in the settlement of California and Utah.

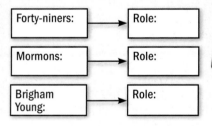

Forty-niners: → Role:

Mormons: → Role:

Brigham Young: → Role:

INDIANA ACADEMIC STANDARDS
United States History

8.1.15 Explain the concept of Manifest Destiny and describe its impact on westward expansion of the United States.

American Diary

From early 1848—when John Sutter discovered gold in California—until late 1849, the population of California increased from 15,000 to more than 100,000. Wild-eyed prospectors came from all over the world. "Farmers left their fields untilled and went off. . . . Workmen quit their jobs without notice. . . . In every town . . . one might buy gold-seekers' manuals, guides and maps."

—*from* The Way Our People Lived

Gold mining in California

California Gold Rush

Main Idea The discovery of gold led to rapid growth and eventual statehood for California.

History and You Do you think searching for treasure would be an exciting life? Read what life was like during the California Gold Rush.

· ·

When gold was discovered in California in 1848, people from all over the world traveled to the region in search of riches. Those who arrived in 1849 were called **forty-niners.** As one official reported, "the farmers have thrown aside their plows, the lawyers their briefs, the doctors their pills, the priests their prayer books, and all are now digging gold." Many people arrived by sea. Others traveled on the Oregon Trail or the Santa Fe Trail.

Americans made up about 80 percent of the forty-niners. Others came from Mexico, South America, Europe, and Australia. About 300 men arrived from China, the first large group of Asian immigrants to settle in America. Although some eventually returned to China, others remained and established California's Chinese American community.

The Californios

The Treaty of Guadalupe Hidalgo ended the war with Mexico and made Californios citizens of the United States. The treaty also guaranteed them the rights to their lands. The Land Law of 1851, however, established a group of reviewers who examined the Californios' land rights. When a new settler claimed a Californio's land, the two parties would go to court, and the Californio had to prove that he or she owned the land. Some Californios were able to prove their claims. Many, however, lost their land.

Life in California

As people rushed to a new area to look for gold, they built new communities, called **boomtowns,** almost overnight. At one site on the Yuba River where only two houses stood in September 1849, a miner arrived the next year to find a town of 1,000 people "with a large number of hotels, stores, groceries, bakeries, and . . . gambling houses."

Cities also flourished during the Gold Rush. As ships arrived daily with gold seekers, San Francisco grew from a tiny village to a city of about 20,000 people.

By the Numbers / Gold Rush Prices

Costs Miners might mine $10 worth of gold one day but $2,000 the next day. Even though their income was unpredictable, miners still had to buy supplies. What did goods cost in San Francisco in 1849?

Gold Rush Era California

Item	Cost
Flour	$18 per pound
Coffee	$16 per pound
Butter	$1 per pound
Rice	$10 per pound
Wood	$20 per cord
Sleeping Room	$12 per week
Labor (earned money)	$6–10 per day

0 100 kilometers
0 100 miles
Albers Equal-Area projection

Critical Thinking

Analyzing San Francisco's prices were 20 times higher than those in the rest of the country. Why would miners pay high prices?

People from all over the world traveled to California in search of gold.

1. **Interpreting** Describe how people in the cartoon acted as they left for California.

2. **Drawing Conclusions** Do you think the cartoonist views the California Gold Rush as favorable? Why or why not?

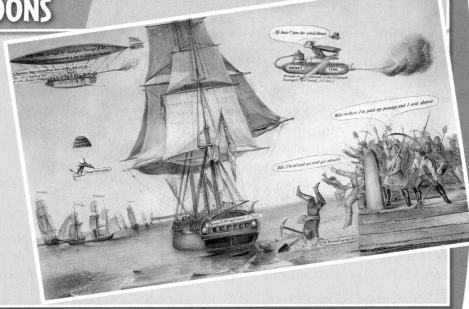

Most forty-niners had no experience in mining. Whenever they heard that gold had been discovered at a particular site, they rushed to it and attacked the hillsides with pickaxes and shovels. They spent hours bent over streambeds, "washing" or "panning" the water for gold dust and nuggets.

The California Gold Rush more than doubled the world's supply of gold. For all their hard work, however, very few forty-niners achieved lasting wealth. Most found little or no gold. Many of those who did lost their riches through gambling or wild spending.

Boomtown merchants, however, made huge profits. They could charge whatever they liked for food and other essential items because there were no other nearby stores that sold these products. For example, an immigrant named **Levi Strauss** sold the miners sturdy pants made of denim. His "Levi's" made him rich.

Gold Rush Society

Mining camps contained men of all backgrounds, but few women. Lonely and suffering hardships, many men spent their free hours drinking, gambling, and fighting. Mining towns had no police or prisons. As a result, citizens formed committees of groups known as **vigilantes** (VIH•juh•LAN•teez) to protect themselves. Vigilantes took the law into their own hands and acted as police, judge, jury, and sometimes executioner.

Economic and Political Progress

The Gold Rush had lasting effects on California. Agriculture, shipping, and trade grew to meet the demand for food and other goods. Many people who had arrived looking for gold stayed to farm or run a business.

Rapid growth brought the need for better government. In 1850, Californians applied for statehood and wrote a **constitution**—a list of laws to support the government. The constitution's ban on slavery, however, caused a crisis in Congress. Southern states opposed California's admission. California did not enter the Union until a compromise was reached later that year.

✓ **Reading Check** **Explaining** Why did the forty-niners travel to California?

A Religious Refuge in Utah

Main Idea The Mormons settled in Utah.

History and You Think about how you would plan to build a city in a desert. Learn how the Mormons created a thriving city in the harsh terrain of a desert.

. . . .

A visitor to the Utah Territory in the 1850s wrote admiringly: "The whole of this small nation occupy themselves as usefully as the working bees of a hive." This account described the **Mormons,** or members of the Church of Jesus Christ of Latter-day Saints. Mormons settled in Utah to fulfill their vision of the godly life.

The First Mormons

The Church of Jesus Christ of Latter-day Saints was among a number of religious movements that sprang up during the religious awakenings of the 1830s and 1840s. The founder of the Mormon Church was **Joseph Smith,** a New Englander living in western New York. Smith claimed that he had received visions that led him to build a new Christian church. He began preaching Mormon ideas in 1830.

Smith published *The Book of Mormon* that year, announcing that it was a translation of words written on golden plates that he had received from an angel. The text told of the coming of God and the need to build a kingdom on Earth to receive him.

Smith hoped to use his visions to build an ideal society. He believed that property should be held in common. He also supported polygamy, the idea that a man could have more than one wife. This angered a large number of people. Mormons eventually gave up this practice.

Smith formed a community in New York, but unsympathetic neighbors disapproved of the Mormons' religion and forced them to leave. The Mormons eventually settled in Illinois. In 1839 they bought the town of Commerce, Illinois, and renamed it Nauvoo. Nauvoo became a prosperous community.

Primary Source / The Mormons

West to Utah Strong anti-Mormon feelings in the United States convinced Brigham Young to lead Mormons west. Young hoped to settle in a place where his people could live and worship freely.

Mormons gave people carts to help them carry their possessions on the journey west. By 1860, about 40,000 Mormons had settled in the Utah Territory. ▼

Mormons minted coins and issued paper money in the 1840s and 1850s.

"In our Mountain home we feel not the withering sources of influence of political or even fashionable [tyranny]. . . . I have found the satisfaction of having been [very] successful, and peace again smiles upon all our settlements, and that too without a resort to arms."

—Brigham Young

The Mormon Temple, Salt Lake City, Utah ▼

Critical Thinking

Analyzing Why did Young feel satisfied after the Mormons' journey west?

Persecution of the Mormons, however, continued. In 1844 a mob of local residents killed Joseph Smith. After Smith's death, **Brigham Young** took over as head of the Mormons. Young decided that the Mormons should move again to escape persecution and find religious freedom. This time, the Mormons would move west to the Great Salt Lake in present-day Utah. Although part of Mexico at the time, no Mexicans had settled in the region because of its harsh terrain.

A Haven in the Desert

The Mormon migration began in 1846. About 12,000 Mormons made the trek. It was the largest single migration in American history. The Mormons forged their way along a path that became known as the Mormon Trail. Like the Oregon Trail, the Mormon Trail served as a valuable route into the western United States.

In 1847 the Mormons finally reached the Great Salt Lake. It was there that Young declared that the Mormons would build a new settlement. The land was dry and wild. Nevertheless, the Mormons staked a claim on the land they called Deseret. Soon they had set up farming communities.

At first life was difficult for the settlers. The Mormons, however, made Deseret flourish because of their hard work and determination to succeed. They planned their towns, such as Salt Lake City, carefully and built irrigation canals to water their farms. Property was taxed, and the use of water, timber, and other natural resources was regulated. Mormons also founded industries so they could be self-sufficient. Mormon merchants sold supplies to the forty-niners who passed through Utah on their way to California.

In 1848 the United States acquired the Salt Lake area as part of the settlement with the war with Mexico. In 1850 Congress established the Utah Territory. President Millard Fillmore made Brigham Young the governor of the Utah Territory.

By 1860 there were numerous Mormon communities throughout the Utah region. Utah was not easily **incorporated,** or included, into the United States. The Mormons often had conflicts with federal officials. In 1857 and 1858, war almost broke out between the Mormons and the United States Army. Utah did not become a state until 1896.

✔ **Reading Check** **Identifying** Who founded the Church of Jesus Christ of Latter-day Saints?

Section 4 Review

History ONLINE
Study Central™ To review this section, go to glencoe.com.

Vocabulary

1. Define each of the following terms and use them in a paragraph about the California Gold Rush: forty-niner, boomtown, vigilante, constitution, incorporate.

Main Ideas

2. Explaining Why was California's entry into the Union delayed?

3. Explaining Why did the Mormons leave New York?

Critical Thinking

4. Making Connections How did the Gold Rush affect California's population?

5. Organizing In a diagram like the one below, list the reasons Deseret was able to flourish.

Success of Deseret

6. Creative Writing You are living in a California boomtown in the mid-1800s. Write a journal entry that describes what your daily life is like.

Answer the
7. Essential Question
What factors affected the settlement of California and Utah in the West?

Visual Summary

Oregon Territory

- The area includes present-day Oregon, Washington, and Idaho and parts of Montana, Wyoming, and British Columbia.
- The United States, Great Britain, Spain, and Russia claim the Oregon Territory.
- Mountain men create east-west passages that are vital for trade and settlement.
- Manifest Destiny is the belief that God has given Americans the right to extend the country's western boundaries.
- In 1846 Britain and the U.S. set the border at latitude 49° N.

Texas

- Americans receive land grants from Mexico and settle in Texas.
- Texas colonists agree to learn Spanish, become Mexican citizens, convert to Catholicism, and obey Mexican law in exchange for land at low prices.
- Texans wins their independence from Mexico in 1836.
- Texas joins the Union in 1845.

New Mexico

- The territory includes all of present-day New Mexico, Arizona, Nevada, and Utah and parts of Colorado and Wyoming.
- The first American trader arrives in New Mexico in 1821.
- The Santa Fe Trail trade route begins near Independence, Missouri, and ends in New Mexico.

Utah Territory

- The Mormons, founded by Joseph Smith, seek to escape religious persecution.
- In 1846 Brigham Young leads the Mormons west; they settle near the Great Salt Lake.
- The Mormons establish successful farming communities.
- Utah becomes a state in 1896.

California

- Spanish explorers and Mexican missionaries settle the region.
- In June 1846, American settlers proclaim California's independence from Mexico.
- After the war with Mexico, the United States buys California and New Mexico for $15 million.
- The Gold Rush fuels settlement and economic growth.
- California becomes a state in 1850.

STUDY TO GO Study anywhere, anytime! Download quizzes and flash cards to your PDA from glencoe.com.

INDIANA STATEWIDE TEST PRACTICE

Reviewing Vocabulary

Directions: Choose the word or words that best completes the sentence.

1 The idea in the early 1800s that the United States should spread across the North American continent to the Pacific Ocean was called _____.

A emigration
B Fifty-Four Forty
C *empresario*
D Manifest Destiny

2 In the early 1800s, Mexicans who had moved north and claimed Texas as their home were known as _____.

A Tejanos
B forty-niners
C Santa Annas
D vigilantes

3 Large estates called _____ were set up by Mexican settlers on mission lands in California.

A *empresarios*
B annexes
C ranchos
D boomtowns

4 Around the 1850 California gold fields, new communities called _____ sprang up almost overnight.

A forty-niners
B Californios
C vigilantes
D boomtowns

Reviewing Main Ideas

Directions: Choose the best answer.

5 In the Adams-Onís Treaty of 1819

A the United States and Britain agreed to jointly occupy Oregon.
B Spain gave up claims to Oregon.
C the United States gained sole possession of the Oregon Territory.
D Russia gave up claims to the Oregon Territory.

6 How did Mexico attract settlers to Texas?

A It restricted the amount of land owned by *empresarios.*
B It removed all taxes on American-made goods.
C It offered land grants to people who agreed to settle.
D It agreed to allow freedom of religion.

7 Why did many Americans in the 1840s want to make California a state?

A to convert Native Americans to Christianity
B to abolish the Spanish missions
C to build ports on the Pacific coast
D to sell Native Americans into slavery

8 Mormons used irrigation to water crops at

A Deseret.
B New York City.
C San Francisco.
D boomtowns in California.

GO ON

Critical Thinking

Directions: Choose the best answer.

9 **How did the phrase "Fifty-Four Forty or Fight" refer to the issue of the Oregon Territory?**

 A It referred to the about 5,000 Americans who lived in the territory.

 B It was another phrase meaning "Manifest Destiny."

 C It referred to the price of an acre of land in the territory.

 D It referred to the line of latitude that some wanted as the territory border.

Base your answer to question 10 on the illustration below and your knowledge of Chapter 12.

Source: Library of Congress

10 **The print above shows the killing of Joseph Smith. Why was Joseph Smith murdered?**

 A He had helped escaped enslaved people to freedom.

 B He pushed for the annexation of Texas as a free state.

 C Local residents objected to his religious views.

 D He cheated forty-niners out of their earnings from gold mining.

Constructed Response

Directions: Write a short response to each of the following questions. In your answer:

 • *address all parts of the question*

 • *use information from the chapter*

 • *include facts, examples, and details relevant to the question*

 • *use clear language*

Base your answer to question 11 on the reading below and your knowledge of Chapter 12.

> After a particular route has been selected to make the journey across the plains . . . their first business should be to organize themselves into a company. . . . The company should be of sufficient [size] to herd and guard animals, and for protection against [Native Americans].
>
> —Advice to travelers heading west, from R.B. Marcy, *The Prairie and Overland Traveler*

11 **Why were the settlers advised to travel west in a relatively large group?**

12 **Name two conditions that the Mexican government wanted American settlers in Texas to agree to when moving there.**

13 **What was the importance of the Gadsden Purchase?**

14 **Why did vigilantes appear in California mining towns?**

Need Extra Help?														
If you missed questions. . .	1	2	3	4	5	6	7	8	9	10	11	12	13	14
Go to page. . .	363	367	374	379	359	367	374	382	363	382	362	367	377	380

Chapter 13

North and South 1820–1860

New York City in 1857

PRESIDENTS

JAMES MONROE 1817–1825

1824 ★
U.S. and Russia settle Northwest coast land claims

JOHN Q. ADAMS 1825–1829

1826 ★
The Last of the Mohicans published

ANDREW JACKSON 1829–1837

1834 ★
McCormick reaper is patented

MARTIN VAN BUREN 1837–1841

PRESIDENTS

U.S. Events

World Events

1820

1830

★ **1820**
Antarctica discovered

★ **1825**
World's first public railroad opens in England

★ **1832**
Greece recognized as independent state

Section 1: The North's Economy

Essential Question What innovations in industry, travel, and communications changed the lives of Americans in the 1800s?

Section 2: The North's People

Essential Question How did immigration have an impact on cities, industry, and culture in the North?

Section 3: Southern Cotton Kingdom

Essential Question How did the South's industry and economy differ from the industry and economy of the North?

Section 4: The South's People

Essential Question How did unique elements of culture develop among enslaved African Americans in the South?

History ONLINE

Chapter Overview Visit glencoe.com and click on **Chapter 13—Chapter Overviews** to preview chapter information.

FOLDABLES® Study Organizer

Organizing Information

Make this Foldable to help summarize what you learn about similarities and differences between the North and the South.

Step 1 Mark the center of a sheet of notebook paper.

Step 2 Fold the sheet of notebook paper into thirds.

Step 3 Sketch a map of the United States on the front and label your Foldable as shown.

North (1820–1860)

South (1820–1860)

Reading and Writing After you finish taking notes in your Foldable, list the causes and effects of the differences that led to conflict between these regions.

◀ California gold miner

WILLIAM HENRY HARRISON 1841

JOHN TYLER 1841–1845

★ **1845** James Marshall discovers gold in California

JAMES POLK 1845–1849

ZACHARY TAYLOR 1849–1850

MILLARD FILLMORE 1850–1853

FRANKLIN PIERCE 1853–1857

JAMES BUCHANAN 1857–1861

1840

1850

1860

★ **1845** Great Irish Famine begins

★ **1848** Johannes Rebmann is first European to see Kilamanjaro

★ **1857** Sepoy Rebellion begins in India

★ **1859** Darwin's *On the Origin of Species* is published

▶ Kilimanjaro in Tanzania

The North's Economy

Essential Question ◄

What innovations in industry, travel, and communications changed the lives of Americans in the 1800s?

Reading Guide

Content Vocabulary

clipper ship (p. 390)
telegraph (p. 391)
Morse code (p. 392)

Academic Vocabulary

innovation (p. 389)   transform (p. 391)

Key People

Elias Howe (p. 389)
Robert Fulton (p. 390)
Peter Cooper (p. 390)
Samuel Morse (p. 391)
John Deere (p. 393)
Cyrus McCormick (p. 393)

Reading Strategy

Taking Notes As you read, use the diagram below to describe the three phases of the development of industrialization in the North.

Development of Industrialization

Phase 1
↓
Phase 2
↓
Phase 3

INDIANA ACADEMIC STANDARDS
United States History

8.1.27 Give examples of scientific and technological developments that changed cultural life in the nineteenth-century United States, such as the use of photography, growth in the use of the telegraph, the completion of the transcontinental railroad, and the invention of the telephone.

8.4.5 Analyze contributions of entrepreneurs and inventors in the development of the United States economy.

American Diary

Railroad travel in the mid-1840s was uncomfortable. English novelist Charles Dickens described what it was like to travel on a train. "There is a great deal of jolting, a great deal of noise, a great deal of wall, not much window, a locomotive engine, a shriek, and a bell. The cars are like shabby omnibusses, but larger; holding thirty, forty, fifty people. . . . In the center of the carriage there is usually a stove, fed with charcoal . . . which is for the most part red-hot. It is insufferably close."

—*from* American Notes for General Circulation

The number of railroad routes increased dramatically from 1840 to 1860.

Technology and Industry

Main Idea Industry, travel, and communications greatly expanded during the 1800s.

History and You How often do you use e-mail or text messaging during any one day? Read to learn about the invention of the telegraph, which greatly improved communications in the 1800s.

. . . .

Early trains differed from and offered few of the comforts of modern-day trains. They were noisy and often dirty. As Charles Dickens noted, they also provided a jolty ride. Locomotives were part of the wave of industrialization during the 1800s. **Innovations**—new ideas or methods—in industry and technology began changing the way Americans worked, traveled, and communicated.

Industrialization

The industrialization of the North developed in three phases. In the first phase, manufacturers made products by dividing the tasks involved among the workers. For example, one worker would spin thread all day, and another would weave cloth. This was faster than having one person spin and then weave. During the second phase, manufacturers built factories to bring specialized workers together. Products could be made more quickly than before.

In the third phase, factory workers used machinery to perform some of their work. Many of the new machines ran on water-power or steam power. For example, power-driven looms took over the task of weaving. The worker's job changed from weaving to tending the machine. This change produced more fabric in less time.

Mass production of cotton textiles began in New England in the early 1800s. **Elias Howe** invented the sewing machine in 1846. Using this machine and machine-made fabrics, workers produced clothing on a large scale. Other types of industries developed during the same period. By 1860, the Northeast's factories produced at least two-thirds of the country's manufactured goods.

Improved Transportation

Transportation improvements contributed to the success of America's new industries. Between 1800 and 1850, construction crews built thousands of miles of roads and canals.

Primary Source / Railroad Expansion, 1860

Major Railroads, 1860

Total Length of Railroad Tracks	
1840	3,000 miles (4,828 km)
1850	9,000 miles (14,484 km)
1860	30,000 miles (48,280 km)

Railroads

ATLANTIC OCEAN

0   200 kilometers
0   200 miles
Albers Equal-Area projection

Making Tracks Trains were important not only for transporting people across the country, but they also allowed goods to be shipped greater distances than ever before. Beginning in the early 1800s, industrialization and technology began to change the way Americans worked, traveled, and communicated.

Critical Thinking

Making Inferences What region might have an advantage for transporting goods and people more easily?

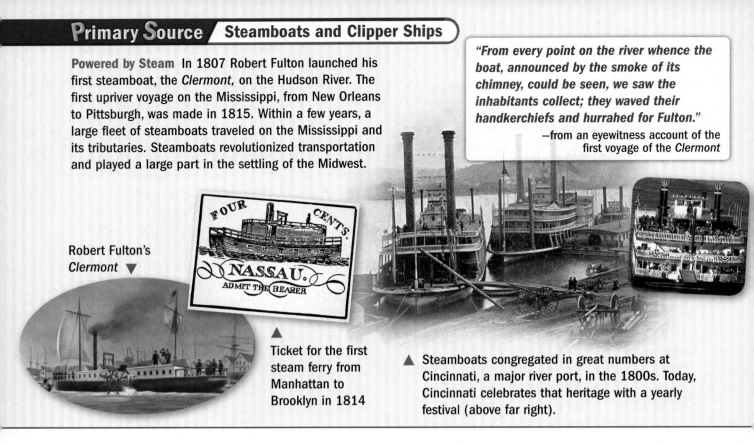

Powered by Steam In 1807 Robert Fulton launched his first steamboat, the *Clermont*, on the Hudson River. The first upriver voyage on the Mississippi, from New Orleans to Pittsburgh, was made in 1815. Within a few years, a large fleet of steamboats traveled on the Mississippi and its tributaries. Steamboats revolutionized transportation and played a large part in the settling of the Midwest.

"From every point on the river whence the boat, announced by the smoke of its chimney, could be seen, we saw the inhabitants collect; they waved their handkerchiefs and hurrahed for Fulton."

—from an eyewitness account of the first voyage of the *Clermont*

Robert Fulton's *Clermont* ▼

FOUR CENTS. NASSAU. ADMIT THE BEARER

▲ Ticket for the first steam ferry from Manhattan to Brooklyn in 1814

▲ Steamboats congregated in great numbers at Cincinnati, a major river port, in the 1800s. Today, Cincinnati celebrates that heritage with a yearly festival (above far right).

Canals opened new shipping routes by connecting many lakes and rivers. Upstream travel against the current was extremely difficult though. That changed in 1807, when inventor **Robert Fulton** demonstrated a reliable steamboat. Steamboats could carry goods and passengers more cheaply and quickly along inland waterways than flatboats or sail-powered vessels.

In the 1840s, builders began to widen and deepen canals to accommodate steamboats. By 1860 about 3,000 steamboats traveled the country's major rivers and canals, as well as the Great Lakes, spurring the growth of cities such as Cincinnati, Buffalo, and Chicago.

Sailing ships also were improved in the 1840s. The clipper ships—with sleek hulls and tall sails—were the pride of the open seas. They could sail 300 miles (483 km) per day, as fast as most steamships at that time. The ships got their name because they "clipped" time from long journeys. Before the clippers, the voyage from New York to Great Britain took about 21 to 28 days. A clipper ship could usually make that trip in half the time.

Locomotives

The development of railroads in the United States began with short stretches of tracks to connect mines with nearby rivers. Horses, rather than locomotives, pulled the early trains. The first steam-powered passenger locomotive, the *Rocket,* began operating in Britain in 1829.

Peter Cooper designed and built the first American steam locomotive in 1830. Called the *Tom Thumb,* it got off to a bad start. In a race against a horse-drawn train in Baltimore, the *Tom Thumb*'s engine failed. Engineers soon improved the engine, and within 10 years steam locomotives were pulling trains in the United States.

A Railway Network

In 1840 the United States had almost 3,000 miles (4,828 km) of railroad track. By 1860, it had almost 31,000 miles (49,890 km), mostly in the North and Midwest areas. One railway linked the cities of New York City and Buffalo. Another connected the Pennsylvania cities of Philadelphia and Pittsburgh.

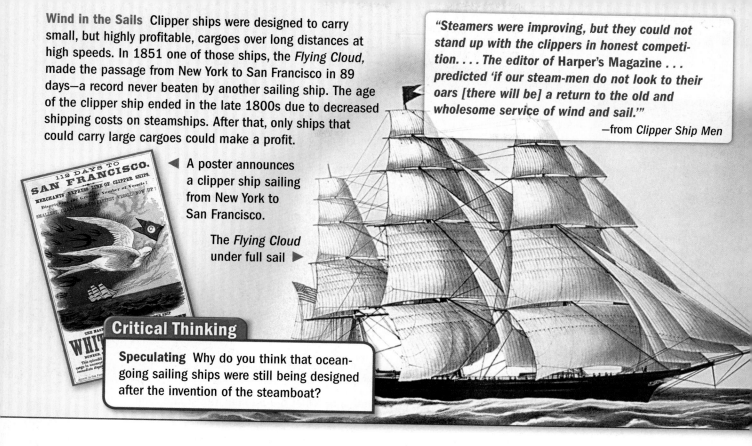

Wind in the Sails Clipper ships were designed to carry small, but highly profitable, cargoes over long distances at high speeds. In 1851 one of those ships, the *Flying Cloud*, made the passage from New York to San Francisco in 89 days—a record never beaten by another sailing ship. The age of the clipper ship ended in the late 1800s due to decreased shipping costs on steamships. After that, only ships that could carry large cargoes could make a profit.

"Steamers were improving, but they could not stand up with the clippers in honest competition. . . . The editor of Harper's Magazine . . . predicted 'if our steam-men do not look to their oars [there will be] a return to the old and wholesome service of wind and sail.'"

—from *Clipper Ship Men*

◀ A poster announces a clipper ship sailing from New York to San Francisco.

The *Flying Cloud* under full sail ▶

Critical Thinking

Speculating Why do you think that ocean-going sailing ships were still being designed after the invention of the steamboat?

Yet another linked Baltimore and Wheeling, Virginia (now West Virginia). Railway builders connected these eastern lines to lines being built farther west in Ohio, Indiana, and Illinois. By 1860, a network of railroad track united the Midwest and the East.

Moving Goods and People

Along with canals, the railways **transformed,** or changed, trade in the nation's interior. The changes began with the opening of the Erie Canal in 1825 and the first railroads of the 1830s. Before this time, agricultural goods were carried down the Mississippi River to New Orleans. From there they were shipped to the East Coast or to other countries.

The development of the east-west canal and the rail network allowed grain, livestock, and dairy products to move directly from the Midwest to the East. Goods could now be moved faster and more cheaply. As a result, manufacturers in the East could offer them at lower prices.

The railroads also played an important role in the settlement and industrialization of the

Midwest. Fast, affordable train travel brought people into Ohio, Indiana, and Illinois. The populations of these states grew. As more people moved into the area, new towns and industries developed.

Faster Communication

The growth of industry and the new pace of travel created a need for faster methods of communication over the vast distances. The **telegraph**—an apparatus that used electric signals to transmit messages—filled that need.

Samuel Morse, an American inventor, was seeking support for a system of telegraph lines. On May 24, 1844, Morse got the chance to demonstrate that he could send messages instantly along wires. As a crowd in the U.S. capital watched, Morse tapped in the words "What hath God wrought!" A few moments later, the telegraph operator in Baltimore sent the same message back in reply. The telegraph worked! Soon telegraph messages were flashing back and forth between Washington, D.C., and Baltimore.

People IN HISTORY

John Deere
Inventor of the Steel-Tipped Plow

Because the heavy Midwestern soil stuck to cast-iron plows, farmers had to stop every few feet to clean the plow blades. Blacksmith John Deere set out to create a polished steel plow that would clean itself. The plows became a successful new business. Within 10 years he was selling 1,000 plows per year. Deere constantly improved his design. He was quoted as saying, *"I will never put my name on a product that does not have in it the best that is in me."*

Samuel Morse
Inventor of the Telegraph

Samuel Morse had trouble convincing Congress to build a telegraph line. When he finally did, however, Americans were thrilled with the telegraph's speed. In a letter to his brother, Sidney, Morse described the scene that day: *"The enthusiasm of the crowd . . . was excited to the highest pitch. . . . They gave the Telegraph three cheers, and I was called to make my appearance at the window where three cheers were given to me by some hundreds present."*

CRITICAL Thinking

1. **Analyzing** What did Samuel Morse and John Deere have in common?
2. **Identifying** What showed the popularity of the telegraph? Of the steel-tipped plow?

Morse transmitted his message in **Morse code.** This code, which Morse developed and which bears his name, is a series of dots and dashes representing the letters of the alphabet. A skilled Morse code operator could rapidly tap out words in the dot-and-dash alphabet.

Americans adopted the telegraph eagerly. A British visitor marveled at the speed with which Americans formed telegraph companies and erected telegraph lines. Americans, he wrote, were driven to "annihilate [wipe out] distance" in their vast country. To speed the transmission of news using the telegraph, the Associated Press was formed in 1848. By 1852, there were about 23,000 miles (37,015 km) of telegraph lines in the United States.

Reading Check **Explaining** How did canals and railways transform trade in the interior of the United States?

Agriculture

Main Idea Revolutionary inventions in the 1830s changed farming methods, and agriculture became more profitable.

History and You Have you or your family ever bought produce from a farmers market? Read to learn how agriculture boomed during the 1800s.

The railroads gave farmers access to new markets far from their homes in which to sell their products. At the same time, advances in agricultural technology allowed farmers to greatly increase the size of the harvests they produced.

In the early 1800s, few farmers had ventured into the treeless Great Plains west of Missouri, Iowa, and Minnesota. Even areas of mixed forest and prairie west of Ohio and Kentucky seemed too difficult for farming.

Settlers worried that their wooden plows could not break the prairie's matted sod. Further, they worried that the soil would not be fertile enough to support fields of crops.

Revolution in Agriculture

Three revolutionary inventions of the 1830s changed farming methods and encouraged settlers to cultivate larger areas of the Midwest. One invention was the steel-tipped plow that **John Deere** invented in 1837. Far sturdier than the wooden plow, Deere's plow easily cut through the hard-packed prairie sod. Equally important were the mechanical reaper, which sped up the harvesting of wheat, and the thresher, which quickly separated the grain from the stalk.

McCormick's Reaper

Born on a Virginia farm, **Cyrus McCormick** became interested in machines that would ease the burden of farmwork. McCormick designed and constructed the mechanical reaper. He made a fortune manufacturing and selling it.

For hundreds of years, farmers harvested grain with handheld sickles, or cutting tools. McCormick's reaper could harvest grain much faster than a person using a sickle.

 History ONLINE
Student Web Activity Visit glencoe.com and complete the Chapter 13 Web Activity about agriculture in the mid-1800s.

Because farmers could harvest wheat so quickly, they began planting more of it. Growing wheat became profitable. McCormick's reaper ensured that raising wheat would remain the main economic activity on the Midwestern prairies.

New machines and the accessibility to railroads allowed farmers to devote more acres to cash crops—crops raised strictly for sale. Midwestern farmers began growing wheat as a cash crop and shipping it east by train and canal barge. Farmers in the Northeast and Middle Atlantic states increased their production of fruits and vegetables.

Despite improvements in agriculture, the North turned away from farming and toward industry. It was difficult to make a living farming the rocky soil of New England. Industry, however, flourished in the area. The number of people working in factories continued to rise.

✓ Reading Check **Identifying** What innovation sped up the harvesting of wheat?

Section 1 Review

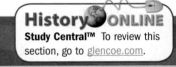 **History ONLINE**
Study Central™ To review this section, go to glencoe.com.

Vocabulary

1. Write a paragraph in which you explain why each of these terms appears in a chapter about American life in the first half of the nineteenth century: innovation, clipper ship, transform, telegraph, Morse code.

Main Ideas

2. Summarizing How were messages sent via telegraph? Why was this invention important?

3. Identifying List innovations in farming methods in the 1830s.

Critical Thinking

4. Making Connections Use a diagram like the one below to show factors that encouraged the settlement of the Midwest.

5. Expository Writing Write a paragraph discussing why industrial growth and the new pace of travel created a desire for faster communication.

Answer the
6. Essential Question
What innovations in industry, travel, and communications changed the lives of Americans in the 1800s?

The North's People

Reading Guide

Content Vocabulary

trade union (p. 396)

discrimination (p. 396)

strike (p. 396)

famine (p. 398)

prejudice (p. 396)

nativist (p. 399)

Academic Vocabulary

community (p. 396)   license (p. 397)

Key People and Events

Henry Boyd (p. 396)

Samuel Cornish (p. 396)

John B. Russwurm (p. 396)

Macon B. Allen (p. 397)

Sarah G. Bagley (p. 397)

Know-Nothing Party (p. 399)

Reading Strategy

Taking Notes As you read, use a diagram like the one below to list two reasons for the growth of cities.

Growth of Cities

INDIANA ACADEMIC STANDARDS
United States History

8.1.10 Compare differences in ways of life in the northern and southern states, including the growth of towns and cities in the North and the growing dependence on slavery in the South.

8.1.25 Give examples of how immigration affected American culture in the decades before and after the Civil War, including growth of industrialism in the North; religious differences; tensions between middle-class and working-class people, particularly in the Northeast; and intensification of cultural differences between the North and the South.

American Diary

"Over there [Germany], alas, common sense and free speech lie in shackles. . . . I invite you to come over here, should you want to obtain a clear notion of genuine public life, freedom of people and sense of being a nation. . . . I have never regretted that I came here, and never! never! again shall I bow my head under the yoke of despotism and folly."

—August Blümner, a German immigrant quoted in
News from the Land of Freedom

Immigrants arriving in New York Harbor

Northern Factories

Main Idea Many workers in the mid-1800s saw the need for reforms in working conditions.

History and You Do you babysit or mow lawns to earn money? Is the pay fair? Read to learn why workers in the mid-1800s wanted to earn more pay and improve their working conditions.

. . . .

For many immigrants like August Blümner, America meant freedom and liberty. Immigrants often settled in cities and found work in the many mills and factories there. Working conditions were harsh, however, and reforms were needed.

Between 1820 and 1860, America's manufacturing increasingly shifted to mills and factories. As numerous machines took over more production tasks, these tasks were brought under one roof—creating the factory system. In addition to textiles and clothing, factories produced items such as shoes, watches, guns, sewing machines, and agricultural machinery.

Working Conditions

As the factory system developed, working conditions worsened. Employees worked long hours, averaging 11.4 hours per day by 1840. Factory work involved many dangerous conditions, and longer workdays caused on-the-job accidents.

For example, long leather belts connected the machines to the factory's water-powered driveshaft. These belts had no protective shields. Workers, especially children, often suffered injuries from the rapidly spinning belts. Many workers lost their fingers or broke their bones.

Employees often labored under unpleasant conditions. Factories were miserably hot and stifling in the summer. The machines gave off heat, and air-conditioning had not yet been invented. Most factories had no heating in the winter, and workers were cold.

Factory owners were often more concerned about profits than about employees' comfort and safety. No laws existed to regulate working conditions or to protect workers.

By the Numbers / Immigration in the Mid-1800s

Sources of Immigration Newcomers came to America from many different countries in the mid-1800s, but the overwhelming majority came from Ireland and Germany.

Sources of U.S. Immigration, 1841–1860

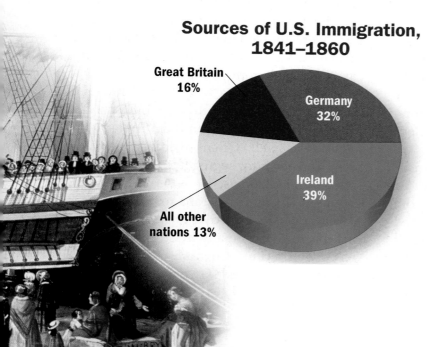

- Great Britain 16%
- Germany 32%
- Ireland 39%
- All other nations 13%

Immigration, 1820–1860

Annual immigration (in thousands) / Year

Critical Thinking

Predicting Why might people leave their homeland for another country?

Lowell Girls In Lowell, Massachusetts, the textile mills were staffed mainly by young female workers known as "Lowell girls." They toiled long hours in a hot, dangerous working environment for low wages. While they sought better working conditions, the girls had opportunities to attend social gatherings and educational programs.

> "Pleasures there are, even in factory life; and we have many. . . . Where can you find a more pleasant place for contemplation?"
> —Sarah G. Bagley, "Pleasures of Factory Life"

Power loom of the type used at the Lowell factories ▶

◀ Cover of the *Lowell Offering*, a magazine published by the women at the Lowell mills

Critical Thinking

Analyzing Refer to the quotation and the pictures, and describe what it was like to work in the Lowell mills.

Workers' Attempts to Organize

By the 1830s, workers began organizing to improve working conditions. Fearing the growth of the factory system, skilled workers formed **trade unions**—organizations of workers with the same trade, or skill. Steadily worsening working conditions also led unskilled workers to organize.

In the mid-1830s, skilled workers in New York City staged a series of **strikes.** They refused to work in order to put pressure on employers. Workers wanted to receive higher wages and to limit their workday to 10 hours. Groups of skilled workers formed the General Trades Union of New York.

In the early 1800s, going on strike was illegal. Striking workers could be punished for breaking the law, or they could be fired from their jobs. In 1842 a Massachusetts court ruled that workers did have the right to strike. It would be many years, however, before workers received other legal rights.

African American Workers

Slavery largely disappeared from the North by the 1830s. However, racial **prejudice**—an unfair opinion not based on facts—and **discrimination**—unfair treatment of a group—remained. For example, New York no longer required white men to own property in order to vote. However, few African Americans were allowed to vote. Rhode Island and Pennsylvania passed laws to keep free African Americans from voting.

Most **communities** would not allow free African Americans to attend public schools. Many communities barred them from public facilities as well. Often African Americans were forced into segregated, or separate, schools and hospitals.

A few African Americans rose in the business world. **Henry Boyd** owned a furniture manufacturing company in Cincinnati, Ohio. In 1827 **Samuel Cornish** and **John B. Russwurm** founded *Freedom's Journal*, the first African American newspaper, in New York City. In 1845 **Macon B. Allen** became the first African American **licensed,** or given official authority, to practice law in the United States. Most African Americans, however, were extremely poor.

Women Workers

Employers also discriminated against women, paying them less than male workers. Men excluded women from unions and wanted them kept out of the workplace.

Some female workers tried to organize in the 1830s and 1840s. **Sarah G. Bagley,** a weaver from Massachusetts, founded the Lowell Female Labor Reform Organization. Her group petitioned for a 10-hour workday in 1845. Because most of the petitioners were women, the legislature did not consider the petition. Women like Sarah Bagley, however, paved the way for later movements to correct the injustices against female workers.

✔ **Reading Check** **Describing** How did conditions for workers change as the factory system developed?

The Rise of Cities

Main Idea European immigrants often faced hardships and discrimination when they settled in Northern cities.

History and You Do you have Irish or German ancestors or know someone who does? Read to learn why many Irish and Germans came to the United States.

. . . .

The growth of factories and immigration—the movement of people into a country—went hand in hand with the growth of Northern cities. Both natural-born citizens and immigrants flocked to the cities, where most of the factories were located. American manufacturers welcomed immigrants, many of whom were willing to work for low pay.

Increase in Urban Population

Between 1820 and 1840, some Midwestern towns that had been small villages located along rivers developed into major cities.

Primary Source / Nativism

Anti-immigrant Sentiment Nativists feared the impact new immigrants would have on American culture. Many of the new immigrants were Catholic, while nativists were mainly Protestant. Nativists from the American Party (also called the Know-Nothing Party) tried to block immigration and limit the political rights of immigrants.

◀ American Party emblem, 1854

"Americans must rule America; *and to this end native-born citizens should be selected for all State, Federal and municipal offices of government employment, in preference to all others.*"
—the American Party platform, from the American National Convention, 1856

◀ Protestants and Catholics battle in the streets of Philadelphia in 1844 over the issue of religious instruction in the schools.

By the Numbers

Immigrants as a Percentage of the Population

1820   1860

99.5%   87%

13%

less than 1%

■ American Citizens
■ Immigrants (not naturalized)

Source: Historical Census Browser, University of Virginia

Critical Thinking

Making Connections How was the issue of religious instruction in schools related to nativism?

Many Irish immigrants journeyed to the United States in the mid-1800s. Castle Garden, the building in the upper left, was the processing facility for immigrants at that time.

1. **Interpreting** According to this cartoon, how do the British feel about the migration? How do you know?

2. **Analyzing** What reason does the cartoon suggest for why the immigrants are leaving? How do you know?

A. Uncle Sam (United States)
B. Irish immigrants
C. John Bull (Britain)
D. British lion

St. Louis, Pittsburgh, Cincinnati, and Louisville profited from their waterfront locations. They became growing centers of trade that linked the farmers of the Midwest with the cities of the Northeast. After 1830, the Great Lakes became a center for shipping, and new urban centers such as Buffalo, Detroit, Milwaukee, and Chicago arose.

The larger cities became even larger. The population of New York City, the nation's largest city, passed 800,000. Philadelphia had more than 500,000 people in 1860.

Immigration

Immigration to the United States increased dramatically between 1840 and 1860. The largest group of immigrants to the United States at that time were from Ireland. Between 1846 and 1860, more than 1.5 million Irish immigrants arrived in the country. They came to the United States because of a potato blight that destroyed most of the Irish potato crops in the 1840s. A **famine,** an extreme shortage of food, struck Ireland. More than a million people died.

Mostly farmers, the Irish immigrants were too poor to buy land. For this reason many settled in the Northeast and took low-paying factory jobs in the cities. Many of the Irish men also worked on the railroads. Accounting for nearly half of the immigrants, Irish women became servants and factory workers in the Northern cities.

The second-largest group of immigrants in the United States between 1820 and 1860 came from Germany. Some sought work and opportunity. Others came because the German democratic revolution had failed. Many arrived with enough money to buy farms or open their own business. They prospered and founded their own communities and self-help organizations. Some German immigrants settled in New York and Pennsylvania, but many moved to the Midwest and the western territories.

The Impact of Immigration

The European immigrants who came to the United States between the years of 1820 and 1860 changed the character of the country.

These people brought their languages, customs, religions, and traditions with them. Some of their ways of life filtered into American culture.

Before the early 1800s, the country had relatively few Catholics. Most of them lived around Baltimore, New Orleans, and St. Augustine. Most Irish immigrants and about one-half of the German immigrants were Roman Catholics. Many Catholic immigrants settled in cities of the Northeast. The Church provided spiritual guidance and served as a center of community life for the newcomers.

The German immigrants brought their language as well as their religion. When they settled, they founded their own publications and established musical societies.

Immigrants Face Prejudice

In the 1830s and 1840s, anti-immigrant feelings rose. Some Americans feared that immigrants were changing the character of the United States too much.

People opposed to immigration were known as **nativists.** They believed that immigration threatened the future of "native"—American-born—citizens. Some nativists accused immigrants of taking jobs from "real"

Americans and were angry that immigrants would work for lower wages. Others accused immigrants of bringing crime and disease to American cities. Immigrants who lived in city slums were likely targets of this prejudice.

The Know-Nothing Party

Nativists formed secret anti-Catholic societies. In the 1850s, they formed a new political party: the American Party. Because members of nativist groups often answered questions about their organization with the statement "I know nothing," their party came to be known as the **Know-Nothing Party.**

The Know-Nothings called for stricter citizenship laws. They wanted to extend the immigrants' waiting period for citizenship from 5 to 21 years and to ban foreign-born citizens from holding office.

In the mid-1850s, the Know-Nothing movement split into a Northern branch and a Southern branch over the question of slavery. At this time the slavery issue was also dividing the Northern and Southern states of the nation.

Reading Check **Identifying** Which two nations did most immigrants come from in the mid-1800s?

Section 2 Review

History ONLINE
Study Central™ To review this section, go to glencoe.com.

Vocabulary

1. Use each of these terms in a sentence that will help explain its meaning: trade union, strike, prejudice, discrimination, community, license, famine, nativist.

Main Ideas

2. **Listing** List some of the early attempts at work reforms in the North.

3. **Discussing** Why did some Americans object to immigration?

Critical Thinking

4. **Classifying** Create a diagram like the one below to identify the two major groups of immigrants to the United States in the first half of the 1800s and show where they settled.

Group		Area Settled
	→	
	→	

5. **Creative Writing** Imagine that you are an African American child living in the North in the mid-1800s. Write a poem in which you describe how you feel about your treatment.

Answer the Essential Question

6. How did immigration have an impact on cities, industry, and culture in the North?

Essential Question

How did the South's industry and economy differ from the industry and economy of the North?

Reading Guide

Content Vocabulary

cotton gin *(p. 401)*   capital *(p. 403)*

Academic Vocabulary

consequence *(p. 402)*   process *(p. 402)*

Key People and Events

Eli Whitney *(p. 401)*

William Gregg *(p. 403)*

Joseph Reid Anderson *(p. 403)*

Reading Strategy

Taking Notes As you read, use a diagram like the one below to show reasons cotton production grew but industrial growth was slower in the South.

Boom in Cotton Production

Slow Industrial Growth

INDIANA ACADEMIC STANDARDS
United States History

8.1.10 Compare differences in ways of life in the northern and southern states, including the growth of towns and cities in the North and the growing dependence on slavery in the South.

8.3.6 Identify the agricultural regions of the United States and be able to give reasons for the type of land use and subsequent land development during different historical periods.

8.4.6 Relate technological change and inventions to changes in labor productivity in the United States in the eighteenth and nineteenth centuries.

American Diary

"*I have just returned from Philadelphia. My business there was to lodge a Model of my machine and receive a Patent for it. I accomplished everything agreeable to my wishes. I had the satisfaction to hear it declared by a number of the first men in America that my machine is the most perfect & the most valuable invention that has ever appeared in this Country. I have received my Patent.*"

—Eli Whitney, letter to his father, March 30, 1794

Cotton gin being used on Southern plantation

Rise of the Cotton Kingdom

Main Idea The economy in the South, unlike that in the North, remained largely agricultural.

History and You What fabric is your favorite T-shirt or pair of sweats made of? Read to learn how cotton was a major economic asset to the Deep South.

. . . .

Eli Whitney transformed cotton production with his new invention, the cotton gin. To the cotton planters of the South, Whitney's cotton gin was indeed the "most perfect and the most valuable invention."

Changes in the South

In 1790 the South seemed to be an underdeveloped agricultural region. Most Southerners lived along the Atlantic coast in Maryland, Virginia, and North Carolina. This area was known as the Upper South.

By 1850 the South had changed. Its population had spread inland to the Deep South—which included Georgia, South Carolina, Alabama, Mississippi, Louisiana, and Texas.

The economy of the South was thriving. That economy depended, however, on slavery. Having all but disappeared from the North, slavery was growing stronger than ever in the South.

Cotton Rules the Deep South

In colonial times, rice, indigo, and tobacco made up the South's main crops. After the American Revolution, demand for these crops decreased. European mills now wanted Southern cotton. However, cotton took time and labor to produce. After harvest, workers had to carefully separate the plant's sticky seeds from the cotton fibers.

Cotton production was revolutionized when **Eli Whitney** invented the cotton gin in 1793. The **cotton gin** was a machine that could remove seeds from cotton fibers, dramatically increasing the amount of cotton that could be processed. A worker could clean 50 times more cotton each day with the machine than by hand. Furthermore, the gin was small enough for one person to carry from place to place.

By the Numbers / **Cotton Production, 1820–1860**

The South's Agricultural Economy Agriculture was very profitable in the South. By 1860, cotton production made up 57.5 percent of U.S. exports.

1820

Missouri / Kentucky / Virginia / North Carolina / South Carolina / Arkansas Territory / Tennessee / Miss. / Georgia / Texas (Spain) / Alabama / Louisiana / Fla. / ATLANTIC OCEAN / Gulf of Mexico

0 200 kilometers
0 200 miles
Albers Equal-Area projection

Major cotton-producing areas, 1820

1860

Missouri / Kentucky / Virginia / North Carolina / South Carolina / Arkansas / Tennessee / Miss. / Georgia / Texas / Alabama / Louisiana / Fla. / ATLANTIC OCEAN / Gulf of Mexico

0 200 kilometers
0 200 miles
Albers Equal-Area projection

Major cotton-producing areas, 1860

Critical Thinking

Predicting How might an agricultural economy increase the need for workers?

Economics & History

Productivity is the amount of goods and services a worker can produce in a given period of time, such as an hour or a day.

▲ Elias Howe's sewing machine enabled workers to make large amounts of clothing in a day.

Productivity in services increased too. The steamboat could move cotton goods to market faster. ▶

Advances in technology increased productivity in the 1800s. Before the invention of the cotton gin, a worker could produce 1 pound of cotton a day by hand. With the cotton gin, a worker could produce 50 pounds of cotton a day. This increase in productivity meant (a) farmers could grow more cotton to sell; and (b) the use of slave labor increased. By the mid-1800s, cotton made up more than one-half of U.S. exports.

Cotton Production as a Percentage of U.S. Exports

1800 — 7.1%

1820 — 32%

1840 — 51.6%

1860 — 57.5%

Source: *Historical Statistics of the United States*

Critical Thinking

1. **Making Inferences** In addition to technology, what other factors might increase productivity?
2. **Determining Cause and Effect** How do you think increases in productivity affected the price consumers paid for a cotton shirt? Why?

Whitney's invention had important **consequences,** or results. Because the cotton gin **processed,** or prepared, cotton fibers so quickly, farmers wanted to grow more cotton to increase their profits. Thus, they needed more laborers. Many Southern planters relied on slave labor to plant and pick their cotton.

By 1860 the economies of the Deep South and the Upper South had developed in different ways. Both parts of the South were agricultural. The Upper South produced tobacco, hemp, wheat, and vegetables. The Deep South was committed to cotton and, in some areas, to rice and sugarcane.

The value of enslaved people increased because of their key role in producing cotton and sugar. The Upper South became a center for the sale and transport of enslaved people throughout the region.

✔ **Reading Check** **Describing** What effect did the cotton gin have on the South's economy?

Industry in the South

Main Idea Industry developed slowly in the South for a variety of reasons.

History and You To get to school, do you take the bus, ride in a car, or walk? Read to learn how the people of the South traveled.

. . . .

The economy of the South became increasingly different from that of the North. The mostly rural South contributed only a small percentage of the nation's manufacturing value by 1860. The entire South had a lower value of manufactured goods than the state of Pennsylvania.

Barriers to Industry

There were many reasons why industry developed so slowly in the South. One reason was the boom in cotton sales. Agriculture, especially cotton, was extremely profitable.

Another stumbling block in the South was the lack of **capital**—money to invest in businesses. Planters would have had to sell enslaved people or land to raise the money to build factories. In addition, the market for manufactured goods in the South was small. The large population of enslaved people had no money to buy merchandise. This limited local market discouraged industries from developing. Yet another reason is that some Southerners simply did not want industry. One Texas politician, Louis Wigfall, summed up that Southern point of view:

PRIMARY SOURCE

"We want no manufactures: we desire no trading, no mechanical or manufacturing classes. As long as we have our rice, our sugar, our tobacco and our cotton, we can command wealth to purchase all we want."
—quoted in *Louis T. Wigfall, Southern Fire-eater*

Southern Factories

Some Southern leaders wanted to develop industry in the region. They argued that the South depended too much on the North for manufactured goods. These leaders also argued that factories would help the less prosperous economy of the Upper South.

Two Southerners shared this view. **William Gregg,** a South Carolina merchant, opened his own textile factory. In Virginia, **Joseph Reid Anderson** took over the Tredegar Iron Works and made it one of the nation's leading iron producers. During the Civil War, Tredegar provided artillery and other iron products for the Southern forces. These industries, however, were the exception rather than the rule in the South.

Southern Transportation

Natural waterways were used to transport goods in the South. Most towns were located on coasts or along rivers. Few canals existed, and roads were poor.

The South had fewer railroads than the North. Southern rail lines were short, local, and not interlinked. Thus Southern cities grew more slowly than Northern cities where railways were major routes of commerce and settlement. By 1860 only about one-third of the nation's rail lines lay within the South. This rail shortage would seriously hinder the South during the Civil War.

Reading Check **Explaining** What is capital? Why is it important for economic growth?

Section 3 Review

History ONLINE
Study Central™ To review this section, go to glencoe.com.

Vocabulary

1. Use cotton gin, consequence, process, and capital in complete sentences to define the terms.

Main Ideas

2. **Discussing** Discuss the similarities and differences between the economies of the Upper South and the Deep South around 1860.

3. **Explaining** Why did some Southerners feel that industrial growth would benefit the region?

Critical Thinking

4. **Identifying** Re-create the diagram below to show the barriers to Southern transportation.

5. **Persuasive Writing** Look again at the words of the Texas politician who said, "We want no manufactures." Add a second paragraph to his quotation that explains, in words you imagine could be his, why he opposes industry for the South.

Answer the
6. **Essential Question**

How did the South's industry and economy differ from the industry and economy of the North?

Meet the Author

Julius Lester (1939–) took inspiration for *Day of Tears* from several sources, one being a photograph of an enslaved girl, about nine years old, holding a white baby. This girl served as Emma, the main character of the novel, and Lester kept her photograph on his desk while he wrote the book.

Building Background

In *Day of Tears,* Julius Lester uses dialogue to tell the story of the largest auction of enslaved people in U.S. history, which took place in Savannah, Georgia, in 1859. More than 400 enslaved people were put up for sale. The readers hear the words and thoughts of more than 20 characters, including the enslaved and their slaveholders, as they describe the horrors of the auction. This was known as the "weeping time." As you read this excerpt from *Day of Tears,* consider how Lester's use of dialogue affects the overall theme of humanity.

Vocabulary

strident high-pitched

verge edge

coach carriage

Slave Market by Eyre Crowe ▶

DAY OF TEARS

Julius Lester

Characters

Emma 12-year-old enslaved girl

Will Emma's father

Mattie Emma's mother

Pierce Butler slaveholder

Sarah Master Butler's daughter

Frances Master Butler's daughter

emma

The lady in the long blue dress and slave-seller were looking in this direction. Ain't nothing over here for them to see. Now the slave-seller say something to Master [Butler] and then Master and the lady start talking. Master shakes his head. She talks some more. Master don't shake his head this time.

She talk some more. This time Master nods slowly. The woman holds out her hand and Master shakes it. The woman turn around and look over here again. Miss Frances is looking over this way, too. Master look like he found something very interesting on the floor to stare at. Master say something to Frances and she starts in this direction.

I see Papa. He's staring at Master and looks angry about something.

FRANCES: (*Calls out loudly as she comes near.*) Sarah! Papa wants you!

SARAH: (*Starts toward her sister, still holding Emma's hand.*) Come on, Emma. It's time to go home.

FRANCES: (*Close enough to Sarah and Emma that she doesn't have to raise her voice.*) Emma can't come.

SARAH: Why not?

FRANCES: Because. . . .

EMMA: (*Beginning to understand what she just witnessed.*) Frances? Did Master Butler sell me to that lady? Is that what they was shaking hands about?

FRANCES: (*Refuses to look at Emma.*) Come on, Sarah! Now! (*Her voice is* **strident** *and she is on the* **verge** *of tears.*) Please, Sarah! Papa wants you to come with me!

SARAH: Emma? Papa wouldn't sell you. I know he wouldn't do that.

EMMA: (*Puts her arms around Sarah and holds her tightly, blinking her eyes rapidly to hold back her own tears.*) You go on with your sister. Your papa wants you. You go on now.

SARAH: But, what about you? I want you to come.

EMMA: You go on. Everything will be all right. (*Takes her arms from* around Sarah, looks at Frances and opens her arms. Frances runs to Emma's embrace, tears trickling down her face. The two hug tightly. After a moment, Emma releases her.) You go on now. You don't want to keep your papa waiting.

* * *

mattie

I knew something terrible had happened the minute I heard that girl [Sarah] screaming. From way down the road I could hear her, and the closer they got, the louder her screaming was. I ran outside and the **coach** had hardly stopped before she was out the door and running to me.

"Papa sold Emma! Papa sold Emma!" she sobbed. . . .

I knew something terrible had happened the minute I heard that girl screaming.

[Will] got down from the coach and come over to where I was outside the door to the kitchen and he hugged me real hard and kept saying over and over, "I'm sorry, Mattie. I'm sorry," like it was his fault. Sarah was there in between us like she wanted as much of the hugging as she could get, and Will picked her up. She put one arm around my neck and one around Will's and the three of us had ourselves a good cry.

Analyzing Literature

1. **Respond** What surprised you most about Master Butler's sale of Emma?

2. **Recall and Interpret** What actions show Master Butler is unhappy about selling Emma?

3. **Evaluate**
   (a) How does the dialogue structure affect point of view in the story?
   (b) In your opinion, which character seems most sympathetic toward the slaves—Sarah, Frances, or Master Butler? Why?

The South's People

Essential Question ◄

How did unique elements of culture develop among enslaved African Americans in the South?

Reading Guide

Content Vocabulary

yeoman *(p. 407)*   spiritual *(p. 409)*

tenant farmer   slave codes
    (p. 407)   *(p. 410)*

overseer *(p. 408)*   literacy *(p. 412)*

Academic Vocabulary

legal *(p. 409)*   brief *(p. 410)*

Key People and Events

Nat Turner *(p. 410)*

Harriet Tubman *(p. 411)*

Frederick Douglass *(p. 411)*

Underground Railroad *(p. 411)*

Reading Strategy

Taking Notes As you read, use a diagram like the one below to describe the work that was done on Southern plantations.

Working on a Plantation

INDIANA ACADEMIC STANDARDS
United States History

8.1.10 Compare differences in ways of life in the northern and southern states, including the growth of towns and cities in the North and the growing dependence on slavery in the South.

8.1.16 Describe the abolition of slavery in the northern states; conflict and compromises associated with westward expansion of slavery, such as the Missouri Compromise (1820), The Compromise of 1850, Kansas-Nebraska Act (1854); and the continued resistance to slavery by people such as Frederick Douglass, Harriet Tubman, William Lloyd Garrison, and Harriet Beecher Stowe.

American Diary

"We lodged in log huts, and on the bare ground. . . . In a single room were huddled, like cattle, ten or a dozen persons, men, women, and children. . . . Our beds were collections of straw and old rags, thrown down in the corners and boxed in with boards; a single blanket the only covering. . . . The wind whistled and the rain and snow blew in through the cracks, and the damp earth soaked in the moisture till the floor was miry [muddy] as a pigsty [enclosed area where pigs live]."

—*from* Father Henson's Story of His Own Life

Former slave quarters on a plantation in South Carolina

Farms and Plantations

Main Idea The South had far more small farms than large plantations.

History and You Would you like to own your own business one day? Read to learn about what it took to keep a plantation operating.

• •

The Southern economy was based on agriculture. Enslaved workers like Josiah Henson were used to farm the land. The South before 1860 is usually portrayed as a land of stately plantations that wealthy white slaveholders owned. In reality most white Southerners were either small farmers without enslaved people or planters with a handful of enslaved workers. Most white Southerners fit into four categories: yeomen, tenant farmers, the rural poor, or plantation owners.

Small Farmers and the Rural Poor

Yeomen—farmers who did not have enslaved workers—made up the largest group of whites in the South. Most yeomen owned land, ranging from 50 to 200 acres (20 to 81 ha). They grew crops for their own use and to sell, trading produce with local merchants. Yeomen lived mostly in the Upper South and in the hilly areas of the Deep South.

Not all Southern whites owned land. Some rented land or worked as **tenant farmers** on landlords' estates. The majority of Southern whites lived in simple homes—cottages or log cabins. Others—the rural poor—lived in crude cabins in wooded areas. Looked down on by other whites, the rural poor were stubbornly independent. They were proud of being self-sufficient and avoided jobs that were normally done by enslaved people.

Plantations

A large plantation might cover several thousand acres. Plantation owners usually lived in comfortable but not luxurious farmhouses. They measured their wealth partly by the number of enslaved people they controlled. Only about 4 percent of plantation owners held 20 or more enslaved workers in 1860. Most slaveholders held fewer than 10 enslaved workers. A few free African Americans also held enslaved workers. Some free African Americans purchased members of their own families to free them.

By the Numbers / **Southern Population, 1860**

A Slaveholding Society In 1860 about 400,000 households in the South held enslaved workers. Nearly 4 million African Americans remained in slavery.

African Americans 32%

17% Whites

2%

49%

African Americans
- Enslaved
- Free

Whites
- Slaveholders
- Not slaveholders

*Total population = 12 million

Source: Geospatial and Statistical Data Center

The Legree Plantation, Capers Island, South Carolina ▶

Critical Thinking

Identifying What percentage of the total Southern population did African Americans make up?

THEN Enslaved people drew on the rhythms of their African homeland to create uniquely American musical forms. One form was the *work song* or *field holler*. A worker led a rhythmic call-and-response song, which sometimes included shouts and moans. The beat set the tempo for their work.

Conversion of enslaved African Americans to Christianity gave rise to *spirituals*, or religious folk songs. Often spirituals combined a longing for freedom with religious themes, as in "Swing Low, Sweet Chariot."

"Swing Low, Sweet Chariot"
Swing low, sweet chariot
Coming for to carry me home.
I looked over Jordan and what did I see
Coming for to carry me home
A band of angels coming after me
Coming for to carry me home

"While on their way [to work], they [the slaves] would make the dense old woods . . . [echo] with their wild songs, revealing at once the highest joy and the deepest sadness."
—Frederick Douglass, *Narrative of the Life of Frederick Douglass*

The main economic goal for large plantation owners was to earn profits. Such plantations had fixed costs. These are regular operating expenses that remain much the same year after year—housing and feeding workers, for example.

Cotton prices, however, varied from season to season, depending on the market. To receive the best prices, planters sold their cotton to agents in large cities, such as New Orleans and Charleston. The cotton exchanges, or trade centers, were of vital importance to the cotton economy. The agents extended credit—a form of loan—to the planters and held the cotton for several months until the price rose. Then the agents sold the cotton. Only at that time were the planters paid for their cotton. This system kept the planters in debt.

Plantation Wives

Wives of plantation owners took charge of their households. They supervised the buildings and the fruit and vegetable gardens. They watched over the enslaved domestic workers and sometimes tended to them when they became ill. In addition, they might keep the plantation's financial records. Their life was often difficult and lonely. Planters were often absent to deal with cotton agents. Their wives spent long periods alone.

Work on the Plantation

Large plantations needed many different kinds of workers. Some enslaved people did domestic work. They cleaned the house, cooked, did laundry and sewing, and served meals. Others were trained as blacksmiths, carpenters, shoemakers, or weavers. Still others worked in the pastures, tending the livestock. Most enslaved African Americans, however, were field hands. They worked from sunrise to sunset to plant, tend, and harvest crops. An **overseer,** or plantation manager, supervised them.

Reading Check **Identifying** What group made up the largest number of whites in the South?

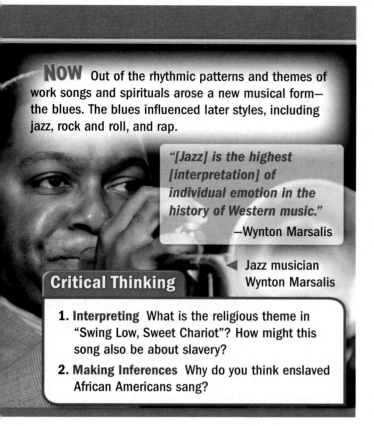

NOW Out of the rhythmic patterns and themes of work songs and spirituals arose a new musical form—the blues. The blues influenced later styles, including jazz, rock and roll, and rap.

"[Jazz] is the highest [interpretation] of individual emotion in the history of Western music."
—Wynton Marsalis

◀ Jazz musician Wynton Marsalis

Critical Thinking

1. **Interpreting** What is the religious theme in "Swing Low, Sweet Chariot"? How might this song also be about slavery?
2. **Making Inferences** Why do you think enslaved African Americans sang?

Life Under Slavery

Main Idea Despite their hardships, enslaved African Americans found methods to help them cope with their lack of freedom.

History and You Can you imagine moving to a foreign land that has different customs? Read to learn how enslaved African Americans coped with their situation.

. . . .

Enslaved African Americans suffered hardships and misery. They worked hard, earned no money, and had little hope of freedom. One of their worst fears was being sold to another planter and separated from their loved ones. In the face of these brutal conditions, they had to cope with their situation. Enslaved African Americans maintained their family life as best they could and developed a culture all their own, blending African and American elements. They resisted slavery through a variety of clever methods and looked ahead to the day when they would be set free.

Family Life

Enslaved people had few comforts beyond the bare necessities. Uncertainty and danger were constant threats in their lives. American laws in the early 1800s did not protect enslaved families. A slaveholder's death could lead to the breakup of an enslaved family. A husband or wife could be sold and moved away. Although not recognized by law, marriages between enslaved people occurred. Their marriage vows included the phrase "until death or separation do us part." Couples recognized and lived with the possibility that one of them could be sold.

Enslaved people needed some measure of stability in their lives. They established a network of relatives and friends who made up their extended family. If a father or mother were sold, an aunt, an uncle, or a close friend could raise the children left behind. Large, close-knit, extended families became a vital feature of African American culture.

African American Culture

In 1808 Congress outlawed the slave trade. Slavery remained **legal,** or permitted by law, but no new enslaved people could enter the United States. By 1860, almost all the enslaved people in the South had been born there.

These native-born African Americans held on to their African customs. They continued to perform African music and dance. They passed traditional African folk stories on to their children. Some wrapped colored cloth around their heads in the African style. Although many enslaved African Americans accepted Christianity, they often followed the religious beliefs and practices of their African ancestors as well.

African American Christianity

For many enslaved African Americans, Christianity became a religion of hope and resistance. They prayed intensely for the day when they would be free from bondage.

The passionate beliefs of the enslaved Southerners found expression in the **spiritual,** an African American religious folk song.

The spiritual below, for example, refers to the biblical story of Daniel, who was saved from the lions' den:

PRIMARY SOURCE

"Didn't my Lord deliver Daniel
Deliver Daniel, deliver Daniel
Didn't my Lord deliver Daniel
An' why not-a every man."
—from "Didn't My Lord Deliver Daniel"

Spirituals enabled enslaved people to communicate secretly among themselves. Many spirituals combined elements related to the enslaved people's Christian faith with laments about earthly suffering.

Slave Codes

Between 1830 and 1860, life under slavery became even more difficult. The **slave codes**—the laws in the Southern states that controlled enslaved people—became more severe. Slave codes had existed since the 1700s. One purpose of the codes was to prevent the event that white Southerners dreaded most—the slave rebellion. For this reason slave codes prohibited enslaved people from assembling in large groups. The codes also required enslaved people to have written passes before leaving the slaveholder's property.

Slave codes made it a crime to teach enslaved people to read or write. White Southerners feared that an educated enslaved person might start a revolt. An enslaved person who could not read and write, whites believed, was less likely to rebel.

Resistance to Slavery

Some enslaved African Americans did rebel openly against their owners. One was **Nat Turner.** He was a popular religious leader among enslaved people. Turner had taught himself to read and write. In 1831 he led a group of followers on a **brief,** or short, violent rampage in Southhampton County, Virginia. Before being captured, Turner and his followers killed at least 55 whites. Nat Turner was hanged, but his rebellion frightened white Southerners. Turner's rebellion led to more severe slave codes.

Primary Source / Slave Codes

Laws Govern Enslaved Persons Slave codes had governed the relationship between slaveholders and enslaved persons since colonial times. After the 1831 slave rebellion led by Nat Turner, harsher slave codes were enacted. Enslaved people could not own property, enter into contracts, or legally marry. Slave codes also spelled out the many restrictions that applied to free African Americans.

"The scenes that I have witnessed are enough to harrow [plow] up the soul; but could the slave be permitted to tell the story of his sufferings, which no white man, not linked with slavery, is allowed to know, the land would vomit out the horrible system, slaveholders and all, if they would not unclinch their grasp upon their defenceless victims."

—Nehemiah Caulkins,
in *American Slavery As It Is*

The punishments used against enslaved people included the use of the whip. Some slaveholders resorted to branding. ▶

Copper slave tags identified enslaved workers when they were hired out. ▶

◀ Title page of the slavery code of Alabama (1833)

Critical Thinking

Speculating What effect do you think harsher slave codes would have on enslaved people?

The Nat Turner Rebellion

Violent Uprising In 1831 Nat Turner saw an eclipse of the sun and took it to be a sign from God commanding him to kill his enemies. He and six of his men killed his slaveholder's family and then went from farm to farm, killing all the whites they encountered. Turner and his followers were caught and executed, but slaveholders lived in fear of another violent uprising.

While in jail, Turner was interviewed by Thomas Gray, who recorded his confession. ▶

Nat Turner and his followers meet in the woods to plan their uprising. ▼

"The course has been by no means a direct one. [Northern traders] began first by making [the slaves] religious . . . telling the blacks . . . the black man was as good as the white; that all men were born free and equal; that they can not serve two masters."

—Governor John Floyd of Virginia, in a letter responding to the rebellion, 1831

"And about this time I had a vision, and I saw white spirits and black spirits engaged in battle, and the sun was darkened; the thunder rolled in the heavens, and blood flowed in streams; and I heard a voice saying, '. . . let it come, rough or smooth, you must surely bear it.'"

—*The Confessions of Nat Turner*

Critical Thinking

1. **Interpreting** To what "two masters" was Governor John Floyd referring?
2. **Determining Cause and Effect** According to Floyd and Nat Turner, what were the causes of the rebellion?

Armed revolts were rare, however. African Americans in the South knew that they would only lose. For the most part, enslaved people resisted slavery by working slowly or by pretending to be ill. Occasionally resistance was more active. Some enslaved workers would set fire to a plantation building or break tools. Resistance helped enslaved African Americans tolerate their lack of freedom. Even if they were not free, they could strike back at the slaveholders. Resistance also helped set boundaries that slaveholders would respect.

Escaping Slavery

Some enslaved African Americans tried to run away to the North. A few succeeded. **Harriet Tubman** and **Frederick Douglass** were two African American leaders who were born into slavery. They both gained their freedom when they fled to the North.

Getting to the North was difficult for most enslaved people. Most who succeeded escaped from the states of the Upper South.

The **Underground Railroad** offered aid to enslaved people who had escaped. It was a network of "safe houses" owned by free blacks and whites who opposed slavery.

Some enslaved people sought to find relatives on plantations or to escape punishment. Rarely did they plan to flee to the North. Moses Grandy, who did escape, spoke about the problems runaways faced:

PRIMARY SOURCE

"They hide themselves during the day in the woods and swamps; at night they travel. . . . In these dangerous journeys they are guided by the north-star, for they only know that the land of freedom is in the north."

—from *Narrative of the Life of Moses Grandy*

Most runaways were caught and returned to their owners. Discipline was severe. The most common punishment was whipping.

✔ **Reading Check** **Explaining** How did the African American spiritual develop?

City Life and Education

Main Idea By the mid-1800s, the South had several large cities, and education had begun to expand throughout the region.

History and You How far do you travel to get to your school? Read to learn why some Southern families may not have been able to send their children to school.

. . . .

The South was primarily agricultural. It had several large cities by the mid-1800s, however, including Baltimore and New Orleans. The ten largest cities in the South were either seaports or river ports.

Life in Southern Cities

Cities located at the crossroads of the railways also began to grow. Among them were Chattanooga, Montgomery, and Atlanta. Whites, enslaved workers, and many free African Americans lived in cities.

In the cities, free African Americans had the opportunity to form their own communities. They practiced trades and founded churches and institutions. Free African Amer-icans' lives were not secure. Their rights were limited. Most states would not allow them to move from state to state. Free African Americans were denied an equal share in economic and political life.

Education

During this era, no statewide public school systems existed. People who could afford to do so sent their children to private schools. Some of the larger cities established public schools. By the mid-1800s, however, education was growing. North Carolina and Kentucky set up and ran public schools.

The South was behind other sections of the country in **literacy,** the number of people able to read and write. One reason for this situation was the South's geography. The South had few people per square mile. Many families could not send their children great distances to attend school. In addition, many Southerners believed that education was a private matter, not a state function.

✓ Reading Check **Identifying** Why did Southern cities such as Atlanta and Montgomery grow?

Section 4 Review

History ONLINE
Study Central™ To review this section, go to glencoe.com.

Vocabulary

1. Using complete sentences, define the following terms: yeoman, tenant farmer, overseer, legal, spiritual, slave code, brief, literacy.

Main Ideas

2. **Describing** Other than plantation owners, what kinds of farmers existed in the South?

3. **Discussing** How did the family structure of enslaved African Americans help them survive life under slavery?

4. **Explaining** Why did education in the South lag behind other areas of the United States?

Critical Thinking

5. **Organizing** Use a diagram like the one below to keep track of key people, events, and practices in resistance to slavery.

Resistance to Slavery

6. **Persuasive Writing** Write a dialogue between an enslaved husband and wife. One wants to try to escape to the North, and the other argues against doing so.

Answer the
7. **Essential Question**
How did unique elements of culture develop among enslaved African Americans in the South?

Visual Summary

Comparing North and South

The North and the South developed differently during the first half of the 1800s. The North built an industrial economy, while the South pursued an agricultural economy based on slavery. Those economies influenced the labor force and the development of transportation in the regions.

Plantation workers using a cotton gin ▶

	North	South
Economy	• Industrial • New technology fuels growth of industry • Industry develops rapidly Power loom ▶	• Agricultural • Revolutionary cotton gin makes cotton crop highly profitable • Industry develops slowly
People	 • Immigrants, including many from Ireland, work factory jobs • Slavery has mostly disappeared by 1830s, but racial prejudice and discrimination remain ◀ Mill workers	• The South had more small farms than large plantations • Most small farmers work land themselves • Slavery on large cotton plantations grows due to increased demand for labor • By 1860 about 4 million African Americans lived under slavery
Transportation	• Roads, canals, and railroads are built for transportation and shipping	• Natural waterways for shipping; fewer railroads are built than in the North

◀ Steamboats in Cincinnati

INDIANA STATEWIDE TEST PRACTICE

TEST-TAKING **TIP**

To understand the questions better, rewrite them in your own words, if you have time. Be careful not to change the meaning.

Reviewing Vocabulary

Directions: Choose the word or words that best completes the sentence.

1 The invention of the _____ in the 1840s greatly improved communications over great distances.

   A telephone
   B telegraph
   C airplane
   D railroad

2 A(n) _____, an extreme shortage of food, struck Ireland in the 1840s.

   A surplus
   B famine
   C accumulation
   D overabundance

3 Money used to invest in business is called _____.

   A stock
   B capital
   C tariffs
   D welfare

4 The South lagged behind other parts of the nation in _____, the number of people able to read and write.

   A media
   B logic
   C grammar
   D literacy

Reviewing Main Ideas

Directions: Choose the best answer.

5 Labor unions were formed for all of the following reasons EXCEPT

   A to improve workers' wages.
   B to protect factory owners from being sued.
   C to make factories safer.
   D to prevent children from working long hours.

6 What was the main reason that the Southern economy remained largely agricultural?

   A Southerners lacked the capital to start industries.
   B Cotton sales were very profitable.
   C Southerners refused to work in factories.
   D Costs to ship goods to markets were too high.

7 The largest group of whites in the South were

   A yeomen.
   B tenant farmers.
   C the rural poor.
   D plantation owners.

8 The Southern laws that controlled enslaved people were called

   A spirituals.
   B overseers.
   C credits.
   D slave codes.

GO ON ▶

History ONLINE

For additional test practice, use **Self-Check Quizzes**—Chapter 13 at glencoe.com.

Critical Thinking

Directions: Choose the best answer.

9 **What happened in the first phase of industrialization in the North?**

   A Factory workers used machinery to perform some of their tasks.

   B Manufacturers made products by dividing the tasks among workers.

   C Water and steam power were used to produce more products in less time.

   D Manufacturers built factories to bring specialized workers together.

Base your answer to question 10 on the map below and your knowledge of Chapter 13.

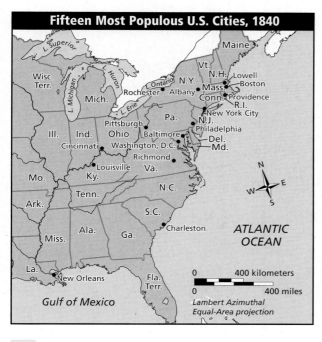

Fifteen Most Populous U.S. Cities, 1840

10 **The information on the map shows that**

   A cities grew more rapidly in the North.

   B Southern rail lines connected all parts of the South.

   C the North Atlantic Coast did not have many cities.

   D Southern cities were growing more quickly than those in the North and Midwest.

Constructed Response

Directions: Write a short response to each of the following questions. In your answer:

- *address all parts of the question*
- *use information from the chapter*
- *include facts, examples, and details relevant to the question*
- *use clear language*

Base your answer to question 11 on the table below and your knowledge of Chapter 13.

Occupational Distribution of American Workers

	1820	1860
Agriculture	79%	53%
Mining	0.4%	1.6%
Construction	—	4.7%
Manufacturing	3%	14%
Trade	—	8%
Transport	1.6%	6.4%
Service	4.1%	6.4%

11 **Explain how the technological innovations of the early 1800s affected the change in the percentage of Americans working in agriculture and manufacturing.**

12 **Discuss two reasons for the rapid growth of Northern cities in the early 1800s.**

13 **What was the Underground Railroad? How would enslaved African Americans view the Underground Railroad? How would Southern slaveholders view it?**

STOP

Need Extra Help?													
If You Missed Questions...	1	2	3	4	5	6	7	8	9	10	11	12	13
Go to Page...	391	398	403	412	396	402	407	410	389	397	389	398	411

The Age of Reform 1820–1860

During the 1800s, most American students attended one-room schools.

PRESIDENTS

U.S. Events

World Events

JAMES MONROE 1817–1825

★ **1821** Sequoya develops Cherokee alphabet

 JOHN Q. ADAMS 1825–1829

★ **1827** New York bans slavery

ANDREW JACKSON 1829–1837

★ **1830** *Book of Mormon* published

 MARTIN VAN BUREN 1837–1841

1820

1830

★ **1821** Mexico becomes independent nation

★ **1837** Victoria becomes queen of England

History ONLINE
Chapter Overview Visit glencoe.com
and click on **Chapter 14—Chapter
Overviews** to preview chapter information.

Section 1: Social Reform

Essential Question How did religion influence the social reforms in the United States during the early and mid-1800s?

Section 2: The Abolitionists

Essential Question How did abolitionists influence the antislavery movement?

Section 3: The Women's Movement

Essential Question What were the effects of the women's rights movement of the middle to late 1800s?

FOLDABLES
Study Organizer

Organizing Information
Make this Foldable to organize what you learn about the reform movements of the 1800s.

Step 1 Fold a sheet of paper in half lengthwise.

Step 2 Fold the paper into three equal sections.

Step 3 Cut the folds on the top flap.

Step 4 Label the tabs as shown.

Reform and Society | Reform and Slavery | Reform and Women

Reading and Writing As you read the chapter, take notes in your Foldable about how reformers addressed problems in society and issues facing enslaved people and women.

Elizabeth Cady Stanton at the Seneca Falls Convention ▶

WILLIAM HENRY HARRISON 1841

JOHN TYLER 1841–1845

JAMES POLK 1845–1849

★ **1848** Seneca Falls Convention held

ZACHARY TAYLOR 1849–1850

MILLARD FILLMORE 1850–1853

FRANKLIN PIERCE 1853–1857

JAMES BUCHANAN 1857–1861

1840   **1850**   **1860**

★ **1843** Maori revolt against British in New Zealand

★ **1847** Liberia claims independence

★ **1850** Taiping Rebellion begins in China

★ **1853** Crimean War begins

★ **1859** Belgian inventor Lenoir builds first practical internal-combustion engine

Social Reform

Essential Question ◄

How did religion influence the social reforms in the United States during the early and mid-1800s?

Reading Guide

Content Vocabulary

revival
(p. 419)

normal school
(p. 420)

utopia
(p. 419)

transcendentalist
(p. 421)

temperance
(p. 419)

civil disobedience
(p. 421)

Academic Vocabulary

lecture (p. 419)   author (p. 421)

Key People and Events

Second Great Awakening (p. 419)

temperance movement (p. 419)

Reading Strategy

Taking Notes As you read, use a diagram like the one below to identify the reformers' contributions.

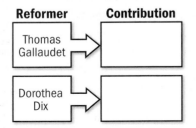

Reformer	Contribution
Thomas Gallaudet →	
Dorothea Dix →	

INDIANA ACADEMIC STANDARDS
United States History

8.1.19 Explain the influence of early individual social reformers and movements.

8.1.24 Identify the influence of individuals on political and social events and movements such as the abolition movement, the Dred Scott case, women's rights, and Native American Indian removal.

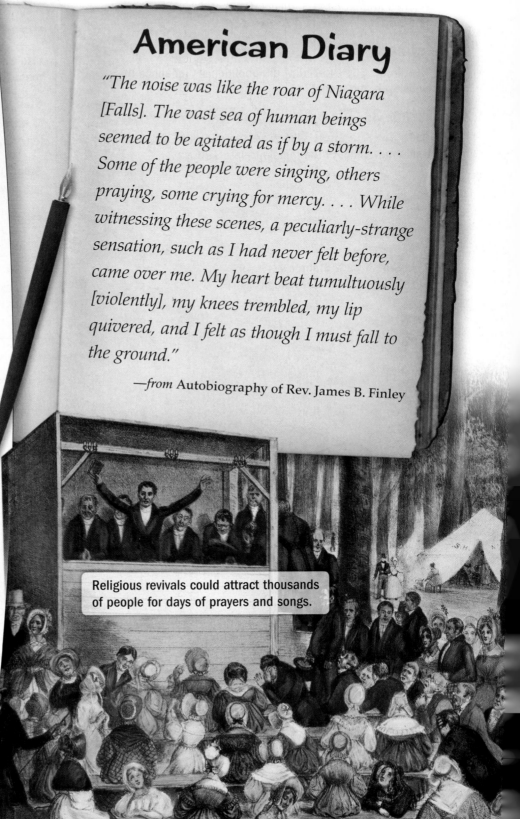

American Diary

"The noise was like the roar of Niagara [Falls]. The vast sea of human beings seemed to be agitated as if by a storm. . . . Some of the people were singing, others praying, some crying for mercy. . . . While witnessing these scenes, a peculiarly-strange sensation, such as I had never felt before, came over me. My heart beat tumultuously [violently], my knees trembled, my lip quivered, and I felt as though I must fall to the ground."

—from Autobiography of Rev. James B. Finley

Religious revivals could attract thousands of people for days of prayers and songs.

Religion and Reform

Main Idea The Second Great Awakening influenced social and educational reforms.

History and You Do you volunteer to help people, such as the elderly, with their daily chores? You are probably familiar with individuals or organizations who help people in need. Read about how reformers felt a responsibility to help others.

. . . .

Religious camp meetings, called **revivals,** were quite common in the early 1800s. People would travel great distances to hear preachers speak and to pray, sing, weep, and shout. This was the time when a wave of religious fervor—known as the **Second Great Awakening**—stirred the nation. The first Great Awakening had spread through the colonies in the mid-1700s.

There was a new spirit of reform throughout America in the early 1800s. This spirit brought changes to American religion, education, and literature. Some reformers sought to improve society by forming **utopias.** These communities were based on a vision of the

perfect society. However, most were founded on impractical ideas and only a few groups, like the Mormons, were able to establish stable, lasting communities.

The Religious Influence

Attending revivals often made men and women eager to reform both their own lives and the world. Some people became involved in missionary work and social reform movements. Among those movements was the push to ban alcohol.

Lyman Beecher, a Connecticut minister, crusaded against the use of alcohol. He wanted to protect society from "rum-selling, tippling folk, infidels [nonbelievers], and ruffscruff." Beecher and other reformers called for **temperance,** drinking little or no alcohol. They used **lectures,** pamphlets, and revival-style rallies to warn people of the dangers of liquor.

The **temperance movement** led to some victories when Maine and other states passed laws banning the manufacture and sale of alcoholic beverages. Most of these laws, however, were later repealed, or canceled.

Primary Source / Responsibility for Others

Helping Others Reformer Dorothea Dix encouraged others to help the less fortunate. She said, "Become the [protectors] of your race, the just guardians of the solemn rights you hold in trust. Raise up the fallen, [aid] the desolate, restore the outcast, defend the helpless, and for your eternal and great reward receive the [blessing].'"

—from *Memorial to the Massachusetts Legislature*

Dorothea Dix ▶

Critical Thinking

Comparing Do you know any people today who share beliefs similar to Second Great Awakening reformers? What are their beliefs?

This cartoon, by Nathaniel Currier, is titled "The Drunkard's Progress." It was created in 1846, during the temperance movement.

1. **Summarizing** How would you describe the "progress" from step 1 through step 9?

2. **Making Inferences** Who do the people under the arch represent? Why are they shown in the cartoon?

Reforming Education

Reformers also wanted to improve education. In the mid-1850s, most schools were poorly funded, and many teachers lacked training. Some people opposed compulsory, or required, education.

In addition, restrictions were placed on who could attend school. Girls were often excluded because parents thought education was wasted on future wives and mothers. Many African Americans were also denied the right to attend school.

Massachusetts lawyer Horace Mann was a leader of educational reform. Partly because of his efforts, in 1839 Massachusetts founded the nation's first state-supported **normal school** where high-school graduates were trained to become teachers. Other states soon adopted Mann's reforms.

Many new colleges and universities were created during the age of reform. Most admitted only men, but gradually, higher education became available to groups that had been denied the opportunity. Oberlin College of Ohio, for example, founded in 1833, admitted both women and African Americans.

People With Special Needs

Some reformers focused on the problem of teaching people with disabilities. Thomas Gallaudet (GA•luh•DEHT) developed a method to educate people who were hearing impaired. He opened the Hartford School for the Deaf in Connecticut in 1817. At about the same time, Samuel Gridley Howe advanced the cause of people who were visually impaired. He developed books with large raised letters that people with sight impairments could "read" with their fingers. Howe headed the Perkins Institute, a school for the blind, in Boston.

Schoolteacher Dorothea Dix began visiting prisons in 1841. She found some prisoners chained to the walls with little or no clothing, often in unheated cells. Dix also learned that some of the inmates were guilty of no crime. They were people who were mentally ill. Dix made it her life's work to educate the public about the poor conditions for prisoners and the mentally ill.

✓ **Reading Check** **Identifying** How did Samuel Howe help the visually impaired?

Cultural Trends

Main Idea A distinct type of American literature emerged in the 1820s.

History and You Have you read works by Thoreau, Emerson, or Dickinson? Read to learn how these writers changed American literature.

· ·

The changes in American society also influenced art and literature. Beginning in the 1820s, American artists developed their own style and explored American themes.

The American spirit of reform influenced the **transcendentalists.** These thinkers and writers stressed the relationship between humans and nature and the importance of the individual conscience. Margaret Fuller, Ralph Waldo Emerson, and Henry David Thoreau were leading transcendentalists.

Through her writings, Fuller supported women's rights. In his works, Emerson urged people to listen to the inner voice of conscience and to overcome prejudice. Thoreau practiced **civil disobedience** by refusing to obey laws he considered unjust. In 1846 Thoreau went to jail rather than pay a tax to support the Mexican War.

Numerous poets also created great works during this period. Henry Wadsworth Longfellow wrote narrative, or story, poems such as the *Song of Hiawatha*. Poet Walt Whitman captured the new American spirit and confidence in his *Leaves of Grass*. Emily Dickinson wrote simple, deeply personal poems. In a poem called "Hope," written in 1861, she compares hope to a bird:

PRIMARY SOURCE

"'Hope' is the thing with feathers—
That perches in the soul—
And sings the tune without the words—
And never stops—at all—"
— from *Emily Dickinson: Selected Poems*

During this time, women were the **authors** of the most popular fiction. Harriet Beecher Stowe wrote the most successful best-seller of the mid-1800s, *Uncle Tom's Cabin*. Stowe's novel explores the injustice of slavery, an issue that took on new urgency during the age of reform.

✓ **Reading Check** Identifying Cause and Effect How did the spirit of reform influence American authors?

Section 1 Review

History ONLINE
Study Central™ To review this section, go to glencoe.com.

Vocabulary

1. Use the following key terms to write a paragraph about social reform: revival, utopia, temperance, lecture, normal school, transcendentalist, civil disobedience, author.

Main Ideas

2. **Identifying** What problems spurred reform in the area of education?

3. **Explaining** What themes did the transcendentalists focus on in their writings?

Critical Thinking

4. **Synthesizing** In what ways did the writers of the mid-1800s demonstrate the American spirit of the times?

5. **Analyzing** What reforms resulted from the Second Great Awakening? Use a diagram like the one below to organize your answer.

Second Great Awakening

6. **Persuasive Writing** Create a brochure about the newly established Oberlin College to send to potential students. Explain why the college differs from others, and describe the advantages of this college experience.

7. **Answer the Essential Question**
How did religion influence the social reforms in the United States during the early and mid-1800s?

TIME NOTEBOOK

What were people's lives like in the past?

These two pages will give you some clues to everyday life in the United States as you step back in time with TIME Notebook.

PHOTO RESEARCHERS

Profile

"My best friends solemnly regard me as a madman." That's what the artist **JOHN JAMES AUDUBON** *writes about himself in his journal. And he does seem to be a bit peculiar. After all, he put a band around a bird's foot so he could tell if it returned from the South in the spring. No one's ever done that before. Audubon is growing more famous thanks to his drawings. His love of the wild and his skill as an artist have awakened a new sense of appreciation for animal life in the United States. Here is what he wrote while on a trip to New Orleans in 1821.*

"I took a walk with my gun this afternoon to see . . . millions of Golden Plovers [medium-sized shorebirds] coming from the northeast and going nearly south—the destruction . . . was really astonishing—the Sportsmen here are more numerous and at the same time more expert at shooting on the wing than anywhere in the United States. . . . 400 Gunners were out. Supposing that each man killed 40 dozen that day, 192,000 plovers must have been destroyed."

PLUVIALIS DOMINICA, AMERICAN GOLDEN PLOVER, DRAWN BY AUDUBON

THE NATURAL HISTORY MUSEUM / ALAMY

Wright & Ditson REGULATION. LEAGUE BALL

SPORTS

Baseball for Beginners

Want to take up the new game of baseball? Keep your eye on the ball— because the rules keep changing!

1845

- bases are set 90 feet (27 m) apart in a diamond shape
- only nine men play on each side
- pitches are thrown underhand
- a ball caught on the first bounce is an "out"

1846

- at first base, a fielder can tag the bag before the runner reaches it and so make an out

1847

- players may no longer throw the ball at a runner to put him out

NORTH WIND PICTURE ARCHIVES / ALAMY

Going for the Gold?

You probably know the 1849 rush of gold seekers to California has given us new phrases like pay dirt, pan out, *and* strike it rich. *But are you aware that the demands of all those people have reduced supplies and sent prices skyrocketing? See if you can match the item below with the price you'd pay for it in California—thanks to the Gold Rush.*

1. Barrel of flour   a. $36
2. Dozen eggs   b. $800
3. A shovel   c. $100
4. Barrel of sugar   d. $400

Pretty steep when you remember that most workers are only making about $2 a day!

Answers: 1. b; 2. a; 3. c; 4. d

NUMBERS

UNITED STATES AT THE TIME

0 Amount of national debt in 1835 and 1836. During the Jackson administration, the United States entirely paid off its national debt

30 Number of minutes a person has to sit to have a photo taken to get the correct exposure in 1839

300 Number of families who traveled with Stephen Austin as the first American colonists to the Mexican state of Texas in 1821 and 1822

3,000 Number of pioneers who took the Overland trails west in 1845; many people headed for the Willamette Valley in Oregon, while others followed the newly improved California Trail over the Sierra Nevada to California

MILESTONES

EVENTS AND PEOPLE OF THE TIME

INVENTED. The first sewing machine in the United States by Walter Hunt in 1834. Too bad Hunt didn't bother to patent his invention—Elias Howe patented his own sewing machine a few years later and grew extremely rich. Hunt *did* patent the first fountain pen and the first repeating rifle. He also invented the safety pin after four hours of twisting wire. It's a billion-dollar idea—so why did he sell the patent rights for only $100?

MARCHED. 17,000 Cherokee forced by federal troops from their Georgia homeland to reservations in the West from 1838 to 1839. About 4,000 Native Americans died on the 116-day-long march, now known as the "Trail of Tears."

EMIGRATED. In 1845, to England, Frederick Douglass, former slave, author, and abolitionist leader, to escape danger in reaction to his autobiography, *Narrative of the Life of Frederick Douglass.*

BETTMANN / CORBIS

ELIAS HOWE'S SEWING MACHINE

CRITICAL THINKING

Theorizing Why do you think pioneers sang or played tunes around campfires? Are those reasons similar to why people play or sing music today? Explain your answer.

Hypothesizing Why do you think prices of everyday items skyrocketed during the Gold Rush?

The Abolitionists

Essential Question

How did abolitionists influence the antislavery movement?

Reading Guide

Content Vocabulary
abolitionist *(p. 425)*
Underground Railroad *(p. 430)*

Academic Vocabulary
route *(p. 430)*   medical *(p. 431)*

Key People and Events
American Colonization Society *(p. 425)*
William Lloyd Garrison *(p. 426)*
Sarah Grimké *(p. 427)*
Angelina Grimké *(p. 427)*
David Walker *(p. 428)*
Frederick Douglass *(p. 428)*
Sojourner Truth *(p. 429)*
Elijah Lovejoy *(p. 431)*

Reading Strategy
Taking Notes As you read, use a diagram like the one below to identify five abolitionists. Below each name, write a brief description of his or her role in the movement.

Abolitionists

INDIANA ACADEMIC STANDARDS
United States History

8.1.16 Describe the abolition of slavery in the northern states; conflict and compromises associated with westward expansion of slavery, such as the Missouri Compromise (1820), The Compromise of 1850, Kansas-Nebraska Act (1854); and the continued resistance to slavery by people such as Frederick Douglass, Harriet Tubman, William Lloyd Garrison, and Harriet Beecher Stowe.

American Diary

Sojourner Truth was an enslaved woman who gained her freedom in 1827. Although she lacked a formal education, her eloquent and deeply religious antislavery speeches attracted huge crowds. Truth believed that just as African Americans deserved equal rights, so too did women. Sojourner Truth's most famous speech, "Ain't I a Woman?", was given in Akron, Ohio, in 1851. Truth asked, "I have plowed and reaped and husked and chopped and mowed, and can any man do more than that?"

—quoted in Sojourner Truth As Orator

Enslaved children work outside their living quarters in Savannah, Georgia.

Early Efforts to End Slavery

Main Idea During the early 1800s, some Americans began to call for an end to slavery.

History and You What issues divide our nation today? Read to learn how the issue of slavery continued to divide the nation in the early 1800s.

· ·

The spirit of reform that swept the United States in the early 1800s was not limited to improving education and expanding the arts. It also included the efforts of **abolitionists** like Sojourner Truth. Abolitionists were among the growing band of reformers who worked to abolish, or end, slavery.

Even before the American Revolution, some Americans had tried to limit or end slavery. At the Constitutional Convention in 1787, the delegates did not agree on this difficult issue. Instead, they reached a compromise by agreeing to let each state decide whether to allow slavery. By the early 1800s, slavery had ended in the Northern states. It continued, however, to be a part of the economy in Southern states.

The reform movement of the early and mid-1800s gave new life to the antislavery movement. Many Americans came to believe that slavery was wrong. Yet not all Northerners shared this view. The conflict over slavery continued to build.

Many who led the antislavery movement came from the Quaker faith. One Quaker, Benjamin Lundy, founded a newspaper in 1821 to spread the abolitionist message. He wrote:

PRIMARY SOURCE

"I heard the wail of the captive, I felt his pang of distress, and the iron entered my soul."
—quoted in "The Underground Railroad in Ohio"

American Colonization Society

The first large-scale antislavery effort was not aimed at abolishing slavery. Its aim was to resettle African Americans in Africa or the Caribbean. The **American Colonization Society,** formed in 1816 by a group of white Virginians, freed enslaved workers by buying them from slaveholders and sending them abroad to start new lives.

Time Line / The Abolition Movement

Early Opposition Early antislavery societies called for a gradual end to slavery. In the 1830s, however, more groups were inspired by the American reform movement and argued that enslaved people should be freed immediately.

★ **1787** States given authority to decide whether to allow slavery

★ **1831** William Lloyd Garrison begins publishing *The Liberator*

★ **1833** American Anti-Slavery Society founded

★ **1816** American Colonization Society founded

★ **1832** New England Anti-Slavery Society founded

★ **1840s** Sojourner Truth's speeches draw huge crowds

Critical Thinking

Making Inferences Why do you think some people supported a gradual end to slavery?

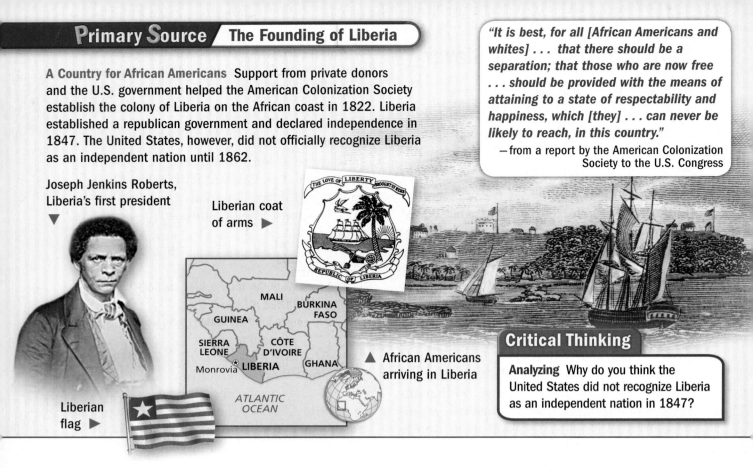

A Country for African Americans Support from private donors and the U.S. government helped the American Colonization Society establish the colony of Liberia on the African coast in 1822. Liberia established a republican government and declared independence in 1847. The United States, however, did not officially recognize Liberia as an independent nation until 1862.

"It is best, for all [African Americans and whites] . . . that there should be a separation; that those who are now free . . . should be provided with the means of attaining to a state of respectability and happiness, which [they] . . . can never be likely to reach, in this country."

—from a report by the American Colonization Society to the U.S. Congress

Joseph Jenkins Roberts, Liberia's first president ▼

Liberian coat of arms ▶

▲ African Americans arriving in Liberia

Liberian flag ▶

Critical Thinking

Analyzing Why do you think the United States did not recognize Liberia as an independent nation in 1847?

The society raised money from private donors, Congress, and a few state legislatures to send several groups of African Americans out of the country. Some traveled to the west coast of Africa, where the society acquired land for a colony. The first African American settlers arrived in this colony, called Liberia—Latin for "place of freedom"—in 1822. Some 12,000 to 20,000 African Americans settled in the new country between 1822 and 1865.

The American Colonization Society did not stop the growth of slavery. The number of enslaved people continued to increase. The society could resettle only a small number of African Americans. Furthermore, most African Americans did not want to go to Africa. Many were from families that had lived in America for generations. They simply wanted to be free in American society. Some African Americans feared that the society might actually strengthen slavery.

Reading Check **Explaining** How did the American Colonization Society fight slavery?

The Movement Changes

Main Idea Beginning in the 1830s, slavery became the most pressing issue for reformers.

History and You Is there a leader or a person whom you admire? Does he or she stand up for others? Read to learn how abolitionists worked to end slavery.

Reformers realized that the gradual approach to ending slavery had failed. Moreover, the numbers of enslaved persons had sharply increased because the cotton boom in the Deep South made planters increasingly dependent on slave labor. Beginning in about 1830, the American antislavery movement took on new life. Slavery became the most pressing social issue for reformers.

William Lloyd Garrison

Massachusetts abolitionist **William Lloyd Garrison** had a great influence on the antislavery movement. In 1831, he started the antislavery newspaper, *The Liberator*.

Garrison was one of the first white abolitionists to call for the immediate freeing of enslaved people. He denounced the slow, gradual approach of other reformers. In the first issue of his paper, he wrote, "*I will be* as harsh as truth, and as uncompromising as justice. . . . I will not retreat a single inch—AND I WILL BE HEARD."

Garrison *was* heard. He attracted enough followers to start the New England Anti-Slavery Society in 1832 and the American Anti-Slavery Society the next year. The abolitionist movement grew rapidly. By 1838, the antislavery societies Garrison started had more than 1,000 chapters, or local branches.

The Grimké Sisters

Among the first women who spoke out publicly against slavery were **Sarah** and **Angelina Grimké.** The sisters were born in South Carolina to a wealthy slaveholding family. The women moved to Philadelphia in 1832. While living in the North, the Grimké sisters lectured and wrote against slavery. At one antislavery meeting, Angelina Grimké exclaimed:

PRIMARY SOURCE

"As a Southerner I feel that it is my duty to stand up . . . against slavery. I have seen it—I have seen it."
—from a speech at Pennsylvania Hall

The Grimkés persuaded their mother to give them their share of the family inheritance. Instead of money or land, the sisters asked for several of the enslaved workers, whom they immediately freed.

The Grimkés and Angelina's husband, abolitionist Theodore Weld, wrote *American Slavery As It Is* in 1839. This book collected firsthand accounts of life under slavery. It was one of the most powerful abolitionist publications of its time.

History ONLINE
Student Web Activity Visit glencoe.com and complete the Chapter 14 Web Activity about African American abolitionists.

People IN HISTORY

Harriet Beecher Stowe

Author of Uncle Tom's Cabin

Stowe wrote many books and stories about social reform. *Uncle Tom's Cabin*, published in 1852, was her most famous work. The novel shows slavery as a cruel and brutal system. Stowe later said that while she was writing it, "My heart was bursting with the anguish excited by the cruelty and injustice our nation was showing to the slave." *Uncle Tom's Cabin* had a major impact on public feelings about slavery. Even President Abraham Lincoln is claimed to have said that Harriet Beecher Stowe wrote the book that started the American Civil War.

CRITICAL Thinking

1. **Analyzing** Why did Stowe write *Uncle Tom's Cabin*?
2. **Evaluating** Why do you think Stowe might be accused of starting a civil war?

Different Views In the 1820s, antislavery sentiment strengthened in the North. Abolitionists formed the American Anti-Slavery Society in 1833. The Society attacked slavery in its literature and speeches. In response, Southerners developed a theory to defend slavery.

"As slaveholders and their apologists are . . . flooding the world with testimony that their slaves are kindly treated; that they are well fed, well clothed, well housed, well lodged, moderately worked, and bountifully provided with all things needful for their comfort. . . . We will prove that the slaves in the United States are treated with barbarous inhumanity."

▲ Theodore Weld —from *American Slavery As It Is*

▲ In an announcement for a meeting of the Massachusetts Anti-Slavery Society, a poem by John Greenleaf Whittier was included:

"On, woman! from thy happy hearth
Extend thy gentle hand to save
The poor and perishing of earth—
The chained and stricken slave!
Oh, plead for all the suffering of thy kind—
For the crushed body and the darkened mind."

African American Abolitionists

African Americans also played a major role in the abolitionist movement. The abolition of slavery was an especially important goal to the free African Americans of the North.

Most African Americans in the North lived in poverty in cities. They were excluded from most jobs. White mobs often attacked them. These African Americans, however, were proud of their freedom, and many wanted to help those who were still enslaved.

African Americans helped organize and direct the American Anti-Slavery Society. They subscribed in large numbers to *The Liberator.* In 1827 Samuel Cornish and John Russwurm started the country's first African American newspaper, *Freedom's Journal.*

Born a free man in North Carolina, writer **David Walker** of Boston published his argument against slavery. He challenged African Americans to rebel and overthrow slavery. He wrote, "America is more our country than it is the whites'—we have enriched it with our blood and tears."

In 1830 free African American leaders held their first convention in Philadelphia. Delegates met "to devise ways and means for the bettering of our condition." They discussed starting an African American college and encouraging free African Americans to emigrate to Canada.

Frederick Douglass

Frederick Douglass, the most widely known African American abolitionist, was born enslaved in Maryland. After teaching himself to read and write, he escaped from slavery in Maryland in 1838. He settled first in Massachusetts and then moved to New York.

As a runaway, Douglass could have been captured and returned to slavery. Still, he joined the Massachusetts Anti-Slavery Society. He traveled widely to address abolitionist meetings. Douglass was a powerful speaker who often moved listeners to tears with his message. At an Independence Day gathering, he told the audience:

◀ Selling enslaved people at auction

▲ Defenders of slavery described plantations as ideal settings where enslaved persons were well treated.

▲ Poster announcing the raffle of a horse and an enslaved female

"In all social systems there must be a class to do the menial duties, to perform the drudgery of life. That is, a class requiring but a low order of intellect and but little skill. . . . Such a class you must have, or you would not have that other class which leads progress, civilization, and refinement. . . . Fortunately for the South, she found a race adapted to that purpose."
—Senator James Henry Hammond in a speech to Congress, 1858

Critical Thinking

Analyzing Primary Sources What pro-slavery arguments are discussed in the quotations from Weld and Hammond?

PRIMARY SOURCE

"What, to the American slave, is your 4th of July? I answer; a day that reveals to him, more than all other days in the year, the gross injustice and cruelty to which he is the constant victim. To him, your celebration is a sham . . . your national greatness, swelling vanity; your sounds of rejoicing are empty and heartless; . . . your shouts of liberty and equality, hollow mockery."
—from *Frederick Douglass: Selected Speeches and Writings*

Douglass was editor of the antislavery newspaper *North Star* and won admiration as a powerful and influential speaker and writer. He even traveled abroad. Douglass spoke to huge antislavery audiences in London and the West Indies.

Douglass returned to the United States because he believed abolitionists must fight slavery at its source. He insisted that African Americans receive not just their freedom but full equality with whites as well. In 1847 friends helped Douglass buy his freedom from the slaveholder from whom he had fled in Maryland.

Sojourner Truth

"I was born a slave in Ulster County, New York," Isabella Baumfree began when she told her story to audiences. Called "Belle," she lived in the cellar of a slaveholder's house. She escaped in 1826 and gained official freedom in 1827 when New York banned slavery. Quaker friends then helped her find her son who had been sold as a slave. She eventually settled in New York City with her two youngest children. In 1843 Belle chose a new name:

PRIMARY SOURCE

"The Lord [named] me Sojourner . . . Truth, because I was to declare the truth to the people."
—from *Sojourner Truth: Slave, Prophet, Legend*

Sojourner Truth worked with a number of other abolitionists, including William Lloyd Garrison and Frederick Douglass, to bring about the end of slavery. She traveled throughout the North and spoke about her experiences as an enslaved person. Sojourner Truth was also an active supporter of the women's rights movement.

Primary Source | Reactions Against Abolitionism

Anti-Abolitionists Opposition to abolitionism was almost as strong in the North as it was in the South. Southerners viewed abolitionism as an attack on their way of life. Many Northerners feared the effect abolition might have upon them. In both areas, anti-abolitionists violently responded to literature that supported abolitionism.

In 1837 in Alton, Illinois, a mob killed abolitionist newspaper editor Elijah Lovejoy, destroyed his press (right), and burned his house (below).

▲ Southerners burn antislavery documents in Charleston, South Carolina, in 1830.

"And men, like the abolitionist . . . [who goes] about meddling with other Peoples' affairs . . . [should] pay attention to his own affairs, & let his neighbor alone. . . . If these matters are going to be [agitated it will] . . . lead to the separation of the Union."

—from a letter by E. W. Taylor (a New Yorker who moved to South Carolina)

Critical Thinking

Analyzing Why did anti-abolitionists destroy pro-abolition literature?

The Underground Railroad

Some abolitionists risked prison—even death—by helping African Americans escape from slavery. The network of escape **routes**—lines of travel—from the South to the North was called the **Underground Railroad.**

Passengers on this "railroad" traveled through the night, often on foot, and went north. The North Star was their guide. During the day passengers rested at "stations"—barns, basements, and attics—until the next night's journey. The railroad's "conductors" were whites and African Americans who helped guide the runaways to freedom in the Northern states or Canada. Harriet Tubman became the most famous conductor on the Underground Railroad.

The Underground Railroad helped only a tiny fraction of the enslaved population. Still, the Railroad gave hope to people who suffered in slavery. It also gave abolitionists a way to help some enslaved people.

 Reading Check **Explaining** What were "stations" on the Underground Railroad?

Clashes Over Abolitionism

Main Idea Many Southerners and Northerners opposed abolition.

History and You Can you think of a time when you feared change, even if it was for the better? Read to learn why many people opposed abolition.

• •

The antislavery movement triggered a strong reaction against abolitionism. Many Southerners opposed the idea of ending slavery. They held that abolitionism threatened the South's way of life, which depended on enslaved labor.

Not all Northerners were abolitionists. The abolitionists in the North made up only a small fraction of the population. Many Northerners saw the antislavery movement as a threat to the nation's social order. They believed that once freed, the African Americans could never blend into American society. Other Northerners feared that the abolitionists could begin a war between the North and South.

Many Northerners also had economic fears. They did not want to lose their jobs to the emancipated workers who might travel to the North and work for cheaper wages.

Opposition to abolitionism sometimes erupted into violence against the abolitionists themselves. Philadelphia's antislavery headquarters was burned, which set off a bloody race riot. A Boston mob attacked and threatened to hang abolitionist William Lloyd Garrison. Authorities saved his life by putting him in jail.

Elijah Lovejoy in Illinois was not so lucky. Angry whites invaded his antislavery newspaper offices and wrecked his presses three times. Each time Lovejoy installed new presses and resumed publication. The fourth time the mob set fire to the building. When Lovejoy came out of the blazing building, he was shot and killed.

The South Reacts

Southerners fought abolitionism with arguments in defense of slavery. They claimed that slavery was essential to the Southern economy and had allowed Southern whites to reach a high level of culture.

Southerners also argued that they treated enslaved people well. They claimed that Northern workers were worse off than enslaved workers because they worked in factories for long hours at low wages. These jobs were repetitious and often dangerous. Also, Northern workers had to pay for their own goods and services from their small earnings, whereas the system of slavery provided food, clothing, and **medical** care to its workers.

Other defenses of slavery were based on racism. Many whites believed that African Americans were better off under white care than on their own.

The conflict between pro-slavery and antislavery groups continued to mount. At the same time, a new women's rights movement was growing.

Reading Check **Explaining** How did many Southerners defend the instituion of slavery?

History ONLINE
Study Central™ To review this section, go to glencoe.com.

Section 2 Review

Vocabulary

1. Write complete sentences that define the following terms: abolitionist, route, Underground Railroad, medical.

Main Ideas

2. Specifying What effect did the American Colonization Society have on slavery? How did enslaved African Americans view that group and its efforts?

3. Discussing Discuss the role of African Americans in the abolitionist movement.

4. Comparing and Contrasting How did Northerners and Southerners view abolitionism differently?

Critical Thinking

5. Outlining Use a format like the one below to make an outline of this section. Write each main heading on a line with a Roman numeral, and then list important facts below it. The number of key facts may vary from this sample.

   I. First main heading
     A. Key fact #1
     B. Key fact #2
  II. Second main heading
     A. Key fact #1
     B. Key fact #2
 III. Third main heading
     A. Key fact #1
     B. Key fact #2

6. Creative Writing Write a conversation that might have taken place between a Southern plantation owner and a Massachusetts abolitionist about the abolition of slavery. Have each character explain his or her point of view.

Answer the Essential Question

7. How did abolitionists influence the antislavery movement?

The Age of Reform **Chapter 14** **431**

The Underground Railroad

The Underground Railroad was a loosely organized system of secret routes for helping enslaved people escape to Canada or to areas of safety in free states. However, the popular notion of lantern-wielding "conductors" guiding families of enslaved people through forests in the South is largely inaccurate. In fact, few Southerners were willing to assist an enslaved person escape. For the most part, fugitives were on their own until they reached border states. There they could find assistance from loosely-connected groups of abolitionists. This network was the true Underground Railroad.

How Did Geography Affect the Underground Railroad?

Few abolitionists escorted runaways from the Deep South into free territory. Most runaways—typically single young men—probably lived in the upper South, close to free territories. Anti-slavery Northerners—mostly free African Americans—in border towns such as Ripley, Ohio, and Wilmington, Delaware, hid escapees from police and professional slave catchers and helped them move farther north.

The Underground Railroad, Charles T. Webber, 1893
The painting portrays a group of enslaved African Americans arriving at a safe house "station" on the Underground Railroad. Three abolitionists, Levi Coffin and his wife, Catharine, as well as Hannah Haddock, are also pictured. The scene most likely takes place at the Coffin farm in Cincinnati, Ohio.

This "hidey hole" built in a safe house in Fountain City, Indiana, was used to conceal fugitives from the police and professional slave catchers. The beds could be moved in front of the hole to conceal it. ▼

A MAN KIDNAPPED!

A PUBLIC MEETING AT

FANEUIL HALL!

WILL BE HELD

THIS FRIDAY EVEN'G,

May 26th, at 7 o'clock,

To secure justice for A MAN CLAIMED AS A SLAVE by a

VIRGINIA KIDNAPPER!

And NOW IMPRISONED IN BOSTON COURT HOUSE, in defiance of the Laws of Massachusetts. Shall he be plunged into the Hell of Virginia Slavery by a Massachusetts Judge of Probate!

BOSTON, May 26th, 1854.

◄ This poster refers to Anthony Burns, a runaway enslaved man. Burns's arrest and trial under the Fugitive Slave Act of 1850 sparked protests by abolitionists in Boston and other Northern cities.

Escape Routes Escapees used two main corridors to flee into the North. Enslaved people from inland Southern states generally made their way toward Ohio, Illinois, Indiana, and Michigan. Runaways from Southern states along the Atlantic coast tended to follow the coastline into Pennsylvania, New Jersey, and New York. Many of these runaways eventually headed into Canada. ▼

Routes to Freedom

Legend:
- Slaveholding regions
- Non-slaveholding regions
- ← Underground Railroad route
- — 1860 boundary

0 400 kilometers
0 400 miles
Albers Equal-Area projection

Ellen Craft (1826–1891) was the daughter of an African American enslaved woman and her slaveholder. Passing as white, Ellen escaped from slavery in Georgia in 1848 by dressing as a Southern male slaveholder (pictured below left). Her darker-skinned husband, **William Craft** (pictured right), accompanied her by pretending to be her valet.

Analyzing Geography

1. **Place** From which state do you think more African Americans successfully escaped slavery to freedom: Kentucky or Alabama? Explain your answer.

2. **Regions** On the map, locate the cities of Toledo, Cleveland, and Buffalo. Why do you think these cities became important points along the Underground Railroad?

Essential Question ◄

What were the effects of the women's rights movement of the middle to late 1800s?

Reading Guide

Content Vocabulary

suffrage *(p. 435)*   coeducation *(p. 437)*

Academic Vocabulary

capable *(p. 437)*   ministry *(p. 438)*

Key People and Events

Lucretia Mott *(p. 435)*

Elizabeth Cady Stanton *(p. 435)*

Susan B. Anthony *(p. 437)*

Catherine Beecher *(p. 437)*

Emma Hart Willard *(p. 437)*

Mary Lyon *(p. 438)*

Elizabeth Blackwell *(p. 438)*

Reading Strategy

Taking Notes As you read, use a diagram like the one below to identify the contributions these individuals made to women's rights.

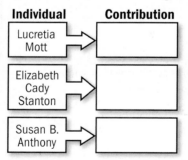

Individual	Contribution
Lucretia Mott →	
Elizabeth Cady Stanton →	
Susan B. Anthony →	

INDIANA ACADEMIC STANDARDS
United States History

8.1.24 Identify the influence of individuals on political and social events and movements such as the abolition movement, the Dred Scott case, women's rights, and Native American Indian removal.

8.1.26 Give examples of the changing role of women and minorities in the northern, southern, and western parts of the United States in the mid-nineteenth century, and examine possible causes for these changes.

American Diary

When Lucy Stone attended college, she faced many challenges. Her daughter, Alice Stone Blackwell, recalled, "At the low wages then paid to women, it took Lucy nine years to save up money enough to enter college." Stone attended Oberlin College in Ohio, which was the first college in the United States to admit women. Stone graduated from Oberlin in 1847 and became a strong supporter of women's rights.

—*from* Lucy Stone: Pioneer of Woman's Rights

Mount Holyoke Female Seminary in South Hadley, Massachusetts, was the first women's college in the United States.

Women and Reform

Main Idea Women organized to win equal rights.

History and You Can you imagine a time when women were not allowed to vote and had limited access to education and jobs? Read to learn how women worked to change their status in America.

Many women abolitionists also worked for women's rights. Like many of the women reformers, **Lucretia Mott** was a Quaker. Quaker women enjoyed a certain amount of equality in their own communities. Mott helped fugitive enslaved workers and organized the Philadelphia Female Anti-Slavery Society. At the world antislavery convention in London, she met **Elizabeth Cady Stanton.** There, they joined forces to work for women's rights.

The Seneca Falls Convention

In July 1848, Stanton, Mott, and other women organized the first women's rights convention in Seneca Falls, New York. About 200 women and 40 men attended.

The convention issued a Declaration of Sentiments and Resolutions. The declaration called for an end to laws that discriminated against women. It also demanded that women be allowed to enter the all-male world of trades, professions, and businesses. The most controversial issue at the Seneca Falls Convention, however, was about **suffrage,** or the right to vote.

Elizabeth Stanton insisted that the declaration include a demand for woman suffrage. The delegates, however, thought the idea of women voting was too radical. Lucretia Mott told her friend, "Lizzie, thee will make us ridiculous." Standing with Stanton, the abolitionist Frederick Douglass argued powerfully for women's right to vote. After a heated debate, the convention voted to include the demand for woman suffrage in the United States.

Growth of the Women's Movement

The Seneca Falls Convention paved the way for the growth of the women's rights movement. During the 1800s women held several national conventions, including the first national women's rights convention, in Worcester, Massachusetts. A number of reformers, both male and female, joined the growing movement.

Time Line / Women's Rights

Struggling for Equality Women who fought to end slavery also began to argue for their own rights and an equal place in society.

★ **1833** Oberlin College admits women and African Americans

★ **1844** Female textile workers in Massachusetts form labor association

★ **1837** Mary Lyon establishes Mount Holyoke Female Seminary

★ **1848** First women's rights convention held in Seneca Falls, New York

◀ Mary Lyon

Critical Thinking

Speculating Why do you think the Declaration of Independence is often referred to by people struggling to gain rights?

The Seneca Falls Declaration

The first women's rights convention adopted resolutions proclaiming women's equality and calling for women's right to vote, to speak publicly, and to run for office. Before the meeting, the women published a "Declaration of Sentiments" in the local newspaper to state their goals.

▲ Elizabeth Cady Stanton

When, in the course of human events, it becomes necessary for one portion of the family of man to assume among the people of the earth a position different from that which they have **hitherto** occupied, but one to which the laws of nature and of nature's God entitle them, a decent respect to the opinions of mankind requires that they should declare the causes that impel them to such a course.

> This document reflects the ideas in the Declaration of Independence. Like the patriots of 1776, women are announcing the need for revolutionary change.

We hold these truths to be self-evident: that all men and women are created equal; that they are **endowed** by their Creator with certain **inalienable** rights; that among these are life, liberty, and the pursuit of happiness. . . .

> Here two important words—*and women*—are added to Thomas Jefferson's famous phrase.

The history of mankind is a history of repeated injuries and **usurpations** on the part of man toward woman, having in direct object the establishment of an absolute tyranny over her. To prove this, let facts be submitted to a candid world. . . .

> During this time, husbands were legal masters of their wives.

> A list of specific grievances follows this paragraph.

Now, in view of this entire **disfranchisement** of one-half the people of this country, their social and religious **degradation**—in view of the unjust laws above mentioned, and because women do feel themselves aggrieved, oppressed, and fraudulently deprived of their most sacred rights, we insist that they have immediate admission to all the rights and privileges which belong to them as citizens of the United States.

> In addition to the right to vote, most educational and employment opportunities at this time were unavailable to women.

> In 1920—more than 70 years after Seneca Falls—American women finally gained the right to vote.

VOCABULARY

hitherto (HIH·thuhr·TOO): before
endowed (ihn·DAU·ehd): provided
inalienable (ih·NAYL·yuh·nuh·buhl): impossible to surrender
usurpations (YOO·suhr·PAY·shuhnz): wrongful seizures of power
disfranchisement (DIHS·FRAN·CHYZ·muhnt): deprivation of rights, especially the right to vote
degradation (DEH·gruh·DAY·shuhn): lowering in status

Critical Thinking

1. **Drawing Conclusions** Why did the authors of this document use the Declaration of Independence as a model?

2. **Speculating** How do you think the authors would have responded to critics who ridiculed them as being too bold?

3. **Making Inferences** How did this document, along with the women's convention, help women acquire more rights?

Maria Mitchell

First professional woman astronomer

Mitchell was educated by her father and became fascinated with astronomy. She discovered the orbit of a new comet in 1847, and her accomplishments became widely known. Mitchell accepted a position at Vassar College when it opened in 1865. She wrote, *"It seems to me that the needle is the chain of woman. . . . Emancipate her from the 'stitch, stitch, stitch,' . . . and she would have time for studies which would engross as the needle never can."*

Mary Lyon

Founder of Mount Holyoke

After working as a teacher for 20 years, Lyon began raising funds for Mount Holyoke Female Seminary in 1834. She became the school's first principal when it opened in 1837. Lyon wrote that women should be educated in order to *"promote human happiness. To advance everything excellent. . . . Promote the best interests of this life & that which is to come. . . . The great secret of the whole in some respects is female education."*

CRITICAL Thinking

1. **Analyzing** What beliefs did Maria Mitchell and Mary Lyon share?
2. **Identifying** What did Mitchell mean by the phrase "the needle is the chain of woman"?

Susan B. Anthony was the daughter of a Quaker abolitionist in New York. Anthony worked for women's rights and temperance. She called for equal pay for women, college training for girls, and **coeducation**—the teaching of males and females together. Anthony organized the country's first women's temperance association, the Daughters of Temperance.

Anthony met Elizabeth Cady Stanton at a temperance meeting in 1851. They became lifelong friends and partners in the struggle for women's rights and suffrage. For the rest of the century, Anthony and Stanton led the women's movement. They worked with other women to win the right to vote. Beginning with Wyoming in 1890, several states granted women suffrage. It would not be until 1920, however, that women would gain the right to vote throughout the United States.

✓ Reading Check **Explaining** What is suffrage?

Progress by Women

Main Idea Women made progress in achieving equality in education, marriage laws, and professional employment.

History and You Are there some laws that you consider unfair or unjust? Read to learn how some women worked to change laws and social customs that they thought were unjust.

Pioneers in women's education began to call for more opportunity. Early champions such as **Catherine Beecher** and **Emma Hart Willard** believed that women should be educated for their traditional roles in life. They also thought that women could be **capable,** or skillful, teachers. The Milwaukee College for Women created courses based on Beecher's ideas "to train women to be healthful, intelligent, and successful wives, mothers, and housekeepers."

Education

Some young women began to make their own opportunities. They broke the barriers to female education and helped other women do the same.

After her marriage, Emma Willard educated herself in subjects considered suitable only for males, such as science and mathematics. In 1821 Willard set up the Troy Female Seminary in upstate New York. Willard's seminary taught mathematics, history, geography, and physics, as well as the usual homemaking subjects.

Mary Lyon established Mount Holyoke Female Seminary in Massachusetts in 1837. She modeled its curriculum on that of nearby Amherst College.

Marriage and Family Laws

During the mid to late 1800s, women made some gains in marriage and property laws. New York, Pennsylvania, Indiana, Wisconsin, Mississippi, and the new state of California recognized the right of women to own property after their marriage.

Some states passed laws permitting divorced women to share the guardianship of their children with their husbands. Indiana was the first of several states that allowed women to seek divorce if their husbands were chronic abusers of alcohol.

Breaking Barriers

In the 1800s, women had few career choices. They could become elementary teachers, but school boards often paid lower salaries to women than to men. Employment in professions that were dominated by men, such as medicine and the **ministry,** or Christian service, was even more difficult. Some strong-minded women, however, succeeded.

For example, **Elizabeth Blackwell's** medical school application was turned down repeatedly. Finally accepted by Geneva College in New York, Blackwell graduated first in her class and achieved fame as a doctor.

Despite the accomplishments of notable women, and their gains in education, state laws, and employment opportunities, women remained limited by social customs and expectations. Women had just begun the long struggle to achieve their goal of equality.

Reading Check **Identifying** What gains were made by women in the field of education?

Section 3 Review

History ONLINE
Study Central™ To review this section, go to glencoe.com.

Vocabulary

1. Write a short paragraph about the women's movement of the middle to late 1800s that uses the following terms correctly: suffrage, coeducation, capable, ministry.

Main Ideas

2. **Listing** What opportunities were reserved for males in the middle to late 1800s?

3. **Explaining** Describe the rights within marriage that women gained in the 1800s.

Critical Thinking

4. **Making Connections** Many reformers in the 1800s focused on abolition and woman suffrage. Use a diagram like the one below to help you consider ways in which the two movements were similar.

5. **Expository Writing** What arguments might have been used by women who supported suffrage? You are a female pioneer traveling west. Write a paragraph explaining why women should have the right to vote.

Answer the Essential Question

6. What were the effects of the women's rights movement of the middle to late 1800s?

What were some social and educational reforms of the early 1800s?

- Temperance movement
- Expansion of higher education
- Education targeting the blind and deaf
- Improving prison conditions
- Transcendentalism in literature

Methodist camp meeting ▶

Abolitionist and reformer Frederick Douglass ▼

How did abolitionists fight slavery?

◀ Meeting notice, Massachusetts Anti-Slavery Society

- Founded African colony for formerly enslaved people
- Published antislavery newspapers and books
- Established antislavery societies
- Spoke publicly against slavery
- Created Underground Railroad to help enslaved people escape to freedom

How did Southerners defend slavery?

- Claimed slavery was essential to Southern economy
- Argued that enslaved workers were treated well
- Argued that system of slavery provided for needs of workers

What were the goals of the women's movement?

Elizabeth Cady Stanton and Susan B. Anthony, leaders in the woman suffrage movement ▶

- Access to all-male professions
- Woman suffrage (the right to vote)
- Equal pay for women
- Higher education for women
- Right to own property

STUDY TO GO

Study anywhere, anytime! Download quizzes and flash cards to your PDA from glencoe.com.

INDIANA STATEWIDE TEST PRACTICE

TEST-TAKING TIP

If you are not sure of the answer, try to narrow the options. First, eliminate any choices that you know are clearly wrong. Then, if necessary, make a guess among the remaining choices.

Reviewing Vocabulary

Directions: Choose the word or words that best completes the sentence.

1 Some reformers of the early and mid-1800s formed _____ based on a vision of the perfect society.

  A revivals
  B utopias
  C commissions
  D ministries

2 Henry David Thoreau practiced _____ by refusing to obey laws he considered unjust.

  A temperance
  B abolitionism
  C civil disobedience
  D representation

3 _____, such as Benjamin Lundy, were reformers who worked to end slavery.

  A Abolitionists
  B Segregationists
  C Utopians
  D Republicans

4 The Seneca Falls Convention in 1848 supported the demand for woman _____, or the right to vote, in the United States.

  A veto
  B emancipation
  C suffrage
  D abolition

Reviewing Main Ideas

Directions: Choose the best answer.

5 Dorothea Dix made it her life's work to

  A ban the manufacture and sale of alcoholic beverages.
  B resettle freed African Americans in Liberia.
  C educate the public about the needs of prisoners and the mentally ill.
  D spread Christianity among workers in urban centers.

6 A major subject of transcendentalist literature was

  A realism.
  B the importance of the human conscience.
  C anti-abolitionism.
  D the relationship between humans and technology.

7 Which of the following arguments did pro-slavery Southerners use against abolitionists?

  A Slave labor was essential, allowing the South to maintain its way of life and culture.
  B Many abolitionists were also secretly slaveholders.
  C Abolitionists wanted to free enslaved workers to send them to South America.
  D Abolitionists wanted to steal Southerners' farms.

8 Which of the following were grievances against women that the Seneca Falls Convention sought to repair?

  A Women could not vote.
  B Women were considered the property of their husbands.
  C Women overall did not have the same legal rights as men.
  D all of the above

GO ON

History ONLINE

For additional test practice, use **Self-Check Quizzes**—Chapter 14 at glencoe.com.

Critical Thinking

Directions: Choose the best answer.

9 **Which of the following statements best expresses the extent of support for abolitionism in the North?**

  A The majority of Northerners strongly supported abolitionism.

  B Abolitionists in the North made up only a small part of the population.

  C Most Northerners were indifferent to the abolitionist cause.

  D Most Northerners favored expelling abolitionists from the country.

Base your answer to question 10 on the reading below and your knowledge of Chapter 14.

> We hold these truths to be self-evident; that all men are created temperate [without the need to drink alcohol]; they are endowed by their Creator with certain natural and innocent desires; that among these are the appetite for cold water and the pursuit of happiness!
>
> —from *Manifesto of the Washington Total Abstinence Societies*

10 **Why does this temperance document imitate the style of the Declaration of Independence?**

  A It intended to associate the movement with the principles of the Declaration.

  B It was written about the time of the Declaration of Independence.

  C It wanted to link the cause to the promotion of religion.

  D It aimed to win support for a temperance amendment to the Constitution.

Constructed Response

Directions: Write a short response to each of the following questions. In your answer:

- *address all parts of the question*
- *use information from the chapter*
- *include facts, examples, and details relevant to the question*
- *use clear language*

11 **List three reform movements of the mid-1800s, and state their effects at that time.**

Base your answer to question 12 on the reading below and your knowledge of Chapter 14.

> A woman who goes out to wash, works as hard in proportion as a wood sawyer, or a coal heaver, but she is not generally able to make more than half as much by a day's work.
>
> —from Sarah Grimké, *Letters on Equality of Sexes*

12 **Explain the reform issue that Sarah Grimké discusses in this excerpt.**

13 **Identify two major themes of American writers during the reform period of the early to mid-1800s.**

Base your answer to question 14 on the reading below and your knowledge of Chapter 14.

> America is more our country than it is the whites—we have enriched it with our blood and tears.
>
> —from David Walker, *Appeal*

14 **What point is the African American abolitionist David Walker making in this excerpt?**

STOP

Need Extra Help?														
If you missed questions. . .	1	2	3	4	5	6	7	8	9	10	11	12	13	14
Go to page. . .	419	421	425	435	420	421	431	435	430	419	439	438	421	428

Civil War and Reconstruction
1840–1896

FIRED FROM FORT MOULTRIE INTO CHARLESTON, S.C. 1861

Spent cannon round from
the attack on Fort Sumter,
April 1861

"*It is well that war is so terrible; we would grow too fond of it.*"
—Robert E. Lee

Union soldiers with a cannon, June 1862

Unit 5

Reading History

Identifying Cause and Effect

Learn It! A *cause* is an action or event that makes something happen. What happens as a result is the *effect*.

> **Cause**
> The slavery issue splits the Democratic Party.

> **Effect**
> Northern Democrats nominate Stephen Douglas.

> **Effect**
> Southern Democrats nominate John C. Breckinridge.

—from Chapter 15, p. 463

The issue of slavery split the Democratic Party. The northern Democrats nominated Stephen Douglas. They supported popular sovereignty. Southern Democrats vowed to uphold slavery. Their candidate was John C. Breckinridge.

Practice It! Read the paragraph and write down the cause and effect(s) on another sheet of paper.

—from Chapter 17, p. 531

In the 1870s, Reconstruction governments created public schools for both races. Within a few years, about 50 percent of white children and 40 percent of African American children in the South were enrolled.

> **Cause**
> _____

> **Effect**
> _____
> _____

> **Effect**
> _____
> _____

Academic Vocabulary Preview

In addition to content vocabulary, you will also find academic vocabulary in this unit. Knowing academic vocabulary will help you understand content that is taught in all of your classes, not just social studies. Learning these words will also help you perform well on tests. Below are the academic vocabulary terms that appear in Unit 5.

Academic Vocabulary	Definition	Practice It!
Chapter 15 Toward Civil War		
temporary (TEHM · puh · REHR · ee) *p. 449*	brief	**Identify** the term from Chapter 15 that best completes the sentences.
regulate (REH · gyuh · LAYT) *p. 450*	to control	
network (NEHT · WUHRK) *p. 453*	an interconnected system	1. The Underground Railroad was a secret _____ of people opposed to slavery.
inevitable (ih · NEH · vuh · tuh · buhl) *p. 455*	unavoidable	
rigid (RIH · juhd) *p. 458*	firm and inflexible	2. When Southern states seceded from the Union, it signaled the _____ coming of the Civil War.
topic (TAH · pihk) *p. 460*	a subject of discussion	
reject (rih · JEHKT) *p. 464*	to refuse to accept	3. The _____ of slavery was one that divided families as well as the nation.
justify (JUHS · tuh · FY) *p. 464*	to find reason(s) to support	
Chapter 16 The Civil War		
contrast (kuhn · TRAST) *p. 476*	completely opposite	**Identify** the term from Chapter 16 that best matches the underlined term or terms.
challenge (CHA · luhnj) *p. 479*	a demanding situation	
abandon (uh · BAN · duhn) *p. 481*	to leave behind	4. Many women collected food, clothing, and medicine to give out to the troops.
impact (ihm · PAKT) *p. 487*	to effect or influence	
distribute (dih · STRIH · byuht) *p. 493*	to divide and give out	5. A person could avoid the draft by hiring a replacement to serve in his place.
substitute (SUHB · stuh · TOOT) *p. 496*	a replacement	
nevertheless (NEH · vuhr · thuh · LEHS) *p. 501*	however	6. Under attack, Union soldiers decided to leave the fort.
encounter (ihn · KAUN · tuhr) *p. 502*	to come upon; meet	
series (SIHR · eez) *p. 507*	sequence	
interpret (ihn · TUHR · pruht) *p. 509*	to explain the meaning of something	
Chapter 17 Reconstruction and the New South		
radical (RA · dih · kuhl) *p. 520*	extreme	**Choose** the synonym that best matches the meaning of each vocabulary word listed below.
adjust (uh · JUHST) *p. 520*	to adapt	
convince (kuhn · VIHNS) *p. 523*	to persuade (someone) that something is true	7. **radical** 9. **suspend** a. method a. believe b. drastic b. eliminate c. envy c. delay
suspend (suh · SPEHND) *p. 526*	to temporarily prevent	
credit (KREH · diht) *p. 530*	extra time to pay for purchased goods	
academy (uh · KA · duh · mee) *p. 531*	a school that provides special training	8. **convince** 10. **outcome** a. bother a. conclusion b. believe b. expense c. persuade c. anew
outcome (AUT · KUHM) *p. 536*	a result	
commission (kuh · MIH · shuhn) *p. 536*	a special group	

Toward Civil War 1840–1861

Confederate forces bombarded Fort Sumter on April 12, 1861. The attack on the fort, located in Charleston Harbor, South Carolina, marked the beginning of the Civil War.

★ **1846** Congress establishes the Smithsonian Institution

WILLIAM HENRY HARRISON 1841

JOHN TYLER 1841–1845

JAMES POLK 1845–1849

ZACHARY TAYLOR 1849–1850

MILLARD FILLMORE 1850–1853

PRESIDENTS

U.S. Events

1840

1845

1850

World Events

1843 ★ Charles Dickens: *A Christmas Carol* published

1845 ★ Many Irish emigrate to escape famine

1848 ★ Marx publishes *The Communist Manifesto*

Section 1: Slavery and the West
Essential Question Did the compromises that Congress made effectively address slavery and sectionalism?

Section 2: A Nation Dividing
Essential Question How did popular sovereignty lead to violence in Kansas?

Section 3: Challenges to Slavery
Essential Question What was the significance of the *Dred Scott* decision?

Section 4: Secession and War
Essential Question What role did the theory of states' rights play in the outbreak of the Civil War?

History ONLINE
Chapter Overview Visit glencoe.com and click on **Chapter 15—Chapter Overviews** to preview chapter information.

FOLDABLES Study Organizer

Organizing Information
Make this Foldable to help organize what you learn about events leading up to the Civil War.

Step 1 Fold an 11" x 17" sheet of paper accordion style.

Step 2 Fold the bottom edge up three inches. Glue the edges to make pockets.

Step 3 Label the panels with the section titles as shown. Use the pockets to hold notes taken on index cards.

Reading and Writing As you read the chapter, take notes on key issues and key events in the years leading up to war.

◀ Edwin Drake drills the first oil well near Titusville, Pennsylvania.

FRANKLIN PIERCE 1853–1857

1854 ★ Kansas-Nebraska Act passes

1857 ★ U.S. Supreme Court makes *Dred Scott* decision

JAMES BUCHANAN 1857–1861

1859 The Drake Well becomes first U.S. oil well

1861 ★ Civil War begins

ABRAHAM LINCOLN 1861–1865

1855

1860

1855 ★ Florence Nightingale improves health care during Crimean War

1856 ★ Henry Bessemer introduces process for making steel inexpensively

1861 ★ Alexander II frees serfs in Russia

Slavery and the West

Essential Question ◄

Did the compromises that Congress made effectively address slavery and sectionalism?

Reading Guide

Content Vocabulary

sectionalism (p. 449)   secede (p. 451)
fugitive (p. 451)   abstain (p. 451)

Academic Vocabulary

temporary (p. 449)   regulate (p. 450)

Key People and Events

Missouri Compromise (p. 449)
Stephen A. Douglas (p. 451)
Compromise of 1850 (p. 451)

Reading Strategy

Taking Notes As you read, use a diagram like the one below to describe how two compromises addressed the issue of slavery in new states.

```
        Slavery in
        New States
       /          \
Missouri        Compromise
Compromise:     of 1850:
```

INDIANA ACADEMIC STANDARDS
United States History

8.1.16 Describe the abolition of slavery in the northern states; conflict and compromises associated with westward expansion of slavery, such as the Missouri Compromise (1820), The Compromise of 1850, Kansas-Nebraska Act (1854); and the continued resistance to slavery by people such as Frederick Douglass, Harriet Tubman, William Lloyd Garrison, and Harriet Beecher Stowe.

8.1.20 Analyze the causes and effects of events leading to the Civil War, including development of sectional conflict over slavery.

American Diary

When Missouri applied for statehood in 1819, controversy arose in Congress. Slavery was legal in Missouri, and Missouri's admission would change the balance between free states and slave states. The Missouri debate became so bitter that Thomas Jefferson wrote: "This momentous question, like a fire bell in the night, awakened and filled me with terror. I considered it at once as the knell [funeral bell] of the Union."

—letter to John Holmes

A riverboat traveling on the Mississippi River at St. Louis

The Missouri Compromise

Main Idea The Missouri Compromise temporarily resolved the issue of whether new states would be slave states or free states.

History and You Do you feel loyalty to your school during a contest with another school? Read how differences between the North and the South created feelings of loyalty to a region.

. . . .

Many settlers brought enslaved African Americans into Missouri with them. When Missouri applied for statehood, its constitution allowed slavery. The request sparked an angry debate in Congress. In 1819, 11 states permitted slavery and 11 did not. The Senate—with two members from each state—was, therefore, evenly balanced between slave and free states. The admission of a new state would upset that balance.

In addition, the North and the South, with their different economic systems, were competing for new lands in the western territories. At the same time, a growing number of Northerners wanted to restrict or ban slavery. Southerners, even those who disliked slavery, opposed these antislavery efforts. They resented the interference by outsiders in Southerners' affairs. These differences between the North and the South grew into **sectionalism**—an exaggerated loyalty to a particular region of the country.

The Senate suggested a way to resolve the crisis—allow Missouri to join as a slave state and admit Maine at the same time as a free state. Maine, formerly part of Massachusetts, had also applied for statehood. The Senate wanted to settle the issue of slavery in the territories for good. It proposed banning slavery in the rest of the Louisiana Purchase north of 36°30' N latitude.

Speaker of the House Henry Clay carefully guided the bill through the House of Representatives, which passed it by a close vote in 1820. Maine joined the union that year. In 1821 Missouri became the twenty-fourth state. The **Missouri Compromise** preserved the balance between slave and free states in the Senate. It also brought about a **temporary,** or brief, lull in the debate over slavery.

Reading Check Explaining Why was the admission of a new state controversial in 1819?

By the Numbers / The Missouri Compromise

The Vote The map shows how the House of Representatives voted on provisions in a law restricting slavery.

For extending slavery
Against extending slavery
Tie vote

N.H.
Vt.
Me.
N.Y.
Mass.
R.I.
Pa.
N.J.
Conn.
Del.
Md.
Ill. Ind. Ohio
Va.
Ky.
N.C.
Tenn.
S.C.
Miss. Ala. Ga.
La.
Fla. Terr.
Gulf of Mexico
ATLANTIC OCEAN

40°N
30°N
70°W
80°W
90°W

0   200 kilometers
0   200 miles
Albers Equal-Area projection

Critical Thinking

Comparing Which region united in favor of extending slavery? Which region opposed extending slavery?

New Territories and the Free-Soil Party

NATIONAL GEOGRAPHIC

A New Party Forms The acquisition of New Mexico and California brought the slavery issue into the open. Many Southern senators argued that Congress had no constitutional power to forbid slavery in the new territories. In 1848, a new party—the Free-Soil Party—formed. Free-Soilers supported the Wilmot Proviso, which banned the spread of slavery into the new territories gained from Mexico.

▲ The Van Buren-Adams Free-Soil ticket received nearly 300,000 votes in 1848. Later the Republican Party would adopt many principles from the Free-Soil Party.

"Gen. [Zachary] Taylor and Gen. [Lewis] Cass are proslavery candidates. Mr. Van Buren and Mr. Adams are antislavery candidates. The former are the shameless tools of the slave-power. The latter bravely resist it."
—Gerrit Smith, New York abolitionist, August 1848

Critical Thinking

Finding the Main Idea What led to the formation of the Free-Soil Party?

A New Compromise

Main Idea The Compromise of 1850 addressed several issues, including slavery in the territories.

History and You Do you engage in some give and take in order to settle an argument? Read how Congress settled its differences in 1850.

· ·

The debate over slavery in new territories erupted again in the 1840s. The annexation of Texas, where slavery already existed, became the main issue in the presidential election of 1844. Democrat James Polk won the election and pressed forward on acquiring Texas. Texas became a state in 1845. At the same time, support grew in the South for taking New Mexico and California from Mexico. Government actions led to war with Mexico.

Conflicting Views

Soon after the Mexican War began, Representative David Wilmot of Pennsylvania introduced a proposal. Called the Wilmot Proviso, it would ban slavery in any lands that might be acquired from Mexico.

Southerners protested. They believed that any antislavery policy about the territories endangered slavery everywhere. They wanted California and New Mexico to remain open to slavery. Senator John C. Calhoun of South Carolina countered with another proposal. It stated that neither Congress nor any territorial government had the authority to ban slavery from a territory or **regulate,** or control, it.

Neither proposal passed, but both caused bitter debate. By the 1848 presidential election, the United States had gained California and New Mexico from Mexico but took no action on slavery in those areas.

The Free-Soil Party

In 1848 the Whigs selected Zachary Taylor, a Southerner and a hero of the Mexican War, as their candidate. The Democrats chose Senator Lewis Cass of Michigan. Both candidates ignored the slavery issue.

This failure to take a stand angered voters. Many opponents of slavery left their parties and formed the Free-Soil Party. Adopting the slogan "Free Soil, Free Speech, Free Labor, and Free Men," they chose former president Martin Van Buren as their candidate. Taylor won, but the Free-Soil Party gained several seats in Congress.

The Compromise of 1850

With the backing of President Taylor, California applied to become a free state in 1849. Meanwhile, antislavery forces wanted to ban slavery in Washington, D.C. Southerners, however, wanted a strong national law that required states to return **fugitive,** or runaway, enslaved people. The key issue, however, remained the balance of power in the Senate. If California entered as a free state, the slaveholding states would be outvoted in the Senate. Southerners talked about **seceding** from, or leaving, the Union.

In 1850 Senator Henry Clay tried to find a compromise. He proposed that California enter as a free state, while the rest of the new territories would have no limits on slavery. In addition, the slave trade, but not slavery itself, would be banned in Washington, D.C. Finally, Clay pushed for a stronger fugitive slave law.

A heated debate began in Congress. Senator Calhoun opposed Clay's plan. He felt that the Union could be saved only by protecting slavery. Senator Daniel Webster supported the plan. He reasoned that slavery had little chance in the new territories because the land was not suited to plantations.

When President Taylor—an opponent of Clay's plan—died unexpectedly, Vice President Millard Fillmore succeeded him and favored a compromise. To end the crisis, Illinois Senator **Stephen A. Douglas** divided Clay's plan into parts that could be voted on separately. Fillmore had several Whigs **abstain,** or not vote, on the parts they opposed. Congress finally passed five bills in 1850. Taken together, these laws became known as the **Compromise of 1850.**

✔ **Reading Check** **Explaining** Who formed the Free-Soil Party and why?

Section 1 Review

History ONLINE
Study Central™ To review this section, go to glencoe.com.

Vocabulary

1. Use each of the following terms in a sentence that clearly expresses its meaning: sectionalism, temporary, regulate, fugitive, secede, abstain.

Main Ideas

2. **Describing** How did the Missouri Compromise preserve the balance of power in the U.S. Senate?

3. **Explaining** How did Stephen Douglas help win approval of the Compromise of 1850?

Critical Thinking

4. **Analyzing** What was the Wilmot Proviso? Why was this amendment to a bill so controversial?

5. **Comparing** Describe what the North and South each gained from the Compromise of 1850. Use a diagram like the one below.

6. **Creative Writing** Write a dialogue in the form of a conversation in which John Calhoun and Daniel Webster express their views on the Compromise of 1850.

Answer the
7. **Essential Question**
Did the compromises that Congress made effectively address slavery and sectionalism?

Essential Question ◄

How did popular sovereignty lead to violence in Kansas?

Reading Guide

Content Vocabulary

popular sovereignty (p. 454)

civil war (p. 455)

border ruffians (p. 455)

Academic Vocabulary

network (p. 453)   inevitable (p. 455)

Key People and Events

Fugitive Slave Act (p. 453)

Kansas-Nebraska Act (p. 454)

John Brown (p. 455)

Reading Strategy

Taking Notes Use a diagram like the one below to note reactions to the Kansas-Nebraska Act. Also, summarize the reasons for these reactions.

```
        Kansas-Nebraska Act
          /            \
  Antislavery:      Pro-slavery:
```

INDIANA ACADEMIC STANDARDS
United States History

8.1.16 Describe the abolition of slavery in the northern states; conflict and compromises associated with westward expansion of slavery, such as the Missouri Compromise (1820), The Compromise of 1850, Kansas-Nebraska Act (1854); and the continued resistance to slavery by people such as Frederick Douglass, Harriet Tubman, William Lloyd Garrison, and Harriet Beecher Stowe.

8.1.20 Analyze the causes and effects of events leading to the Civil War, including development of sectional conflict over slavery.

8.3.1 Read maps to interpret symbols and determine the landforms and human features that represent physical and cultural characteristics of areas in the United States.

American Diary

On May 24, 1854, the people of Boston erupted in outrage. Federal officers had seized Anthony Burns, a runaway enslaved African American who lived in Boston, to return him to slavery. Abolitionists tried to rescue Burns from the federal courthouse, and city leaders attempted to buy his freedom. All efforts failed. Federal troops escorted Burns to a ship that would carry him back to Virginia and into slavery. In a gesture of bitter protest, Bostonians draped buildings in black and hung the American flag upside down.

The Underground Railroad by James Michael Newell

The Fugitive Slave Act

Main Idea The Fugitive Slave Act required all citizens to help catch runaways, yet many Northerners refused to cooperate.

History and You Have you ever tried to protect someone from a bully? Read how Northerners tried to thwart the efforts of slave hunters.

. . . .

As part of the Compromise of 1850, Senator Henry Clay of Kentucky convinced Congress to pass the **Fugitive Slave Act** as an attempt to pacify slaveholders. The Fugitive Slave Act of 1850 required all citizens to help catch runaways. Anyone who aided a fugitive could be fined or imprisoned. People in the South believed the law would force Northerners to recognize the rights of Southerners. Instead, enforcement of the law convinced more people in the North of the evils of slavery.

After the passage of the Fugitive Slave Act, slaveholders stepped up their efforts to catch runaway enslaved people. They even tried to capture runaways who had lived in freedom in the North for years. Sometimes they seized African Americans who were not trying to escape and forced them into slavery.

History ONLINE

Student Web Activity Visit glencoe.com and complete the Chapter 15 Web Activity about the Underground Railroad.

In spite of the penalties, some Northerners refused to cooperate with the law. They justified their opposition on moral grounds. In his 1849 essay "Civil Disobedience," Henry David Thoreau wrote that if the law "requires you to be the agent [cause] of injustice to another, then I say, break the law."

The Underground Railroad, a **network,** or interconnected system, of free African Americans and whites, helped runaways make their way to freedom. Antislavery groups tried to rescue African Americans who were being pursued or to free those who were captured. In Boston, members of one such group followed federal agents shouting, "Slave hunters—there go the slave hunters." People contributed funds to buy the freedom of African Americans. Northern juries refused to convict those accused of violating the Fugitive Slave Act.

Reading Check **Explaining** What was the purpose of the Underground Railroad?

Primary Source / Reward Poster

A poster advertises a substantial reward for a runaway enslaved man.

Critical Thinking

Making Inferences Under the Fugitive Slave Act of 1850, any citizen might be required to help capture a runaway slave. Why do you think some people condemned this law?

Slavery and Sectionalism   NATIONAL GEOGRAPHIC

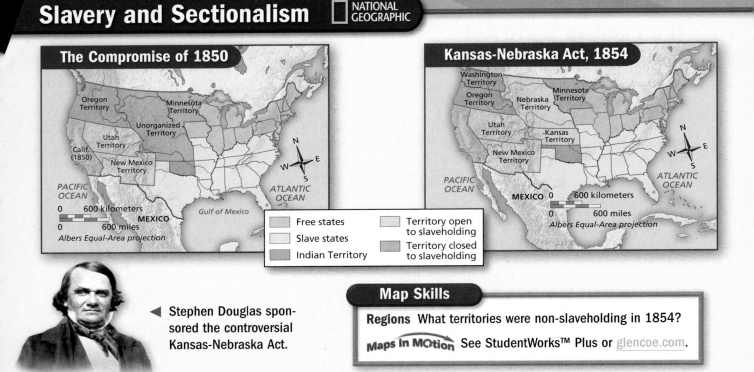

The Compromise of 1850

Kansas-Nebraska Act, 1854

Free states
Slave states
Indian Territory
Territory open to slaveholding
Territory closed to slaveholding

◀ Stephen Douglas sponsored the controversial Kansas-Nebraska Act.

Map Skills

Regions What territories were non-slaveholding in 1854?

Maps In Motion See StudentWorks™ Plus or glencoe.com.

The Kansas-Nebraska Act

Main Idea The Kansas-Nebraska Act resulted from another dispute over slavery in Congress.

History and You Do you recall how the Missouri Compromise limited slavery in the territories? Read how this agreement fell apart in the 1850s.

Franklin Pierce, a New Hampshire Democrat, became president in 1853. Pierce intended to enforce the Fugitive Slave Act.

In 1854 Stephen A. Douglas, the Illinois senator who forged the Compromise of 1850, introduced a bill in Congress. He proposed organizing the region west of Missouri and Iowa as the territories of Kansas and Nebraska. Douglas hoped his plan to expand the nation would be acceptable to both the North and the South.

Because of their location, Kansas and Nebraska seemed likely to become free states. Both lay north of 36°30′N latitude, the line set in the Missouri Compromise as the limit of slavery. Douglas knew Southerners would object to admitting Kansas and Nebraska as

free states because it would give free states more votes in the Senate. As a result, Douglas proposed abandoning the Missouri Compromise and letting the settlers in each territory vote on whether to allow slavery. He called this **popular sovereignty**—allowing the people to decide.

Passage of the Act

Many Northerners protested. Douglas's plan to repeal the Missouri Compromise would allow slavery into areas that had been free for more than 30 years. Southerners in Congress, however, supported the bill. They expected Kansas to be settled mostly by slaveholders from Missouri who would vote to keep slavery legal. With some support from Northern Democrats and the backing of President Pierce, Congress passed the **Kansas-Nebraska Act** in 1854.

Conflict in Kansas

Right after the law passed, pro-slavery and antislavery groups rushed into Kansas. When elections took place, a pro-slavery legislature was elected.

Although only about 1,500 voters lived in Kansas at the time, more than 6,000 people cast ballots. Thousands of pro-slavery supporters from Missouri crossed the border just to vote in the election. These Missourians traveled in armed groups and became known as **border ruffians.**

Soon, the new Kansas legislature passed laws supporting slavery. One law even restricted political office to pro-slavery candidates.

The antislavery people refused to accept these laws. Instead they armed themselves, held their own elections, and adopted a constitution that banned slavery. By January 1856, rival governments existed in Kansas—one for and one against slavery.

"Bleeding Kansas"

With both sides arming themselves, an outbreak of violence became **inevitable,** or unavoidable. In May 1856, 800 slavery supporters attacked the town of Lawrence, a stronghold of antislavery settlers. The attackers burned the Free State Hotel and destroyed two newspaper offices and many homes. Soon after, antislavery forces retaliated.

John Brown, a fervent abolitionist, believed God chose him to end slavery. The attack on Lawrence enraged Brown. He vowed to "strike terror in the hearts of the pro-slavery people." One night Brown led a group along Pottawatomie Creek, where they seized and killed five supporters of slavery.

Armed bands soon roamed the territory. Newspapers referred to "Bleeding Kansas" and "the Civil War in Kansas." A **civil war** is a conflict between citizens of the same country. In October 1856 the territorial governor sent federal troops to stop the bloodshed.

Violence also broke out in Congress. Senator Charles Sumner of Massachusetts lashed out against pro-slavery forces in Kansas. He also criticized pro-slavery senators, such as Andrew P. Butler of South Carolina. Two days later, Butler's cousin, Representative Preston Brooks, walked into the Senate chamber and hit Sumner with a cane. Sumner fell to the floor, unconscious and bleeding. This incident and the Kansas feud revealed the rising hostility between North and South.

Reading Check **Explaining** What events led to "Bleeding Kansas"?

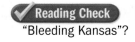

History ONLINE
Study Central™ To review this section, go to glencoe.com.

Section 2 Review

Vocabulary

1. Use each of these terms in a sentence that will help explain its meaning: network, popular sovereignty, border ruffians, inevitable, civil war.

Main Ideas

2. Listing What were some ways that Northerners defied the Fugitive Slave Act?

3. Explaining How would the issue of slavery in Kansas and Nebraska be decided under the Kansas-Nebraska Act?

Critical Thinking

4. Contrasting How did Southerners expect Northerners to react to the Fugitive Slave Act? How did Northerners actually react?

5. Sequencing Use a diagram like the one below to list the steps leading to bloodshed in Kansas.

6. Persuasive Writing Decide whether you would have been for or against the Kansas-Nebraska Act and the concept of popular sovereignty. Then write a newspaper editorial arguing your position.

Answer the
7. Essential Question
How did popular sovereignty lead to violence in Kansas?

Challenges to Slavery

Essential Question ◄

What was the significance of the *Dred Scott* decision?

Reading Guide

Content Vocabulary
arsenal (p. 461)   martyr (p. 461)

Academic Vocabulary
rigid (p. 458)   topic (p. 460)

Key People and Events
Republican Party (p. 457)
John C. Frémont (p. 457)
James Buchanan (p. 457)
Dred Scott (p. 458)
Abraham Lincoln (p. 460)

Reading Strategy
Taking Notes As you read, use a diagram like the one below to note each party's candidate and platform in the 1856 presidential election. Also record the election result.

Republican:	—	Platform:
Democrat:	—	Platform:
American Party:	—	Platform:

⬇

(Election Result:)

INDIANA ACADEMIC STANDARDS
United States History

8.1.20 Analyze the causes and effects of events leading to the Civil War, including development of sectional conflict over slavery.

8.1.24 Identify the influence of individuals on political and social events and movements such as the abolition movement, the Dred Scott case, women's rights, and Native American Indian removal.

American Diary

A few years after the attacks in Kansas, John Brown led a raid in Harpers Ferry, Virginia. Many people considered Brown and his followers to be ruthless murderers. The Fredericksburg Herald declared that, "shooting is a mercy they should be denied." Others viewed Brown as a freedom fighter. When Brown was executed in 1859, writer Henry David Thoreau wrote, "He is not Old Brown any longer, [but] an angel of light."

—quoted in "John Brown at Harpers Ferry" and from Thoreau's "A Plea for Capt. John Brown"

John Brown leaving Charleston jail on his way to his execution

A New Political Party

Main Idea Opponents of slavery from different political parties came together to form the new Republican Party.

History and You Which of today's political issues is most important to your family? Read to learn how the parties stood on key issues of the 1854 and 1856 elections.

· ·

Even before Brown's raid, other events drove the North and South further apart. After the Kansas-Nebraska Act, the Democratic Party began to divide along sectional lines, with Northern Democrats leaving the party. Differing views over the slavery issue destroyed the Whig Party.

The Election of 1854

In 1854 additional antislavery Whigs and Democrats joined forces with Free-Soilers to form the **Republican Party.** The Republicans challenged the pro-slavery Whigs and Democrats, choosing candidates to run in the state and congressional elections of 1854. Their main message was that the government should ban slavery from new territories. The Republican Party quickly showed its strength in the North. In the election, the Republicans won control of the House of Representatives and of several state governments. In the South, the Republican Party had almost no support.

Almost three-fourths of the Democratic candidates from free states lost in 1854. The Democrats were increasingly becoming a Southern party.

The Election of 1856

Democrats and Republicans met again in the presidential election of 1856. The Whig Party, disintegrating over the slavery issue, did not offer a candidate of its own.

The Republicans chose **John C. Frémont** of California as their candidate for president. Frémont gained fame as an explorer in the West. The party platform called for free territories, and its campaign slogan became "Free soil, Free speech, and Frémont."

The Democratic Party nominated **James Buchanan** of Pennsylvania, an experienced diplomat and former member of Congress. Buchanan wanted to appease the South in order to save the Union. As a result, the party endorsed the idea of popular sovereignty.

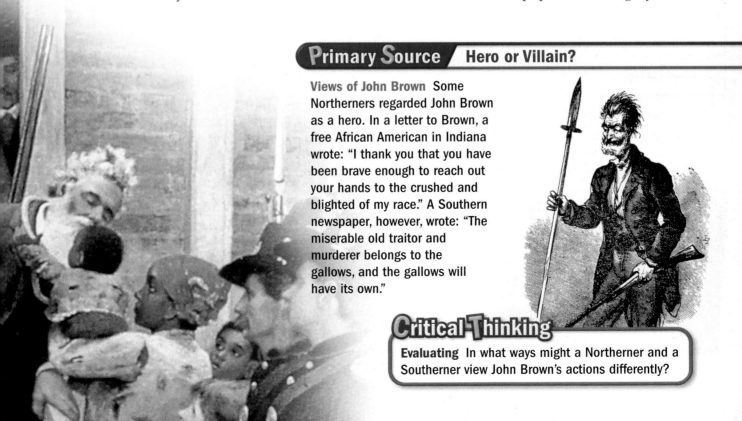

Primary Source / Hero or Villain?

Views of John Brown Some Northerners regarded John Brown as a hero. In a letter to Brown, a free African American in Indiana wrote: "I thank you that you have been brave enough to reach out your hands to the crushed and blighted of my race." A Southern newspaper, however, wrote: "The miserable old traitor and murderer belongs to the gallows, and the gallows will have its own."

Critical Thinking

Evaluating In what ways might a Northerner and a Southerner view John Brown's actions differently?

The Election of 1856

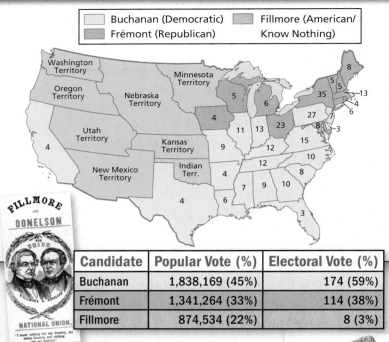

Legend:
- Buchanan (Democratic)
- Frémont (Republican)
- Fillmore (American/ Know Nothing)

Candidate	Popular Vote (%)	Electoral Vote (%)
Buchanan	1,838,169 (45%)	174 (59%)
Frémont	1,341,264 (33%)	114 (38%)
Fillmore	874,534 (22%)	8 (3%)

Northern States for Buchanan The presidential election of 1856 was decided in the swing states of Pennsylvania, Illinois, and Indiana. Democratic candidate James Buchanan won all three. Only 1,200 of Republican John Frémont's 1.34 million popular votes came from slaveholding states.

The Republican ticket of John C. Frémont and William L. Dayton opposed slavery's expansion into the territories. ▶

▲ Third-party candidate Fillmore appealed to voters concerned about immigration and Catholicism.

Democrats stressed that Buchanan was the candidate of conciliation and stability and believed that a Frémont victory would lead to civil war. ▶

Map Skills

Regions In which region was Frémont most successful? Which states in that area did he not win?

Maps In Motion See StudentWorks™ Plus or glencoe.com.

The American Party, or Know Nothings, grew quickly between 1853 and 1856 by attacking immigrants. The Know Nothings nominated former president Millard Fillmore. Most of the Northern delegates, however, walked out of the convention when the party refused to call for the repeal of the Kansas-Nebraska Act.

The presidential vote divided along **rigid**— firm and inflexible—sectional lines. Buchanan won the election. He took all Southern states except Maryland and received 174 electoral votes compared to 114 for Frémont and 8 for Fillmore. Frémont did not receive a single electoral vote south of the Mason-Dixon line, but he carried 11 of the 16 free states.

Reading Check **Identifying** Which political party was emerging as the party of the South in the 1854 and 1856 elections?

The *Dred Scott* Case

Main Idea The Supreme Court's decision in the *Dred Scott* case dealt a severe blow to antislavery forces and further divided the country.

History and You How would you feel if the Supreme Court decided that you were "property"? Read to find out how the decision in the *Dred Scott* case shocked the nation.

. . . .

Dred Scott was an enslaved African American bought by an army doctor in Missouri, a slave state. In the 1830s, the doctor moved his household to Illinois, a free state, and then to the Wisconsin Territory, where slavery was banned by the Northwest Ordinance of 1787. Later the family returned to Missouri, where the doctor died. In 1846, with the help of antislavery lawyers, Scott sued for his freedom.

458   Chapter 15   *Toward Civil War*

Scott claimed he should be free because he once lived in areas of the North where slavery was prohibited.

Eleven years later, as anger grew over the slavery issue, the case reached the Supreme Court. The case attracted enormous attention across the country. While the immediate issue was Dred Scott's status, the Court also had the opportunity to rule on the question of slavery in the territories.

The Court's Decision

The Court's decision electrified the nation. Chief Justice Roger B. Taney (TAW•nee) said that Dred Scott was still an enslaved person. As such, Scott was not a citizen and had no right to bring a lawsuit. Taney continued on, addressing broader issues.

Taney wrote that Scott's residence on free soil did not make him free. An enslaved person was property, and the Fifth Amendment prohibits Congress from taking away property without "due process of law."

Finally, Taney wrote that Congress had no power to prohibit slavery in any territory. The Missouri Compromise—which banned slavery north of 36°30'N latitude—was unconstitutional. For that matter, so was popular sovereignty. Not even the voters in a territory could prohibit slavery because that would amount to taking away a person's property. In effect, the decision meant that the Constitution protected slavery.

Reaction to the Decision

Rather than settling the issue, the decision divided the country even more. The Court upheld what many in the South had always maintained: Nothing could legally stop the spread of slavery. The Republicans' main issue—limiting the spread of slavery—was ruled unconstitutional.

Republicans and other antislavery groups were outraged. They called the *Dred Scott* decision "a wicked and false judgment" and "the greatest crime" ever committed in the nation's courts.

Reading Check **Applying** Based on the *Dred Scott* decision, could voters ban slavery? Explain.

Primary Source / The *Dred Scott* Decision

A Controversial Ruling In his ruling in the *Dred Scott* case, Chief Justice Roger B. Taney declared the Missouri Compromise unconstitutional because it deprived slaveholders of their property without due process or compensation. Southerners praised the decision, which opened all U.S. territory to slavery.

Supreme Court Chief Justice Roger B. Taney ▶

◀ Newspaper announcing the *Dred Scott* decision

▲ The Old Courthouse in St. Louis where the *Dred Scott* case was heard

"They [African Americans] had for more than a century before been regarded as beings of an inferior order and altogether unfit to associate with the white race . . . and so far inferior that they had no rights which the white man was bound to respect. . . . No one . . . should induce the Court to give to the words of the Constitution a more liberal construction in their favor than they were intended to bear when the instrument was framed and adopted."

—Roger Taney, *Dred Scott* v. *Sandford* decision, March 1857

Critical Thinking

Assessing How do you think the *Dred Scott* decision affected sectional tensions in the country?

A Raid to Fight Slavery John Brown gained notoriety fighting against pro-slavery forces in Kansas in the mid-1850s. Financed by wealthy abolitionists, Brown led a raid in 1859 to capture the federal arsenal at Harpers Ferry, Virginia. Brown hoped to use the weapons at the arsenal to spark an uprising by enslaved people in Virginia.

John Brown and his men barricaded themselves in this brick engine house to fight off attacks from federal troops. ▼

"Now if . . . I should forfeit my life for the furtherance of the ends of justice and MINGLE MY BLOOD . . . with the blood of millions in this slave country whose rights are disregarded by wicked, cruel, and unjust enactments—I submit; so LET IT BE DONE."
—John Brown's statement to the Virginia Court

▲ Federal troops commanded by Colonel Robert E. Lee crushed Brown's raid. More than half of Brown's force, including two of his sons, died in the fighting. Brown and his surviving men were captured and Brown was later hanged.

Critical Thinking

Drawing Conclusions Was the raid on Harpers Ferry a success for abolitionists? Why or why not?

Lincoln and Douglas

Main Idea The Lincoln-Douglas debates placed the little-known Lincoln into the national spotlight.

History and You Do you like to root for the underdog? Read how Abraham Lincoln skillfully debated against the powerful Stephen Douglas.

. . . .

In the congressional election of 1858, the Senate race in Illinois was the center of national attention. The contest pitted the current senator, Democrat Stephen A. Douglas, against Republican challenger **Abraham Lincoln.** People considered Douglas a likely candidate for president in 1860. Lincoln was nearly an unknown.

Douglas, a successful lawyer, joined the Democratic Party and won election to the House in 1842 and to the Senate in 1846. Short, stocky, and powerful, Douglas was called "the Little Giant." He disliked slavery but thought that the controversy over it would interfere with the nation's growth. He believed the issue could be resolved through popular sovereignty.

Born in the poor backcountry of Kentucky, Abraham Lincoln moved to Indiana as a child, and later to Illinois. Like Douglas, Lincoln was intelligent, ambitious, and a successful lawyer. He had little formal education—but excellent political skills. He had served in the Illinois legislature and in the U.S. House of Representatives. Lincoln saw slavery as morally wrong but admitted there was no easy way to end slavery where it existed. He was certain, though, that slavery should not be allowed to spread.

The Lincoln-Douglas Debates

Not as well-known as Douglas, Lincoln challenged the senator to a series of debates. Douglas reluctantly agreed. The two met seven times in August, September, and October of 1858 in cities and villages throughout Illinois. Thousands came to these debates. The main **topic,** or subject of discussion, was slavery.

During the debate at Freeport, Lincoln pressed Douglas about his views on popular sovereignty. Could the people of a territory legally exclude slavery before becoming a state? Douglas replied that the people could exclude slavery by refusing to pass laws protecting slaveholders' rights. Douglas's response, which satisfied antislavery followers but lost him support in the South, became known as the Freeport Doctrine.

Douglas claimed that Lincoln wanted African Americans to be fully equal to whites. Lincoln denied this. Still, Lincoln said, "in the right to eat the bread . . . which his own hand earns, [an African American] is my equal and the equal of [Senator] Douglas, and the equal of every living man." The real issue, Lincoln said, is "between the men who think slavery a wrong and those who do not think it wrong. The Republican Party think it wrong."

Following the debates, Douglas won a narrow victory in the election. Lincoln lost the election but did not come away empty-handed. He gained a national reputation as a man of clear thinking who could argue with force and persuasion.

The Raid on Harpers Ferry

After the 1858 election, Southerners felt threatened by Republicans. In late 1859, an act of violence added to their fears. On October 16 the abolitionist John Brown led a group on a raid on Harpers Ferry, Virginia. His target was an **arsenal,** a storage site for weapons. Brown hoped to arm enslaved African Americans and start a revolt against slaveholders. Abolitionists had paid for the raid.

Brown's raid was defeated by local citizens and federal troops. Convicted of treason and murder, Brown was sentenced to hang. His execution shook the North. Some antislavery Northerners denounced Brown's use of violence. Others saw Brown as a **martyr**—a person who dies for a great cause.

John Brown's death rallied abolitionists. When Southerners learned of Brown's abolitionist ties, their fears of a great Northern conspiracy against them seemed to be confirmed. The nation was on the brink of disaster.

Reading Check **Identifying** Why did John Brown raid the arsenal at Harpers Ferry?

Section 3 Review

History ONLINE
Study Central™ To review this section, go to glencoe.com.

Vocabulary

1. Define each of the following terms, and use each in a sentence: rigid, topic, arsenal, martyr.

Main Ideas

2. **Specifying** What issue led to the formation of the Republican Party, and what stand did the new party take on that issue?

3. **Explaining** What reasons did Taney give for Dred Scott's status as an enslaved person?

4. **Identifying** How did the Lincoln-Douglas debates benefit Lincoln?

Critical Thinking

5. **Identifying Points of View** Use a diagram like the one below to compare the views of Lincoln and Douglas on the issue of slavery.

Slavery

Douglas's Views:

Lincoln's Views:

6. **Making Inferences** Why do you think the raid on Harpers Ferry by a mere 18 men seemed so threatening to Southerners?

7. **Persuasive Writing** Write a rebuttal, or response, to Roger B. Taney on the *Dred Scott* decision. Address the points he made in his remarks on the Court's decision.

Answer the Essential Question

8. What was the significance of the *Dred Scott* decision?

Essential Question ◄

What role did the theory of states' rights play in the outbreak of the Civil War?

Reading Guide

Content Vocabulary
secession (p. 463)   states' rights (p. 464)

Academic Vocabulary
reject (p. 464)   justify (p. 464)

Key People and Events
John Crittenden (p. 463)
Confederate States of America (p. 464)
Jefferson Davis (p. 464)
Fort Sumter (p. 466)

Reading Strategy
Taking Notes As you read, list the major events on a time line like the one below.

Nov. 1860	Feb. 1861	April 1861

Dec. 1860	March 1861

INDIANA ACADEMIC STANDARDS
United States History

8.1.20 Analyze the causes and effects of events leading to the Civil War, including development of sectional conflict over slavery.

8.1.21 Describe the importance of key events and individuals in the Civil War.

American Diary

The events at Harpers Ferry inflamed slaveholders. In 1859 the Charleston Mercury *declared "The day of compromise is passed. . . . There is no peace for the South in the Union." Republicans argued that the South leaving the Union was a tactic to frighten voters from casting their ballots for Abraham Lincoln. To many Southerners, however, Lincoln's election would signal that their position in the Union was hopeless.*

—from the Charleston Mercury

The Wigwam in Chicago was the site of the 1860 Republican Convention.

Secession

Main Idea Fearing that President Lincoln would not protect Southern rights, first South Carolina and then other states voted to leave the Union.

History and You Have you ever been so angry that you needed to leave a room? Read to learn about the South's decision to secede.

· ·

Would the Union break up? That was the burning question as the presidential election of November 1860 approached.

The Election of 1860

The issue of slavery split the Democratic Party. The northern Democrats nominated Stephen Douglas. They supported popular sovereignty. Southern Democrats vowed to uphold slavery. Their candidate was John C. Breckinridge. Moderates from the North and the South who formed the Constitutional Union Party chose John Bell. This party took no position on slavery.

The Republicans nominated Abraham Lincoln. Their platform was that slavery should be left undisturbed where it existed, but that it should be excluded from the territories.

Many Southerners feared, however, that a Republican victory would encourage slave revolts.

With the Democrats divided, Lincoln won a clear majority of the electoral votes. The vote was along purely sectional lines. Lincoln's name did not even appear on the ballot in most Southern states, but he won every Northern state. In effect, the more populous North outvoted the South.

Attempt at Compromise

The Republicans promised not to disturb slavery where it already existed. Many Southerners, though, did not trust the Republican Party to protect their rights. On December 20, 1860, South Carolina voted to secede from the Union.

As other Southern states debated the question of **secession,** or withdrawal from the Union, leaders in Congress worked frantically to fashion a compromise. Senator **John Crittenden** of Kentucky proposed a series of amendments to the Constitution. Central to his plan was a provision to protect slavery south of 36°30′N latitude—the line set by the Missouri Compromise—in all territories "now held or hereafter acquired."

Primary Source / **Secession Ribbon**

PALMETTO.

LIBERTY OR DEATH!

DON'T TREAD ON ME

Supporting Separation *Secession* means "separation from the Union." Some Southerners wore ribbons like this one to show their support for separating from the United States. The words on the ribbon are mottoes, or well-known expressions, from the American Revolution.

Critical Thinking

Analyzing What did the mottoes mean during the American Revolution? Why do you think secessionists used these mottoes?

This cartoon was created in 1861, just before the outbreak of the Civil War. Secession was breaking up the United States.

1. **Interpreting** What do the men in the cartoon represent?

2. **Analyzing** Look at each person's expression. How would you describe their expressions?

3. **Identifying Points of View** What does the cartoonist think will result from the men's action?

SECESSIONISTS LEAVING THE UNION

Republicans **rejected,** or refused to accept, this provision. They had just won an election on the principle that slavery would not be extended in any territories. "Now we are told . . ." Lincoln wrote, "the government shall be broken up unless we surrender to those we have beaten." Leaders in the South also rejected the plan. "We spit upon every plan to compromise," exclaimed one Southern leader. "No human power can save the Union," wrote another.

The Confederacy

By February 1861, Texas, Louisiana, Mississippi, Alabama, Florida, and Georgia joined South Carolina and also seceded. On February 4, delegates from these states and South Carolina met to form a new nation. Calling themselves the **Confederate States of America,** they chose **Jefferson Davis** as their president.

Southerners **justified,** or found reasons to support, secession with the theory of **states' rights.** The states, they argued, had voluntarily chosen to enter the Union. They defined the Constitution as a contract among the independent states. They believed the national government violated that contract by refusing to enforce the Fugitive Slave Act and by denying the Southern states equal rights in the territories. As a result, they argued, the states had a right to leave the Union.

Reactions to Secession

Many Southerners welcomed secession, ringing church bells and celebrating in the streets. Other Southerners, however, were alarmed. Virginian Robert E. Lee expressed concern about the future. "I only see that a fearful calamity is upon us," he wrote.

In the North, some abolitionists preferred to allow the Southern states to leave. If the Union could be kept together only by compromising on slavery, they declared, then let the Union be destroyed. Most Northerners, however, believed that the Union must be preserved. For Lincoln the issue was "whether in a free government the minority have the right to break up the government whenever they choose."

Lincoln Takes Office

Lincoln had won the election, but he was not yet president. James Buchanan's term ran until March 4, 1861. In December 1860, Buchanan sent a message to Congress saying that the Southern states had no right to secede from the Union. Then he added that he had no power to stop them from doing so.

As Lincoln prepared for his inauguration on March 4, 1861, people throughout the United States wondered what he would say and do. They wondered, too, what would happen in Virginia, North Carolina, Kentucky, Tennessee, Missouri, and Arkansas. These slave states chose to remain in the Union, but the decision was not final. If the United States used force against the Confederate States of America, the remaining slave states also might secede.

In his Inaugural Address, Lincoln spoke to the seceding states directly, mixing tough-ness with words of peace. He said that secession would not be permitted, that "the Union of these States is perpetual [forever]." He vowed to hold federal property in the South, including a number of forts and military installations, and to enforce the laws of the United States. At the same time, Lincoln pleaded with the South:

PRIMARY SOURCE

"In your hands, my dissatisfied fellow countrymen, and not in mine, are the momentous issues of *civil war*. The Government will not assail you. You can have no conflict without being yourselves the aggressors. . . . We are not *enemies*, but *friends*. *We must not be enemies.* Though passion may have strained, it must not break our bonds of affection."

—Abraham Lincoln, on reconciliation

✓ **Reading Check** **Explaining** What was John Crittenden's proposal to save the Union?

Seceding States, 1860–1861

NATIONAL GEOGRAPHIC

West Virginia separated from Virginia in 1861 and was admitted to the Union in 1863.

Jefferson Davis ▶

On February 4, 1861, delegates met in Alabama to form a new nation.

South Carolina was the first state to secede from the Union.

Washington Territory, Ore., Nevada Terr., Calif., Utah Territory, Dakota Territory, Minn., Wis., Mich., Nebraska Territory, Iowa, Ill., Ind., Ohio, Colorado Territory, Kans., Mo., Ky., W. Va., Va., N.C., Tenn., S.C., Ark., Miss., Ala., Ga., Tex., La., Fla., New Mexico Territory, Indian Terr., N.H., Vt., Me., Mass., N.Y., R.I., Pa., N.J., Conn., Washington, D.C., Del., Md.

PACIFIC OCEAN

ATLANTIC OCEAN

0 600 kilometers
0 600 miles
Lambert Azimuthal Equal-Area projection

Union territories
Union free state
Union slave state
Slave state seceding before siege of Ft. Sumter, April 1861
Slave state seceding after siege of Ft. Sumter, April 1861
Boundary between Union & Confederacy

Map Skills

1. **Regions** Which states seceded before the attack on Fort Sumter?

2. **Regions** Which states did not secede until after the attack on Fort Sumter?

Maps In Motion See StudentWorks™ Plus or glencoe.com.

Fort Sumter

Main Idea The Civil War began when Confederate forces attacked Fort Sumter in South Carolina.

History and You Have you ever argued with a family member over an item that you each felt you owned? Read to learn about events at Fort Sumter.

· ·

Confederate forces had already seized some U.S. forts within their states. Although Lincoln did not want to start a war by trying to take the forts back, allowing the Confederates to keep them would amount to admitting their right to secede.

The day after taking office, Lincoln received a message from the commander of **Fort Sumter,** a U.S. fort on an island guarding Charleston Harbor. The message warned that the fort was low on supplies and the Confederates demanded its surrender.

Lincoln responded by sending a message to Governor Francis Pickens of South Carolina. He informed Pickens that he was sending an unarmed expedition with supplies to Fort Sumter. Lincoln promised that Union forces would not "throw in men, arms, or ammunition" unless they were fired upon. The president thus left the decision to start shooting up to the Confederates.

Jefferson Davis made a fateful choice. He ordered his forces to attack Fort Sumter before the Union supplies could arrive. Confederate guns opened fire early on April 12, 1861. Union captain Abner Doubleday witnessed the attack from inside the fort:

PRIMARY SOURCE

"Showers of balls . . . and shells . . . poured into the fort in one incessant stream, causing great flakes of masonry to fall in all directions."

—quoted in *Fort Sumter*

High seas kept Union relief ships from reaching the fort. Fort Sumter surrendered on April 14. Thousands of shots were fired during the siege, but there was no loss of life.

President Lincoln issued a call for troops, and volunteers quickly signed up. Meanwhile, Virginia, North Carolina, Tennessee, and Arkansas voted to join the Confederacy. The Civil War had begun.

✓ **Reading Check** **Explaining** Why did Lincoln decide not to send armed troops to Fort Sumter?

Section 4 Review

History ONLINE
Study Central™ To review this section, go to <u>glencoe.com</u>.

Vocabulary

1. Use each of the following vocabulary terms in a sentence that will help explain its meaning: secession, reject, justify, states' rights.

Main Ideas

2. **Specifying** What action did South Carolina take after Lincoln won the election of 1860? Why?

3. **Explaining** What was the significance of the attack on Fort Sumter?

Critical Thinking

4. **Drawing Conclusions** How would you describe President Lincoln's priorities as he took office in March 1861?

5. **Sequencing** In a diagram like the one below, trace the events leading to the surrender of Fort Sumter.

6. **Descriptive Writing** Imagine that you are a Confederate journalist. Write a brief announcement about the attack on Fort Sumter for your newspaper. Then write another brief announcement of the event—this time from a Union journalist's point of view.

7. **Answer the Essential Question**
What role did the theory of states' rights play in the outbreak of the Civil War?

1848–1854

1848 The Free-Soil Party forms to oppose slavery in territories.

Van Buren-Adams poster, 1848 ▶

1850

- The Compromise of 1850 temporarily eases debate on slavery in Congress.
- The Fugitive Slave Act stirs up antislavery feelings in North.

1854

- The Kansas-Nebraska Act declares popular sovereignty in territories.
- Missouri voters help elect proslavery legislature in Kansas.
- The Republican Party forms as antislavery party.

1855–1859

1856

Jan. Kansas antislavery forces set up a rival government.

May Slavery supporters unleash violence in Kansas.

Oct. Federal troops are sent to end violence in "Bleeding Kansas."

1857 The *Dred Scott* decision rules that slavery is protected by the Constitution.

1858 Lincoln-Douglas debates focus on slavery and give Lincoln national recognition.

1859

Oct. John Brown raids Harpers Ferry arsenal uniting abolitionists.

1860–1861

1860

Nov. Lincoln is elected president.

Dec. South Carolina secedes; other Southern states follow.

1861

Feb. Southern states form Confederate States of America.

March Lincoln speaks of preserving the Union and preventing war in his Inaugural Address.

April The Confederate attack on Fort Sumter begins the Civil War.

◀ Fighting at Harpers Ferry

▲ Confederate attack on Fort Sumter

STUDY TO GO Study anywhere, anytime! Download quizzes and flash cards to your PDA from glencoe.com.

Did the South Have the Right to Secede?

Building Background

When Abraham Lincoln was inaugurated to his first term as president, on March 4, 1861, the unfinished Capitol dome seemed to reflect the uncertain future of the United States. Seven Southern states had already voted to secede from the Union and form the Confederate States of America.

The Confederate president, Jefferson Davis, had been inaugurated earlier, on February 18. Each man's inauguration address presented a different view on the basic question of whether a state had the right to secede from the Union.

NO

ABRAHAM LINCOLN

One section of our country believes slavery is right and ought to be extended, while the other believes it is wrong and ought not to be extended. This is the only substantial dispute. . . .

The [President] derives all his authority from the people, and they have referred none upon him to fix terms for the separation of the States. The people themselves can do this if also they choose, but the Executive as such has nothing to do with it. His duty is to administer[1] the present Government as it came to his hands and to transmit it unimpaired[2] by him to his successor. . . .

We are not enemies, but friends. We must not be enemies. Though passion may have strained it must not break our bonds of affection. The mystic chords of memory, stretching from every battlefield and patriot grave to every living heart and hearthstone all over this broad land, will yet swell the chorus of the Union, when again touched, as surely they will be, by the better angels of our nature.

Abraham Lincoln's first inauguration, March 4, 1861

---

[1] **administer** manage
[2] **unimpaired** unharmed

YES

JEFFERSON DAVIS

An agricultural people, whose chief interest is the export of a commodity required in every manufacturing country, our true policy is peace, and the freest trade which our necessities will permit. . . . There can be but little rivalry between ours and any manufacturing or navigating community, such as the Northeastern States of the American Union. It must follow, therefore, that a mutual interest would invite good will and kind offices. If, however, passion or the lust of dominion[3] should cloud the judgment or inflame the ambition of those States, we must prepare to meet the emergency and to maintain, by the final arbitrament[4] of the sword, the position which we have assumed among the nations of the earth. We have entered upon the career of independence, and it must be inflexibly pursued. . . . As a necessity, not a choice, we have resorted to the remedy of separation; and henceforth our energies must be directed to the conduct of our own affairs, and the perpetuity[5] of the Confederacy which we have formed.

---

[3] **dominion** territory

[4] **arbitrament** power to decide

[5] **perpetuity** lasting life

DBQ Document-Based Questions

1. **Identifying** What are Abraham Lincoln's and Jefferson Davis's basic arguments against or in favor of secession?

2. **Making Inferences** What issue seems most important to Lincoln? To Davis?

3. **Analyzing** Did either president refer to the economies of the different regions? If so, how were they described?

4. **Evaluating** In your opinion, which of the two addresses makes the more powerful appeal to emotions? Explain your answer in a short essay.

Jefferson Davis's inauguration in Montgomery, Alabama, February 18, 1861

INDIANA STATEWIDE TEST PRACTICE

Reviewing Vocabulary

Directions: Choose the word or words that best completes the sentence.

1 Southerners supported a strong national law that required states to return _____ enslaved people.

A transitory
B exiled
C fugitive
D injured

2 To counter opposition to slavery, Southern states often threatened to _____ from the Union.

A secede
B abstain
C subvert
D retaliate

3 A(n) _____ is an armed conflict between citizens of the same country.

A uprising
B civil disobedience
C civil war
D skirmish

4 Many abolitionists saw John Brown as a _____, a person who dies for a great cause.

A saint
B martyr
C fugitive
D debtor

Reviewing Main Ideas

Directions: Choose the best answer.

5 Which of the following was a proposal to ban slavery in any lands obtained from Mexico?

A Compromise of 1850
B Wilmot Proviso
C Missouri Compromise
D Freeport Doctrine

6 What resulted from the Fugitive Slave Act?

A The law's passage quieted violence in Kansas and Nebraska.
B Most Northerners believed Southern slaveholders' rights should be upheld.
C Abolitionists were jailed in the North.
D The law convinced many Northerners of the evils of slavery.

7 The Supreme Court decision in the *Dred Scott* case stated that

A enslaved people could bring lawsuits.
B Congress could not ban slavery in any territory.
C the slave trade should be abolished.
D the Missouri Compromise was unconstitutional.

8 Which idea was included in the Republican 1860 election platform?

A Slavery should be decided by popular sovereignty.
B The minority has the right to break up the government.
C Slavery should be left where it existed but banned from the territories.
D Slavery should be protected in all territories south of 36°30'N latitude.

GO ON

History ONLINE

For additional test practice, use **Self-Check Quizzes**—Chapter 15 at glencoe.com.

Critical Thinking

Directions: Choose the best answer.

Base your answer to question 9 on the cartoon below and your knowledge of Chapter 15.

SOUTHERN CHIVALRY — ARGUMENT VERSUS CLUB'S.

Source: Bettman/CORBIS

9 **This cartoon shows the attack on Senator Sumner over the issue of slavery. What emotions did the event in this cartoon stir up in the North?**

A Angry Northerners thought the attack showed the violence of Southern ways.

B Ashamed Northerners believed that the attack showed Northern weakness.

C Northerners celebrated because they thought the attack was justified.

D Northerners were indifferent because the attack involved two Southerners.

10 **Why did the addition of new territories after 1848 cause a problem for the United States?**

A War with Mexico would occur if the United States added the new territories.

B The new territories would add non-English speaking people to the country.

C Taxes would have to be raised to support the new territories.

D Their admission as slave or free states might upset the balance of power in Congress.

Constructed Response

Directions: Write a short response to each of the following questions. In your answer:

- *address all parts of the question*
- *use information from the chapter*
- *include facts, examples, and details relevant to the question*
- *use clear language*

11 **Explain why Kansas became an area of civil war.**

Base your answer to question 12 on the reading below and your knowledge of Chapter 15.

> We are not enemies, but friends. We must not be enemies. Though passion may have strained, it must not break our bonds of affection.
>
> —from Abraham Lincoln, *Inaugural Address*, 1861

12 **Why did Lincoln make this appeal in his 1861 Inaugural Address?**

13 **Identify where and under what circumstances the American Civil War began.**

14 **Discuss how public reactions to secession differed in the North and the South.**

STOP

Need Extra Help?														
If you missed questions. . .	1	2	3	4	5	6	7	8	9	10	11	12	13	14
Go to page. . .	451	451	455	461	450	453	458	463	455	448	454	465	466	464

The Civil War
1861–1865

Civil War: First at Vicksburg, 1863 by H. Charles McBarron, Jr.

PRESIDENTS

ABRAHAM
LINCOLN

U.S. Events

World Events

1861
Conflict at Fort Sumter,
South Carolina, begins
Civil War

★ **1861**
Robert E. Lee
named commander
of Confederate armies

1861

★ **1861**
• Russia emancipates serfs
• First ironclad warship
completed in England

1862

★ **1862**
International Red Cross
established; American
Red Cross organized 10
years later

Section 1: The Two Sides
Essential Question What were the strengths and weaknesses of the North and the South?

Section 2: Early Stages of the War
Essential Question Why did neither the Union nor the Confederacy gain a strong advantage during the early years of the war?

Section 3: Life During the War
Essential Question What social, political, and economic changes resulted from the war?

Section 4: The Strain of War
Essential Question How did the events at Gettysburg and Vicksburg change the course of the war?

Section 5: The War's Final Stages
Essential Question What events led to the end of the war?

History ONLINE
Chapter Overview Visit glencoe.com and click on **Chapter 16—Chapter Overviews** to preview chapter information.

FOLDABLES®
Study Organizer

Organizing Information
Make this Foldable to help organize what you learn about the Civil War.

Step 1 Fold a sheet of paper in half from side to side.

> Fold it so the left edge lies about $\frac{1}{2}$ inch from the right edge.

Step 2 Turn the paper and fold it into thirds.

> This will make three tabs.

Step 3 Unfold and cut the top layer only along both folds.

Step 4 Label your Foldable as shown.

Before the War | During the War | After the War
The Civil War

Reading and Writing As you read the chapter, list events that occurred before, during, and after the Civil War under the appropriate tabs of your Foldable.

ANDREW JOHNSON

★ **1863**
- Emancipation Proclamation issued
- Grant named commander of Union armies

★ **1864**
Sherman's March to the Sea begins

★ **1865**
Civil War ends

1863 ——————— **1864** ——————— **1865**

★ **1863**
London subway opens

★ **1864**
First Geneva Convention establishes rules for treatment of prisoners of war

★ **1865**
French writer Jules Verne publishes a novel about a trip to the moon

The Two Sides

Essential Question ◄

What were the strengths and weaknesses of the North and the South?

Reading Guide

Content Vocabulary
border state *(p. 475)* export *(p. 477)*
blockade *(p. 477)*

Academic Vocabulary
contrast *(p. 476)*   challenge *(p. 479)*

Key People and Events
Abraham Lincoln *(p. 475)*
Anaconda Plan *(p. 477)*

Reading Strategy
Taking Notes As you read, take notes on the differences and similarities between the two sides.

North   South

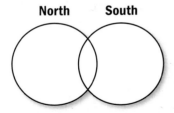

INDIANA ACADEMIC STANDARDS
United States History

8.1.10 Compare differences in ways of life in the northern and southern states, including the growth of towns and cities in the North and the growing dependence on slavery in the South.

8.1.21 Describe the importance of key events and individuals in the Civil War.

American Diary

At the Battle of Malvern Hill in 1862, a Union sergeant named Driscoll shot a young Confederate soldier. Hurrying forward, Driscoll turned the soldier's face up to see if the young man was dead. But when he looked at the dying soldier's face, he received a terrible shock. Looking up, the boy murmured, "Father," and then closed his eyes forever. The soldier was his son, who had gone south before the war.

Goals and Strategies

Main Idea The North and the South had many different strengths, strategies, and purposes in the Civil War.

History and You Is it better for an army to have plenty of soldiers or a powerful will to fight? Why? Read to learn how these characteristics affected the Civil War.

. . . .

Like the Driscolls, many families were divided by the war. Neither side imagined, however, that the war would cost such a terrible price in human life. During the four years of fighting, hundreds of thousands of Americans had lost their lives. Many thousands more were wounded in battle.

The Border States

For most states, choosing sides in the Civil War was easy. The **border states** of Delaware, Maryland, Kentucky, and Missouri, however, were bitterly divided. Slavery was legal in all four states, though none had many enslaved people. All four had ties to the North and the South.

These states were vital to the Union because of their strategic locations. Missouri could control parts of the Mississippi River and major routes to the West. Kentucky controlled the Ohio River. Delaware was close to Philadelphia.

Maryland, perhaps the most important of the border states, was close to Richmond, the Confederate capital. Most significantly, Washington, D.C., lay within the state. If Maryland seceded, the North's government would be surrounded.

President **Abraham Lincoln** worked tirelessly to keep the four border states in the Union. In the end, he was successful.

Still, many border state residents supported the Confederacy. The president had his hands full trying to restrain these opponents of the war. In September 1861, Lincoln wrote:

PRIMARY SOURCE

"I think to lose Kentucky is nearly the same as to lose the whole game. . . . We would as well consent to separation at once, including the surrender of this capitol."

—from *Abraham Lincoln: His Speeches and Writings*

More than 400,000 Union and Confederate soldiers were wounded in battle during the Civil War.

By the Numbers / The Fighting Forces

Organization of the Armies The smaller Confederate army and the larger Union army were organized in roughly the same way.

1861–1865

Union soldiers
2,100,000

Confederate soldiers
900,000

50 Soldiers	= 1 Platoon
2 Platoons	= 1 Company
10 Companies	= 1 Regiment
4–6 Regiments	= 1 Brigade
4–5 Brigades	= 1 Division
3 Divisions	= 1 Corps

Critical Thinking

Concluding Why do you think the armed forces were divided into units?

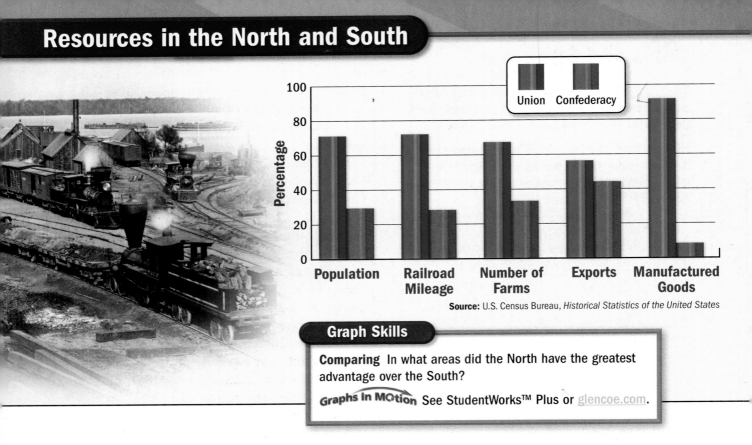

Source: U.S. Census Bureau, *Historical Statistics of the United States*

Graph Skills

Comparing In what areas did the North have the greatest advantage over the South?

Graphs In Motion See StudentWorks™ Plus or glencoe.com.

Comparing North and South

When the war began, both sides had advantages and disadvantages. How they would use those strengths and weaknesses would determine the war's outcome.

The North had a larger population and better resources than the South. The South had other advantages, such as excellent military leaders and a strong fighting spirit. Also, because most of the war was fought in the South, the Confederacy knew the land and had the will to defend it.

War Aims

The North and the South had different aims in fighting the Civil War. The South's goal was to establish itself as an independent nation. To do this, the South did not have to invade the North or destroy the Union army. The Confederacy needed only to fight hard enough and long enough to convince Northerners that the war was not worth its cost.

In **contrast,** the Northern goal was to restore the Union. That meant invading the South and forcing the breakaway states to give up their quest for sovereignty. Although slavery helped drive a wedge between Northerners and Southerners, President Lincoln's original aim was not to defeat slavery. He wrote in 1862:

PRIMARY SOURCE

"If I could save the Union without freeing *any* slave I would do it."

—from *Abraham Lincoln: His Speeches and Writings*

Confederate Strategies

The South expected support from Britain and France, whose supply of Southern cotton was being disrupted by the war. Southerners reasoned that these nations might pressure the North to end the war.

The South's basic strategy, however, was to conduct a defensive war. This meant that the South would hold on to as much territory as possible. Southerners felt that if they showed determination to be independent, Northerners would tire of the war. The only exception to this defensive strategy was a plan to attack Washington, D.C.

Union Strategies

The North's war plan came from General Winfield Scott, hero of the war with Mexico. Knowing that the North would have to subdue the South completely, he proposed three main strategies for winning the war.

First, the Union should **blockade,** or close, Southern ports. This strategy would prevent supplies from reaching the Confederacy. It also would keep the South from **exporting** its cotton crop—or selling it to other countries.

Second, the North intended to gain control of the entire Mississippi River, which would split the Confederacy in two and cut Southern supply lines. Scott's plan was called the **Anaconda Plan,** after the snake that squeezes its prey to death.

Third, the North planned to capture Richmond, Virginia, the Confederate capital.

✓ Reading Check **Explaining** Why was it to the South's advantage to fight a defensive war?

Americans Against Americans

Main Idea Soldiers in the Civil War came from every region, and each side expected an early victory.

History and You What motivates men and women to join the armed forces today? Read to find out about the backgrounds of the Civil War soldiers.

· ·

The Civil War was more than a war between the states. It pitted brother against brother and neighbor against neighbor. Kentucky senator John Crittenden had two sons who became generals. One fought for the Confederacy, the other for the Union. Even President Lincoln's wife, Mary Todd Lincoln, had relatives in the Confederate army.

Many left their homes and families to enlist in the Union or Confederate armies. Soldiers on both sides had many reasons for signing up. Some were motivated by patriotism and loyalty to their causes.

Economics & History

Enlisted men in both the Union and Confederate armies were paid monthly. Compare the pay rates to those in later wars.

Army Salaries (monthly)

Rank	Civil War	World War II 1942	Vietnam War 1965	Iraq War 2007
Private	*$13	$50	$85	$1,203 – 1,543.20
Corporal	$14	$66	$210	$1,699.50
Sergeant	$17	$78	$261	$1,854 – 2,339.10
Sergeant Major	$21	$138	$486	$4,110

*Until 1864, African Americans in the Civil War were paid only $7.00 per month.

Source: *Bureau of Economic Analysis*; Princeton Review; www.militaryfactory.com

To get more men to enlist, Union recruiters put up posters offering a sign-up bonus or bounty.

$7.20	Overcoat	$1.14	Pair of Shoes
$6.71	Dress Coat	$1.35	Hat
$2.95	Blanket	$0.88	Undershirt
$2.63	Blouse	$0.55	Underwear
$3.03	Trousers	$0.26	Socks

Soldiers had to replace any of the clothing they lost out of their own pay.

Union soldier's cap ▲

Critical Thinking

Calculating What was a private's weekly salary in the Civil War?

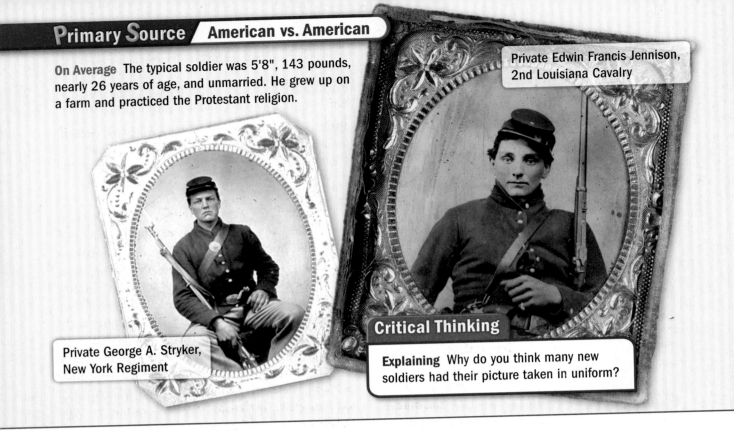

On Average The typical soldier was 5'8", 143 pounds, nearly 26 years of age, and unmarried. He grew up on a farm and practiced the Protestant religion.

Private Edwin Francis Jennison, 2nd Louisiana Cavalry

Private George A. Stryker, New York Regiment

Critical Thinking

Explaining Why do you think many new soldiers had their picture taken in uniform?

Others thought they would be called cowards if they did not serve. Still others yearned for excitement. The sister of William Stone of Louisiana wrote that her brother was:

PRIMARY SOURCE

"wild to be off to Virginia [to join the Confederate army]. He so fears that the fighting will be over before he can get there."
—from *Brokenburn: The Journal of Kate Stone*

The quest for excitement was especially strong among younger soldiers. Many recruits on both sides were hardly adults. Tens of thousands of soldiers were under 18, and some were younger than 14. To get into the army, many teenagers ran away from home or lied about their ages.

Although teenage boys were accepted into military service, one group of men was not permitted to fight during the early days of the war. Unwilling to provide enslaved people with weapons, the Confederacy barred African Americans from the army. The Union also refused to let freed people enlist. Northern leaders worried that white troops would not accept African American soldiers. Later in the war, though, this policy was changed.

False Hopes

When the war began, each side expected an easy victory. Northerners could not imagine the Confederates holding out for long against the Union's greater resources. They boasted that the war would end in a quick and glorious triumph for the Union.

Confederates found it impossible to believe that the North could ever subdue the fighting spirit of the South. Both sides were wrong. In the end, the war lasted far longer than most Americans could have guessed.

Who Were the Soldiers?

Soldiers came from every region and all walks of life. Most, though, came from farms. Almost half of the North's troops and more than 60 percent of the South's had owned or worked on farms. Lincoln's early terms of enlistment asked governors to supply soldiers for 90 days. When the conflict did not end quickly, soldiers' terms became longer.

By the summer of 1861, the Confederate army had about 112,000 soldiers, who were sometimes called Rebels. The Union had about 187,000 soldiers, or Yankees, as they were also known. By the end of the war, about 900,000 men fought for the Confederacy and about 2.1 million men for the Union. The Union army included just under 200,000 African Americans and about 10,000 Latino soldiers.

The Life of a Soldier

In both the North and the South, civilians and soldiers suffered terrible hardships and faced new **challenges.** In letters to their families and friends at home, soldiers described what they saw and how they felt. Many wrote about their boredom, discomfort, sickness, fear, and horror.

Most of the time the soldiers lived in camps. Camp life had its pleasant moments of songs, stories, letters from home, and baseball games. Often, however, a soldier's life was dull—a seemingly unchanging routine of drills, bad food, marches, and rain.

During lulls between battles, Confederate and Union soldiers sometimes forgot they were enemies. A private described his wartime experiences:

PRIMARY SOURCE

"A part of Co K and some of the enemy came together and stacked arms and talked for a long time. Our men cooked coffee and treated them and [afterward] . . . each one took up his position again and they began to fire at each other again, but not as hard as before."
—from *The Life of Billy Yank*

The Reality of War

In spite of fleeting moments of calm, the reality of war was never far away. Both sides suffered terrible losses. The new rifles used during the Civil War fired with greater accuracy than the muskets of earlier wars.

Medical facilities were overwhelmed by the thousands of casualties. After the Battle of Shiloh, the wounded lay in the rain for more than 24 hours waiting for treatment. A Union soldier recalled, "Many had died there, and others were in the last agonies as we passed. Their groans and cries were heart-rending."

Faced with such horrors, many men deserted. About one of every 11 Union soldiers and one of every 8 Confederates ran away because of fear, hunger, or sickness.

Reading Check Explaining Why did both sides think the war would end quickly?

Section 1 Review

History ONLINE
Study Central™ To review this section, go to glencoe.com.

Vocabulary

1. Write a short paragraph in which you use all the following vocabulary terms: border state, contrast, blockade, export, challenge.

Main Ideas

2. **Explaining** Why were the border states important to both the North and South?

3. **Evaluating** What was the purpose of the Anaconda Plan?

Critical Thinking

4. **Predicting** What do you think would be the South's greatest advantage in the war?

5. **Comparing** Create a diagram to compare Northern and Southern aims and strategies.

	North	South
Aims		
Strategies		

6. **Descriptive Writing** You are a Southerner or Northerner in 1861. Write a journal entry that explains your reasons for joining the Confederate or Union army.

**Answer the
Essential Question**

7. What were the strengths and weaknesses of the North and the South?

Early Stages of the War

Essential Question

Why did neither the Union nor the Confederacy gain a strong advantage during the early years of the war?

Reading Guide

Content Vocabulary

tributary *(p. 482)* casualty *(p. 483)*
ironclad *(p. 483)*

Academic Vocabulary

abandon *(p. 481)* impact *(p. 487)*

Key People and Events

Stonewall Jackson *(p. 481)*
Ulysses S. Grant *(p. 482)*
Battle of Shiloh *(p. 483)*
Robert E. Lee *(p. 485)*
Battle of Antietam *(p. 486)*
Frederick Douglass *(p. 487)*
Emancipation Proclamation *(p. 487)*

Reading Strategy

Taking Notes As you read, place the early Civil War battles described in the text on a time line and take notes on what happened during each one.

INDIANA ACADEMIC STANDARDS
United States History

8.1.21 Describe the importance of key events and individuals in the Civil War.

8.1.24 Identify the influence of individuals on political and social events and movements such as the abolition movement, the Dred Scott case, women's rights, and Native American Indian removal.

8.3.1 Read maps to interpret symbols and determine the landforms and human features that represent physical and cultural characteristics of areas in the United States.

American Diary

Captain Van Brunt, of the U.S. Navy, described the historic first battle between metal-plated ships in 1862: "[The Monitor*] laid herself right alongside of the* Merrimack, *and the contrast was that of a pigmy to a giant. Gun after gun was fired by the* Monitor, *which was returned with whole broadsides from the rebels with no more effect, apparently, than so many pebblestones thrown by a child."*

—*quoted in* Official Records of the Union and Confederate Navies in the War of the Rebellion, *1898*

War on Land and Sea

Main Idea The Confederates decisively won the First Battle of Bull Run.

History and You Would you eat a picnic lunch while a battle was raging all around you? Read to learn what happened in 1861 when many people did exactly that.

. . . .

The Civil War was fought on sea as well as on land. While the Union and Confederacy mobilized their armies, the Union navy began operations against the South. In April 1861, President Lincoln proclaimed a blockade of all Confederate ports.

Southerners hoped to break the Union blockade with a secret weapon—the *Merrimack*, an **abandoned** Union warship. The Confederates rebuilt and covered the wooden ship in iron. The armored vessel, renamed the *Virginia*, could withstand Union cannon fire.

First Battle of Bull Run

Pressure mounted in the summer of 1861, leading to the first major battle of the Civil War. On July 21, about 30,000 inexperienced Union troops commanded by General Irvin McDowell attacked a smaller, equally inexperienced Confederate force led by General P. G. T. Beauregard. The fighting took place in northern Virginia, about 5 miles (8 km) from the town of Manassas Junction near a small river called Bull Run. Hundreds of Washington, D.C., residents went to the battle site to picnic and watch.

The Yankees drove the Confederates back at first. Then the Rebels rallied, inspired by reinforcements under General Thomas Jackson. Jackson was seen holding out heroically, "like a stone wall," and became known thereafter as **"Stonewall" Jackson.** The Confederates unleashed a savage counterattack that forced Union lines to break. The Union retreat turned into a mad stampede when retreating Union troops collided with the civilians, fleeing in panic back to Washington, D.C.

The outcome shocked Northerners. They began to understand that the war could be a long, difficult, and costly struggle. President Lincoln appointed a new general, George B. McClellan, to head and organize the Union army of the East—called the Army of the Potomac—and to train the troops.

Primary Source | Naval Warfare

The Ironclads The *Monitor* was small for a warship—about 172 feet (52 m) long—and constructed almost entirely of iron. A revolving armored tower called a turret housed the guns.

The Union's *Monitor* (below) battled the ironclad *Merrimack* (left), called the *Virginia* by the Confederates, on March 9, 1862.

iron turret rotates on a pivot

11-inch (28-cm) cannon housed inside rotating turret

layered armor plating

Critical Thinking

Making Inferences What advantages would an iron warship have over a wooden ship? Explain.

The loss at Bull Run discouraged Union supporters. Although dismayed by the results, President Lincoln was also determined. Within days he issued a call for more volunteers for the army. He signed two bills requesting a total of 1 million soldiers to serve for three years. Victories in the West raised Northern spirits and also increased enlistment.

The War in the West

In the West, the major Union goal was to control the Mississippi River and its **tributaries,** the smaller rivers that flow into a larger river. With control of the river, Union ships on the Mississippi could prevent the states of Louisiana, Arkansas, and Texas from supplying the rest of the Confederacy. Control would also let Union gunboats and troops move into the heart of the South.

The battle for the rivers began in February 1862 when Union forces captured Fort Henry on the Tennessee River. The assault was led by naval commander Andrew Foote and army general **Ulysses S. Grant.** Soon afterward, Grant and Foote moved against Fort Donelson on the Cumberland River. The Confederates in Fort Donelson realized that they had no chance of winning the battle, so they asked Grant what terms, or incentives, he would give them to give up the fort. Grant said:

PRIMARY SOURCE

"No terms except an unconditional and immediate surrender can be accepted."
—General Grant to General Buckner, February 1862

"Unconditional Surrender" Grant became the North's new hero.

War of the Ironclads

As conflict was raging on the rivers of the West, ships of the Union and Confederate navies were fighting in the Atlantic Ocean.

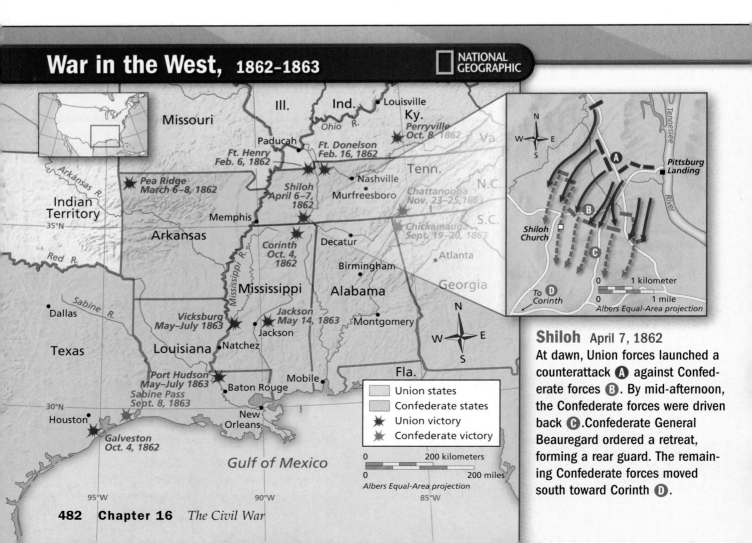

War in the West, 1862–1863

NATIONAL GEOGRAPHIC

Union states
Confederate states
★ Union victory
✷ Confederate victory

0   200 kilometers
0   200 miles
Albers Equal-Area projection

0   1 kilometer
0   1 mile
Albers Equal-Area projection

Shiloh April 7, 1862
At dawn, Union forces launched a counterattack Ⓐ against Confederate forces Ⓑ. By mid-afternoon, the Confederate forces were driven back Ⓒ.Confederate General Beauregard ordered a retreat, forming a rear guard. The remaining Confederate forces moved south toward Corinth Ⓓ.

On March 8, 1862, the *Merrimack*, renamed the *Virginia*, attacked a group of Union ships off the coast of Virginia. The North's wooden warships could not damage the Confederate ship—shells simply bounced off its iron sides. Some Northern leaders feared the South would use the **ironclad** warship to destroy the Union navy, steam up the Potomac River, and bombard Washington, D.C.

The North, though, had an ironclad ship of its own, the *Monitor,* and this ship rushed toward Virginia. On March 9, the two ironclads met in battle. Neither ship could sink the other. Although the battle was indecisive, it was also historic because it was the first ever between metal-covered ships.

The Battle of Shiloh

Meanwhile, in the West, General Grant and about 40,000 troops headed south along the Tennessee River toward Corinth, Mississippi, an important railroad junction. In early April 1862, the Union army camped at Pittsburg Landing, 20 miles (32 km) from Corinth. Nearby was a church named Shiloh. Additional Union forces came from Nashville to join Grant.

Confederate leaders decided to strike first, before the reinforcements arrived. Early in the morning of April 6, Confederate forces led by Albert Sidney Johnston and P. G. T. Beauregard launched a surprise attack on the Union troops. The **Battle of Shiloh** lasted two days, with some of the most bitter, bloody fighting of the war. Even though Shiloh was a narrow victory for the Union forces, the losses were enormous. Together the two armies suffered more than 23,000 **casualties**—people killed or wounded.

After Shiloh, Union forces gained control of Corinth on May 30. Memphis, Tennessee, fell to Union armies on June 6. The North seemed well on its way to controlling the Mississippi River.

The Battle of Shiloh

More than 23,000 troops were killed or wounded in the Battle of Shiloh. This was the highest number of casualties of any Civil War battle to date. The Union victory was an important step toward the goal of controlling the Mississippi River.

Critical Thinking

Analyzing Did either Beauregard or Sherman accept the fact that his side might lose the Battle of Shiloh? Do you think their statements reflect what most military leaders would say in this situation? Explain.

Day One

A surprise attack by the Confederate army gave it an early advantage. Union general William T. Sherman remarked to General Grant, *"Well, Grant, we've had the devil's own day of it, haven't we?"*

"Yes," Grant replied, *"Lick 'em tomorrow, though."*

◀ William T. Sherman

Day Two

With Union reinforcements, the battle changed direction, resulting in a Union victory. Confederate general P. G. T. Beauregard lamented, *"I thought I had General Grant just where I wanted him and could finish him up in the morning."*

P. G. T. Beauregard ▶

Battle Dates

Monitor & Virginia
Mar. 9, 1862

Seven Days
June 25–July 1, 1862

Bull Run
(2nd Battle)
Aug. 29–30, 1862

Antietam
Sept. 17, 1862

Fredericksburg
Dec. 13, 1862

Chancellorsville
May 1–4, 1863

Gettysburg
July 1–3, 1863

Union advance
Union retreat
Confederate advance
Confederate retreat
Union victory
Confederate victory
Inconclusive battle

New Orleans Falls

A few weeks after Shiloh, the North won another important victory. On April 25, 1862, Union naval forces under David Farragut captured New Orleans, Louisiana, the largest city in the South. Farragut, who was of Spanish descent, grew up in the South but remained loyal to the Union. His capture of New Orleans, near the mouth of the Mississippi River, meant that the Confederacy could no longer use the river to carry its goods to sea. Together with Grant's victories to the north, the capture of New Orleans gave the Union control of most of the Mississippi River. Only the city of Vicksburg, Mississippi, blocked Union control of the river and the success of the Union's western strategy.

Reading Check **Comparing and Contrasting**
How was the Battle of Shiloh like the First Battle of Bull Run? How were the two battles different?

War in the East

Main Idea The South won several important victories in the East during 1862, but the Union responded with a vital triumph of its own.

History and You What is the most valuable thing you have lost? Read to learn what happened when a Confederate officer lost some important papers.

W hile Union and Confederate forces were struggling for control of Tennessee and the Mississippi River, another major campaign was being waged in the East to capture Richmond, Virginia. Richmond, the capital of the Confederacy, was close to the northern Confederate border and vulnerable to attack. Yet it was a matter of pride to defend it at all costs. Repelling one Union advance after another, Confederate armies prevented the fall of Richmond until the end of the war.

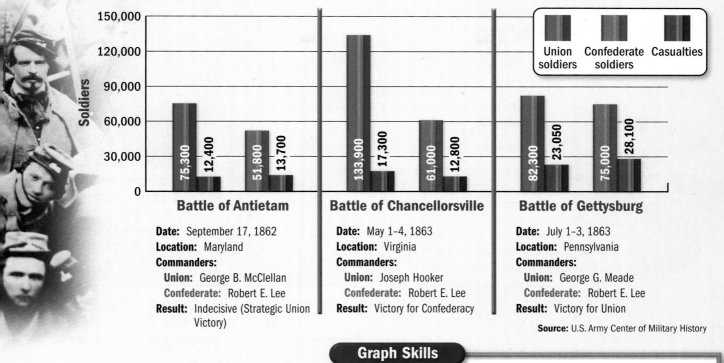

By the Numbers

The Battle of Antietam was the bloodiest one-day battle in the war and in American history. Several battles in the East were costly in terms of total casualties (killed, wounded, missing, and captured).

Soldiers

150,000
120,000
90,000
60,000
30,000
0

Union soldiers | Confederate soldiers | Casualties

Battle of Antietam
75,300 12,400

Date: September 17, 1862
Location: Maryland
Commanders:
  Union: George B. McClellan
  Confederate: Robert E. Lee
Result: Indecisive (Strategic Union Victory)

Battle of Chancellorsville
133,900 17,300 61,000 12,800

Date: May 1–4, 1863
Location: Virginia
Commanders:
  Union: Joseph Hooker
  Confederate: Robert E. Lee
Result: Victory for Confederacy

Battle of Gettysburg
82,300 23,050 75,000 28,100

Date: July 1–3, 1863
Location: Pennsylvania
Commanders:
  Union: George G. Meade
  Confederate: Robert E. Lee
Result: Victory for Union

Source: U.S. Army Center of Military History

Graph Skills

Calculating About how many soldiers fought at Chancellorsville?

Graphs In Motion See StudentWorks™ Plus or glencoe.com.

Victories for the Confederacy

Southern victories in the East were largely the result of the leadership of General **Robert E. Lee** and Stonewall Jackson. Through knowledge of the terrain, speed of movement, and the ability to inspire their troops, Confederate forces managed to defeat Union forces sometimes twice as large as their own.

In 1862 Confederate forces turned back General George B. McClellan at the Seven Days' Battle, General John Pope at the Second Battle of Bull Run, and General Ambrose Burnside at Fredericksburg. In May 1863, at Chancellorsville, Virginia, Lee's army defeated a Union army twice its size. "My God, my God," Lincoln said when he learned of the defeat, "What will the country say!"

Victories in the East did not include victories outside the Confederacy. Lee's two attempts to invade the North failed. In September 1862,

Lee's army was turned back at the Battle of Antietam. Less than a year later, Confederate forces would face the same fate at Gettysburg. You will read about the Battle of Gettysburg in Section 4.

Invasion of the North

Washington, D.C., presented a tempting target for the Confederates, but the city was too well guarded for Lee to consider an attack. On the urging of Confederate president Jefferson Davis, Lee moved his troops instead into western Maryland—Union territory. His goal now was to sweep into Pennsylvania and carry the war into the Northern states. Lee knew that McClellan was pursuing him with a sizable force, so he concentrated on moving forward. Lee's forces crossed into Maryland and began an invasion of the North.

Lincoln declared in the Emancipation Proclamation that:

"all persons held as slaves within any state . . . in rebellion against the United States, shall be then, thenceforward and forever free."

Results of the Proclamation

✔ It sent a clear message to enslaved people and the Confederacy that slavery would no longer be tolerated.

✔ African American military units were formed.

✔ Europe was strongly opposed to slavery. No European government would defend the South in its war to protect the institution of slavery.

"If my name ever goes into history, it will be for this act."
—Abraham Lincoln, 1863

"The white man's happiness cannot be purchased by the black man's misery."
—Frederick Douglass, 1849

Critical Thinking

Explaining What political reasons did Lincoln have for issuing the Emancipation Proclamation?

The Battle of Antietam

Once in Maryland, Lee split his army in four parts and instructed them to move in different directions. He hoped to confuse McClellan about the size and destination of his army. A Confederate officer, however, lost his copy of Lee's orders describing this plan. The paper was found by two Union soldiers, who brought it to McClellan.

McClellan did not attack immediately. Lee reassembled his troops, and on September 17, 1862, the two sides met in the **Battle of Antietam** near Sharpsburg, Maryland.

About 6,000 soldiers were killed. About 17,000 more were badly wounded. It was the deadliest single day of fighting during the war. Antietam was an important victory for the Union. Because of the great losses, Lee chose to retreat to Virginia after the fighting. At least for the time being, his strategy of invading the North had failed. The Union could breathe a little more easily.

Reading Check **Summarizing** What was the outcome of the Battle of Antietam?

The Emancipation Proclamation

Main Idea Lincoln's Emancipation Proclamation had an enormous effect in America and abroad.

History and You How do you make difficult decisions? Read to learn about the debate over the war's purpose and how Lincoln eventually settled on a course of action.

At first, Abraham Lincoln cast the Civil War as a battle for the Union rather than as a fight against slavery. As the conflict progressed, however, Lincoln changed the way he thought about slavery and its role in the war.

The Debate

Lincoln hated slavery, yet he was reluctant to make the Civil War a battle to end it. He feared that many Union supporters would strongly oppose such a decision. At the beginning of the war, Lincoln hesitated to move against slavery because of the border states.

Even many Northerners who disapproved of slavery were not eager to risk their lives to end it. Other Americans held a different opinion, however.

From the start of the war, abolitionists, including orator **Frederick Douglass** and newspaper editor Horace Greeley, urged Lincoln to make the war a fight to end slavery. These Northerners made several arguments to support their position. First, they argued, slavery was a moral wrong that needed to be abolished. Second, they pointed out that slavery was the root of the divisions between North and South. Therefore, the nation could never be fully restored if slavery continued.

Finally, Douglass and others brought up the issue of foreign policy. Britain and France each sympathized with the South for economic reasons. Southern leaders were trying to persuade Britain and France to recognize the Confederacy's independence.

Public opinion in England and France was strongly antislavery. By casting the war as a fight for freedom, Douglass pointed out, Lincoln would make Britain and France less willing to support the South. That, in turn, would help the Union cause.

Lincoln Decides

Lincoln knew that the Constitution did not give him the power to end slavery. The Constitution did, however, give him the power to take property from an enemy in wartime—and, by law, enslaved people were property. On September 22, 1862, soon after the North's victory at Antietam, Lincoln announced that he would issue the **Emancipation Proclamation**—a decree freeing all enslaved people in rebel territory on January 1, 1863.

Effects of the Proclamation

The Emancipation Proclamation did not actually free a single enslaved person. The proclamation applied only to enslaved people in areas held by the Confederacy. There Lincoln had no power to enforce the new policy.

The proclamation had an important **impact** in America, however. By issuing the Emancipation Proclamation, the government declared slavery to be wrong. If the Union won the war, slavery would be banned forever.

✔ **Reading Check** **Summarizing** Why did abolitionists believe that Lincoln should make the end of slavery a goal of the war?

Section 2 Review

History ONLINE
Study Central™ To review this section, go to glencoe.com.

Vocabulary

1. Use each of these terms in a sentence that will help explain its meaning: abandon, tributary, ironclad, casualty, impact.

Main Ideas

2. Analyzing What factors helped the Confederates win the First Battle of Bull Run?

3. Summarizing What was the final outcome of the Battle of Shiloh?

4. Explaining What did the Emancipation Proclamation state?

Critical Thinking

5. Analyzing Why was controlling the Mississippi River vital to the North and the South? Explain your answer in a diagram like the one shown here.

Control of the Mississippi

6. Evaluating Which of Frederick Douglass's arguments for making the abolition of slavery an aim of the war do you find most convincing? Why?

7. Expository Writing You read about General Lee's lost battle orders. Write a short paragraph explaining the role of chance and error in this discovery, as well as General McClellan's use of the information.

Answer the
8. Essential Question
Why did neither the Union nor the Confederacy gain a strong advantage during the early years of the war?

America's LITERATURE

Meet the Author

Stephen Crane (1871–1900) had never seen a battlefield when he wrote *The Red Badge of Courage,* which he based on accounts of the Confederate victory at Chancellorsville. Even so, he described the experience of war so realistically that even combat veterans admired his work.

Building Background

The American novelist Stephen Crane, who created the most famous depiction of Civil War combat in his 1895 novel *The Red Badge of Courage,* did not describe warfare in traditional, heroic terms. Instead, he tried to present an objective, almost scientific examination of the effect of battle on individuals. As you read this excerpt from *The Red Badge of Courage,* be aware of how Crane creates an effect of realism.

Vocabulary

careering speeding

exasperation extreme irritation

impotency powerlessness

imprecations curses

pummeling beating

exultant very joyful

THE RED BADGE OF COURAGE

Stephen Crane

He was at a task. He was like a carpenter who has made many boxes, making still another box, only there was furious haste in his movements. He, in his thought, was **careering** off in other places, even as the carpenter who as he works whistles and thinks of his friend or his enemy, his home or a saloon. And these jolted dreams were never perfect to him afterward, but remained a mass of blurred shapes.

Presently he began to feel the effects of the war atmosphere—a blistering sweat, a sensation that his eyeballs were about to crack like hot stones. A burning roar filled his ears.

Following this came a red rage. He developed the acute **exasperation** of a pestered animal, a well-meaning cow worried by dogs. He had a mad feeling against his rifle, which could only be used against one life at a time. He wished to rush forward and strangle with his fingers. He craved a power that would enable him to make a world-sweeping gesture and brush all back. His **impotency** appeared to him, and made his rage into that of a driven beast.

A burning roar filled his ears.

Buried in the smoke of many rifles his anger was directed not so much against the men whom he knew were rushing toward him as against the swirling battle phantoms which were choking him, stuffing their smoke robes down his parched throat. He fought frantically for respite for his senses, for air, as a babe being smothered attacks the deadly blankets.

There was a blare of heated rage mingled with a certain expression of intentness on all faces. Many of the men were making low-toned noises with their mouths, and these subdued cheers, snarls, **imprecations,** prayers, made a wild, barbaric song that went as an undercurrent of sound, strange and chantlike with the resounding chords of the war march. The man at the youth's elbow was babbling. In it there was something soft and tender like the monologue of a babe. . . .

The lieutenant of the youth's company had encountered a soldier who had fled screaming at the first volley of his comrades. Behind the lines these two were acting a little isolated scene. The man was blubbering and staring with sheeplike eyes at the lieutenant, who had seized him by the collar and was **pummeling** him. He drove him back into the ranks with many blows. The soldier went mechanically, dully, with his animal-like eyes upon the officer. Perhaps there was to him a divinity expressed in the voice of the other—stern, hard, with no reflection of fear in it. He tried to reload his gun, but his shaking hands prevented. The lieutenant was obliged to assist him.

The men dropped here and there like bundles. The captain of the youth's company had been killed in an early part of the action. His body lay stretched out in the position of a tired man resting, but upon his face there was an astonished and sorrowful look, as if he thought some friend had done him an ill turn. . . .

At last an **exultant** yell went along the quivering line. The firing dwindled from an uproar to a last vindictive popping. As the smoke slowly eddied away, the youth saw that the charge had been repulsed. The enemy were scattered into reluctant groups. He saw a man climb to the top of the fence, straddle the rail, and fire a parting shot. The waves had receded, leaving bits of dark *débris* upon the ground.

Analyzing Literature

1. **Respond** What surprised you most about Stephen Crane's description of combat?

2. **Recall and Interpret**
   (a) What is the "dark *débris*" left on the battlefield?
   (b) What is the effect of using this phrase?

3. **Evaluate and Connect**
   (a) In your opinion, which details in this passage contribute most powerfully to the effect of realism Crane was striving to create?
   (b) What conclusions can you draw from Crane's depiction of battle?

Essential Question

What social, political, and economic changes resulted from the war?

Reading Guide

Content Vocabulary

habeas corpus (p. 495)

greenback (p. 497)

draft (p. 496)

inflation (p. 497)

bounty (p. 496)

Academic Vocabulary

distribute (p. 493)   substitute (p. 496)

Key People and Events

Mary Edwards Walker (p. 492)

Dorothea Dix (p. 492)

Clara Barton (p. 492)

Sally Tompkins (p. 492)

bread riots (p. 494)

Reading Strategy

Taking Notes As you read the section, complete a diagram like the one below by describing three ways that women in the North and the South contributed to the war effort.

Contributions

INDIANA ACADEMIC STANDARDS
United States History

8.1.21 Describe the importance of key events and individuals in the Civil War.

8.1.26 Give examples of the changing role of women and minorities in the northern, southern, and western parts of the United States in the mid-nineteenth century, and examine possible causes for these changes.

American Diary

Drummer boy Delavan Miller, who served in a New York Regiment, recalls: "The day after a battle is always a sad one in a regiment. Men search for missing comrades and some are found cold in death who were full of life the day before. No jests are spoken. The terribleness of war has been forcibly impressed on all participants."

—*from* Drum Taps in Dixie

Men with the 36th Pennsylvania Infantry Regiment drill at their winter quarters near Langley, Virginia.

A Different Way of Life

Main Idea The Civil War affected civilians as well as soldiers.

History and You How does war change the everyday life of citizens? Read on to find out how Americans tried to adjust to wartime conditions.

. . . .

Thirteen-year-old Delavan Miller served as a drummer for a New York regiment. He recalls that:

PRIMARY SOURCE

"The great majority of the men really felt that the war would be ended before we had a chance to take a hand in. I may say that the drummer boys, full of young red blood, were as eager for [battle] as the older men, but most of us had got enough of war before we reached Appomattox."

—from *Drum Taps in Dixie*

Life at Home

When the Civil War began, Miller, like many other teenagers, left everything that was familiar to him to serve in the military. This meant leaving family, friends, and school.

Almost everyone who stayed home was touched in some way by the war. Only about one-half of the 12 million school-age children attended school. Many of those who did not worked to help support their families. Schools closed during the war in some areas, especially those near the scenes of battles and skirmishes. Many schools and churches served as hospitals for the wounded.

Shortages in the South

Although the war affected everyone, life in the South changed most dramatically. Both armies spent most of their time on Southern soil, and the South therefore suffered the greatest destruction. Southerners who lived in the paths of marching armies lost crops and homes. Thousands became refugees, and even those who lived outside the war zones suffered. As one observer noted, the South depended on the outside world "for everything from a hairpin to a toothpick, and from a cradle to a coffin." As the war dragged on, shortages of food, supplies, and even household items became commonplace.

✔ **Reading Check** **Explaining** What problems did the Southern people face during the war?

If You Were There / Drummer Boys in the Civil War

Duties and Tasks At 13, you join the army and train as a drummer. Your day begins at 5 A.M. Your drums call the soldiers to meals, roll call, drills, bed, and lights out. You also do chores for officers and surgeons. Your meals, when you can eat, are usually plain biscuits called hardtack and barely cooked bacon.

◄ "Drummer" Jackson served with an African American regiment.

Critical Thinking

Making Inferences What is your daily routine like? How do you think you would have handled the life of a drummer?

New Roles for Women

Main Idea Many Northern and Southern women took on new responsibilities during the war.

History and You Think of ways that your family would be affected by a war in your backyard. Read to learn the many ways families were affected by the Civil War.

. . . .

Against the advice of family and friends, Kate Cumming, a young woman from Mobile, Alabama, left home to begin a career as a nurse with the Confederate Army of the Mississippi. Cumming was one of the many women whose lives changed greatly because of the Civil War.

In both the North and the South, women kept the farms and factories going. They ran offices, taught school, and kept government records. Women suffered the stress of having husbands away at war and the pain of losing family members. They scrimped and saved to make do without many things they were used to, and they prayed to keep their families together.

Treating the Sick and Wounded

In the Civil War, for the first time, thousands of women served as nurses. At first many doctors did not want women nurses, saying that women were too delicate for the grisly work required on the battlefields. Men thought of nursing as work for males and believed it was improper for women to tend the bodies of unknown men.

Strong-minded women disregarded these objections. **Mary Edwards Walker** became the first woman army surgeon and later received the Congressional Medal of Honor. **Dorothea Dix** convinced officials to let women work as nurses and recruited large numbers of women to serve. Another Northerner, **Clara Barton,** became famous for her work with wounded soldiers. In the South, **Sally Tompkins** established a hospital for soldiers in Richmond, Virginia.

Kate Cumming, who nursed the wounded in Corinth after the Battle of Shiloh, wrote, "Nothing that I had ever heard or read had given me the faintest idea of the horrors witnessed here."

Primary Source / **Women in the War**

New Roles Women filled many roles during the Civil War. Many offered their services as nurses. A few were spies, and as many as 400 disguised themselves as men to serve as Union or Confederate soldiers. They cut their hair, donned men's clothing, and changed their names to fight alongside men in battle. Many were following brothers or husbands to war, but some wanted to fight because they believed in the cause.

"Francis Clailin" ▶

Nurse in field hospital ▼

Frances Louisa Clayton changed her name to Francis Clailin and enlisted as a Union soldier to be with her husband. Like the woman described below, Clayton's identity was revealed in a hospital.

"Maybe she would have remained undiscovered for a long time if she hadn't fainted. She was given a warm bath which gave the secret away."

Frances Clayton ▶

Spies

Some women were spies. Rose O'Neal Greenhow entertained Union leaders in Washington, D.C. She gathered information about Union plans that she passed to the South. Greenhow eventually was caught, convicted of treason, and exiled. Belle Boyd, of Front Royal, Virginia, informed Confederate generals of Union army movements in the Shenandoah Valley.

Some women disguised themselves as men and became soldiers. Loretta Janeta Velázquez fought for the South at the First Battle of Bull Run and at the Battle of Shiloh. Later she became a Confederate spy.

Harriet Tubman, an important "conductor" on the Underground Railroad, also served as a spy and scout for the Union. In 1863 Tubman led a mission that freed hundreds of enslaved people and disrupted southern supply lines.

Reading Check **Making Inferences** How do you think women felt about how the war changed their lives?

Elizabeth Van Lew lived in Richmond and secretly sent information about Confederate activities to President Lincoln.

"For my loyalty to my country I have two beautiful names— here I am called 'Traitor,' farther North a 'Spy.'"

Elizabeth Van Lew ▲

Critical Thinking

Analyzing Did the Civil War change the traditional roles of women? How?

Prison Camps and Field Hospitals

Main Idea When Americans went to war, most were not prepared for the horrors of battle.

History and You What goes through the mind of a doctor or nurse in the middle of battle? Read to learn about battlefield medicine.

. . . .

After the terror on the battlefield, many men suffered the agony of their wounds. Still others faced the humiliation and suffering of being taken prisoner.

In the Hands of the Enemy

Throughout the war, each side treated its enemy soldiers with a mixture of sympathy and hostility. At first, the two sides exchanged prisoners. However, when each realized that the men simply returned to fight again, they set up prison camps. Prisoners were generally allowed to keep their blanket and a cup or canteen when they were captured. These few provisions were all they had during their imprisonment. Food shortages also added to the suffering. Volunteers **distributed,** or gave out, bread and soup among the wounded, but in the prisons there was little or nothing to eat.

Andersonville prison, in Georgia, was opened in early 1864. It was built to hold 10,000 prisoners, but by August, 33,000 were crammed into it. The men slept in shallow holes dug in the ground and daily received a teaspoon of salt, three tablespoons of beans, and eight ounces of cornmeal. They drank and cooked with water from a stream that also served as a sewer. Almost 13,000 Union prisoners died there, mostly from disease.

The Union prison in Elmira, New York, was no better. Captured soldiers from the sunny South suffered through the winter months without blankets and warm clothes. The hospital was in a flooded basement, and a pond within the compound served as both toilet and garbage dump. Almost one quarter of all prisoners at Elmira died.

Field Hospitals

Surgeons traveled with the troops and set up hospitals near battlefields. There, with bullets and cannonballs flying past their heads, they bandaged wounds and amputated limbs. A nurse recalls:

PRIMARY SOURCE

"We have to walk, and when we give the men anything kneel, in blood and water; but we think nothing of it."
—from Kate: The Journal of a Confederate Nurse

The war produced many casualties, and doctors struggled to tend to the wounded. Disease was a constant threat, and some regiments lost half their men to illness before ever going into battle. Crowded together in army camps and drinking from unsanitary water supplies, many soldiers became sick. Smallpox, when it erupted, could be deadly, as could a number of other diseases, including dysentery, typhoid, and pneumonia.

✓ **Reading Check** Comparing and Contrasting
How were the prison camps at Andersonville and Elmira alike, and how were they different?

Political and Economic Change

Main Idea The Civil War led to political change and strained the economies of the North and the South.

History and You Can you think of a time when you disagreed with or opposed something? Did you take action? Read to learn why and how people opposed the Civil War, and how Presidents Lincoln and Davis responded.

．．．．．．．．．．．．．．．．．．．．．．．．．．．．．．．．．

Throughout the Civil War, numerous smaller "civil wars" raged in the North and the South.

In the South

Many Southerners opposed the war in the first place. After two years, the war had taken huge amounts of food, materials, and money, and shortages were widespread.

Bread riots erupted throughout the South as hungry people took to the streets. In Richmond, a mob, mostly made of women and

LINKING PAST TO PRESENT   Battlefield Medicine

THEN At the time of the Civil War, medicine was still relatively primitive. Doctors for the most part had two years of medical school. Battlefield physicians used extreme measures in treating casualties. Faced with appalling wounds, doctors often amputated arms and legs to prevent gangrene and other infections from spreading.

▲ Civil War amputation kit

children, gathered peacefully to protest but soon started smashing shop windows and stealing food.

In the North

The Union, too, had its war opponents. The Democratic Party, which always opposed Lincoln, was split down the middle. The War Democrats were sharply critical of how the Republican administration was running the war. The Peace Democrats, in contrast, argued for an immediate end to fighting. They called for reuniting the states through negotiation. Mostly from the Midwestern states of Ohio, Illinois, and Indiana, the Peace Democrats were viewed by some as traitors. This earned them the nickname Copperheads, after the poisonous snake. However, by 1863, they proudly embraced this label and wore copper pennies as badges because the coins had "Lady Liberty" on them.

As in the South, some Northerners who opposed the war discouraged enlistment. Occasionally they went further, helping Confederate prisoners of war escape. Some histo-rians claim that the activities of the Peace Democrats encouraged the South and that the war dragged on because the South believed that the North would abandon the struggle.

Jail Without Trial

As a way of dealing with war opponents in the North, President Lincoln suspended **habeas corpus.** This legal proceeding is a protection against unlawful imprisonment. A prisoner uses it to ask for a court hearing to determine if he or she is being held lawfully. The Constitution provides that habeas corpus can be suspended only "when in cases of rebellion or invasion, the public safety may require it."

As a result of Lincoln's action, thousands of Northerners were jailed without trials. When people—even supporters of the war—spoke out against the suspension, they were labeled treasonous Copperheads. Lincoln's critics were right to be concerned. Although many who were in jail actively helped the enemy, others were simply political leaders who had stated their opinions.

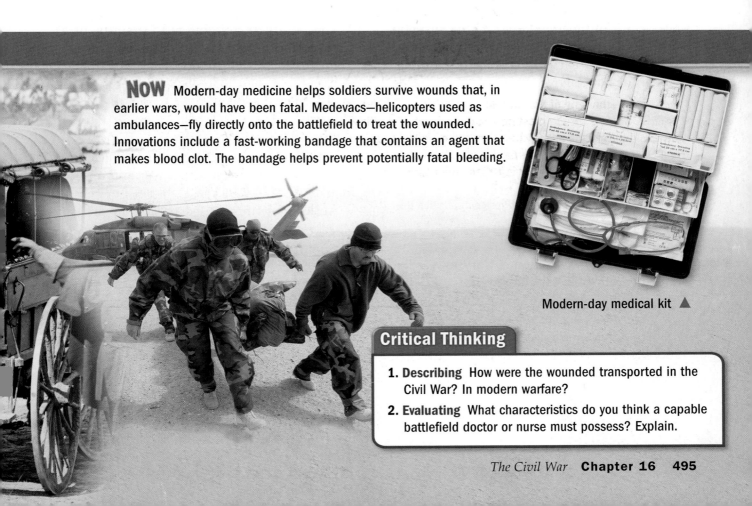

NOW Modern-day medicine helps soldiers survive wounds that, in earlier wars, would have been fatal. Medevacs—helicopters used as ambulances—fly directly onto the battlefield to treat the wounded. Innovations include a fast-working bandage that contains an agent that makes blood clot. The bandage helps prevent potentially fatal bleeding.

Modern-day medical kit ▲

Critical Thinking

1. **Describing** How were the wounded transported in the Civil War? In modern warfare?

2. **Evaluating** What characteristics do you think a capable battlefield doctor or nurse must possess? Explain.

Primary Sources
INTERPRETING
POLITICAL CARTOONS

A Northern newspaper ran this cartoon in 1863. It shows Lady Liberty warding off an attack of the Peace Democrats, or Copperheads.

1. **Identify** Who does the woman represent?
2. **Points of View** What is the cartoonist expressing about the Peace Democrats? How can you tell?

A. Lady Liberty   B. Copperheads

THE COPPERHEAD PARTY—IN FAVOR OF A VIGOROUS PROSECUTION OF PEACE!

In the South, President Jefferson Davis also suspended the right of habeas corpus. He, too, believed he needed to deal harshly with opponents of the war. However, by suspending habeas corpus, Davis upset many loyal supporters. In early 1864, North Carolina's Governor Vance wrote him:

PRIMARY SOURCE

"I hear with deep regret that a bill is certainly expected to pass . . . suspending the writ of habeas corpus, throughout the Confederacy, and that certain arrests will immediately be made."
—letter to Confederate President Jefferson Davis

Draft Laws

After the initial excitement of the war had disappeared, both the North and the South had trouble recruiting troops. In 1862 the Confederate Congress passed a **draft** law requiring able-bodied white men between 18 and 35 to serve for three years. Later the range was extended to cover men between 17 and 50. There were several exceptions. If he could afford it, a man could hire a **substitute,** or replacement, to serve for him. Later, if a man had 20 or more enslaved people, he did not have to serve.

The North, at first, offered a **bounty,** or a sum of money paid to encourage volunteers. Then, in March 1863, it too passed a draft law. All men from age 20 to 45 had to register. As in the South, a man could avoid the draft, either by hiring a substitute or by paying $300. Such exceptions met with great protest. In both the North and the South, people complained it was "a rich man's war and a poor man's fight."

Antidraft sentiment led to riots in several Northern cities. The worst disturbance was the New York City draft riots in July 1863. Members of the working class, many of them Irish immigrants, attacked government and military buildings. Then mobs turned their attacks against African Americans. Many white workers had opposed the Emancipation Proclamation, fearing that freed blacks would take their jobs. After four days of terror, more than 100 people were dead. Federal troops had to be rushed in to stop the riots.

Economic Effects

The war strained the economies of the North and the South. However, the North, with its greater resources, was better able to cope with the immense costs of the war.

The two governments had three ways of paying for the war:

1. They borrowed money by selling war bonds that promised high interest.
2. They imposed new taxes, including income taxes.
3. They printed money. Northern money was called **greenbacks** because of its color.

The North Prospers

Northern industry profited from the war effort. It produced guns, ammunition, shoes, and uniforms. Farmers prospered as they sold their crops to provide a steady supply of food for the troops. However, prices rose faster than wages because goods were in high demand. This **inflation,** or general increase in prices, caused a great hardship for working people. Still, the Northern economy boomed during the war years.

Economic Troubles in the South

The war's economic strain was felt more sharply in the South, where warfare destroyed farmland and railroad lines. Also, the blockade prevented the shipping of trade goods. Vital materials could not reach the Confederacy. Salt was so desperately needed that women scraped the floors of smokehouses to recover it. Food shortages led to riots in Atlanta, Richmond, and other cities.

Inflation, too, was much worse in the South. As early as 1862, citizens begged Confederate leaders for help. In North Carolina, citizens wrote desperate letters to the governor:

PRIMARY SOURCE

"If it is Constitutional, and if your position . . . gives you the power to do so, in the name of . . . suffering humanity, of the cries of widows and orphans, *do* put down the Speculation and extortion in this . . . State."
—R. L. Abernethy to Governor Zebulon Vance, 1862

Reading Check Determining Cause and Effect Describe at least three causes of discontent among people in the North and the South.

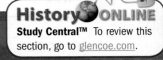

History ONLINE
Study Central™ To review this section, go to glencoe.com.

Section 3 Review

Vocabulary

1. Use each of these terms in a complete sentence that will help explain its meaning: distribute, habeas corpus, draft, substitute, bounty, greenback, inflation.

Main Ideas

2. **Describing** What role did Sally Tompkins play in the war effort? Which women played a similar role in the North?

3. **Summarizing** Who were the Copperheads? What was their position on fighting the war?

4. **Explaining** Why did the Union and the Confederacy institute drafts?

Critical Thinking

5. **Describing** Explain three ways that the governments raised money for the war effort.

Raising Funds

6. **Persuasive Writing** President Lincoln suspended writs of habeas corpus to prevent interference with the draft. Do you think suspending civil liberties is justified in some situations? Write a short essay explaining your position and defend it.

7. Answer the **Essential Question**
What social, political, and economic changes resulted from the war?

The Strain of War

Essential Question ◄

How did the events at Gettysburg and Vicksburg change the course of the war?

Reading Guide

Content Vocabulary
entrench (p. 499)   siege (p. 505)

Academic Vocabulary
nevertheless (p. 501)   encounter (p. 502)

Key People and Events
54th Massachusetts (p. 501)
Pickett's Charge (p. 503)
Gettysburg Address (p. 505)

Reading Strategy
Taking Notes As you read, use a chart like the one shown below to write at least one important fact about each of these battles.

Battle	Importance
Fredericksburg	
Chancellorsville	
Gettysburg	
Siege of Vicksburg	

INDIANA ACADEMIC STANDARDS
United States History

8.1.21 Describe the importance of key events and individuals in the Civil War.

8.1.28 Recognize historical perspective and evaluate alternative courses of action by describing the historical context in which events unfolded and by avoiding evaluation of the past solely in terms of present-day norms.

8.3.1 Read maps to interpret symbols and determine the landforms and human features that represent physical and cultural characteristics of areas in the United States.

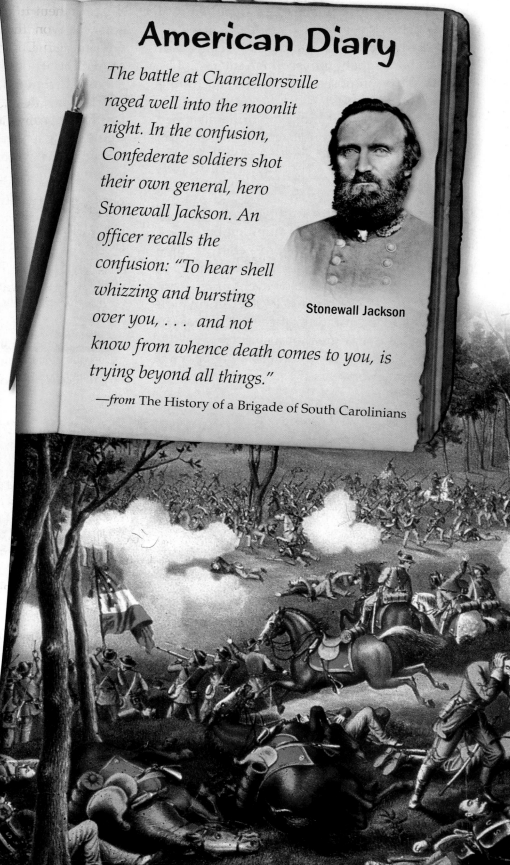

American Diary

The battle at Chancellorsville raged well into the moonlit night. In the confusion, Confederate soldiers shot their own general, hero Stonewall Jackson. An officer recalls the confusion: "To hear shell whizzing and bursting over you, . . . and not know from whence death comes to you, is trying beyond all things."

Stonewall Jackson

—*from* The History of a Brigade of South Carolinians

Southern Victories

Main Idea In the winter of 1862 and the spring of 1863, the South seemed to be winning the Civil War.

History and You How do leadership qualities make a difference to what happens in life? Read to learn the qualities of some Civil War battle commanders that led to victories and to defeat.

· ·

Southern victories in the East were largely the result of the military leadership of generals Robert E. Lee and Stonewall Jackson. Through knowledge of the terrain and the ability to inspire troops, these two managed to defeat larger Union forces. Jackson's death at Chancellorsville not only removed one of the South's great strategists, it affected the morale of its army and its citizens. As Jackson lay dying, Lee said, "He has lost his left arm; I have lost my right."

Battle of Fredericksburg

After Antietam, Robert E. Lee moved his army out of Maryland into Virginia. This encouraged Union leaders to attack. The new Union commander, General Ambrose Burnside, boldly marched his troops toward the Confederate capital at Richmond.

Lee chose to intercept the Union troops near the town of Fredericksburg. He moved his forces to hills south of the town and ordered them to dig trenches so they could fire down on the enemy from a protected position. On December 13, 1862, the Union army attacked. Lee's **entrenched** forces drove the Union troops back soundly. Devastated by his failure, General Burnside resigned and was replaced by General Joseph Hooker.

Battle of Chancellorsville

In May 1863, Lee again used strategy brilliantly. He divided his forces in Virginia in response to General Hooker's having done the same thing—even though Hooker had twice as many men. Some Confederate troops stayed to defend Fredericksburg, and some confronted the main Union force at Chancellorsville. A third group made a daring maneuver that caught the Union army by surprise. Under the leadership of Stonewall Jackson, Confederate troops marched around the side of Hooker's position.

Stonewall Jackson mortally wounded at the battle of Chancellorsville in Virginia

Critical Thinking

Speculating What do you think is the main reason some leaders decided to fight for the Confederacy? For the Union?

Then, suddenly, Jackson's army turned and attacked the Union forces in the rear. At the same time, Lee struck from the front. Sandwiched between the two Confederate forces, Hooker eventually withdrew his men. One of the Confederate companies fired on Stonewall Jackson's company by mistake, wounding the general in the left arm. Jackson's arm had to be amputated, and he died a week later.

Weak Union Generals

In less than a year, three different generals led the Union forces. Lincoln was frustrated by their conduct of the war. Major General George McClellan commanded the Union forces at the Battle of Antietam in March 1862. He prepared well but was reluctant to engage the enemy. Said Lincoln, "If McClellan doesn't want to use the army, I'd like to borrow it for awhile."

The last straw came when, after victory at Antietam, McClellan failed to obey Lincoln's order to follow the retreating Confederate troops and "destroy the rebel army."

Lincoln pushed his next commander, General Ambrose Burnside, to take aggressive action. Burnside quickly lost the president's favor after a crushing loss at Fredericksburg.

Next, Lincoln appointed Major General Joseph Hooker, who had often been critical of other generals. Hooker's attitude matched the president's.

PRIMARY SOURCE

"May God have mercy on General Lee, for I will have none."

—General Joseph Hooker to his staff, April 1863

Words, however, were not enough to defeat Lee, who crushed Hooker's forces at Chancellorsville. Within two months, Hooker resigned.

Lincoln's next commander needed to prove himself quickly. Major General George Meade assumed command three days before one of the most important battles of the war.

Reading Check **Synthesizing** What strategies did General Lee use to defeat Union armies that were much larger than his?

Primary Source / African American Soldiers

Union Recruits Of the more than 2 million soldiers who served in the Union army and navy, nearly 200,000 were African American. As news of the Emancipation Proclamation spread, many African Americans from the North and the South enlisted. More than half were formerly enslaved.

▼ Union soldiers

Union Army

Nearly 10% of the soldiers in the Union army were African American.

Union Navy

About 18% of sailors in the Union navy were African American.

African Americans in the War

Main Idea African Americans showed courage and skill as soldiers in the Union army.

History and You What does it mean to act bravely? Read to learn about the 54th Massachusetts regiment and the battle for Fort Wagner.

. . . .

At first, both the North and the South barred African Americans from serving in their armies. As time passed, the North relaxed its rules.

In the South

African Americans made up more than 30 percent of the Southern population, but Confederate leaders never seriously considered allowing them to enlist. Confederate leaders feared that African American soldiers, once armed, would attack their fellow troops or even begin a general revolt. The Confederates felt that the advantage of having more soldiers in their army did not justify this risk.

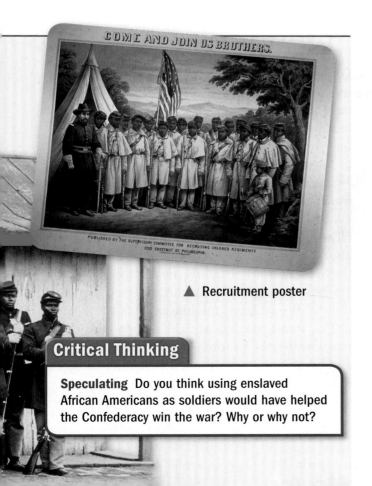

COME AND JOIN US BROTHERS.

PUBLISHED BY THE SUPERVISORY COMMITTEE FOR RECRUITING COLORED REGIMENTS
1210 CHESTNUT ST. PHILADELPHIA.

▲ Recruitment poster

Critical Thinking

Speculating Do you think using enslaved African Americans as soldiers would have helped the Confederacy win the war? Why or why not?

History ONLINE
Student Web Activity Visit glencoe.com and complete the Chapter 16 Web Activity about African Americans in the war.

In the North

President Lincoln at first resisted appeals to enlist African Americans in the Union army. He feared that such a policy would be resented in the border states. By 1862, though, it was evident that the North needed more soldiers, and many Union African Americans were eager to fight. As a result, Congress decided to allow the formation of all-African American regiments.

These new soldiers were in a tough position. Many white regiments from the North doubted their fighting ability. Others resented their presence. Many Southern troops hated the African American soldiers and often focused their fiercest gunfire on African American Northern regiments.

Still, African Americans joined. By the end of the war, they comprised about 10 percent of the Union army. Some were freed people from the North; others were runaway enslaved African Americans from the South. These men fought hard and effectively, too. As one white Union officer wrote about an all-African American Kansas regiment:

PRIMARY SOURCE

"They make better soldiers in every respect than any troops I have ever had under my command."
—Union general James G. Blunt

The 54th Massachusetts

The best-known African American regiment was the **54th Massachusetts.** In 1863 this regiment took part in an assault on Fort Wagner in South Carolina. The 54th served in the front lines of this battle. Confederate gunfire battered the men, causing nearly 300 casualties in this regiment alone. **Nevertheless,** the soldiers bravely fought on. Though the Union could not capture the fort, the 54th became famous for the courage and sacrifice of its members.

✔ **Reading Check** Comparing and Contrasting
How were Union and Confederate policies regarding African American soldiers alike and different?

YOU DECIDE

Should Lee Have Invaded the North?

The war was fought in Southern territory for the most part. Lee's first invasion was turned back at Antietam. In 1863 he tried again.

The Alternatives

Play it safe

Should the South continue its defensive strategy?

Be bold

Should Lee launch a second invasion of the North?

Considering the Consequences

If the invasion fails

- The Confederacy makes no further attempt to invade the North.
- The tide of war turns in favor of the North.

If the invasion succeeds

- The Confederacy likely gains support from Europe.
- Union antiwar feeling grows.

The Decision

Could Lee's forces conquer the army of the Potomac on its own soil? Confident after the brilliant victory at Chancellorsville, Lee decided to invade the North.

The Results

- Lee's army in northern Virginia is defeated.
- The Confederacy makes no further attempt to invade the North.
- The tide of war turns in favor of the North.

DBQ Document-Based Questions

1. **Analyzing** In your opinion, did Lee have valid reasons for invading the North?
2. **Explaining** What do you think was the best reason for not invading the North?

The Tide of War Turns

Main Idea The Battle of Gettysburg marked a turn in the war as the Union forces defeated the Confederates.

History and You Have you ever made a decision that seemed right at the time but turned out to be disastrous? Read to learn what happened when General Lee decided to invade the North.

In spring of 1863, the South had the upper hand, but that was soon to change. The Confederate victory at Chancellorsville ruined Union plans for attacking Richmond. Robert E. Lee, emboldened by his victories, decided to take the war into the North. A win there might impress France and Britain.

The South's strategy recalled that of the colonies in the Revolutionary War—though far outnumbered, they were aided by France and had won. Now, France and Britain missed the goods—especially cotton—they were accustomed to buying from Southern planters. If the Confederates appeared to be winning, those nations might help.

The Battle of Gettysburg

In July 1863, a small town in southern Pennsylvania became the site of one of the most decisive battles in the Civil War. Gettysburg was not a capital, a strategic port, or the location of an important fort. That such serious fighting took place there was almost an accident.

The Confederates entered the town for much-needed supplies. General Lee hoped to avoid fighting troops in an unfamiliar area. However, the two sides **encountered** one another. When Lee's armies crawled out of Gettysburg four grueling days later, it was after sustaining 25,000 casualties. The Union—the victor—suffered the loss of 23,000.

The battle started at 5:30 A.M. on July 1. Outnumbered, Union troops retreated to a section of high ground called Cemetery Ridge. Reinforcements for both sides arrived, and on the second day of fighting, Southern generals tried to dislodge Union forces from hills named Round Top and Little Round Top. However, after furious fighting, Union forces under the command of General George Meade held their positions.

That night, Meade made the decision not to retreat. The next day, Lee also made an important decision. He ordered an attack designed to "create a panic and virtually destroy the [Union] army."

The Confederates started by firing nearly 140 cannons at the Union lines. Then, under the leadership of General George Pickett, thousands of Confederate troops attacked the Union's center position at Cemetery Ridge. Putting themselves directly in the way of musket and artillery fire, they advanced across open land.

At first, it seemed that **Pickett's Charge** might work—the Confederates broke the first line of Union defense. In the end, however, three-quarters of those who started the attack lay dead or wounded on the ground. Lee later wrote:

PRIMARY SOURCE

"The army did all it could. I fear I required of it impossibilities."

—from *Memoirs of Robert E. Lee*

Gettysburg put an end to one goal of Confederate foreign policy: gaining help from Britain and France. The South hoped to receive from the British two ironclads that would be used to sweep Union shipping from the Atlantic. However, in October 1863, the British government decided not to release the ships.

The Vicksburg Siege

On July 4, the day that Lee retreated from Gettysburg, the Confederacy suffered another major military blow. The important river city of Vicksburg, Mississippi, fell under the control of Union troops led by Ulysses S. Grant.

The Battle of Gettysburg, Day 3 NATIONAL GEOGRAPHIC

Gettysburg

General Lee

Cemetery Hill

Culp's Hill

Pickett's Charge

Cemetery Ridge

General Meade

- Confederate troops
- Union troops
- Confederate troop movements

Little Round Top

Big Round Top

Willoughby Run

Seminary Ridge

Pitzer's Run

Plum Run

Rock Creek

0   1 kilometer
0   1 mile
Albers Equal-Area projection

Pickett's Charge came at the height of the three-day battle. More than 12,000 Confederate troops marched across an open field to attack the Union's center position. The effort ended in disaster.

▲ Today, the Gettysburg battlefield's 1,400 monuments commemorate "the great deeds of valor."

"The sacrifice of life on that blood soaked field . . . was too awful for the heralding of victory, even for our victorious foe."

—George E. Pickett, in a letter to his fiancée

Critical Thinking

Concluding Why did Pickett think that the North did not want to celebrate the victory?

The Gettysburg Address

On November 19, 1863, President Abraham Lincoln gave a short speech at the dedication of a national cemetery on the battlefield of Gettysburg. His simple yet eloquent words expressed his hopes for a nation divided by civil war.

▲ Monument at Gettysburg

Four **score** and seven years ago our fathers brought forth on this continent a new nation, conceived in liberty, and dedicated to the **proposition** that all men are created equal.

> Lincoln is referring to the nation declaring its independence in 1776—87 years before.

Now we are engaged in a great civil war, testing whether that nation, or any nation so conceived and so dedicated, can long **endure**. We are met on a great battlefield of that war. We have come to dedicate a portion of that field as a final resting place for those who here gave their lives that that nation might live. It is altogether fitting and proper that we should do this.

> Union soldiers were fighting to keep the nation (North and South) together.

But, in a larger sense, we can not dedicate—we can not **consecrate**—we can not **hallow**—this ground. The brave men, living and dead, who struggled here, have consecrated it far above our poor power to add or detract. The world will little note nor long remember what we say here, but it can never forget what they did here. It is for us, the living, rather, to be dedicated here to the unfinished work which they who fought here have thus far so nobly advanced. It is rather for us to be here dedicated to the great task remaining before us—that from these honored dead we take increased devotion to that cause for which they gave the last full measure of devotion; that we here highly **resolve** that these dead shall not have died in vain; that this nation, under God, shall have a new birth of freedom; and that government of the people, by the people, for the people, shall not perish from the earth.

> The soldiers who died made the supreme sacrifice. Lincoln believes it is up to those who are still living to carry on their unfinished work.

> The U.S. government was created to serve the people. People are the source of the government's power.

Vocabulary

score: twenty

proposition (PRAH·puh·ZI·shun): an idea or a belief

endure: to continue or last

consecrate (KAHN·suh·KRAT): to dedicate to a sacred purpose

hallow (HA·LOH): to respect greatly

resolve: to make a firm decision

Critical Thinking

1. **Making Inferences** How is the Civil War going to "test" whether or not the United States can endure?

2. **Interpreting** Why do you think Lincoln thought it was so important to honor those who fought and died at Gettysburg?

3. **Finding the Main Idea** According to Lincoln, why was the war being fought?

Grant first launched his attack in April, surrounding the 30,000 Confederate troops holding Vicksburg. In May, Grant began a **siege** against the town, blockading it to prevent food and supplies from entering. Union gunships on the river supported Grant's 77,000 troops by firing thousands of mortar shells into the city.

During the 47-day siege, both sides suffered heavy casualties. More than 9,000 Confederate and 10,000 Union troops died, many of disease or starvation. Remarkably, fewer than 20 civilians were killed in the siege.

The bad news did not end there for the South, though. A few days later, it lost Port Hudson in Louisiana, its last stronghold on the vital Mississippi River. The Union strategy to split the South in two had succeeded. Arkansas, Louisiana, and Texas were now cut off. In a single month, July 1863, the Civil War reached a major turning point.

Lincoln's Gettysburg Address

On November 19, 1863, Soldiers' National Cemetery was dedicated at Gettysburg. At the ceremony, former governor of Massachusetts Edward Everett delivered a two-hour speech. After him, President Abraham Lincoln spoke for about two minutes. In 272 words, Lincoln was able to honor the soldiers and the cause for which they had fought and died, as well as state his vision for the country.

PRIMARY SOURCE

"These dead shall not have died in vain.... Government of the people, by the people, for the people shall not perish from the earth."

—from the Gettysburg Address

Reactions to Lincoln's **Gettysburg Address** in the press were mixed. Everett, along with the *New York Times, Chicago Tribune,* and *Springfield* (Mass.) *Republican,* thought the speech was a success. The *Republican* wrote, "His little speech is a perfect gem; deep in feeling, compact in thought and expression, and tasteful . . . in every word and comma."

✔ **Reading Check** **Explaining** How do the events of this section demonstrate that the "tide" of war turned?

Section 4 Review

History ONLINE
Study Central™ To review this section, go to glencoe.com.

Vocabulary

1. Define each of these terms in a sentence that will help explain its meaning: entrench, nevertheless, encounter, siege.

Main Ideas

2. **Explaining** Why was the battle of Chancellorsville important?

3. **Contrasting** How were African American soldiers treated differently than white soldiers?

4. **Explaining** In the Gettysburg Address, what did Lincoln say was the duty of "the living" to accomplish?

Critical Thinking

5. **Making Inferences** Why do you think many leaders called for African Americans to be allowed to fight in the Civil War?

6. **Organizing** Using a graphic organizer similar to the one below, list the results of the Battle of Gettysburg.

7. **Expository Writing** Refer to Lincoln's Gettysburg Address in this section. Write an essay discussing Lincoln's ideas on freedom and the importance of saving the Union.

Answer the
8. **Essential Question**
How did the events at Gettysburg and Vicksburg change the course of the war?

Essential Question ◄

What events led to the end of the war?

Reading Guide

Content Vocabulary

total war *(p. 507)*   resistance *(p. 509)*

Academic Vocabulary

series *(p. 507)*   interpret *(p. 509)*

Key People and Events

David Farragut *(p. 509)*

March to the Sea *(p. 510)*

Appomattox Court House *(p. 512)*

Reading Strategy

Taking Notes As you read, take notes on the significance of battles late in the war.

Battle	Importance

INDIANA ACADEMIC STANDARDS
United States History

8.1.21 Describe the importance of key events and individuals in the Civil War.

8.3.1 Read maps to interpret symbols and determine the landforms and human features that represent physical and cultural characteristics of areas in the United States.

American Diary

After Union forces took control of Atlanta on September 2, 1864, General William Sherman ordered the city burned and the citizens to leave. When the mayor of Atlanta pleaded with Sherman to change his mind, Sherman refused. He responded: "War is cruelty, and you cannot refine it. . . . You might as well appeal against the thunderstorm as against these terrible hardships of war."

—from Memoirs of General William T. Sherman

Atlanta and many other Southern cities, including Richmond as shown here, suffered large-scale destruction as the war continued.

Total War Strikes the South

Main Idea After a long, bloody summer, Union forces captured major Southern strongholds, and as a result, Lincoln won reelection.

History and You Have you ever had a goal that was difficult to reach? Did you have a strategy to reach your goal? Read to learn how Grant and the Union forces executed their plan.

General William Sherman's destruction of Atlanta and other areas of the South was part of a deliberate strategy to bring the horrors of war—terror, starvation, violence, and homelessness—to the Southern people. This systematic destruction of an entire land—not just its army—is called **total war.**

Union Strategy

By 1864, Union forces surrounded the South. Union ships blocked the Confederate coast, strangling its export economy and cutting off supplies. The Union controlled the Mississippi River, and the western Confederate states were cut off. A bold plan of attack was needed. General Grant would be the one to draw up such a plan.

Grant in Charge

Ulysses S. Grant was only an average student and a failure as a farmer and businessperson. At soldiering, however, he was brilliant. He chalked up victories at Shiloh and Vicksburg and at another important battle in Chattanooga, Tennessee. In March 1864, President Lincoln put General Grant in charge of all the Union armies.

Grant then devised his plan. He would deliver killing blows from all sides. His armies would move on to Richmond, the Confederate capital. At the same time, William Tecumseh Sherman would lead his troops in attacks across the Deep South.

Grant soon put his strategy into effect. In May and June of 1864, Grant's army of 115,000 men smashed into Lee's 64,000 troops in a **series** of three battles near Richmond, Virginia—the battles of the Wilderness, Spotsylvania Courthouse, and Cold Harbor. Each time Confederate lines held, but each time Grant quickly resumed the attack.

"Whatever happens, there will be no turning back," Grant promised Lincoln. He was determined to march southward, attacking Lee's forces relentlessly until the Confederacy surrendered.

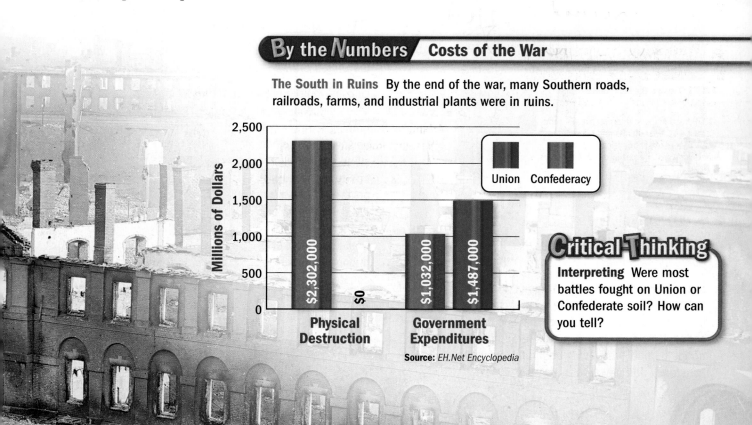

By the Numbers / Costs of the War

The South in Ruins By the end of the war, many Southern roads, railroads, farms, and industrial plants were in ruins.

Millions of Dollars

Union   Confederacy

Physical Destruction: $2,302,000 (Union), $0 (Confederacy)

Government Expenditures: $1,032,000 (Union), $1,487,000 (Confederacy)

Source: *EH.Net Encyclopedia*

Critical Thinking

Interpreting Were most battles fought on Union or Confederate soil? How can you tell?

The Wilderness Campaign

In the northeast corner of the Confederacy, about halfway between Washington, D.C., and Richmond, Virginia, lay an area of dense woods called the Wilderness. Here, on May 5, 1864, the six bloodiest weeks of the war began. For two days, the forces of Grant and Lee struggled among a tangle of trees through which they could scarcely see. Said a Union private, "It was a blind and bloody hunt to the death."

Lee had only about 60,000 men to Grant's more than 100,000. Both sides suffered huge casualties. Grant, who lost 17,000 men, cried in his tent at the end of the second day. Meanwhile, brushfires raged through the forest, burning alive 200 wounded men. On the morning of the third day, with no clear winner, Grant moved his forces south toward Richmond.

The next battles were fought at nearby Spotsylvania Courthouse and at Cold Harbor. On June 2, the night before this third battle began, a Union general observed that men were "writing their names and home addresses on slips of paper and pinning them to the backs of their coats" to help people identify their bodies. The war seemed hopeless. Grant, however, was determined. He explained to the White House:

PRIMARY SOURCE

"I propose to fight it out on this line, if it takes all summer."
—Dispatch to Washington, May 11, 1864

Grant's critics in the North called him a "butcher" because of the huge loss of life among his own troops—50,000 in 30 days. Lincoln, however, said, "I can't spare this man. He fights."

People IN HISTORY

Robert E. Lee

General, commander in chief of the Confederate armies

Lee, a brilliant scholar and a daring soldier, was willing to take risks. However, when his orders caused enormous loss of lives, he was filled with sadness. When he finally surrendered, he told his troops he had *"unceasing admiration of your constancy and devotion to your country."*

Abraham Lincoln

Sixteenth president of the United States

Lincoln would not give up. He lost seven elections on the way to winning the presidency. His perseverance helped him stand against all opposition to the war. He believed, *"A house divided against itself cannot stand."* He would see the war through until the country was reunited.

The Petersburg Siege

Continuing his movement south, Grant went on to Petersburg, a railroad center that was vital to the Confederate movement of troops and supplies. If Grant could take Petersburg, then Richmond would be cut off from the rest of the Confederacy. Grant laid siege. The Confederates defended the city, but they could not win. Trains brought food and reinforcements to the Union troops. The Confederates could get neither. For nine long months, however, they held out.

Sherman in Georgia

Meanwhile, William Tecumseh Sherman took off for Georgia. In early July, his troops circled Atlanta. There they faced the brilliant Confederate general, John Hood, whose forces put up major **resistance.** Sherman laid siege. Finally, on September 1, Hood abandoned the city. The mood in the South was desperate. Mary Chesnut, a Georgian who kept a diary throughout the war, wrote, "There is no hope, but we will try to have no fear."

Farragut at Mobile Bay

The highest-ranking officer in the Union navy was **David Farragut,** the son of a Latino military man. Young David Farragut joined the navy when he was only 12 years old. Now, in August 1864, he was leading a fleet of 18 ships through a narrow channel into Mobile Bay in Alabama. The Confederates had two forts on either side of the channel, and they had mined the waters with torpedoes. Guns were firing from both forts. What was Farragut to do? He gave his famous order, "Damn the torpedoes, full speed ahead!"

Farragut, who was suffering from dizziness, had himself tied to the ship's rigging so he could stay in the battle. His invasion was a success, and the last Southern port east of the Mississippi was blocked.

The Election of 1864

Through most of 1864, opposition to the war in the North grew stronger. A presidential election was coming up in November, and it looked unlikely that Lincoln would win reelection. His loss could mean an end to the war and recognition of the Confederate government as an independent country. Southerners clung to this hope.

After Atlanta fell and Mobile Bay was blocked, Northerners began to believe again that they could win. Lincoln won a second term handsomely—with 55 percent of the popular vote, 212 to 21 electoral votes.

Lincoln **interpreted,** or explained, his reelection as a clear sign from the voters to end slavery permanently by amending the Constitution. On January 31, 1865, Congress passed the Thirteenth Amendment, which banned slavery in the United States.

Reading Check Summarizing What was the Union strategy in 1864, and what were the results?

Ulysses S. Grant

General of the United States Army and eighteenth president of the United States

Grant was a fearless soldier and an expert horseman at a time when soldiers rode horses in battle. Grant's strategy seemed ruthless at times, but he said, *"I have never advocated [war] except as a means of peace."*

CRITICAL Thinking

1. **Synthesizing** What characteristics do you think these three men shared?

2. **Describing** Select a quote from one of the men described. What does the quote reveal about that person?

Battle Dates

The Wilderness
May 5–6, 1864

Cold Harbor
June 3, 1864

Petersburg siege
June 5, 1864–April 3, 1865

Kennesaw Mountain
June 27, 1864

Atlanta
July 20–Sept. 2, 1864

Franklin
Nov. 30, 1864

Nashville
Dec. 15–16, 1864

Wilmington
Feb. 12–22, 1865

Bentonville
March 19–21, 1865

Appomattox Court House
April 9, 1865

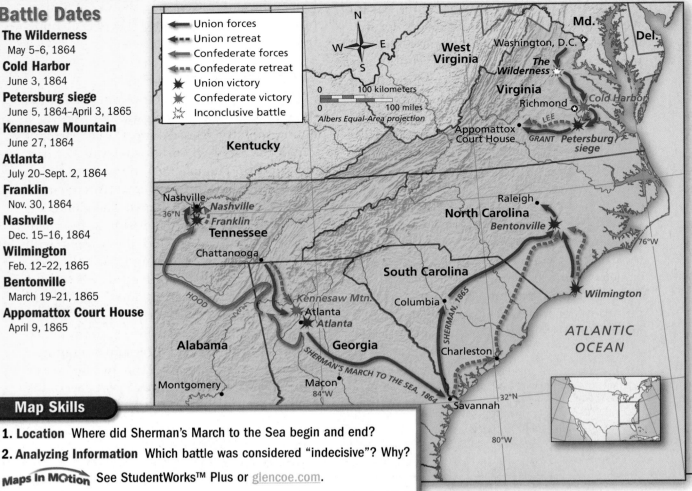

Map Skills

1. **Location** Where did Sherman's March to the Sea begin and end?
2. **Analyzing Information** Which battle was considered "indecisive"? Why?

Maps In Motion See StudentWorks™ Plus or glencoe.com.

The War's End

Main Idea After four years of fighting against unfavorable odds, the South finally surrendered.

History and You How would you treat an enemy who said, "I give up"?

From the beginning of the war, the Union army wanted to capture the Confederate capital. When Grant finally drove Lee's army out of Petersburg, Virginia, Jefferson Davis knew that Richmond was doomed.

Sherman's March to the Sea

The last months of the war saw the Union determined to break the will of the South. Sherman and his men became destroyers.

Before Sherman's army left Atlanta in November, it burned much of this beautiful city. From Atlanta, Sherman's troops burned cities and farmlands as they marched across Georgia to the Atlantic coast. This trail of destruction is known as Sherman's **March to the Sea.**

Sherman continued his path of destruction through the Carolinas to join Grant's forces near Richmond. Union troops took what food they needed, tore up railroad lines and fields, and killed livestock in an effort to destroy anything that was useful to the South.

White Southerners deplored Sherman's march, but thousands of African Americans left their plantations to follow the protection of his army. For them, this was a march to freedom.

The Union Advances

1861

Early Stages Confederate troops won most of the battles in the first year of the Civil War.

1863

Union Gains Union control of the Mississippi River cut off Texas and Arkansas, the South's leading food producers, from the Confederacy.

1865

Final Stages By 1865, the Union controlled large parts of the Confederacy.

By the Numbers

Lives Lost More lives were lost in the Civil War than in any other major American conflict. Deadly weapons, poor medical practices, infection, and disease all contributed.

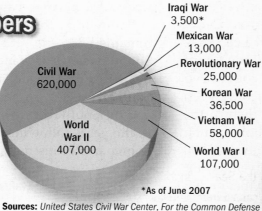

Civil War 620,000

World War II 407,000

Iraqi War 3,500*

Mexican War 13,000

Revolutionary War 25,000

Korean War 36,500

Vietnam War 58,000

World War I 107,000

*As of June 2007

Sources: *United States Civil War Center, For the Common Defense*

Unknown Soldiers A gravestone in Gettysburg Cemetery commemorates the loss of 425 Civil War soldiers who were never identified.

The Fall of Richmond

Meanwhile, Grant continued the siege of Petersburg. Lee and his troops defended the town, but sickness, casualties, and desertion weakened them. Finally, on April 2, 1865, the Confederate lines broke and Lee withdrew.

Word of Lee's retreat came to the Confederate president. As the Union army marched toward Richmond, Davis and his cabinet gathered documents, gave orders that bridges and weapons useful to the enemy be set on fire, and fled the city. An observer wrote:

PRIMARY SOURCE

"The trains came and went, wagons, vehicles, and horsemen rumbled and dashed to and fro. . . . As night came on . . . rioting and robbing took place."
—from *Battles and Leaders of the Civil War*

The armory, with its stores of ammunition, exploded. Boom after boom rang through the city, and fires raged out of control.

Two days later, President Lincoln and his son Tad arrived to tour the fallen capital. Said Lincoln, "Thank God I have lived to see this. It seems to me that I have been dreaming a horrid nightmare for four years, and now the nightmare is over."

Joyful African Americans followed Lincoln everywhere, singing, laughing, and reaching out to touch him. When one man knelt down to thank him, Lincoln replied, "Don't kneel to me. You must kneel to God only, and thank Him for your freedom."

At the Confederate president's house, Lincoln sat in a chair in Davis's office and "looked far off with a dreamy expression."

At Libby Prison, where the Union held Confederate prisoners of war, Lincoln was asked what to do with the prisoners and replied, "If I were in your place, I'd let 'em up easy, let 'em up easy."

Surrender at Appomattox

The formal end of the war came a few days later, on April 9, 1865. Two days earlier, Grant asked Lee to surrender, writing, "The result of last week must convince you of the hopelessness of further resistance."

Yet Lee believed he must fight on. However, when the Union captured the train carrying food to his troops and Lee was completely surrounded, he knew it was over.

In the little town of **Appomattox Court House,** Virginia, Grant met with Lee. They shook hands and talked a little. Then Grant offered his terms. Lee's soldiers could keep their small firearms, the officers could keep their horses, and no one would disturb the soldiers as they made their way home. In an act of generosity, Grant also gave 25,000 rations to feed Lee's troops. Dignity and compassion were the order of the day that ended America's deadliest war.

The Toll of War

More lives were lost in the Civil War than in any other conflict in American history. More than 600,000 soldiers died. The war cost billions of dollars. In the South, cities and farmlands were destroyed, and it would take years and a massive national effort to rebuild.

The war had other consequences as well. The North's victory saved the Union. The federal government was strengthened and was now clearly more powerful than the states. Finally, the war freed millions of African Americans. The end of slavery, however, did not solve the problems that the newly freed African Americans were to face.

Following the war, many questions remained. No one yet knew how to bring the Southern states back into the Union, nor what the status of African Americans would be in Southern society. Americans from the North and the South tried to answer these questions in the years following the Civil War—an era known as Reconstruction.

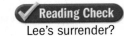 **Reading Check** **Evaluating** What events led to Lee's surrender?

Section 5 Review

History ONLINE
Study Central™ To review this section, go to glencoe.com.

Vocabulary

1. Define each of the following terms, and use them in a paragraph about the last year of the Civil War: total war, series resistance, interpret.

Main Ideas

2. **Explaining** How did events on the battlefield affect Lincoln's reelection?

3. **Describing** Why did Sherman burn and destroy the South's land?

4. **Explaining** What were Grant's terms of surrender at Appomattox Court House?

Critical Thinking

5. **Analyzing** Complete a graphic organizer similar to the one below to explain the effects of the Civil War on the nation.

ended slavery

Effects of the Civil War

6. **Descriptive Writing** Take on the role of a reporter living in Georgia during Sherman's March to the Sea. Write a brief article describing the Union's actions and their effects on the people living there.

Answer the
7. **Essential Question**
What events led to the end of the war?

Visual Summary

1861

Feb. Southern states form the Confederacy

Apr. Union surrenders Fort Sumter

June Four border states stay in the Union

July First major battle fought at Bull Run in Virginia

1862

Mar. The *Monitor* and the *Virginia* fight the first battle between ironclad ships

Ironclad gunboat

Apr. Farragut's naval forces capture New Orleans

Sept. Antietam is the first major battle on Northern soil

1863

Jan. Lincoln issues Emancipation Proclamation

July Lee's invasion of the North turned back at Gettysburg

July Fall of Vicksburg results in Union control of the Mississippi River

1864

Mar. General Ulysses Grant assumes command of all Union armies

Nov. Lincoln reelected to second term

1865

Feb. Sherman's forces march through the Carolinas

Apr. 2 Lee evacuates Richmond; Union forces capture capital

Apr. 9 Surrender at Appomattox Court House

Apr. 14 Lincoln is assassinated

▲ A Union soldier with his family in a Washington, D.C., camp in 1862

STUDY TO GO Study anywhere, anytime! Download quizzes and flash cards to your PDA from glencoe.com.

INDIANA STATEWIDE TEST PRACTICE

TEST-TAKING TIP

Answer the questions you know first and go back to those left unanswered in the remaining time.

Reviewing Vocabulary

Directions: Choose the word or words that best completes the sentence.

1 **One of the Union's goals was to _____, or close Southern ports.**

A draft
B siege
C blockade
D abandon

2 **To _____ is to sell or trade a good to another country.**

A stock
B import
C export
D distribute

3 **_____, or a general increase in prices, brought hardship to both the Confederacy and the Union.**

A Bounty
B Inflation
C Habeas corpus
D Injunction

4 **Union General William Sherman used a strategy called _____, or the systematic destruction of land and resources of the South.**

A total war
B guerrilla war
C Pickett's Charge
D the Anaconda Plan

Reviewing Main Ideas

Directions: Choose the best answer.

5 **What was one advantage the Southern states had during the Civil War?**

A They received military support from Britain and France.
B Many battles occurred on lands more familiar to Southerners.
C The largest weapons factories were located in the South.
D Most people in the country agreed with the Southern states' ideas.

6 **By gaining control of the Mississippi and Tennessee rivers, what was the Union able to do?**

A capture Fort Sumter
B force the Confederacy to surrender
C split the Confederacy
D defeat the Confederate forces at Gettysburg

7 **During the war, the economy of the South**

A was severely strained from the blockade instituted by the North.
B remained unchanged because most of the battles took place on Northern soil.
C was strengthened due to inflation.
D was strengthened because bounties were paid to army recruits.

8 **The battles of _____ in July 1863 were major turning points in the war.**

A Bull Run and Washington
B Shiloh and Second Bull Run
C Antietam and Fredericksburg
D Gettysburg and Vicksburg

GO ON ➡

Critical Thinking

Directions: Choose the best answer.

9 **One result of the Battle of Antietam was that**

A the Confederacy was split in two.
B David Farragut became a hero in the North.
C Lincoln issued the Emancipation Proclamation.
D Great Britain decided to support the Confederacy.

Base your answer to question 10 on the political cartoon below and your knowledge of Chapter 16.

LINCOLN'S TWO DIFFICULTIES.
Lin. "WHAT! NO MONEY! NO MEN!"

Source: Corbis

10 **What are the challenges that Lincoln is facing?**

A The people do not support the war.
B Lincoln is worried that he will lose his reelection campaign.
C The Confederacy is winning the war.
D There is not enough money or soldiers to fight the war.

11 **The purpose of Sherman's destructive March to the Sea was to**

A anger Southern citizens.
B destroy anything that was useful to the South.
C persuade the British not to aid the South.
D destroy Native American resistance in the area.

Constructed Response

Directions: Write a short response to each of the following questions. In your answer:

- *address all parts of the question*
- *use information from the chapter*
- *include facts, examples, and details relevant to the question*
- *use clear language*

12 **Describe the impact that civilians had on the war effort. Include references to both the South and the North.**

13 **How did the Civil War affect the economies of the North and the South?**

Base your answer to question 14 on the reading below and your knowledge of Chapter 16.

> With malice toward none, with charity for all, with firmness in the right as God gives us to see the right, let us strive on to finish the work we are in, to bind up the nation's wounds, to care for him who shall have borne the battle and for his widow and his orphan—to do all which may achieve and cherish a just and lasting peace among ourselves and with all nations.
>
> —from Abraham Lincoln's second Inaugural Address

14 **In his address, Lincoln describes what he sees as the country's major tasks following the Civil War. What are these tasks?**

STOP

Need Extra Help?														
If you missed questions. . .	1	2	3	4	5	6	7	8	9	10	11	12	13	14
Go to page. . .	477	477	497	507	476	482	497	502	486	500	510	491	494	509

Reconstruction and the New South 1865–1896

FREEDMEN'S SCHOOL.

A teacher and her students in front of the Freedmen's School in North Carolina

PRESIDENTS

ABRAHAM LINCOLN 1861–1865

ANDREW JOHNSON 1865–1869

ULYSSES S. GRANT 1869–1877

U.S. Events

★ **1867**
• Alaska purchased
• First Recon-struction Act passed

★ **1870**
Fifteenth Amendment ratified

1877 ★
Reconstruction ends

1860

1870

World Events

★ **1866**
First transatlantic cable connects North America to Europe

★ **1868**
Meiji era begins in Japan

★ **1871**
Bismarck unifies Germany

★ **1874**
First major exhibit of impressionist art in Paris

Section 1: Reconstruction Plans

Essential Question How did plans to unify the nation differ after the Civil War?

Section 2: Radicals in Control

Essential Question What were the results of Radical Reconstruction?

Section 3: The South During Reconstruction

Essential Question In what ways did government in the Southern states change during Reconstruction?

Section 4: Change in the South

Essential Question How did the South change politically, economically, and socially when Reconstruction ended?

History ONLINE
Chapter Overview Visit glencoe.com and click on **Chapter 17—Chapter Overviews** to preview chapter information.

Organizing Information Make this Foldable to help you summarize what you learn about Reconstruction and the New South.

Step 1 Fold an 11" x 17" piece of paper lengthwise to create a shutterfold.

Step 2 Fold a 3-inch tab along the bottom, and glue or staple the seams to create four pockets.

Step 3 Label the Foldable as shown.

Reading and Writing As you read the chapter, take notes on notecards about key events and issues covered in each section. Use your Foldable to store the cards, and then answer the Essential Questions for each section.

Jane Addams, founder of Hull House ▶

RUTHERFORD B. HAYES 1877–1881

JAMES GARFIELD 1881

CHESTER ARTHUR 1881–1885

GROVER CLEVELAND 1885–1889

★ **1890** Hull House opens in Chicago

BENJAMIN HARRISON 1889–1893

GROVER CLEVELAND 1893–1897

1880

1890

1900

★ **1882** Beginning of British occupation of Egypt

★ **1886** First May Day celebration held in Paris

★ **1891** Famine spreads throughout Russia

★ **1896** Ethiopia defeats invading Italians

Essential Question

How did plans to unify the nation differ after the Civil War?

Reading Guide

Content Vocabulary

Reconstruction (p. 519)

amnesty (p. 519)

Academic Vocabulary

radical (p. 520)

adjust (p. 520)

Key People and Events

Ten Percent Plan (p. 519)

Radical Republicans (p. 520)

Thaddeus Stevens (p. 520)

Wade-Davis Bill (p. 520)

Freedmen's Bureau (p. 520)

John Wilkes Booth (p. 521)

Andrew Johnson (p. 521)

Reading Strategy

Taking Notes As you read, use a diagram like the one below to describe each Reconstruction plan.

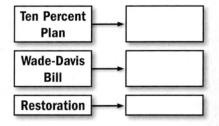

INDIANA ACADEMIC STANDARDS
United States History

8.1.22 Explain and evaluate the policies, practices, and consequences of Reconstruction, including the Thirteenth, Fourteenth, and Fifteenth Amendments to the Constitution.

8.2.7 Explain the importance in a democratic republic of responsible participation by citizens in voluntary civil associations/nongovernmental organizations that comprise civil society.

American Diary

Major Henry Rathbone tried to seize John Wilkes Booth after Booth shot President Lincoln at Ford's Theater. As Booth leaped over the railing of the presidential box onto the stage, Rathbone cried, "Stop that man." Rathbone later stated: "I then turned to the President. . . . I saw that he was unconscious, and, supposing him mortally wounded, rushed to the door for the purpose of calling medical aid."

—*from* The Assassination of President Lincoln and the Trial of the Conspirators

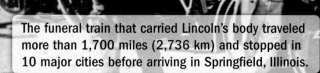

The funeral train that carried Lincoln's body traveled more than 1,700 miles (2,736 km) and stopped in 10 major cities before arriving in Springfield, Illinois.

Reconstruction Debate

Main Idea Government leaders disagreed about how Southern states could rejoin the Union.

History and You Have you ever had an argument with a friend? How did you resolve your differences? Read to learn how the North and South tried to work out their problems after the Civil War.

. . . .

Major Henry Rathbone and the rest of the nation were deeply shocked by Abraham Lincoln's assassination. Four years of civil war, followed by the president's death, shook the nation. The Union was saved, but Americans still faced the difficult challenges of reuniting and rebuilding their country.

Southern states, because they had left the Union in 1861, needed to be readmitted. The economy and society of the devastated South also needed to be rebuilt. Americans disagreed bitterly, however, about how to accomplish these tasks. This period of rebuilding is called **Reconstruction.** This term also refers to the various plans for readmitting Southern states to the Union.

Lincoln's Plan

Before his assassination, President Lincoln offered the first plan for accepting the Southern states back into the Union. In December 1863, during the Civil War, the president announced what came to be known as the **Ten Percent Plan.** When 10 percent of the voters of a state took an oath of loyalty to the Union, the state could form a new government and adopt a new constitution that banned slavery.

Lincoln wanted to encourage Southerners who supported the Union to take charge of the state governments. He believed that punishing the South would serve no useful purpose and would only delay healing the torn nation. Lincoln offered **amnesty**—a pardon—to all white Southerners who were willing to swear loyalty to the Union, except Confederate leaders. In 1864 three states under Union occupation—Louisiana, Arkansas, and Tennessee—set up governments under the plan. These states then became caught in controversy when Congress refused to seat the states' representatives.

If You Were There / Viewing Lincoln's Funeral Train

Springfield, Illinois At 9 P.M. on Wednesday, May 3, you stand with a large crowd at Springfield's railroad station. The funeral train carrying President Lincoln's body arrives from Chicago. A horse-drawn carriage takes the president's coffin to the state capitol. Once the coffin is placed on an elaborate platform, thousands of people walk past it, paying their last respects.

ABRAHAM LINCOLN'S
FUNERAL MARCH,
Dedicated to the
PEOPLE OF THE UNITED STATES

Composed by
W.J. ROBJOHN.
DETROIT
Published by J. Henry Whittemore.

Route of Lincoln's Funeral Train

CANADA
Lake Michigan
Lake Huron
Lake Ontario
Lake Erie
New York
Albany
Buffalo
Chicago
Cleveland
New York City
Ohio
Harrisburg
Penn.
ATLANTIC OCEAN
Columbus
Philadelphia
Baltimore
Springfield Ill.
Indianapolis
Ind.
Washington, D.C.
Md.
Ohio River
N
W   E
S

0   200 kilometers
0   200 miles
Albers Equal-Area projection

Critical Thinking

Identifying Central Issues
As a resident of Springfield, how might you feel about Lincoln's death? If you were a Southerner, would you feel the same way? Explain.

Course of Study African Americans who were enrolled in freedmen's schools learned practical skills such as sewing as well as academic subjects. A popular textbook was Lydia Maria Child's *Freedmen's Book*, a collection of essays and poems used to teach and inspire freed African Americans.

▼ Freedmen's Bureau School, Edisto Island, South Carolina

"Yesterday . . . my sister and I formally opened school. . . . We had more than one thousand (1,000) children, and seventy-five adults; and found time, after disciplining them, to hear the readers, to instruct the writers, and to teach the multitude from the blackboard."

—Lucy Chase, April 1865

"We have glorious schools in full blast—And I am so satisfied with the work here that nothing in the world could make me wish to be in another place, or doing anything else."

—Sarah Chase, February 1866

Critical Thinking

Analyzing Why do you think practical skills and academic subjects were taught at freed people's schools?

The Radicals' Plan

Some Republicans considered Lincoln's plan too forgiving. They favored a more **radical**, or extreme, approach and were called **Radical Republicans.** Radical Republican **Thaddeus Stevens** declared that Southern institutions "must be broken up and relaid, or all our blood and treasure have been spent in vain." Congress was controlled by the Radical Republicans and voted to deny seats to representatives from any state that was readmitted under Lincoln's plan.

In July 1864, Congress passed the **Wade-Davis Bill.** To rejoin the Union, a state had to meet several requirements. First, a majority of the state's white males had to swear loyalty to the Union. Second, only white males who swore they had not fought against the Union could vote for delegates to a state constitutional convention. Finally, any new state constitution had to ban slavery. The bill would also bar former Confederates from holding public office.

Lincoln refused to sign the bill, but he wanted new state governments to form quickly so that order could be restored in the South as soon as possible. Lincoln realized that he would have to compromise with the Radical Republicans.

The Freedmen's Bureau

In March 1865, Lincoln and Congress set up the **Freedmen's Bureau.** The bureau helped African Americans **adjust**, or adapt, to freedom. It provided food, clothing, and medical services. It helped freed people acquire land or find work for fair wages.

The bureau also set up schools, staffed mostly by teachers from the North. It gave aid to new African American institutions of higher learning, such as Atlanta University, Howard University, and Fisk University.

Reading Check **Contrasting** What were the differences between Lincoln's views and the Radical Republicans' views concerning Reconstruction?

Johnson's Plan

Main Idea After Lincoln was assassinated, Andrew Johnson became president and announced his plan of "Restoration."

History and You How do you think Abraham Lincoln's death might affect plans to unify the nation? Read about President Johnson's Reconstruction plan.

. . . .

Shortly after the Freedmen's Bureau was founded, a tragic event took place that shocked the nation. On April 14, 1865, President Lincoln attended a play at Ford's Theater in Washington, D.C. **John Wilkes Booth,** an actor and Confederate sympathizer, entered the private box and shot Lincoln in the head. Lincoln died several hours later.

News of the president's assassination swept across the nation. African Americans mourned the man who helped them win their freedom. Northern whites grieved for the leader who had saved the Union.

When Lincoln died, Vice President **Andrew Johnson** became president. Johnson was born in the South but supported the Union during the war. Johnson soon revealed his plan for Reconstruction. Called "Restoration," his plan would grant amnesty to most Southerners once they swore loyalty to the Union. High-ranking Confederates could be pardoned only by appealing to the president. This provision revealed Johnson's desire to humiliate the leaders who he believed had tricked the South's people into seceding.

Johnson also allowed only loyal, pardoned whites to vote for delegates to the state constitutional conventions. Stating that "white men alone must manage the South," Johnson opposed equal rights for African Americans.

Before a state could reenter the Union, it had to denounce secession and ban slavery. States also had to ratify the Thirteenth Amendment to the Constitution, passed by Congress in January 1865. This amendment abolished slavery throughout the United States. By the end of 1865, all former Confederate states, except Texas, had new governments and were ready to rejoin the Union.

Reading Check **Specifying** What did the Thirteenth Amendment accomplish?

Section 1 Review

History ONLINE
Study Central™ To review this section, go to glencoe.com.

Vocabulary

1. Write a short paragraph in which you use all of the following vocabulary terms:
Reconstruction, amnesty, radical, adjust.

Main Ideas

2. **Explaining** Why did Lincoln disagree with the harsh Reconstruction plan of the Radical Republicans?

3. **Specifying** Under Johnson's Restoration plan, how could high-ranking or wealthy Confederates gain a pardon?

Critical Thinking

4. **Contrasting** Using a diagram like the one below, compare the Reconstruction plans of Lincoln and the Radical Republicans.

Reconstruction Plans

Lincoln	Radical Republicans

5. **Drawing Conclusions** Do you think President Johnson's Southern heritage influenced his Reconstruction plan? Explain your answer.

6. **Persuasive Writing** Write a one-paragraph response to the Radical Republicans' plan for Reconstruction from Abraham Lincoln's point of view. Explain why you think the South should be treated less harshly.

Answer the Essential Question

7. How did plans to unify the nation differ after the Civil War?

Essential Question ◄

What were the results of Radical Reconstruction?

Reading Guide

Content Vocabulary

black codes *(p. 523)*   impeach *(p. 527)*

override *(p. 524)*

Academic Vocabulary

convince *(p. 523)*   suspend *(p. 526)*

Key People and Events

Civil Rights Act of 1866 *(p. 523)*

First Reconstruction Act *(p. 525)*

Second Reconstruction Act *(p. 526)*

Tenure of Office Act *(p. 526)*

Edwin Stanton *(p. 526)*

Ulysses S. Grant *(p. 527)*

Reading Strategy

Taking Notes As you read, use a diagram like the one below to answer the questions about impeachment.

Impeachment

What Is It?

Who Was Impeached?

Outcome of Trial?

INDIANA ACADEMIC STANDARDS
United States History

8.1.22 Explain and evaluate the policies, practices, and consequences of Reconstruction, including the Thirteenth, Fourteenth, and Fifteenth Amendments to the Constitution.

8.1.26 Give examples of the changing role of women and minorities in the northern, southern, and western parts of the United States in the mid-nineteenth century, and examine possible causes for these changes.

American Diary

For three days in May 1866, white mobs in Memphis, Tennessee, burned African American churches, schools, and homes. An army officer investigating the causes of the riot later reported: "Three [African American] churches were burned, also . . . about fifty (50) private dwellings, owned, occupied or inhabited by freedmen as homes, and . . . in many instances containing the hard earnings of months of labor."

—from the report on Memphis riot investigation, by Charles F. Johnson, 1866

Memphis rioters set fire to an African American schoolhouse built by the Freedmen's Bureau.

African Americans' Rights

Main Idea When Northerners realized that African Americans in the South were still being mistreated, they worked to find a way to help them.

History and You Think about the rights American citizens have. Read to find out how Congress made sure that formerly enslaved African Americans became citizens.

• •

Many Northerners saw the Memphis riot as an attempt by whites to terrorize African Americans and keep them from enjoying and practicing their new freedoms. The Memphis incident and similar riots in other Southern cities helped **convince,** or persuade, Radical Republicans that President Johnson's Reconstruction plan was not strong enough.

During the fall of 1865, Southern states created new governments based on Johnson's plan. They also elected new representatives to Congress. When the Southern representatives arrived in Washington, D.C., however, Congress refused to seat them. Many Republicans refused to readmit the Southern states on such easy terms.

Black Codes

By early 1866, Southern states had passed **black codes,** or laws to control freed men and women. The black codes trampled the rights of African Americans. They allowed plantation owners to exploit African American workers and allowed officials to arrest and fine jobless African Americans. The codes also banned African Americans from owning or renting farms. To freed men and women and many Northerners, the black codes resembled slavery.

In early 1866, Congress passed a bill giving the Freedmen's Bureau new powers. The agency could now set up special courts to try individuals charged with violating the rights of African Americans. African Americans could also serve on juries in these courts.

Congress then passed the **Civil Rights Act of 1866.** This act granted full citizenship to African Americans and gave the federal government the power to intervene in state affairs to protect their rights. The law overturned the black codes. It also contradicted the 1857 *Dred Scott* decision of the Supreme Court, which had ruled that African Americans were not citizens.

Primary Source / Freed People's Schools

Freedom to Learn Throughout the South, African Americans of all ages attended freed men and women's schools to learn basic reading, writing, and mathematical skills. As one freed person declared, education was "the next best thing to liberty." Many white Southerners, however, opposed schooling for African Americans. During the Memphis riots, white mobs burned down freed people's schools and attacked teachers and students. Despite the violence, African Americans continued to enroll in the schools.

—from *Forever Free: The Story of Emancipation and Reconstruction*

▲ Freed people's school, Richmond, Virginia, 1866

Critical Thinking

Hypothesizing Why do you think freed African Americans were eager to receive an education?

Protection of Rights The Fourteenth Amendment gave African American males their citizenship and tried to prevent the Southern states from taking away their rights. Since its ratification in 1868, the Supreme Court has written several landmark decisions related to the Fourteenth Amendment.

"All persons born or naturalized in the United States, and subject to the jurisdiction thereof, are citizens of the United States and of the State wherein they reside. No State shall make or enforce any law which shall abridge the privileges or immunities of citizens of the United States; nor shall any State deprive any person of life, liberty, or property, without due process of law; nor deny to any person within its jurisdiction the equal protection of the laws."

—Fourteenth Amendment, Section I

▲ The Supreme Court limited the Fourteenth Amendment in a series of rulings in the late 1800s. These rulings led to segregation and voter restrictions in the South.

In 1954 the Supreme Court ruled in *Brown* v. *Board of Education, Topeka, Kansas* that the equal protection clause forbade segregation. The Court ordered the desegregation of the nation's public schools. ▶

During the 2000 presidential election, the Supreme Court ruled in *Bush* v. *Gore* that the Florida recount violated the equal protection clause. The Court argued that since vote counters used different standards to count the votes, the recount did not treat all voters equally.

Responding to an ▶ appeal by Clarence Gideon, the Supreme Court in 1963 ruled in *Gideon* v. *Wainwright* that all defendants were entitled to legal counsel in cases involving possible jail time, including those who were too poor to hire a lawyer.

Critical Thinking

Assessing How has the Fourteenth Amendment influenced the rights of individual Americans?

President Johnson vetoed both bills. He argued that the federal government was overstepping its authority. He also argued that the Freedmen's Bureau bill and the Civil Rights Act were unconstitutional because they were approved by a Congress that did not include representatives from all of the states. By raising this issue, Johnson indirectly threatened to veto any law passed by this Congress.

Republicans in Congress had enough votes to **override,** or defeat, both vetoes, and the bills became law. The chances of the president and Congress working together faded. The Radical Republicans abandoned the idea of compromise and drafted a new Reconstruction plan—one created by Congress.

The Fourteenth Amendment

Fearing that the Civil Rights Act might be overturned in court, Congress passed a new amendment to the Constitution in 1866. The Fourteenth Amendment was enacted in 1868. It granted full citizenship to all people born in the United States. Because most African Americans in the United States had been born in the country, they became full citizens.

The amendment also stated that no state could take away a citizen's life, liberty, or property "without due process of law." In addition to this, every citizen was entitled to "equal protection of the laws." If a state prevented any adult male citizen from voting, then it could lose some of its representation in Congress.

The amendment also barred former Confederate leaders from holding national or state office unless pardoned by Congress. The Fourteenth Amendment also excluded Native Americans from citizenship.

Congress declared that Southern states had to ratify the amendment to rejoin the Union. Of the 11 Southern states, only Tennessee ratified it. The refusal of the other Southern states to ratify delayed the amendment's adoption until 1868.

Republican Victory

In the congressional elections of 1866, President Johnson campaigned vigorously against the Radical Republicans. Many Northerners objected to the nasty tone of Johnson's campaign and feared clashes between whites and African Americans. The Republicans won a solid victory, giving Congress the signal to take Reconstruction into its own hands.

Reading Check **Explaining** Why did Johnson consider the civil rights bill unconstitutional?

Radical Reconstruction

Main Idea Radical Republicans were able to put their version of Reconstruction into action.

History and You If you were a member of Congress at this time, what changes would you like to see in a Reconstruction plan? Read to find out how the Radical Republicans shaped Reconstruction.

President Johnson could do little to stop Republicans because they could easily override his vetoes in Congress. Thus began a period known as Radical Reconstruction.

Reconstruction Acts of 1867

The **First Reconstruction Act** passed in 1867 called for the creation of new governments in the 10 Southern states that had not ratified the Fourteenth Amendment. Tennessee, which ratified, kept its government and rejoined the Union.

History ONLINE
Student Web Activity Visit glencoe.com and complete the Chapter 17 Web Activity about Reconstruction.

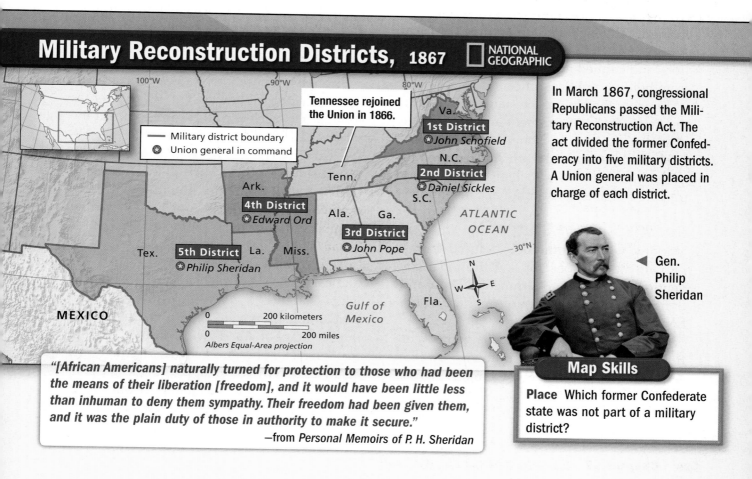

Military Reconstruction Districts, 1867 NATIONAL GEOGRAPHIC

Tennessee rejoined the Union in 1866.

— Military district boundary
⊛ Union general in command

1st District
⊛ John Schofield

2nd District
⊛ Daniel Sickles

4th District
⊛ Edward Ord

3rd District
⊛ John Pope

5th District
⊛ Philip Sheridan

Va. N.C. S.C. Ark. Tenn. Ala. Ga. Tex. La. Miss. Fla.

ATLANTIC OCEAN

Gulf of Mexico

MEXICO

0   200 kilometers
0   200 miles
Albers Equal-Area projection

In March 1867, congressional Republicans passed the Military Reconstruction Act. The act divided the former Confederacy into five military districts. A Union general was placed in charge of each district.

◄ Gen. Philip Sheridan

"[African Americans] naturally turned for protection to those who had been the means of their liberation [freedom], and it would have been little less than inhuman to deny them sympathy. Their freedom had been given them, and it was the plain duty of those in authority to make it secure."
—from *Personal Memoirs of P. H. Sheridan*

Map Skills

Place Which former Confederate state was not part of a military district?

Chance & Error in History

What If Lincoln Had Survived?

Abraham Lincoln wanted the South to be treated compassionately when the war ended. The Radicals expected that the new president, Andrew Johnson, would adopt a firm policy toward the South.

◀ Lincoln's funeral procession, Columbus, Ohio

◀ President Johnson and the Radicals had little in common, and Johnson had little popular support. Many people thought Johnson was self-righteous, hot-tempered, stubborn, and crude.

Second Inaugural Address, March 1865

"With malice toward none, with charity for all, with firmness in the right as God gives us to see the right, let us strive on to finish the work we are in, to bind up the nation's wounds, to care for him who shall have borne the battle and for his widow and his orphan."

—Abraham Lincoln

Critical Thinking

1. **Contrasting** Describe the leadership qualities of Abraham Lincoln and Andrew Johnson.
2. **Speculating** How do you think Reconstruction might have been different if Lincoln had not been assassinated? Explain.

The act divided the 10 Southern states into 5 military districts, each run by a military commander until new governments were formed. The act also guaranteed African American men the right to vote in state elections and banned former Confederate leaders from holding political office.

To rejoin the Union, the states had to ratify the Fourteenth Amendment and submit new state constitutions to Congress for approval. A **Second Reconstruction Act** required the military commanders to register voters and prepare for state constitutional conventions.

Readmission of States

Many white Southerners refused to take part in the elections for constitutional conventions and state governments. Thousands of newly registered African American voters, however, voted.

In the elections, Republicans gained control of Southern state governments. By 1868, seven Southern states—Alabama, Arkansas, Florida, Georgia, Louisiana, North Carolina, and South Carolina—had established new governments and met the requirements for readmission. By 1870, Mississippi, Virginia, and Texas were restored to the Union.

Impeaching the President

Strongly opposed to Radical Reconstruction, President Johnson had the power as commander in chief of the army to direct the actions of the military governors. For this reason, Congress passed a series of laws to limit the president's power, such as the **Tenure of Office Act.** It prohibited the president from removing government officials, including members of his own cabinet, without the Senate's approval.

The conflict between Johnson and the Radicals grew more intense. In August 1867—when Congress was not in session—Johnson **suspended** (removed from office temporarily) Secretary of War **Edwin Stanton** without the Senate's approval. When the Senate met again and refused to approve the suspension, Johnson removed Stanton from office.

This action was a deliberate violation of the Tenure of Office Act. Johnson also appointed people who the Radical Republicans opposed to command some of the Southern military districts.

Outraged by Johnson's actions, the House of Representatives voted to **impeach** the president, or formally charge him, with wrongdoing. In 1868 the case went to the Senate for a trial that lasted almost three months. Johnson's defenders claimed that the president was exercising his right to challenge laws he considered unconstitutional. They argued that Congress impeached the president because of politics, without accusing him of a crime. Johnson's critics disputed that Congress held supreme power to make the laws and that Johnson's use of the veto improperly interfered with this function.

The senators failed to achieve the two-thirds majority required for conviction. Some moderate Republicans supported the president, arguing that Johnson should not be removed from office because of political differences. As a result, Johnson stayed in office until the end of his term in March 1869.

The Fifteenth Amendment

By the presidential election of 1868, most Southern states had rejoined the Union, and many Americans hoped that Reconstruction was over. Abandoning Johnson, the Republicans nominated **Ulysses S. Grant,** the Civil War hero. The Democrats chose Horatio Seymour. Grant received most of the African American votes in the South and won the presidency. The 1868 election showed that voters supported the Republican approach to Reconstruction.

In 1869 Congress passed the Fifteenth Amendment. It prohibited the state and federal governments from denying the right to vote to any male citizen because of "race, color, or previous condition of servitude."

African American men won the right to vote when the amendment was ratified and became law in 1870. Republicans thought the power of the vote would enable African Americans to protect themselves. That belief, however, was too optimistic.

Reading Check **Explaining** How did Republicans organize the South during Reconstruction?

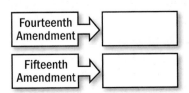

Section 2 Review

History ONLINE
Study Central™ To review this section, go to glencoe.com.

Vocabulary
1. Define each of the following terms and use it in a sentence: convince, black codes, override, suspend, impeach.

Main Ideas
2. **Specifying** What requirement was necessary for African Americans to become citizens under the Fourteenth Amendment?

3. **Explaining** Why was President Johnson unable to stop Radical Republicans from putting their Reconstruction plan into action?

Critical Thinking
4. **Comparing** How were black codes similar to slavery?

5. **Determining Cause and Effect** Describe the impact of the Fourteenth and Fifteenth Amendments on African Americans. Use a diagram like the one below.

Fourteenth Amendment → [ ]

Fifteenth Amendment → [ ]

6. **Persuasive Writing** Assume the role of Andrew Johnson. Write a short speech to give at your trial, explaining why the senators should not convict you of wrongdoing.

Answer the
7. **Essential Question**
What were the results of Radical Reconstruction?

Essential Question ◄····

In what ways did government in the Southern states change during Reconstruction?

Reading Guide

Content Vocabulary

scalawag (p. 529)

carpetbagger (p. 530)

corruption (p. 530)

integrate (p. 531)

sharecropping (p. 531)

Academic Vocabulary

credit (p. 530)   academy (p. 531)

Key People and Events

Hiram Revels (p. 529)

Blanche K. Bruce (p. 529)

Reading Strategy

Taking Notes As you read, use a diagram like the one below to describe improvements in the South in the field of education.

Improvements in Education

INDIANA ACADEMIC STANDARDS
United States History

8.1.22 Explain and evaluate the policies, practices, and consequences of Reconstruction, including the Thirteenth, Fourteenth, and Fifteenth Amendments to the Constitution.

8.2.7 Explain the importance in a democratic republic of responsible participation by citizens in voluntary civil associations/nongovernmental organizations that comprise civil society.

American Diary

John Roy Lynch, once enslaved, ran a business in Mississippi. In the 1869 election—the first in which African Americans could vote—Lynch was elected to the Mississippi state legislature. Lynch later recalled that "the campaign was aggressive . . . the election resulted in a sweeping Republican victory. That party not only elected the state ticket . . . but also had a large majority in . . . the state legislature."

—*from* Reminiscences of an Active Life: The Autobiography of John Roy Lynch

Newly freed African Americans from rural areas moved to Southern cities, such as Richmond, where they sought jobs, voted for the first time, and joined local branches of the Republican Party.

Reconstruction Politics

Main Idea As African Americans began to take part in civic life in the South, they faced resistance, including violence, from whites.

History and You Do some people today use mean names to refer to someone they don't like? Read to learn what former Confederates called Republican supporters in the South.

· ·

During Reconstruction, Republicans dominated Southern politics. Support for the Republican Party came from African Americans, white Southerners who supported Republican policies, and white settlers from the North. These groups were in charge of the state governments.

African Americans in Government

African Americans played an important role in Reconstruction politics, both as voters and as elected officials. In some states they contributed heavily to Republican victories. African Americans did not control any state government, although they briefly held a majority in the lower house of the South Carolina legislature. In other Southern states,

they held important positions, but never in proportion to their numbers.

At the national level, 16 African Americans served in the House of Representatives and 2 in the Senate between 1869 and 1880. **Hiram Revels,** one of the African American senators, was an ordained minister who had recruited African Americans for the Union army. He also started a school for freed African Americans in Missouri and served as chaplain of an African American regiment in Mississippi. Revels remained in Mississippi after the war and was elected to the U.S. Senate in 1870.

Blanche K. Bruce, the other African American senator, also came from Mississippi. A former escaped slave, Bruce taught in a school for African Americans in Missouri when the war began. In 1869 he went to Mississippi, entered politics, and was elected to the U.S. Senate in 1874.

Scalawags and Carpetbaggers

Some Southern whites—such as pro-Union business leaders and non-slaveholding farmers—backed the Republicans. Former Confederates called them **scalawags,** a term meaning "scoundrel" or "worthless rascal."

Primary Source / The African American Church

Creating a Community After the Civil War, many African Americans formed their own churches free of white control. In addition to providing a place of worship, churches supported schools, social events, and political meetings. Elias Campbell Morris was a popular African American preacher and a leader of the Republican Party in Arkansas. He encouraged African Americans to participate in politics, saying that improvements in society "will depend in a large measure upon what we prove able to do for ourselves."

—from *This Far by Faith: Stories from the African American Religious Experience*

◀ In many African American homes, the social, political, and economic life of the family centered around religion.

Critical Thinking

Analyzing Information Why do you think churches played such an important political and social role in the African American community?

People IN HISTORY

Blanche K. Bruce

African American senator from Mississippi

In Mississippi, the election of 1876 was controversial. Many people thought that African Americans were pressured to vote for white Democrats. Bruce stated: *"The conduct of the late election in Mississippi . . . put in question and jeopardy the sacred rights of the citizen."*

Hiram Revels

First African American senator

Revels wanted to find common ground between African Americans and white Southerners. He felt that in most places in Mississippi, *"white people . . . accept as a fact that all men are born free and equal, and . . . are ready to guarantee to my people every right and privilege guaranteed to an American citizen."*

CRITICAL Thinking

1. **Analyzing** How do Revels and Bruce differ in their views of Mississippi politics?
2. **Evaluating** Which view of Mississippi politics do you think is more accurate? Explain your answer.

Many Northern whites who moved to the South after the war also supported the Republicans. Critics called these Northerners **carpetbaggers** because they arrived with all their belongings in cheap suitcases made of carpet fabric. Although some carpetbaggers were dishonest, most were not. Many were reformers who wanted to help the South.

Many Southerners accused Reconstruction governments of **corruption**—or dishonest or illegal actions. Although some officials made money illegally, probably less corruption occurred in the South than in the North.

Resistance to Reconstruction

Most Southern whites opposed efforts to expand African Americans' rights. Life soon became difficult for African Americans. Most white landowners refused to rent land to freed people. Store owners refused them **credit**—extra time to pay for goods—and employers would not hire them.

Secret societies, such as the Ku Klux Klan, used fear and violence to deny rights to freed men and women. Wearing white sheets and hoods, Klan members killed thousands of African Americans and their white friends. They beat and wounded many more and burned African American homes, schools, and churches. Many Southerners, especially planters and Democrats, backed the Klan. These people, who had the most to gain from the return of white supremacy, saw violence as a defense against Republican rule.

In 1870 and 1871, Congress passed several laws to try to stop the growing violence of the Klan. These laws met with limited success. Most white Southerners refused to testify against those who attacked African Americans and their white supporters.

✓ **Reading Check** Explaining Who were the scalawags and carpetbaggers? Why did many Southerners resent them?

Education and Farming

Main Idea Education improved for both races in the South, but the sharecropping system limited economic opportunities for African Americans.

History and You If you could not attend school, how would the course of your life change? Read about advances in education in the South.

· ·

During Reconstruction, African Americans created their own schools. The Freedmen's Bureau also helped spread education. Northern women and African Americans came south to teach in schools. In the 1870s, Reconstruction governments created public schools for both races. Within a few years, about 50 percent of white children and 40 percent of African American children in the South were enrolled. Northern missionary societies set up **academies**—schools for special training. These academies grew into a network of African American colleges and universities, including Fisk University in Tennessee and Morehouse College in Georgia.

Generally, African American and white students attended different schools. Only a very few states required that schools be **integrated**—include both whites and African Americans—but the laws were not enforced.

Along with education, most freed people wanted land. Some African Americans purchased land with the help of the Freedmen's Bank, but most failed to get their own land. The most common form of farmwork for freed people was **sharecropping.** In this system, a landowner rented a plot of land to a sharecropper, or farmer, along with a crude shack, some seeds and tools, and perhaps a mule. In return, sharecroppers shared a percentage of their crops with the landowners.

After paying the landowners, sharecroppers often had little left to sell. Sometimes there was barely enough to feed their families. For many, sharecropping was little better than slavery.

Reading Check Describing What was the relationship between sharecroppers and landowners?

Section 3 Review

History ONLINE
Study Central™ To review this section, go to glencoe.com.

Vocabulary

1. Use each of these terms in a sentence that will help explain its meaning: scalawag, carpetbagger, corruption, credit, academy, integrate, sharecropping.

Main Ideas

2. **Specifying** What kinds of resistance did African Americans face as they tried to exercise their rights as citizens in the South?

3. **Describing** How did Reconstruction governments reform education in the South?

Critical Thinking

4. **Organizing** Use a diagram like the one below to identify the three main groups that made up the Southern Republican Party.

5. **Analyzing** How did the sharecropping system work to keep African Americans from improving their lives?

6. **Expository Writing** Imagine that you are a journalist in 1869. You are preparing to interview an African American senator from Mississippi, a carpetbagger, and a white Southern planter. Write three questions you would ask each about Reconstruction. Suggest how each person would respond.

Answer the
Essential Question

7. In what ways did government in the Southern states change during Reconstruction?

What were people's lives like in the past?

These two pages will give you some clues to everyday life in the United States as you step back in time with TIME Notebook.

PHOTO RESEARCHERS

New Railway Crosses the Country

GETTING THERE

By now, you have probably heard that the tracks of the Union Pacific and Central Pacific railways met up in Utah on May 10, 1869—completing the first transcontinental railroad in the United States. A pioneer named **ALEXANDER TOPONCE** *wrote about the events that day:*

"When they came to drive the last spike, Governor Stanford, president of the Central Pacific, took the sledge, and the first time he struck he missed the spike and hit the rail.

"What a howl went up! Irish, Chinese, Mexicans, and everybody yelled with delight. 'He missed it. Yee.' The engineers blew the whistles and rang their bells. Then Stanford tried it again and tapped the spike and the telegraph operators had fixed their instruments so that the tap was reported in all the offices east and west, and set bells to tapping in hundreds of towns and cities. . . . Then Vice President T. C. Durant of the Union Pacific took up the sledge and he missed the spike the first time. Then everybody slapped everybody else again and yelled, 'He missed it too, yow!'

"It was a great occasion, everyone carried off souvenirs and there are enough splinters of the last tie in museums to make a good bonfire."

VERBATIM

WHAT PEOPLE ARE SAYING

❝I will never pay a dollar of your unjust fine.❞

> **SUSAN B. ANTHONY,**
> *after being arrested and fined $100*
> *for voting in the 1872 election*

❝Mr. Watson, come here. I want you!❞

> **ALEXANDER GRAHAM BELL,**
> *in 1876, making the first*
> *phone call to his assistant*

❝The shouts, groans, curses, smashing of seats, screams of women, shuffling of feet, and cries of terror created a pandemonium that will stand out in my memory as the hell of hells.❞

> **HELEN TRUMAN,**
> *an audience member*
> *at Ford's Theater the night*
> *Lincoln was shot in 1865*

❝It seemed like it took a long time for freedom to come. Everything just kept on like it was.❞

> **MILLIE FREEMAN,**
> *former enslaved African American,*
> *about life after the Civil War*

❝Forty miles away we still saw the brilliant flames looming above the doomed city.❞

> **JOHN CHAPIN,**
> *a witness to the Great Chicago Fire*
> *in 1871, which killed 250 people*
> *and destroyed 18,000 buildings*

NORTH WIND PICTURE ARCHIVES / ALAMY

VIRGINIA STATS
State of the Union

Richmond had been the capital of the Confederacy—and Virginia paid the price after the Civil War. One of the states most ravaged by battles, Virginia's farm values sank from fifth in the country to tenth. The state tried to get new business by lowering taxes. That led to more factories, but they produced less than in the past.

CORBIS

	1860	1870
Number of Farms	86,468	73,849
Value of Farm Land	$371.8 million	$213 million
Number of Factories	5,385	5,933
Value of Manufactured Products	$50.7 million	$38.4 million

MILESTONES
EVENTS AND PEOPLE OF THE TIME

DRAWN. An elephant to represent jittery Republican voters by Thomas Nast before the presidential election in 1874. Looks like his symbol for Republicans might stick—after all, Nast is the artist who drew a mule to represent Democrats.

STRETCHED. Baseball fans in 1882 in what is becoming known as the "seventh inning stretch." The athletic director of New York's Manhattan College baseball team felt sorry for fidgety students in the crowd and told them to stand up and stretch during a game. Word has it that New York Giants fans will copy the practice.

DRIVEN OUT. African American members of the Georgia legislature in 1868, after white members claimed that African Americans might vote but not hold office.

THE REPUBLICAN VOTE

BETTMANN / CORBIS

NUMBERS
UNITED STATES AT THE TIME

2 cents About the price per acre the United States paid for Alaska in 1867—the total price is $7.2 million

600,000 Approximate number of African Americans in the South who had enrolled in school by 1877

$125 Price of a typewriter, invented by Christopher Sholes in 1868

120,000,000,000 Number of locusts in a swarm that reached a mile high, 100 miles wide (161 km), and up to 300 miles long (483 km), wiping out crops in the West in 1874

MARY EVANS PICTURE LIBRARY / ALAMY

10,000 Number of people who went to the first Kentucky Derby horse race in 1875

CRITICAL THINKING

Speculating Based on Susan B. Anthony's reaction to her voting fine, what personal and philosophical qualities do you think she had?

Assessing How might the values of Virginia's farm and manufacturing economies have affected the lives of its citizens after the Civil War? Use the table to help explain your answer.

Change in the South

Essential Question

How did the South change politically, economically, and socially when Reconstruction ended?

Reading Guide

Content Vocabulary

cash crop
(p. 539)

grandfather clause
(p. 539)

poll tax
(p. 539)

segregation
(p. 540)

literacy test
(p. 539)

lynching
(p. 540)

Academic Vocabulary

outcome
(p. 536)

commission
(p. 536)

Key People and Events

Amnesty Act *(p. 535)*

Rutherford B. Hayes *(p. 536)*

Compromise of 1877 *(p. 536)*

Jim Crow laws *(p. 540)*

Plessy v. Ferguson *(p. 540)*

Reading Strategy

Taking Notes As you read, use a diagram like the one below to summarize the goals for industry and for agriculture that leaders hoped to achieve in the "New South."

```
          The New South
          /           \
   Goal for        Goal for
   Industry:       Agriculture:
```

INDIANA ACADEMIC STANDARDS
United States History

8.1.22 Explain and evaluate the policies, practices, and consequences of Reconstruction, including the Thirteenth, Fourteenth, and Fifteenth Amendments to the Constitution.

8.3.6 Identify the agricultural regions of the United States and be able to give reasons for the type of land use and subsequent land development during different historical periods.

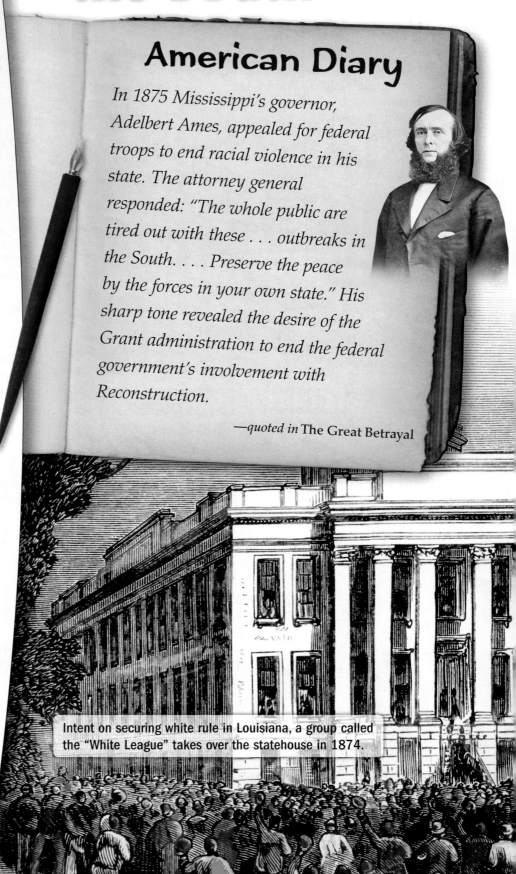

American Diary

In 1875 Mississippi's governor, Adelbert Ames, appealed for federal troops to end racial violence in his state. The attorney general responded: "The whole public are tired out with these . . . outbreaks in the South. . . . Preserve the peace by the forces in your own state." His sharp tone revealed the desire of the Grant administration to end the federal government's involvement with Reconstruction.

—quoted in The Great Betrayal

Intent on securing white rule in Louisiana, a group called the "White League" takes over the statehouse in 1874.

The End of Reconstruction

Main Idea Democrats steadily regained control of Southern governments as support for Radical Reconstruction policies decreased.

History and You Would you lose respect for a famous sports star if you learned he or she was cheating? Read how scandals weakened public support for the Radical Republicans.

. . . .

During the Grant administration, Northerners began losing interest in Reconstruction. Many believed it was time for the South to solve its own problems.

Reconstruction declined for other reasons as well. The old Radical leaders began to disappear from politics. Thaddeus Stevens died in 1868. Others retired or lost elections.

Opponents of Reconstruction also exploited racial prejudice in the North. They argued that only Southerners really knew how to deal with African Americans and that the fate of the freed people should be left to the South. Southerners protested what they called "bayonet rule"—the use of federal troops to support Reconstruction governments. Grant tried to avoid any clashes with the South.

Republican Revolt

In the early 1870s, reports of corruption in Grant's administration and in Reconstruction governments spread. Some Republicans split with the party over the issue of corruption. Another group broke with the party over Reconstruction, proposing peaceful reconciliation—coming together again—with Southern whites. Calling themselves Liberal Republicans, these two groups nominated Horace Greeley, a newspaper editor, to run against Grant in 1872. Despite the split among Republicans, Grant was reelected.

Democrats Regain Power

In 1872 Liberal Republicans helped pass the **Amnesty Act,** which pardoned most former Confederates. Nearly all white Southerners could vote and hold office again. The amnesty changed the political balance in the South by restoring full rights to people who supported the Democratic Party.

In Southern states where a majority of voters were white, Democrats soon regained control of state governments. In states where African Americans held a majority, the Ku Klux Klan helped the Democrats take power by terrorizing Republican voters.

Mississippi House of Representatives

1870

82 Republicans

25 Democrats

1875

97 Democrats

20 Republicans

By the Numbers / Politics in Mississippi

End of Reconstruction After the Civil War, Republican state governments in Mississippi and other Southern states set up schools, built hospitals, and ended racial discrimination laws. By 1880, these reforms that began under Reconstruction came to an end as the more conservative Democrats returned to power throughout the South.

Mississippi State Budgets	
1870	$1,061,250
1871	$1,729,046
1876	$518,709
1877	$697,019
1880	$803,191

Source: *Cyclopaedia of Political Science, 1899.*

Critical Thinking

Interpreting Why do you think state government spending in Mississippi declined around 1876? How do you think the state's African American population was affected by this and other changes?

The Republicans had other problems as well. In 1873 a series of political scandals came to light. Investigations uncovered top government officials making unfair business deals, scheming to withhold public tax money, and accepting bribes. One scandal involved the vice president and another the secretary of war. These scandals further damaged the Grant administration and the Republicans.

In addition to political scandals, Grant and the nation endured a severe economic depression. The crisis began in 1873 when a series of bad railroad investments forced the powerful banking firm of Jay Cooke and Company to declare bankruptcy. A wave of fear known as the Panic of 1873 quickly spread through the nation's financial community. The panic forced small banks to close and the stock market to plummet. Thousands of businesses shut down, and tens of thousands of Americans were thrown out of work. Blame for the hard times fell on the Republicans.

In the congressional elections of 1874, Democrats gained seats in the Senate and won control of the House. For the first time since the Civil War, the Democratic Party controlled a part of the federal government. This situation further weakened Congress's commitment to Reconstruction and protecting the rights of African Americans.

The Election of 1876

President Grant considered running for a third term in 1876. Most Republican leaders preferred a new candidate—one who could win back the Liberal Republicans and unite the party. The Republicans nominated **Rutherford B. Hayes,** governor of Ohio. A champion of political reform, Hayes had a reputation for honesty, and he held moderate views on Reconstruction. The Democrats nominated New York governor Samuel Tilden. Tilden gained fame for fighting political corruption in New York City.

After the election, Tilden appeared to be the winner, receiving almost 250,000 more votes than Hayes. However, disputed returns from four states—representing 20 electoral

Struggle of Reconstruction

Extending Liberties Laws and amendments were passed during Reconstruction to extend civil liberties to African Americans.

Civil Rights Amendments and Laws

Civil Rights Act of 1866

Granted citizenship and equal rights to all persons born in the United States (except Native Americans)

Fourteenth Amendment (1870)

Granted citizenship and equal protection of the laws to all persons born in the United States (except Native Americans)

Fifteenth Amendment (1870)

Protected the voting rights of African Americans

Civil Rights Act of 1875

Outlawed racial segregation in public services
Ensured the right of African Americans to serve as jurors

votes—kept the **outcome,** or results, in doubt. Tilden had 184 electoral votes, only 1 short of what he needed to win. Yet if Hayes received all 20 of the disputed votes, he would have the 185 electoral votes required for victory.

To review the election results, Congress created a special **commission,** or group, of 15 persons made up equally of members of the House of Representatives, the Senate, and the Supreme Court. The commission had 7 Republicans, 7 Democrats, and 1 independent. But the independent resigned, and a Republican took his place. The commission voted 8 to 7 to award all 20 electoral votes, and the election, to Hayes. The vote followed party lines.

Compromise of 1877

Democrats in Congress threatened to fight the commission's decision. Republican and Southern Democratic leaders reportedly met in secret to work out an agreement. On March 2, 1877, Congress declared Hayes the winner.

The agreement—called the **Compromise of 1877**—included some favors to the South.

Disputed Election of 1876 NATIONAL GEOGRAPHIC

Rutherford B. Hayes ▶

One of Oregon's three electoral votes was in doubt.

▨ Disputed electoral vote

Washington Territory — 3

Montana Territory

Dakota Territory — 5

Idaho Territory

Wyoming Territory

3

Utah Terr. — 3

6

Arizona Territory

New Mexico Territory

Unorg. Terr.

10

11

11

5

21 15 22

5

15 12

11

6

8 10 11

8

8

7

35

7

5 5

13

4

6

29

9

8

3

10

12

7

4

Northern troops still occupied three states.

People living in territories could not vote in national elections.

Candidate	Electoral Vote	Popular Vote	Political Party
Hayes	185	4,036,572	Republican
Tilden	184	4,284,020	Democrat

Critical Thinking

Comparing Which laws are most similar to each other?

The new government would give more aid to the South. Republicans agreed to withdraw all remaining troops from Southern states. Without soldiers to support them, the remaining Republican governments in South Carolina and Louisiana quickly collapsed. The Democrats, in turn, promised to maintain African American rights.

A New Policy

In his Inaugural Address, Hayes declared that what the South needed most was the restoration of "wise, honest, and peaceful local self-government." During a goodwill trip to the South, Hayes announced his intention of letting Southerners handle racial issues. Hayes's message was clear. The federal government would no longer attempt to reshape Southern society. Reconstruction had come to an end.

✓ **Reading Check** **Summarizing** How did the Compromise of 1877 affect Reconstruction?

Change in the South

Main Idea After Reconstruction, the South experienced a political shift and industrial growth.

History and You Do you recall that lack of industry put the South at a disadvantage during the Civil War? Read to learn how Southerners vowed to create a strong industrial "New South."

• •

Many Southern whites hated Republicans for their role in the Civil War and in Reconstruction. When Reconstruction ended, power in the South shifted to the Democrats.

Democrats in Control

In some regions, the ruling Democrats were the large landowners and other groups that held power before the Civil War. In many areas, however, new leaders took charge. Among their ranks were merchants, bankers, and other business leaders who supported economic development.

Change in Politics

These Democrats called themselves "Redeemers" because they had "redeemed," or saved, the South from Republican rule. The Redeemers adopted conservative policies, such as lower taxes and reduced government spending. They drastically cut, or even eliminated, many social services started during Reconstruction, including public education. Their one-party rule and conservative policies dominated Southern politics well into the 1900s.

Rise of the "New South"

By the 1880s, forward-looking Southerners were convinced that their region must develop a strong industrial economy. They argued that the South lost the Civil War because its industry did not match the North's. Henry Grady, editor of the *Atlanta Constitution*, headed a group that urged Southerners to "out-Yankee the Yankees" and build a "New South." This "New South" would have industries based on the region's abundant coal, iron, tobacco, cotton, and lumber. Southerners would create this new economy by embracing a spirit of hard work and regional pride.

Industry in the South made dramatic gains in the 1880s. Textile mills sprang up across the South. The American Tobacco Company, developed largely by James Duke of North Carolina, eventually controlled almost all tobacco manufacturing in the nation. By 1890, Southern mills produced nearly 20 percent of the nation's iron and steel. Much of the industry was in Alabama near deposits of iron ore.

Southern industry grew as a result of a cheap and reliable workforce. Most factory workers put in long hours for low wages. A railroad-building boom also aided industrial development. By 1870, the Southern railroad system, which had been destroyed during the war, was largely rebuilt. The miles of rail track more than doubled between 1880 and 1890. Still, the South did not develop an industrial economy as strong as the North's. Agriculture remained the South's main economic activity.

Primary Source | Sharecropping

Denied Land During the Civil War, formerly enslaved African Americans hoped to acquire abandoned or confiscated Confederate lands. The government under President Johnson, however, returned Southern plantations to their former slaveholders.

Formerly enslaved African Americans often ended up working as sharecroppers on land that belonged to their former owners. ▼

Southern laws forced sharecroppers to work the land until they paid off their debts. A system emerged in the South that closely resembled slavery. ▼

Typical sharecropper contract ▶

To secure payment of said rent and supply bill, the said Dawson [the sharecropper] grants unto said Solid South [the landowner] a special privilege and right of pledge on all the products raised on said land, and on all his stock, farming implements, and personal property, and hereby waives in favor of said Solid South the benefit of any and all homestead laws and exemption laws now in force, or which may be in force, in Louisiana, and agrees that all his property shall be seized and sold to pay said rent and supply bill in default of payment thereof as herein agreed. Any violation of this contract shall render the lease void.

Rural Economy

Supporters of the New South hoped to change Southern agriculture as well as industry. Their goal was small, profitable farms raising a variety of crops rather than large plantations devoted to cotton. A different economy emerged, however. Some plantations were broken up, but many large landowners held on to their land. When estates were divided, much of the land went to sharecropping and tenant farming, neither of which was profitable.

Debt also caused problems. Poor farmers used credit to buy supplies. Merchants who sold on credit charged high prices, and farmers' debts rose. To repay debts, farmers grew **cash crops**—crops that could be sold for money. As in the past, the main cash crop was cotton. Too much cotton forced prices down, however. Farmers then had to grow even more cotton to try to recover their losses. Sharecropping and reliance on one cash crop kept Southern agriculture from advancing.

✔ **Reading Check** **Describing** Why did industry in the South grow during this period?

Agricultural Production in the South, 1850–1890

Increased production lowered cotton prices and left much of the rural South in poverty after the Civil War. ▶

Source: *Historical Statistics of the South*

Critical Thinking

Comparing and Contrasting How was the South after the Civil War similar to and different from the South before the Civil War?

Graphs In Motion See StudentWorks™ Plus or glencoe.com.

A Divided Society

Main Idea As Reconstruction ended, true freedom for African Americans became a distant dream.

History and You How would you feel if you had to pass a test on a subject you never studied in order to graduate? Read to learn about a test African Americans in the South had to pass in order to vote.

· ·

As Reconstruction ended, African Americans' dreams for justice faded. In the last 20 years of the 1800s, racism became firmly set in the culture. Individuals took steps to keep African Americans separated from whites and to deny them basic rights.

Voting Restrictions

The Fifteenth Amendment prohibited any state from denying an individual the right to vote because of race. Southern leaders, however, found ways to get around the amendment and prevent African Americans from voting.

Many Southern states required a **poll tax,** a fee people had to pay to vote. Because many African Americans could not afford the tax, they could not vote. The tax also kept many poor whites from voting.

Another approach was to make prospective voters take a **literacy test** in which they had to read and explain difficult parts of state constitutions or the federal Constitution. Because most African Americans had little education, literacy tests prevented many from voting.

Literacy tests could also keep some whites from voting. For this reason some states passed **grandfather clauses.** These laws allowed people who did not pass the literacy test to vote if their fathers or grandfathers voted before Reconstruction. Because African Americans could not vote until 1867, they were excluded. By the end of the 1800s, such laws and the constant threat of violence caused African American voting to decline drastically.

Jim Crow Laws

By the 1890s, **segregation,** or the separation of the races, had become a common feature of the South. Southern states passed so-called **Jim Crow laws** that required African Americans and whites to be separated in almost every public place.

In 1896 the Supreme Court upheld segregation laws in ***Plessy v. Ferguson.*** The case involved a Louisiana law requiring separate sections on trains for African Americans. The Court ruled that segregation was legal as long as African Americans had access to public places equal to those of whites.

One problem, however, was that the facilities were separate but in no way equal. Southern states spent much more money on schools and other facilities for whites than on those for African Americans. This "separate but equal" doctrine gave legal support to Southern segregation for more than 50 years. White violence against African Americans also rose. One form of violence was **lynching,** in which an angry mob killed a person by hanging. African Americans were lynched because they were suspected of crimes—or because they did not behave as whites thought they should behave.

Reconstruction's Impact

Reconstruction was both a success and a failure. It helped the South rebuild its economy. Yet much of the South remained agricultural and poor. African Americans gained greater equality, created their own institutions, and shared in government with whites. Their advances, however, did not last. In the words of African American writer and civil rights leader W.E.B. Du Bois, "The slave went free; stood a brief moment in the sun; then moved back again toward slavery."

✔ Reading Check **Describing** How was segregation applied?

Section 4 Review

History ONLINE
Study Central™ To review this section, go to glencoe.com.

Vocabulary

1. Use each of these terms in a sentence that will help explain its meaning: outcome, commission, cash crop, poll tax, literacy test, grandfather clause, segregation, lynching.

Main Ideas

2. **Explaining** How did the Amnesty Act help Democrats regain control of Southern state governments?

3. **Describing** How did forward-thinking Southerners want to change the South's economy?

4. **Explaining** Why did African American voting in the South decline drastically by the late 1800s?

Critical Thinking

5. **Determining Cause and Effect** Use a diagram like the one below to describe the two issues that split the Republican Party for the 1872 election. Then name the group these dissatisfied Republicans came together to form.

Issues That Divided Republicans

New Group:

6. **Analyzing** Did agriculture in the New South achieve the shift envisioned by its supporters? Why or why not?

7. **Descriptive Writing** You are an African American in 1899. When you took a seat on a train, the white conductor told you to move to a separate section. Write a letter to W.E.B. Du Bois, describing the incident and your feelings about it.

Answer the Essential Question

8. How did the South change politically, economically, and socially when Reconstruction ended?

◀ Freedmen's school

Reconstruction Plans

- The South is rebuilt and readmitted to the Union during Reconstruction.
- Lincoln's Ten Percent Plan is designed to heal the Union quickly.
- The Radical Republicans' Wade-Davis Bill has strict requirements for states to be readmitted.
- The Freedmen's Bureau helps African Americans adjust to freedom.
- Abraham Lincoln is assassinated in April 1865.
- President Johnson's "Restoration" plan calls for states to ratify the amendment to abolish slavery.

Lincoln's funeral ▼

Radical Reconstruction

- Radical Republicans believe Johnson's plan is too easy on the South.
- Southern states pass black codes to control freed African Americans, but Congress passes the Civil Rights Act of 1866 to protect their freedoms.
- The Fourteenth Amendment gives African Americans citizenship and equal protection of the laws.
- Radical Republicans win Congress and enact their own Reconstruction plans.
- Congress impeaches Johnson but fails to convict him.
- The Fifteenth Amendment gives African American men the right to vote.

Andrew Johnson ▲

Reconstruction in the South

- African Americans vote and take part in Southern politics.
- Some whites resist the expansion of African Americans' rights and form the Ku Klux Klan.
- Sharecropping limits economic opportunities for African Americans.

Reconstruction Ends

- Republicans lose power as a result of political corruption and economic crisis.
- Democrats regain control of Southern state governments.
- Southern Democrats encourage economic growth but limit the rights of African Americans.

STUDY TO GO Study anywhere, anytime! Download quizzes and flash cards to your PDA from glencoe.com.

Southern Industry After the Civil War

Before the Civil War, the backbone of the Southern economy was agriculture. After Reconstruction, industry in the South made dramatic gains.

How Did Geography Affect Southern Industry?

Many Southern industries after the Civil War centered around regional agricultural products such as tobacco and cotton. In the 1880s textile mills sprang up throughout the South. Additionally, Southern forests provided lumber for new homes, factories, railroad ties, and above all, furniture.

Other Southern industries centered on the region's rich reserves of coal and iron. By 1900, the South led the world in coal production; this same period saw a large growth in iron and steel mills.

		Coal		Lumber
		Cotton		Textiles
		Iron		Tobacco

▲ While the economy of the Old South focused on cotton and tobacco production, distinct industrial regions began to develop after the Civil War.

Manufacturing in the Southern States, 1860–1900*

State	1860	1880	1900
Alabama	1,459	2,070	5,602
Arkansas	518	1,202	4,794
Florida	185	426	2,056
Georgia	1,890	3,593	7,504
Louisiana	1,744	1,553	4,350
Mississippi	976	1,479	4,772
North Carolina	3,689	3,802	7,226
South Carolina	1,230	2,078	3,762
Tennessee	2,572	4,326	8,016
Texas	983	2,996	12,289
TOTAL	**15,246**	**23,525**	**60,371**

*Number of Manufacturing Establishments

Thomas Nast's illustration for an 1882 cover of *Harper's Weekly* compares the Old South's "King Cotton" of 1861 to the New South's "Queen of Industry." ▶

What they were saying . . .

Atlanta *Constitution* editor Henry Grady was one of the leaders calling for a "New South," a South that is industrialized and part of a modern national economy.

"We are going to take a noble revenge . . . by invading every inch of your territory [the North] with iron, as you invaded ours twenty-nine years ago."

After the Civil War, Southerners built a number of iron and steel mills. Many mills were located near the iron ore deposits around Birmingham, Alabama. Founded in 1871, Birmingham became a prime industrial center of the New South. Between 1880 and 1900, the area in and around Birmingham was second only to Pittsburgh, Pennsylvania, in the number of new furnaces for making iron.

Although tobacco was grown in the South before the Civil War, it was rarely processed there. By 1900, tobacco processing had become a major Southern industry. ▶

One of the first industries to gain strength in the "New South" was the textile industry. Textile mills produced cotton cloth.

▲ The lumber industry thrived in many parts of the South.

Analyzing Geography

1. **Location** In which parts of the "New South" did coal mining predominate? Textile manufacturing? Tobacco?

2. **Human-Environment Interaction** In what ways did Southern agriculture influence the types of industries that arose in the New South?

INDIANA STATEWIDE TEST PRACTICE

TEST-TAKING TIP

Be sure to pay attention to specific words in a question. Words can act as clues to help you identify the correct answer.

Reviewing Vocabulary

Directions: Choose the word or words that best completes the sentence.

1 President Lincoln offered _____, or a pardon, to all white Southerners who were willing to swear loyalty to the Union.

A funds
B representation
C decorations
D amnesty

2 The House of Representatives voted to _____ President Andrew Johnson, or formally charge him with wrongdoing.

A annex
B impeach
C commission
D segregate

3 Very few states required that schools be _____, or include both whites and African Americans.

A integrated
B segregated
C coeducational
D documented

4 Many Southern states required a(n) _____, in which people had to read and explain difficult parts of state constitutions or the federal Constitution in order to vote.

A poll tax
B override
C literacy test
D Ten Percent Plan

Reviewing Main Ideas

Directions: Choose the best answer.

5 Which of the following was a provision of the 1864 Wade-Davis bill?

A African American males had to swear loyalty to the Union.
B Ex-Confederates could not hold public office.
C Confederate states could be readmitted to the Union even if they kept slavery.
D Delegates to a constitutional convention had to be formerly enslaved people.

6 What was Andrew Johnson's reaction to the Civil Rights Act of 1866?

A He supported the law.
B He threatened to override the veto.
C He persuaded Congress to pass the bill.
D He said it was unconstitutional.

7 Southern whites who supported the Republicans were called

A scalawags.
B sharecroppers.
C carpetbaggers.
D freed men and women.

8 The series of laws known as "black codes"

A helped the South to rebuild.
B pardoned high-ranking Confederate officials.
C severely limited the rights of African Americans.
D established colleges to train African American teachers.

GO ON

Critical Thinking

Directions: Choose the best answer.

9 **What did the Thirteenth, Fourteenth, and Fifteenth Amendments have in common?**

   A They were all passed after the end of the Civil War.
   B They extended civil liberties to African Americans.
   C They were popular in the Southern states.
   D They had the support of President Andrew Johnson.

Base your answer to question 10 on the reading below and your knowledge of Chapter 17.

> The right of citizens of the United States to vote shall not be denied or abridged by the United States or any State on account of race, color, or previous condition of servitude.
>
> —from the Fifteenth Amendment to the U.S. Constitution

10 **The main idea of the Fifteenth Amendment is that**

   A poll taxes are constitutional.
   B slavery is illegal.
   C a person's right to vote cannot be denied on the basis of race.
   D grandfather clauses are constitutional.

Base your answer to question 11 on the reading below and your knowledge of Chapter 17.

> A citizen of the United States who is at least eighteen (18) years of age and who has been a resident of a precinct thirty (30) days immediately preceding an election may vote in that precinct at the election.
>
> —Article 2, Section 2(A), the Indiana Constitution

11 **To be eligible to vote in Indiana, you must be at least 18 years of age and a resident of a precinct for at least 30 days before an election. You must also**

   A own property.
   B have voted in previous elections.
   C be a citizen of the United States.
   D vote in primary elections.

Constructed Response

Directions: Write a short response to each of the following questions. In your answer:

   • *address all parts of the question*
   • *use information from the chapter*
   • *include facts, examples, and details relevant to the question*
   • *use clear language*

12 **List three services provided by the Freedmen's Bureau.**

Base your answer to question 13 on the reading below and your knowledge of Chapter 17.

> The slave went free; stood a brief moment in the sun; then moved back again toward slavery.
>
> —from *Black Reconstruction*

13 **Explain what civil rights leader W.E.B. Du Bois meant by these words.**

14 **Identify two drawbacks to sharecropping.**

15 **What was the result of the Compromise of 1877?**

STOP

Need Extra Help?															
If you missed questions. . .	1	2	3	4	5	6	7	8	9	10	11	12	13	14	15
Go to page. . .	519	527	531	539	520	523	529	523	536	527	539	520	540	531	536

Overview

An epilogue is a conclusion that appears at the end of a text. It provides additional or up-to-date information about what you have read and studied earlier. After your study of the early period of American history, this epilogue describes what happened in the United States and the world from 1877 to the present day. During this period, the United States developed a strong economy and became a major player in world affairs. Meanwhile, the nation worked to ensure equal rights and a better life for all of its citizens.

Looking Ahead: 1877 to the Present

During the late 1800s, the United States became an industrial and world power. Waves of immigrants provided workers for the growing American economy. The first part of the 1900s saw Americans involved in fighting two world wars. Then, from 1945 to 1991, the United States competed with the Soviet Union for world leadership. During this period, a movement for civil rights swept the country and led to social changes. Since 2000, the United States has faced challenges from the growth of terrorism both at home and throughout the world.

▲ Following the Civil War, many formerly enslaved people moved west and worked on the cattle drives.

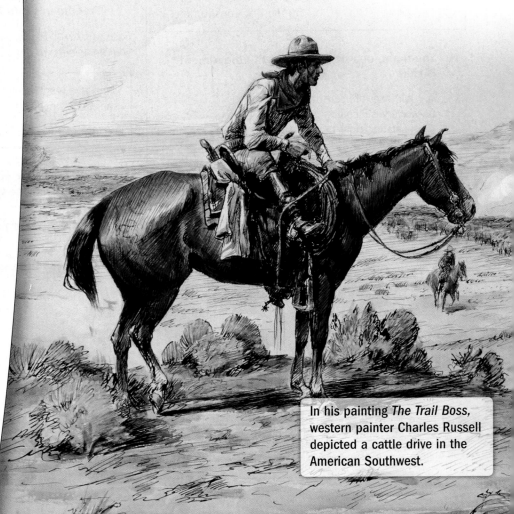

In his painting *The Trail Boss*, western painter Charles Russell depicted a cattle drive in the American Southwest.

Reshaping the Nation

Main Idea New technology and a growing workforce made the United States a world industrial power.

History and You Imagine you want to start your own business. What is needed to get the business up and running? Read to learn how industries in America were able to succeed during the late 1800s.

· ·

The Civil War left lasting effects on the United States. The North's victory united the country. Millions of African Americans were freed from slavery but still faced discrimination. The federal government was strengthened.

With the war's end, Americans began seeking new ventures. During the late 1800s, the nation finally tamed the lands that extended beyond the Mississippi River to the Pacific Ocean. At the same time, new factories, railroads, and cities were built at an ever-increasing speed.

The Western Frontier

In the mid-1800s, one last frontier remained for Americans to settle—the land west of the Mississippi River. By the end of the century, miners, ranchers, and farmers had settled the American West.

Growth of the Mining Industry By the mid-1800s, mineral discoveries had drawn miners to the West. Gold strikes in Colorado and Nevada created boomtowns—towns that grew up almost overnight near mining sites—as thousands of prospectors headed to the region.

The discovery of valuable minerals helped bring the railroads west. A major goal was the building of a transcontinental rail line—one that would span the continent and connect the Atlantic and Pacific coasts. The railroads brought a wave of new settlers to the West—ranchers and farmers.

Ranchers and Farmers The demand for beef in the east led Texas ranchers to organize cattle drives—herding hundreds of thousands of cattle north to the railroad. At the end of the trail, the cattle crowded the stockyards in flourishing railroad cities, such as Omaha, Abilene, Kansas City, and Chicago. This open-range cattle industry, however, collapsed very quickly due to overgrazing, overproduction, new western settlers, and severe winters.

With the end of the "Cattle Kingdom," farmers settled the Great Plains, turning this "wilderness" to productive farmland. To survive on the Plains, farmers found new ways of doing things. Lacking wood, they cut sod into bricks to build houses. They used windmills to pump scarce water and barbed wire to fence in their property.

Native Americans

The arrival of miners, cowhands, and farmers changed the Western frontier dramatically. No one felt these changes more keenly than the Native Americans who had lived on the Great Plains for centuries.

As white settlers moved west, however, vast numbers of buffalo, on which the Native Americans depended, were slaughtered. With the loss of the buffalo, the federal government set out to move Native Americans to reservations, tracts of land set aside for them.

Many Native Americans opposed the reservation policy and began to clash with settlers and the United States Army. By 1886, however, U.S. troops had confined every Native American group to reservations.

In 1887 the Dawes Act changed government policy toward Native Americans, proposing to break up the reservations and encouraging Native Americans to farm. Over the next 50 years, the government divided up the reservations, but land dealers grabbed most of the valuable land. With Native American resistance at an end, nothing remained to stop white settlers. The last frontier had finally disappeared.

The Growth of Industry

As settlers moved westward, farmers in other parts of the country moved to the cities. They took jobs in the new urban industries. The United States was changing from a rural nation into a modern, industrial nation.

The United States had all the necessary ingredients for industry to grow—abundant natural and human resources, investment money, a free enterprise economic system, and new inventions and technology.

By 1900, huge companies dominated the economy. Their efficiency resulted in cheaper production, higher quality, and lower prices that drove smaller competitors out of business. Corporations, monopolies, and trusts became common.

Industrial Workers Industrial growth in the late 1800s created new jobs and raised the standard of living for many workers. Laborers,

Primary Source / Conflicts With Native Americans

Cultures Under Pressure Westward migration of white settlers in the mid-1800s caused conflicts with Native Americans on the Great Plains. White settlers fought with many groups, including the Sioux, Cheyenne, Apache, and Navajo. After the Civil War, the U.S. government implemented a reservation policy. Some Native Americans agreed to move to reservations; others resisted.

Native American Population

Source: Paul Stuart, *Nations Within a Nation*

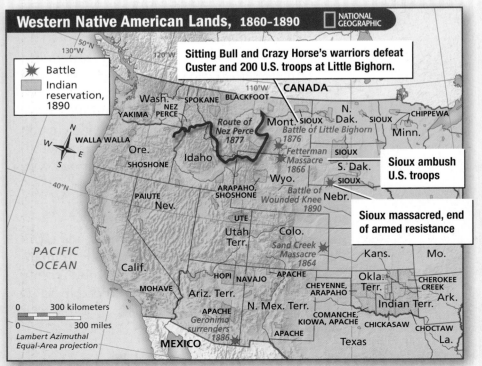

Western Native American Lands, 1860–1890   NATIONAL GEOGRAPHIC

Sitting Bull and Crazy Horse's warriors defeat Custer and 200 U.S. troops at Little Bighorn.

Sioux ambush U.S. troops

Sioux massacred, end of armed resistance

"You might as well expect all rivers to run backward as that any man who was born a free man should be contented when penned up and denied liberty to go where he pleases."

—Chief Joseph of the Nez Perce, on a visit to Washington, D.C., 1879 however, worked 10 to 12 hours-a-day, six days-a-week. Factories and mines were often noisy, polluted, and unsafe.

Dissatisfied workers organized into groups, called labor unions, to demand better pay and working conditions. In 1886 a group of unions joined together to form the American Federation of Labor (AFL). The AFL represented skilled workers. Its first leader was Jewish immigrant Samuel Gompers. The AFL pushed for higher wages, better working conditions, and the right to bargain collectively. In collective bargaining, unions represent workers in bargaining with management.

Many workers used strikes to achieve their goals. They refused to do their jobs until their employers agreed to certain demands. In 1877 a national railroad strike became the first of many violent confrontations between workers and employers.

Toward an Urban America

As people moved to the cities to take factory jobs, they transformed America from a rural country into an urban nation. The cities also grew because of immigration.

The New Immigrants After the Civil War, many immigrants arrived from southern and eastern Europe. Others came from China, Japan, and Mexico. When they arrived they were processed at government reception centers, such as Ellis Island in New York harbor and Angel Island in San Francisco Bay.

Most immigrants settled in cities and looked for factory work. People of the same ethnic group—with the same language and customs—tended to form communities. Neighborhoods of Jewish, Italian, Polish, Chinese, and other groups developed in large cities.

In the late 1800s, hostility grew toward many of the new racial and ethnic groups coming into the country. Immigrants became easy targets of hostility for Americans already disturbed by rapid social changes. Some people, especially workers, blamed immigrants for low wages. Employers found that immigrants would accept lower wages than native-born Americans. Others resented the different cultures and religions of many immigrants.

Life in the Cities Cities were exciting places that offered jobs, stores, and entertainment. They had a growing middle class of professional people, managers, and salaried office clerks. At the top of the economic and social ladder stood the very rich, who lived differently than most Americans.

The term "Gilded Age"—*gilded* refers to something covered with a thin layer of gold—became associated with America in the late 1800s. The Gilded Age suggested both the extravagant wealth of the time and the terrible poverty that lay underneath. The rapid growth of cities produced serious problems, including disease, crime, little or no sanitation, and overcrowding.

> *"When I look back now from this high hill of my old age, I can still see the butchered women and children [at Wounded Knee]. . . . And I can see that something else died there in the bloody mud. . . . A people's dream died there."*
>
> —Black Elk, *Black Elk Speaks* (1932)

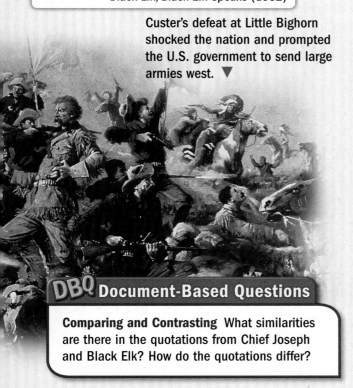

Custer's defeat at Little Bighorn shocked the nation and prompted the U.S. government to send large armies west. ▼

DBQ Document-Based Questions

Comparing and Contrasting What similarities are there in the quotations from Chief Joseph and Black Elk? How do the quotations differ?

In major cities, the poor often lived in tenements—huge apartment buildings—with as many as four people living in each of the small, dark rooms. Help was provided by religious groups, such as the Salvation Army, and settlement houses. These houses offered education, medical care, playgrounds, nurseries, and libraries to the poor. One famous settlement house was Hull House in Chicago, founded by Jane Addams in 1889.

During the 1880s and 1890s, many city reformers campaigned for clean water and better sewage systems. They demanded better ventilation, plumbing in all new buildings, and mandatory vaccinations. These improvements meant that fewer people died of diseases like typhoid and smallpox.

A Changing American Culture Toward the end of the 1800s, education became more widely available to Americans. By 1914, nearly every state required children to have at least some schooling. More than 80 percent of all children between the ages of 5 and 17 were enrolled in elementary and secondary schools.

Many Americans began to enjoy increasing amounts of leisure time. The large crowds in the cities increased the popularity of spectator sports—including baseball, football, basketball, and boxing. People also flocked to nickelodeon theaters, which charged five cents to see a movie. New types of music and literature developed at the turn of the century. Band music, jazz, and ragtime became popular. Writers such as Mark Twain, Stephen Crane, and Jack London produced stories that described the real lives of people. More and more people began to read newspapers and magazines.

✓ **Reading Check** **Describing** What did settlement houses provide?

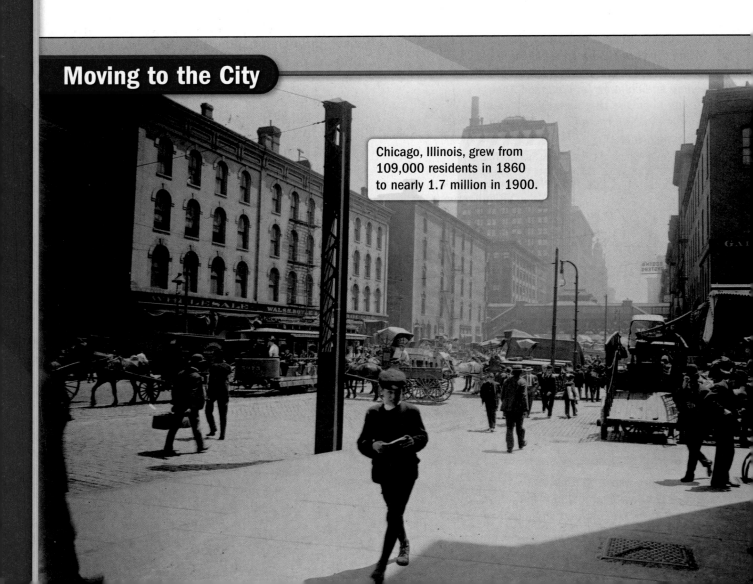

Moving to the City

Chicago, Illinois, grew from 109,000 residents in 1860 to nearly 1.7 million in 1900.

Reform, Expansion, and War

Main Idea Americans reformed society at home and played a major role in events abroad.

History and You Have you ever joined a group that worked toward a common cause? Read to learn how Americans acted together to change American society during the early 1900s.

· ·

During the late 1800s and early 1900s, American reformers believed that they could make society better and more just. They passed laws that affected business practices, public health, and government employees. During this era, the United States became a world leader. United States armies fought in two overseas conflicts: the Spanish-American War and World War I. These years of domestic change and foreign conflict provided foundations for the world you live in today.

By the Numbers

Urban and Rural Population Growth, 1860–1900

[Bar graph: Population (in millions) on y-axis from 0 to 50, Year on x-axis showing 1860, 1870, 1880, 1890, 1900, with Urban and Rural bars]

Source: *Historical Statistics of the United States*

Graph Skills

Summarizing In a sentence, describe the trend in rural and urban population between 1860 and 1900.

Progressive Reforms

Industrialization changed American society. Cities were often crowded, working conditions were often bad, and the old political system was breaking down. These conditions gave rise to the Progressive movement. Progressives campaigned for political and social reforms. Some journalists, nicknamed muckrakers, helped progressives by exposing injustices.

Making Government Efficient Progressives promoted reforms in government. Political machines—powerful organizations linked to political parties—controlled many cities. To break the power of political machines, reformers worked to make city governments more honest and efficient. They supported the commission system, a plan that placed city governments in the hands of business-minded officials called commissioners. By 1917 commissions governed nearly 400 American cities.

Democracy and Progressivism In the early 1900s, progressives backed reforms to expand the people's direct control of government. The initiative allowed citizens to place a measure or issue on the ballot in a state election. The referendum gave voters the opportunity to accept or reject measures that the state legislature enacted. The recall enabled voters to remove unsatisfactory elected officials from their jobs.

Progressives also changed the way United States senators are elected. The Constitution had given state legislatures the responsibility to select those who would represent their state in the U.S. Senate, but party bosses and business interests often controlled the process. The Seventeenth Amendment provided for the direct election of senators. Ratified in 1913, the amendment gave the people the right to vote directly for their senators.

Reforming Business and Banking Progressives also believed that government had to keep large companies and corporations from becoming too powerful. In 1890 Congress passed the Sherman Antitrust Act, making it illegal for companies to limit competition.

The Woman Suffrage Movement

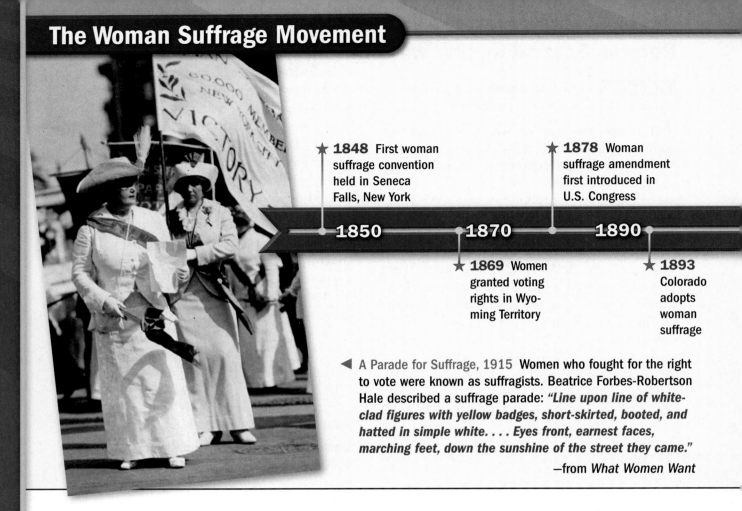

1848 First woman suffrage convention held in Seneca Falls, New York

1878 Woman suffrage amendment first introduced in U.S. Congress

1850 — 1870 — 1890

1869 Women granted voting rights in Wyoming Territory

1893 Colorado adopts woman suffrage

◄ **A Parade for Suffrage, 1915** Women who fought for the right to vote were known as suffragists. Beatrice Forbes-Robertson Hale described a suffrage parade: *"Line upon line of white-clad figures with yellow badges, short-skirted, booted, and hatted in simple white. . . . Eyes front, earnest faces, marching feet, down the sunshine of the street they came."*

—from *What Women Want*

In 1902 President Theodore Roosevelt began to take action against companies that had violated the Sherman Antitrust Act. His administration sued trusts in the railroad, beef, tobacco, and oil industries.

Reformers also called for regulations to control railroad rates. In 1887 Congress passed the Interstate Commerce Act, which required railroads to charge "reasonable and just" rates. The act also created the Interstate Commerce Commission (ICC) to supervise the railroad industry and, later, the trucking industry.

The Federal Reserve System Other progressive reforms in the nation's economy followed. In 1914 President Woodrow Wilson convinced Congress to create the Federal Reserve—a system of 12 regional banks supported by a central board based in Washington. The new banking system was authorized to issue Federal Bank Notes

as official U.S. paper currency. President Wilson also established the Federal Trade Commission to investigate corporations for unfair trade practices.

Votes for Women During the early 1900s, the cause of women's rights gained more support. Suffragists—men and women who fought for woman suffrage, or women's right to vote—won their first victories in the West. Wyoming led the nation in giving women the right to vote. Between 1910 and 1913, five other states adopted woman suffrage. In the meantime, suffragists continued their struggle to win the right to vote everywhere.

In 1919 the Senate voted in favor of the Nineteenth Amendment, which allowed woman suffrage. The amendment was ratified in 1920, in time for women to vote in that year's presidential election. For the first time, American women were able to participate in the election of their national leaders.

1919 House and Senate pass the federal woman suffrage amendment

1910 — 1920 →

1920 Nineteenth Amendment, granting women the right to vote, is ratified

Chart Skills

Identifying In what state or territory were women first granted the right to vote?

Seeking Justice Despite progressive reforms, many Americans still faced discrimination—unequal treatment because of their race, religion, ethnic background, or place of birth. African Americans were denied basic rights and restricted to second-class citizenship. In 1896 the Supreme Court, in *Plessy* v. *Ferguson*, legalized segregation when it recognized the legality of "separate but equal" facilities.

African Americans rose to the challenge of achieving equality. Booker T. Washington founded the Tuskegee Institute to teach African Americans technical skills to help them escape poverty. George Washington Carver joined the faculty there in 1896. Stating that his research "was to help the farmer and fill the poor man's empty dinner pail," Carver transformed agricultural development in the South. From the peanut, which was formerly of little use, Carver developed hundreds of products, including plastics, shaving cream, and paper. Entrepreneur

Madam C.J. Walker made a fortune in marketing hair care and beauty products to African American women. Ida B. Wells, editor of an African American newspaper, began a campaign to end lynching. W.E.B. Du Bois helped found the National Association for the Advancement of Colored People (NAACP) in 1909. This interracial group has remained at the forefront of efforts to gain legal and economic equality for African Americans.

Mexican Americans also encountered discrimination and violence. Between 1900 and 1914, the Mexican American population grew dramatically as people crossed the border to escape revolution and economic troubles in Mexico. Within their communities, Mexican Americans formed self-defense associations to raise money for insurance and legal help.

In California and other western states, Asians struggled against prejudice and resentment. White Americans claimed that Chinese immigrants, who worked for lower wages, were taking away jobs. Legislation limited the rights of immigrants from Japan as well as China.

Overseas Expansion

The late 1800s were an age of imperialism—a time when powerful European nations, as well as Japan, created large empires. The search for markets and raw materials in Asia and Africa drove imperialism. Many Americans wanted the United States to also expand its trade and power and to spread Western civilization.

In 1898 during the presidency of William McKinley, the United States annexed—took control of—the Hawaiian Islands. The islands provided a base for the American navy. From Hawaii, the United States could oversee its trade in Japan and China.

The Spanish-American War That same year, the United States went to war with Spain. The American press had aroused intense anger by reporting the brutal way that Spain crushed a rebellion in Cuba.

Almost immediately, fighting extended to Spanish colonies in the Pacific Ocean, as well as in Cuba. When the Spanish-American War ended, not only did Cuba gain its independence, but the United States also gained Guam, the Philippines, and Puerto Rico.

The Panama Canal The Spanish-American War had shown how important it was for the nation's navy to move quickly between the Atlantic and Pacific Coasts. The trip around South America took a long time and slowed trade between the coasts. As a result, President Theodore Roosevelt decided to build a canal across Panama to connect the Atlantic and Pacific Oceans. At that time, Panama was part of the country of Colombia.

Because Colombia was unwilling to give up its land, in 1903 Americans helped Panamanians rebel against Colombia. After winning independence, Panama signed a treaty allowing the United States to build the canal. The Panama Canal opened in 1914, greatly shortening the route between the Atlantic and Pacific Oceans.

World War I

In 1914 Europe went to war. The United States tried to remain neutral, but it was eventually drawn into the fighting. Over the next few years, nearly 30 countries participated in what became known as World War I. The main campaigns were fought in Europe, but armed forces also clashed in the Middle East, Africa, and Asia.

War Erupts in Europe World War I arose from the tensions that engulfed European nations as they sought empires and built up their armies. To protect themselves, European nations began to form alliances—defense agreements among nations.

When World War I began, President Wilson declared the United States to be neutral. As the war went on, however, Americans began to side with the Allies. At the same time, American trade with the Allies soared.

To stop American assistance to the Allies, Germany began using submarines, known as U-boats, to sink cargo ships headed to Britain. After the sinking of the passenger ship *Lusitania* in May 1915, Germany promised to warn ships before attacking. In early 1917, Germany broke its promise, sinking six American ships without warning. President Woodrow Wilson asked Congress to declare war on Germany on April 2, 1917.

American Troops in Battle Shortly after declaring war, Congress established a military draft. By war's end, about 3 million American men had been drafted, and another 2 million had volunteered.

In the spring of 1918, troops from the American Expeditionary Force, under the command of General John J. Pershing, arrived in France and were greeted enthusiastically by war-weary French citizens. On May 28, 1918, American troops helped slow the German march toward Paris when about 4,000 American soldiers captured the German

The Human Cost of War

President Woodrow Wilson leads the procession after the signing of the Treaty of Versailles.

position at the village of Cantigny. Days later, the U.S. Army again engaged the Germans in battle at Belleau Woods. For 24 hours-a-day over a period of three weeks, the Americans faced a solid barrage of German machine-gun fire. The Americans won, but casualties were in the thousands.

A month later, the Germans launched a major attack on Allied forces at Chateau-Thierry along the Marne River. The American and French armies pushed the Germans back and for the first time in the war, the momentum switched to the Allies.

In late September, Pershing's troops attacked the Germans in the Argonne Forest of northeastern France. After weeks of heavy fighting in rough terrain, German lines finally crumbled. When the Germans realized they had little chance of winning the war, they appealed to President Wilson for an armistice, or an agreement to end the war. The armistice was signed on November 11, 1918, a day that came to be called Armistice Day and is now known as Veterans' Day.

Searching for Peace In January 1919, President Wilson and other world leaders met in Paris to negotiate a treaty ending the war. The Treaty of Versailles, as it was known, set up the League of Nations—an international organization to preserve the peace. The treaty required Germany to make reparations, or pay war damages. The treaty also created new nations including Czechoslovakia, Yugoslavia, and Poland.

When Wilson presented the Treaty of Versailles to the Senate for ratification, Republicans argued that the League of Nations would limit America's independence. The Senate rejected the treaty. The United States never joined the League of Nations.

Reading Check **Describing** How did the Seventeenth Amendment advance democracy?

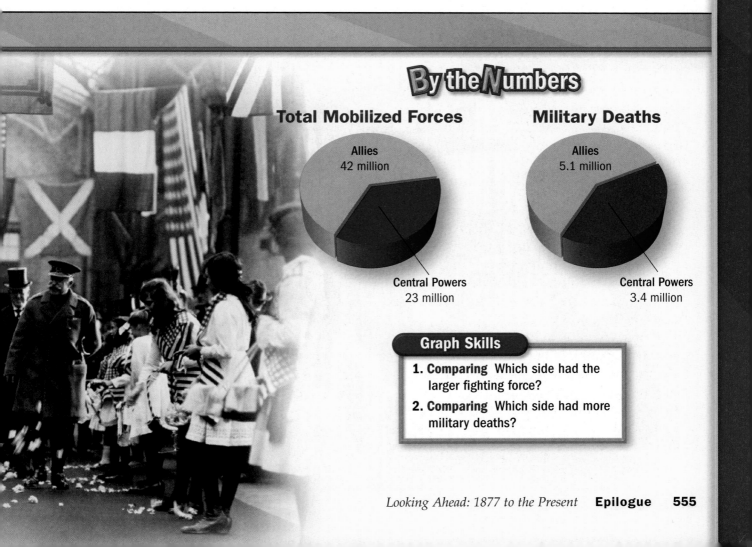

By the Numbers

Total Mobilized Forces

Allies
42 million

Central Powers
23 million

Military Deaths

Allies
5.1 million

Central Powers
3.4 million

Graph Skills

1. **Comparing** Which side had the larger fighting force?
2. **Comparing** Which side had more military deaths?

Turbulent Decades

Main Idea From the 1920s to the 1940s, the United States experienced prosperity, a severe economic downturn, and a second world war.

History and You How would you be affected if travel by car did not exist? Read to learn how the automobile began to transform American life during the 1920s.

· ·

After World War I, many Americans enjoyed the economic prosperity of the 1920s. When economic troubles brought rises in unemployment and homelessness in the 1930s, frustration and fear gripped many people. Government programs helped restore public confidence, but war loomed on the horizon. During the early 1940s, the United States fought in World War II to halt the expansion of aggressive dictatorships in Europe and Asia.

The Jazz Age

Tired of war and world responsibilities, Americans were ready to seek enjoyment when World War I ended. As a result, the 1920s became an era of new ideas and pastimes. People danced to the beat of a new kind of music called jazz. Jazz, a distinctly American music that developed from ragtime and the blues, captured the spirit of the era so well that the 1920s is often referred to as the Jazz Age.

A Time of Turmoil After World War I, conflict flared anew between business management and labor unions. Workers in general wanted to preserve and, if possible, raise the wages paid to them during the war. When management refused to cooperate, many workers resorted to strikes. In 1919 alone, there were more than 3,600 strikes involving millions of workers.

The 1920s Economy

1920s Innovation During the 1920s, the auto industry led the way in adopting mass-production techniques. Companies also produced and consumers also acquired electric appliances—toasters, stoves, vacuum cleaners, and radios.

Nativism Many Americans feared a link between labor union activities and communism. Communism is an idea that advocates an end to private property. It also supports a form of government in which a single political party controls the economy and society as a whole. American concerns about communism led to the Red Scare, a period when the government went after "Reds"—as Communists were known—and others with views that were considered too anti-American.

The fears many Americans felt also led to an increase in nativism—or anti-immigrant feelings. World War I had dramatically slowed the huge flow of immigration that had begun in the 1880s. After the war ended, heavy immigration resumed. Many Americans saw the newcomers as a threat to their jobs and their security.

Prohibition The early 1920s also saw increased efforts to enforce traditional moral values.

By the Numbers

Industry (Percentage Increase, 1922–28)	
Industrial production	70%
Gross national product	40%
Corporate profits	62%

Workers (Percentage Increase, 1922–28)	
Workers' incomes	11%
Average workweek	-4%

Source: Jules Tygiel, "The 1920s Economy: A Statistical Portrait"

Invented in the 1920s

- Push-button elevators
- Electric razors
- Spiral-bound notebooks
- Pop-up toasters
- Car radios
- Adhesive tape
- Self-winding wristwatch
- Band-Aid™

Critical Thinking

Identifying Cause and Effect How did standardized mass production change the American economy?

The Eighteenth Amendment (1919) established Prohibition. This was a total ban on the manufacture, sale, and transportation of alcohol. However, some people began making and selling alcohol illegally. Prohibition also contributed to the rise of organized crime. Prohibition was finally repealed in 1933 with the passage of the Twenty-first Amendment.

A Booming Economy The end of World War I and the start of the 1920s brought another industrial revolution. As investments and talent poured into industry, goods poured out. Among the products that gained popularity in the 1920s were automobiles, telephones, vacuum cleaners, refrigerators, and canned goods. The automobile especially changed American society. It provided jobs, strongly influenced American buying habits, led to highway construction, and promoted travel.

A Mass Culture During the 1920s, the mass media—forms of communication, such as newspapers and radio—began to reach millions of people. Laborsaving devices and fewer working hours gave Americans more leisure time. People enjoyed tabloid-style newspapers, large-circulation magazines, phonograph records, the radio, and movies.

Interest in sports and entertainment grew, and, as a result, people sought new heroes. Athletes like baseball's Babe Ruth and golf's Bobby Jones were widely popular. Americans celebrated Charles Lindbergh's completion of the first nonstop solo flight across the Atlantic Ocean.

Meanwhile, new forms of art and literature flourished. In the 1920s, Harlem, an African American section of New York City, witnessed a flowering of African American culture. Known as the Harlem Renaissance, this movement included writers such as Langston Hughes and Zora Neale Hurston. Other American writers, such as Gertrude Stein and F. Scott Fitzgerald, left the country and settled in Paris, France. Known as the "lost generation," these writers questioned American ideals and sought new sources of inspiration.

In the 1930s, the Great Plains got a double dose of catastrophe: the Depression coupled with severe drought and dust storms. This area was labeled the "Dust Bowl." The storms, called "dusters" or "black blizzards," swept across the dry, fine soil of the area, blocking out the sun and burying fences, farm equipment, houses, and even animals.

Lawrence Svobida waited as long as he could for the rains to come to his Kansas wheat farm.

"With my financial resources at last exhausted and my health seriously, if not permanently impaired, I am at last ready to admit defeat and leave the Dust Bowl forever."

—from *An Empire of Dust*

▲ Dust storm in Oklahoma, 1935

Migrant workers in California ▲

The Great Depression

During the 1930s, the United States and the world's other industrialized countries were hit by an economic depression. The 1930s depression was so severe that it became known as the Great Depression. It marked the longest, deepest, and most devastating economic depression ever experienced by the United States.

The Economy Crumbles In October 1929, stock prices fell dramatically. Investors panicked and began selling their stocks. Since many investors purchased stock with borrowed money, they could not pay back their loans, which weakened the banks. The stock market crash exposed many problems in the economy. Millions of people lost their savings and their jobs. By 1932, more than one out of four Americans were out of work. People who had been put out of their homes lived in shacks built out of cardboard or tin.

Roosevelt's New Deal During the 1932 presidential election, Democratic candidate Franklin Delano Roosevelt promised a "new deal for the American people." With the nation's economy crumbling, the American people elected him president. Roosevelt sent Congress proposals to fight the Depression. These proposals collectively became known as the New Deal.

To create jobs and to provide people with money to buy food and housing, the federal government set up several different agencies. One of these, the Civilian Conservation Corps (CCC), gave jobs mostly to young people, who planted trees and built facilities in the nation's parks.

The Works Progress Administration (WPA) paid jobless workers to build dams, roads, bridges, and hospitals. It also created projects for artists and writers. Other new government agencies tried to help farmers, small businesses, and homeowners.

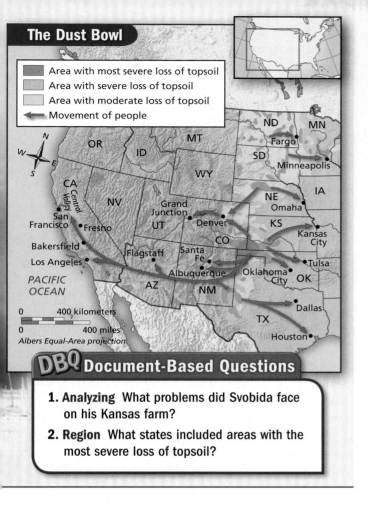

The Dust Bowl

- Area with most severe loss of topsoil
- Area with severe loss of topsoil
- Area with moderate loss of topsoil
- Movement of people

ND
MN
Fargo
MT
OR
ID
SD
Minneapolis
WY
NE
IA
CA Central Valley
NV
Grand Junction
Omaha
San Francisco
Fresno
UT
Denver
KS
Kansas City
Bakersfield
CO
Flagstaff
Santa Fe
Los Angeles
Albuquerque
Oklahoma City
Tulsa
PACIFIC OCEAN
AZ
NM
OK
Dallas
TX
Houston

0   400 kilometers
0   400 miles
Albers Equal-Area projection

DBQ Document-Based Questions

1. **Analyzing** What problems did Svobida face on his Kansas farm?
2. **Region** What states included areas with the most severe loss of topsoil?

Effects of the New Deal The New Deal produced lasting effects. It greatly increased the power of the presidency and the size of the federal government. It also established the idea that the federal government is responsible for the welfare of needy Americans. In 1935 Congress passed the Social Security Act. This program gave pensions, or payments, to citizens after they turned 65 and retired. It also provided Americans with unemployment insurance. If people lost their jobs, they received money from the government until they found a new one.

In terms of its main goal of ending the Depression, the New Deal was only a limited success. Unemployment remained high, and economic recovery was not complete until after World War II.

World War II

Less than 25 years after World War I, the United States found itself at war again. This war, though, was different from World War I. It was a fight for survival, and, before it was over, it involved almost every country in the world. By the end of 1941, 22 countries had already declared their support for the Allies—the United States, Great Britain, France, China, and the Soviet Union. The Axis powers—Germany, Italy, and Japan—were supported by Romania, Bulgaria, and Hungary.

The Road to War The events leading to World War II began in the 1920s. Several dictators—leaders who control their nations by force—seized power by playing on the fear and anger people felt after World War I and during the Great Depression.

The first dictator to take power was Benito Mussolini in Italy. In Germany, many people rallied around Adolf Hitler—leader of the National Socialist Workers' Party, or Nazi Party. The Depression also brought military leaders to power in Japan. In 1940 Germany, Italy, and Japan signed a pact and became allies.

In September 1939, Hitler sent his armies into Poland. Two days later, Britain and France declared war on Germany. World War II had begun. Germany's armed forces quickly overran Poland. The following spring, Hitler's troops invaded France, which surrendered a few weeks later. Then, in June 1941, Hitler ordered a massive attack on the Soviet Union.

Maintaining Neutrality Americans watched the war in Europe with concern but did not want to become involved. Roosevelt promised to stay neutral. However, he asked Congress to pass the Lend-Lease Act, allowing America to sell, lease, or lend weapons to nations whose security was vital to America's defense. Britain and the Soviet Union began receiving lend-lease aid.

While Roosevelt tried to help Britain, Japan expanded into Southeast Asia. The United States tried to stop Japan by applying economic pressure. Desperate for resources and confident of their military might, the Japanese government began planning an attack on the United States.

Pearl Harbor On December 7, 1941, Japanese warplanes attacked the American naval base at Pearl Harbor, Hawaii. The attack enraged Americans. The next day, President Roosevelt went before Congress. Calling December 7 "a day which will live in infamy," he asked for a declaration of war on Japan. On December 11, Germany and Italy declared war on the United States. The United States then joined the Allies against the Axis Powers.

The Home Front After Pearl Harbor, millions of Americans rushed to enlist in the armed forces. Those who remained at home worked hard to provide resources for food, shelter, training, and medical care for all those in uniform.

During the war, industry expanded rapidly. Incomes rose and unemployment fell. For the first time, a large number of women—about 350,000—served in the military. At the same time, far more women than ever before entered the work force.

The war also created new opportunities for African Americans—in the armed forces and in the nation's war factories. Japanese Americans, however, experienced discrimination after the attack on Pearl Harbor. Worried about their loyalty, the government forced Japanese Americans on the West Coast to relocate to internment camps.

The War in Europe In late 1942, American and British troops landed in North Africa and drove out the Germans. The following year, the western Allies reached Italy. As the Allies advanced, the Italians overthrew Mussolini and surrendered. However, German forces in Italy resisted. After bitter fighting, the western Allies finally broke through German lines and liberated Rome in June 1944.

While fighting raged in North Africa and Italy, the western Allies launched an air war against Germany. The bombings killed thousands of civilians and caused massive destruction, but it did not crack Germany's will to win. Meanwhile, the Germans suffered severe defeats in eastern Europe. There, in early 1943, Soviet forces freed the

The War and Social Change

Mexican Farmworkers ▶ In 1942 the federal government arranged for Mexican farmworkers to help with the harvest in the Southwest. The laborers were part of the Bracero Program. *Bracero* is a Spanish word meaning "worker." More than 200,000 Mexicans came to help harvest fruit and vegetables and to build and maintain railroads.

◀ **Women Take New Roles** The need for defense workers changed traditional patterns of American society. As millions of men joined the armed services, more women than ever before entered the labor force.

city of Leningrad and forced the German army at Stalingrad, exhausted by months of heavy fighting, to surrender.

D-Day As the Soviets pushed toward Germany from the east, the western Allies carried out a massive invasion of continental Europe from the west. General Dwight Eisenhower, the commander of Allied forces in Europe, directed this invasion, known as Operation Overlord. On June 6, 1944—D-Day—Allied ships landed thousands of troops at Normandy, on the Atlantic coast of France. From Normandy, the western Allies pushed toward Paris and ultimately, Germany.

The Holocaust As the Allies entered Germany and other parts of Europe, they found horrifying evidence of Nazi brutality. The Nazis hated Jews and committed genocide—the killing of an entire group of people. Not until Allied troops reached the Nazi death camps—at Auschwitz, Dachau, Buchenwald, and elsewhere—and found the survivors and the gas chambers in which so many had died was the horrible truth fully realized. The Nazis had killed thousands of Jews every day in gas chambers. As many as 6 million, two-thirds of Europe's Jews, were murdered in the Holocaust.

Victory in Europe By April 1945, Soviet troops had reached Berlin, and British and American forces met at the Elbe River in eastern Germany. One week later, Germany surrendered. President Roosevelt did not share in the Allied victory celebration. Less than four weeks earlier, he had died. His vice president, Harry S. Truman, succeeded him.

War in the Pacific Soon after the Pearl Harbor attack in December 1941, Japanese forces moved forward in the Pacific. They forced American soldiers under General Douglas MacArthur to surrender the Philippines. With Japan's quick offensive, American morale was low. However, in June 1942, the American navy destroyed four Japanese aircraft carriers and hundreds of airplanes at the Battle of Midway, northwest of Hawaii. This was the first major Japanese defeat.

The United States then adopted a strategy known as island hopping—seizing an island and using it as a base to attack the next island. Between August 1942 and March 1945, American forces engaged in fierce campaigns for control of Pacific islands such as Guadalcanal, Guam, Iwo Jima, and Okinawa. With superior air and naval power, the Americans finally secured the islands.

The War Ends By the summer of 1945, American forces were closing in on Japan. When Japan refused to surrender, President Truman ordered the use of a secret weapon—the atomic bomb. The United States dropped two atomic bombs in August 1945. The first destroyed the city of Hiroshima. The second destroyed the city of Nagasaki. After the bombings, Japan agreed to surrender, marking the end of the war.

✔ **Reading Check** **Identifying** What event occurred on December 7, 1941? What did this event lead to?

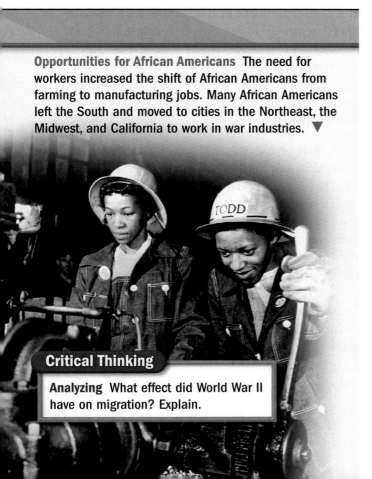

Opportunities for African Americans The need for workers increased the shift of African Americans from farming to manufacturing jobs. Many African Americans left the South and moved to cities in the Northeast, the Midwest, and California to work in war industries. ▼

Critical Thinking

Analyzing What effect did World War II have on migration? Explain.

Turning Points

Main Idea After World War II, Americans enjoyed prosperity, worked for a more just society, and struggled to halt the spread of communism abroad.

History and You Have you ever wanted to stop someone from doing something without having a fight? Read to learn how the United States tried to stop communism without fighting another global war.

. . . .

Beginning in 1945, the United States and the Soviet Union entered a bitter rivalry known as the Cold War. Each side tried to gain allies and prove that its system—democracy and free enterprise or communism—was better. International tensions rose as the United States and the Soviet Union built up their arsenals of nuclear weapons.

Cold War Beginnings

The problems leading to the Cold War began when the Soviet Union refused to allow promised free elections in eastern Europe. Instead, the Soviets set up Communist governments in the region. In response, in 1947 President Truman pledged U.S. help to nations that wanted to rebuild their economies and resist communism.

A year later, the United States, Britain, and France united their occupied areas of Germany to form West Germany. Protesting this decision, the Soviets sealed off democratic West Berlin, which was surrounded by the Soviet-run East German area. President Truman responded with an airlift to bring supplies, including food, medicine, and fuel, to West Berlin. In April 1949, the United States and other Western nations created the North Atlantic Treaty Organization (NATO)—a mutual defense alliance.

The Korean War The Cold War was not limited to Europe. In 1949 Mao Zedong formed a new Communist government in China. In June 1950, the Communist nation of North Korea invaded South Korea. American and United Nations (UN) forces came to South Korea's defense. As they pushed the North Koreans back, China intervened. Huge numbers of Chinese troops drove the UN troops back into South Korea.

The UN forces eventually stopped the Chinese and then pushed them back to the border between North and South Korea. The war then became a stalemate—a situation in which neither side could win. A cease-fire agreement was finally reached in July 1953. Korea remained divided. By intervening in Korea, the United States showed that it would act firmly to halt Communist expansion.

Fear and Prosperity During the Cold War, a "red scare" swept the country. The fear of "the enemy within" helped launch an effort to uncover suspected Communists. In the early 1950s, Senator Joseph McCarthy charged that Communists were active in the federal government and in the military. He never proved a single case, but even the suspicion of being Communist was enough to cause many people to lose their jobs.

In 1952 Republican Dwight D. Eisenhower won the presidential election. During Eisenhower's two terms, from 1953 to 1961, the United States economy grew rapidly.

Divided Germany   NATIONAL GEOGRAPHIC

Critical Thinking

Speculating What might have happened to Germany and other parts of Europe if the Allies had not conducted the airlift?

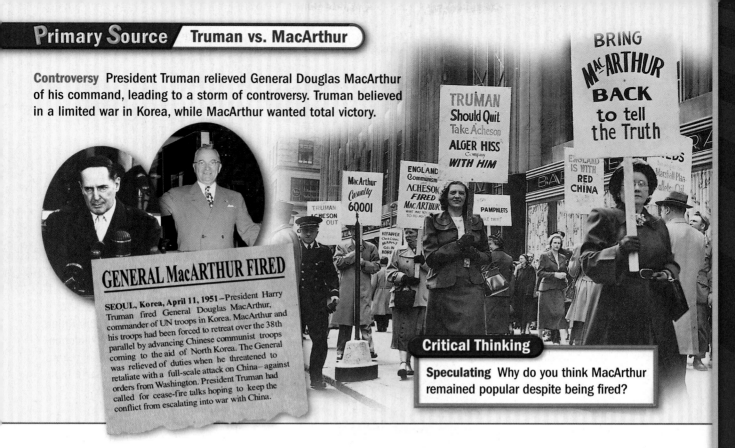

Controversy President Truman relieved General Douglas MacArthur of his command, leading to a storm of controversy. Truman believed in a limited war in Korea, while MacArthur wanted total victory.

BRING
MacARTHUR
BACK
to tell
the Truth

TRUMAN
Should Quit
Take Acheson
ALGER HISS
Company
WITH HIM

ENGLAND
Communism
ACHESON
FIRED
MacARTHUR

PAMPHLETS

ENGLAND
IS WITH
RED
CHINA

Marshall Plan

MacArthur
Casualty
60001

TRUMAN
ACHESON
OUT

GENERAL MacARTHUR FIRED

SEOUL, Korea, April 11, 1951—President Harry Truman fired General Douglas MacArthur, commander of UN troops in Korea. MacArthur and his troops had been forced to retreat over the 38th parallel by advancing Chinese communist troops coming to the aid of North Korea. The General was relieved of duties when he threatened to retaliate with a full-scale attack on China—against orders from Washington. President Truman had called for cease-fire talks hoping to keep the conflict from escalating into war with China.

Critical Thinking

Speculating Why do you think MacArthur remained popular despite being fired?

Americans earned higher wages and purchased more consumer goods than ever before. As a result, factory production soared. The postwar "baby boom," or increased birthrate, promised even more economic growth in the future.

Cuba and the Cold War During the 1950s, the Cold War reached Latin America. In 1959 Fidel Castro seized power in Cuba. The following year, Castro allied with the Soviet Union. In April 1961, the new U.S. President John F. Kennedy allowed approximately 1,500 Cubans, trained by the Central Intelligence Agency (CIA), to land in Cuba at the Bay of Pigs. Their mission to overthrow Castro's government failed. The Bay of Pigs embarrased Kennedy, who took blame for the failure.

Two months later, Soviet leader Nikita Khrushchev told Kennedy that the West must get out of Berlin. Kennedy refused. Shortly afterward, the East German government, with Soviet support, built a wall dividing Communist East Berlin from democratic West Berlin. The Berlin Wall became a symbol of Communist repression.

In October 1962, Kennedy decided to blockade—or close off—Cuba, until the Soviets removed the nuclear missiles they were installing there. As Soviet ships headed toward the blockade, the world waited to see if nuclear war would break out. Abruptly, the Soviet ships turned back. After days of negotiations, the Soviets agreed to pull their missiles out of Cuba.

Civil Rights

After World War II, many Americans worked to advance equal rights. They focused attention on discrimination, or unfair treatment, of African Americans, Latinos, Native Americans, women and others in jobs, housing, and education. They also called for an end to segregation—the separation of people of different races.

New Push for Civil Rights In 1954 the U.S. Supreme Court ruled in the case of *Brown v. Board of Education of Topeka, Kansas,* that segregation in public schools was unconstitutional. In the 1950s, President Eisenhower used federal agencies to make sure that

Sit-in at a lunch counter ▶

★ **May 1954**
Brown decision declares segregated schools unconstitutional

★ **Sept. 1957**
Federal troops escort African American students to desegregate Little Rock's Central High School

★ **December 1955**
Rosa Parks is arrested and Montgomery bus boycott begins

★ **Feb. 1960**
Sit-in movement spreads after students stage sit-in at North Carolina lunch counter

★ **May 1961**
Freedom Riders brave violence to desegregate interstate bus travel

Rosa Parks ▶

states ended segregation in their schools. The *Brown* decision was an important victory for African Americans, who had been working hard to gain civil rights.

In December 1955, an African American woman named Rosa Parks was arrested in Montgomery, Alabama, for refusing to leave a section of a bus reserved for white people. Shortly afterward, African Americans in Montgomery began to boycott—to refuse to use—the city's buses. Finally, in 1956 the Supreme Court ruled that all segregated buses were unconstitutional.

At the meeting to organize the boycott, a young minister named Dr. Martin Luther King, Jr., emerged as one of the leaders of the civil rights movement. King believed that African Americans should use nonviolent protests and civil disobedience, or the refusal to obey laws that are considered unjust, to achieve their goals.

Kennedy and Johnson President Kennedy had expressed support for African Americans before he was assassinated in 1963. However, his successor, Lyndon Johnson, was the one who pushed a new Civil Rights Act and a Voting Rights Act through Congress. Johnson also outlined a set of programs called the "Great Society." Perhaps the most important laws passed as part of the Great Society were those establishing Medicare and Medicaid. Medicare helped pay for medical care for senior citizens. Medicaid helped poor people pay their hospital bills.

By the mid-1960s, the civil rights movement had won many victories. Yet a growing number of African Americans grew tired of the slow pace of change. On April 4, 1968, racial tensions took a tragic turn. An assassin shot and killed Dr. Martin Luther King, Jr. Dr. King's legacy remained, however, to

Birmingham police use hoses to force civil rights protestors to stop their marches. ▶

Sept. 1962 James Meredith tries to register at University of Mississippi

★ **Aug. 1963** King delivers "I Have a Dream" speech during March on Washington

★ **March 1965** King leads march in Selma, Alabama, to build support for new voting rights law

★ **May 1963** Police use force to stop Birmingham marchers

★ **July 1964** President Johnson signs Civil Rights Act of 1964 into law

★ **Aug. 1965** Congress passes Voting Rights Act of 1965

◀ National Guard escorts Freedom Riders

Critical Thinking

Analyzing What action did African Americans take in 1960 in the struggle for equal rights?

inspire Americans to continue his struggle for equal rights.

Women's Rights During the 1960s, concern over inequality in the workplace united women. In 1963 supporters of women's rights won passage of the Equal Pay Act, which outlawed paying men more than women for the same job.

In 1966 activists for women's rights formed the National Organization for Women, which campaigned for equal rights for women in all areas of life. NOW backed an Equal Rights Amendment (ERA) to the Constitution but was unable to get the states to ratify it.

Despite the ERA's defeat, women did make progress. In 1972 the federal government banned discrimination against women in schools and educational programs that received federal funds.

Latino Rights Meanwhile, the nation's rapidly growing Latino population sought equal rights. In the early 1960s, migrant workers formed unions to fight for better wages and working conditions. Their leader, César Chávez, organized thousands of laborers into the United Farm Workers (UFW). The efforts of Chávez called attention to the migrant workers' cause.

Others besides Chávez worked to secure equal rights for Latinos. Latino men and women organized to fight discrimination and to elect Latinos to government posts. The League of United Latin American Citizens won suits in federal courts to guarantee Latinos the right to serve on juries and to send their children to unsegregated schools. An independent Mexican American political party formed in 1969. *La Raza Unida,* or "the United People," mobilized voters, promoted bilingual education, and worked to end job discrimination.

Native Americans In the 1960s Native Americans demanded political power. In 1968 Congress passed the Indian Civil Rights Act, which protected Native American constitutional rights and allowed Native American nations to make laws on their own reservations.

Believing the process of change too slow, some Native Americans began taking stronger action. In February 1973, the American Indian Movement (AIM) took control of part of a large Sioux reservation in South Dakota. The people there suffered from poverty and poor health care. After several months, the siege ended, but it focused national attention on the terrible living conditions of many Native Americans.

People With Disabilities People with disabilities also sought equal treatment in the 1960s and 1970s. Congress responded by passing laws that improved access to public facilities, offered more opportunities for disabled people in the workplace, and provided greater educational opportunities for disabled people.

The Vietnam Era

Even as the civil rights movement remade American society at home, the United States continued to struggle against communism abroad, particularly in Vietnam.

Vietnam War Begins In the late 1950s, President Eisenhower had sent military supplies and advisers to South Vietnam. President Kennedy continued this policy. Despite American aid, the Vietcong—the Communist forces in South Vietnam—grew stronger. The Vietcong received weapons and supplies from North Vietnam.

In August 1964, North Vietnam was accused of attacking American ships in the Gulf of Tonkin. In response, Congress authorized President Johnson to use force. Gradually, the American troops shifted from defending their bases to trying to find and destroy the Vietcong. In mid-February 1965, Johnson ordered sustained bombing of North Vietnam. Then, on March 8, the first United States combat troops landed in Vietnam. In April Johnson decided to increase American forces in South Vietnam and to use combat troops.

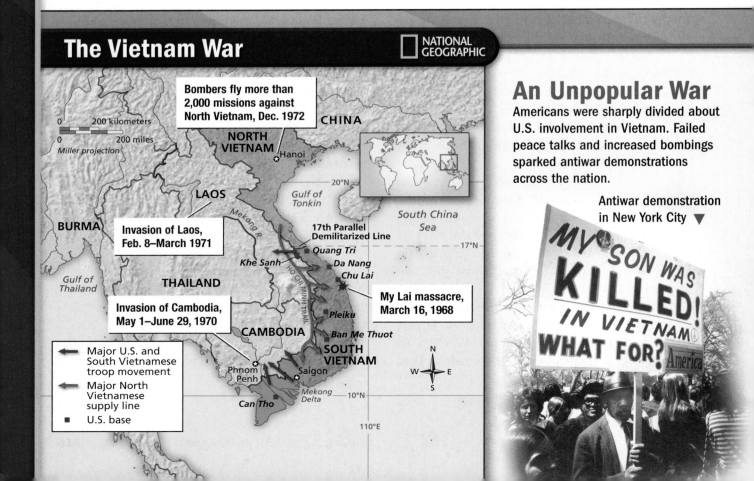

The Vietnam War

NATIONAL GEOGRAPHIC

Bombers fly more than 2,000 missions against North Vietnam, Dec. 1972

CHINA

NORTH VIETNAM

Hanoi

0 200 kilometers
0 200 miles
Miller projection

20°N

Gulf of Tonkin

LAOS

Mekong R.

South China Sea

BURMA

Invasion of Laos, Feb. 8–March 1971

17th Parallel Demilitarized Line

17°N

Quang Tri

Khe Sanh

Da Nang

Chu Lai

Gulf of Thailand

THAILAND

My Lai massacre, March 16, 1968

Invasion of Cambodia, May 1–June 29, 1970

Pleiku

CAMBODIA

Ban Me Thuot

SOUTH VIETNAM

N
W   E
S

Phnom Penh

Saigon

Mekong Delta

10°N

Can Tho

110°E

Major U.S. and South Vietnamese troop movement

Major North Vietnamese supply line

U.S. base

An Unpopular War
Americans were sharply divided about U.S. involvement in Vietnam. Failed peace talks and increased bombings sparked antiwar demonstrations across the nation.

Antiwar demonstration in New York City ▼

MY SON WAS KILLED! IN VIETNAM WHAT FOR?

An Increase in Troops North Vietnam increased its support of the Vietcong. To meet the situation, American commander General William Westmoreland asked for additional troops. By the end of 1965, there were more than 180,000 U.S. troops in Vietnam. By the end of 1968, the total had increased to more than 500,000.

Opposition to the War The American people disagreed sharply over the Vietnam War. Many young people opposed the war, especially the draft. However, opposition to the war was not limited to the young. Members of Congress and the news media became critical of Johnson's policies, too.

As the 1968 election approached, President Johnson announced he would not run for reelection. The Republican Party nominated Richard Nixon, Eisenhower's vice president. Nixon defeated Democrat Hubert Humphrey, winning 301 electoral votes to Humphrey's 191. Nixon promised to find a way to end the Vietnam War, pledging America would have "peace with honor."

President Nixon's plan to achieve "peace with honor" was called Vietnamization. As American troops were withdrawn, the United States would step up efforts to train and equip South Vietnamese forces. In time these forces would take over all the fighting.

Nixon's hope was that ultimately the North Vietnamese would grow tired of the war and negotiate peace. To hasten that end, Nixon secretly ordered the bombing of Cambodia because the Vietcong and North Vietnamese were using sanctuaries—safe places—there as springboards for offensives into South Vietnam. Then in the spring of 1970 Nixon announced the invasion of Cambodia.

The Cambodian invasion sparked demonstrations on college campuses throughout the nation. Many demonstrations were accompanied by violence. Four students were killed at Kent State University in Ohio and two were killed at Jackson State College in Mississippi.

American Involvement Ends Previous attempts to end the Vietnam War through negotiations had stalled. Then in late 1972 a breakthrough came. The final agreement was reached in January 1973. The last American troops pulled out of South Vietnam. Despite the peace agreement, North Vietnam's army launched a full-scale invasion of South Vietnam in early 1975. By May 1975, South Vietnam had fallen. Vietnam was united into one country, under the control of a Communist government.

The Vietnam War took a staggering toll of lives and caused great suffering. More than 58,000 Americans were dead. Over 1 million Vietnamese civilians and soldiers died between 1965 and 1975. The relatives of the American soldiers who had been classified as missing in action, or as MIAs, continued to demand that the government press the Vietnamese for information. As the years passed, however, the likelihood of finding anyone alive faded.

By the Numbers

United States Troops in Vietnam, 1965–1973

Source: *Statistical Abstract of the United States*

Map Skills

1. **Location** Along what line of latitude did the demilitarized zone run?

2. **Regions** Most of the Ho Chi Minh Trail runs through which countries?

Reading Check Analyzing What did the Supreme Court rule in *Brown* v. *Board of Education?*

Modern America

Main Idea After the 1970s, Americans experienced prosperity, change, and conflict.

History and You Why do things change in the world? Do you think people make a difference, or are big developments in economics and technology responsible? Read to learn about the challenges affecting modern America.

. . . .

During the late 1900s, the United States and the world experienced sweeping changes. Communism in Europe collapsed, the Cold War ended, and new technology transformed societies. As the twenty-first century dawned, however, Americans came to realize that they were not isolated from the dangers of a violent world.

Search for Stability

During the early 1970s, relations improved between the United States and the two Communist powers—the Soviet Union and China. As the Cold War thawed, the Americans and Soviets agreed to sign an arms control treaty limiting the number of nuclear missiles both sides could have. Meanwhile, the United States became involved in the Middle East. Angry at America's support for Israel, the oil-producing Arab states imposed an embargo—a ban on shipments—of crude oil. This crisis, which lasted from 1973 to 1974, caused gasoline prices to skyrocket.

The Watergate Scandal Shortly after President Nixon's reelection in 1972, a scandal rocked his presidency. During the election campaign, burglars had been caught trying to break into the Democratic Party offices at the Watergate apartment complex. Nixon denied that his staff had ordered the break-in. After a Senate committee uncovered his staff's involvement, Nixon denied ordering a cover-up.

The House of Representatives began proceedings to impeach, or formally accuse, the president of abusing his power. On August 9, 1974, Richard Nixon resigned as president. He expressed hope that his resignation would begin the process of healing the nation. Nixon's vice president, Gerald Ford, succeeded him.

The Path of Watergate

The Watergate scandal rocked the nation's trust in its elected officials but ultimately illustrated that America's system of government works.

Security guard Frank Willis discovered the Watergate break-in ▶

June 1972 ★
Watergate break-in reported

June 1973 ★
Counsel to the president John Dean implicates Nixon in cover-up

1972 — **1973** — **1974**

Nov. 1972 ★
Nixon reelected

May 1973 ★
Senate hearings begin

Oct. 1973 ★
White House refuses to release tapes; the president fires special prosecutor; Attorney General Richardson resigns

April 1974 ★
Nixon releases edited tapes

Gerald Ford's administration faced growing economic problems, caused in part by the oil embargo. This, as well as Ford's pardon of Richard Nixon, turned many people against Ford. In 1976, voters elected the Democratic candidate, Jimmy Carter, to the presidency.

The Carter Presidency

When Jimmy Carter took office, his first task was to fix the economy. Carter tried to speed economic growth by cutting taxes and increasing government spending, but his policies did little to bring improvements.

Carter spent much of his time dealing with foreign policy problems. He arranged new talks between Israeli and Egyptian leaders at Camp David. These negotiations led to an Egyptian-Israeli peace treaty signed at the White House in March 1979. The treaty marked the first time that an Arab nation recognized Israel's right to exist.

Carter based much of his foreign policy on human rights—a concern that governments around the world grant more freedom to their people. He withdrew economic and military aid from some of the worst offenders, including Argentina, South Africa, and Iran. In 1979, a revolution brought an Islamic government to power in the Middle Eastern country of Iran. Later that year, Iranian students with the support of government officials seized the American embassy in Tehran. They held 52 Americans hostage for 444 days.

The hostage crisis and the nation's ongoing economic problems damaged President Carter politically. In the 1980 election, the Republican candidate, Ronald Reagan, easily defeated Carter. Shortly afterward, Iran released the American hostages.

The Reagan Revolution

By the 1980s, many Americans were discontented with government and concerned about the direction in which society was going. Some began to call for a return to "traditional" values, such as family life, hard work, respect for the law, and patriotism.

Appealing to the nation's growing conservative mood, Ronald Reagan promised to reduce the role of the government in people's lives. He slashed taxes and cut back on government programs. Reagan also began a rapid buildup of American military forces. By cutting taxes while increasing military spending, Reagan greatly increased the federal debt—the amount of money the government had to borrow to pay for its programs.

The American military buildup forced the Soviet Union to respond, and it simply could not afford to keep up. A new Soviet leader, Mikhail Gorbachev, saw that the time had come to reform the Communist system. In 1987 Reagan and Gorbachev agreed to reduce the number of nuclear missiles under their control. A major step had been taken toward reducing the threat of nuclear war.

The Collapse of Communism

Ronald Reagan's popularity enabled his vice president, George Bush, to win the 1988 presidential election. During Bush's presidency, calls for democracy swept the Communist world.

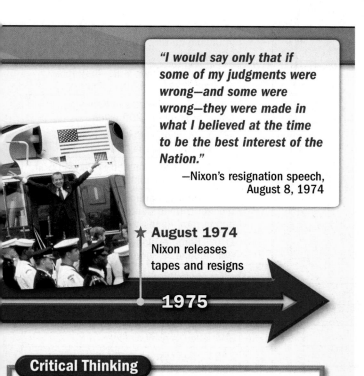

"I would say only that if some of my judgments were wrong—and some were wrong—they were made in what I believed at the time to be the best interest of the Nation."
—Nixon's resignation speech, August 8, 1974

★ **August 1974**
Nixon releases tapes and resigns

1975

Critical Thinking

Analyzing Visuals Look at the photo above. What thoughts or feelings do you think President Nixon was having at the time he left the White House?

In 1989 Communist governments in eastern Europe crumbled one by one. The Berlin Wall was torn down, and the following year East Germany and West Germany reunited. By the end of 1991, the Communist Party had been outlawed in Russia, and the Soviet Union had broken up into separate republics.

While communism collapsed in Europe, a serious crisis developed in the Middle East. In 1990, Iraq invaded Kuwait. President Bush persuaded European and Arab nations to join the United States in an effort to free Kuwait. Bush then launched Operation Desert Storm—a massive attack on Iraqi forces that freed Kuwait and destroyed much of Iraq's army.

The Clinton Years

Despite success in the Middle East, the Bush administration was hurt by an economic recession. Democrat Bill Clinton, governor of Arkansas, defeated Bush in the 1992 presidential race. After assuming office, Clinton cut government spending to reduce the deficit. In 1993 Clinton and the leaders of Canada and Mexico signed the North American Free Trade Agreement (NAFTA), which created a free-trade area for the three countries of North America.

After Clinton won reelection in 1996, the economy continued to grow rapidly. For the first time in many years, the government balanced the budget and ran a surplus—it took in more money than it spent. During Clinton's second term, a scandal emerged involving a personal relationship between the president and a White House intern. Some evidence suggested that the president had obstructed justice and committed perjury, or lied under oath, to conceal the relationship. The House of Representatives voted to impeach President Clinton. The Senate then held a trial and acquitted the president.

Global Terrorism

NATIONAL GEOGRAPHIC

7	1995 Bombing of federal office building in Oklahoma City, 168 killed, more than 500 injured
8	1996 U.S. complex in Saudi Arabia bombed, 19 U.S. soldiers killed
9	1998 U.S. embassies in Kenya and Tanzania bombed, 200 killed
10	1999 Chechen separatists bomb apartments in Russia, 300 killed
11	2000 USS *Cole* bombed in Persian Gulf, 17 U.S. soldiers killed
12	2001 Hijacked airliners crash into the World Trade Center, the Pentagon, and in rural Pennsylvania
13	2002 Bomb explodes at resort in Bali, Indonesia, more than 200 killed
14	2002–present Attacks in Afghanistan
15	2003–present Attacks in Iraq against coalition troops and civilians
16	2004 Beslan school hostage crisis, 344 killed, mostly children
17	2004 Train system in Madrid, Spain, bombed, 191 killed
18	2004 U.S. Consulate in Jeddah, Saudi Arabia, attacked, 5 killed
19	2005 London subway bombed, 52 killed

1	1979 Fifty-two Americans held hostage in Iran
2	1983 U.S. Marine barracks in Lebanon bombed, 241 killed
3	1985 TWA flight hijacked; hostages held in Lebanon
4	1988 Pan Am flight explodes over Scotland, 270 killed
5	1993 World Trade Center bombed in New York, 6 killed
6	1994–present Over 160 suicide bombing attacks in Israel, hundreds killed

The George W. Bush Presidency

The impeachment scandal left the country divided. For the 2000 election, the Democrats nominated Vice President Al Gore. The Republicans nominated Governor George W. Bush of Texas, son of former President Bush. The election was one of the closest in history. Gore led in the popular vote, but the results in Florida were disputed and on election night no one knew who won. The dispute was finally resolved by the Supreme Court. On January 20, 2001, George W. Bush became the 43rd president of the United States.

Bush faced major challenges in winning over public and congressional support after the election controversy. Some of Bush's major policies included a $1.6 trillion tax cut and the No Child Left Behind Act, an overhaul of federal education legislation. During his first term in office, the terrorist attacks of September 11, 2001, led to his call for a war on terrorism.

Disrupting Terror Plots

Law-enforcement officials such as the officer watching the banks of monitors (above) work to uncover threats from terrorist activity. Highlights of their success:

- **December 2001** Would-be bomber stopped by passengers while on trans-Atlantic flight
- **2003** Disrupted a plot to use hijacked commercial airplanes to attack Heathrow Airport in London
- **2004** Disrupted plot to conduct large-scale bombings in cities in the United Kingdom
- **July 2005** Attempt to bomb the London subway is stopped
- **August 2006** Uncovered plot to smuggle liquid explosives onto trans-Atlantic airline flights
- **June 2007** Vehicles packed with explosives are discovered in London; suspects arrested

Critical Thinking

Analyzing Which attack took place in the U.S. Southwest?

New Challenges

On September 11, 2001, terrorists from the Middle East seized four American passenger planes. Two planes were deliberately crashed into New York City's World Trade Center. A third plane was flown into the Pentagon, the U.S. military headquarters in Washington, D.C. A fourth plane was seized, but the passengers heroically fought back. This plane crashed in Pennsylvania.

Fighting Terrorism The terrorists were later found to be part of al-Qaeda (al KY·duh), a terrorist group created by a Saudi Arabian named Osama bin Laden. Al-Qaeda grew out of the Muslim struggle against the Soviets in Afghanistan. Osama was one of the fighters there. Using his family's wealth, bin Laden formed al-Qaeda to recruit new fighters.

After the 9/11 attacks, the United States declared war on terrorism. It first focused on Afghanistan. There, bin Laden and al-Qaeda hid out with the help of the militant Muslim government called the Taliban. The Taliban was defeated, and the United States helped set up a new Afghan government.

In the United States, President Bush acted to protect Americans from further terrorist attacks. In October 2001, Congress passed and the President signed into law the USA Patriot Act of 2001. This new measure gave federal officials new powers to investigate those who plot or carry out terrorism.

The Iraq War The attacks of 9/11 raised fears that terrorist groups might acquire nuclear, chemical, or biological weapons. These weapons of mass destruction could kill thousands of people at a time. President Bush believed that Iraq's government had these weapons and was an immediate threat.

In 2003 a group of countries led by the United States invaded Iraq. The Iraqi army was quickly defeated, and Iraq's leader Saddam Hussein was overthrown. Later, an Iraqi court found Hussein guilty of ordering mass executions. He was executed in 2006. The United States and its allies set out to rebuild Iraq's economy and create a democracy.

U.S. Foreign-Born Population, 1850–2005

Legend:
- Foreign-born (in millions)
- Percentage of total population

Three generations of the Solano family from San Antonio, Texas ▶

Source: U.S. Census Bureau; Urban Institute

Graph Skills

1. **Identifying** In what year did the foreign-born population reach its all-time high?
2. **Analyzing** What was the percentage of foreign-born population in 2005?

The quick victory over the Iraqi army did not end the fighting. Insurgents, or rebel groups, battled U.S. forces. Iraq also was torn apart by disputes among Iraq's Muslim communities.

Many Americans had expected the war to be over quickly. As the fighting dragged on, support for the war declined. The failure to find weapons of mass destruction also caused many Americans to wonder if the war in Iraq was a mistake.

Bush's Second Term During the 2004 presidential race between President Bush and Democratic challenger Senator John Kerry of Massachusetts, the war was a major issue. Economic issues such as the budget deficit and job losses, and moral debates over medical research and the definition of marriage divided citizens. President Bush was elected for a second term, winning the popular vote by a margin of 51 to 48 percent. In his Inaugural Address, Bush expressed his commitment to the war in Iraq. Soon after the election, he announced a surge, or rapid increase, of more troops to Iraq. Whether the surge could work was unclear. However, by the summer of 2007, what was clear was that Americans remained divided over the Iraq war and that its outcome remained uncertain.

Challenges Ahead

Since the 1980s, the United States and other countries have experienced a technological revolution driven in many ways by the computer. Through their personal computers, people are now able to go on the Internet. This is a huge web of linked computer networks. The Internet has made global communications almost instant.

The technology revolution has tied together people and nations more closely. It has led to the rise of globalism, the idea that the world's economies and societies are part of one big system. Globalism has boosted trade and has made people aware of issues that affect the world as a whole.

Controlling Weapons Preserving peace remains a global issue for the United States. In the late 1990s and early 2000s, acts of terror multiplied at home and abroad. Another major issue is nuclear proliferation, or the spread of nuclear weapons. The number of countries owning or seeking nuclear weapons is growing. New dangers also lurk with the development of new kinds of warfare, including chemical weapons and biological weapons, which deliberately spread disease among humans.

The Environment In recent years, Americans have become aware of dangers to the world's environment. For example, many people fear that Earth's resources will soon be unable to support a rapidly rising world population. Air and water pollution also are major concerns. Many scientists think that the Earth is getting warmer and believe that this may be caused by pollution. They think that this global warming will lead to changing weather patterns. For example, some experts claim that hurricanes and other storms have grown stronger and longer-lasting as Earth has warmed. On August 25, 2005, Hurricane Katrina struck the Gulf of Mexico's coast. Storm conditions raged from Florida to Louisiana. The hurricane destroyed buildings, roads, and electrical lines. Thousands of people were left homeless, and at least 1,800 people died. Hurricane Katrina was one of the worst natural disasters in American history.

A Changing Society As America enters the twenty-first century, its population has begun to change significantly. The number of older Americans has risen. Ways of living and working have been altered. Above all, changes in U.S. laws and unstable conditions worldwide have led to a rise in the number of immigrants to the United States. By 2007, nearly half of all the country's immigrants came from Latin America and Canada, and another third from Asia.

Despite their many differences, Americans are united in affirming their democratic way of life. They are committed to passing on the ideal of liberty and justice for all to future generations.

Reading Check **Analyzing** Why did President George W. Bush call for military action against Iraq?

Epilogue Review

Main Ideas

1. **Identifying** What was the transcontinental railroad? How did it influence settlement?

2. **Describing** What actions were taken by African Americans to secure civil rights?

3. **Making Connections** How were the terrorist attacks on September 11, 2001, related to the war in Afghanistan?

Critical Thinking

4. **Organizing Information** Re-create the diagram below and write three ways in which cities were changing in the early 1900s.

5. **Drawing Conclusions** Do you think the expansion of the federal government during Franklin Roosevelt's presidency was necessary? Why or why not?

6. **Making Inferences** Do you think President Nixon succeeded in attaining "peace with honor" in the Vietnam War?

7. **Analyzing** What are two major challenges Americans face today? Explain why you made your choices.

8. **Expository Writing** How will world events affect your future? Write an essay entitled "The World's Future and My Own" identifying important issues and explaining how events could affect your life.

Appendix

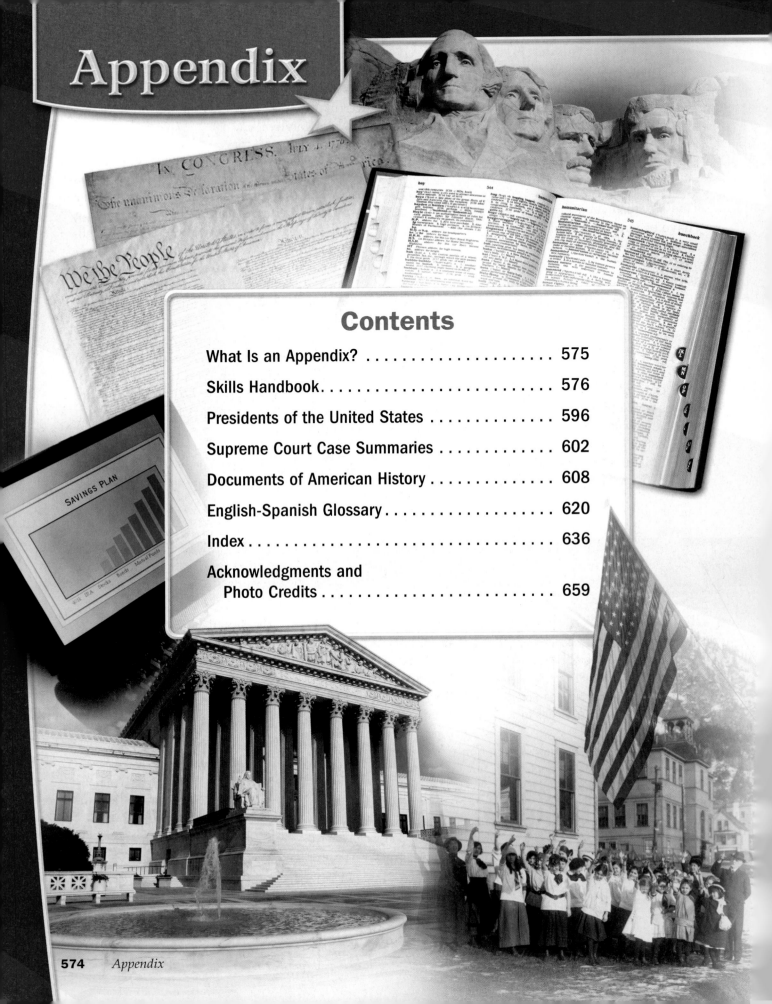

Contents

What Is an Appendix?

An appendix is the additional material you often find at the end of books. The following information will help you learn how to use the appendix in The American Journey.

Skills Handbook

The Skills Handbook offers you information and practice using critical thinking and social studies skills. Mastering these skills will help you in all your courses.

Presidents of the United States

The presidents have served as our nation's leaders. In this resource you will find information of interest on each of the nation's presidents, including their term in office, their political affiliation, and their occupations before they became president.

Supreme Court Case Summaries

The Supreme Court Case Summaries provide readable discussions of important Supreme Court cases. The summaries are listed in alphabetical order and include a summary of the facts of the case and its impact.

Documents of American History

This is a collection of some of the most important writings and speeches in American history. Each document begins with an introduction describing the author and placing the selection within its historical context.

English-Spanish Glossary

A glossary is a list of important or difficult terms found in a textbook. The glossary gives a definition of each term as it is used in the book. The glossary also includes page numbers telling you where in the textbook the term is used. Since words sometimes have other meanings, you may wish to consult a dictionary to find other uses for the term.

In *The American Journey,* the Spanish glossary is included with the English glossary. The Spanish term is located directly across from the English term. A Spanish glossary is especially important to bilingual students or those Spanish-speaking students who are learning the English language.

Index

An index is an alphabetical listing that includes the subjects of the book and the page numbers where those subjects can be found. The index in this book also lets you know that certain pages contain maps, graphs, charts, photos, paintings, or cartoons about the subject.

Acknowledgments and Photo Credits

This section lists photo credits and literary credits for the book. You can look at this section to find out where the publisher obtained the permission to use a photograph or to use excerpts from other books.

Test Yourself

Find the answers to these questions by using the Appendix on the following pages.

1. What does *ironclad* mean?
2. Who was the sixth president of the United States?
3. Which section of the Appendix would help you find out about "bleeding Kansas"?
4. What was the purpose of issuing the Seneca Falls Declaration?
5. What was the Supreme Court's decision in *Marbury* v. *Madison*?

Skills Handbook

Contents

Understanding Cause and Effect

Why Learn This Skill?

Cause-and-effect relationships are important in the study of history. To understand cause and effect, consider *why* an event occurred. A *cause* is an action or situation that produces an event. What happens as a result of a cause is an *effect*.

Marco Polo ▶

Learn It!

To identify cause-and-effect relationships, follow these steps:

1. Identify two or more events or developments.

2. Decide whether one event caused the other. Look for "clue words" such as *because, led to, brought about, so that, after that, produced, as a result of, since,* or *in the wake of.*

3. Identify the outcomes of events. Remember that some effects have more than one cause, and some causes lead to more than one effect. Also, an effect can become the cause of yet another effect.

The Crusades brought western Europeans into contact with the Middle East. Arab merchants sold spices, sugar, silk, and other goods from China and India to Europeans. As a result, European interest in Asia grew.

That interest grew even more after Marco Polo returned from China. In 1296 he began writing an account of his trip. He described Asia's marvels in his book Travels, *which was widely read in Europe. Little did Marco Polo realize that 200 years later* Travels *would inspire Christopher Columbus to sail in the opposite direction to reach the East.*

Practice It!

Categorize the items below as either *cause, effect,* or *both.*

1. The Crusades brought western Europeans to the Middle East.

2. European interest in Asia grew.

3. Marco Polo wrote *Travels,* an account of his trip to China.

4. *Travels* inspired Christopher Columbus to sail in the opposite direction to reach the East.

Apply It!

In a newspaper, read an article describing a current event. Determine at least one cause and one effect of that event, and complete a flowchart like the one below.

| Cause | → | Event | → | Effect |

Classifying and Categorizing Information

Why Learn This Skill?

As a student, it is important to know how to organize large quantities of information in an understandable way. *Classifying* helps you to arrange facts into broad groups. *Categorizing* helps you to organize that information into more detailed groups according to common characteristics.

Rudolph Valentino movie poster (left) and King Kong movie poster (right) ▶

1 Learn It!

Follow these steps to learn how to classify and categorize:

1. To classify information, look for topics and facts that have common broad characteristics. In the first paragraph, a broad topic might be *Reasons for Cultural Change in America.* Under this topic, further classifications might be *The Growth of Mass Media* and *Increase in Leisure Time.*

2. Divide the information further into categories, based on more specific characteristics. For example, under *Mass Media*, categories could be *Movies* and *Radio.* Each of those categories could contain more examples and details and could become column heads in a chart.

3. As you read, look for examples that fit into the categories you created.

Cultural changes spread quickly because of the growth of mass media—forms of communication, such as newspapers and radio, that reach millions of people. Laborsaving devices and fewer working hours gave Americans more leisure time to enjoy newspapers, magazines, phonograph records, the radio, and the movies.

In the 1920s, the motion picture industry in Hollywood, California, became a major business. For millions of Americans the movies offered entertainment and escape. The first movies were black and white and silent, with the actor's dialogue printed on the screen. In 1927 Hollywood introduced movies with sound. The first "talkie," The Jazz Singer, created a sensation.

The radio brought entertainment into people's homes in the 1920s. Radio networks broadcast popular programs that included news, concerts, sporting events, and comedies.

2 Practice It!

1. What are two further classifications for the topic *Increase in Leisure Time?*

2. What details/examples from the paragraphs above could you place under the categories *Movies* and *Radio?*

3 Apply It!

Look at the Geographic Dictionary on pages Ref 30–Ref 31. In a chart, list the terms that would fall into the classifications "Landforms" or "Bodies of Water." Can you identify other categories in which to group the information?

Making Comparisons

Why Learn This Skill?

When you make comparisons, you determine similarities among ideas, objects, or events. You should also examine qualities that make each of the ideas, objects, or events unique. Making comparisons is an important skill because it can help you to choose among several possible alternatives.

1 Learn It!

To make comparisons, follow these steps:

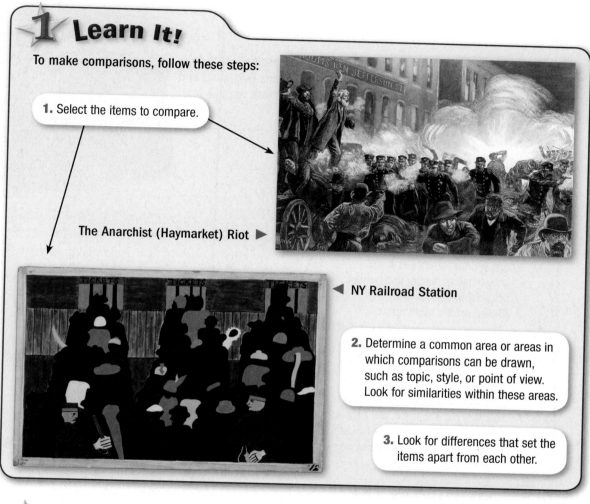

1. Select the items to compare.

The Anarchist (Haymarket) Riot ▶

◀ NY Railroad Station

2. Determine a common area or areas in which comparisons can be drawn, such as topic, style, or point of view. Look for similarities within these areas.

3. Look for differences that set the items apart from each other.

2 Practice It!

After studying the paintings above, answer the following questions:

1. How are the subjects of the paintings similar?

2. How are they different?

3. What can you tell about the two artists' attitudes toward their subject?

3 Apply It!

Survey 10 of your classmates about an issue in the news, and summarize their responses. Then write a paragraph or two comparing their opinions.

Predicting Consequences

Why Learn This Skill?

Predicting future events is difficult, but the more information you have, the more accurate your predictions will be. Making good predictions will help you to make better decisions. Using these skills can also help you to understand the consequences of historical events.

The assassination of Archduke Franz Ferdinand and Archduchess Sophie ▶

 Learn It!

To help you make predictions, follow these steps:

1. Gather information about the topic.

2. Use your experience and your knowledge of history and human behavior to predict what consequences could result.

3. Analyze each of the possible consequences by asking yourself: How likely is it that this will happen?

On the morning of June 28, 1914, Archduke Franz Ferdinand, the heir to the throne of the Austro-Hungarian Empire, and his wife Sophie were assassinated while visiting Bosnia, an Austrian province.

Gavrilo Princip, Franz Ferdinand's assassin, belonged to a Serbian nationalist group that had plotted Ferdinand's murder to bring down the Austro-Hungarian Empire and unite the Slavs.

 Practice It!

Read the excerpt above and answer the following questions:

1. What outcome is most likely to occur between Austria-Hungary and Serbia?

2. On what do you base your prediction?

3. Do you think a situation similar to the one described in the passage is likely to occur again?

Apply It!

Analyze three newspaper articles about an event affecting your community or the nation. Make an educated prediction about what will happen, and explain your reasoning. Then write a few paragraphs summarizing your prediction. You may want to check back later to see if your prediction came true.

Analyzing and Interpreting Information

Why Learn This Skill?

Have you ever heard someone say, "Don't believe everything you read"? To be an informed citizen, you have to analyze and interpret information carefully as you read to make sure you understand the meaning and the intent of the writer. Doing so helps you decide what you think about a subject.

Andrew Carnegie ▶

1 Learn It!

To analyze and interpret information, use the following steps:

1. Identify the topic being discussed.

2. Examine how the information is organized. What are the main points?

3. Think about how reliable the source of the information is.

4. Summarize the information in your own words. Does the information agree with or contradict something you believe?

> [T]he surplus wealth of the few will become, in the best sense, the property of the many. . . . [T]his wealth, passing through the hands of the few, can be made a much more potent [strong] force for the elevation of our race than if it had been distributed in small sums to the people themselves. Even the poorest can be made to see this, and to agree that great sums gathered by some of their fellow-citizens and spent for public purposes, from which the masses reap the principal benefit, are more valuable to them than if scattered among them through the course of many years in trifling amounts.
>
> —Andrew Carnegie, "Wealth"

2 Practice It!

Read the excerpt above and answer the following questions:

1. What topic is being discussed?

2. What is the main point?

3. Summarize the information in this excerpt, and then provide your analysis, based on this information and what you already know about the subject.

3 Apply It!

Select an issue that is currently in the news, such as gasoline prices, global warming, or taxation. Read an article or watch a news segment about the issue. Analyze the information and make a brief statement of your own about the topic. Explain your thinking.

Distinguishing Fact From Opinion

Why Learn This Skill?

To make reasonable judgments about what others say or write, it is important to distinguish facts from opinions. Facts can be checked for accuracy and proven. They answer specific questions such as: What happened? Who did it? When and where did it happen? Opinions are based on people's differing values and beliefs. Opinions often begin with phrases such as *I believe* or *It seems to me*. They also frequently contain words such as *should* or *ought* or judgment words such as *best, worst,* or *greatest.*

▶ Louise Slaughter speaks at National Press Club June 2007

 Learn It!

To learn how to separate facts from opinions, follow these steps:

1. Identify the facts. Ask: which statements can be proved? Where would I find information to verify this statement? If the information is a statistic, it may sound impressive, but you won't know if it's accurate unless you check the source.

2. Identify opinions by looking for statements of feelings or beliefs. Opinions sometimes contain words like *should, would, could, best, greatest, all, every,* or *always.*

All of my colleagues understand that the PATRIOT Act has provided the law enforcement agencies with many valuable tools which facilitate their work in the struggle against terrorism. But with these new tools comes a very real danger that the liberty we seek to protect could be easily compromised in the overzealous pursuit of greater security. . . .

We have evidence which suggests, in contrast to information coming out of the Justice Department, that many of these measures have resulted in the violation of the civil liberties of American citizens. In addition, we understand that some of the extended search and seizure powers used by the law enforcement are apparently not being used for their intended purpose, which is strictly to fight terrorism, and that is unacceptable.

—Congresswoman Louise McIntosh Slaughter, July 21, 2005

 Practice It!

The excerpt above is from a speech delivered to Congress by U.S. Representative Louise McIntosh Slaughter concerning the reauthorization, or renewal, of the Patriot Act. Reread the excerpt and answer the questions that follow.

1. Which statements in the passage are factual?

2. Which statements are opinions? Explain.

 Apply It!

Watch a television interview. Then list three facts and three opinions that you hear.

Drawing Inferences and Conclusions

Why Learn This Skill?

When you make an *inference,* you "read between the lines," or use clues to figure something out that is not stated directly in the text. A *conclusion* is a logical understanding that you reach based on details or facts that you read or hear. By drawing inferences and conclusions you can formulate ideas and make decisions.

Jefferson Davis ▶

1 Learn It!

Follow these steps to draw inferences and conclusions:

1. Read carefully for facts and ideas, and list them.

2. Summarize the information.

3. Consider what you may already know about the topic.

4. Use your knowledge and insight to develop some logical conclusions based on the facts.

There can be but little rivalry between ours and any manufacturing or navigating community, such as the Northeastern States of the American Union. It must follow, therefore, that a mutual interest would invite good will and kind offices. If, however, passion or the lust of dominion [power] should cloud the judgment or inflame the ambition of those States, we must prepare to meet the emergency and to maintain, by the final [deciding power] of the sword, the position which we have assumed among the nations of the earth. We have entered upon the career of independence, and it must be inflexibly pursued. . . . As a necessity, not a choice, we have resorted to the remedy of separation; and henceforth our energies must be directed to the conduct of our own affairs, and the [lasting life] of the Confederacy which we have formed.

—Jefferson Davis's inaugural speech, February 18, 1861

2 Practice It!

After reading the passage above, answer the following questions:

1. What points does the author make?

2. Which point does your experience contradict?

3. What inference can you make about the Confederate states' reasons for declaring their independence?

4. What conclusions can you draw about Davis' beliefs about a possible war?

3 Apply It!

Read an editorial printed in today's newspaper. What can you infer about the importance of the topic being addressed? Can you tell how the writer feels about the topic? Explain your answer.

Writing a Paragraph

Why Learn This Skill?

Paragraphs are the building blocks of an essay or other composition. Each paragraph is a unit—a group of sentences about a single topic or idea.

Washington observes Von Steuben drilling troops at Valley Forge ▶

 Learn It!

Most well-written paragraphs share four characteristics:

At first glance the British had an overwhelming advantage in the war. They had the strongest navy in the world. They also had an experienced, well-trained army and the wealth of a worldwide empire. Britain also had a much larger population than the United States. There were over 8 million people in Britain, compared with only 2.5 million in the United States.

1. A paragraph expresses one main idea or is about one subject. A topic sentence states the main idea, and may be located at the beginning, middle, or end of the paragraph.

2. The rest of the sentences support the main idea. The main idea may be developed by facts, examples, or reasons.

3. The sentences are arranged in a logical order.

4. Transitional words link sentences within the paragraph. Examples include *next, then, finally, also, because, however,* and *as a result.*

 Practice It!

Use the following sentences to build a paragraph containing a topic sentence and other sentences that give supporting details. Put the sentences in a logical order and add transitional words if you need to. Underline your topic sentence.

1. They were forced to ship soldiers and supplies thousands of miles across the Atlantic.

2. They were fighting on their own ground and fought with great determination to protect it.

3. The Americans possessed some advantages.

4. The British, in contrast, had to wage war in a faraway land.

 Apply It!

Choose a topic from the era of the Revolutionary War and write a paragraph about it. Then rewrite the paragraph with its sentences out of order. Exchange papers with a classmate. Can he or she find the topic sentence? Does it read logically?

Taking Notes and Outlining

Why Learn This Skill?

Taking notes and outlining are ways of recording important information about what you read. Both methods also help you recall information. Writing down information in a brief and orderly form helps you remember key points and makes it easier to study.

Outlining is similar to sketching a scene. First, you draw the rough shape, or outline, of the picture. Then you fill in the details. Outlining helps you identify main ideas and group related facts.

 Learn It!

To learn how to take notes, use the following steps:

1. **Identify** the subject and write it at the top of your page.

2. **Select** specific details that support the main subject and include them in your notes. Look for topic sentences of paragraphs and words in bold or italics.

3. **Paraphrase** the information. Putting it in your own words helps you understand the meaning of the information.

4. **Condense** words into a personal shorthand, such as dropping vowels ("develop" becomes "dvlp"), and use symbols ("and" becomes "+") to save time.

> In 1776 the Second Continental Congress appointed a committee to draw up a plan for a new government. After much debate the Congress adopted the **Articles of Confederation** in November 1777. The Articles, America's first constitution, provided for a new central government under which the states kept most of their power. For the states, the Articles of Confederation were "a firm league of friendship" in which each state retained "its sovereignty, freedom and independence." Under the Articles of Confederation, Congress had the authority to conduct foreign affairs, maintain armed forces, borrow money, and issue currency.

 Practice It!

Read the excerpt above. Then, on a separate sheet of paper, take notes on the paragraph. Be sure to consider the following questions.

1. What is the subject of the paragraph?
2. What is the main point of the paragraph?
3. What details are especially important to write down?

 Apply It!

Read a short article from a local newspaper about a governmental issue. Outline the important information. Write a short summary of the article using only your outline.

Summarizing Information

Why Learn This Skill?

Imagine you have been assigned a long chapter to read. How can you remember the important facts? Summarizing information means that you reduce large amounts of information to a few key phrases. Being able to summarize can help you remember the main ideas and key details.

Statue of Liberty ▶

 Learn It!

To summarize information, follow these guidelines when you read:

1. Read through the selection. Determine the main idea and the most important supporting details.

2. A summary can be a sentence or a short paragraph that includes the main ideas. In your summary, restate the text using your own words. Be brief—do not include many supporting details.

3. For the first paragraph, a summary statement might be: By the early 1900s, immigration patterns were changing and most new immigrants came from southern and eastern Europe.

In the mid-1880s, the pattern of immigration started to change. Large groups of "new" immigrants arrived from eastern and southern Europe. Greeks, Russians, Hungarians, Italians, Turks, and Poles were among the newcomers. At the same time, the number of "old" immigrants from northern and western Europe started to decrease. By 1907, 80 percent of immigrants came from southern and eastern Europe.

Many of these newcomers were Catholics or Jews. Few spoke English. Because of this, they did not blend into American society as easily as the "old" immigrants had. Often, they clustered together in neighborhoods made up of people of the same nationality.

 Practice It!

After reading the excerpt above, answer the following questions:

1. In a summary of the first paragraph, would you include the statement, "The number of 'old' immigrants decreased"? Why or why not?

2. Write a summary statement for the second paragraph.

 Apply It!

Read the section titled "Citizen Participation" of the Constitution Handbook of this book. Summarize the information in two or three sentences.

Reading a Time Line

Why Learn This Skill?

Knowing the relationship of time to events is important in studying history. A time line is a visual way to show the flow of dates and events in the correct order that they occurred. On many time lines, the years are evenly spaced. For example, a time line showing 1,000 years might be divided into ten 100-year intervals. Each event on a time line is described beside the date when the event took place.

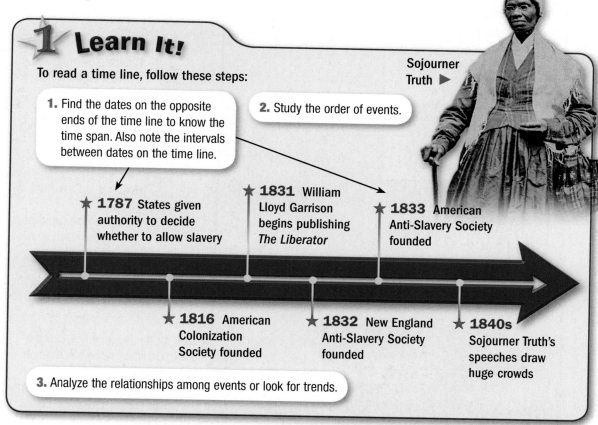

1 Learn It!

To read a time line, follow these steps:

1. Find the dates on the opposite ends of the time line to know the time span. Also note the intervals between dates on the time line.

2. Study the order of events.

Sojourner Truth ▶

1787 States given authority to decide whether to allow slavery

1831 William Lloyd Garrison begins publishing *The Liberator*

1833 American Anti-Slavery Society founded

1816 American Colonization Society founded

1832 New England Anti-Slavery Society founded

1840s Sojourner Truth's speeches draw huge crowds

3. Analyze the relationships among events or look for trends.

2 Practice It!

Analyze the time line about the Abolition movement. Use it to answer the questions that follow.

1. What time span is represented?

2. Which occurred first: the founding of the American Colonization Society or the founding of the American Anti-Slavery Society?

3. How many years after states were allowed to decide the issue of slavery did William Lloyd Garrison begin publishing *The Liberator?*

3 Apply It!

List 10 key events that have occurred in your life and the dates on which these events occurred. Write the events in chronological order on a time line.

Understanding Parts of a Map

Why Learn This Skill?

Maps can direct you down the street or around the world. There are as many different kinds of maps as there are uses for them. Being able to read a map begins with learning about its parts.

1 Learn It!

To understand the parts of a map, follow these steps:

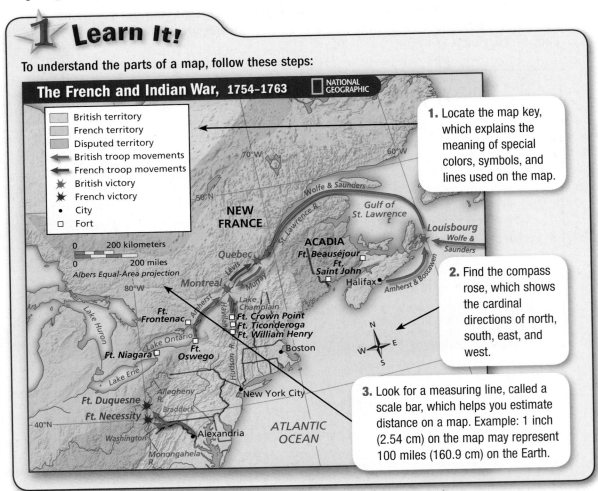

The French and Indian War, 1754–1763 NATIONAL GEOGRAPHIC

British territory
French territory
Disputed territory
British troop movements
French troop movements
British victory
French victory
City
Fort

1. Locate the map key, which explains the meaning of special colors, symbols, and lines used on the map.

2. Find the compass rose, which shows the cardinal directions of north, south, east, and west.

3. Look for a measuring line, called a scale bar, which helps you estimate distance on a map. Example: 1 inch (2.54 cm) on the map may represent 100 miles (160.9 cm) on the Earth.

2 Practice It!

The map above shows the territories held by Great Britain and France in North America, as well as the battles between these two countries in their quests to control the North American continent. Look at the parts of the map and then answer the following questions:

1. What color shows the disputed territory?

2. Which direction would you travel to go from Fort Oswego to Boston?

3. About how many miles was it from New York City to Fort Ticonderoga?

4. Who won the battle in Quebec?

3 Apply It!

Create a mental image of your house. Draw a map showing the location of various areas. Include a map key to explain any symbols or colors you use, as well as a scale bar to explain the size of your map compared to the real area. Finally, add a compass rose and title to your map.

Recognizing Historical Perspectives

Why Learn This Skill?

As you study historical events or read primary sources from the past, you may be surprised by the actions taking place or the beliefs being expressed. To accurately evaluate the event or statement, you must carefully consider the time period and the experiences and viewpoints of the people involved.

 Learn It!

To learn how to recognize historical perspectives, ask yourself these questions:

1. When was the statement made? To what event or time does the statement refer, and what other related events had occurred before or were occurring at the time?

2. Who is the author or speaker of the statement? What past experiences or current considerations might influence that person's viewpoint?

3. Why is it important to think critically about historical perspectives?

An 1868 treaty was supposed to bring peace, but tensions remained and erupted in more fighting. This time the conflict arose over the Black Hills of the Dakotas. The government had promised that "No white person or persons shall be permitted" to settle on the Black Hills. However, the hills were rumored to contain gold, and white prospectors swarmed into the area.

The Sioux protested against the trespassers. Instead of protecting the Sioux's rights, the government tried to buy the hills. Sitting Bull, an important leader of the Lakota Sioux, refused. "I do not want to sell any land. Not even this much," he said, holding a pinch of dust.

 Practice It!

Read the excerpt above and answer the following questions:

1. What conflict is being discussed in the excerpt above?

2. What past events and beliefs may have influenced Sitting Bull's statement? How did white and Native American beliefs about land differ at that time?

3. How does recognizing historical perspectives help you better understand the events and statements related to a historical period?

 Apply It!

Look in a current newspaper or news-magazine to find an example of a conflict between two or more groups of people. Write a short summary of how their perspectives of each other have determined their historical and current relationships.

Analyzing News Media

Why Learn This Skill?

Every citizen needs to be aware of current issues and events to make good decisions when exercising citizenship rights. To get an accurate profile of current events, you must learn to think critically about the news.

Herbert Hoover ▶

Learn It!

The following steps will help you think critically:

1. Think about the source of the news story. Reports that reveal sources are more reliable than those that do not. If you know the sources, you can evaluate them for reliability and bias.

2. Many news stories also interpret events. Such analyses may reflect a reporter's biases. Look for biases as you read or listen to news stories.

3. Ask yourself whether the news is even-handed and thorough. Is it reported on the scene or secondhand? Does it represent both sides of an issue?

AIM TO PACK COURT, DECLARES HOOVER

President Roosevelt's message to Congress asking for authority to appoint new Federal judges whenever existing ones were over 70 years old was characterized last night by Herbert Hoover, his predecessor in the White House, as a proposal for "packing" the Supreme Court to get through New Deal measures. . . .

"The Supreme Court has proved many of the New Deal proposals as unconstitutional. Instead of the ample alternatives of the Constitution by which these proposals could be submitted to the people through constitutional amendment, it is now proposed to make changes by 'packing' the Supreme Court. It has the implication of subordination of the court to the personal power of the Executive."

Practice It!

The excerpt above is from the *New York Times* newspaper of February 6, 1937. Read the passage; then answer the following questions:

1. What point is the article trying to make?
2. Is the article reporting something on the scene or secondhand?
3. Does the article reflect bias or strong opinion about the issue?
4. Is only one side of the issue presented? Explain.

Apply It!

Think of a current issue in the news that is controversial or in which public opinion is divided. Read newspaper features and editorials and watch television reports on the issue. Can you identify biases? Which reports more fairly represent the issue and the solutions? Which reports are the most reliable?

Analyzing Primary and Secondary Sources

Why Learn This Skill?

To determine what happened in the past, historians do some detective work. They comb through bits of written and illustrated evidence from the past to reconstruct events. These bits of evidence are called *primary sources.* They are records of events made by people who witnessed them. Primary sources include letters, diaries, photographs, newspaper articles, and legal documents.

This textbook, like many other history books, is a secondary source. It was written by using primary sources to explain the topics covered. The value of a secondary source depends on how well the author has used primary sources. Learning to analyze secondary sources will help you figure out whether they are presenting topics completely and accurately.

Dr. Martin Luther King, Jr. ▶

1 Learn It!

To analyze a **primary source,** follow these steps:

> *We have waited for more than 340 years for our constitutional and God-given rights . . . [W]e still creep at horse and buggy pace toward gaining a cup of coffee at a lunch counter. Perhaps it is easy for those who have never felt the stinging darts of segregation to say, 'Wait.'. . . Let us all hope that the dark clouds of racial prejudice will soon pass away.*
>
> —Dr. Martin Luther King, Jr.
> Letter from Birmingham Jail, April 1963

1. Identify the author, the publication, or the document.

2. Determine when and where the document was written or illustrated.

3. Read the document or study the illustration for its content. Try to answer the five "W" questions:
Whom is it about?
What is it about?
When did it happen?
Where did it happen?
Why did it happen?

2 Practice It!

The primary source above is a small part of a letter written by civil rights leader Dr. Martin Luther King, Jr., while he was in an Alabama jail.

1. When was the letter written?

2. To whom do you think the letter was written?

3. Why do you think Dr. King wrote the letter?

4. How do you know this is a primary source and not a secondary source?

3 Apply It!

Find a primary source and a secondary source related to a single historical topic. In several paragraphs, compare and contrast the information presented in the two sources.

Analyzing Historical Maps

Why Learn This Skill?

Historical maps show a portion of the world at a specific time in history. These maps can show physical, political, economic, climatic, or cultural information as it relates to that time period. They are useful because of the concise, visual way they present information.

1 Learn It!

To read a historical map, follow these steps:

1. Read the title to see what topic is illustrated. The specific time period is often referenced in the title.

2. Read the legend and any other text.

3. Notice how any movement, routes, or other information is indicated on the map.

Candidate	Electoral Vote	Popular Vote	Political Party
Hayes	185	4,036,572	Republican
Tilden	184	4,284,020	Democrat

2 Practice It!

Answer the following questions about the map above:

1. What event and time in history does the map cover?

2. For whom did most Northern states vote?

3. In which states were the electoral votes disputed?

4. Why are there no numbers for electoral votes in the territories?

3 Apply It!

Study the United States Territorial Growth maps on pages Ref 10–Ref 11 in the front of your textbook. Then answer these questions:

1. In which general direction did growth take place?

2. What time period is covered in the last map?

Researching on the Internet

Why Learn This Skill?

Imagine that your teacher has sent you to the Internet to research and write a report about the current makeup of the United States Congress. Knowing how to locate and choose sources that contain accurate and current information will help save you time. You will also be able to write a better and more accurate report.

Joint meeting of Congress ▶

1 Learn It!

Information on the Internet varies widely in its relevance and quality. Not all sources will be useful for your report on members of the Senate and House of Representatives. After choosing a search engine and typing in your topic, follow these steps to help you evaluate and select Internet resources:

1. Locate the author of the Web site and assess his/her qualifications. Is the person or organization credible and legitimate?

2. Evaluate the accuracy of the information. Are the facts on the site documented? Does the site contain a bibliography?

3. Judge whether the information is biased. Does the author present only one point of view?

4. Determine how the information is presented. Are there helpful visuals? Does the text skim the surface or offer in-depth details?

5. Review when the site was last updated. Is the information current?

6. Look for a list of links to other useful resources. Is the information on those sites appropriate and reliable?

2 Practice It!

Look at the following list of sources. Which would be most helpful in writing a report on the United States Congress? Explain your choices.

1. An online encyclopedia written by anyone who wants to contribute

2. www.senate.gov, the home page for the U.S. Senate

3. A student's notes on the Internet about a family trip to Washington, D.C.

4. A government site on Congressional documents drawn up between 1774 and 1785

3 Apply It!

Log onto the Internet to create a bibliography of six sources you might use to write your report. Explain why you would choose each source. Make sure you include information about both the House of Representatives and the Senate, including a breakdown of the membership of each.

Interpreting a Political Cartoon

Why Learn This Skill?

Political cartoons express opinions through art. The cartoons appear in newspapers, magazines, books, and on the Internet. Political cartoons usually focus on public figures, political events, or economic or social conditions. This type of art can give you a summary of an event or circumstance, along with the artist's opinion in an entertaining way.

 Learn It!

Follow these steps to interpret a political cartoon:

1. Read the title, caption, or conversation balloons. They help you identify the subject of the cartoon.

2. Identify the characters, people, or symbols shown. Symbols are objects that stand for something else.

3. Examine the actions in the cartoon. Ask yourself: What is happening and why?

4. Identify the cartoonist's purpose; is it to persuade, criticize, or just make people think? What statement or idea is he or she trying to express?

SECESSIONISTS LEAVING THE UNION

 Practice It!

Study the cartoon above. Then answer these questions:

1. What is the subject of the cartoon?
2. What words give clues to the meaning of the cartoon?
3. What is happening in the cartoon?
4. What message do you think the cartoonist is trying to send?

Apply It!

Bring a newsmagazine to class. With a partner, analyze the message in each political cartoon you find.

Writing a Case Study

Why Learn This Skill?

Have you ever wondered what can be done to help keep your community clean? A case study on environmental clean-up and recycling would help define the issue and propose various solutions to the problem.

A case study is an in-depth analysis of a particular situation or problem that could apply to a broader field. It involves thorough research and interviews to gain a better understanding of a problem and to suggest solutions. In this example, a case study might be done on the placement of recycling bins for aluminum cans to determine that action's effect on the community. This type of research tool can help both the writer and reader gain a more extensive understanding of a situation.

1 Learn It!

To learn how to write a case study, follow these steps:

1. Treat the case study like a story: introduce the problem at the very beginning of the study in a manner intended to grab the reader's attention.

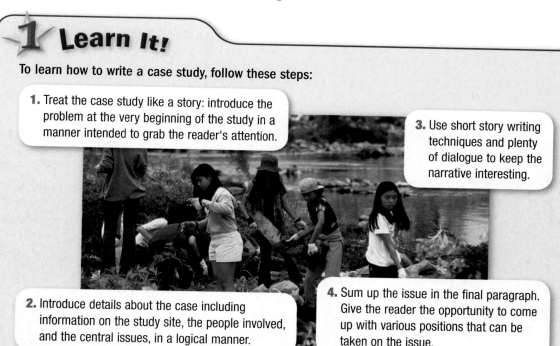

3. Use short story writing techniques and plenty of dialogue to keep the narrative interesting.

2. Introduce details about the case including information on the study site, the people involved, and the central issues, in a logical manner.

4. Sum up the issue in the final paragraph. Give the reader the opportunity to come up with various positions that can be taken on the issue.

2 Practice It!

Identify a situation or event described in this book that you think could be investigated as a case study. Write a case study in which you answer the following questions:

1. Is there a problem/issue that could apply to a broader group of people?

2. What are the major issues, and who is involved?

3. What solutions have been attempted and what others could be tried?

3 Apply It!

Research to find two sources of information on the topic of banning teenagers from using cell phones while driving. Create fictional characters that might be affected by a law like this. Use your sources and your imagination to write a one-page case study on the topic.

Presidents of the United States

In this resource, you will find portraits of the individuals who served as presidents of the United States, along with their occupations, political party affiliations, and other interesting facts.

George Washington ★1

Presidential term: 1789–1797
Lived: 1732–1799
Born in: Virginia
Elected from: Virginia
Occupations: Soldier, Planter
Party: None
Vice President: John Adams

John Adams ★2

Presidential term: 1797–1801
Lived: 1735–1826
Born in: Massachusetts
Elected from: Massachusetts
Occupations: Teacher, Lawyer
Party: Federalist
Vice President: Thomas Jefferson

Thomas Jefferson ★3

Presidential term: 1801–1809
Lived: 1743–1826
Born in: Virginia
Elected from: Virginia
Occupations: Planter, Lawyer
Party: Republican**
Vice Presidents: Aaron Burr, George Clinton

James Madison ★4

Presidential term: 1809–1817
Lived: 1751–1836
Born in: Virginia
Elected from: Virginia
Occupation: Planter
Party: Republican**
Vice Presidents: George Clinton, Elbridge Gerry

James Monroe ★5

Presidential term: 1817–1825
Lived: 1758–1831
Born in: Virginia
Elected from: Virginia
Occupation: Lawyer
Party: Republican**
Vice President: Daniel D. Tompkins

John Quincy Adams ★6

Presidential term: 1825–1829
Lived: 1767–1848
Born in: Massachusetts
Elected from: Massachusetts
Occupation: Lawyer
Party: Republican**
Vice President: John C. Calhoun

Andrew Jackson ★7

Presidential term: 1829–1837
Lived: 1767–1845
Born in: South Carolina
Elected from: Tennessee
Occupations: Lawyer, Soldier
Party: Democratic
Vice Presidents: John C. Calhoun, Martin Van Buren

Martin Van Buren ★8

Presidential term: 1837–1841
Lived: 1782–1862
Born in: New York
Elected from: New York
Occupation: Lawyer
Party: Democratic
Vice President: Richard M. Johnson

William H. Harrison ★9

Presidential term: 1841
Lived: 1773–1841
Born in: Virginia
Elected from: Ohio
Occupations: Soldier, Planter
Party: Whig
Vice President: John Tyler

** *The Republican Party during this period developed into today's Democratic Party. Today's Republican Party originated in 1854.*

John Tyler 10

Presidential term: 1841–1845
Lived: 1790–1862
Born in: Virginia
Elected as V.P. from: Virginia
Succeeded Harrison
Occupation: Lawyer
Party: Whig
Vice President: None

James K. Polk 11

Presidential term: 1845–1849
Lived: 1795–1849
Born in: North Carolina
Elected from: Tennessee
Occupation: Lawyer
Party: Democratic
Vice President: George M. Dallas

Zachary Taylor 12

Presidential term: 1849–1850
Lived: 1784–1850
Born in: Virginia
Elected from: Louisiana
Occupation: Soldier
Party: Whig
Vice President: Millard Fillmore

Millard Fillmore 13

Presidential term: 1850–1853
Lived: 1800–1874
Born in: New York
Elected as V.P. from: New York
Succeeded Taylor
Occupation: Lawyer
Party: Whig
Vice President: None

Franklin Pierce 14

Presidential term: 1853–1857
Lived: 1804–1869
Born in: New Hampshire
Elected from: New Hampshire
Occupation: Lawyer
Party: Democratic
Vice President: William R. King

James Buchanan 15

Presidential term: 1857–1861
Lived: 1791–1868
Born in: Pennsylvania
Elected from: Pennsylvania
Occupation: Lawyer
Party: Democratic
Vice President: John C. Breckinridge

Abraham Lincoln 16

Presidential term: 1861–1865
Lived: 1809–1865
Born in: Kentucky
Elected from: Illinois
Occupation: Lawyer
Party: Republican
Vice Presidents: Hannibal Hamlin, Andrew Johnson

Andrew Johnson 17

Presidential term: 1865–1869
Lived: 1808–1875
Born in: North Carolina
Elected as V.P. from: Tennessee
Succeeded Lincoln
Occupation: Tailor
Party: Republican
Vice President: None

Ulysses S. Grant 18

Presidential term: 1869–1877
Lived: 1822–1885
Born in: Ohio
Elected from: Illinois
Occupations: Farmer, Soldier
Party: Republican
Vice Presidents: Schuyler Colfax, Henry Wilson

Rutherford B. Hayes 19

Presidential term: 1877–1881
Lived: 1822–1893
Born in: Ohio
Elected from: Ohio
Occupation: Lawyer
Party: Republican
Vice President: William A.
Wheeler

James A. Garfield 20

Presidential term: 1881
Lived: 1831–1881
Born in: Ohio
Elected from: Ohio
Occupations: Laborer, Professor
Party: Republican
Vice President: Chester A.
Arthur

Chester A. Arthur 21

Presidential term: 1881–1885
Lived: 1830–1886
Born in: Vermont
Elected as V.P. from: New York
Succeeded Garfield
Occupations: Teacher, Lawyer
Party: Republican
Vice President: None

Grover Cleveland 22

Presidential term: 1885–1889
Lived: 1837–1908
Born in: New Jersey
Elected from: New York
Occupation: Lawyer
Party: Democratic
Vice President: Thomas A.
Hendricks

Benjamin Harrison 23

Presidential term: 1889–1893
Lived: 1833–1901
Born in: Ohio
Elected from: Indiana
Occupation: Lawyer
Party: Republican
Vice President: Levi P. Morton

Grover Cleveland 24

Presidential term: 1893–1897
Lived: 1837–1908
Born in: New Jersey
Elected from: New York
Occupation: Lawyer
Party: Democratic
Vice President: Adlai E.
Stevenson

William McKinley 25

Presidential term: 1897–1901
Lived: 1843–1901
Born in: Ohio
Elected from: Ohio
Occupations: Teacher, Lawyer
Party: Republican
Vice Presidents: Garret Hobart,
Theodore Roosevelt

Theodore Roosevelt 26

Presidential term: 1901–1909
Lived: 1858–1919
Born in: New York
Elected as V.P. from: New York
Succeeded McKinley
Occupations: Historian, Rancher
Party: Republican
Vice President: Charles W. Fairbanks

William H. Taft 27

Presidential term: 1909–1913
Lived: 1857–1930
Born in: Ohio
Elected from: Ohio
Occupation: Lawyer
Party: Republican
Vice President: James S.
Sherman

Presidents of the United States

Woodrow Wilson 28

Presidential term: 1913–1921
Lived: 1856–1924
Born in: Virginia
Elected from: New Jersey
Occupation: College Professor
Party: Democratic
Vice President: Thomas R. Marshall

Warren G. Harding 29

Presidential term: 1921–1923
Lived: 1865–1923
Born in: Ohio
Elected from: Ohio
Occupations: Newspaper Editor, Publisher
Party: Republican
Vice President: Calvin Coolidge

Calvin Coolidge 30

Presidential term: 1923–1929
Lived: 1872–1933
Born in: Vermont
Elected as V.P. from: Massachusetts; succeeded Harding
Occupation: Lawyer
Party: Republican
Vice President: Charles G. Dawes

Herbert C. Hoover 31

Presidential term: 1929–1933
Lived: 1874–1964
Born in: Iowa
Elected from: California
Occupation: Engineer
Party: Republican
Vice President: Charles Curtis

Franklin D. Roosevelt 32

Presidential term: 1933–1945
Lived: 1882–1945
Born in: New York
Elected from: New York
Occupation: Lawyer
Party: Democratic
Vice Presidents: John N. Garner, Henry A. Wallace, Harry S. Truman

Harry S. Truman 33

Presidential term: 1945–1953
Lived: 1884–1972
Born in: Missouri
Elected as V.P. from: Missouri Succeeded Roosevelt
Occupations: Clerk, Farmer
Party: Democratic
Vice President: Alben W. Barkley

Dwight D. Eisenhower 34

Presidential term: 1953–1961
Lived: 1890–1969
Born in: Texas
Elected from: New York
Occupation: Soldier
Party: Republican
Vice President: Richard M. Nixon

John F. Kennedy 35

Presidential term: 1961–1963
Lived: 1917–1963
Born in: Massachusetts
Elected from: Massachusetts
Occupations: Author, Reporter
Party: Democratic
Vice President: Lyndon B. Johnson

Lyndon B. Johnson 36

Presidential term: 1963–1969
Lived: 1908–1973
Born in: Texas
Elected as V.P. from: Texas Succeeded Kennedy
Occupation: Teacher
Party: Democratic
Vice President: Hubert H. Humphrey

Richard M. Nixon 37

Presidential term: 1969–1974
Lived: 1913–1994
Born in: California
Elected from: New York
Occupation: Lawyer
Party: Republican
Vice Presidents: Spiro T. Agnew,
Gerald R. Ford

Gerald R. Ford 38

Presidential term: 1974–1977
Lived: 1913–2006
Born in: Nebraska
Appointed as V.P. upon Agnew's
resignation; succeeded Nixon
Occupation: Lawyer
Party: Republican
Vice President: Nelson A. Rockefeller

James E. Carter, Jr. 39

Presidential term: 1977–1981
Lived: 1924–
Born in: Georgia
Elected from: Georgia
Occupations: Business, Farmer
Party: Democratic
Vice President: Walter F.
Mondale

Ronald W. Reagan 40

Presidential term: 1981–1989
Lived: 1911–2004
Born in: Illinois
Elected from: California
Occupations: Actor, Lecturer
Party: Republican
Vice President: George H.W. Bush

George H.W. Bush 41

Presidential term: 1989–1993
Lived: 1924–
Born in: Massachusetts
Elected from: Texas
Occupation: Business
Party: Republican
Vice President: J. Danforth Quayle

William J. Clinton 42

Presidential term: 1993–2001
Lived: 1946–
Born in: Arkansas
Elected from: Arkansas
Occupation: Lawyer
Party: Democratic
Vice President: Albert Gore, Jr.

George W. Bush 43

Presidential term: 2001–
Lived: 1946–
Born in: Connecticut
Elected from: Texas
Occupation: Business
Party: Republican
Vice President: Richard B. Cheney

Presidents of the United States

Supreme Court Case Summaries

CONTENTS

Brown v. Board of Education
1954

In *Brown* v. *Board of Education of Topeka, Kansas,* the Supreme Court overruled *Plessy* v. *Ferguson* (1896) making the separate-but-equal doctrine in public schools unconstitutional. The Supreme Court rejected the idea that truly equal but separate schools for African American and white students would be constitutional. The Court explained that the Fourteenth Amendment's requirement that all persons be guaranteed equal protection of the law is not met simply by ensuring that African American and white schools "have been equalized . . . with respect to buildings, curricula, qualifications and salaries, and other tangible factors."

The Court then ruled that racial segregation in public schools violates the Equal Protection Clause of the Constitution because it is inherently unequal. In other words, the very fact of separation marks the separated race as inferior. The Court's decision has been extended beyond public education to virtually all public facilities and activities.

George E.C. Hayes, Thurgood Marshall, and James Nabrit, Jr., were attorneys who argued the case against segregation in *Brown* v. *Board of Education.*

Bush v. Gore
2000

The 2000 presidential election was hanging in the balance as the state of Florida recounted their disputed ballots. Candidates George W. Bush, Republican, and Al Gore, Democrat, were so close in the polls that there was a manual recount of the votes.

Bush went to the Court to stop the recount, stating that it violated the Fourteenth Amendment. The Court ruled that since the manual recount had no uniform way to judge each disputed vote equally, it did violate the Constitution and had to be stopped. As a result, Bush won Florida's electoral votes and became president.

Dred Scott v. Sandford
1857

Dred Scott was taken by slaveholder John Sanford to the free state of Illinois and to the Wisconsin Territory, which had also banned slavery. Later they returned to Missouri, a slave state. Several years later, Scott sued for his freedom under the Missouri legal principle of "once free, always free." In other words, under Missouri law enslaved people were entitled to freedom if they had lived in a free state at any time. Missouri courts ruled against Scott, but he appealed the case all the way to the United States Supreme Court.

The Supreme Court decided this case before the Fourteenth Amendment was added to the Constitution. (The Fourteenth Amendment provides that anyone born or naturalized in the United States is a citizen of the nation and of his or her state of residence.) The Court held that enslaved African Americans were property, not citizens, and thus had no rights under the Constitution. The decision also overturned the Missouri Compromise of 1820, which

Dred Scott

had outlawed slavery in territories north of 36° 30' latitude. Many people in the North were outraged by the decision, which moved the nation closer to civil war.

Furman v. Georgia
1972

This decision put a halt to the application of the death penalty under state laws then in effect. For the first time, the Supreme Court ruled that the death penalty amounted to cruel and unusual punishment, which is outlawed in the Constitution. The Court explained that existing death penalty laws did not give juries enough guidance in deciding whether or not to impose the death penalty. As a result, the death penalty in many cases was imposed arbitrarily, that is, without a reasonable basis in the facts and circumstances of the offender or the crime.

The *Furman* decision halted all executions in the 39 states that had death penalty laws at that time. Since the decision, 38 states have rewritten death penalty laws to meet the requirements established in the *Furman* case.

Gibbons v. Ogden
1824

Thomas Gibbons had a federal license to operate a steamboat along the coast, but he did not have a license from the state of New York to travel on New York waters. He wanted to run a steamboat line between Manhattan and New Jersey that would compete with Aaron Ogden's company. Ogden had a New York license. Gibbons sued for the freedom to use his federal license to compete against Ogden on New York waters.

Gibbons won the case. The Supreme Court made it clear that the authority of Congress to regulate interstate commerce (among states) includes the authority to regulate intrastate commerce (within a single state) that bears on, or relates to, interstate commerce.

Before this decision, it was thought a state could close its borders to interstate commerce. The Court affirmed, however, that a state can regulate purely internal commerce, but only Congress can regulate commerce having both intrastate and interstate dimensions.

Gideon v. Wainwright
1963

After being accused of robbery, Clarence Gideon, a poor man, could not afford to hire a lawyer. Gideon defended himself in a Florida court because the judge in the case refused to appoint a free lawyer. The jury found Gideon guilty. Eventually, Gideon appealed his conviction to the United States Supreme Court, claiming that, by failing to appoint a lawyer, the lower court had violated his rights under the Sixth and Fourteenth Amendments.

The Supreme Court agreed with Gideon. In *Gideon* v. *Wainwright* the Supreme Court held for the first time that poor defendants in criminal cases have the right to a state-paid attorney under the Sixth Amendment. The rule announced in this case has been refined to apply whenever the defendant, if convicted, can be sentenced to more than six months in jail or prison.

Hamdan v. Rumsfeld
2006

In 2004 the Bush administration began holding captured terrorist suspects at the American military base in Guantanamo Bay, Cuba. It insisted that these prisoners, as illegal enemy fighters, did not have the right of appeal to American courts. Instead, the president as commander in chief would create special military courts to hear their cases.

In 2006 the Supreme Court struck down this plan in *Hamdan* v. *Rumsfeld*. It argued that Bush's military courts, as they stood, violated both U.S. military law and international law regarding the treatment of prisoners of war. President Bush then asked Congress to pass legislation setting up military courts that met the Court's objections. Prisoners would have the right to see evidence against them, and any evidence obtained by torture would not be accepted in court. However, prisoners could be held indefinitely without trial if the military courts had determined they were being lawfully held.

In 1988 Congress officially apologized for the internment of Fred Korematsu (center) and other Japanese Americans.

Korematsu v. United States
1944

After the Japanese bombing of Pearl Harbor in 1941, thousands of Japanese Americans on the West Coast were forced to abandon their homes and businesses, and they were moved to internment camps in California, Idaho, Utah, Arizona, Wyoming, Colorado, and Arkansas. The prison-like camps offered poor food and cramped quarters.

The Supreme Court's decision in *Korematsu* v. *United States* upheld the authority of the federal government to move Japanese Americans, many of whom were citizens, from designated military areas that included almost the entire West Coast. The government defended the so-called exclusion orders as a necessary response to Japan's attack on Pearl Harbor. Only after his reelection in 1944 did President Franklin Roosevelt rescind the evacuation orders, and by the end of 1945 the camps were closed.

Marbury v. Madison
1803

During his last days in office, President John Adams commissioned William Marbury and several other men as judges. This action by Federalist president Adams angered the incoming Democratic-Republican president Thomas Jefferson. Jefferson then ordered James Madison, his secretary of state, not to deliver the commissions, thus blocking the appointments. William Marbury sued, asking the Supreme Court to order Madison to deliver the commission that would make him a judge.

The Court ruled that the Judiciary Act—the law that gave Marbury his appointment—was unconstitutional. More importantly, the *Marbury* decision established one of the significant principles of American constitutional law. The Supreme Court held that it is the Court itself that has the final say on what the Constitution means. The Court had secured for itself the power to review acts of Congress—the power of judicial review. It is also the Supreme Court that has the final say in whether or not an act of government—legislative or executive at the federal, state, or local level—violates the Constitution.

McCulloch v. Maryland
1819

Following the War of 1812, the United States experienced years of high inflation and general economic turmoil. In an attempt to stabilize the economy, the United States Congress chartered a Second Bank of the United States in 1816. Maryland and several other states, however, opposed the competition that the new national bank created and passed laws taxing its branches. In 1818 James McCulloch, head of the Baltimore branch of the Second Bank of the United States, refused to pay the tax to the state of Maryland. The case worked its way through the Maryland state courts all the way to the United States Supreme Court.

The Supreme Court declared the Maryland tax unconstitutional and void. More importantly, the decision established the foundation for expanded congressional authority. The Court held that the necessary and proper clause of the Constitution allows Congress to do more than the Constitution expressly authorizes it to do. The decision allows Congress to enact nearly any law that will help it achieve any of its duties as set forth in the Constitution. For example, Congress has the express authority to regulate interstate commerce. The necessary and proper clause permits Congress to do so in ways not actually specified in the Constitution.

Minnesota v. Mille Lacs Band of Chippewa Indians
1999

An 1855 Treaty with the United States set aside lands in present-day Minnesota and Wisconsin to several Chippewa bands as reservations at Mille Lacs but made no mention of, among other things, whether it abolished rights guaranteed by previous treaties. Minnesota was admitted to the Union in 1858. In 1990 the Mille Lacs Band and several members sued Minnesota, its Department of Natural Resources, and state officials (collectively State), seeking, among other things, a declaratory judgment that they retained their ownership rights to the land without state interference. The District Court ultimately concluded that the Chippewa retained their claim under the 1837 Treaty and resolved several resource allocation and regulation issues. The State's argument under the "equal footing doctrine," that Minnesota's entrance into the Union in 1855 extinguished any Indian treaty rights, was considered void. The Supreme Court ruled in favor of the Chippewa and the existing 1837 treaty.

In 1963 the arrest of Ernesto Miranda (left) led to a landmark decision.

Miranda v. Arizona
1966

In 1963 police in Arizona arrested Ernesto Miranda for kidnapping. The court found Miranda guilty on the basis of a signed confession. The police admitted that neither before nor during the questioning had Miranda been advised of his right to consult with an attorney before answering any questions or of his right to have an attorney present during the interrogation. Miranda appealed his conviction, claiming that police had violated his right against self-incrimination under the Fifth Amendment by not informing him of his legal rights during questioning.

Miranda won the case. The Supreme Court held that a person in police custody cannot be questioned unless told that he or she has: 1) the right to remain silent, 2) the right to an attorney (at government expense if the accused is unable to pay), and 3) that anything the person says after stating that he or she understands these rights can be used as evidence of guilt at trial. These rights have come to be called the Miranda warning. They are intended to ensure that an accused person in custody will not unknowingly give up the Fifth Amendment's protection against self-incrimination.

New York Times v. United States
1971

In June 1971, the *New York Times* published its first installment of the "Pentagon Papers," a classified document about government actions in the Vietnam War era. The secret document had been leaked to the *Times* by antiwar activist Daniel Ellsberg, who had previously worked in national security for the government. President Richard Nixon went to court to block further publication of the Pentagon Papers. The *New York Times* appealed to the Supreme Court to allow it to continue publishing without government interference.

The Supreme Court's ruling in this case upheld earlier decisions establishing the doctrine of prior restraint. This doctrine protects the press (broadly defined to include newspapers, television and radio, filmmakers and distributors, etc.) from government attempts to block publication. Except in extraordinary circumstances, the press must be allowed to publish.

Plessy v. Ferguson
1896

In the late 1800s, railroad companies in Louisiana were required by state law to provide "separate-but-equal" cars for white and African American passengers. In 1890 a group of citizens in New Orleans selected Homer Plessy to challenge that law. In 1892 Plessy boarded a whites-only car and refused to move. He was arrested. Plessy appealed to the Supreme Court, arguing that the Louisiana separate-but-equal law violated his right to equal protection under the Fourteenth Amendment.

Homer Plessy lost the case. The *Plessy* decision upheld the separate-but-equal doctrine used by Southern states to perpetuate segregation following the Civil War. The court ruled that the Fourteenth Amendment's equal protection clause required only equal public facilities for the two races, not equal access to the same facilities. This decision was overruled in 1954 by *Brown* v. *Board of Education of Topeka, Kansas* (discussed previously).

Roe v. Wade
1973

Roe v. *Wade* challenged restrictive abortion laws in both Texas and Georgia. The suit was brought in the name of Jane Roe, an alias used to protect the privacy of the plaintiff.

In this decision, the Supreme Court ruled that females have a constitutional right under various provisions of the Constitution—most notably, the due process clause—to decide whether or not to terminate a pregnancy. The Supreme Court's decision in this case was the most significant in a long line of decisions over a period of 50 years that recognized a constitutional right of privacy, even though the word "privacy" is not found in the Constitution.

Tinker v. Des Moines School District
1969

During the Vietnam War, some students in Des Moines, Iowa, wore black armbands to school to protest American involvement in the conflict. Two days earlier, school officials had adopted a policy banning the wearing of armbands to school. When the students arrived at school wearing armbands, they were suspended and sent home. The students argued that school officials violated their First Amendment right to free speech.

The Supreme Court sided with the students. In a now-famous statement, the Court said that "it can hardly be argued that either students or teachers shed their constitutional rights of freedom of speech or expression at the schoolhouse gate." The Supreme Court went on to rule that a public school could not suspend students who wore black armbands to school to symbolize their opposition to the Vietnam War. In so holding, the Court likened the students' conduct to pure speech and decided it on that basis.

United States v. Nixon
1974

In the early 1970s, President Nixon was named an unindicted co-conspirator in the criminal investigation that arose in the aftermath of a break-in at the offices of the Democratic Party in Washington, D.C. A federal judge had ordered President Nixon to turn over tapes of conversations he had with his advisers about the break-in. Nixon resisted the order, claiming that the conversations were entitled to absolute confidentiality by Article II of the Constitution.

The decision in this case made it clear that the president is not above the law. The Supreme Court held that only those presidential conversations and communications that relate to performing the duties of the office of president are

confidential and protected from a judicial order of disclosure. The Court ordered Nixon to give up the tapes, which revealed evidence linking the president to the conspiracy to obstruct justice. He resigned from office shortly thereafter.

Worcester v. Georgia
1832

State officials in Georgia wanted to remove the Cherokee from land that was guaranteed to them in earlier treaties. Samuel Worcester was a congregational missionary who worked with the Cherokee people. He was arrested for failure to have a license that the state required to live in Cherokee country and for refusing to obey an order from the Georgia militia to leave Cherokee lands. Worcester then sued the state of Georgia. He claimed that Georgia had no legal authority on Cherokee land because the United States government recognized the Cherokee in Georgia as a separate nation.

The Supreme Court agreed with Worcester by a vote of 5 to 1. Chief Justice John Marshall wrote the majority opinion, which said that Native American nations were a distinct people with the right to have independent political communities and that only the federal government had authority over matters that involved the Cherokee.

President Andrew Jackson supported Georgia's efforts to remove the Cherokee to Indian Territory and refused to enforce the Court's ruling. After the ruling Jackson remarked, "John Marshall has made his decision. Now let him enforce it." As a result of Jackson's refusal to enforce the Court's order, thousands of Cherokee died on the long, forced trek to Indian Territory, known as the "Trail of Tears."

President Nixon encounters angry protesters in 1974 during the Watergate scandal.

The Magna Carta

The Magna Carta, signed by King John in 1215, marked a decisive step forward in the development of constitutional government in England. Later, it became a model for colonists who carried the Magna Carta's guarantees of legal and political rights to America.

1. . . . [T]hat the English Church shall be free, and shall have its rights entire, and its liberties unimpaired. . . . we have also granted for us and our heirs forever, all the liberties written out below, to have and to keep for them and their heirs, of us and our heirs:

39. No free man shall be seized or imprisoned, or stripped of his rights or possessions, or outlawed or exiled, or deprived of his standing in any other way, nor will we proceed with force against him, or send others to do so, except by the lawful judgment of his equals, or by the law of the land.

40. To no one will we sell, to no one deny or delay right or justice.

41. All merchants may enter or leave England unharmed and without fear, and may stay or travel within it, by land or water, for purposes of trade, free from all illegal exactions, in accordance with ancient and lawful customs. This, however, does not apply in time of war to merchants from a country that is at war with us. . . .

42. In future it shall be lawful for any man to leave and return to our kingdom unharmed and without fear, by land or water, preserving his allegiance to us, except in time of war, for some short period, for the common benefit of the realm. . . .

60. All these customs and liberties that we have granted shall be observed in our kingdom in so far as concerns our own relations with our subjects. Let all men of our kingdom, whether clergy or laymen, observe them similarly in their relations with their own men. . . .

63. . . . Both we and the barons have sworn that all this shall be observed in good faith and without deceit. Witness the abovementioned people and many others. Given by our hand in the meadow that is called Runnymede, between Windsor and Staines, on the fifteenth day of June in the seventeenth year of our reign.

Illuminated manuscript, Middle Ages

The Mayflower Compact

*On November 21, 1620, forty-one colonists aboard the **Mayflower** drafted this agreement. The Mayflower Compact was the first plan of self-government ever put in force in the English colonies.*

In the Name of God, Amen. We, whose names are underwritten, the Loyal Subjects of our dread Sovereign Lord King James, by the Grace of God, of Great Britain, France, and Ireland, King, Defender of the Faith, etc. Having undertaken for the Glory of God, and Advancement of the Christian Faith, and the Honour of our King and Country, a Voyage to plant the first Colony in the northern Parts of Virginia; Do by these Presents, solemnly and mutually, in the Presence of God and one another, covenant and combine ourselves together into a civil Body Politick, for our better Ordering and Preservation, and Furtherance of the Ends aforesaid: And by Virtue hereof do enact, constitute, and frame, such just and equal Laws, Ordinances, Acts, Constitutions, and Officers, from time to time, as shall be thought most meet and convenient for the general Good of the Colony; unto which we promise all due Submission and Obedience. In Witness whereof we have hereunto subscribed our names at Cape-Cod the eleventh of November, in the Reign of our Sovereign Lord King James, of England, France, and Ireland, the eighteenth, and of Scotland, the fifty-fourth, Anno Domini, 1620.

The Federalist, No. 10

James Madison wrote several articles supporting ratification of the Constitution for a New York newspaper. In the excerpt below, Madison argues for the idea of a federal republic.

By a faction, I understand a number of citizens . . . who are united and actuated by some common impulse . . . adverse to the rights of other citizens. . . .

The inference to which we are brought is that the causes of faction cannot be removed and that relief is only to be sought in the means of controlling its effects. . . .

A republic, by which I mean a government in which the scheme of representation takes place . . . promises the cure for which we are seeking. . . .

The two great points of difference between a democracy and a republic are: first, the delegation of the government, in the latter, to a small number of citizens elected by the rest; secondly, the greater number of citizens, and greater sphere of country, over which the latter may be extended.

James Madison

The effect of the first difference is . . . to refine and enlarge the public views, by passing them through the medium of a chosen body of citizens, whose wisdom may best discern the true interest of their country, and whose patriotism and love of justice will be least likely to sacrifice it to temporary or partial considerations. . . .

Washington's Farewell Address

At the end of his second term as president, George Washington spoke of the dangers facing the young nation. He warned against the dangers of political parties and sectionalism, and he advised the nation against permanent alliances with other nations.

. . . Citizens by birth or choice of a common country, that country has a right to concentrate your affections. The name of American, which belongs to you in your national capacity, must always exalt the just pride of patriotism more than any appellation derived from local discriminations. With slight shades of difference, you have the same religion, manners, habits, and political principles. You have in a common cause fought and triumphed together. . . .

In contemplating the causes which may disturb our union it occurs as matter of serious concern that any ground should have been furnished for characterizing parties by geographical discriminations. . . .

No alliances, however strict, between the parts can be an adequate substitute. They must inevitably experience the infractions and interruptions which all alliances in all times have experienced. . . .

George Washington

The great rule of conduct for us in regard to foreign nations is, in extending our commercial relations to have with them as little political connection as possible. . . .

. . . I anticipate with pleasing expectation that retreat in which I promise myself to realize . . . the sweet enjoyment of partaking in the midst of my fellow citizens the benign influence of good laws under a free government—the ever-favorite object of my heart, and the happy reward, as I trust, of our mutual cares, labors, and dangers.

"The Star-Spangled Banner"

During the British bombardment of Fort McHenry during the War of 1812, a young Baltimore lawyer named Francis Scott Key was inspired to write the words to "The Star-Spangled Banner." Although it became popular immediately, it was not until 1931 that Congress officially declared "The Star-Spangled Banner" as our national anthem.

O! say can you see by the dawn's early light,
What so proudly we hailed at the twilight's last gleaming,
Whose broad stripes and bright stars through the perilous fight,
O'er the ramparts we watch'd, were so gallantly streaming?
And the Rockets' red glare, the Bombs bursting in air,
Gave proof through the night that our Flag was still there;
O! say does that star-spangled Banner yet wave,
O'er the Land of the free, and the home of the brave!

Documents of American History

The Monroe Doctrine

In 1823 President James Monroe proclaimed the Monroe Doctrine. Designed to end European influence in the Western Hemisphere, it became a cornerstone of United States foreign policy.

. . . With the existing colonies or dependencies of any European power we have not interfered and shall not interfere. But with the Governments who have declared their independence and maintained it, and whose independence we have, on great consideration and on just principles, acknowledged, we could not view any interposition for the purpose of oppressing them, or controlling in any other manner their destiny, by any European power in any other light than as the manifestation of any unfriendly disposition toward the United States. . . .

Our policy in regard to Europe, which was adopted at an early stage of the wars which have so long agitated that quarter of the globe, nevertheless remains the same, which is, not to interfere in the internal concerns of any of its powers; to consider the government de facto as the legitimate government for us; to cultivate friendly relations with it, and to preserve those relations by a frank, firm, and manly policy, meeting in all instances the just claims of every power, submitting to injuries from none. . . .

James Monroe

Memorial of the Cherokee Nation

The Indian Removal Act of 1830 called for the relocation of Native Americans to territory west of the Mississippi River. Cherokee leaders protested the policy.

We are aware that some persons suppose it will be for our advantage to remove beyond the Mississippi. We think otherwise. Our people universally think otherwise. . . .

We wish to remain on the land of our fathers. We have a perfect and original right to remain without interruption or molestation. The treaties with us, and laws of the United States made in pursuance of treaties, guaranty our residence and our privileges, and secure us against intruders. Our only request is, that these treaties may be fulfilled, and these laws executed. . . .

. . . We have been called a poor, ignorant, and degraded people. We certainly are not rich; nor have we ever boasted of our knowledge, or our moral or intellectual elevation. But there is not a man within our limits so ignorant as not to know that he has a right to live on the land of his fathers, in the possession of his immemorial privileges, and that this right has been acknowledged by the United States; nor is there a man so degraded as not to feel a keen sense of injury, on being deprived of his right and driven into exile. . . .

The Seneca Falls Declaration

One of the first documents to express the desire for equal rights for women is the Declaration of Sentiments and Resolutions, issued in 1848 at the Seneca Falls Convention in Seneca Falls, New York. Led by Lucretia Mott and Elizabeth Cady Stanton, the delegates adopted a set of resolutions that called for woman suffrage and opportunities for women in employment and education. Excerpts from the Declaration follow.

When, in the course of human events, it becomes necessary for one portion of the family of man to assume among the people of the earth a position different from that which they have hitherto occupied, but one to which the laws of nature and of nature's God entitle them, a decent respect to the opinions of mankind requires that they should declare the causes that impel them to such a course.

We hold these truths to be self-evident: that all men and women are created equal; that they are endowed by their Creator with certain inalienable rights; that among these are life, liberty, and the pursuit of happiness; that to secure these rights governments are instituted, deriving their just powers from the consent of the governed. Whenever any form of government becomes destructive of these ends, it is the right of those who suffer from it to refuse allegiance to it, and to insist upon the institution of a new government, laying its foundation on such principles, and organizing its powers in such form as to them shall seem most likely to effect their safety and happiness. Prudence, indeed, will dictate that governments long established should not be changed for light and transient causes; . . . But when a long train of abuses and usurpations, pursuing invariably the same object, evinces a design to reduce them under absolute despotism, it is their duty to throw off such government, and to provide new guards for their future security. . . .

The history of mankind is a history of repeated injuries and usurpations on the part of man toward woman, having in direct object the establishment of an absolute tyranny over her. To prove this, let facts be submitted to a candid world. . . .

Now, in view of the entire disfranchisement of one-half the people of this country, their social and religious degradation—in view of the unjust laws above mentioned, and because women do feel themselves aggrieved, oppressed, and fraudulently deprived of their most sacred rights, we insist that they have immediate admission to all the rights and privileges which belong to them as citizens of these United States. . . .

Elizabeth Cady Stanton

The Emancipation Proclamation

On January 1, 1863, President Abraham Lincoln issued the Emancipation Proclamation, which freed all enslaved people in states under Confederate control. The Proclamation was a step toward the Thirteenth Amendment (1865), which ended slavery in all of the United States.

. . . That on the 1st day of January, in the year of our Lord 1863, all persons held as slaves within any state or designated part of a state, the people whereof shall then be in rebellion against the United States, shall be then, thenceforward, and forever free; and the Executive Government of the United States, including the military and naval authority thereof, will recognize and maintain the freedom of such persons, and will do no act or acts to repress such persons, or any of them, in any efforts they may make for their actual freedom.

That the Executive will, on the 1st day of January aforesaid, by proclamation, designate the states and parts of states, if any, in which the people thereof, respectively, shall then be in rebellion against the United States; and the fact that any state, or the people thereof, shall on that day be in good faith represented in the Congress of the United States, by members chosen thereto at elections wherein a majority of the qualified voters of such states shall have participated, shall, in the absence of strong countervailing testimony, be deemed conclusive evidence that such state, and the people thereof, are not then in rebellion against the United States. . . .

And, by virtue of the power and for the purpose aforesaid, I do order and declare that all persons held as slaves within said designated states and parts of states are, and henceforward shall be, free; and that the Executive Government of the United States, including the military and naval authorities thereof, will recognize and maintain the freedom of said persons.

And I hereby enjoin upon the people so declared to be free to abstain from all violence, unless in necessary self-defense; and I recommend to them that, all cases when allowed, they labor faithfully for reasonable wages.

And I further declare and make known that such persons, of suitable condition, will be received into the armed service of the United States. . . .

And upon this act, sincerely believed to be an act of justice, warranted by the Constitution upon military necessity, I invoke the considerate judgement of mankind and the gracious favor of Almighty God. . . .

Abraham Lincoln

The Gettysburg Address

On November 19, 1863, President Abraham Lincoln gave a short speech at the dedication of a national cemetery on the battlefield of Gettysburg. His simple yet eloquent words expressed his hopes for a nation divided by civil war.

Four score and seven years ago our fathers brought forth on this continent a new nation, conceived in liberty, and dedicated to the proposition that all men are created equal.

Now we are engaged in a great civil war, testing whether that nation, or any nation so conceived and so dedicated, can long endure. We are met on a great battlefield of that war. We have come to dedicate a portion of that field as a final resting place for those who here gave their lives that that nation might live. It is altogether fitting and proper that we should do this.

But, in a larger sense, we can not dedicate—we can not consecrate—we can not hallow—this ground. The brave men, living and dead, who struggled here, have consecrated it far above our poor power to add or detract. The world will little note nor long remember what we say here, but it can never forget what they did here. It is for us, the living, rather, to be dedicated here to the unfinished work which they who fought here have thus far so nobly advanced. It is rather for us to be here dedicated to the great task remaining before us—that from these honored dead we take increased devotion to that cause for which they gave the last full measure of devotion; that we here highly resolve that these dead shall not have died in vain; that this nation, under God, shall have a new birth of freedom; and that government of the people, by the people, for the people, shall not perish from the earth.

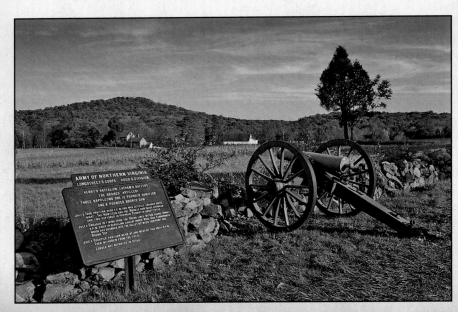

Current day photo of Gettysburg battlefield

I Will Fight No More

In 1877 the Nez Perce fought the government's attempt to move them to a smaller reservation. After a remarkable attempt to escape to Canada, Chief Joseph realized that resistance was hopeless and advised his people to surrender.

Tell General Howard I know his heart. What he told me before I have in my heart.

I am tired of fighting. . . . The old men are all dead. It is the young men who say yes or no. He who led the young men is dead. It is cold and we have no blankets. The little children are freezing to death. My people, some of them have run away to the hills, and have no blankets, no food; no one knows where they are—perhaps freezing to death. I want to have time to look for my children and see how many of them I can find. Maybe I shall find them among the dead. Hear me, my chiefs.

I am tired; my heart is sick and sad. From where the sun now stands I will fight no more forever.

Cheyenne shield

The Pledge of Allegiance

In 1892 the nation celebrated the 400th anniversary of Columbus's landing in America. In connection with this celebration, Francis Bellamy, a magazine editor, wrote and published the Pledge of Allegiance. The words "under God" were added by Congress in 1954 at the urging of President Dwight D. Eisenhower.

I pledge allegiance to the Flag of the United States of America and to the Republic for which it stands, one Nation under God, indivisible, with liberty and justice for all.

Students in a New York City school recite the Pledge of Allegiance.

The American's Creed

William Tyler Page of Friendship Heights, Maryland, wrote The American's Creed. This statement of political faith summarizes the true meaning of freedom available to all Americans. The U.S. House of Representatives adopted the creed on behalf of the American people on April 3, 1918.

I believe in the United States of America as a Government of the people, by the people, for the people; whose just powers are derived from the consent of the governed; a democracy in a republic; a sovereign Nation of many sovereign States; a perfect union, one and inseparable; established upon those principles of freedom, equality, justice, and humanity for which American patriots sacrificed their lives and fortunes.

I therefore believe it is my duty to my Country to love it, to support its Constitution, to obey its laws, to respect its flag, and to defend it against all enemies.

The Fourteen Points

On January 8, 1918, President Woodrow Wilson went before Congress to offer a statement of aims called the Fourteen Points. Wilson's plan called for freedom of the seas in peace and war, an end to secret alliances, and equal trading rights for all countries. The excerpt that follows is taken from the president's message.

. . . We entered this war because violations of right had occurred which touched us to the quick and made the life of our own people impossible unless they were corrected and the world secured once for all against their recurrence. What we demand in this war, therefore, is nothing peculiar to ourselves. It is that the world be made fit and safe to live in; and particularly that it be made safe for every peace-loving nation which, like our own, wishes to live its own life, determine its own institutions, be assured of justice and fair dealing by the other peoples of the world as against force and selfish aggression. All the peoples of the world are in effect partners in this interest, and for our own part we see very clearly that unless justice be done to others it will not be done to us. The program of the world's peace, therefore, is our program; and that program, the only possible program, as we see it, is this:

I. Open covenants of peace, openly arrived at, after which there shall be no private international understandings of any kind but diplomacy shall proceed always frankly and in the public view.

II. Absolute freedom of navigation upon the seas, outside territorial waters, alike in peace and in war, except as the seas may be closed in whole or in part by international action for the enforcement of international covenants.

XIV. A general association of nations must be formed under specific covenants for the purpose of affording mutual guarantees of political independence and territorial integrity to great and small states alike. . . .

Brown v. Board of Education

On May 17, 1954, the Supreme Court ruled in **Brown** *v.* **Board of Education of Topeka, Kansas,** *that racial segregation in public schools was unconstitutional. This decision provided the legal basis for court challenges to segregation in every aspect of American life.*

. . . The plaintiffs contend that segregated public schools are not "equal" and cannot be made "equal" and that hence they are deprived of the equal protection of the laws. Because of the obvious importance of the question presented, the Court took jurisdiction. . . .

Our decision, therefore, cannot turn on merely a comparison of these tangible factors in the Negro and white schools involved in each of the cases. We must look instead to the effect of segregation itself on public education.

In approaching this problem, we cannot turn the clock back to 1868 when the Amendment was adopted, or even to 1896 when *Plessy* v. *Ferguson* was written. We must consider public education in the light of its full development and its present place in American life throughout the Nation. Only in this way can it be determined if segregation in public schools deprives these plaintiffs of the equal protection of the laws.

Today, education is perhaps the most important function of state and local governments. Compulsory school attendance laws and the great expenditures for education both demonstrate our recognition of the importance of education to our democratic society. . . . In these days,

it is doubtful that any child may reasonably be expected to succeed in life if he is denied the opportunity of an education. Such an opportunity, where the state has undertaken to provide it, is a right which must be made available to all on equal terms.

We come then to the question presented: Does segregation of children in public schools solely on the basis of race, even though the physical facilities and other "tangible" factors may be equal, deprive the children of the minority group of equal educational opportunities? We believe that it does.

. . . We conclude that in the field of public education the doctrine of "separate but equal" has no place. Separate educational facilities are inherently unequal. Therefore, we hold that the plaintiffs and others similarly situated for whom the actions have been brought are, by reason of the segregation complained of, deprived of the equal protection of the laws guaranteed by the Fourteenth Amendment. . . .

Armed guards escort African American students.

John F. Kennedy's Inaugural Address

President Kennedy's Inaugural Address on January 20, 1961, set the tone for his administration. In his address Kennedy stirred the nation by calling for "a grand and global alliance" to fight tyranny, poverty, disease, and war.

We observe today not a victory of party but a celebration of freedom—symbolizing an end as well as a beginning—signifying renewal as well as change. For I have sworn before you and Almighty God the same solemn oath our forebears prescribed nearly a century and three-quarters ago.

The world is very different now. For man holds in his mortal hands the power to abolish all forms of human poverty and all forms of human life. And yet the same revolutionary beliefs for which our forebears fought are still at issue around the globe— the belief that the rights of man come not from the generosity of the state but from the hand of God.

We dare not forget today that we are the heirs of that first revolution. Let the word go forth from this time and place, to friend and foe alike, that the torch has been passed to a new generation of Americans—born in this century, tempered by war, disciplined by a hard and bitter peace, proud of our ancient heritage—and unwilling to witness or permit the slow undoing of those human rights to which this nation has always been committed, and to which we are committed today at home and around the world.

Let every nation know, whether it wishes us well or ill, that we shall pay any price, bear any burden, meet any hardship, support any friend, oppose any foe to assure the survival and the success of liberty.

This much we pledge—and more.

To those old allies whose cultural and spiritual origins we share, we pledge the loyalty of faithful friends. United, there is little we cannot do in a host of cooperative ventures. Divided, there is little we can do. . . .

Let us never negotiate out of fear. But let us never fear to negotiate.

Let both sides explore what problems unite us instead of belaboring those problems which divide us. . . .

Let both sides seek to invoke the wonders of science instead of its terrors. Together let us explore the stars, conquer the deserts, eradicate disease, tap the ocean depths, and encourage the arts and commerce. . . .

And so, my fellow Americans: ask not what your country can do for you—ask what you can do for your country.

My fellow citizens of the world: ask not what America will do for you, but what together we can do for the freedom of man. . . .

President Kennedy speaking at his inauguration

"I Have a Dream"

On August 28, 1963, while Congress debated wide-ranging civil rights legislation, Dr. Martin Luther King, Jr., led more than 200,000 people in a march on Washington, D.C. On the steps of the Lincoln Memorial he gave a stirring speech in which he eloquently spoke of his dreams for African Americans and for the United States. Excerpts of the speech follow.

. . . There are those who are asking the devotees of civil rights, "When will you be satisfied?"

We can never be satisfied as long as the Negro is the victim of the unspeakable horrors of police brutality. . . .

We cannot be satisfied as long as the Negro's basic mobility is from a smaller ghetto to a larger one. . . .

We can never be satisfied as long as a Negro in Mississippi cannot vote and a Negro in New York believes he has nothing for which to vote. . . .

I say to you today, my friends, that in spite of the difficulties and frustrations of the moment I still have a dream. It is a dream deeply rooted in the American dream. I have a dream that one day this nation will rise up and live out the true meaning of its creed: "We hold these truths to be self-evident, that all men are created equal."

I have a dream that one day on the red hills of Georgia the sons of former slaves and the sons of former slaveowners will be able to sit down together at the table of brotherhood.

I have a dream that one day even the state of Mississippi, a desert state sweltering with the heat of injustice and oppression, will be transformed into an oasis of freedom and justice.

I have a dream that my four little children will one day live in a nation where they will not be judged by the color of their skin but by the content of their character. . . .

. . . When we let freedom ring, when we let it ring from every village and every hamlet, from every state and every city, we will be able to speed up that day when all of God's children, black men and white men, Jews and Gentiles, Protestants and Catholics, will be able to join hands and sing in the words of the old Negro spiritual: "Free at last! Free at last! Thank God Almighty, we are free at last!"

Dr. Martin Luther King, Jr.

Glossary/Glosario

Content vocabulary are words that relate to American history content. Words that have an asterisk (*) are academic vocabulary. They help you understand your school subjects. All vocabulary words are **boldfaced and highlighted in yellow** in your textbook.

A

· · · · · · · · · · ENGLISH · · · · · · · · · ·

*abandon give up (pp. 189, 481)

abolitionist a person who strongly favors doing away with slavery (p. 425)

abstain to not take part in some activity, such as voting (p. 451)

*academy a private high school; school that provides specialized training (p. 531)

*access the ability to get to (p. 359)

*accumulate collect; gather together (p. 256)

*acquire to come to have as a new or added characteristic, trait, or ability (p. 31)

*adjust adapt (p. 520)

*aid to help (p. 161)

alien an immigrant living in a country in which he or she is not a citizen (p. 269)

alliance a close association of nations or other groups, formed to advance common interests or causes (p. 109)

*alter to change (p. 40)

ambush a surprise attack (p. 178)

*amend to alter; improve (pp. 199, 218)

amendment an addition to a formal document such as the Constitution (p. 210)

American System policies devised by Henry Clay to stimulate the growth of industry (p. 323)

amnesty the granting of pardon to a large number of persons; protection from prosecution for an illegal act (p. 519)

annex to add a territory to one's own territory (p. 371)

*approach move toward (p. 135)

archaeology the study of ancient peoples (p. 7)

arsenal a storage place for weapons and ammunition (p. 461)

· · · · · · · · · · ESPAÑOL · · · · · · · · · ·

*abandonar renunciar (págs. 189, 481)

abolicionista persona que apoya convincentemente la abolición de la esclavitud (pág. 425)

abstenerse no formar parte de algunas actividades, como votar (pág. 451)

*academia escuela secundaria privada; escuela que brinda capacitación especializada (pág. 531)

*acceder capacidad de alcanzar (pág. 359)

*acumular juntar; reunir (pág. 256)

*adquirir tener una característica, un rasgo o una aptitud nueva o adicional (pág. 31)

*ajustar adaptar (pág. 520)

*ayudar asistir (pág. 161)

extranjero inmigrante que vive en un país en el que no es ciudadano (pág. 269)

alianza asociación estrecha de las naciones u otros grupos, formada para fomentar intereses o causas comunes (pág. 109)

*alterar modificar (pág. 40)

emboscada ataque sorpresa (pág. 178)

*enmendar modificar; mejorar (págs. 199, 218)

enmienda adición a un documento formal como la Constitución (pág. 210)

Sistema estadounidense políticas creadas por Henry Clay para estimular el crecimiento de la industria (pág. 323)

amnistía otorgamiento del perdón a un gran número de personas; protección para no ser procesado por un acto ilegal (pág. 519)

anexar agregar un territorio al territorio propio (pág. 371)

*acercarse dirigirse hacia (pág. 135)

arqueología el estudio de pueblos antiguos (pág. 7)

arsenal lugar para el almacenaje de armas y municiones (pág. 461)

artifact an item left behind by early people that represents their culture (p. 7)

astrolabe an instrument used by sailors to observe positions of stars (p. 31)

***author** writer (p. 421)

***authority** power to decide; power to give orders and make decisions (p. 283)

artefacto artículos provenientes de antiguas civilizaciones que representan su cultura (pág. 7)

astrolabio instrumento usado por los marineros para observar las posiciones de las estrellas (pág. 31)

***autor** escritor (pág. 421)

***autoridad** poder para decidir; poder para dar órdenes y tomar decisiones (pág. 283)

backcountry a region of hills and forests west of the Tidewater (p. 94)

bicameral consisting of two houses, or chambers, especially in a legislature (p. 187)

black codes laws passed in the South just after the Civil War aimed at controlling freedmen and enabling plantation owners to exploit African American workers (p. 523)

blockade cut off an area by means of troops or warships to stop supplies or people from coming in or going out; to close off a country's ports (pp. 170, 477)

bond a note issued by the government, which promises to pay off a loan with interest (p. 256)

boomtown a community experiencing a sudden growth in business or population (p. 379)

border ruffian Missourian who traveled in armed groups to vote in Kansas's election during the mid-1850s (p. 455)

border state state between the North and the South that was divided over whether to stay in the Union or join the Confederacy (p. 475)

bounty money given as a reward, such as to encourage enlistment in the army (p. 496)

boycott to refuse to buy items from a particular country (p. 125)

***brief** short in duration (p. 410)

burgess elected representative to an assembly (p. 61)

zona rural región de colinas y bosques al oeste de Tidewater (pág. 94)

bicameral que consiste en dos cámaras, en especial en una asamblea legislativa (pág. 187)

códigos negros leyes aprobadas en el Sur después de la Guerra Civil que apuntaban al control de los libertos y permitían que los dueños de plantaciones explotaran a los trabajadores afroamericanos (pág. 523)

bloqueo aislamiento de un área por medio de tropas o barcos de guerra para impedir el ingreso o el egreso de suministros o personas; cierre de los puertos de un país (págs. 170, 477)

bono título emitido por el gobierno con la promesa de pagar un préstamo con intereses (pág. 256)

pueblo en bonanza comunidad que experimenta un crecimiento repentino en los negocios o la población (pág. 379)

rufianes fronterizos hombres de Missouri que viajaban en grupos armados para votar en las elecciones de Kansas a mediados de la década de 1850 (pág. 455)

estado fronterizo estado ubicado entre el Norte y el Sur dividido teniendo en cuenta si formaba parte de la Unión o de la Confederación (pág. 475)

recompensa dinero otorgado como premio, por ejemplo, para incentivar el enrolamiento en el ejército (pág. 496)

boicot negarse a comprar artículos de un país en particular (pág. 125)

***breve** de duración corta (pág. 410)

representante electo representante electo de una asamblea (pág. 61)

cabinet a group of advisers to the president (p. 253)

Californio Mexican who was one of the original settlers of California (p. 376)

canal an artificial waterway (p. 315)

gabinete grupo de consejeros del presidente (pág. 253)

californio mexicano que fue uno de los primeros pobladores de California (pág. 376)

canal vía artificial de agua (pág. 315)

Glossary/Glosario

*capable having the necessary abilities (p. 437)

capital money for investment (pp. 307, 403)

capitalism an economic system based on private property and free enterprise (p. 307)

carbon dating a scientific method used to determine the age of an artifact (p. 9)

carpetbagger northerner who moved to the South after the Civil War (p. 530)

cash crop farm crop raised to be sold for money (pp. 92, 539)

casualty a military person killed, wounded, or captured (p. 483)

caucus a meeting held by a political party to choose their party's candidate for president or decide policy (pp. 268, 340)

cede to give up by treaty (p. 377)

census official count of a population (p. 313)

*challenge demanding situation (pp. 261, 479)

*channel a trench or groove to allow the passage of water (p. 17)

*chart to map (p. 51)

charter a document that gives the holder the right to organize settlements in an area (p. 60)

charter colony colony established by a group of settlers who had been given a formal document allowing them to settle (p. 101)

checks and balances the system in which each branch of government has a check on the other two branches so that no one branch becomes too powerful (p. 208)

circumnavigate to sail around the world (p. 41)

civil disobedience refusal to obey laws that are considered unjust as a nonviolent way to press for changes (p. 421)

civilization a highly developed culture, usually with organized religions and laws (p. 11)

civil war conflict between citizens of the same country (p. 455)

clan a group united by a common interest or characteristic (p. 22)

classical relating to ancient Greece and Rome (p. 30)

*clause a condition added to a document (p. 191)

clipper ship a fast sailing ship with slender lines, tall masts, and large square sails (p. 390)

*capaz tener las habilidades necesarias (pág. 437)

capital dinero disponible para inversiones (págs. 307, 403)

capitalismo sistema económico basado en la propiedad privada y en la libre empresa (pág. 307)

datación por carbono método científico usado para determinar la antigüedad de un artefacto (pág. 9)

carpetbagger norteño que se trasladó al Sur después de la Guerra Civil (pág. 530)

cultivo comercial producto agrícola que se vende por dinero (págs. 92, 539)

víctima persona del ejército asesinada, herida o capturada (pág. 483)

caucus reunión celebrada por un partido político para elegir el candidato presidencial de su partido o definir una política (págs. 268, 340)

ceder renunciar por tratado (pág. 377)

censo registro oficial de una población (pág. 313)

*desafiar situación difícil (págs. 261, 479)

*canal fosa marina o surco para permitir el pasaje de agua (pág. 17)

*trazar un mapa hacer un mapa (pág. 51)

carta de privilegio documento que le otorga al poseedor el derecho de organizar los asentamientos en un área (pág. 60)

colonia con carta de privilegio colonia formada por un grupo de colonos que recibieron un documento formal que establece que pueden establecerse (pág. 101)

controles y balances sistema en que cada rama del gobierno controla a las otras dos ramas, de manera que ninguna de éstas pueda adquirir demasiado poder (pág. 208)

circunnavegar navegar por el mundo (pág. 41)

desobediencia civil rehusarse a obedecer las leyes que se consideran injustas, forma no violenta de exigir cambios (pág. 421)

civilización cultura muy evolucionada, generalmente con leyes y religiones organizadas (pág. 11)

guerra civil conflicto entre ciudadanos de un mismo país (pág. 455)

clan grupo unificado por un interés o una característica en común (pág. 22)

clásico relativo a las antiguas Grecia y Roma (pág. 30)

*cláusula condición anexada a un documento (pág. 191)

velero barco de vela rápido con líneas delgadas, mástiles altos y amplias velas cuadradas (pág. 390)

coeducation the teaching of male and female students together (p. 437)

Columbian Exchange exchange of goods, ideas, and people between Europe and the Americas (p. 51)

commence to begin (p. 375)

*__commission__ a group of persons directed to perform some duty (p. 536)

committee of correspondence an organization that spread political ideas through the colonies (p. 128)

*__community__ group of people living in a particular place (p. 396)

*__complex__ complicated; highly detailed (p. 11)

compromise agreement between two or more sides in which each side gives up some of what it wants (p. 200)

concurrent powers powers shared by the states and the federal government (p. 216)

Conestoga wagon large, broad-wheeled, canvas-covered wagon used by western settlers (p. 281)

*__conflict__ disagreement (p. 279)

conquistador Spanish explorer in the Americas in the 1500s (p. 43)

*__consequence__ result or effect of (p. 402)

constitution a list of fundamental laws to support a government (pp. 79, 187, 380)

*__contrast__ large degree of difference (p. 476)

*__contribute__ help to cause an event or situation (p. 305)

*__convention__ formal meeting (p. 198)

*__convert__ change religious beliefs (p. 105)

*__convince__ to persuade (someone) that something is true (p. 523)

corruption dishonest or illegal actions (p. 530)

cotton gin a machine that removed seeds from cotton fiber (pp. 306, 401)

coureur de bois French trapper living among Native Americans (p. 52)

*__credit__ a form of loan; ability to buy goods based on future payment (p. 530)

culture a way of life of a group of people who share similar beliefs and customs (p. 9)

customs duty tax on foreign imported goods (p. 278)

coeducación enseñanza conjunta de hombres y mujeres (pág. 437)

Intercambio Colombino intercambio de mercancías, ideas y gente entre Europa y las Américas (pág. 51)

comenzar empenzar (pág. 375)

*__comisión__ grupo de personas dirigidas para realizar tareas (pág. 536)

comité de correspondencia organización que divulga ideas políticas a través de las colonias (pág. 128)

*__comunidad__ grupo de personas que viven en un lugar en particular (pág. 396)

*__complejo__ complicado; sumamente detallado (pág. 11)

compromiso acuerdo entre dos o más partes en el que cada una de ellas renuncia a algo de lo que desea (pág. 200)

poderes concurrentes poderes compartidos por los estados y el gobierno federal (pág. 216)

carreta Conestoga carreta grande de ruedas anchas, cubierta con lona que usaban los colonos del oeste (pág. 281)

*__conflicto__ desacuerdo (pág. 279)

conquistador explorador español en las Américas en los años 1500 (pág. 43)

*__consecuencia__ resultado o efecto de (pág. 402)

constitución lista de leyes fundamentales para sostener un gobierno (págs. 79, 187, 380)

*__contraste__ amplio grado de diferencia (pág. 476)

*__contribuir__ ayudar a provocar un evento o una situación (pág. 305)

*__convención__ reunión formal (pág. 198)

*__convertir__ cambiar de creencias religiosas (pág. 105)

*__convencer__ persuadir (a alguien) de que algo es verdadero (pág. 523)

corrupción acciones ilegales o deshonestas (pág. 530)

desmotadora de algodón máquina que sacaba las semillas de las fibras de algodón (págs. 306, 401)

coureur de bois cazador francés que vivía entre nativoamericanos (pág. 52)

*__crédito__ una forma de préstamo; capacidad de comprar bienes en función de un pago futuro (pág. 530)

cultura estilo de vida de un grupo de personas que comparten creencias y costumbres similares (pág. 9)

derecho aduanero impuesto sobre los productos extranjeros importados (pág. 278)

D

*debate discussion by opposing points of view (p. 141)

debtor person or country that owes money (p. 80)

decree an order given by one in authority (p. 368)

depreciate to fall in value (p. 191)

depression a period of low economic activity and widespread unemployment (pp. 195, 350)

desert to leave without permission (p. 162)

*design a plan or course of action (p. 106)

*devote to commit by a solemn act (p. 39)

*diminish to lessen the authority, dignity, or reputation of (p. 223)

discrimination unfair treatment of a group; unequal treatment because of a person's race, religion, ethnic background, or place of birth (p. 396)

dissent disagreement with or opposition to an opinion (p. 65)

*distribute give out (p. 493)

draft the selection of persons for military service (p. 496)

*debate discusión al oponer puntos de vista (pág. 141)

deudor persona o país que debe dinero (pág. 80)

decreto orden otorgada por una autoridad (pág. 368)

desvalorizar reducir el valor (pág. 191)

depresión período de actividad económica baja y desempleo generalizado (págs. 195, 350)

desertar abandonar sin permiso (pág. 162)

*diseño plan o instrucciones para realizar algo (pág. 106)

*dedicarse comprometerse por un acto solemne (pág. 39)

*aminorar disminuir la autoridad, la dignidad o la reputación de (pág. 223)

discriminación trato injusto de un grupo; trato desigual debido a la raza, la religión, el origen étnico o el lugar de nacimiento de una persona (pág. 396)

disentimiento desacuerdo con una opinión u oposición a ésta (pág. 65)

*distribuir repartir (pág. 493)

llamamiento a filas selección de personas para el servicio militar (pág. 496)

E

effigy rag figure representing an unpopular individual (p. 125)

Electoral College a special group of voters selected by their state's voters to vote for the president and vice president (p. 207)

*element one part of a larger whole (p. 307)

embargo an order prohibiting trade with another country (p. 290)

emigrant a person who leaves a country or region to live elsewhere (p. 362)

empresario a person who arranged for the settlement of land in Texas during the 1800s (p. 367)

encomienda system of rewarding conquistadors with tracts of land and the right to tax and demand labor from Native Americans who lived on the land (p. 47)

*encounter to come upon; meet (pp. 127, 502)

entrenched occupying a strong defensive position (p. 499)

efigie figura que representa a un individuo impopular (pág. 125)

Colegio Electoral grupo especial de votantes seleccionados por los votantes de su estado para elegir al presidente y al vicepresidente (pág. 207)

*elemento parte de un entero (pág. 307)

embargo una orden que prohíbe el comercio con otro país (pág. 290)

emigrante persona que abandona un país o región para vivir en otro país (pág. 362)

empresario persona que disponía el asentamiento de la tierra en Texas durante los años 1800 (pág. 367)

encomienda sistema de recompensa a los conquistadores con extensiones de tierra y el derecho de cobrar impuestos y exigir trabajo de los nativoamericanos que vivían en el territorio (pág. 47)

*encuentro topar con; reunirse con (págs. 127, 502)

atrincherado que ocupa una fuerte posición defensiva (pág. 499)

Glossary/Glosario

enumerated powers powers belonging only to the federal government (p. 216)

*__establish__ to set up (p. 367)

*__estate__ property; land (p. 77)

*__estimate__ approximate number (p. 9)

*__ethnic__ pertaining to a group sharing a common culture (p. 74)

executive branch the branch of government, headed by the president, that carries out the nation's laws and policies (p. 207)

*__expand__ to increase in size or scope (p. 61)

export to sell goods abroad (pp. 99, 477)

poderes enumerados poderes que pertenecen sólo al gobierno federal (pág. 216)

*__establecer__ instalar (pág. 367)

*__propiedad__ finca, tierra (pág. 77)

*__estimación__ número aproximado (pág. 9)

*__étnico__ que pertenece a un grupo que comparte una cultura en común (pág. 74)

poder ejecutivo rama del gobierno, encabezada por el presidente, que maneja las leyes y las políticas de la nación (pág. 207)

*__expandir__ aumentar en tamaño o alcance (pág. 61)

exportar vender bienes en el exterior (págs. 99, 477)

factory system system bringing manufacturing steps together in one place to increase efficiency (p. 306)

famine an extreme shortage of food (p. 398)

*__federal__ the national or central governing authority (p. 343)

federalism the sharing of power between federal and state governments (pp. 206, 216)

federation a type of government that links different groups together (p. 21)

forty-niner person who went to California during the gold rush of 1849 (p. 379)

*__found__ establish or set up (p. 46)

free enterprise the freedom of private businesses to operate competitively for profit with minimal government regulation (p. 307)

frigate small warship (p. 296)

fugitive running away or trying to run away (p. 451)

*__function__ operate (p. 75)

Fundamental Orders of Connecticut the first written plan for a government in America (p. 68)

sistema de fábrica sistema que reúne las categorías de fabricación en un solo lugar para aumentar la eficiencia (pág. 306)

hambre escasez extrema de alimentos (pág. 398)

*__federal__ autoridad del gobierno nacional o central (pág. 343)

federalismo posesión conjunta del poder entre los gobiernos centrales y estatales (págs. 206, 216)

federación tipo de gobierno que une a diferentes grupos (pág. 21)

hombres del cuarenta y nueve persona que se trasladó a California durante la Fiebre del Oro de 1849 (pág. 379)

*__fundar__ instaurar o establecer (pág. 46)

libre empresa libertad de los negocios privados de operar de forma competitiva para obtener ganancias con regulación gubernamental mínima (pág. 307)

fragata buque de guerra pequeño (pág. 296)

fugitivo que se fuga o está tratando de fugarse (pág. 451)

*__funcionar__ operar (pág. 75)

Órdenes Fundamentales de Connecticut primer plan escrito para un gobierno de Estados Unidos (pág. 68)

*__globe__ the planet Earth (p. 51)

*__goal__ aim or purpose (p. 297)

*__mundo__ planeta Tierra (pág. 51)

*__meta__ objetivo o propósito (pág. 297)

Glossary/Glosario

grandfather clause a clause that allowed individuals who did not pass the literacy test to vote if their fathers or grandfathers had voted before Reconstruction began; an exception to a law based on preexisting circumstances (p. 539)

*grant special privilege or authority (p. 43)

greenback a piece of U.S. paper money first issued by the North during the Civil War (p. 497)

guerrilla tactics referring to surprise attacks or raids rather than organized warfare (p. 347)

guerrilla warfare a hit-and-run technique used in fighting a war; fighting by small bands of warriors using tactics such as sudden ambushes (p. 172)

cláusula del abuelo cláusula que permitía que los individuos que no aprobaban la prueba de alfabetización pudieran votar si sus padres o abuelos habían votado antes de que se iniciara la Reconstrucción; una excepción a la ley basada en circunstancias preexistentes (pág. 539)

*concesión privilegio o autoridad especial (pág. 43)

verdes billete estadounidense emitido por primera vez por el Norte durante la Guerra Civil (pág. 497)

tácticas de guerrilla se refiere a ataques sorpresa en lugar de técnicas militares organizadas (pág. 347)

guerra de guerrillas técnica de golpear y huir que se usaba para pelear una guerra; lucha de pequeños grupos de guerreros que usaban tácticas como emboscadas repentinas (pág. 172)

habeas corpus a legal order for an inquiry to determine whether a person has been lawfully imprisoned (p. 495)

headright a 50-acre grant of land given to colonial settlers who paid their own way (p. 61)

hieroglyphics an ancient form of writing using symbols and pictures to represent words, sounds, and concepts (p. 12)

hábeas corpus orden legal para una indagación con el fin de determinar si una persona ha sido arrestada injustamente (pág. 495)

interés concesión de 50 acres de tierra que se les dio a los colonos que pagaron a su manera (pág. 61)

jeroglíficos forma antigua de escritura con el uso de símbolos e imágenes para representar palabras, sonidos y conceptos (pág. 12)

*impact effect or influence (pp. 171, 487)

impeach to formally charge a public official with misconduct in office (p. 527)

implied powers powers not specifically mentioned in the Constitution (pp. 219, 266)

import to buy goods from foreign markets (p. 99)

*impose to establish or imply by authority (p. 32)

impressment forcing people into service, as in the navy (pp. 263, 289)

incorporate to include (p. 382)

indentured servant laborer who agreed to work without pay for a certain period of time in exchange for passage to America (p. 77)

*inevitable unavoidable (p. 455)

inflation a continuous rise in the price of goods and services (pp. 164, 497)

*innovation introduce something new (p. 389)

*institution an organization (p. 349)

*impacto efecto o influencia (págs. 171, 487)

impugnar denunciar formalmente a un funcionario público por mala conducta en el desempeño de su cargo (pág. 527)

poderes implícitos poderes no mencionados específicamente en la Constitución (págs. 219, 266)

importar comprar bienes de los mercados extranjeros (pág. 99)

*imponer establecer o inculpar por autoridad (pág. 32)

requisición captura de personas para el servicio militar, como en la armada naval (págs. 263, 289)

incorporar incluir (pág. 382)

sirviente por contrato trabajador que acepta trabajar sin que le paguen durante un período a cambio del pasaje a Estados Unidos (pág. 77)

*inevitable ineludible (pág. 455)

inflación aumento continuo en el precio de los bienes y los servicios (págs. 164, 497)

*innovación introducción de algo nuevo (pág. 389)

*institución organización (pág. 349)

Glossary/Glosario

integrate to end separation of different races and bring into equal membership in society (p. 531)

***intense** exhibiting strong feeling (p. 322)

interchangeable parts uniform pieces that can be made in large quantities to replace other identical pieces (p. 306)

***internal** within a location such as a nation or state (p. 322)

***interpret** to explain the meaning of (p. 509)

***involve** include (p. 221)

ironclad armored naval vessel (p. 483)

Iroquois Confederacy a powerful group of Native Americans in the eastern part of the United States made up of five nations: the Mohawk, Seneca, Cayuga, Onondaga, and Oneida (p. 105)

***issue** point or matter of discussion (p. 165)

integrar terminar la separación de diferentes razas e implantar la pertenencia igualitaria en la sociedad (pág. 531)

***intenso** que expresa sentimientos fuertes (pág. 322)

partes intercambiables partes uniformes que pueden fabricarse en grandes cantidades para reemplazar otras partes idénticas (pág. 306)

***interno** dentro de un lugar, como una nación o un estado (pág. 322)

***interpretar** explicar el significado de (pág. 509)

***implicar** incluir (pág. 221)

acorazado barco naval blindado (pág. 483)

Confederación Iroquesa grupo poderoso de nativoamericanos en la parte este de Estados Unidos compuesto de cinco naciones: mohawk, seneca, cayuga, onondaga y oneida (pág. 105)

***asunto** punto o tema de discusión (pág. 165)

joint occupation the possession and settling of an area shared by two or more countries (p. 359)

joint-stock company a company in which investors buy stock in the company in return for a share of its future profits (p. 60)

judicial branch the branch of government, including the federal court system, that interprets the nation's laws (p. 208)

judicial review the right of the Supreme Court to determine if a law violates the Constitution (p. 279)

***justify** find reason to support (p. 464)

ocupación en común posesión y asentamiento de un área compartida por dos o más países (pág. 359)

sociedad por acciones compañía en la que los inversores compran acciones en la compañía a cambio de una parte de sus ganancias futuras (pág. 60)

poder judicial rama del gobierno, incluido el sistema de tribunales federales, que interpreta las leyes de una nación (pág. 208)

revisión judicial derecho de la Corte Suprema a determinar si una ley viola la Constitución (pág. 279)

***justificar** encontrar razones para apoyar (pág. 464)

laissez-faire policy that government should interfere as little as possible in the nation's economy (pp. 278, 351)

***lecture** talk or speech given to an individual or a group for education or as a gentle scolding (p. 419)

***legal** permitted by law (p. 409)

legislative branch the branch of government that makes the nation's laws (p. 207)

***license** to grant official authority (p. 397)

line of demarcation an imaginary line running down the middle of the Atlantic Ocean from the North Pole to the South Pole dividing the Americas between Spain and Portugal (p. 41)

laissez-faire **(dejar hacer)** política que establece que el gobierno no debe interferir en la economía de una nación (págs. 278, 351)

***sermón** charla o discurso dirigido a un individuo o grupo con fines educativos o como reprimenda gentil (pág. 419)

***legal** permitido por ley (pág. 409)

poder legislativo rama del gobierno que dicta las leyes de una nación (pág. 207)

***autorizar** otorgar autoridad oficial (pág. 397)

línea de demarcación línea imaginaria a lo largo del océano Atlántico desde el Polo Norte al Polo Sur que divide a las Américas entre España y Portugal (pág. 41)

Glossary/Glosario

link join or connect (p. 13)

literacy ability to read and write (p. 412)

literacy test a method used to prevent African Americans from voting by requiring prospective voters to read and write at a specified level (p. 539)

lock in a canal, an enclosure with gates at each end used in raising or lowering boats as they pass from level to level (p. 316)

Loyalists American colonists who remained loyal to Britain and opposed the war for independence (p. 137)

lynching putting to death a person by the illegal action of a mob (p. 540)

vincular unir o conectar (pág. 13)

alfabetización capacidad de leer y escribir (pág. 412)

prueba de alfabetización método usado para impedir que los afroamericanos votaran al exigirles a los votantes futuros un nivel específico de lectura y escritura (pág. 539)

esclusa en un canal, un cercamiento con puertas en cada extremo usadas para elevar o bajar barcos al pasar de un nivel a otro (pág. 316)

partidarios colonos americanos que permanecieron leales a Gran Bretaña y se opusieron a la guerra por la independencia (pág. 137)

linchamiento muerte de una persona por la acción ilegal de una banda (pág. 540)

maintain keep or uphold (p. 261)

maize an early form of corn grown by Native Americans (p. 9)

majority more than half (p. 337)

Manifest Destiny the idea popular in the United States during the 1800s that the country must expand its boundaries to the Pacific (p. 363)

manumission the freeing of some enslaved persons (p. 197)

martyr a person who sacrifices his or her life for a principle or cause (p. 461)

Mayflower Compact a formal document, written in 1620, that provided law and order to the Plymouth colony (p. 66)

medical health; pertaining to the practice of medicine (p. 431)

mercantilism the theory that a state's or nation's power depended on its wealth (p. 50)

mercenary paid soldier who serves in the army of a foreign country (p. 155)

Middle Passage a part of the Triangular trade when enslaved Africans were shipped to the West Indies (p. 91)

migration a movement of a large number of people into a new homeland (p. 8)

militia a group of civilians trained to fight in emergencies (pp. 107, 133)

ministry the office, duties, or functions of a minister (p. 438)

mantener conservar o preservar (pág. 261)

millo forma antigua de grano que cultivaban los nativoamericanos (pág. 9)

mayoría más de la mitad (pág. 337)

Destino Manifiesto idea popular en Estados Unidos durante los años 1800 que establecía que el país debía extender sus fronteras al Pacífico (pág. 363)

manumisión liberación de algunos esclavos (pág. 197)

mártir persona que sacrifica su vida por un principio o una causa (pág. 461)

Convenio de Mayflower documento formal, redactado en 1620, que le otorgó ley y orden a la colonia de Plymouth (pág. 66)

médico salud; perteneciente a la práctica de la medicina (pág. 431)

mercantilismo teoría que sostiene que el poder de una nación o un estado depende de su riqueza (pág. 50)

mercenario soldado pago que presta sus servicios en el ejército de un país extranjero (pág. 155)

Travesía intermedia parte del comercio triangular cuando los esclavos africanos se embarcaban hacia las Antillas (pág. 91)

migración traslado de un gran número de personas a una nueva tierra (pág. 8)

milicia grupo de civiles entrenados para luchar en emergencias (págs. 107, 133)

clerecía oficio, deberes o funciones de un pastor (pág. 438)

minutemen companies of civilian soldiers who boasted that they were ready to fight on a minute's notice (p. 134)

mission religious settlement (pp. 46, 82)

Morse code a system for transmitting messages that uses a series of dots and dashes to represent the letters of the alphabet, numbers, and punctuation (p. 392)

mosque a Muslim house of worship (p. 33)

mountain man a frontiersman living in the mountain wilderness (p. 360)

minutemen compañías de soldados civiles que se jactaban de estar listos para pelear de un momento a otro (pág. 134)

misión asentamiento religioso (págs. 46, 82)

código Morse sistema de transmisión de mensajes que utiliza una serie de puntos y rayas para representar letras del alfabeto, números y puntuación (pág. 392)

mezquita casa de culto musulmana (pág. 33)

hombre montañés colonizador que vive en áreas montañosas naturales (pág. 360)

N

national debt the amount of money a national government owes to other governments or its people (p. 255)

nationalism intense loyalty to one's nation or group and promotion of its interests above all others (p. 293)

nativist a person who favors those born in his country and is opposed to immigrants (p. 399)

*network an interconnected system of people or things (p. 453)

neutral rights the right to sail the seas and not take sides in a war (p. 289)

neutrality a position of not taking sides in a conflict (p. 262)

*nevertheless however (p. 501)

nomad person who moves from place to place in search of food or grazing land (p. 8)

nominating convention system in which delegates from the states selected the party's presidential candidate (p. 340)

nonimportation the act of not importing or using certain goods (p. 125)

normal school a two-year school for training high school graduates as teachers (p. 420)

Northwest Passage water route to Asia through North America sought by European explorers (p. 51)

nullify to cancel or make ineffective (pp. 270, 341)

deuda nacional cantidad de dinero que un gobierno nacional debe a otros gobiernos o a su población (pág. 255)

nacionalismo lealtad intensa a una nación o a un grupo y promoción de los intereses por encima de todos (pág. 293)

nativista persona que apoya a las personas nacidas en su país y que se opone a los inmigrantes (pág. 399)

*red sistema interconectado de personas o cosas (pág. 453)

derechos neutrales derecho a navegar en el mar sin tomar partido en una guerra (pág. 289)

neutralidad no tomar partido en un conflicto (pág. 262)

*no obstante sin embargo (pág. 501)

nómada persona que se traslada de un lugar a otro en búsqueda de alimentos o tierras para pastoreo (pág. 8)

convención nominadora sistema en el que los delegados de los estados seleccionaban el candidato presidencial del partido (pág. 340)

no importación no importar o usar ciertos bienes (pág. 125)

escuela normal escuela de dos años para capacitar a los graduados de preparatoria par ser maestros (pág. 420)

Pasaje del Noroeste ruta marítima a Asia a través de América del Norte que buscaban los exploradores europeos (pág. 51)

anular cancelar o hacer inefectivo (págs. 270, 341)

O

*occupy to control (p. 127)

ordinance a law or regulation (p. 190)

*ocupar controlar (pág. 127)

ordenanza ley o regulación (pág. 190)

Glossary/Glosario

*outcome result (p. 536)

override to overturn or defeat, as a bill proposed in Congress (p. 524)

overseer person who supervises a large operation or its workers (pp. 94, 408)

*resultado desenlace (pág. 536)

anular revocar o derrotar, como un proyecto de ley propuesto en el Congreso (pág. 524)

capataz persona que supervisa una operación importante o a sus trabajadores (págs. 94, 408)

P

pacifist person opposed to the use of war or violence to settle disputes (p. 75)

*participate take part in (p. 340)

partisan favoring one side of an issue (p. 265)

patent a document that gives an inventor the sole legal right to an invention for a period of time (p. 306)

Patriot American colonist who favored American independence (p. 137)

patroon landowner in the Dutch colonies who ruled like a king over large areas of land (p. 73)

petition a formal request (pp. 140, 190)

Pilgrim Separatist who journeyed to the colonies during the 1600s for a religious purpose (p. 65)

pilgrimage a journey to a holy place (p. 33)

plantation a large estate run by an owner or manager and farmed by laborers who lived there (p. 47)

plurality largest single share (p. 337)

*plus in addition (p. 359)

*policy plan of action (p. 68)

poll tax a tax of a fixed amount per person that had to be paid before the person could vote (p. 539)

popular sovereignty political theory that government is subject to the will of the people (p. 215); before the Civil War, the idea that people living in a territory had the right to decide by voting if slavery would be allowed there (p. 454)

prairie schooner a covered wagon used by pioneers in cross-country travel (p. 362)

preamble the introduction to a formal document, especially the Constitution (pp. 142, 215)

precedent a tradition (p. 253)

prejudice an unfair opinion not based on facts (p. 396)

*previous earlier; coming before (p. 155)

pacifista persona que se opone al uso de guerras o violencia para solucionar conflictos (pág. 75)

*participar formar parte de (pág. 340)

partidista favorece un punto de vista de un asunto (pág. 265)

patente documento que le otorga al inventor el derecho exclusivo legal de una invención durante un período determinado (pág. 306)

patriota colono americano a favor de la independencia de Estados Unidos (pág. 137)

patroon terrateniente en las colonias holandesas que gobernaba como un rey en grandes extensiones de tierra (pág. 73)

petición solicitud formal (págs. 140, 190)

peregrino separatista que visitó las colonias durante los años 1600 para un propósito religioso (pág. 65)

peregrinación viaje a un lugar sagrado (pág. 33)

plantación propiedad extensa dirigida por un propietario o un administrador y cultivada por los trabajadores que vivían allí (pág. 47)

pluralidad parte mayor (pág. 337)

*más en suma (pág. 359)

*política plan de acción (pág. 68)

impuesto de votación impuesto de una cantidad fija por persona que debía pagarse para que una persona pudiera votar (pág. 539)

soberanía popular teoría política acerca de que el gobierno está sujeto a la voluntad de las personas (pág. 215); antes de la Guerra Civil, la idea de que las personas que vivían en un territorio tenían el derecho de decidir por votación si se permitiría la esclavitud en dicho lugar (pág. 454)

goleta de pradera una carreta cubierta usada por los pioneros en los viajes por el país (pág. 362)

preámbulo introducción a un documento formal, especialmente la Constitución (págs. 142, 215)

precedente tradición (pág. 253)

prejuicio opinión injusta no basada en los hechos (pág. 396)

*previo anterior, que antecede (pág. 155)

Glossary/Glosario

*principal** most important (p. 93)

principle basic or fundamental reason, truth, or law (p. 270)

privateer armed private ship licensed to attack merchant ships (pp. 170, 296)

process prepare (p. 402)

prohibit stop; disallow (p. 123)

propaganda ideas or information designed and spread to influence opinion (p. 127)

proportional to be the same as or corresponding to (p. 199)

proprietary colony colony run by individuals or groups to whom land was granted (pp. 74, 101)

prospect chance for success; outlook (p. 110)

pueblo home or community of homes built by Native Americans (pp. 17, 46)

purchase something bought and paid for (p. 283)

Puritans Protestants who, during the 1600s, wanted to reform the Anglican Church (p. 65)

pursue to continue (p. 177)

principal más importante (pág. 93)

principio razón básica o fundamental, verdad o ley (pág. 270)

corsario buque privado armado autorizados a atacar a barcos mercantes (págs. 170, 296)

procesar preparar (pág. 402)

prohibir detener; desaprobar (pág. 123)

propaganda ideas o información diseñadas y difundidas para influenciar la opinión (pág. 127)

proporcional ser lo mismo que o corresponder a (pág. 199)

colonia propietaria colonia dirigida por personas o grupos que recibían las tierras (págs. 74, 101)

perspectiva oportunidad de éxito; visión (pág. 110)

pueblo casa o comunidad de casas construidas por nativoamericanos (págs. 17, 46)

compra algo adquirido y pagado (pág. 283)

puritanos protestantes que, durante los años 1600, deseaban reformar la Iglesia Anglicana (pág. 65)

perseguir perseverar (pág. 177)

Q

Quechua language spoken by the Inca (p. 15)

quipu calculating device developed by the Inca (p. 15)

Quran the book composed of sacred writings accepted by Muslims as revelations made to Muhammad by Allah through the angel Gabriel (p. 33)

quechua idioma hablado por los incas (pág. 15)

kipu dispositivo para calcular diseñado por los incas (pág. 15)

Corán libro compuesto de escrituras sagradas aceptadas por los musulmanes como revelaciones hechas a Mahoma por Alá a través del ángel Gabriel (pág. 33)

R

radical extreme (p. 520)

ranchero Mexican ranch owner (p. 374)

rancho huge properties for raising livestock set up by Mexican settlers in California (p. 374)

ratify to give official approval to (p. 177)

react respond (p. 289)

Reconstruction the reorganization and rebuilding of the former Confederate states after the Civil War (p. 519)

recruit to enlist soldiers in the army (p. 155)

region an area inside a larger area (p. 314)

regulate to control (p. 450)

reject refuse to accept (p. 464)

radical extremo (pág. 520)

ranchero dueño de un rancho mexicano (pág. 374)

rancho vastas propiedades para la cría de ganado establecidas por pobladores mexicanos en California (pág. 374)

ratificar otorgar aprobación oficial a (pág. 177)

reaccionar responder (pág. 289)

reconstrucción reorganización y reconstrucción de los antiguos estados de la Confederación después de la Guerra Civil (pág. 519)

reclutar enrolar soldados al ejército (pág. 155)

región área dentro de un área más amplia (pág. 314)

regular controlar (pág. 450)

rechazar negarse a aceptar (pág. 464)

Glossary/Glosario

relocate to force a person or group of people to move (p. 343)

*rely depend (p. 89)

*remove take away (p. 368)

rendezvous a meeting (p. 360)

repeal to cancel an act or law (p. 125)

republic a government in which citizens rule through elected representatives (p. 188)

republicanism favoring a republic, or representative democracy, as the best form of government (p. 215)

reserved powers powers retained by the states (p. 216)

*reside to exist or live within (p. 208)

*resistance an opposing force (p. 509)

resolution a formal expression of opinion (p. 125)

*resolve bring to an end (p. 269)

*resource something used by people (p. 374)

*restriction limitation (p. 291)

*reveal show something that was hidden (p. 313)

revenue incoming money (p. 123)

revival a series of meetings conducted by a preacher to arouse religious emotions (p. 419)

*rigid firm and inflexible (p. 458)

*route line of travel (p. 430)

royal colony colony run by a governor and a council appointed by the king or queen (p. 101)

trasladar obligar a una persona o grupo de personas a trasladarse (pág. 343)

*confiar depender (pág. 89)

*quitar arrebatar (pág. 368)

encuentro reunión (pág. 360)

revocar cancelar una ley (pág. 125)

república gobierno en que los ciudadanos gobiernan a través de representantes electos (pág. 188)

republicanismo a favor de un república, o democracia representativa, como mejor forma de gobierno (pág. 215)

poderes reservados poderes conservados por los estados (pág. 216)

*residir existir o vivir dentro (pág. 208)

*resistencia fuerza opuesta (pág. 509)

resolución expresión formal de opinión (pág. 125)

*resolver poner fin (pág. 269)

*recurso algo usado por la gente (pág. 374)

*restricción limitación (pág. 291)

*revelar mostrar algo que estaba oculto (pág. 313)

ingresos dinero entrante (pág. 123)

renacimiento religioso serie de reuniones dirigidas por un predicador para incitar emociones religiosas (pág. 419)

*rígido firme e inflexible (pág. 458)

*ruta línea de viaje (pág. 430)

colonia real colonia dirigida por el gobernador y un consejo designado por el rey o la reina (pág. 101)

S

saga a long detailed story (p. 38)

scalawags name given by former Confederates to Southern whites who supported Republican Reconstruction of the South (p. 529)

secede to leave or withdraw (pp. 285, 341, 451)

secession withdrawal from the Union (p. 463)

sectionalism loyalty to a region (pp. 322, 449)

sedition activities aimed at weakening established government (p. 270)

segregation the separation or isolation of a race, class, or group (p. 540)

*select choose (p. 337)

Separatists Protestants who, during the 1600s, wanted to leave the Anglican Church in order to found their own churches (p. 65)

saga historia larga y detallada (pág. 38)

scalawags nombre otorgado por los primeros confederados a los blancos del Sur que apoyaban la Reconstrucción Republicana del Sur (pág. 529)

separarse abandonar o retirarse (págs. 285, 341, 451)

secesión retiro de la Unión (pág. 463)

seccionalismo lealtad a una región (págs. 322, 449)

sedición actividades dirigidas a debilitar un gobierno establecido (pág. 270)

segregación separación o aislamiento de una raza, clase o grupo (pág. 540)

*seleccionar elegir (pág. 337)

separatistas protestantes que, durante los años 1600, deseaban dejar la Iglesia Anglicana para fundar sus propias iglesias (pág. 65)

Glossary/Glosario

series a number of events coming in order (p. 507)

sharecropping system of farming in which a farmer works land for an owner who provides equipment and seeds and receives a share of the crop (p. 531)

siege military blockade (p. 505)

*****similar** having common qualities (p. 278)

slave codes laws passed in the Southern states that controlled and restricted enslaved people (pp. 94, 410)

*****source** a supply (p. 8)

speculator person who risks money in order to make a large profit (p. 112)

spiritual an African American religious folk song (p. 409)

spoils system practice of handing out government jobs to supporters; replacing government employees with the winning candidate's supporters (p. 340)

states' rights rights and powers independent of the federal government that are reserved for the states by the Constitution (p. 270); the belief that states' rights supersede federal rights and law (p. 464)

state sovereignty the concept that states have the right to govern themselves independent of the federal government (p. 322)

*****status** rank or position (p. 142)

strait a narrow passageway connecting two larger bodies of water (p. 41)

*****strategy** plan of action (p. 175)

strike a stopping of work by workers to force an employer to meet demands (p. 396)

*****structure** something that is constructed or built (p. 17)

subsistence farming farming in which only enough food to feed one's family is produced (p. 89)

*****substitute** replacement (p. 496)

*****successor** one who follows another in order (p. 99)

suffrage the right to vote (p. 435)

surplus excess; amount left over after necessary expenses are paid (p. 93)

*****survive** continue to live (p. 347)

*****suspend** to prevent or bar from carrying out official duties (p. 526)

serie un número de eventos que van en orden (pág. 507)

aparcería sistema de agricultura en el que el agricultor trabaja la tierra para un propietario que aporta el equipo y las semillas y recibe una parte de los cultivos (pág. 531)

sitio bloqueo militar (pág. 505)

*****similar** con las mismas cualidades (pág. 278)

códigos de esclavitud leyes aprobadas en los estados sureños que controlaban y clasificaban a los esclavos (págs. 94, 410)

*****fuente** un suministro (pág. 8)

especulador persona que arriesga dinero para obtener grandes ganancias (pág. 112)

espiritual canción popular religiosa afroamericana (pág. 409)

sistema de despojo práctica de repartir puestos gubernamentales a los defensores; reemplazo de empleados del gobierno con defensores del candidato triunfador (pág. 340)

derechos estatales derechos y poderes independientes del gobierno federal que se reservan para los estados a través de la Constitución (pág. 270); creencia acerca de que los derechos de los estados superan los derechos y las leyes federales (pág. 464)

soberanía estatal concepto acerca de que los estados tienen derecho a gobernarse independientemente del gobierno federal (pág. 322)

*****estatus** rango o posición (pág. 142)

estrecho pasadizo estrecho que conecta dos masas de agua mayores (pág. 41)

*****estrategia** plan de acción (pág. 175)

huelga cese laboral de los trabajadores para imponerle a un empleador el cumplimiento de las exigencias (pág. 396)

*****estructura** algo construido o fabricado (pág. 17)

agricultura de subsistencia agricultura en la que sólo se producen alimentos suficientes para abastecer a una familia (pág. 89)

*****sustituto** reemplazo (pág. 496)

*****sucesor** persona que sigue a otra en orden (pág. 99)

sufragio derecho a votar (pág. 435)

superávit exceso; cantidad que queda después de pagar los gastos necesarios (pág. 93)

*****sobrevivir** continuar con vida (pág. 347)

*****suspender** detener o prohibir la continuidad de las tareas de un funcionario (pág. 526)

Glossary/Glosario

*sustain to suffer or experience (p. 173)

*symbol an object that represents something else (p. 352)

*sufrir experimentar o sobrellevar (pág. 173)

*símbolo objeto que representa una cosa (pág. 352)

tariff a tax on imports or exports (pp. 257, 341)

*technology the use of science in commerce and industry (p. 31)

Tejano a Mexican who claims Texas as his home (p. 367)

telegraph a device or system that uses electric signals to transmit messages by a code over wires (p. 391)

temperance the use of little or no alcoholic drink (p. 419)

*temporary not lasting (p. 449)

tenant farmer farmer who works land owned by another and pays rent either in cash or crops (pp. 81, 407)

terrace a raised piece of land with the top leveled off to promote farming (p. 15)

theocracy a form of government in which the society is ruled by religious leaders (p. 12)

Tidewater a region of flat, low-lying plains along the seacoast (p. 94)

*topic subject of discussion (p. 460)

total war war on all aspects of the enemy's life (p. 507)

trade union organization of workers with the same trade or skill (p. 396)

*tradition cultural beliefs and practices (p. 205)

transcendentalist any of a group of New England writers who stressed the relationship between human beings and nature, spiritual things over material things, and the importance of the individual conscience (p. 421)

*transfer to move from one place to another (p. 155)

*transform to change (p. 391)

triangular trade a trade route that exchanged goods between the West Indies, the American colonies, and West Africa (p. 90)

tributary a smaller river that flows into a larger river (p. 482)

arancel impuesto sobre las importaciones o las exportaciones (págs. 257, 341)

*tecnología uso de ciencia en el comercio y la industria (pág. 31)

tejano mejicano que reclama Texas como su patria (pág. 367)

telégrafo dispositivo o sistema que usa señales eléctricas para transmitir mensajes mediante códigos y cableado (pág. 391)

templanza consumo de pocas bebidas alcohólicas o ninguna (pág. 419)

*temporal que no dura (pág. 449)

arrendatario agricultor que trabaja la tierra de otra persona y paga un alquiler en efectivo o mediante cultivos (págs. 81, 407)

terraza terreno elevado con el extremo superior nivelado para promover la agricultura (pág. 15)

teocracia forma de gobierno en la que la sociedad es gobernada por líderes religiosos (pág. 12)

Tidewater región de llanuras planas de baja altura a lo largo de la costa marina (pág. 94)

*tema objeto de discusión (pág. 460)

guerra total guerra en todos los aspectos de la vida del enemigo (pág. 507)

gremio organización de trabajadores con el mismo oficio o destreza (pág. 396)

*tradición creencias y prácticas culturales (pág. 205)

transcendentalista cualquier grupo de escritores de Nueva Inglaterra que enfatizaba la relación entre los seres humanos y la naturaleza, las cosas espirituales en lugar de las cosas materiales; y la importancia de la conciencia del individuo (pág. 421)

*transferir llevar de un lugar a otro (pág. 155)

*transformar modificar (pág. 391)

comercio triangular ruta comercial que intercambia bienes entre las Antillas, las colonias estadounidenses, y África Occidental (pág. 90)

afluente un río más pequeño que desemboca en un río más grande (pág. 482)

tribute money paid for protection (p. 287)

turnpike a road that one must pay to use; the money is used to pay for the road (p. 313)

tributo dinero que se paga a cambio de protección (pág. 287)

autopista ruta cuyo uso debe pagarse; el dinero se utiliza para pagar la ruta (pág. 313)

unconstitutional not agreeing or consistent with the Constitution (p. 257)

*****underestimate** misjudge; disbelieve the abilities of others (p. 295)

Underground Railroad a system that helped enslaved African Americans follow a network of escape routes out of the South to freedom in the North (p. 430)

*****uniform** identical; unchanging (p. 255)

utopia community based on a vision of a perfect society sought by reformers (p. 419)

inconstitucional que no concuerda ni concuerda con la Constitución (pág. 257)

*****subestimar** juzgar mal; desacreditar las capacidades de otros (pág. 295)

Ferrocarril Subterráneo sistema que ayudó a los esclavos afroamericanos a seguir una red de rutas de escape del Sur para obtener libertad en el Norte (pág. 430)

*****uniforme** que es idéntico; no se modifica (pág. 255)

utopía comunidad basada en una visión de la sociedad perfecta deseada por los reformadores (pág. 419)

veto to reject a bill and prevent it from becoming a law (p. 349)

vigilantes people who take the law into their own hands (p. 380)

*****violate** disturb or disregard (p. 124)

*****volunteer** willingly step forward (p. 136)

veto rechazar un proyecto de ley y evitar que se convierta en ley (pág. 349)

vigilantes personas que toman la ley en sus propias manos (pág. 380)

*****violar** alterar o hacer caso omiso (pág. 124)

*****voluntario** que tiene voluntad de avanzar (pág. 136)

writ of assistance legal document that enabled officers to search homes and warehouses for goods that might be smuggled (p. 123)

escritos de asistencia documento legal que le permitía a los funcionarios buscar casas y depósitos para almacenar los posibles productos de contrabando (pág. 123)

yeoman Southern owner of a small farm who did not have enslaved people (p. 407)

terrateniente menor propietario sureño de una pequeña granja que no tuvo esclavos (pág. 407)

Glossary/Glosario

Index

The following abbreviations are used in the index: m=map, c=chart, p=photograph or picture, g=graph, crt=cartoon, ptg=painting, q=quote.

A

Index

Index

Index

Index

Index

Index

Index

Index

Index

Index

Index

Index

Acknowledgments

Text Acknowledgments

Grateful acknowledgment is given authors, publishers, and agents for permission to reprint the following copyrighted material. Every effort has been made to determine copyright owners. In case of any omissions, the Publisher will be pleased to make suitable acknowledgments in future editions.

70 Excerpt from *The Witch of Blackbird Pond* by Elizabeth George Speare. Copyright © 1958, renewed 1986 by Elizabeth George Speare. Reprinted by permission of Houghton Mifflin Company. All rights reserved.; **130** From *My Name is America: The Journal of William Thomas Emerson—A Revolutionary War Patriot* by Barry Denenberg. Copyright © 1998 by Barry Denenberg. Reprinted by permission of Scholastic, Inc.; **310** Reprinted by permission of Simon & Schuster Books for Young Readers, an imprint of Simon & Schuster's Publishing Division, from *Fever, 1793* by Laurie Halse Anderson. Copyright © 2000 by Laurie Halse Anderson.; **404** From *Day of Tears* by Julius Lester. Copyright © 2005 by Julius Lester. Reprinted by permission of Hyperion Books for children. All rights reserved.; **421** "Hope is the thing with feathers" reprinted by permissions of the publishers and the Trustees of Amherst College from *The Poems of Emily Dickinson*, Thomas H. Johnson, ed., Cambridge, Mass.: The Belknap Press of Harvard University Press, copyright © 1951, 1955, 1979, 1983 by the President and Fellows of Harvard College.

Glencoe would like to acknowledge the artists and agencies who participated in illustrating this program: SettingPace; American Artists Reps Inc.; GeoNova LLC.

Photo Credits

Cover (t)Rubberball/Jupiterimages, (b)Museum of the City of New York/CORBIS; **IN4** Bettmann/CORBIS; **IN5** (l)Francis G. Mayer/CORBIS, (r)Tom Grill/CORBIS; **IN6** (l)David Muench/CORBIS, (r)CORBIS; **IN7** (tl)Getty Images, (tr)Brand X/CORBIS, (bl)The Granger Collection, New York, (br)The British Museum/HIP/The Image Works; **IN8** (t)Bettmann/CORBIS, (b)Hulton-Deutsch Collection/CORBIS; **IN9** (t)Bill Heinsohn/Alamy Images, (c)The Granger Collection, New York, (b)North Wind Picture Archives; **IN10** Art Archive/National Palace, Mexico City/Dagli Orti; **IN12** Collection of the New-York Historical Society/Bridgeman Art Library; **IN14** The Granger Collection, New York; **IN15** National Portrait Gallery, Smithsonian Institution/Art Resource, NY; **IN19** Getty Images; **IN38** (t)tompiodesign.com/Alamy Images, (b)Steve Vidler/SuperStock; **IN39** (l)Geoffrey Bryant/Photo Researchers, (r)age fotostock/SuperStock; **IN42–IN43** Richard Cummins/CORBIS; **Ref 16** (t)ThinkStock/SuperStock, (cl)Janet Foster/Masterfile, (cr)Mark Tomalty/Masterfile, (bl)age fotostock/SuperStock, (br)Jurgen Freund/Nature Picture Library; **Ref 18** (t)Dorling Kindersley/Getty Images, (b)Steve Skjold/Alamy Images; **0** Pilgrim Hall Museum; **0-1** Peabody Essex Museum, Salem, MA/Bridgeman Art Library; **4** (t)Frank Lukasseck/CORBIS, (c)Werner Forman/Topham/The Image Works (b)Liu Jianmin/Panorama/The Image Works; **5** (tl)Werner Forman/Topham/The Image Works, (tr)Indianapolis Museum of Art/Bridgeman Art Library, (b)The British Museum/Heritage-Images/The Image Works; **6-7** Kenneth Garrett; **8** Gianni Dagli Orti/CORBIS; **10-11** Jon Davison/Lonely Planet Images, Werner Forman/Topham/The Image Works; **12** Scala/Art Resource, NY; **13** (l)Archivo Iconografico, S.A./CORBIS; **14** (l)Craig Lovell/Eagle Visions Photography/Alamy Images, (r)Danita Delimont/Alamy Images; **16-17** Art Archive/Musée du Nouveau Monde La Rochelle/Dagli Orti; **17** Liu Jianmin/Panorama/The Image Works, Peabody Essex Museum, Salem, MA/Bridgeman Art Library; **18-19** Richard A. Cooke/CORBIS; **19** (t)Werner Forman/Topham/The Image Works, (c)Werner Forman/Art Resource, NY, (b)Michael S. Lewis/CORBIS; **20-21** Stock Montage/Alamy Images; **21** (t)Art Archive/Buffalo Bill Historical Center, Cody, WY/Mireille Vautier, (b)Werner Forman/Topham/The Image Works; **23** (t)Kenneth Garrett, (c)The British Museum/Heritage-Images/The Image Works, (b)Art Archive/Buffalo Bill Historical Center, Cody, WY/Mireille Vautier; **26** (t)Bettmann/CORBIS, (c)Kazuyoshi Nomachi/CORBIS, (b)Universitatsbibliothek, Gottingen, Germany, Bildarchiv Steffens/Bridgeman Art Library; **27** (t)Bettmann/CORBIS, (b)HIP/Art Resource, NY; **28** Roger-Viollet/The Image Works; **28-29** Bruno Morandi/Getty Images; **30** (l)Art Archive/Marine Museum, Lisbon/Dagli Orti, (r)akg-images; **30-31** Lockheed Martin; **31** Comstock/SuperStock; **32** (t)Heini Schneebeli/Bridgeman Art Library, (b)David Morris/Alamy Images; **34-35** Bettmann/CORBIS; **35** CORBIS; **36** Jack Sullivan/Alamy Images; **38** (t)Werner Forman/Art Resource, NY, (b)Bettmann/CORBIS; **39** (l)Art Archive/General Archive of the Indies, Seville/Dagli Orti, (r)Bridgeman-Giraudon/Art Resource, NY; **42-43** Ned Seidler/National Geographic Image Collection; **43** George H. H. Huey/CORBIS; **45** (tl)World History Archive/Alamy Images, (tr)The Granger Collection, New York, (b)Schomburg Center/Art Resource, NY, (br)Wendell Metzen/Index Stock Imagery; **46** (l)North Wind Picture Archives, (r)Art Archive/National Palace, Mexico City/Dagli Orti; **48-49** Musée des Ursulines de Québec, collection of the Monastère des Ursulines de Québec; **49** Hudson's Bay Company Archives, Provincial Archives of Manitoba; **50** C Squared Studios/Getty Images; **50-51** Pixtal/age fotostock; **53** (t)Art Archive/Marine Museum Lisbon/Dagli Orti, (cl)CORBIS, (c)Private Collection, Photo © Heini Schneebeli/Bridgeman Art Library, (r)Art Archive/General Archive of the Indies, Seville/Dagli Orti, (b)The Granger Collection, New York; **56** (t)Stock-Brazil/Alamy Images, (b)Musée de l'Armée/Dist. Réunion des Musées Nationaux/Art Resource, NY; **57** (t)Darrell Gulin/CORBIS, (b)Werner Forman/Art Resource, NY; **58-59** Private Collection/Bridgeman Art Library; **60** (l)North Wind Picture Archives, (r)The Granger Collection, New York; **62-63** David Muench/CORBIS; **63** The Granger Collection, New York; **64** Mary Evans Picture Library; **64-65** Swerve/Alamy Images; **65** Collection of the New-York Historical Society/Bridgeman Art Library; **66-67** The Granger Collection, New York; **70** Bettmann/CORBIS; **72** Stapleton Collection/CORBIS; **72-73** Library of Congress, Prints & Photographs Division, LC-USZC4-12217; **73** Henry Francis Dupont Winterthur Museum, Delaware/Bridgeman Art Library; **74** (l)The Granger Collection, New York, (r)Art Resource, NY; **76-77** The Granger Collection, New York; **78** (t)The Granger Collection, New York, (b)StockBrazil/Alamy Images; **79** The Granger Collection, New York; **80** (l)Schlesinger Library, Radcliffe Institute, Harvard University/Bridgeman Art Library, (r)Louis S. Glanzman/National Geographic Image Collection; **81** akg-images; **83** (tl)Swerve/Alamy Images, (tc)Collection of the New-York Historical Society/Bridgeman Art Library, (tr)MPI/Getty Images, (b)The Granger Collection, New York; **86** (t)SuperStock, (c)SSPL/The Image Works, (b)Art Archive/Lucien Biton Collection, Paris/Dagli Orti; **87** (t)National Portrait Gallery, London/Bridgeman Art Library, (b)The Granger Collection, New York; **88-89** Collection of the New-York Historical Society/Bridgeman Art Library; **89** James Leynse/CORBIS; **90** (l)Collection of the New-York Historical Society/Bridgeman Art Library, (c)SSPL/The Image Works, (r)North Wind Picture Archives; **92** Mary Evans Picture Library/The Image Works; **92-93** SuperStock; **93** Chicago History Museum/Bridgeman Art Library; **94** The Granger Collection, New York; **96** (l)North Wind Picture Archives/Alamy Images, (r)Mary Evans Picture Library/Alamy Images; **97** (t)North Wind Picture Archives/Alamy Images, (c)Jack Carey/Alamy Images, (b)CORBIS; **98-99** age fotostock/SuperStock; **99** The Colonial Williamsburg Foundation; **100** (l)Courtesy American Antiquarian Society, (r)The Granger Collection, New York; **100-101** The Granger Collection, New York; **102** Topham/The Image Works; **104-105** Artist Robert Griffing/Paramount Press Inc.; **106** Art Archive; **108-109** Art Archive/General Wolfe Museum, Quebec House/Eileen Tweedy; **109** (l)Stapleton Collection/CORBIS, (r)The Granger Collection, New York; **110** Geography & Map Division/Library of Congress; **110-111** SuperStock; **111** National Gallery of Canada, Ottawa, Ontario/Bridgeman Art Library; **113** (t)The Granger Collection, New York, (bc)Geography & Map Division/Library of Congress, (b)Collection of the New-York Historical Society/Bridgeman Art Library; **116** The National Archives/HIP/The Image Works; **116-117** SuperStock; **120** (t)SuperStock, (c)The Granger Collection, New York, (b)Ironbridge Gorge Museum, Telford, Shropshire, UK/Bridgeman Art Library; **121** (t)Maya Barnes Johansen/The Image Works, (tc)Massachusetts Historical Society, Boston/Bridgeman Art Library, (bc)Kevin Fleming/CORBIS, (b)Réunion des Musées Nationaux/Art Resource, NY; **122** Topham/The Image Works; **122-123** 126 Courtesy of the Massachusetts Historical Society; **126-127** Historic New England, Boston/Bridgeman Art Library; **127** Bettmann/CORBIS; **128** (l)Bettmann/CORBIS, (r)Massachusetts Historical Society, Boston/Bridgeman Art Library; **130** Library of Congress, Prints & Photographs Division, LC-USZC4-4971; **132-133** North Carolina Museum of Art/CORBIS; **133** Kevin Fleming/CORBIS; **134** Nichipor Collection, Courtesy Minuteman National Historical Park/Rob Huntley/Lightstream; **135** (l)Geoffrey Clements/CORBIS, (c)Kevin Fleming/CORBIS, (r)Bettmann/CORBIS; **136** (l)National Portrait Gallery, Smithsonian Institution/Art Resource, NY, (r)Collection of the New-York Historical Society/Bridgeman Art Library; **138-139** Francis G. Mayer/CORBIS; **139** CORBIS; **140** (t)American Antiquarian Society, Worcester, MA/Bridgeman Art Library, (b)National Portrait Gallery, London; **141** (l)Collection of the New-York Historical Society/Bridgeman Art Library, (c)Private Collection, Peter Newark American Pictures/Bridgeman Art Library, (r)SuperStock; **145** Art Archive; **147** CORBIS; **149** (l)CORBIS, (r)Bettmann/CORBIS; **150** (t)American Illustrators Gallery, NYC/Bridgeman Art Library, (c)Collection of the New-York Historical Society/Bridgeman Art Library, (b)Blanc Kunstverlag/SV-Bilderdienst/The Image Works; **151** (t)Painting by Don Troiani, photo courtesy Historical Art Prints, Ltd., (c)Former Grandidier collection Musée national des Arts asiatiques-Guimet G 956/Thierry Ollivier/RMN/Art Resource, NY; **152-153** The Granger Collection, New York; **153** Bob Krist/CORBIS; **154** The Granger Collection, New York; **155** Drew Crawford/The Image Works; **156-157** Bettmann/CORBIS; **157** The Granger Collection, New York; **158** 160-161 SuperStock; **161** The Metropolitan Museum of Art/Art Resource, NY; **162** (l)SuperStock, (r)Collection of the New-York Historical Society/Bridgeman Art Library; **163** (l)JG Photography/Alamy Images, (r)SuperStock; **164** Bettmann/CORBIS; **166** (l)TIME, (r)Stock Montage/Getty Images; **167** (l)Lebrecht Music and Arts Photo Library/Alamy Images, (r)Old Paper Studios/Alamy Images; **168** National Gallery of Canada, Ottawa, Ontario/Bridgeman Art Library; **168-169** Painting by Don Troiani, Military & Historical Image Bank; **169** The Granger Collection, New York; **170** (l)Guardian Royal Exchange Insurance Collection/The Bridgeman Art Library, (c)Bettmann/CORBIS, (r)National Trust Photographic Library/David Levenson/The Image Works; **171** The Granger Collection, New York; **172** 174-175 SuperStock; **175** Library of Congress, Prints & Photographs Division, LC-DIG-ppmsca-05936; **176** (l)Yale University Art Gallery/Art Resource, NY, (c)Ann Ronan Picture Library/HIP/The Image Works, (r)Art Media/HIP/The Image Works; **177** Stapleton Collection/CORBIS; **179** (tl)JG Photography/Alamy Images, (tr)SuperStock, (b)The Granger Collection, New York; **180** (l)Atwater Kent Museum of Philadelphia/Courtesy of Historical Society of Pennsylvania/Bridgeman Art Library, (c)Archivo Iconografico, SA/CORBIS, (r)Visual Arts Library (London)/Alamy Images; **181** (t)Visual Arts Library (London)/Alamy Images, (b)North Wind Picture Archives; **184** (t)Private Collection/Bridgeman Art Library, (b)Mervyn Rees/Alamy Images; **185** (t)Joseph Sohm; Visions of America/CORBIS, (tc b)The Granger Collection, New York, (bc)Bridgeman-Giraudon/Art Resource, NY; **186** Courtesy of the Massachusetts Historical Society; **186-187** The Granger Collection, New York; **187** Tom Grill/CORBIS; **188** 189 The Granger Collection, New York; **190-191** North Wind Picture Archives; **191** The Granger Collection, New York; **192** (t)Atwater Kent Museum of Philadelphia, Courtesy of Historical Society of Pennsylvania Collection/Bridgeman Art Library, (tc)StockBrazil/Alamy Images, (tr)The Granger Collection, New York, (bl)M Stock/Alamy Images, (br)The British Museum/HIP/The Image Works; **194-195** Stock Montage/Getty Images; **196** (l)NPS, (r)The Granger Collection, New York; **197** Museum of the City of New York/CORBIS; **198** 199 200 The Granger Collection, New York; **202** (l)Maya Barnes Johansen/The Image Works, (r)Bettmann/CORBIS; **203** (l)Smithsonian American Art Museum, Washington, DC/Art Resource, NY, (r)Joe Sohm/The Image Works; **204** SuperStock; **204-205** Michael Ventura/PhotoEdit; **205** The Granger Collection, New York; **206** (l)Getty Images, (r)The Granger Collection, New York; **207** Brand X/CORBIS; **208** The Granger Collection, New York; **209** (l)Réunion des Musées Nationaux/Art Resource, NY, (r)The Granger Collection, New York; **211** (t)Tom Grill/CORBIS, (tc)The Granger Collection, New York, (bc)Joseph Sohm; Visions of America/CORBIS, (b)Stock Montage/Getty Images; **214** PhotoDisc/Getty Images; **214-215** Steve Allen/Brand X Pictures/Jupiterimages; **215** Mark Wilson/Getty Images; **218** Private Collection, Peter Newark American Pictures/Bridgeman Art Library; **219** (l)Library of Congress, Prints & Photographs Division, LC-USZ62-8422, (r)Hassan Ammar/AFP/Getty Images; **221** Matthew Cavanaugh/epa/CORBIS; **224** (t)Bettmann/CORBIS, (c)Joe Sohm/Pan America/Jupiter Images, (b)Comstock/PunchStock; **226** White House Historical Association; **227** Herminio Rodriguez/AP Images; **228** Bettmann/CORBIS; **230** Boltin Picture Library; **244** Dennis Brack/Black Star/Time Life Pictures/Getty Images; **245** Sandy Schaeffer/Mai/Mai/Time Life Pictures/Getty Images; **246** Jeff Greenberg/The Image Works; **246-247** SuperStock; **250** (t)SuperStock, (c)The Granger Collection, New York, (b)akg-images; **251** (tl)The Granger Collection, New York, (tc)Roy Ooms/Masterfile, (tr)Hulton-Deutsch Collection/CORBIS, (bl)Free Agents Limited/CORBIS, (br)The Gallery Collection/CORBIS; **252-253** The Granger Collection, New York; **253** Charles Dharapak/AP Images; **256** Peabody Essex Museum, Salem, MA/Bridgeman Art Library; **258** (t bc)The Granger Collection, New York, (tc)North Wind Picture Archives/Alamy Images, (b)Private Collection/Stapleton Collection/Bridgeman Art Library; **259** (t)Uyen Le/Alamy Images, (tc)Julia Robertson/Aero Imaging, (bc)The New York Public Library/Art Resource, NY, (b)CORBIS; **260-261** Metropolitan Museum of Art, New York/Lauros/Giraudon/Bridgeman Art Library; **261** 262 The Granger Collection, New York; **264-265** The New York Public Library/Art Resource, NY; **265** Bettmann/CORBIS; **266** The Granger Collection, New York; **267** (l)The Granger Collection, New York, (r)Christie's Images/SuperStock; **268** Library of Congress, Prints & Photographs Division, LC-USZC4-2711; **269** American Antiquarian Society, Worcester,

MA/Bridgeman Art Library; **271** (t)The Granger Collection, New York, (c)The Granger Collection, New York, (b)Tom Grill/CORBIS; **273** CORBIS; **274** (t)imagebroker/Alamy Images, (bl)Library of Congress, Prints & Photographs Division, LC-USZC4-6051, (br)Borromeo/Art Resource, NY; **275** (t)Library of Congress, (b)The Granger Collection, New York; **276** Private Collection, Peter Newark American Pictures/Bridgeman Art Library; **276-277** Library of Congress, Prints & Photographs Division, LC-DIG-ppmsca-07708; **278** (l)Index Stock Imagery, (r)Monticello/Thomas Jefferson Foundation, Inc.; **280-281** David David Gallery/SuperStock; **282** Brown Brothers; **283** The Granger Collection, New York; **284** (l)Hulton Archive/Getty Images, (r)Clark Family Collection, William Clark Papers/Missouri Historical Society, St. Louis; **286** Smithsonian Institution; **286-287** Courtesy of the Naval Historical Foundation, Washington, DC; **287** US Navy Photo; **288** (l)The Mariners' Museum, Newport News, VA, (c)US Naval Academy Collection, (r)North Wind Picture Archives; **289** Private Collection, Photo © Christie's Images/Bridgeman Art Library; **290** The Granger Collection, New York; **292** (l)The Granger Collection, New York, (c)Ohio Historical Society, (r)Getty Images; **294-295** The Granger Collection, New York; **295** Collection of the New-York Historical Society/Bridgeman Art Library; **296** Troiani Collection; **297** The Granger Collection, New York, (c)Stock Montage/Getty Images; **299** (tl)Private Collection, Peter Newark American Pictures/Bridgeman Art Library, (tr c)The Granger Collection, New York, (cl)Brown Brothers, (cr)Troiani Collection, (b)U.S. Naval Academy Collection; **302** (t)Collection of the New-York Historical Society/Bridgeman Art Library, (c)The Granger Collection, New York, (b)Hermitage, St. Petersburg, Russia/Bridgeman Art Library; **303** (t)Smithsonian Institution/CORBIS, (bl)Clive Barda/PAL/The Image Works, (br)North Wind Picture Archives; **304-305** Bettmann/CORBIS; **305** University of Massachusetts Lowell, Center for Lowell History; **306** Smithsonian Institution, Washington DC/Bridgeman Art Library; **307** SSPL/The Image Works; **308** The Granger Collection, New York; **310** (l)Joyce Tenneson, (r)The Granger Collection, New York; **312-313** The Granger Collection, New York; **314** North Wind Picture Archives; **315** Brand X Pictures/PunchStock; **316** The Granger Collection, New York; **318** (t b)Bettmann/CORBIS, (c)North Wind Picture Archives/Alamy Images; **319** (t)Illustration Works/Getty Images, (c)Bettmann/CORBIS, (b)North Wind Picture Archives/Alamy Images; **320** Bettmann/CORBIS; **320-321** Fourth of July Celebration in Center Square by John Lewis Krimmel, 1819, India ink and watercolor, 31.5 x 46cm, (Bc882 K897), The Historical Society of Pennsylvania; **321** Gibson Stock Photography; **322** (l)The Corcoran Gallery of Art/CORBIS, (r)Massachusetts Historical Society, Boston/Bridgeman Art Library; **323** Christie's Images/Bridgeman Art Library; **325** (l)The Granger Collection, New York, (r)SuperStock; **327** (tl)Smithsonian Institution, Washington DC/Bridgeman Art Library, (tr)North Wind Picture Archives, (bl)SSPL/The Image Works, (br)The Granger Collection, New York; **330** Historical & Military Archive; **330-331** The Granger Collection, New York; **334** (t)Woolaroc Museum, Bartlesville, OK/SuperStock, (b)Taxi/Getty Images; **335** (t)Bettmann/CORBIS, (bl)Museum of London/HIP/The Image Works, (b)Hulton-Deutsch Collection/CORBIS; **336** Archivo Iconografico, S.A./CORBIS; **336-337** CORBIS SYGMA; **338** (l)David J. & Janice L. Frent Collection/CORBIS, (r)The Granger Collection, New York; **339** David J. & Janice L. Frent Collection/CORBIS; **340** Bettmann/CORBIS; **342** James Robinson/Earth Scenes; **342-343** North Wind Picture Archives; **344** Bettmann/CORBIS; **344-345** SuperStock; **345** (l)Library of Congress, Prints & Photographs Division, LC-USZC4-11120, (r)Buddy Mays/CORBIS; **346** (l)Print Collector/HIP/The Image Works, (r)North Wind Picture Archives; **348-349** The Granger Collection, New York; **350** Collection of the New-York Historical Society/Bridgeman Art Library; **351** (t b)The Granger Collection, New York, (c)Ohio Historical Society; **353** (t)Woolaroc Museum, Bartlesville, OK/SuperStock, (b)Bettmann/CORBIS; **355** National Museum of American History, Smithsonian Institution, Behring Center; **356** (t)Butler Institute of American Art, Youngstown, OH/Gift of Joseph G. Butler III 1946/Bridgeman Art Library, (bl)Unicorn Productions, (br)Photo Courtesy of the U.S. House of Representatives; **357** (tl)New Haven Colony Historical Society and Adams National Historic Site, (tr)CORBIS, (bl)Alinari Archives/The Image Works, (br)NASA; **358-359** Private Collection/Bridgeman Art Library; **359** Tria Giovan/CORBIS; **360** (l)Museum of the Mountain Man, (r)Walters Art Museum, Baltimore/Bridgeman Art Library; **361** (l)Courtesy National Park Service, (r)The Granger Collection, New York; **362** The Granger Collection, New York; **364** (l)The Granger Collection, New York, (r)Bettmann/CORBIS; **365** (l)The Granger Collection, New York, (r)Bettmann/CORBIS; **366-367** **367** The Center for American History, The University of Texas at Austin; **368** (l)Archives and Information Services Division, Texas State Library and Archives Commission, (r)The Granger Collection, New York; **368-369** Bettmann/CORBIS; **369** Bill Heinsohn/Alamy Images; **370** (l)The Granger Collection, New York, (r)Photo Courtesy of Beth Griggs/First Capitol Historical Foundation; **372-373** Art Archive/Bill Manns; **374** (l)Michael T. Sedam/CORBIS, (r)Painting by William Henry Jackson; William Henry Jackson Collection. Catalog No.SCBL_155. Scotts Bluff National Monument; **375** The Granger Collection, New York; **376** (l)Library of Congress, Prints & Photographs Division, LC-USZC2-2744, (r)From the collection of the Old State House Museum; **378-379** Bettmann/CORBIS; **380** The Granger Collection, New York; **381** (tl)Government Transfer: US DOTT, USM, (tr)Bettmann/CORBIS, (bl)Private Collection, Peter Newark Western Americana/Bridgeman Art Library, (br)Barry Howe/CORBIS; **383** Butler Institute of American Art, Youngstown, OH/Gift of Joseph G. Butler III 1946/Bridgeman Art Library, (cl)From the collection of the Old State House Museum, (c)Michael T. Sedam/CORBIS, (cr)Bettmann/CORBIS, (b)Private Collection, Peter Newark Western Americana/Bridgeman Art Library; **385** The Granger Collection, New York; **386** (t)Museum of the City of New York/Bridgeman Art Library, (c)The Granger Collection, New York, (b)Fritz Polking/The Image Works; **387** (t)The Granger Collection, New York, (b)SuperStock; **388-389** The Granger Collection, New York; **390** (l)Private Collection, Peter Newark American Pictures/Bridgeman Art Library, (tr)CORBIS, (bl)Bettmann/CORBIS, (br)Mike Simons/CORBIS; **391** (l)Collection of the New-York Historical Society/Bridgeman Art Library, (r)Ann Ronan Picture Library/Heritage-Images/The Image Works; **392** (l)The Granger Collection, New York, (r)The Image Works; **394-395** Museum of the City of New York/Bridgeman Art Library; **396** (l)The Granger Collection, New York, (r)age fotostock/SuperStock; **397** (t)David J. & Janice L. Frent Collection/CORBIS, (b)The Granger Collection, New York; **398** The Granger Collection, New York; **400-401** Private Collection, Peter Newark American Pictures/Bridgeman Art Library; **402** (l)SSPL/The Image Works, (r)The Granger Collection, New York; **404** (l)Julius Lester, (r)The Granger Collection, New York; **406-407** Reinhard Eisele/CORBIS; **407** Collection of the New-York Historical Society/Bridgeman Art Library; **408** The Granger Collection, New York; **409** Carlos Barria/Reuters/CORBIS; **410** (l)Alabama Department of Archives and History, Montgomery, Alabama, (c)CORBIS, (r)Louie Psihoyos/CORBIS; **411** (l)CORBIS, (r)The Granger Collection, New York; **413** (t)Private Collection, Peter Newark American Pictures/Bridgeman Art Library, (cl)The Granger Collection, New York, (cr)age fotostock/SuperStock, (b)CORBIS; **416** (t)City Art Museum, St. Louis, MO/Bridgeman Art Library, (b)Masterfile Royalty Free; **417** (t)Bettmann/CORBIS, (bl)Werner Forman/Art Resource, NY, (br)Snark/Art Resource, NY; **418-419** The Granger Collection, New York; **419** National Portrait Gallery, Smithsonian Institution/Art Resource, NY; **420** The Granger Collection, New York; **422** (t)Photo Researchers, (c)The Natural History Museum/Alamy Images, (b)TIME; **423** (l)North Wind Picture Archives/Alamy Images, (c)Bettmann/CORBIS, (r)D. Hurst/Alamy Images; **424-425** New York Historical Society; **425** Library of Congress, Prints & Photographs Division, LC-USZ62-119343; **426** (l)Library of Congress, Prints & Photographs Division, LC-USZC4-4609, (r)The Granger

Collection, New York; **427** Hulton-Deutsch Collection/CORBIS; **428 429** The Granger Collection, New York; **430** (l r)North Wind Picture Archives, (c)The Granger Collection, New York; **432** (t)Bettmann/CORBIS, (br)Louie Psihoyos/CORBIS, (bl)The Granger Collection, New York; **433** **434-435** **435** The Granger Collection, New York; **436** National Portrait Gallery, Smithsonian Institution/Art Resource, NY; **437** The Granger Collection, New York; **439** (t)The Granger Collection, New York, (b)National Portrait Gallery, Smithsonian Institution/Art Resource, NY; **441** Library of Congress, Prints & Photographs Division, LC-USZC4-2525; **442** Dave King/Dorling Kindersley/DK Images; **442-443** Bettmann/CORBIS; **446** (t)Library of Congress, Washington DC/Bridgeman Art Library, (tr)Chicago Historical Society, (b)SuperStock; **447** (t)SuperStock, (b)Roger-Viollet/The Image Works; **448-449** The Granger Collection, New York; **450** The Granger Collection, New York; **452-453** Smithsonian American Art Museum, Washington, DC/Art Resource, NY; **453** The Granger Collection, New York; **454** SuperStock; **456-457** The Granger Collection, New York; **457** Private Collection, Peter Newark American Pictures/Bridgeman Art Library; **458** (l) David J. & Janice L. Frent Collection/CORBIS, (c)CORBIS, (r)The Granger Collection, New York; **459** (l)CORBIS, (c)Andre Jenny/The Image Works, (r)Topham/The Image Works; **460** (l)Andre Jenny/The Image Works, (c)CORBIS, (r)Mary Evans Picture Library/The Image Works; **462-463** Mary Evans Picture Library; **463** Lee Snider/Photo Images/CORBIS; **464** The Granger Collection, New York; **465** Topham/The Image Works; **467** (tl)The Granger Collection, New York, (bl)Mary Evans Picture Library/The Image Works, (br)Library of Congress, Washington DC/Bridgeman Art Library; **468** CORBIS; **469** (l)Medford Historical Society Collection/CORBIS, (r)Bettmann/CORBIS; **470** Bettmann/CORBIS; **471** David J. & Janice L. Frent Collection/CORBIS; **472** (t)The Granger Collection, New York, (b)National Portrait Gallery, Smithsonian Institution/Art Resource, NY; **473** (t)Library of Congress, Prints & Photographs Division, LC-DIG-cwpb-03379, (b)CORBIS; **474-475** Bettmann/CORBIS; **476** CORBIS; **477** (t)Library of Congress, (b)Military and Historical Image Bank; **478** (l)Library of Congress, Prints & Photographs Division, LC-B8184-10575, (r)Bettmann/CORBIS; **480-481** **481** Bettmann/CORBIS; **483** (t)CORBIS, (c)MPI/Getty Images, (b)Hulton-Deutsch Collection/CORBIS; **484-485** Omikron/Photo Researchers; **486** (l)PhotoDisc, (r)Bettmann/CORBIS; **488** (t)Bettmann/CORBIS, (b)Historical Art Prints; **490** Courtesy Dennis M. Keesee Collection; **490-491** Medford Historical Society Collection/CORBIS; **491** CORBIS; **492** (t)Published courtesy of the Trustees of the Boston Public Library, (b)CORBIS; **493** The Granger Collection, New York; **494** Dr. Michael Echols, American Surgical Antiques; **494-495** Library of Congress, Prints & Photographs Division, LC-DIG-cwpb-03950; **495** (l)Michael Macor/San Francisco Chronicle/CORBIS, (r)Irish Gant/Getty Images; **496** (t)David A. Northcott/CORBIS, (b)The Granger Collection, New York; **498** Bettmann/CORBIS; **498-499** MPI/Getty Images; **499** (t)Old Paper Studios/Alamy Images, (b)Library of Congress, Prints & Photographs Division, LC-DIG-cwpb-05665; **500-501** CORBIS; **501** Kean Collection/Getty Images; **502** National Portrait Gallery, Smithsonian Institution/Art Resource, NY; **503** (t)David Muench/CORBIS, (c)The Granger Collection, New York, (b)Military and Historical Image Bank; **504** **506** CORBIS; **506-507** Library of Congress; **508** **509** CORBIS; **511** Eliot Elisofon/Time Life Pictures/Getty Images; **513** (tl)Michigan Capitol Committee, photography by Peter Glendinning, (tr)The Museum of the Confederacy, Richmond, Virginia/Photography by Katherine Wetzel, (c)CORBIS, (bl)Library of Congress, (br)Creatas Images/Jupiterimages; **515** **516** (t)The Granger Collection, New York, (bl)Chris Willson/Alamy Images, (br)Musee Marmottan, Paris/Giraudon/Bridgeman Art Library; **517** (t)National Portrait Gallery, Smithsonian Institution/Art Resource, NY, (b)Hulton-Deutsch Collection/CORBIS; **518** Bettmann/CORBIS; **518-519** Picture History; **519** CORBIS; **520** (l)CORBIS, (r)The Granger Collection, New York; **522-523** North Wind Picture Archives; **523** The Granger Collection, New York; **524** (others)Bettmann/CORBIS, (tr)Larry Downing/newscom/REUTERS; **525** Bettmann/CORBIS; **526** The Granger Collection, New York; **528** Courtesy of Special Collections, LSU Libraries, Louisiana State University; **528-529** Bettmann/CORBIS; **529** Brooklyn Museum/CORBIS; **530** (l)Time Life Pictures/Getty Images, (r)Hulton Archive/Getty Images; **532** (l)Photo Researchers, (r)North Wind Picture Archives/Alamy Images; **533** (t)CORBIS, (c)Mary Evans Picture Library/Alamy Images, (b)Bettmann/CORBIS; **534** Library of Congress, Prints & Photographs Division, LC-DIG-cwpbh-04425; **534-535** North Wind Picture Archives; **537** Bettmann/CORBIS; **538** (l)Bettmann/CORBIS, (r)The Granger Collection, New York; **541** (l)Bettmann/CORBIS, (r)The Granger Collection, New York; **542** Bettmann/CORBIS; **543** (t)Library of Congress, Prints & Photographs Division, LC-USZ62-104925, (tc)CORBIS, (b)CORBIS; **545** CORBIS; **546** The Granger Collection, New York; **546-547** SuperStock; **549** Private Collection, Peter Newark American Pictures/Bridgeman Art Library; **550** Alvah C. Roebuck/CORBIS; **552** Paul Thompson/Topical Press Agency/Getty Images; **553** David J. & Janice L. Frent Collection/CORBIS; **554-555** Bettmann/CORBIS; **556** (l)National Motor Museum/HIP/The Image Works, (r)Image courtesy of The Toaster Museum Foundation, www.toaster.org; **558** (inset)Library of Congress, Prints & Photographs Division, LC-USZ62-69109, (bkgd)AP Images; **560** (l)Bernard Hoffman/Time Life Pictures/Getty Images, (r)National Archives/CORBIS; **560-561** CORBIS; **563** (l)CORBIS, (c)Library of Congress/Getty Images, (r)Hulton-Deutsch Collection/CORBIS; **564** Don Cravens/Time Life Pictures/Getty Images; **564-565** Hulton Archive/Getty Images; **565** (t)Charles Moore/Black Star, (b)Paul Schutzer/Time Life Pictures/Getty Images; **566** Charles Gatewood/The Image Works; **568** (tl)Dennis Brack/Black Star, (tr)Steve Northup/Time Life Pictures/Getty Images, (b)Wally McNamee/CORBIS; **569** Alex Webb/Magnum Photos; **571** Matt Cardy/Getty Images; **572** Bob Daemmrich/Photo Edit; **574** (cw from top)Joseph Sohm/Jupiterimages, dynamicgraphics/Jupiterimages, Library of Congress, Brand X/Punchstock, PhotoDisc/Getty Images, National Archives; **576** (cw from top)PhotoDisc/Getty Images, Clark Family Collection, William Clark Papers/Missouri Historical Society, St. Louis, The Granger Collection, New York, PhotoDisc/Getty Images, Image Source/Jupiterimages, (bkgd)Fototeca Storica Nazionale/Getty Images; **577** Roger-Viollet/The Image Works; **578** (l)Billy Rose Theater Collection, The New York Public Library for the Performing Arts, Astor, Lenox and Tilden Foundations, (r)The Granger Collection, New York; **579** (t)Bettmann/CORBIS, (b)Digital Image © The Museum of Modern Art/Licensed by SCALA/Art Resource, NY; **580** The Granger Collection, New York; **581** Bettmann/CORBIS; **582** AP Images; **583** Topham/The Image Works; **584** Superstock; **586** The Granger Collection, New York; **587** Library of Congress, Prints & Photographs Division, LC-USZ62-119343; **590** White House Historical Association; **591** Bettmann/CORBIS; **593** (t)Sandy Schaeffer/Mai/Mai/Time Life Pictures/Getty Images, (b)Erin Patrice O'Brien/Getty Images; **594** The Granger Collection, New York; **595** Jonathan Nourok/PhotoEdit; **596** Henry T. Kaiser/Index Stock Imagery; **597 through 601** White House Historical Association; **601** (b)Official White House Photo by Eric Draper; **602** **603** (l)C. Sherburne/PhotoLink/Getty Images, (r)Bettmann/CORBIS; **604** (t)CORBIS, (b)C. Sherburne/PhotoLink/Getty Images, **605** (t)C. Sherburne/PhotoLink/Getty Images, (b)Bettmann/CORBIS; **606** C. Sherburne/PhotoLink/Getty Images; **607** (t)C. Sherburne/PhotoLink/Getty Images, (b)Wally McNamee/CORBIS; **608** North Wind Picture Archives; **609** **610** **611** Bettmann/CORBIS; **612** **613** National Portrait Gallery, Smithsonian Institution/Art Resource, NY; **614** Mark Burnett; **615** (t)Shield, Unknown Southern Cheyenne, about 1880; Painted rawhide, cloth, feathers, brass bells, cowtail; Denver Art Museum Collection: Native Arts acquisition funds, 1968.330ab; © Denver Art Museum; (b)CORBIS; **617** UPI/Bettmann/CORBIS; **618** Bettmann/CORBIS; **619** Flip Schulke/CORBIS; Timeline Official Presidential Portraits White House Historical Association.

Election 2008

A New President

Table of Contents

The Candidates

Because of the power and influence of the United States, the president, as our leader, has one of the most important roles in the world. Although the president is the head of just one of the three branches of government, the president—with the exception of the vice president—is the only official elected by the entire nation. As a result, the president stands as a symbol not only of the federal government, but of the entire country as well.

The Constitution lists rules about who can become president of the United States. By law, anyone who meets these qualifications is eligible.

Qualifications for U.S. President

✓ natural-born citizen

✓ at least 35 years of age

✓ a resident of the U.S. for at least 14 years

 As you read about the different political candidates, what other qualities or characteristics do you think a president should have?

Notable Candidates in History

1789 — George Washington runs unopposed for election as president.

1796 — Presidential candidates representing two rival political parties compete for the first time: Federalist John Adams and Democratic-Republican Thomas Jefferson.

1828 — Andrew Jackson and John Quincy Adams exchange personal attacks in the first true "mud-slinging" campaign.

1844 — Democrat James K. Polk is the first "dark horse," or unexpected candidate, to win the presidency.

1872 — Equal Rights Party nominates the first woman, Victoria Woodhull, to run for president and the first African American, Frederick Douglass, as vice president.

John McCain

Present position:
U.S. senator from Arizona

Born: August 29, 1936;
Panama Canal Zone

Lives in: Phoenix, Arizona

Education:
U.S. Naval Academy, B.S., 1958
National War College, 1974

John McCain comes from a distinguished military family. His father and grandfather were U.S. Navy admirals. McCain served as a naval pilot in the Vietnam War. His plane was shot down, and he was held prisoner by Vietnamese Communists for five years. After his release, McCain was honored as a war hero. Leaving the Navy, McCain was elected as a U.S. representative to Congress from Arizona in 1982. Four years later, he won election as a U.S. senator from Arizona. He is serving his fourth term in the Senate.

Sarah Palin

Present position:
Governor of Alaska

Born: February 11, 1964;
Sandpoint, Idaho

Lives in: Wasilla, Alaska

Education:
University of Idaho, B.S., 1987

Raised in Alaska, Sarah Palin worked as a sports reporter for local television and newspapers. In the 1990s, she served on the Wasilla, Alaska, city council and was elected the city's mayor in 1996. She later served as chairperson of the Alaska Oil and Gas Conservation Commission. In 2006 Palin was elected governor of Alaska, the first woman to hold the post. She became known for her efforts to fight corruption in Alaskan politics.

Barack Obama

Present position:
U.S. senator from Illinois

Born: August 4, 1961;
Honolulu, Hawaii

Lives in: Chicago, Illinois

Education:
Columbia University, B.A., 1983
Harvard University Law School, J.D., 1991

Of multiethnic background, Barack Obama was born in Hawaii to a white American mother from Kansas and a black father from Kenya, East Africa. After his parents divorced and his father returned to Africa, Obama stayed with his mother and was raised in Indonesia and Hawaii. Completing his higher education, Obama worked as a civil rights lawyer and taught law at the University of Chicago. In 1996 Obama was elected to the Illinois Senate and then to the U.S. Senate in 2004.

Joseph Biden

Present position:
U.S. senator from Delaware

Born: November 20, 1942;
Scranton, Pennsylvania

Lives in: Wilmington, Delaware

Education:
University of Delaware, B.A., 1965
Syracuse University, J.D., 1968

Born to a working-class family, Joseph Biden was raised in the suburbs of Wilmington, Delaware. After serving in local politics, Biden was elected to the Senate from Delaware at age 29. Through six terms in the Senate, Biden has become a skilled legislator. Having served on the Senate Judiciary and Foreign Relations Committees, Biden is known as an expert on issues related to foreign affairs, national security, drug policy, and crime.

1928 — Al Smith of New York is the first Roman Catholic to gain a major party's nomination for president.

1964 — Senator Margaret Chase Smith (R-Maine) becomes the first woman to seek a major party's nomination for president.

1972 — Shirley Chisholm (D-New York) is the first African American woman to seek a major party's presidential nomination.

1984 — Democrat Geraldine Ferraro is the first woman nominated for the vice presidency by a major party.

2000 — Connecticut senator Joseph Lieberman becomes the first Jewish American to run on a national ticket.

2008 — Barack Obama becomes the first African American to be elected president.

The Issues

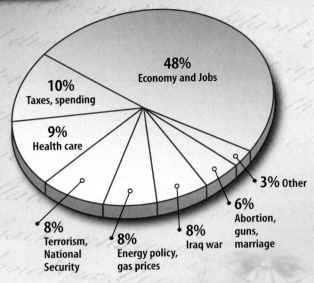

A host of issues—the economy, health care, and the Iraq war, for example—grabbed the attention of voters in the 2008 presidential race. When asked what issue was the most important in determining their vote for president, here is how registered voters responded one month before the election.

48% Economy and Jobs

10% Taxes, spending

9% Health care

8% Terrorism, National Security

8% Energy policy, gas prices

8% Iraq war

6% Abortion, guns, marriage

3% Other

VOTERS AND THE ISSUES

Source: *Newsweek* Poll conducted by Princeton Survey Research Associates International. Oct. 8-9, 2008

How the Candidates Voted

McCain's and Obama's voting records on selected issues, 2005-2008

	McCain	Obama
Trade		
Pass Central America Free Trade Agreement (2005)	Y	N
Economy and Jobs		
Increase minimum wage to $7.25 per hour (2007)	Y	Y
Pass $700 billion financial rescue package (2008)	Y	Y
Education		
Provide $52 million for community learning centers (2005)	N	Y
Shift $11 billion from corporate tax loopholes to education (2005)	N	Y
Immigration		
Allow illegal aliens to take part in Social Security (2006)	Y	Y
Begin comprehensive immigration reform (2007)	Y	Y
Declare English as the official language of the U.S. (2007)	Y	N
War on Terror		
Restrict business with foreign countries with links to terrorism (2005)	N	Y
Allow a phased withdrawal of troops from Iraq (2006)	N	Y
Reauthorize the Patriot Act (2006)	Y	Y
Preserve habeas corpus for Guantanamo detainees (2006)	N	Y
Redeploy non-essential U.S. troops out of Iraq in 9 months (2007)	N	Y

Where the Candidates Stand

 ## REPUBLICAN

 ## DEMOCRAT

Economy and Taxes

★ Lobbyists' influence blamed for financial crisis; favors greater government oversight

★ End taxes on unemployment benefits

★ Cut capital gains tax to raise incentive to save and invest

★ Treasury Department to guarantee 100 percent of savings for 6 months

★ Lower tax rates on retirement savings plans

★ Increase tax deductions for people selling stock at a loss

Energy

★ No taxes on windfall profits

★ No drilling in the Arctic, but support for offshore drilling

★ No ethanol subsidies

★ Expand nuclear power

Health Care

★ Free-market, consumer-based

★ $5,000 refundable tax credit for health insurance to every family

Education

★ Federal government should play a limited role in public education; education primarily a state and local concern

★ Keep No Child Left Behind Act's emphasis on standards and achievement; focus on individual achievement rather than group averages

Foreign Policy

★ Iraq—early and continuing supporter of war; favors troop increase; against timetable for troop withdrawal but projects all troops home by 2013

★ Iran—use economic and diplomatic pressure, work closely with European allies

★ Trade—honor NAFTA and other agreements; international reduction of trade barriers

Economy and Taxes

★ Federal rollback of regulations blamed for financial crisis; calls for greater government oversight

★ Tax breaks for businesses that create new jobs

★ Penalty-free withdrawals allowed from retirement savings

★ A 90-day reprieve for homeowners facing foreclosures

★ Suspend unemployment taxes and extend benefits

★ Federal lending agency to help financially-ailing cities and states

Energy

★ Tax windfall profits

★ No drilling in the Arctic and offshore

★ Provide ethanol subsidies

★ No support for nuclear power

Health Care

★ No requirements on small businesses

★ Reform of Medicare and Medicaid to reduce fraud

Education

★ Federal spending of $18 billion a year on early childhood classes, teacher recruitment, and other initiatives

★ Rewrite No Child Left Behind Act; keep emphasis on standards and accountability but offer aid to high-need schools

Foreign Policy

★ Iraq—early opponent of war; opposes troop increase; withdraw 1 or 2 brigades a month to finish within 16 months

★ Iran—use direct diplomacy; tighten economic sanctions

★ Trade—amend NAFTA to favor U.S. workers; end tax breaks for companies that outsource jobs

Historic Elections

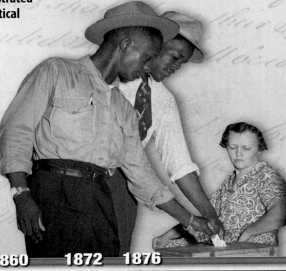

CHANGE
WE NEED

The Election of **2008** is historic with the election of Barack Obama, the nation's first African American president. Read about other significant elections.

1800 Peaceful Transfer of Power

The election of Thomas Jefferson marked an important event in American history. At the time, the Federalists controlled the presidency and the Congress. They could have refused to step down and overthrown the Constitution. Instead, they respected the people's right to choose the president. The election of 1800 demonstrated that the power to govern could be peacefully transferred from one political party to another.

1860 Secession and War

Republican Abraham Lincoln won every Northern state and a clear victory in the Electoral College. Many Southerners did not trust a Republican president to protect their interests. For them, the only choice was to leave the Union. By March 1861, seven Southern states had seceded to form the Confederate States of America. With the Union split in two, the threat of civil war loomed on the horizon.

Election Milestones

1800	1824	1840	1860	1872	1876
Peaceful Transfer of Power	John Quincy Adams wins the presidency, but it requires a vote in Congress; supporters of Andrew Jackson make charges of a corrupt deal.	William Henry Harrison is the first president to die in office; Vice President John Tyler assumes the presidency, establishing a precedent that later becomes law.	Secession and War	With the passage of the Fifteenth Amendment (1870), African American males vote for the first time in a presidential election.	Reconstruction Ends

1876 Reconstruction Ends

On Election Day, Democrat Samuel Tilden had 184 electoral votes, 1 short of a majority. Republican Rutherford B. Hayes won 165 electoral votes, leaving 20 votes in dispute. When a special commission awarded all 20 disputed votes to Hayes, many people concluded that a deal had been made. The Democrats accepted Hayes as president in exchange for the removal of federal troops from the South. The era of Reconstruction was over.

1932 Government Expands

As the effects of the Great Depression worsened, Democratic candidate Franklin D. Roosevelt was elected president, promising "a new deal for the American people." Roosevelt persuaded Congress to create many new social and economic programs. When Roosevelt became president in 1933, about 600,000 people worked in the federal government. By the time he died in 1945, more than 3 million workers served in the federal government.

We Want F.D.R. Again

1960 Television Campaigns

Compared to earlier campaigns, the 1960 campaign made new use of television. Both major parties spent large amounts of money on television ads. The televised presidential debates may have been the turning point in one of the closest elections in American history. Kennedy seemed relaxed and outgoing, while Nixon struck many as formal and stiff in manner.

2000 Supreme Court Resolves Election

When the polls closed, neither Democrat Al Gore nor Republican George W. Bush had the necessary 270 electoral votes to be declared the winner. Bush held a narrow lead in Florida, but a dispute arose over ballot recounts in the state. Bush asked the Supreme Court to stop a hand recount of ballots. In *Bush* v. *Gore*, the Court ruled the election results should stand as counted. As a result, Bush won Florida and the presidency.

Chicago Daily Tribune
DEWEY DEFEATS TRUMAN

1912 **1920** **1932** **1948** **1960** **2000 2008**

Third party candidate Theodore Roosevelt wins 27 percent of the popular vote —the highest percentage ever for a third party.

With the passage of the Nineteenth Amendment, women vote in a presidential election for the first time.

Government Expands

Harry Truman is elected in one of the most surprising upsets in political history; early polls showed Thomas Dewey, the Republican candidate, with a big lead.

Television Campaigns

Supreme Court Resolves Election

First African American President

The Results

Presidential Candidate	Popular Vote	% of Popular Vote	Electoral Votes
■ Obama	66,882,230	53	365
■ McCain	58,343,671	46	173

*Numbers on map show electoral votes per state.

WA 11
OR 7
MT 3
ND 3
MN 10
WI 10
MI 17
NH 4
VT 3
ME 4
MA 12
NY 31
RI 4
CT 7
NJ 15
DE 3
MD 10
DC 3
ID 4
SD 3
IA 7
PA 21
NV 5
WY 3
NE 5
IL 21
IN 11
OH 20
WV 5
VA 13
CA 55
UT 5
CO 9
KS 6
MO 11
KY 8
NC 15
AZ 10
NM 5
OK 7
AR 6
TN 11
SC 8
TX 34
LA 9
MS 6
AL 9
GA 15
FL 27
AK 3
HI 4

CONGRESSIONAL PARTY AFFILIATION*

House

Democrat 257   Republican 178

Senate

Democrat 56   Republican 41

Undecided 1
Independent 2

Source: www.senate.gov, www.house.gov

* All figures represent total number of voting members of Congress. Totals may change due to undecided races as of February 5, 2009.